GS

GENTILE REACTIONS TO JEWISH IDEALS

GENTILE REACTIONS
TO
JEWISH IDEALS

With Special Reference to Proselytes

by

JACOB S. RAISIN

Published Posthumously under the Editorship of
HERMAN HAILPERIN

Philosophical Library
New York

Printed in the United States of America

iv

FOREWORD

I HAVE been asked to write a few lines as a Foreword to this posthumous work of my unforgettable brother Jacob Salmon Raisin, and I confess that I am doing it with some misgivings. This stems from the cognizance that I am little deserving of this honor, having done practically nothing to make possible the publication of this volume. The fullest credit for it goes to our sister, Mrs. Isaac H. Levin, who worked so hard to bring it about, and, of course, to Doctor Herman Hailperin of Pittsburgh, who, at the request of the family, edited the manuscript and brought to his task not only a ready fund of extensive rabbinic and mediaeval scholarship but a painstaking zeal for accuracy as to details and data. To him we are all greatly indebted for the final form of the book which brother Jacob would himself have revised had not death overtaken him in the very midst of his labors.

Despite the above mentioned reluctance, I am quite happy to have these words of mine preface the volume. For Jacob S. Raisin was my brother not only in the flesh but in spirit as well. We had in common ever so many interests of a moral and spiritual nature, both of us being rabbis in the Reform wing of Judaism which appealed so greatly to us, and both of us sharing in the basic ideals of our Jewish people and glorying in its marvelous past, its unequalled capacity for martyrdom, and its unquenchable hope for a noble future for the Jews as for the whole of mankind. Essentially optimistic by nature, Jacob found great comfort in the shaping of events which led to the rise of the new Jewish State and which, prophet-like, he foresaw in our last conversation just prior to his passing in 1946.

As for this volume which I saw growing in size and scope in the course of many years, it is the swan-song of one who

v

for more than forty years served our people as preacher, teacher and writer, enriching our literature with works of great excellence on a variety of themes in both English and Hebrew. In itself this work bears testimony to a profound scholarship zealously cultivated during a life-time of study of Jewish history and lore. I am convinced that not only his own age but future generations will find themselves indebted to Jacob S. Raisin for his unusual contribution to the store-house of Jewish learning.

MAX RAISIN
Paterson, New Jersey
May, 1951

EDITOR'S PREFACE

THE task of editing this work was a labor of love. The editor was attracted to the task originally because of his desire to pay homage to one whose whole life was consecrated to the ministry, to scholarship, and to the practice, in public duty and private thinking, of those ideals which are the heritage of the Judeo-Christian tradition. The prompting to undertake the work went deeper still. Upon first reading even of the chapter headings, I was lured to accept the commission because I sensed immediately that Doctor Raisin's work was cognate to the field of research to which I had been devoting all my mature years.[1]

Rabbi Raisin set out to show that Judaism, in its own nature and enthusiasm, was, almost from its beginnings, a missionary religion; that the Jews for centuries, carried on propaganda to effect the consummation of their belief in the ultimate acceptance by all the peoples of the world of the one and only God; that though the Jews suffered much from suppression and degradation, there was never a time when some non-Jews did not knock for admission into the household of Israel.

It is very evident from our author's method and spirit that he felt the necessity of traversing many by-paths in order to set forth his thesis in true historic perspective. Unlike other special studies in Jewish proselytism,[2] Raisin's work is not episodic. His unique contribution consists of the wide sweep and epic treatment—the very materials which some others mistakenly might judge to be extraneous and far afield from the major theme.

It seems, therefore, necessary for the editor to offer a statement of the scope of the author's thesis such as he himself might have done had he lived to complete his work for

vii

publication. For a long time, historians, Jewish and Christian, have been studying incidental and transient cases of non-Jews who have accepted the Jewish religion, and of Jews who have converted to the Christian religion. It may even be said that such incidental cases as have been described have most often not been recognized to be elements that produced any historic effect worth noting. Doctor Raisin is the first to make the subject taken up in his work a part of world history. Our author felt the necessity of presenting the course of Jewish proselyting in its true historic continuity. In reading Raisin's work one finds points of contact between Jews and non-Jews so frequent, and meanings of relations so cumulative, and the location and description of these contacts so detailed, that one is persuaded of the continuous nature of this history. We feel that what can be proven to be so continuous through so many centuries and in so many parts of the world must be regarded as a major topic of history worthy of treatment in a work of such magnitude as the present one.

In order to avoid the pitfalls of scholars who have dealt with proselytes and converts in isolated cases, Doctor Raisin set out to give an account of the history of Gentile-Jewish relations with an eye to the bearing of these economic, social and intellectual relations upon proselytes—*from earliest times to the present*. Our author has sensed correctly that the historian must likewise be cognizant of the ubiquity of the Jews, in the ancient, mediaeval, and modern worlds. 'Tis no wonder that Raisin's treatment of the presence of the Jews is so far flung. Even when we reckon with the Jews on their own soil, we must remember that Palestine itself was successively made part of the Assyrian, Hellenistic-Egyptian, Hellenistic-Syrian, Parthian and Roman Empires. A people scattered everywhere and among all peoples, the Jews are described by our author as a group *at home*, now among Canaanites, and later among Babylonians and Greeks and Romans, and then among Christian peoples, and Arab speaking peoples, and North-African, and in Europe and in the Western Hemisphere, and back to India and even China. This work is, in a sense, a history of the Jews in relation to other peoples.

Why was it necessary to make the story so "long"? It is true that popular forum lecturers pride themselves on making long stories short. There are times, however, when short stories should be made long! A book is never too large or too long if it states what must be stated, and has something to say. Since it is a fact that there never was a time wherein there were not some Gentiles who accepted Judaism, then it is the duty of the historian to tell us something about these people known as Jews. What are their ideals and what are their mores? More especially, for our purpose here, what is their outlook on humanity? How early in their thinking did they think in terms of *humanity* and *universality*? So Doctor Raisin's introductory chapters (I and II) deal with "The Idea of One Humanity" in the light of the Bible, Apocrypha and Talmud. It is also necessary to describe in detail the Judaism to which proselytes turned, and likewise to delineate the Christianity and the Christian peoples to whom Jews turned. One cannot, for example, possibly begin to understand the Christian-Jewish relations in western and eastern Europe after the year 1500 unless one knows in detail the history and nature of the Reformation and Renaissance. Our author, therefore, finds it obligatory to give a detailed explication of Luther's role and contribution to the Reform movements (Ch. 24).

It is now necessary to say a word about Raisin's method in the use of the documents. Almost at the beginning of his opus, Doctor Raisin reveals a tendency to ignore much of the knowledge we now have of the development of the biblical text and of higher criticism. The present editor had to reckon in his own mind with the cry of those who will contend that it is impossible to follow the chronology in so many places or the historical placement and area of documents. Is it possible that our author was unfamiliar with the whole field of biblical literary and historical criticism? Certainly not.

Let us refer briefly to Chapter 3, "In the Days of the Baalim". There he freely mixes Bible and Talmud. He also accepts, (without even a bare mention of the problem), the historicity of Abraham. In the judgment of the present writer, Doctor Raisin's procedure was basically and essentially historic—*in the context of his treatise*. The critical reader must bear in mind two things: one, the mental habit of the biblical-rabbinic world of thought, and two, the mental habit of the Christian world of thought in its acceptance of the Hebrew materials. The literature of the Bible and of the Talmud and Midrash expresses *organic* thinking,[3] not categorical. There is, of course, a coherence in rabbinic thought but it is not our coherence. Rabbinic theology is a real thing though it must be noted that it is a theology *in solution,*— not a "system" or "order" of religious thought. Rabbinic literature is, in the form of the written word, a reflection of organic thinking intact.

Because the material in rabbinic thought consists of interpretations of concrete situations with consequent innumerable repetition of concepts, rabbinic theology cannot be put into a systematic, classified form so far as its concepts are concerned. And therefore, the deductions which the Rabbis draw from biblical texts in order to prove their own statements are reasonable, if we remember that their statements have to do with the organic concepts. What the Rabbis read into Scripture is not so foreign to the biblical text as it was conceived by the Jewish folk, who naturally attached fable, story, exaggeration and parable,—taken out of their mental organic complex and framework. If the objection be raised that the biblical period be not a unit, still it does not invalidate the fact that the Bible did *represent* a single organic unit. The biblical period may not be a unit, but the Bible itself, the selected books, edited and put into one collection, certainly is. It is therefore true to say that rabbinic theology and the Bible have many features in common, and that an intimate relationship exists between rabbinic thought and Scripture.

With reference to the problem facing us at this point, it is important to bear in mind that, when the biblical and rabbinic materials reached the Christians, the Bible and Talmud were not the objects of historical, critical analysis. The body of Jewish ideas came into the non-Jewish world as an organic body of ideas, and not in literary strands or fragmentary documents. The Hebrew Scriptures had been inherited with a vast commentary which had grown up out of a *civilization,* and, therefore, the Christian civilization could not help but meet Scripture and Talmud in their entirety. The Christians did accept the historicity of Abraham even as did the Jews. Christians (and Mohammedans later likewise) believed the Old Testament account to be authentic even as did the most faithful Jew—from Genesis to Chronicles it was the word of God. With the believing Jew, Christianity taught that there was a future world where human life, so bitter in this world, will there attain its fulfillment. Both religions believed that the only way in which man can attain such salvation is by conducting himself in accordance with the supernaturally revealed word of God. The main point at issue turned on the question as to which group was in possession of the authoritative revelation of God's will. In any case, Christian scholars could never forget or readily ignore the naturalized relation of the Christian beliefs to the literature and wider milieu of the Old Testament. In short, the Christians reckoned with the whole corpus of the Jewish writings. Our author, for the purpose of laying out his thesis, was right in not adhering to strict historical and critical canons when applied with our logic and categories to ancient documents.

Thus, a word must be said about Raisin's use of legends. Legendary accounts of biblical heroes were not mere imaginative fancies to the Rabbis. To them neither fact nor fiction, the legends belonged to another category, provided for by organic thinking, that is, the category of significance.[4] We do the same thing. We read about a certain event; then we ask, what is its deeper significance or meaningfulness. One never can separate into strict categories legend from historic fact in documents of Bible literature. Dr. Raisin himself says, in discussing an account of Moslem proselytes, that legends frequently conceal a germ of fact (Vol. II, p. 406). Chapter 5, "Bible Proselytes in Rabbinic Lore", gives evidence of the continuity of the mission idea among the Jews and the growth of the Jewish missionary program. And even if we still maintain that the legends about good relations between Gentiles and Jews are mere "legends", no scholar can deny that they at least reflect clearly the sentiments of those who first uttered the legends, and most certainly the ideas of those who recorded them.

Raisin's work is, in general, an excellent corrective of much of what has been written about Jews in their relation to the non-Jewish world. One recurrent theme of traditional Jewish historiography is the emphasis on the isolation of the Jews. It is true that Jews and Gentiles did live in an atmosphere of deepening hatreds. But this was not a constant. Jewish history is not one long, uninterrupted account of persecution. History studies all contacts and measures the forces and results of contacts of minds in agreement as well as of minds in conflict. Not only are there emergences of relations between Christians and Jews that provide positive contributions and influences, but in the very time of persecution one often finds that non-Jews seek to join the Jewish religion, or that Jews and Christians fraternize simply because they are humanly normal and friendly. The story, as our author tells it, is not one uniform and consistent pattern of persecution, or of conversion (of Jews to Christianity), or of proselytism, or of pogroms. Raisin's work establishes firmly that Jews were never completely isolated, not even in periods of suppression and degradation.

Our author goes deeper. Because of the traditional view of Jewish history as an even pattern of persecution, and because this information has led to a distorted view as to Jewish cohesiveness, and as to the opinion which Jews had of their own corporate strength, Raisin's several excursuses on the presence of the Jews constitute a sound corrective. Without these treatments, our work would be a bare account of sporadic conversions to Judaism. Chapter 3 sets forth an account of the heroic struggle to establish the Jewish religion and the ever growing Jewish loyalties resulting therefrom. Chapter 10, "From Iraq to Iran" delineates the power and force of the communal, corporate existence of the Jews in their own eyes. Without Chapter 11, "The Jewish Enlightenment in Egypt", one cannot possibly understand the curious and unique role of Jewish Hellenism in the history of proselytism. And so much of Volume 2 is devoted to the Jew as European, as constituting for centuries, a state within a state, as living in proximity to Christian and Islamic peoples under the same governments, in a nexus of daily economic, social, legal and even intellectual relations—that one must conclude that proselytism and conversions, too, are part of an inexorable historic process. The documents which Doctor Raisin presents speak for themselves. They give evidence that certainly in Western Europe, for ten centuries, at least, the Jews and Christians lived in relatively peaceful relations. The Crusades herald a new era in the application of disabilities against the Jews. Previously, outbreaks were sporadic and incidental, not part of an ecclesiastical program for the purpose of inquisition or of a state's policy for the purpose of annihilation.

Our author goes deeper still. In the very period of "The Church Triumphant" (Chapter 19), when certain historical developments seemed to sound the death knell of the Jews for all time, there were forces at work among servants of the State and of the Church which challenge the historian to trace out the threads of proselytism and conversion in the web of the thirteenth century European history. It is true that Raisin by no means glosses over the bitter conflicts of social and intellectual antagonisms of the twelfth and thirteenth centuries. Yet our author presents material which clearly shows that Christian scholarship turned positively to the intellectual heritage of its opponents for argumentation upon its own ideas. The scholarship of the thirteenth century had greatly widened the intellectual horizon. Raisin points out that the interest which Christian scholars had in reestablishing the correct text of the Latin Bible with the help of the Jews was great enough to make them ignore the ban against associating with Jews. And still wider horizons ap-

peared. If the material of the Kabbalah became known in
the first place to Christian scholars as material for Christian
apologetic and polemic for the conversion of Jews, it continued also and at the same time to contribute motives and
content for an ever enlarging commentary on the Bible for
the Christians. Our author then describes the Jews as intellectual intermediaries between the Moslems and the Christians.
He also shows that many of the disputations between Jews
and Christians, were, at times, friendly and often academic
in form—though all the public disputations were really aimed
at ultimate conversion. The present editor has often asked the
question, If we imagine that all the Jews of the world
had already been converted, would Christian scholars then
bring to an end their interest in Hebrew and other Jewish
intellectual materials? True to the whole historical pano-
rama of the thirteenth century, our author completes the
chapter with an account of Jews who joined the Christian
Church, either under duress or voluntarily, and with reference
to the edict of expulsion from France, 1394. The Jews had
been banished from England in 1290.

In a work so large and as surcharged in its own original
material content with hate as is the present one, one can
expect to find occasional outbursts of deep feeling and passion
on the part of the writer. The treatise is, after all, a study in
great part, of differences, of bitter polemics, and of perpetuated
hatreds. The present editor is of the opinion that our author
permitted himself to accept uncritically the traditional view
of the Church as the institution par excellence to take over
the legacy of hate and raise that hate to the dignity of a
dogma (p. XIV). It is, however, a tribute to the Church that it
did not do what it had political and ecclesiastical power to
do, that is, readily and easily to ignore the status and presence
of the Jew and thus exclude him altogether from the mediaeval
world. In justice to our author it must be said that Raisin
does set down details of the Church legislation which made
repeated attempts to protect the Jews and to define their
rights (Chapter 14). We miss, however, the proper and careful emphasis in general. If the Jew was excluded from Chris-

tian society, he was but one in a system of secluded groups. Because of the tendency to segregate and to isolate events, historians have been guilty of concluding that in the Middle Ages only the Jewish people suffered. Out of respect for the original work of our author, the editor did not consider it proper to make major changes. Yet, it can be safely said that Raisin does have all the materials present in the facts and offers sufficient information impliedly as correctives of his own generalizations on this point.

Illustrative of our author's tendency to offer his own correctives is, for example, his statement: "To the credit of the papacy be it said that many of the pontiffs were more tolerant than the inferior clergy, and did not favor forced conversion." (Vol. II, p. 363). He sees in the very prohibition against social relations between Jews and Christians the evidence of normal, happy relations. "The constant exhortations of the clergy to shun the society of the Jews are in themselves proof that not all Christians followed the example of the frenzied monks and the fanatic mobs." (Ibid. p. 374). On intermarriage during the so-called "Dark Ages", Raisin says: "Contrary to what we might expect, the Middle Ages were not altogether free from intermarriages, if we may judge by the enactments of the Church and the Synagogue. The issue of such marriages, were, as a rule, raised as Jews, and the Rabbis frequently decry any discrimination against them." (*Ibid.*, p. 494). With reference to the question of dating the beginnings of the missionary idea among the Hebrews, our author gives evidence of critical historical acumen in sensing the germs of Israel's mission as present already in the Mosaic legislation (Chapter 4, "Early Missionaries and Converts", pp. 84f.). It is also philosophically sound for the historian to realize that any people in possession of a great enthusiasm will want to share that enthusiasm with others—and that is the basis for all missionary movements. Another corrective is Raisin's continual and recurrent references to the Judaic leaven in historical Christianity and in the many Christian sects. This is significant as one necessary historical condition for the "natural" turning of Christians to the religion of

Israel. Chapter 8, "At the Cradle of Christianity" gives a detailed account of nascent Christianity and thereby helps to explain historically why Jews were not satisfied with the traditional Christian interpretation of the Judaeo-Christian heritage. Many mediaeval Jewish scholars were rather well acquainted with the activities of Jesus, Peter and Paul. All historical material, which reveals again and again the dissatisfactions and ferment within Christianity has a real bearing on the major theme, as, for example, the Crusades and the twelfth century Renaissance. In this same category we think of our author's detailed descriptions of the reform movements before the Reformation with their many economic, social and intellectual disturbances—all historical preparations for dissent and schism (Chapter 22, "The Aftermath of the Renaissance"). It is no exaggeration to say that all of Raisin's by-paths and seeming departures from the main topic are related organically in the light of his thesis development. To the unhistorical mind such topics as the English claim of descent from ancient Israel, proselytism, conversion, the American inquisition, Russian Sabbatarianism, Messianism, anti-semitism, philo-semitism, Christian sectarianism, the black Jews of the United States, or the Reformation—all would seem so disparate. But when seen within the framework of the present treatise and when examined within the context of the documentary material here presented, these topics belong to a coherent, solid mass. Raisin's wide range of factual material and the cumulative evidence lend power and veracity to his thesis.

In closing this Preface I wish to express my deepest gratitude to Mrs. Isaac H. Levin, sister of the late Rabbi Raisin, whose devotion and love for her brother led her to see this book through the press. She is responsible for many corrections in style and in expression. Her critical insight and discernment have been of great aid in the editing of this work.

HERMAN HAILPERIN

May, 1951.

CONTENTS

VOLUME II

GENTILE REACTIONS
AFTER THE RISE OF CHRISTIANITY

I. JUDAISM'S ATTITUDE TOWARDS
NON-JEWS

OF THE innumerable calumnies invented to justify the persecution of the Jews, from the worshipping of a consecrated ass to the use of human blood for ritual purposes, perhaps the most common and malicious is that the Jews are misanthropic. Balaam, the wizard who managed to curse even when he was coerced to bless, hinted at it when he exclaimed: "Lo, it is a people that dwelleth alone and is not reckoned among the nations." Haman of Persia implied it in his indictment that the Jews' laws "are diverse from every other people, neither keep they the king's laws." Apion, the Egyptian, boldly affirmed it in his declaration that "Jews swear by God the Maker of heaven, earth and the sea, to bear no good will to any foreigner, and particularly to none of the Greeks"; while Cicero, the Roman, asserts the same concerning his countrymen, adducing as evidence their stubborn refusal to allow the Romans to become the masters of Palestine! This legacy of hate was taken over by Christianity and raised almost to the dignity of a dogma; and its effect is felt to this day.

As a corollary of this it has recently become the fashion to absolve Paganism of all prejudice and to put the blame upon its victims, the Jews. Pagans, we are told, were tolerant; if Christianity has turned out to be most intolerant it is because it has imbibed its intolerance from Judaism, the religion which mothered it. As proof of this we are referred to the passages in the Bible where Jehovah is proclaimed to be a jealous and vengeful God who "hath indignation every day"; and to those verses where the early Israelites are called upon to show no quarter to the native Canaanites. Sayings of some talmudic sages are also quoted wherein the heathen persecutors are condemned as inhuman and deserving of extermination. These "higher critics" do not care to consider that documents are of value only if interpreted in the light of the times and conditions which produced them. They ignore the fact that in every known instance these hateful utterances of a few individuals were not shared by the rest; that they were the poisonous product of excruciating personal experiences, and are therefore as alien to normal Judaism as the songs of hate inspired by the late war are to the spirit of true Christianity. The Rabbis had a better insight into human nature when they laid down the law,—"No one should be condemned for an expression uttered in a moment of agony."[1]

The refinement of vilification, however, and the unfairest construction of Jewish history is found in the claim that Jews were averse to proselytism, as if they were afraid lest the Gentiles "return, and be healed." Ernest Renan[2] asserts that after the loss of their political independence:

> Proselytism disappears by degrees from amongst that people who had been its most ardent followers... It renounced heroism and made martyrdom useless by those clever distinctions between the precepts that may be transgressed in order to save one's life and those for which he must suffer death. And from this sprung a singular spectacle: Judaism, which had given the first martyrs to the world, now left the monopoly of it to Christianity, so much so that in certain persecutions Christians might be seen figuring as Jews, so that they might enjoy the immunities of Judaism.

Edward Gibbon,[3] too, has this to say:

> The Jewish religion was admirably fitted for defense, but it was never designed for conquest, and it seems probable that the number of proselytes was never much superior to that of apostates. The divine promise was originally made, and the distinguishing rite of

circumcision was enjoined to a single family. The obligation of preaching to the Gentiles the faith of Moses had never been inculcated as a precept of the Law, nor were the Jews inclined to impose it on themselves as a voluntary duty. The descendants of Abraham were flattered by the opinion that they alone were heirs of the covenant, and they were apprehensive of diminishing the value of their inheritance by sharing it too easily with strangers of the earth. A larger acquaintance with mankind extended their knowledge without correcting their prejudices; and wherever the God of Israel acquired any new votaries, He was much more indebted to the inconstant humor of Polytheism than to the active zeal of His own missionaries.

An unbiased study of Jewish history will, it is hoped, show these assertions to be the reverse of the truth. Far from miserlike, holding on to their spiritual treasure, the Jews grasped every opportunity to impart it to others. The singularity of the Jews consisted in this—that they cared more for the good of mankind as a whole than for the greater glory of Israel as a people. They were zealous not that mankind should call itself by the name of Jacob, but that it should subscribe its hand unto the Lord and accept at least the rudimentary moral precepts of Judaism. They did not insist, as did the Church, that *Nulla salus extra ecclesiam* ("No salvation outside of the Church"). They believed that all who observed what the Rabbis called the "Seven Noahian Laws" were as certain of salvation as if they were Jews observing the whole Law. But these they felt in duty bound to spread all over the world.

That after the rise of Christianity and Mohammedanism their efforts at conversion gradually diminished is no more evidence that Judaism is not a missionary religion than lytism because they no longer proselytize in Bolshevik Russia or in Nazified Germany. The fact is that even when Jewish that Christianity and Mohammedanism are opposed to prose-

missionary efforts were necessarily diminished, they were not altogether abandoned. The wall with which the Jews surrounded themselves in order to prevent their own absorption among the nations of the earth was not intended to keep the nations of the earth without. The gate was always open to those who knocked and sought admittance; and while 'the left hand pushed away, the right hand in reality extended a cordial welcome.' The motto of the synagogue might well have been: "Whosoever will may come and partake of the waters of life freely." It was never limited only to those of the seed of Abraham according to the flesh.

Certainly, if wish is father to thought, the Jews were the most missionary-minded people in history. It was their undying hope that ultimately all mankind would cast away their idols, and all God's erring and wayward children would acknowledge Him as the only God. This hope mitigated the misery of their exile and imbued them with courage to bear the hate and persecution of a hostile and pitiless environment. It formed the burden of the Prophets while Israel was still a nation in its own land, inspired the yearning Psalmists during the Babylonian exile, inflamed the Hellenized Judeans of Egypt, and prompted the Talmudists to debate about the status of the proselytes at a time when to be a Jew, not to say a convert to Judaism, was hazardous in the extreme. All through the vicissitudes of their eventful history there was hardly a period when the Jews did not prove the truth of Isaiah's assertion:

> This people I have formed for Myself
> That they might tell My praise.[4]

To show what the Jews did to effect the consummation of this ardent hope and how the Gentiles reacted to their active or passive propaganda is the object of the following chapters. Suffice it here to state that while the Church did not hesitate to resort to the most inhuman means to degrade the Jews, and while, as a consequence, many Jews joined the camp of the enemy, there was never a time when some non-Jews did not knock for admission into the household of Israel. Some, indeed, stressed only the human, universal ideals in Judaism, and others, while accepting most of the teachings of Judaism, bit the hand that fed them and repaid their benefactors with the most absurd slanders and most fiendish persecutions. But there were not lacking also those who became completely integrated with the "Congregation of the Lord," produced saints and scholars in whom Israel gloried. These not infrequently set an example for their new co-religionists by dying the death of martyrs "for the sanctification of the Name." They were indeed, as so many preferred to call themselves after their conversion, Abrahams, for, like the first Hebrew Patriarch, they were Jews not by the accident of birth but by the compulsion of conviction and like him they fully deserved the veneration and affection Jews always cherished for their "Proselytes of Righteousness."

Before, however, we proceed to describe the various attitudes of Gentiles to Jewish ideals we shall take a bird's-eye view of the attitude of Judaism to non-Jews.

CHAPTER I

THE IDEA OF HUMANITY AS
ONE FELLOWSHIP

IN THE LIGHT OF THE BIBLE AND APOCRYPHA

THE Bible does not begin with the history of Israel, nor with Moses, but with the story of Creation. This in itself indicates the interest displayed by the early Hebrews in the world around them. At the same time it is revealing of the ideals cherished by them on their first emergence from the obscurity of the past. Whether the cosmogonic descriptions of the Book of Genesis were borrowed from the Babylonians, as some claim, or not, they already show in their biblical form the foundation upon which the later Prophets, Psalmists, and rabbis were to build. They tell us that God "saw everything that He had made and, behold, it was very good," and blessed it; they say that all men are descended from the same aboriginal pair which God made in His own image, and all are therefore equally precious in His sight. These ideas were amplified or embellished with the passing of the years. Job introduces the element of joy, and reminds us that at the dawn of the Creation "The morning stars sang together, and all the sons of God shouted for joy." To the Psalmists God not only created the world but rejoiced in His work, filled it with strength and beauty, and established it so that it shall never be moved.

These primitive sagas, where God is still depicted as walking in the garden in the cool of day, afraid lest man, by eating of the Tree of Knowledge, "will become like one of us," and as uncertain whether the Sodomites "have done altogether

1

according to the cry of it which is come unto Me," show Him
to be superhumanly merciful and gracious. He does not let
the guilty Cain escape, but hears the cry of innocent Hagar,
the Egyptian slave, and bestows upon her the same blessing
wherewith He blessed her master, the Hebrew Patriarch. He
refrains from punishing Abimelech when he sins "in the simplicity of his heart." It "grieves Him" to behold man's wickedness upon the earth, yet would He rather let a whole nation
escape because of the righteous few than see the few righteous
perish by reason of the wicked many. If he shows partiality
to Abraham, the Hebrew, it is because he keeps "the way of
the Lord to do righteousness and justice (to all)." There is
nothing arbitrary about Him, nor is He a respecter of persons.
The fact that Ishmael was the son of Abraham and Esau the
son of Isaac, and that both were circumcised, did not count
in their favor:

> Was not Esau Jacob's brother? says the Lord;
> Yet I loved Jacob, and Esau I hated.[1]

But we are not left to learn the God-concept of the Bible
merely by inference. We find that already Abraham conceived
Him as "The Judge of all the earth" and Moses described
Him as:

> The Rock, Whose work is perfect,
> For all His ways are justice.

He is, moreover, full of mercy and lovingkindness (hesed),
even toward the undeserving. He pities and hears the cry
not only of the sufferer but of the sinner who returns to
Him in truth. This is strikingly illustrated in the vision wherein God passes before Moses, after the people worshiped the
Golden Calf, and proclaims:

> The Lord, the Lord God, merciful and gracious, long-
> suffering, and abundant in goodness and truth; keep-
> ing mercy unto the thousandth generation, forgiving
> iniquity, transgression and sin; and that will by no

means clear the guilty; visiting the iniquity of the fathers upon the children, and upon the children's children, unto the third and fourth generation.

This is the theme of all the Prophets and of the Psalmists. None of them saw any inconsistency between God's justice and His mercy or lovingkindness, nor did they apply these attributes only in His relation to Israel. The biblical writers, in many instances, use the general term *adam* (man) or *hai* (living being), in describing God's dealing with the world. Ezekiel reiterates that God has no pleasure in the death of the wicked but rather that he should return from his ways and live. The Psalmists in particular never tire of singing of God's mercy and lovingkindness to all. He "renders to every man according to his work," He judges the world with righteousness and people in His faithfulness. More than that:

As the heaven is high above the earth,
So great is His mercy toward them that
    fear Him...
Like as a father hath compassion upon
    his children,
So hath the Lord compassion upon them
    that fear Him.

The Psalm which through the ages has been most often recited in the synagogue is the one which declares:

The Lord is gracious and full of compassion;
Slow to anger, and of great mercy...
The Lord is good to all,
And His tender mercies are over all His
    works...
The Lord is nigh unto all them that call
    upon Him,
To all that call upon Him in truth.[2]

The Bible furnishes us with life-size pictures of the worthies who are portrayed in the Bible with all their goodness and

all their weaknesses. In none of them can we detect a trace of
a different standard of morality toward those who were not
of the "seed of Abraham." All of them reveal the same
considerateness for those of another race, country, or religion, as for their own. Abram refused to accept "from a
thread to a shoe-latchet" from the king of Sodom for his
services in his behalf, and consented to receive remuneration only for his allies who were not related to him. His
intercession for the sinful cities, and his intercourse with
Melchizedek and the Children of Heth are evidence of the
humanism and universalism which characterized the "rock"
whence the Hebrews were hewn. Isaac bore no grudge against
Abimelech, the king of the Philistines, and readily yielded
to his proposals for peace. Jacob would not retain the money
his sons found in their corn-sacks, since "peradventure it was
an oversight" on the part of the Egyptians, and, though they
were not altogether blameworthy for their behavior, he dis-
owned Simeon and Levi for their treatment of the Hivites.
Judah's most faithful friend was Hirah the Adullamite, and
Onan his son performed his levirate duty toward Tamar,
the Canaanite. While still a slave, Joseph resisted the advances of his pagan mistress, protesting that he would not
"do this great wickedness and sin against God," and, even
when cast into the dungeon, made no effort to clear himself of his mistress' accusation. Nor did he bear a grudge
against the ungrateful chief butler for having forgotten him
so soon after he had been restored to his office.

These traits are conspicuous also in the lives of the other
worthies of the Bible. Moses is as courteous to the pagan
shepherdess of Midian as Jacob was to his cousin Rachel;
and he is as happy to meet Jethro, the heathen priest, as he
is to meet Aaron, his own brother. Joshua keeps faith with
Rahab, and would not abrogate his treaty with the Gibeonites though "they did work wilily." Saul does not forget that
the Kenites showed kindness to the Children of Israel when
they came up out of Egypt, nor does he conceal his compunction at taking the life of Agag, the Amalekite. David
is attached to Hiram of Tyre; cherishes the memory of

Nahash, king of Moab; and metes out justice to the Gibeon-
ite foreigners against the royal house of Saul. That the reputation of the kings of Israel for kindness to all was well
deserved is illustrated in the episode of Ahab, who was by
no means a model of piety. On receiving a letter from the
defeated king of Aram praying for his life, Ahab's immediate reply is: "Is he yet alive? He is my brother." Nor is
there a nobler example of true chivalry than that of Elisha
in the sequel of the story, where, despite Ahab's magnanimity, the same king sends another host against Israel.
When the enemy is suddenly stricken with blindness, the
Prophet would not permit the king to take advantage of
this affliction. "Hast thou taken captive with thy sword and
thy bow those whom thy bow would smite? Set bread and
water before them, that they may eat and drink, and send
them to their master." This was only on a par with the
magnanimity of Pekah, king of Israel, who, at the solicitation
of Oded, fed, clothed, and anointed his Judean captives
and had them carried back to their country.[3]

Even when the ancient Israelites felt themselves called
upon to wage war they saw to it that justice and humanity were
not violated. We hear of no punitive or retaliatory measures
taken against a vanquished enemy. The stringent laws enacted against the Canaanites were due to the constant dread
lest "they become a snare" and teach their conquerors "to
do after all their abominations." Overtures of peace were never
to be abandoned, and the brunt of the battles was to be borne
by none but the combatants. No enemy property was to be
destroyed, nor trees cut down. The only privilege the soldiers
had was that of helping themselves to the enemy's fruit and
fuel. Neither was a neighboring nation to suffer because
of its proximity to the enemy nation. "Thus saith thy brother
Israel," reads a message sent by Moses to the king of Edom:
"Let us pass, I pray thee, through thy land; we will not
pass through field or through vineyard, neither will we drink
of the water of the wells ... We will go up the highway; and
if we drink thy water, I and my cattle, then will I give the
price thereof; let me only pass through on my feet; I will

do thee no hurt." That every nation was entitled to the free possession and enjoyment of its territory seems to have been with the Hebrews a maxim of international law. Jephthah alludes to it in his negotiation with the King of Ammon, and Moses implies it in his farewell address:

When the Most High gave to the nations their
  inheritance,
When He separated the children of men,
He set the borders of the peoples
According to the number of the Children of
  Israel.[4]

When the biblical lawgiver deemed it advisable to legislate against any peoples it was not on account of race. The Amalekites were, according to tradition, kin to the Israelites. They were the offspring of Isaac through Esau. The Draconian measures taken against them were a consequence of their savagery. "He smote the hindmost of thee, all that were enfeebled in the rear when thou wast faint and weary, and he feared not God." He violated the very rudiments of humanity; hence he is to be blotted out from the face of the earth. As the Rabbis explain: "So long as the seed of Amalek exists, the face of God is, as it were, covered (with shame)."[5]

The same is true as regards the Ammonites and Moabites whose peace and prosperity Israel was not to seek. They were assumed to have been the offspring of Lot, Abraham's nephew. It was not, therefore, race prejudice that prompted this prohibition. "They met you not with bread and with water in the way, when ye came forth out of Egypt." What was worse, "they hired against thee Balaam ... to curse thee." Worst of all, the Rabbis add, they made a coalition with the Midianites to seduce Israel to sin, a crime which to them was more reprehensible than murder: since "the slayer deprives his victim only of temporal life, the tempter deprives him of life eternal." Israel is, however, not allowed to hate them permanently. After the tenth generation they are to be admitted into the "assembly of the Lord." As to the Edomites and the Egyptians, the danger of the contagion of their paganism being remote, the Bible ordains that all their wrongs and animosities be forgotten, and nothing but forbearance and fellowship be accorded them. "Thou shalt not abhor an Edomite, for he is thy brother; thou shalt not abhor an Egyptian, because thou wast a stranger in his land. The children of the third generation that are born unto them may enter into the assembly of the Lord."[6]

To be sure, Israel did not always live up to these high ideals. During the long history of Israel's martyrdom there were some of even the saintliest who gave expression to words of hate and bitter denunciation of their oppressors. It is a fact, however, that whenever the wrath of God was invoked in the Bible, in the Talmuds or the ritual, against an individual or a nation, it was evoked by some special atrocity or outrage. It was the cry of pain at the sight of the destruction of his nation that made Jeremiah exclaim: "Pursue them in anger, and destroy them from under the heavens of the Lord." When the Psalmist prayed: "Pour out Thy wrath upon the nations that know Thee not," it was because "they have devoured Jacob, and laid waste his habitation." The much maligned utterance of R. Simeon ben Yohai: "The best of the Gentiles, kill," could be understood when we consider the fiendish persecution he as well as his people had endured at the hands of the Romans. Yet even he qualified his statement with the phrase "in times of war." How little he was prejudiced against gentiles in general can be seen from his declaration that "pagan proselytes are dearer to God than Jewish saints."[7]

Search the Scriptures as we may, we find no ground for the assertion attributed to Jesus in the Sermon on the Mount "Ye have heard that it hath been said, Thou shalt love thy neighbor, and hate thine enemy." Leviticus contains only the first clause, and, as if to assure that no such inference be made, it declares explicitly: "Thou shalt not hate thy brother in thy heart... Thou shalt not take vengeance," etc. Exodus states specifically: "If thou meet thine enemy's ox or his ass going astray, thou shalt surely bring it back to him again ... If thou see the ass of him that hateth thee lying under its burden, thou shalt forbear to pass by him; thou shalt surely release it with him." In Deuteronomy, where the same law is repeated, the word "brother" is substituted for "enemy," so as to make its application as wide as possible. Similarly, the Book of Proverbs enjoins:

> Rejoice not when thine enemy falleth,
> And let not thy heart be glad when he
>   stumbleth ...
> If thine enemy be hungry, give him bread
>   to eat,
> And if he be thirsty, give him water to
>   drink.

Nor were these mere pious counsels. Solomon is said to have been approved by God for not asking the life of his enemies, and the wholehearted Job pleads his cause by testifying:

> If I rejoiced in the destruction of him
>   that hated me,
> Or exulted when evil found him—
> Yea, I suffered not my mouth to sin
> By asking his life with a curse.[8]

Especially noteworthy is the sympathy the Bible displays for those whom we would now call "the forgotten man"—the slave. The Children of Israel were the only people who did not regard the slave as an outcast without human rights. They were also the only people who never sought to conceal the fact that they themselves were sometime slaves. They felt that a slave may morally be the equal of, if not superior to, his owner; that the disgrace was not in being a faithful slave but a cruel master. Whatever, therefore, was hateful to a freeman was not to be exacted of a bondman. The only one who could be sold as a slave was he who had been caught stealing and could not make good his theft. Yet even this practice was denounced by the Prophets, and even in his abject condition the Hebrew slave was better off than many a wage earner of modern times.[9]

This humane legislation was not limited to those of the Hebrew race. It was applied also, with few exceptions, to gentile slaves who fled to Palestine, or were recruited from the ranks of captives of war, or purchased from their own countrymen. These, aliens by nationality and pagans by religion, were not deprived of their rights as human beings. If a slave was struck by his master and thereby lost a tooth or an eye, he obtained his freedom; if he was killed, the master was guilty of manslaughter. During his servitude he was entitled, like his master, to enjoy the rest of the Sabbath. Nor could he be deprived of his rights by being sold or pawned to a Gentile, or exchanged for another slave. In the event of his escape, he might not be returned to his master, but could "dwell in the place ... where it liketh him best." Of course, if he consented to submit to the Abrahamic rite he became a bona fide member of the family, partook of the Paschal lamb, and, if he was the slave of a priest, the slave was permitted to eat of the consecrated food.[10]

The amicable relation between master and servant is reflected in the narratives of Abraham and Eliezer, Jacob and Deborah the nurse of Rebecca, and Boaz and his reapers. Nor was it regarded beneath a master's dignity to marry his slave, or give his daughter in marriage to a slave. Genesis does not gloss the fact that Abraham and Jacob married their slaves, and the Chronicler informs us that, Sheshan "seeing that he had no sons, but daughters ... gave his daughter to Jarha his (Egyptian) servant to wife." As in the case of Abraham and Jacob, the issue of such marriages became, as a rule, integrated with the Children of Israel, and their descendants were forever after regarded as genuine "seed of Abraham."[11]

Such being the attitude of the Israelites toward enemy nationals and declassed foreigners, we need not wonder at their just and fair treatment of those with whom they came in contact in the peaceful pursuits of trade and industry. The Hebrews had no term corresponding to "barbarian" which the Greeks and Romans applied to people of other countries, even as they had no exact equivalent for "slave." To designate a Gentile, the Scriptures use the word *arel* (uncircumcised), *nokhri* or *zar* (stranger). It is significant that the word *ger,* which in Phoenician denoted *slave,* assumed in Palestine the meaning of *resident alien* and in Babylonia that of *proselyte.* In none of these terms is there the implication of inferiority. They were applied by the Hebrews to their own people. This is true also of the word *goi* (nation) which later replaced *nokhri* and *zar.* Thus, God promised Abraham that He would make him "a great *goi.*" It is likewise indiscriminately used in connection with Isaac and Ishmael, Jacob and Esau, and at the revelation of Mount Sinai when the Children of Israel were pledged to constitute themselves "a kingdom of priests, and a holy *goi.*" The Prophets call Israel *goi* both when they praise him for his self-sacrificing loyalty or castigate him for dealing corruptly. The term came to denote a non-Jew exclusively only after the loss of Israel's nationhood. Yet the old usage persisted and is still preserved in the Sabbath afternoon prayer: "Thou are One, and Thy name is One; and who is like Thy people Israel, a unique (or one) *goi* on earth!"[12]

Neither does the Bible arrogate for Palestine a sanctity denied to other countries. It refers to it mostly as the "Land of Canaan," the "Land of the Hebrew," or the "Land of Israel." It regards its soil as sacred only as long as they that dwell upon it serve the Holy One of Israel, and Jerusalem, its capital, as holy only when it is a city of righteousness and full of justice. The God of Scripture is no more limited to space than to time. He appears to Abraham in Chaldea, to Isaac in Philistia, to Jacob in Haran, to Moses in Midian, to Ezekiel in Babylon, to all in Egypt and the Wilderness. "In every place where I will cause My name to be mentioned I will come to thee and bless thee," says Moses in the name of the Lord, and Isaiah in his rapturous vision hears one cherub call unto another:

> Holy, holy, holy is the Lord of Hosts;
> The whole earth is full of His glory!

The children of Israel were quite pleased to learn that the altar erected by the two tribes and a half in the land of Gilead was intended as a witness that they served the same God as their brethren in the land of Canaan (Josh. 22:9f.). In fact, the most ardent hope of the Prophets was that some day there will be "an altar to the Lord in the land of Egypt, and a pillar at the border thereof," and that "all the isles of the nations shall worship Him, every one from his place."[13]

It is interesting to note that the finest expression of God's universality is found in the Psalm attributed to David, whose complaint about being compelled to serve other gods when driven out from the inheritance of the Lord is construed by some to indicate that he believed that God's presence was limited to the Land of Israel:

> Whither shall I go from Thy spirit?
> Or whither shall I flee from Thy presence?
> If I take the wings of the morning,
> And dwell in the uttermost parts of the sea;
> Even there would Thy hand lead me,
> And Thy right hand would hold me.

The great Prophets were no extremists for ritual as ritual, but had an overmastering passion for justice to all. Their righteous indignation was kindled whenever they found man's inhumanity to man; their outcries were the loudest against those who regard the acts and sacrifices as ends in themselves.

> To obey is better than sacrifice,
> And to hearken than the fat of rams,

declares Samuel, and Isaiah protests:

> Bring no more vain oblations,
> It is an offering of abomination unto Me;
> New moon and sabbath, the holding of
>   convocations—
> I cannot endure iniquity along with the
>   solemn assembly.

And in his clarion call which is still heard in every synagogue on the holiest day of the Jewish year, Isaiah reminds his people that the fast which is acceptable to the Lord is

> To loose the fetters of wickedness,
> To undo the bands of the yoke,
> And to let the oppressed go free...
> To deal thy bread to the hungry
> And to bring the poor that are cast out
>   to thy house,
> When thou seest the naked that thou cover
>   him,
> And that thou hide not thyself from thine
>   own flesh.

Hosea, too, asserts that the Lord demands

> ...mercy and not sacrifice,
> And the knowledge of God rather than
>   burnt-offerings.

Amos denies that God ever asked for sacrifices. Micah sums up all the Law and the Prophets when he affirms:

> It hath been told thee, O man, what is good, and
>   what the Lord doth require of thee:
> Only to do justly, and to love mercy, and to walk
>   humbly with Thy God.

Jeremiah reminds the King of Judah that his sin consisted not in his luxurious living but in his wrong doing:

> Did not thy father eat and drink, and do
>   justice and righteousness?
> Then it was well with him.
> He judged the cause of the poor and needy
> Then it was well.
>   Is not this to know Me? saith the Lord.

These ideas are repeatedly reinforced by the Psalmists who sing:

> Sacrifice and meal-offering Thou hast no
>   delight in; ...
> Burnt-offering and sin-offering dost Thou
>   not require. ...
> The sacrifices of God are a broken spirit;
> A broken and a contrite heart, O God, Thou
>   wilt not despise.

These Psalmists declare that he alone will find favor in His sight,

> That hath clean hands, and a pure heart;
> Who hath not taken My name in vain,
> And hath not sworn deceitfully.

It was perhaps with these views in mind that the Prophet of the Restoration, in opposition to those who saw in the rebuilding of the Temple the main object of their repatriation, exclaimed:

> Thus saith the Lord:
> The heaven is My throne,
> And the earth is My footstool;
> Where is the house that he may build
>   unto Me,
> And where is the place that may be
>   My resting-place?[14]

When the Prophets speak scathingly of individuals or nations, it is not because of their race but because of their immorality and inhumanity. They inveigh no less furiously against those of their own people "who hear their words but do them not" than against their heathen contemporaries. In fact, no hate-crazed anti-Semite ever damned Israel more devastatingly than did the Prophets. The Hebrew prince who perverts justice, though he be a scion of the house of David; the Hebrew priest who profanes God's Name, though he be a lineal descendant of the house of Aaron, is equally condemned by these social reformers who believed themselves the mouthpiece of Him who "is of eyes too pure to behold evil." They never condoned or connived at a crime committed by anyone merely because he was an Israelite or a Judean, or because it was perpetrated against a gentile. They drew the line of demarkation not between Jew and non-Jew, but between the righteous and the wicked. It was the gravamen of their teaching that not because of racial preference did God choose the Hebrews, for were not the Patriarchs themselves of gentile and heathen origin?

It is especially in the legal enactments of the Bible that we obtain a glimpse of the genius of Israel in its concern for the welfare of all mankind. Reference has been made to the humane laws governing the treatment in Israel of the under-privileged slave. Needless to say, the "stranger within the gate," whether transient or resident, is put in almost every respect on a par with the rest of the population. He is not to be oppressed, nor humiliated. Any unethical conduct or unsocial act committed against him is as reprehensible as if committed against an Israelite. He, too, is to be loved, even as God loveth him, and gives him His special protection. Every precaution is taken by the legislators to make him feel at home and to guard him against falling a prey to the unscrupulous. "There shall be," enjoins the Bible, "one statute both for you and for the stranger that sojourneth with you, a statute for ever throughout your generations; as ye are, so shall the stranger be before the Lord. One law and one ordinance shall be both for you and for the stranger that sojourneth with you." And again, "The stranger that sojourns with you shall be unto you as the home-born among you, and thou shalt love him as thyself." This is constantly repeated in positive and negative form, and applied to ethical and civic conduct. Magistrates are warned "to judge righteously between man and his brother, and the stranger that is with him," and a curse is pronounced against him "who perverteth the justice due to the stranger."[15]

Speaking generally, the gentile who settled in Palestine, unless he formerly belonged to the nobility or priesthood, was probably better off in his adopted country than in his native land. He could acquire property, and impress even an Israelitish debtor into his service. If employed as a domestic, he was usually integrated into the family and enjoyed, like the rest of the household, Sabbath rest and joy (oneg). If destitute, he was put on an equal footing with the Israelitish poor, fatherless, and widow. If he inadvertently committed a capital crime, the gates of the Cities of Refuge were open for him also; and if he was a repentant sinner, he had the comforting assurance that his fasts and prayers would obtain his forgiveness. So little prejudice was there against the foreigners that Ezekiel, ardent nationalist though he was, provided land-grants for the stranger, too, in his social plan for the reconstruction of his people. The only privilege denied the stranger was that of the royal and priestly prerogatives, probably on the ground that he could not be expected to uphold and defend the national faith. These disabilities, however, did not apply to his children, and he could, by marriage, become the ancestor of the anointed princes and high priests of Israel.[16]

This considerateness for the gentiles was prompted by no utilitarian motive. As we have seen, Abraham interceded in behalf of Abimelech and his wife and his maidservants, and pleaded with God to avert the doom of Sodom and Gomorrah. Solomon, on the occasion of the dedication of the Temple, besought God to hear and do according to all that the stranger calls to Him for. God's house, says Isaiah, was intended to be "a house of prayer for all peoples." Many ceremonials and ordinances connected with the Temple ritual were instituted in behalf of the Gentiles as well as for the Jews, such as the sacrifice of seventy bullocks on Sukkoth (Feast of Tabernacles) to atone for the sins of the seventy nations, and the High Priest's invocation on Yom Kippur (Day of Atonement) of God's blessing upon all mankind.[17]

Perhaps even more illustrative of the universalism of Judaism is the dream of, and faith in, the new world-order, later known as the Kingdom of God, which the Prophets were confident would come to pass in the end of days. This Hope Magnificent, first kindled and never extinguished in the living heart of Israel, was not, as some maintain, the result of oppression, nor were its benefits limited to Israel. Hosea, who lived at a time when the northern kingdom was at the height of its greatness, dreamed of an era when God would renew His covenant even with the beast of the field and the fowls of heaven, and the creeping things of the ground, and would

> Break the bow and the sword, and the battle out
>   of the land,
> And will make them lie down in safety.

Micah and Isaiah, who flourished in Judea during the changing fortunes of the reigns of Uzziah, Jotham, Ahaz, and Hezekiah, both saw visions of a warless, hateless world when

> They shall beat their swords into plowshares,
> And their spears into pruning-hooks;
> Nation shall not lift up sword against nation,
> Neither shall they learn war any more.
> But they shall sit every man under his vine
>   and under his fig-tree;
> And none shall make them afraid.

And Jeremiah, who was fated to drink of the bitter cup of his people's humiliation, anticipated the dawning of a day when everyone would experience God in his heart and strive to serve his fellowman. But for the finest description of this glorious consummation we must go again to Isaiah. Israel's Golden Age, he predicted, would embrace and merge in the Golden Era all of God's handiwork. Nature itself would then cease to be red in talon and claw:

> And the wolf shall dwell with the lamb,
> And the leopard shall lie down with the kid;
> And the calf and the young lion and the
>   fatling together;
> And a little child shall lead them ...
> They shall not hurt nor destroy
> In all My holy mountain;
> For the earth shall be full of the knowledge
>   of the Lord,
> As the waters cover the sea.[18]

These flowers of humanitarianism were produced by the Jews while yet a nation in their own land; these they continued to cultivate even after God seemed to have forsaken them. No change of environment, no vicissitude of fortune, could shake their faith in the Fatherhood of God and the Brotherhood of Man. In fact, like the legendary jewel in Noah's Ark, the humanitarian proclivities of Israel emitted, if possible, an even more brilliant light the more intense became the gloom in which they were steeped and the persecution to which they were exposed. It was when Israel found himself "like a little lamb among seventy wolves" that he most avidly indulged in visions of a world in which political liberty, economic equality, and civic righteousness would transcend the limitations of color, race, and religion.

As Israel never confined his interest exclusively to his own weal, neither did he hesitate to accept, with grateful acknowledgment, the truth and beauty he found in the possession of other people. When the "Men of the Great Assembly" sought to determine which scrolls should be included in the canon of the Bible their acid test was neither the land or the language in which they were produced nor the race or the religion of the authors by whom they were composed. They did not confine themselves to writings which were of undoubted Jewish origin, or which dealt exclusively with the Jewish faith. They took cognizance of the whole range of human thought, and included in their sacred volume not only the laws "which, if a man do, he shall live by them," but the scepticism of Ecclesiastes, the Proverbs of Agur ben Jakeh, and the unorthodox asseverations of Job. It was enough for them, as Carlyle remarks on the Book of Job, that "a noble universality, different from noble patriotism or sectarianism, reigns in it, that it is an epic of sublime sorrow." That none of the authors or *dramatis personae* was seemingly of their kin or conviction did not concern them.[19]

No less revealing of the spirit of Judaism are the books which are excluded from the Canon, but remained popular among the Jews. These apocryphal and pseudepigraphic works, which form the link between what is now called the Old and the New Testaments, bear the hallmarks of the different times and environments in which they were composed. Some of them are saturated with the superstitions of the Babylonians, others with the philosophy of the Grecians. Some were written in Hebrew, others in Aramaic or Greek. But all are pervaded with the spirit of universalism, all of them teach that to obtain favor from God one must love his fellowman and his fellow-creatures; all of them stress the sanctity of all life and hold out the hope of salvation to the whole human race.

Take for instance the Book of Tobit, which Renan calls an "idyl *par excellence* of Jewish piety and domestic happiness." Its scene is laid in Nineveh, the capital of Babylonia, but its hero's inspiration is derived from Jerusalem. He believes in prayer, but it must be associated with alms and righteousness. He insists on honesty and loving-kindness towards all. His parting instructions to his son are: "Turn not away thy face from any poor man, and the face of God shall not be turned away from thee ... Let not the wages of any man, which shall work for thee, tarry with thee, but render it to him out of hand ... And what thou thyself hatest, do to no man." And even when the shadows of death close around him his last moments are brightened not only by the hope that God will again have mercy upon His people, but that

> all nations shall turn to fear the Lord God truly, and shall bury their idols. And all the nations shall bless the Lord, and His people; and all they that love the Lord God in truth and righteousness shall rejoice, showing mercy to our brethren.[20]

The Book of Enoch belongs to another class. It is one of the Apocalypses, written by and for those who would pry into "what is above and what below, what was in the past and what will transpire in the future." But unlike the Gnostics, Enoch does not condemn those who are ignorant of the divine mysteries. He sympathizes with everyone, even with the Fallen Angels in whose behalf he intercedes, and his heart goes out in surpassing pity for all suffering fellowmen. "O, that mine eyes were a cloud of water, that I might weep over you and shed my tears as a cloud of water," he moans. He takes up the cause of all the oppressed and chastises all who are guilty of inhumanity. "Who has permitted you to practice hate and wickedness? . . . Woe to you who love the deeds of unrighteousness . . . Woe to you who hope for misfortune to your neighbor . . . Woe to you who build your houses through the grievous toil of others!" But, like the Prophets of old, Enoch also does not despair. He is sure that in the end of days all wrong will be righted, the earth shall be cleansed from all corruption and every crime, and from all punishment, and from all suffering, and peace and equity shall associate with the sons of men all the days of the world, in every generation of it.[21]

In accordance with a Hebrew custom, which may be traced back to Abraham, it was usual for the head of a family to "command his children and his household after him." Such commands (*zavaot*), or ethical wills, were in the course of time attributed not only to the Patriarchs but to their sons. About the second century, B.C.E., there appeared a collection of *The Testaments of the Twelve Patriarchs,* in which each of the sons of Jacob makes confession of his particular weakness, recommends his favorite virtue, and instructs his posterity how to accumulate treasures in heaven. Reuben warns against jealousy and unchastity, Simeon against envy, Levi against pride, Judah against intemperance and covetousness. On the other hand, Issachar, the husbandman, points to his simple life as a model for his children's imitation:

> I sighed along with all that were heavy-laden, and to the poor I gave my bread. I loved the Lord with all my might, and mankind I also loved, even as my children. Do ye likewise, my children, and all the spirits of Belial will flee from you, and no deed of the wicked will prevail against you; and ye shall subdue every wild beast, for ye will have with you the Lord of Heaven Who walketh with men of simple heart.

Zebulun, the simple fisherman, stresses kindness to all of God's creation:

> And now, my children, hearken unto me. I exhort you to observe the commands of the Lord, and have mercy upon your neighbors, and act compassionately not only toward men, but also toward dumb brutes. . . . For ye must know that I was the first to build a boat for rowing upon the sea, and I plied along the coasts in it, and caught fish for my father's household, until we went down into Egypt. Out of pity I would share my haul with the poor stranger, and if he was sick, or well on in years, I would prepare a savory dish for him, and I gave unto each according to his needs, sympathizing with him in his distress and having pity upon him. . . .

Zebulun cannot recall any sin of which he was guilty, save that he did not disclose to his father what his brothers did to Joseph. Yes, and one other. He saw a man freezing, and having himself nothing to spare, he stole a garment from his father's house, and gave it to him who was in distress. This reminiscence serves him as a text for his exhortation:

> Do ye, therefor, my children, from that which God bestows upon you, show compassion and mercy without hesitation to all men, and give to every man with a good heart. For, in the measure in which man has mercy with his fellowmen God has mercy with him.

The same traits mark the wills of the other Patriarchs. None of them is concerned about his material possessions; all of them even as God foretold of Abraham, command their children and their household after them "to keep the way of the Lord, to do righteousness and justice" to all, even to an enemy.[22]

Perhaps the most influential of the extra-canonical writings was the Book of *Ecclesiasticus,* or the Wisdom of Jesus ben Sira. The author was well versed in the "Law, and the Prophets, and the other books of our fathers." His humanitarianism is on a par with his patriotism, and his constant admonition is for us to be God-like in our love for all:

> The mercy of man is upon his neighbor,
> But the mercy of the Lord is upon all flesh;
> Reproving, and chastening, and teaching,
> And bringing again, as a shepherd doeth his flock.

He urges:

> Be not wroth with thy neighbor for every wrong;
> And do nothing by works of violence. . . .
> Forgive thy neighbor the hurt that he hath done thee,
> And then thy sins shall be pardoned when thou prayest.
> Man cherishes anger against man;
> And doth he seek healing from the Lord?
> Upon man like himself he hath no mercy;
> And doth he make supplication for his own sins? . . .

Ben Sira holds the opinion that the slave is entitled to humane treatment, and whosoever leads the good life is to be honored:

> Entreat not evil a servant that worketh truly
> Nor a hireling that giveth thee his life.
> Let thy soul love a wise servant;
> Defraud him not of liberty. . . .[23]

CHAPTER II

THE IDEA OF HUMANITY AS
ONE FELLOWSHIP

ACCORDING TO THE TALMUD AND AFTER

STRICTLY speaking, the Dispersion refers to the period after
the Jews lost their political independence and became forcibly
scattered among the peoples of the earth. There really never
was a time when there were not some more or less voluntary and permanent Hebrew settlements outside of Palestine.
The ancient bard had already prophesied that Zebulun would
rejoice in his going out and Issachar in his tents. Under Solomon, Judean entrepreneurs reached out thousands of miles
in all directions. In company with the Phoenicians they tra-
versed the Red Sea, and made contacts with India where,
according to some, they left their mark in the formation of
the Indian alphabet. They followed the trade routes through
Arabia and Abyssinia (Ethiopia) as far as Spain, so that
"Canaanite" became synonymous with trader. Joel speaks of
the children of Judah who were sold by the Tyreans "unto
the sons of Jevanim" (Ionians, or Greeks). Jeremiah refers to
Judeans in the land of the North, possibly on the shores of
the Caspian and Black Seas, where, Zechariah tells us, they
have "caused God's spirit to rest." At a later time Sargon,
Sennacherib, and their successors enlisted hundreds of thousands of Israelites into the armies which kept guard over their
conquered provinces. After the Restoration, Artaxerxes Ochus,
Antiochus, Alexander the Great, and Demetrius transported
thousands of families from Babylonia to other countries. By the

23

beginning of the Christian era there were probably three times as many Jews in the lands outside of Palestine as there were in Palestine itself.[1]

No doubt many of these expatriates were assimilated with their neighbors, and became pagans among pagans. But the vast majority clung to the heritage of their fathers, and what is more, they continued to "increase the Torah and glorify it." This was true of the four centuries which elapsed between the conclusion of the "Old Testament" and the commencement of the "New." Indeed, it was during these centuries that the genius of Israel produced most of the Apocrypha and Pseudepigrapha noted above, which, in turn, inspired many of the best parts of the Gospels. It was these centuries which witnessed the development of the Talmud or oral Torah which, even more than the Bible, assured the existence of the Jews as a religious entity amidst the most ruthless enemies that rose up against them.

The sages who came after the Prophets did not think that Judaism received its final touch in the Scriptures. They loved their Bible, pondered over it, counted every letter of it, but they were no bibliolaters. The very reverence which they entertained for their spiritual treasure spurred them on to dig deep into its gold mine of social justice, polish up its nuggets of morality, and by means of their exegesis and hermeneutics palliate or take off the edge of what it still contained of anthropomorphism and racial exclusiveness.

These sages who gave post-biblical Judaism its character and direction were doomed to live in the tragic days preceding the *Hurban* and the centuries of persecution which followed. But the misery in which they were engulfed did not affect the buoyancy and optimism which run like a golden thread through the Bible. Theirs was a "cheerful Godliness." They felt that whatever God made was very good, and said with Ecclesiastes (3:11): "He hath made every thing beautiful in its time." They even ventured to assert that "the Holy One, praised be He, built worlds and destroyed them before he found the present creation according to His liking." Moreover, in God's world nothing is imperfect or superfluous, not even snakes, hornets, and scorpions; and whatever happens, even death and torture, is for the best. They were convinced that God "rejoiced in His work," and they would join with the author of the Wisdom of Solomon in saying:

Thou lovest all things that are
And abhorrest none of the things which Thou didst make;
For never wouldst Thou have formed anything if Thou didst hate it
And how could anything have endured except Thou hadst willed it,
O, Sovereign Lord, Thou Lover of Life![2]

As a lover of life God desires that the world He created be a happy one. Indeed the Rabbis maintain that joyousness is a religious duty. "He causes His Shekinah to rest," they claim, "only on those who are happy because they experienced the joy of goodness (simhah shel mizvah), and will hold man accountable if he failed to indulge in any decent pleasure." Elijah is said to have pointed out to the austere R. Baroka his two companions in the world to come. They were two jesters, who by their funny antics made prisoners forget their misery. When some ultra-pious Jews gave up eating meat and drinking wine because these articles could no longer be used for sacrifices, R. Joshua b. Hananiah reprimanded them, saying that for the same reason they should cease to eat bread and drink water. They also pointed to the many synonyms for joy which abound in Hebrew. Among the seven benedictions which are to be recited at a marriage celebration there is one in which God is praised for creating "joy and gladness, bridegroom and bride, mirth and exultation, pleasure and delight, love, brotherhood, peace and fellowship."[3]

This joyous attitude the Rabbis introduced into the ritual and the various prayers they composed for public and private devotion. Out of the Psalms they selected mostly those which sing of praise, of hope and cheerfulness, but their most favored one was the 145th. This doxology which begins with the exclamation, "How happy are they who dwell in Thy house," and culminates in the call to "all flesh" to bless God's holy name forever and ever, was recommended to be recited thrice daily, with the assurance that he who does so will be rewarded with a special share in the world to come. But the Rabbis did not stop here. A thousand years before St. Francis of Assisi immortalized himself with his *Creatures' Song,* they composed the *Pereḳ Shirah* (Chapter of Song), in which all nature is summoned to join the jubilant praise which pervades the universe. The importance attached to it was so great that it found its way into the Prayerbook, and it, too, was said to be efficacious in bestowing a share of the world to come on those who read it.

The Sages were, as a rule, hesitant about delving into the mystery of the Godhead. They even regarded it as fruitless speculation which has nothing to do with morality, and can lead only to paganism and Gnosticism. With Ben Sira they warned:

> Seek not things that are too hard for thee,
> And search not out things that are above thy strength;
> The things that have been commanded thee, think
>   thereupon,
> For thou hast no need of the things that are secret.

But while they would not argue about God's "Person" they stressed and expatiated upon His attributes, chief among which was His universality, or omnipresence. They sometimes even spoke of Him as "the Space." "There is no place devoid of the Divine Presence." "Wherever thou findest a trace of the footprints of man," they make God say, "there I stand before thee"; and "Whithersoever thou goest, Thy God goeth with thee." God follows those who love Him and receives their prayers even in the house of idolatry.[4]

But their choicest divine attribute was that of mercy. The favorite rabbinic reference to God is *Rahmana,* or *Ab Harahmim* (the Father of Mercies). He is, they declared, not only the Maker but "Defender, Redeemer, and Friend" of all. He created the world in grace, and conducts and renews it in loving-kindness. He is paternally interested in everything which He has made. But His special love is for man. "Beloved is man," says Rabbi Akiba, "for he is created in the image of God; a special love is evinced for him because he is created in the image of God; as it is said, 'For in the image of God made He man.'" Though God is unaffected by the limits of corporeality, the Rabbis depict Him as a Personality, possessing every virtuous excellence, and regardful even of those social amenities which are not directly associated with morality. He clothes the naked, visits the sick, buries the dead, consoles the mourners, returns good for evil, takes counsel with His creatures, adorns the bride, rises before the aged, teaches little children, avoids uncouth expressions, and does not interrupt anyone who addresses Him. Mercy, however, is His "profession." His people are the poor, and "when a beggar stands at your door the Holy One, praised be He, stands at his right hand. He also bestows His gifts even as He sends His rain upon those who know Him and those who know Him not."[5] Nor did the Rabbis regard God's mercy as incompatible with His attribute of justice. On the contrary, they claimed that mercy is but another, even a higher form of justice, because it is "five hundredfold more efficacious." "The Holy One, praised be He, desires to do justice to all." He therefore considers not the crime but the criminal and exacts of everyone "according to his ability." While He exacts of the saints perfection "even to a hair's breadth," He rewards the incorrigible for only a dignified expression or for refraining from doing evil. Accordingly, when He sits in judgment upon idolaters, He uses a different standard from the one He applies to the Jews who, by reason of their longer moral discipline, should be a spiritually stronger people. He judges them by their best representatives, and at night when they abstain from their evil pursuits, He also accepts their prayers even if motivated by material prospects. Because the "Generation of the Flood" mourned for Methuselah, He added seven years to their existence. He rewarded Og for notifying Abraham about the capture of Lot, and Lot's younger daughter for giving her son a more seemly name than her elder sister gave to hers. The rabbinic roster of those who earned God's rewards contains such names as Balak, Balaam, Egypt, Moab, Ashur, Edom (Rome), and Japheth (Greece). This is the motif of the hymn recited during the Ten Days of Repentance:

> And all believe that He lives and exists eternally,
>   He Who is Good, and doeth good to the evil
>   as to the good;
> And all believe that He is good to all,
>   He Who knoweth the inclination of all creatures.[6]

Indeed, God is so anxious to see all His children happy that He shows His displeasure with the elect who did not exert themselves by prayer to save their fellowmen from their inevitable doom. He reproved Noah for not pleading with Him to avert the Flood, and led on Moses to intercede in behalf of those who worshipped the Golden Calf. He yearned for Cain, the Sodomites, and Egyptians to repent, and it was only when all hope for their reformation was gone that He finally resorted to the attribute of strict justice. Yet "even in wrath He remembers mercy." He mourned over those who were destroyed by the Flood "as a father mourns over the loss of his son." When the ministering angels burst forth in hymns of praise at the drowning of the Egyptians He rebuked them, saying, "My handiwork is sinking in the sea, will ye sing My praises?" It grieved Him to have to punish the Egyptians even though the wrongs they perpetrated were against the Israelites, saying, "These are my creatures as well as those, alas that I must destroy these because of those."[7]

Because God is so inexpressibly merciful, He hates to see even the guilty suffer, and weeps over their failings and suffering. According to Rabbi Meir: "When a man is in trouble the Shekinah exclaims: 'He hath caused Me to blush for My head (reason), he hath caused Me to blush for My arm (power).'" In other words, God, as it were, feels ashamed that He did not make him better and did not enable him to avoid his self-incurred punishment. He would save the whole world for the sake of a single man who is righteous; and if there be but one defender against ninety and nine accusers, He would clear the guilty. His sympathy is always with the suffering. He pities them like a father and feels for them like a mother. He is especially susceptible to tears. Thus He presented Esau with Mount Seir, upon which fertilizing showers never cease to fall, because Esau shed two tears when Jacob deprived him of his blessing; and granted Orpah four giant descendants for shedding four tears when she parted with Naomi. He is always on the side of the poor and persecuted: "If a wicked man persecutes a just man, God is on the side of the persecuted just man; if a wicked man persecutes a wicked man, God is on the side of the persecuted wicked man; and even if a just man persecute a wicked man, God is on the side of the persecuted wicked man." Hence, maintain the Rabbis, it is better to be cursed than to curse, for whoever even unintentionally contributes to a fellowman's suffering will not be admitted into the presence of the Shekinah![8]

That God is not a respecter of Jews merely because they are the offspring of Abraham, Isaac, and Jacob was to the Rabbis a truism. They remind us that every gift which He bestowed upon Israel He also bestowed upon the nations. He raised up kings and Prophets for the Gentiles as He did for Israel. He appointed Balaam for the former as He did Moses for the latter. He is ready lovingly to embrace in His eternal arms all the children of men. His first Covenant He made long before the one at Sinai. He made it with Adam and confirmed it with Noah—the progenitors of the entire human race. This Covenant, known as the Noahian Code, consisted of seven articles of rudimentary morality: the prohibition of blasphemy, of disrespect for authority, of murder, incest, robbery, theft, and cruelty to animals. It was the original Torah, and all that the Lord required at that stage of civilization of all mankind. Again, before He presented the Torah to the children of

Israel He offered it first to the children of Esau, to Ammon and Moab, and the children of Ishmael. All of them, however, rejected it. Only as a last resort did God approach the more spiritually inclined seed of Abraham, and they entered with Him into the new, more exacting Covenant with its numerous duties and obligations in order to train them for the arduous task of teaching the human race to attain the same high level of spirituality as Israel. These duties, however, will be discontinued in the time of the Messiah, when humanity will attain its ethical maturity, and the only ceremony that will remain will be the Sacrifice of Thanksgiving.[9]

Even the belief in the Unity of God, which is at the very core of Judaism, the Rabbis did not regard as essential for the salvation of the soul. The righteous Gentiles are as dear to Him as His own priests, and idolatry is far less offensive to Him than immorality. "Would they had forsaken Me, but observed My Commandments" is the interpretation a rabbi boldly gives to the Prophet's outcry: "They have forsaken Me, and have not kept My Commandments." "Ye are Mine," God is represented by the Rabbis as saying, "when ye are as holy as I am," and "only when ye sanctify My Name will I sanctify it over you," or, as R. Judah b. Ilai puts it, "Ye are the children of God when Ye conduct yourselves in a manner becoming His Children."

Judaism is thus not a matter of birth, but of behavior. It is written, says R. Levi, " 'and I have separated you from the nations,' not the nations from you: as one selects the good from the bad. God picks His children wherever they appear, like the gardener his flowers." "I call heaven and earth to witness," states a Midrash, "that whether one be Jew or Gentile, man or woman, bondman or bondwoman, the Divine Spirit will rest upon him according to his deeds." Equally emphatic is the following: "The husband prefers his wife, the son his father, the servant his master, and the maid her mistress. Peradventure, ye think I prefer you to any other? It is taught: 'For the whole earth is Mine.' "[10]

As Israel is God's son only if and when he chooses to be Godlike, so are his national accessories,—his laws and his

GENTILE REACTIONS TO JEWISH IDEALS   31

language,—holy only if they are holy unto the Lord. Neither
of them possesses any intrinsic sanctity. "The Lord did not
choose the nation for the place's sake, but the place for the
nation's sake." "He is present wherever the righteous are
present," says R. Johanan b. Zakkai. The Talmudists seldom
speak of Hebrew as a holy tongue, and still more seldom of
Palestine as the Holy Land. They even previsioned a day
when "all Palestine will be (as holy) as Jerusalem, and all
countries (as holy) as Palestine." One of them did not hesitate to declare that with the fall of the Temple there fell
the iron wall which separated God from Israel. Nor did they
regard Hebrew as the only language worthy to serve as a
vehicle for prayers to God. Prayer should be offered in whatever language one understands. God Himself showed His
respect for Aramaic in the Torah, the Prophets, and the Hagi-
ographa; and for Egyptian when He began the Decalogue
with the word *Anokhi* (I am). He also proclaimed the Torah
in all the seventy languages spoken by man. The translation
of the Bible into the Greek was hailed by many sages as
the fulfillment of Noah's prophecy that the "beauty of Japheth
will adorn the tents of Shem."[11]

The universalism of rabbinic Judaism is reflected also in its
eschatology. As in this world so in the world to come, the
Sages taught, no Jew will be favored because of his race,
nor will the virtuous Gentile be condemned because of his
idolatry. If anything, it will go worse with the former
than with the latter. Jewish scoffers, liars, and hypocrites will
be excluded from the presence of the Shekinah. On Jewish
agnostics, apostates, and informers, "the Gehinnom will shut
its doors," but Gentiles who violate the moral code will suffer
only for a period of twelve months. Some maintain that the
uncircumcised deceased infants of the wicked Jews will have
no share in Paradise, while those of Gentile parents will
"neither live nor be judged." Idolaters will also be saved
through the merits of their children, even as was Terah
through the righteousness of Abraham, and the Ammonites
and Moabites for the sake of Ruth and Naamah. Among those
who are said to have entered Paradise while still alive are

Enoch, Methuselah, Eliezer (the servant of Abraham), Bith-iah, the daughter of Pharaoh, Hiram, the king of Tyre, a slave of R. Judah Hannasi, and a bird by the name of Milham.[12]

No matter who the sinner, God is ever ready to receive him if he but repents. That "repentance, prayer and charity avert the evil decree" was not meant to apply only to Jews. These were available to all. Indeed, "The Holy One, praised be He, looks to (or bids) the nations of the earth to repent, so that He may bring them near beneath His wings." Moses, it is said, was grieved to find many of his people expiating their sins in the lower regions. God explained to him: "Moses, with Me there is no respecting of persons nor taking of gifts; whoever doeth rightly enters Paradise and whoever doeth evilly must descend into hell." On the other hand, when he was amazed to see many Gentiles rewarded in Paradise God pacified him saying:

> Am I not He Whose children you are and Whose Fa-ther I am; Whose brothers you are, and Whose Brother I am; Whose friends you are, and Whose Friend I am; Whose beloved you are, and whose Lover I am? . . . Is there any discrimination before Me between Jew and Gentile, man and woman, male slave and female slave? He who doeth a good deed enters upon his reward!

It is said that R. Judah Hannasi wept when he reflected that God Who is so exacting with Jews permitted a Roman officer "instantaneously to acquire a share in the world to come" when he merely eased the agony of a martyr, or con-tributed to a worthy cause. Yet he should hardly have been surprised. It was in perfect keeping with Jewish tradition about God's way, which transcends, that of the philosopher, the Prophet, and the priest:

> They asked Wisdom what is the punishment of the sinner? Said she, 'Evil pursueth sinners.' They asked Prophecy. She answered, 'The soul that sinneth, it shall die.' They asked the Torah (or the Priestly

Code) and received the reply: 'He shall lay his hand
upon the head of the burnt-offering, and it shall be
accepted for him to make atonement for him.' When
they asked the Holy One, praised be He, He answered:
'Let him repent and he will be forgiven; as it is written:
Good and upright is the Lord, therefore will He
teach sinners in the way.'[13]

Thus, unlike Christianity and Mohammedanism, Judaism
never claimed to be "the only power of God unto salvation."
This must be obtained by character. True, the Scribes and
Pharisees did believe in tithing "mint and anise and cummin,"
and discussed in detail every possible (and impossible) application of the biblical laws. But this was out of an exuberance
of love for their sacred heritage. They did not ignore the
weightier matters of the law, judgment, mercy, and faith.
On the contrary, like the Prophets, like Jesus himself, they
denounced hypocrisy wherever found. "Every person in
whom is hypocrisy," they declared, "brings wrath upon the
world, his prayer remains unheard, is cursed even by the
embryos in their mothers' womb, and will fall into Gehinnom.
A community that is addicted to hypocrisy is loathsome like
an unclean thing and will be driven into exile." Similarly,
"The Holy One, praised be He, hates the person who speaks
one thing with his mouth and another with his heart." The
imitatio Dei, which the Rabbis conceived as the beginning
and end of Judaism, was to be undefiled by selfish motives.[14]

The most heinous offense a Jew can commit against God is
by sinning against his fellowmen. The fast and prayers on
the Day of Atonement expiate for transgressions between man
and God, but for transgressions between man and man the
Day of Atonement brings no expiation until he becomes
reconciled to his fellowman. God is represented as saying,
"More beloved, by Me, are the justice and righteousness
which you perform than all the sacrifices." Again, "Greater
is he who practices charity than he who offers all the sacrifices." "Thy deeds will bring thee near (to God), and thy
deeds will remove thee (from God)," says one of them, while

another declares, "Dearer to God is he who doeth charity than he who offers all the sacrifices, and whoever is just and righteous fills the world with lovingkindness." Others deduce the same doctrines from the verse, "For I desire mercy and not sacrifice." Special favorites were the texts which do not allude specifically to the priests, Levites, or Israel, but to man or the righteous in general, such as "Ye shall keep My statutes and Mine ordinances which, if a man do, he shall live by them"; "Rejoice, ye righteous, in the Lord"; "Do good, O Lord, to the good"; or "Open the gates, that the righteous nation that keepeth faithfulness may enter in." This conviction became so ingrained in Jewish consciousness that no storms of persecution could shake it. Even R. Joshua b. Hananiah, who witnessed the destruction of the Temple and experienced the brutality of Hadrian, asserted: "the righteous of the nations of the earth have a portion in the world to come."[15]

In these views all the Jewish sages concurred through the long centuries of oppression that followed. It was adopted as the authoritative teaching of Judaism by Maimonides, both in his Code and in his Commentary. "Whoever," says he, "accepts the Seven (Noahian) Commandments, and is careful in the observance of them, belongs to the righteous of the nations of the world, and has a portion in the world to come." And again in his reply to an inquirer he states:

> As to your inquiry concerning the nations, know that God requireth the heart, and that all depends upon the intent. Hence the ancient sage stated: 'The righteous of the nations of the world have a portion in the world to come'; if they have acquired what they are capable of acquiring of the knowledge of the Creator, and have ennobled their souls by means of good qualities. There is no doubt that every one who ennobles his soul through the integrity of his personal qualities, through a sound apprehension of the Creator, assuredly has a share in the world to come. Therefore our sages have said, 'A heathen who is engaged

in the study of the Torah is to be regarded like unto the High Priest.'[16]

Even for the unrepentant gentiles, no less than for the unrepentant Jews, some rabbis did not withhold God's all-embracing mercy. There is no "All hope abandon ye who enter here" on the portal of the rabbinic Inferno. According to an apocalyptic Midrash attributed to R. Akiba (who died "for the sanctification of the Name" at the hands of the Romans), at the advent of the Messiah God will sit at the gate of Paradise and deliver a discourse on His new Torah before the saints and the angels. At its conclusion Zerubbabel will rise and recite the *Kaddish* in a voice that will be heard from one end of the earth to the other, and all souls, of Jews and Gentiles, who will be undergoing purification in Gehinnom, will burst out with one grand Amen. At this, God's lovingkindness will be aroused as never before, and He will give the keys of Gehinnom to Michael (the patron angel of Israel) and Gabriel (the patron angel of the Gentiles), saying: "Open ye the gates that the righteous nation that keepeth faithfulness may enter in!" Whereupon the forty thousand gates of Gehinnom will be thrown open and all the denizens of hell will be ushered into Paradise.

Concerning the Messianic age which is to follow the Resurrection, most Rabbis agree that "Every nation and every kingdom which did not oppress Israel will enjoy the bliss of the Millennium." Some, however, like Mar Samuel, were of the opinion that the only difference between the present order and that of the "days of the Messiah" will be in the cessation of prejudices and persecutions. A tradition which goes back to "Moses from Sinai" has it that Elijah, the harbinger of the Messiah, will come "to separate those who are compelled to be near, and to bring together those who were forced apart," including the *mamzerim,* or the illegitimate progeny of Gentile fathers, who were ostracized from the community for no fault of their own. Of them God will say, "Their fathers have sinned, but these unfortunates what have they done? . . . The Sanhedrin hath put them apart because the

Torah commands that a *mamzer* shall be excluded from the assembly of the Lord, but I will comfort them, and make of them pure gold." As for the enemies of Israel they will all be purified of their dross of animosity and will become reconciled to God and God to them, even as it is written:

> 'Moab is My washpot,... Upon Edom do
> I cast my shoe,
> Philistia, will cry aloud unto Me.'

Thereafter there will be neither Jews nor Gentiles; and all the *Mitzvot* (rites) which were intended to discipline them will be abandoned; neither will people say any more *our* God and *their* God; but there will be one humanity on earth, as there is One God in heaven: and all will speak one language, and serve God with the "Sacrifices of Thanksgiving." There will be only this difference between Jews and Gentiles or those who suffered and those who caused suffering: The happiness of the former will be unalloyed with regrets and hence they will worship joyously, the latter will serve Him shamefacedly and tremblingly:

> The Jews will feel like a son who waits upon his father, who thinks 'if I default somewhat in my duty he will not be wroth with me, for he loveth me;' the Gentiles will feel like the servant who saith 'if I default my master may be wroth with me,' and hence he serves with trembling.

It is with them in mind that David composed the second Psalm, which begins:

> 'Why are the nations in an uproar?
> And why do the people mutter in vain?'

and ends:

> 'Serve the Lord with fear, and rejoice
> with trembling,
> Do homage in purity, lest He be angry.'[17]

Accordingly, what the Rabbis required of their people besides faith were "righteousness, justice, loving-kindness, mercy,
truth and peace." These constituted the underlying motif of
the legalistic interpretations of the Halakists (jurists), the
moral disquisitions of the Agadists (preachers), the hymns
and prayers of the liturgists, and the folk-lore and phantasies
which frequently embellish and complement them. Mercy,
however, they seem to have regarded as the greatest of the
qualities which prevail before the Throne of Glory. The Torah,
they maintained, is "from beginning to end mercy," and
"every Prophet was filled with the attribute of mercy both
upon Israel and the nations of the earth." Some of them even
ventured to explain, amplify, and modify the letter of the
Law when it appeared to them to be in conflict with the
spirit of the Law. Thus the Rabbis pronounced the statutes
imposing the death penalty on a *ben sorer* (a stubborn and
rebellious son), and the destruction of an *ir hanidahat* (an
apostate city) as intended merely for academic disquisitions.
Likewise, the *lex talionis,* "an eye for an eye, a tooth for a
tooth," they construed to mean an exaction of pecuniary
satisfaction. In these instances the denunciation attributed
to Jesus is eminently true: namely, the Pharisees "made the
commandments of God of none effect" by their traditions.[18]
The deep humanitarianism of rabbinic Judaism is also
evidenced in the talmudic interpretation of the martial regulations found in the Bible. They were construed to have been
intended only for the wars waged before the conquest of
Palestine, or only in case of defense (*milhemet mitzvah*).
Even then, however, it was pointed out, peace proposals had
to be made before the sword was resorted to, and those who
surrendered were not to be penalized for their resistance.
A war of aggression (*Milhemet reshut*) was surrounded
with so many "sanctions" as to make it almost prohibitory. It
could be declared only by the unanimous decision of the
Great Sanhedrin of seventy-one members. The soldiers might
take their wood and food only in such quantities as they
actually needed, and the besieged city could be invested only
on three sides, so that whoever wished could escape through

the fourth side! Noncombatants, especially women, young girls and boys, were not to be molested.[19]

When these legal and ethical opinions were enunciated, Jews had already been deprived of their nationhood and could no longer wage war against the Gentiles even if they would. Their criminal jurisdiction, too, was very limited, if not abolished altogether. It is, therefore, in the treatment of their slaves, over whom they could exercise complete control, that their humanitarianism appears at its best. These human chattel in which Jews were allowed to traffic in the Middle Ages found among the Jews their only champions and protectors. Ben Sira's plea during the Second Commonwealth found a responsive echo in the talmudic academies of the Diaspora. The Rabbis pleaded the slave's cause on every occasion and legislated against his humiliation and exploitation. They taught that a promise to him is as binding as a promise to a freeman, a wrong done to him is as sinful as a wrong to his master, and threatened those who would violate the chastity of their female slaves with inevitable punishment in the world to come. The Israelites, they maintained, were enslaved by the Egyptians because the offspring of Jacob's free matriarchs lorded it over those of his bondwomen. A rabbinic legend has it that, as a mark of divine approval, the Prophet Elijah appeared to one who shared his meals with his slaves as if they were his equals.

The Rabbis did not indeed abolish slavery altogether, but they recommended emancipation as a deed of great merit and taught that just as it is obligatory to redeem a freeman, so it is to redeem a bondman, and they seized at any trivial pretext to liberate the bondman. R. Eliezer freed his slave because he needed a tenth man to complete the quorum required for religious service. They furthermore insisted on the slave's right to be treated as if he were a free being. If he was manumitted partly, his master could be compelled to complete the manumission to enable him to marry a free woman. If he preferred his own religion he could not be forced to embrace Judaism. These ideas dominated the entire Jewish world. In Egypt, Philo included considerateness for slaves

among his four cardinal virtues and preached: "Behave well
to your servants, as you pray to God that He should behave
toward you. For as we hear them, so shall we be heard, and
as we regard them, so shall we be regarded. Let us show
pity for pity, so that we may receive back like for like." In
Babylonia, Mar Samuel, whose dictum concerning the slave
was: "You may use him but not abuse him," went in search
of a kidnapped female slave, paid her ransom, and then
emancipated her. Abaye remained so attached to his nurse
that he always referred to her as "my mother." In Palestine,
R. Johanan b. Zakkai gave his slave the same meat and
wine that he used for himself, saying, "Did not He that
made me in the womb make him?" Rabban Gamaliel II of
the first century showed utmost consideration for his erudite
slave Tabi, who was quite a scholar, and for Tabita, his bondwoman. So did R. Assi II who lived three centuries later.
Of R. Jose, it is reported that when his wife reproved her
slave, he sided with the latter, quoting from Job:

> If I did despise the cause of my man-servant,
> Or of my maid servant, when they contended with me—
> What then shall I do when God riseth up?[20]

The Rabbis stressed particularly the virtue of truth, with
its corollaries, justice and honesty. "Truth is the seal of the
Holy One, praised be He." He hateth anyone who says "one
thing with the mouth, and another in his heart," for such
a one puts to no effect the whole Torah, whose beginning,
middle, and end is truth. One must not mislead even a
child because he thus teaches him to prevaricate. One's No
or Yes is as binding as his bond, or his oath. This is appli-
cable also to justice, which, however, must not be stern and
vengeful but should be mixed or tempered with mercy. Jerusalem, they claimed, was destroyed because its inhabitants insisted upon the strict letter of the Torah. In all this, the
Gentile is put in a class with the Jew; in some instances he
is even given the advantage over a Jew. Thus a heathen, according to R. Simeon b. Gamaliel, might choose to be tried

either in a Jewish or non-Jewish court, while a Jew is denied such privilege. Jewish enactments are not enforceable on Gentiles, but any laws passed by Gentiles which are not discriminatory, or subversive of the Jewish faith, are as binding upon the Jew as if they were proclaimed by the teachers of the Torah. The legal maxim of Mar Samuel, "The law of the Government is law," became part of the Jewish religion. To render unto Caesar his due is a sacred obligation no matter how intolerant Caesar's Government might be. "He who steals, or conceals, a tax, is like one who sheddeth blood, committeth adultery, and profaneth the Sabbath!"[21]

No less exacting were the Rabbis in their demand for strict honesty in all business transactions. The first question, they said, that one is asked by the heavenly tribunal is, "Didst thou deal honestly with thy fellowman?" They prohibited even those practices which we regard as commonplace. "Of them that monopolize produce, take usury, give short measure, and upset the market, Scripture declares, 'The Lord hath sworn by the pride of Jacob, surely I will never forget any of their works.' " That this applied to Gentiles no less than to Jews is corroborated by the several anecdotes in which the Rabbis refused to benefit by the mistakes made by their non-Jewish tradesmen, and by the laws they laid down for their people's behavior. Though the Gentile is not particular about the dietary laws, it is forbidden to misrepresent to him as permissible, food not permitted to Jews. A Jew who finds aught belonging to a Gentile must restore it to him; if the object is an animal he must take care of it; if he is in the employ of a Gentile, he must not shirk his duty; and he must care for his Gentile neighbor's property as if it were his own. The observant Jew must warn the Gentile against another Jew who might take advantage of him. To maltreat a Gentile is more repugnant to Judaism than to maltreat a Jew, for in addition to the wrong there is also the offense of *hillul Hashem* (profaning the Name of God), which is more heinous than idolatry, and should such a malefactor escape human justice, severe punishment will be meted out to him in the world to come. Even where there is no likelihood of a "profanation of the Name," a Jew must not treat a Gentile unlike a fellow-Jew, and must not take advantage of his weaknesses. This was illustrated by the story that when Joseph was tempted by his pagan mistress, the shades of his father appeared in the window and he heard him say: "The names of thy brothers will be engraven on the jewels of the Ephod. Wilt thou have thy name erased from among theirs?" Whereupon Joseph said to her: "If unmarried women of Gentiles are prohibited to us, how much more their married ones!"[22]

These doctrines were perpetuated in all countries and incorporated into all Jewish legal codes. R. Sherira Gaon, of Babylon, in the tenth century, makes it incumbent on a Jew to testify against his co-religionist who is guilty of an offense against a Gentile. Maimonides, who lived in Egypt in the twelfth century, declares:

> It is forbidden to defraud or deceive any person, even if it be merely in words and will cause no pecuniary loss. . . . The Almighty, praised be His Name, instructed us that on redeeming a Hebrew slave from a Gentile 'He shall reckon with him that bought him,' meaning that he should be careful in his calculations not to cheat the Gentile. . . . Deception, duplicity, cheating and circumvention, are despicable to the Almighty: 'For all that do these things, even all that do unrighteously, are an abomination unto the Lord thy God.'

A Jew, writes R. Judah Hehasid, of Germany, in the same century,

> . . . should never take advantage of the mistake of a Gentile, though the latter may never notice it; and he should put himself out to save him from sustaining a loss by warning him against a suspicious character, even if that person be himself a Jew. . . .

The Holy One, praised be He, executes the judgment of the oppressed, whether Jew or Christian, hence cheat not anybody.

His countryman of the fourteenth century, R. Salman, left an injunction in his last will and testament:

Be honest and conscientious in all your dealings with men, with Gentiles as well as Jews; be kind and obliging to them; do not speak what is superfluous.

Similarly, R. Moses of Coucy, France, in the thirteenth century declares:

It behooves Israel to separate themselves from worldly vanities, and cleave to the seal of the Holy One, which is Truth, and not lie either to a Jew or a Gentile, nor deceive him in the least thing; and to consecrate themselves above others; as it is said: 'The remnant of Israel shall do no iniquity (nor speak lies).'

So also Bahya b. Asher, of Spain, in the thirteenth century:

'Justice, justice shalt thou pursue': justice whether to your benefit or loss; justice in word and in action; justice to Jew and Gentile.

Such statements could be adduced' ad libitum. One more excerpt may not be superfluous. It is from the writing of R. Shneor Zalman, a Polish Jewish sage of the eighteenth century, and author of the very popular Tanya:

It is a sin to rob or steal the merest trifle from a Jew or a Gentile, an adult or a minor; even when the Gentile maltreated the Jew, and the matter involved is not worth a mite. Piety forbids the taking of a thing even when nobody cares for it; such as a splinter from a fence, or a piece of wood for the use of a toothpick![23]

Finally, R. Israel Lipschutz, when explaining the talmudic regulation concerning the ox of an idolater which gored the ox of an Israelite, remarks:

> It is needless to say that we are under obligation to deal justly with our brothers of the nations, who acknowledge God and revere His Torah, and believe that it is divine, and call it Sacred Scripture, and observe of it as much as it is incumbent upon them according to the requirements of our Torah, that is the Seven Commandments, and do not tolerate that even the greatest of their great should do us the least injustice, and do not quench the dimly burning wick; and not only this but they also show great mercy and do kindnesses to our poor, for many and many of them make a livelihood through their generosity; hence how can we be ungrateful, and not say with Joseph: 'How can I do this great wickedness, and sin against God?'[24]

The good life, however, is made up of more than justice and honesty. An important part thereof must be devoted to thoughtfulness for others. A Jew who is not considerate of his fellowman will obtain no mercy from God, and loses his distinction as one of the seed of Abraham, whose chief traits were mercy, modesty, and philanthropy. Noah and Joseph were called righteous, because they were kind to all, even to animals. The three angels whom Abraham entertained appeared to him, one in the guise of a Saracen, one in the guise of a Nabathean, and the third in the guise of an Arab; yet Abraham extended his hospitality to them all. God would not leave even Romulus and Remus, the twins of the Vestal Virgin, who was not only a pagan priestess but an immoral woman, to perish when they had been exposed, and provided a wolf to nurse them till they were rescued by a herdsman.[25] Such conduct is expected also of the faithful Israelite. In deeds of lovingkindness, no less than in the sphere of justice, he must draw no line of demarcation between Jews and Gentiles. In sickness he may profane the Sabbath and discard all religious restrictions for the one as well as for the other; and he must extend a helping hand to all in the hour of distress.

> The poor strangers (Gentiles) must be supported with the poor Israelites; the sick strangers must be visited with the sick Israelites; the dead strangers must be buried with the dead Israelites, on account of the ways of peace.

To this the Talmud Yerushalmi adds: "The Gentile dead are to be eulogized; the Gentile mourners are to be comforted." These injunctions are re-stated in the code of Maimonides:

> Even concerning idolaters our sages have ordained to visit their sick, and to bury their dead with the dead of Israel, on account of the ways of peace. For thus the Scripture saith: 'The Lord is good to all; and His tender mercies are over all His works'; and further we read in the Bible: 'Her ways are ways of pleasantness, and all her paths are peace.' [26]

That most Jews lived up to these requirements is evident by the record of Gentiles represented on Jewish charitable institutions the better to carry out the work of benevolence to all, and by the many stories of sympathy and relief extended by Jews to non-Jews from talmudic times to this day.

The ideal of universal justice and equity which motivated the Rabbis in their capacity as jurists, was still further accentuated by the Aggadists and the authors of books of edification. These teachers of Jewish ethics constantly called on their people to adopt God's attributes and to cooperate with Him in the practice of His "profession," regardless of race or creed. "Be like unto Him," exhorts Abba Saul. "As he is merciful and gracious, be thou also merciful and gracious!" R. Meir makes God Himself plead with His children: "Be like unto Me; as I reward good for evil, so do thou reward good for evil." [27]

The Aggadists or Moralists drew, according to their hermeneutic skill, both upon the popular stories of the Bible and the folk-lore of the people. To them the scriptural cosmogony furnished an inexhaustible source of indoctrination in the equality and brotherhood of all men. Taking the verse "And God made man in His image" as his text, Philo states that every man's intellect is connected with Divine Reason, being an impression from, or a fragment or ray of, that blessed Nature. Less philosophically, the sages of Palestine interpreted it to teach that God's image is to be respected in every man. All souls that came or will come into the world since Adam are, like his, made in the image of God, and were present at the Revelation on Mt. Sinai. All came pure from God, all are alike before Him, and for all of them He yearns when they leave their celestial abode like a father for a daughter who leaves to join her husband. God put one man in the world at the beginning to impress upon us that whoever destroys one life is as if he destroys the whole world, and whoever saves one life is as if he saves the whole world. It was also done to prevent people from boasting of their ancestry, and to caution us that one act of any man may "tip the scales of justice to the side of guilt or the side of merit." [28]

Man, according to the Psalmist is "a little lower than God," and any act, good or evil, done to him is done unto God. To take a human life is deicidal, for it "diminisheth the stature of God; to deny him justice is to disrupt the justice of God; to despise him is to despise Him who spake and the world became." One must not hate even an evil doer, or return evil for evil. "Say not," warns R. Tanhuma, " 'Inasmuch as I have been despised my fellow shall be despised; inasmuch as I have been cursed, my fellow shall be cursed.' Reflect whom thou dost despise: 'In the Image of God created He him.' "
The motto of Ben Azzai was: "Shame not any man," while Ben Zoma used to say: "He who honors God's creatures is honored by Him; he who despises them is despised by Him,

as it is written: 'Them that honor Me will I honor, and they that despise Me shall be lightly esteemed.' "

In general, the pious taught: "Let man love all creatures and envy none." To one who came to a rabbi to ask him how to treat his son who left the faith the answer was given: "Love him. The influence of thy love will lead him to salvation." They also urged that one should pray for the wicked among the Gentiles, even for those who did us wrong. To put anyone to shame was declared to be a cardinal sin to avoid which one should prefer death. Whoever insults a fellowman in public, even if he himself be proficient in the Torah and performs good deeds, will have no share in the world to come; and he who spreads, or even listens to, slanderous reports, is in danger of being classed with idolaters, adulterers, and murderers. Even Moses and Isaiah were severely criticized for speaking illy of their people. Slander indeed was held in such abomination that some rabbis put it on a par with the three cardinal sins (idolatry, unchastity, and murder) for which God "exacts punishment in this world and retains the principal for the world to come." On the other hand, to disregard slander and insult was recommended as a supreme virtue:

> They who are despised, but do not despise; hear themselves maligned, but do not malign; persist in their good deeds out of love; and are happy in spite of their suffering concerning such the Scriptures say 'They that love Him are as the sun when he goeth forth in his might.'[29]

These sentiments were reflected also in the ritual. The *Hallel* (Psalm 113:8) was not recited during the latter part of Passover, because it might seem like rejoicing not only over the liberation of Israel but also over the destruction of the Egyptians. In Palestine, objection was made to the celebration of Purim because it commemorates the evil designs of the Persians. Of Mar Zutra and Rab Ada it is reported that they

never retired before they asked for forgiveness for their enemies. Mar bar Abina's favorite prayer was introduced into
the ritual and is repeated to this day at the three regular
daily services:

> O My God, guard my tongue from evil, and my
> lips from speaking guile; and to such as curse me,
> let my soul be dumb, yea, let my soul be dumb unto
> all as the dust. ... And if any design evil against
> me, speedily make their counsel of no effect, and frus-
> trate their designs.

Prayers intended specially for forgiveness of enemies are
recommended also in various manuals. One of them to be recited before the regular morning devotions is:

> Lo, I solemnly set myself to obey the command 'Thou
> shalt love thy neighbor as thyself.'—O God, forgive,
> I pray Thee, those that have wronged me; forgive
> them in this world and in the next! [30]

Forgiveness, however, is of little ethical value if it is
prompted by a sense of superiority. It must flow from a feeling of humility. Humility is the *sine qua non* of saintliness.
The greatest tribute paid to Hillel was that he, like Moses,
was very humble *(anav)*. God, Himself, is very humble, and
"cannot live in the same world with the haughty and arrogant." He indicated His special love for the lowly and humble
of spirit by selecting Mt. Sinai, the lowest of mountains, for
the scene of the Revelation, and Moses, "the meekest of
men," as the agent through whom the Torah was given,
and by selecting only the gentle animals for His sacrifices.
The "sandal of the Torah is humility; its crown, reverence."
In the saint's ascent to ever higher levels of spirituality the
progressive steps are heedfulness, cleanliness, purity, holiness,
humility, and fear of sin. This is what is meant by "walking
humbly with God." The Jew should pray every day for protection "from arrogance, and the arrogant, whether he be a

Son of the Covenant or not a Son of the Covenant." The
Yalkut admonishes:

> Let one always be unassuming concerning his knowl-
> edge of the Torah and his performance of good deeds
> and his fear of Heaven, not only towards his father
> and his mother, his wife and his children . . . but with
> all those who are near as well as those who are far,
> and even with the Gentile in the market-place.

At the Academy of Yamnia the disciples were taught to say:

> I am (God's) creature, so is my fellowman. I work
> in the city, he works in the field. I hasten to my labor,
> he to his. As he does not boast of his work, neither
> should I of my work. Wilt thou say, I accomplish
> more, and he less, we are taught: 'Whether much or
> little, it matters not, so long as the heart is attuned
> Heavenward.'

In general it was recommended:

> If you have done your fellowman a little wrong, let
> it be in your eyes great; if you have done him much
> good, let it be in your eyes little; if he has done
> you a great wrong, let it be in your eyes little. [31]

The Rabbis enjoined proper respect for all as a religious
duty. Among their various pronouncements are: "Thy neighbor's honor must be as dear to thee as thine own," and "Receive all men with a cheerful, joyous countenance." "Though
he be Esau (a Gentile) remember he is the brother of Jacob."
Thou shalt rise before a hoary head, even if he be an aged
heathen. The High Priest Aaron, according to tradition, never
failed to salute even a sinner. R. Johanan b. Zakkai, it is reported, was always foremost in greeting even a pagan in the
market place, so were Rabban Gamaliel, Abaye, Raba, Rav
Hisda, and others. The last words of R. Eliezer were: "Be
considerate of the dignity of thy fellowman." [32]

For those upon whom their fellowmen have conferred offices of honor or authority, the sages demanded the respect due to their rank: R. Haninah, the Vice High-Priest, taught it as a religious duty to invoke God's blessing upon the Government, for without it "men would swallow each other alive." A special prayer, to be recited at the sight of a king, thanks God for "having imparted of His glory to flesh and blood." It was pointed out that Jacob, Joseph, Elijah, and others paid respect to the powers that were, that Moses and Aaron showed honor to Pharaoh, and that the Shekinah departed from Esther when she called Ahasuerus an abusive name. Since all dignity comes from God, Jews exalt Him by revering it in man. For the same reason they must not rebel against constituted authority, no matter how oppressive, unless they are bidden to deny Him and give up the Torah. [33]

While the sages recommended reasoning with one of another faith, they were averse to ridiculing the honest convictions of anyone, even in the exclusive circle of Jews, "since one who speaks derogatorily of others will ultimately come to speak derogatorily of his own brethren, even of Moses." In this the naive rabbis of Palestine and Babylonia were at one with their more sophisticated co-religionists of Alexandria and Rome. Philo interprets "Thou shalt not curse the gods" to mean, literally, the gods of the heathen. Josephus affirms: "Our legislator hath expressly forbidden us to laugh at and revile those that are esteemed gods by other people." He also includes among the doctrines of Judaism:

> Let not one blaspheme those gods which other cities esteem such; nor may any one steal what belongs to strange temples, nor take away the gifts that are dedicated to other gods.

This is likewise the opinion of Maimonides who states that the harsh biblical prescriptions against idolaters were prompted by the immoral abomination with which they worshiped their gods, and were to apply only to the pagans of Palestine in biblical times. R. Asher b. Yehiel, in his ethical will, entreats his children to be courteous to all, and never speak disparagingly of anyone's faith. According to R. Menahem Meiri: "He who honors God in any righteous manner whatever, even if we do not agree with his belief, should be respected the same as a Jew." During the darkest period of medieval persecution, we hear a Jewish poet sing:

> Thou art Lord,
> And all things are Thy servants, Thy domain,
> And through those that serve idols vain,
> Thine honor is not detracted from,
> For they all aim to Thee to come.

It is a remarkable fact that, notwithstanding the horrors which both Christians and Mohammedans perpetrated against the helpless Jews, the leading spirits of Israel never visited the sins of their followers upon their founders, or minimized the good their religions accomplished. It was during the Crusades that the silence of Jewish history concerning them is first broken. Yet, Judah Halevi (d. 1145), the contemporary Judeo-Spanish poet and philosopher, states in his *Kuzari:*

> The wise providence of God towards Israel may be compared to the planting of a seed of corn. It is placed in the earth, where it seems to be changed into soil, and water, and rottenness, so that it can no longer be recognized. But in very truth it is the seed that has changed the earth and water into its own nature, and raises itself from one stage to another, transforming the elements, and throwing out shoots and leaves. . . . Thus it is with Christians and Moslems. The Torah of Moses has changed them that came into contact with it, even though they seem to have cast the Torah aside. These religions are the preparation and the preface to the Messiah we expect, who is himself the fruit, and whose fruit all will become when they acknowledge Him and all become one tree.

About fifty years later, Maimonides, a victim of Moslem fanaticism, has this to say concerning Christianity and Mohammedanism:

'God is concerned with the Heart,' and as long as their intentions are good it matters little whether their belief be right..... The teachings of Christ, and of Mohammed who arose after him, tend to bring to perfection all mankind, so that they may serve God with one consent. For through them the whole world is full of the words of the Holy Writ and the Commandments—even if they deny the binding character of them now. And when the Messiah doth come, all will return from their errors.

Bahya ibn Pakuda did not hesitate to approve the monastic institutions of the Christians and Mohammedans and to recommend them to his people. "There should be," writes the saintly author of the *Duties of the Heart,* "a class of men who retire from the world to set an example how human passions may be subdued." In southern France the famous scientist and preacher, Jacob Anatoli, at the beginning of the thirteenth century, censured those of his people who believed that Christians have no souls, even though "the foolish Gentiles" claimed, on the authority of the Church, that Jews are possessed of the Devil. The souls of Gentiles are also a portion of the Divine. Every nation has a special mission allotted to it by God, "the Greek for wisdom, the Romans for rulership, as He has chosen Israel for religion."

Similar views were held by Jews in all the centuries that followed and in all the countries in which they lived or found a more or less temporary home. Don Isaac Abravanel, the statesman and commentator, a victim of the Inquisition and an exile from Spain, asserted that the term *nakri* (stranger) should not be applied either to Christians or Moslems, since they also are included in the commandment "Thou shalt love thy neighbor as thyself." R. Isaac Arama, the author of the very popular homiletical *Akedat Yizhak,* himself one of those who, while in Spain, had been compelled to listen to the harangues of conversionary monks, and witnessed, as he wrote, "the smoke of the martyrs' pyres rising incessantly to heaven in all the Spanish kingdoms and the isles," preached:

> We should be grateful to them (Christians) for having accepted so much of the Law and the Prophets through their Messiah ... This, to me, is the best evidence that a divine Providence watches over us in our exile ... seeing that through them our sacred Torah becomes known and accepted among many nations ... and even certain Moslem sects appropriate from it one thing or another ... Hence also it is not likely that the Jews who dwell in their midst will abandon it, since they see Gentiles exalt and extol it, and testify to its truthfulness.

Similarly, R. Jacob Jabez, the opponent of Maimonides' philosophy, who escaped from Portugal to Italy, expressed himself favorably about Christianity. It teaches the nations of the world, he reminds us, about the creation, the merits of the Patriarchs, the Revelation, future reward and punishment, and the resurrection of the dead. "Had the belief in idols continued to this day as it did in times of old, our feet would have, God forfend, long ago have slipped from our own faith." Rabbi Moses Alsheck, of the sixteenth century, in his popular commentary on the Bible, thanks God both for the Christians and the Mohammedans:

> They are indeed two distinct camps, and their laws are different. The one observes the (Abrahamic) covenant ... the other has nothing to do with it ... They are alike in this: Both acknowledge and believe in the Lord Who created the heavens and the earth, the Omniscient and All-Powerful Who rewards and punishes ... give honor to the holy Torah, the Hagiographa and the Prophets ... Their merciful kings

protect us and our religion ... and be it like children
or like slaves, it is our duty to seek their peace and
welfare all the days of our exile. For who knows not
the culture of these men, their grace and kindness and
gentleness in morals and manners, and if we are persecuted it is not they who are to blame but we who
suffer for our sins.

Jacob Emden living in the eighteenth century, a time of
great Jewish suffering and degradation writes in the same
vein:

Christians have many excellent habits and correct
morals. Their pious ones guard themselves from vengeance and hatred, and even from returning evil to an
enemy. They and we would indeed be happy if they
would treat us in accordance with the teaching of
their Evangels which enjoins them: 'Unto him that
smiteth thee on the one cheek offer also the other;
and him that taketh away thy cloak forbid not to
take thy coat also.' For then there would not so many
thousands and tens of thousands of our holy ones be
burned and buried alive for having done no wrong and
spoken no evil; and their masses would not hate us
for loving our Father Who is in heaven, and keeping
the Torah which is the word of the Living God ...
The Nazarene and his disciples themselves, observed
the Sabbath and circumcision, because they were Israelites by birth, but they did not impose these on the
nations because they were not bound to keep them.
The Nazarene has accomplished much good in the
world ... He reinforced and preserved the teachings
of Moses with all his might, and no one of our sages
endeavored more in this regard than he. He would
bring great benefit to the nations of the world, if they
would only not pervert his good intentions, and grasp
the significance of his doctrines in the Evangels.[34]

With the dawn of emancipation and the closer rapprochement which followed in many lands, Jews began to forget the horrors which followed the Crusades, and devoted themselves more and more frequently to an appraisal of Christianity and the founder thereof. Not only in the exhaustive histories of Jost, Graetz, and in special volumes, but also in the textbooks intended for the religious schools, the life of Jesus and the contributions made by Christianity to the spiritual progress of mankind were popularized among the Jews. C. G. Montefiore's *Rabbinic Literature and Gospel Teaching* is generally acknowledged as not only the first of its kind written by a Jew, but one of the best treatises on the subject and is recommended in Christian seminaries as a valuable help for those who are preparing for the Christian ministry. So is *Yeshu Hannozri,* written in Hebrew by the Palestinian scholar, Joseph Klausner. Not that the dogmas of the Church are any more acceptable among Jews today than they had ever been among their ancestors; but Jews have come to recognize that Christianity is playing an important role in the propagation of Jewish ideals and that Jesus lived the life and died the death of a Jewish martyr "for the sanctification of the Name." Says Dr. Kaufmann Kohler, the late great American Jewish theologian:

> It cannot be denied that Paulinian Christianity, while growing into a world-conquering Church, achieved the dissemination of the Sinaitic doctrines as neither Judaism nor the Judeo-Christian sect would have done. The missionary zeal of the Apostle to the heathen caused a fermentation and dissolution in the entire neo-Jewish world, which will not end until all pagan elements are eliminated. Eventually the whole of civilization will accept, through a purified Christianity, the Fatherhood of God, the only Ruler of the world, and the brotherhood of all men as His children...
> We must not be blind to the fact that only her alliance with Rome, her holding in one hand the sword of Esau and in the other the Scriptures of the house of Jacob,

made the Church able to train the crude heathen nations for a life of duty and love, for the willing subordination to a higher power, and caused them to banish vice and cruelty from their deep hold on social and domestic life. Only the powerful Church was able to develop the ancient Jewish institutions of charity and redeeming love into magnificent systems of beneficence, which have led civilization forward toward ideals which will take centuries to develop.

As for Jesus, many Jewish scholars and thinkers of the last century gladly paid tribute to him as one of the greatest of teachers in whom Israel should glory. The modern Jew, writes Dr. Enelow, cannot fail to glory in what Jesus has done for the growth of the ethical and spiritual life of humanity:

The love he has inspired, the solace he has given, the good he had engendered, the hope and joy he has kindled—all that is unequalled in human history. Among the great and the good that the human race has produced, none has even approached Jesus in universality of appeal and sway. He has become the most fascinating figure in history. In him is combined what is best and most mysterious and most enchanting in Israel—the eternal people whose child he was. The Jew cannot help glorying in what Jesus thus has meant to the world; nor can he help hoping that Jesus may yet serve as a bond of union between Jew and Christian, once his teaching is better known and the bane of misunderstanding at last is removed from his words and his ideal.[35]

How free the Sages were from the bias of race and religion is attested by the dictum of R. Johanan b. Napaha: "The heathen in the lands outside of Palestine are not to be classed with idolaters; they only follow the customs of their fathers." Mar Samuel showed more confidence in the faith of some

"Cuthites" than in that of some of his co-religionists. The testimony of a Gentile of good reputation they accepted as readily as that of a Jew, and urged their people to follow the example of the good among the Gentiles. In reply to a question as to what extent one should honor his parents, R. Eliezer cited the behavior of a certain heathen, Dama bar Natina.

The Rabbis also readily paid due homage to the "sages of the Gentiles." They related that King Solomon, when outwitted by the servant of Hiram, King of Tyre, admitted that the Edomites and the Greeks excelled in intelligence. "Who is wise?" asks Ben Zoma and answers, "He who learns from every man." Moreover, "Whoever says a wise thing, is a sage, and should be honored as a *haham,* or *rabbi*"—titles conferred by Jews upon their own sages.[36] Maimonides, himself a great admirer of Aristotle, is of the opinion that "Every idea which seems to be reasonable, and the truth of which is demonstrable, we should not hesitate to accept, whether it be uttered by the Prophets, or by those of the nations of the world." At sight of a wise man, one should thank God for having "imparted of His wisdom to flesh and blood." This is in the *Siddur*—the traditional prayer-book. In the prayer book of the Reform wing of Judaism there is the invocation:

> O Lord, open our eyes that we may see and welcome all truth, whether shining from the annals of ancient revelations or reaching us through the seers of our own time; for Thou hidest not Thy light from any generation of Thy children that feel after Thee and seek Thy guidance.[37]

Besides justice, mercy, and respect for truth and wisdom wherever found, rabbinic Judaism inculcates a profound and abiding interest in, and sympathy with, every human being. "Thou shalt love thy neighbor as thyself," teaches R. Akiba, "is the all-embracing principle of Judaism." R. Simeon b. Eleazar, referring to the second phrase of the same verse, explains: " 'I am the Lord,' I created him, as well as thee:

If thou show love to him, I will surely reward thee; if not, I will surely punish thee." This had already been enunciated by Hillel who taught that "Thou shalt love thy neighbor as thyself" constitutes the whole Torah. With this verse in mind, a Midrash which was edited probably a thousand years later declares: "The heathen is thy neighbor, thy brother; to do him wrong is a sin." During that millennium the fortune of the Jews changed much for the worse, but the attitude of Judaism toward mankind was not altered. The Sages continued to teach that it is the sacred duty of every Jew to love all, help all, and be grateful for the bounties God has bestowed upon the human race as a whole; for "favoring man with knowledge and mortals with understanding"; for "the goodly creatures and the goodly plants which give delight to the children of men"; for "feeding the whole world with His goodness, with grace, with lovingkindness and tender mercies." Of some rabbis it is told that they exchanged gifts with, and participated in, the festive occasions of their pagan friends.[38]

Especially is it the duty of the Jews to seek peace and pursue it not only for themselves but for all humanity, and not only among individuals but, as far as possible, among the nations. Peace, points out R. Hizkiah, is the one commandment to which is added the exhortation "pursue it" (Ps. 34:15) everywhere, any time (Lev. R. 9:15). "The object which the holy Prophet (Moses) is endeavoring to bring to pass throughout the whole of his code of laws," declares Philo, "is to create unanimity and fellowship and agreement and that admixture of differing dispositions by which homes and altars, and nations and countries, and the whole human race, may be conducted to the highest happiness." The Rabbis, too, continually emphasized the merit and importance of peace. For the sake of peace (*mipne darkhe shalom*) they permitted the doing of things, where gentiles are concerned, which otherwise they prohibited. So consecrated were they to this ideal that, they said God would rather have His people sacrifice some truth, or even worship idols, than break the bonds of peace. They lauded even the mimics and clowns of the

Greek and Roman circuses and theatres because, during their entertainments the populace was kept from quarreling with one another! The conversion of an enemy into a friend they held as one of the greatest merits (*mitzvot*). Hence, one should come to the assistance of an enemy before that of a friend. A chapter of the tractate *Derekh Erez* (Good Behavior), which characteristically is included in the talmudic order dealing with damages (*Nezikin*), is devoted exclusively to the ideal of peace:

> Great is peace, for peace is to the world what yeast is to dough. Had not the Holy One, praised be He, given peace on earth, the sword and the beast would demolish it....Great is peace, for in all the commandments of the Torah it is written: 'If thou wilt see,' 'If thou wilt meet,' 'If there will happen,' 'If thou wilt build'... but concerning peace what is written? 'Seek peace and pursue it'—seek it in thy place, pursue it in every other place.... Great is peace, for thus we find even the Torah dissimulate so as to maintain peace between Abraham and Sarah.... Great is peace, for thus we find that the Prophet prevaricated in order not to disturb the peace of Manoah and his wife.... Great is peace, for Israel is called the 'seed of peace.' ... And whosoever loveth peace and pursueth it, and is beforehand in the salutation of peace, the Holy One praised be He, causes him to inherit this world and the world to come; (as it is written):
>
> 'The humble shall inherit the land,
> And delight themselves in the
>   abundance of peace.'[39]

To this it may not be amiss to add the prayer for peace recited on the Sabbath in many modern synagogues:

> Grant us peace, Thy most precious gift, O thou eternal source of peace, and enable Israel to be a messenger of peace unto the peoples of the earth. Bless our

country that it may ever be a stronghold of peace, and its advocate in the councils of nations. May contentment reign within its borders, health and happiness within its homes. Strengthen the bonds of friendship and fellowship among all the inhabitants of our land. Plant virtue in every soul, and may the love of Thy name hallow every home and every heart. Praised be Thou, Giver of peace.

But the Jew was not to be content with merely the peace of non-resistance. One of the directive moral principles of Hillel is "Separate not thyself from the community." Nay, the Jew must ceaselessly strive to make the community a better place in which to live. This solicitude about the well being of his fellow citizens should extend to gentiles as well as to Jews, and to the spiritual as well as to the economic life of the community: "If one see a Gentile about to commit a sin he should restrain him, if it be in his power to do so; for did not the Holy One, praised be He, send the Prophet Jonah to the Ninevites to turn them from their evil ways?" Above all, the Rabbis ordained that one should always pray and hope for the regeneration of mankind and the speedy and final establishment of the Kingdom of God on earth. "A benediction which makes no reference to the Divine Kingdom (of the universe) is no benediction." Furthermore, they introduced the reading of the Book of Ruth on Shabuot, the day of giving of the Torah, and the Book of Jonah on Yom Kippur, the holiest day of the Jewish calendar, to indicate that the conversion of the noble Moabitess and the repentant Ninevites was an earnest of the "far off great event," the larger, universal conversion, which they never doubted was bound to come, "not by power nor by might" but by the spirit of God.[40] This Golden Dream was given expression in the *Alenu* prayer which concludes every Jewish public service:

We therefore hope in Thee, O Lord our God, that we may speedily behold the glory of Thy might, when

Thou wilt remove the abominations from the earth, and the idols will be utterly cut off, when the world will be perfected under the kingdom of the Almighty, and all the children of flesh will call upon Thy name, when Thou wilt turn unto Thyself all the wicked of the earth. Let all the inhabitants of the world perceive and know that unto Thee every knee must bend, every tongue must swear. Before Thee, O Lord our God, let them bow and fall, and unto Thy glorious Name let them give honor; let them all accept the yoke of Thy kingdom, and do Thou reign over them for ever and ever. For the kingdom is Thine, and to all eternity Thou wilt reign in glory.

Similarly in the ritual for Rosh Hashanah God is implored:

Reign Thou in Thy glory over the whole universe, and be exalted above all the earth in Thine honor, and shine forth in the splendor and excellence of Thy might, upon all the inhabitants of the world; that whatsoever hath been made may know that Thou hast made it, and whatsoever hath been created may understand that Thou hast created it, and whatsoever hath breath in its nostrils may say, The Lord God of Israel is King, and His dominion ruleth over all.

And finally in that magnificent hymn of R. Eleazar Kalir, probably of the seventh century, which Israel Zangwill has translated as follows:

> May all the world come to serve Thee,
> And bless Thy glorious Name,
> And Thy righteousness triumphant
> May all the isles acclaim;
> And the peoples may go seeking
> Who knew Thee not before,
> And may the ends of earth praise Thee
> And tell Thy greatness o'er.
> May they build for Thee their altars

Their idols overthrown,
And their graven gods may shame them,
As they turn to Thee alone;
May they worship Thee at sunrise,
And feel Thy kingdom's might;
And impart their understanding
To those astray in night.[41]

GENTILE REACTIONS DURING
THE AGE OF PAGANISM

CHAPTER III

IN THE DAYS OF THE BAALIM

THE HISTORY of Israel begins with a Patriarch who was a proselyte. The "rock" whence they claimed they were hewn was not Shem and certainly not Terah, who was a consistent heathen, but Abraham who abjured the faith of his fathers, and made a covenant with God for himself and his seed forever. His was not quite the religion preached and practiced by his descendants and those who joined and claimed to be his seed in later times. The attribute of God as Jehovah, the Everliving Redeemer, was, according to the Book of Exodus, still unknown to Abraham. His God was the Almighty Judge, the *El Shaddai*. It is as *El Shaddai* that He blesses Abram and changes his name to Abraham; and it is with *El Shaddai* that Isaac blesses Jacob and Jacob blesses his sons. Not until the days of Moses do we find any names compounded with Yah as we find with the popular El or even Shaddai. Abraham, it would seem, believed in a Supreme but not necessarily an Only God, the most high Maker of the heaven and earth, and his only specifically Hebrew rite was the rite of circumcision.[1]

But while his creed may have been elementary, his morality was already of a high order. He practiced the seven Noahian laws. He was brave and fought, but only in self-defense. He preferred peace without victory, and when victory crowned his efforts he refused to take "a thread nor a shoe-latchet" for himself. All he asked was the restitution of what was spent by his friends and the young men who went with him, though they were not of his clan, and his motto was "Let there be no strife, I pray thee, between me and thee, and between my herdsmen and thy herdsmen." He was extraordinarily hospitable without distinction of race or creed. And his heart went out to all mankind. Thus he prayed for the sinful Sodomites, who maltreated his nephew, and for Abimelech the King of Gerar who had designs upon Sarah. In him were embodied the ideals which the Rabbis claimed were to be the characteristic traits of those who would regard themselves as his seed,—the qualities of mercy, modesty, and generosity.[2]

According to the Rabbis, Abraham was one of the very few who reasoned their way into righteousness and the belief in a Supreme Being. Some Semites did it before him. The Chaldeans who subjugated the Sumerians a thousand years previously, and imposed upon them their Semitic language, also left their impress upon their religion. So also did the Hyksos upon that of the Egyptians, and as the latter set up Aten, or Aden, in place of the original divinities, so did the former introduce a belief in a Bel or Baal which resembled the Lord of the Hebrew immigrants. Sumerian records have been discovered in which the god of Eridu is pictured as the Lord of all wisdom and of all mankind, and whatever we may think of the code of Hammurabi, the Semitic king who raised Babylon to the pinnacle of civilization, his insistence on justice has hardly been surpassed by any other code of laws framed by priests and potentates thousands of years afterward. Whether Hammurabi was the biblical Amraphel, against whom Abraham found himself compelled to join battle or not, we know of one contemporary of the Patriarch whose idea of God was similar to that of Abraham, Melchizedek, King of Salem, who met Abraham with bread and wine on his triumphal return, and blessed him in the name of "God Most High, maker of Heaven and earth."[3]

Perhaps it was the call of the country which already in those remote days was known as the land of the Hebrews, that prompted Abraham to leave his native Chaldea for Palestine; and perhaps it was because he was the first of his clan to return from across the river, that he acquired the surname Hebrew. To this cognomen his descendants clung when they left for parts other than Palestine, nor were they mistaken for any other group. Joseph and his brothers were recognized as Hebrews, and the daughter of Pharaoh seemed to have no difficulty in discovering at a glance that Moses, whom the Midianite maidens later took for an Egyptian, was "one of the Hebrews' children." This distinctiveness singled Abraham out from the rest of the Chaldeans, and his higher standard of morality may have made him as unpopular among his countrymen as was Lot among the Sodomites: "This one fellow came in to sojourn, and he will needs play the judge!"[4]

When Abraham arrived at this "old-new Land" of his clan, Palestine was no longer the homogeneous country it probably was when his remote ancestors dwelt in it. Many, if not most, of its autochthonous inhabitants left voluntarily or by compulsion for prosperous Phoenicia, fertile Egypt, or progressive Chaldea. It was penetrated peacefully, or by force of arms, by merchants and soldiers from various parts of Asia, Africa, and Europe. There were the tall, fair mountaineers, known as the Amorites, who swooped down in large numbers from the summits of the Lebanons, a "sinful people" according to the Book of Jubilees "whose wickedness surpassed that of any other," whose "folkways" came to be denounced by the Rabbis. There were the Canaanites from the sea coasts who invaded not only Palestine but Phoenicia, and gave to both the name "the Land of Canaan." There were the Mongoloid Hittites who wrested part of the country from the Amorites, and became the rivals of the Egyptians. There were, of course, the Philistines, because of whom the land acquired also the name of Palestine. These are believed to have come from Crete, and like the Hivites were of the Indo-Germanic derivation.[5]

But this heterogeneous mass, split up in little city-states, most of the time paid tribute either to Chaldea or Egypt, and became in the course of time marked with a certain amount of uniformity. Except for some local variations they spoke the Semitic language, and had a passion for all the gods of the nations with whom they came in contact. By the fifteenth

century before the Christian era, their pantheon was already
full to overflowing with *Baalim* (lords) of every description, big and small, male and female, human, beasts, birds,
and fish, good and evil. They had gods of the sun, the moon,
the storm, and the lightning; gods of the hills and gods of
the valleys, and gods for every locality. The "Lord of the
Gods," however, was the Baal whose consort was Ishtar or
Ashtart, the goddess of love and fecundity. Men and women
worshiped these gods with all sorts of beastliness and cruelty.
To attract their attention they would indulge in all manner
of obscene rites, and to placate them they would gash their
own bodies and tear their hair or submit to castration. "Consecrated" women were found in every temple; the symbols
of Baal and Asherah, sacred poles and tree-stems, were seen
in every place. "If one wished to write all the gods the heathen
worship, all the skins would be insufficient," declares a Midrash
of a much later date. The most brutal worship of all was
that of Moloch, who exacted human sacrifices. Jars containing the skeletons of his infant victims are still in existence.[6]

Into this crowded assemblage of deities Abraham introduced
his newly discovered, or long forgotten, God of righteousness
and mercy. That Abraham at first attracted little attention
we may take for granted, and we may also take it for granted
that those who heard him hardly understood him. *El* or
Shaddai was to them only one more deity among a myriad
of others, probably the protector or progenitor of the Hebrew's
clan. Nor was Abraham fired with the missionary zeal which
characterized his children a thousand years later. His proselytizing must have been rather of the passive than of the
dynamic kind. He circumcised those that were born in his
house and those whom he bought with money, and commanded his children and his household after him, "that
they might keep the way of the Lord, to do righteousness
and justice." At Haran, Shechem, Beth-el, Beer-sheba, the
hotbeds of idolatry, he calls on the name of the Lord, the
God of the universe. To preserve his faith for his posterity he
makes his servant swear by the God of the heaven and the

God of the earth not to take a wife for his son of the daughters of the idolatrous Canaanites.[7]

The posterity of Abràham, however, did not always live up to the hopes entertained by their first Patriarch. Very often they found themselves too weak to resist the allurements of the cults followed by the people among whom they dwelt. Even Jacob had to purge his family of the strange gods which were sacred to Rachel. Nor was the experience of the Children of Israel calculated to deepen their faith in the God of their fathers. Indeed, in the course of time they appear to have forgotten Him, even as He seemed to have forgotten them. Thus when Moses was ordered to inform them that the God of their fathers had sent him unto them, he feared that they would ask, "What is His name?" and Aaron his brother needed but little persuasion to fashion the golden calf before which the people offered sacrifices as the god who brought them out of the land of Egypt.[8]

It was the same with regard to intermarriage. Abraham himself married Hagar, the Egyptian, and Keturah, probably an "Aryan." Jacob married Bilhah and Zilpah and thus supplied four of the twelve Patriarchs with non-Hebraic mothers. Reuben, Simeon, and Judah married Canaanites, Dan a Moabite, Zebulun a Midianite, and Joseph an Egyptian. Dinah, Jacob's only daughter, after her unfortunate experience with her Hivite lover was, according to a midrashic tradition, given in marriage to Job, the Edomite. It is, of course, well known that Moses, too, took as his wife an Ethiopian. According to a rabbinic tradition Eliezer, Aaron's son and his successor to the high priesthood, also married a daughter of Jethro. Such inter-ethnic marriages must have been quite frequent in Egypt. Indeed, the Rabbis tell us that all the tribes, save those of Reuben, Simeon, and Levi, were given to intermarriage. Of the one who was condemned for blasphemy, soon after the Exodus, it is recorded that he was the son of an Israelitish woman by an Egyptian father.[9]

The tendency to intermarry increased with the entrance of the Israelites into the Promised Land. Here they had no

longer to confine themselves to captives or slaves. Most of
them were military adventurers looking for a place in which
to settle. Under such circumstances it was natural that they
should seek mates among the women of the land. "And the
children of Israel dwelt among the Canaanites, the Hittites,
the Amorites, the Perizzites, the Hivites, and the Jebusites;
and they took their daughters to be their wives, and gave
their own daughters to their sons, and served their gods."
The tribe of Benjamin was saved from extinction by the seizure
of the maidens of Jabesh-Gilead, outside of Canaan, when
they crossed over to Shiloh to participate in a religious dance.[10]

The commingling with the *Am Haaretz,* or natives, did
not, however, exhaust the mixture of the Israelites with non-
Israelites. With the gradual development of the monarchic
institutions mercenaries were hired as soldiers of the nobility to fight for the nation. There were Amalekites in the
army of Saul; and it was a warrior son of one of them who
carried the sad news of his death to David. It was also a
"Cushi" who later brought him the tidings of the fate of
Absalom. Ammonites and Moabites occupied positions of
prominence in the reign of David, some of them constituting
his *Gibborim,* or "chief mighty men of valor." Neither Sheba,
who during the civil war led the army of the loyalists, nor
Amasa, who was at the head of the rebels, was an Israelite
by descent. For many years Hittites, Cretans, and Philistines
played such an important role in Israel's political life that
they sometimes decided the fate of the kingdom.

So little prejudice was there against these foreigners that
they never were tempted to deny their national origin. Among
those who fought under Deborah against Jabin, King of
Canaan, were soldiers who were known as having had their
"roots in Amalek," and one of their clan, Abdon the Pira-
thonite, was elevated to the rank of judge. Nor did marriage
with them contaminate their blood. Such marriages as those
of the two sons of Naomi to Ruth and Orpah, daughters of
Moab, and of Ruth to Boaz after her return to the land of
Judah, were of no rare occurrence. In the genealogical lists
of the Book of Chronicles we find that Sheshan gave his

daughter to Jarha his Egyptian servant, and that Mered had a number of children by Bithiah, the daughter of a Pharaoh. It is claimed that Bath-sheba, one of David's wives, was a Hittite, her name being a Semitic slurring of Kuti-Kheba. This would make Solomon a Moabite on his father's side and a Hittite on his mother's. David also married Maachah, the daughter of the King of Geshur, by whom he had Absalom. Had Absalom succeeded to the kingship his dynasty would have been partly Moabite and partly Aramean. Fate, however, decreed that in the veins of the Davidic dynasty should course the blood of more than one of the nations that was traditionally tabooed. Besides the daughter of Pharaoh, Solomon's favorite queen, the mother of Rehoboam who succeeded Solomon was Naamah the Ammonite. A little later, by marrying into the family of Jezebel, daughter of Ethbaal of Sidon, Athaliah became the mother of Ahijah, whose heart "was not with the Lord his God as the heart of David his father." She was also grandmother of Asa who, on the contrary, "did that which was right in the eyes of the Lord, as did David his father."[11]

The gradual change from the nomadic to the agricultural state brought with it also a steadily increasing infiltration into Palestine of merchants and adventurers who spoke Arabic, Aramaic, Syriac, Ethiopic, Egyptian, and various other dialects, Aryan and Semitic. These worshiped all sorts of idols, and practiced all manner of customs. Chief among them were the inhabitants of the coast, especially, the Phoenicians of the north and the Philistines of the south, who offered the services of their artists and artisans for hire, or exchanged their merchandise for the products of the Palestinian soil. As the Israelites lagged behind in the handicrafts, the Philistines obtained a monopoly of the manufacture of agricultural and military instruments. Once during a war with the latter, "there was no smith found throughout the land of Israel. ... So it came to pass in the day of the battle, that there was neither sword nor spear found in the hand of any of the people that were with Saul and with Jonathan." This scarcity of skilled laborers attracted so many of the Philistines that according to certain ethnologists one-fourth of the Palestinian Jews show Philistine lineaments.[12]

But the greatest danger to the religion of Israel lurked in the people they found on their entry into the Land of Israel. "I will not drive them out from before thee in one year.... By little and little I will drive them out from before thee," proved true of the gods even more than of the natives. They surrendered very slowly. In not a few instances the conquerors were lost to the conquered, even as the half tribe of Menasseh on the east of the Jordan was almost entirely swallowed up by the Arameans, the tribe of Reuben by the Moabites, and the tribes of Dan and Asher by the Phoenicians. The Baalim had so long been gods of the country that it was against all the rules of primitive religious ideology to eject them. Many who worshiped Jehovah also worshiped Baal. Others halted between two opinions, and were undecided as to the true God. The result was religious anarchy, or rather synchretism. "Every man did that which was right in his own eyes." *Bamoth* (high places) to Baalim which existed before were left undisturbed, and new ones were erected in their honor. Shechem and Shiloh, Beth-el, Hebron, and Beer-Sheba retained their ancient sanctuaries. The worship of the heavenly bodies continued to be as popular as ever. A grandson of Moses established a pagan shrine in Galilee. Gideon who, in his youth, had endangered his life in fighting Baal and was given the title Jerubaal as a consequence, in his old age, like Solomon after him, fashioned an ephod out of the golden earrings of his subjects, and placed it in Orpah: "and all Israel went astray after it there."[13]

To judge of the extent of idol worship we need but recall the numerous cities which bore a name compounded with "Baal" or with the name of some other god or goddess. The worship of golden calves also continued to be quite common, as was the practice of the obscene rites of the Baal Peor. One of the main centres of idolatry was Baal Brit, in Shechem, which as its name indicates, must have been the symbol of the covenant made between the Israelites and the Canaanites in that section. The Rabbis identify it with *Baal*

Zbub, the god of Ekron, and state that his image, in the shape of a fly (or beetle, reminiscent of the Egyptian scarab), was carried on one's person, and adoringly kissed on frequent occasions. In course of time Jehovah Himself came to be indistinguishable from the Baalim and was worshiped with the same rites, even to the extent of "consecrating" to Him captive and native men and women, and the sacrifice of little boys and girls. The religious condition of the people is thus described in the historic Psalm 106:

> They did not destroy the peoples,
> As the Lord commanded them;
> But mingled themselves with the nations
> And learned their works;
> And they served their idols,
> Which became a snare unto them;
> Yea, they sacrificed their sons and
> their daughters unto demons,
> And shed innocent blood, even the blood
> of their sons and their daughters,
> Whom they sacrificed unto the idols of
> Canaan;
> And the land was polluted with blood.[14]

The thoroughness of the assimilation of the qualities of the native population was evidenced by the names which they gave to their children. In the lengthy lists of Hebrew nomenclature preserved in the Bible we meet with the names of all sorts of unclean animals, the horse, the ass, the dog, the mouse, and the swine; the last was worshiped among the Babylonians as the god of the hunt and war. There are such appellations as crab, shrimp, horseleech, snake, and other forbidden creeping things which were regarded as sacred among the heathen, and of such unclean birds as the raven, the ostrich, and the vulture. Even the few Jah-phoric names would, to a true Hebrew, sound blasphemous, such as, for instance, Abijah or Joab (father of God), Ahijah or Joah, or Ahjo (brother of God), and Benaiah (son of God). Some names among some of the leading personalities of Israel are undisguisedly idolatrous. Saul called his son Eshbaal, Jonathan gave his son the name of Meribaal, and at least one of David's sons bears the suspicious name Beeliada. Perhaps Nun, the name of the father of Joshua, was the metonym for Dagon (fish) the god of the Philistines. This was changed by later scribes, even as they substituted Boshet Gaal for Baal, and Heres (destruction) for Kheres (Sun).[15]

The extent to which idolatry was tolerated is shown in Joshua's assigning the Gibeonites to be hewers of wood and drawers of water for the house of his God. Nor did David see the impropriety of placing the Ark of the Lord in the house of Obed-Edom of Gath, of turning the shrine of the Jebusites into the chief sanctuary of the God of Israel, and of appointing the children of Obed-Edom to serve as priests. Indeed, according to Ezekiel, it continued to be quite the thing to bring in "aliens, uncircumcised in heart and uncircumcised in flesh" to officiate at the Sanctuary. Solomon, the builder of the Temple, was even more than tolerant. He not only did not take away the high places but

> went after Ashtoreth the goddess of the Zidonians, and after Milcom the detestation of the Ammonites. And ... built a high place for Chemosh the detestation of Moab, in the mount that is before Jerusalem, and for Moloch, the detestation of the children of Ammon. And so did he for all the foreign wives, who offered and sacrificed unto their gods.[16]

This royal sanction emboldened the queen mother, who was an Ammonite princess, to impose her religion upon the Israelites. Circumstances greatly favored her efforts. David not only purged his court of those whose loyalty he suspected, but carried his policy of the spoils of office even into the sanctuary. He degraded the Aaronides, the rightful successors to the high-priesthood. A certain Zadok who helped him win the crown of all Israel was made High Priest at the great Bamah at Gibeon, while the sons of Eli were transferred to the then smaller shrines of Jerusalem and Shiloh. Ira, the Jairite, likely a half-breed, was made his "Cohen" or private chaplain. The conservative element was thus eliminated from the courtly and priestly circles. The *Am Haaretz* became ascendant. They refused to pay the taxes imposed upon them by Joshua. They were especially embittered after the Jehovah Temple on Mount Zion began to dominate the older Baal shrines of Palestine.[17]

With the death of Solomon there began the schism which threatened the victory of Baal over Jehovah. The secession of the North from the South was due only partly to the heavy taxes. It was as much religious as economic. The Chronicler plainly states that the trouble arose because Rehoboam "forsook the law of the Lord, and all Israel with him. And ... they had dealt treacherously with the Lord." Yet Rehoboam differed in no way from David and Solomon. His chief offense was that he yielded to the popular demand to continue the ancient shrines of Shechem and Beth-el and Dan, and to encourage the worship at the smaller oracles. As an Ephraimite, the tribe whose root was in Amalek and who was "joined to idols" perhaps more than that of any other tribe, and as one who spent the years of his exile in Egypt, Jeroboam's sympathies were naturally with the natives.[18]

Several strenuous attempts were made by the northern Prophets to regain the waning faith in the God of Israel. Of these the most zealous was Elijah, who hailed from the mountainous district of Gilead. He would brook no compromise. Everywhere he went he called to the people: "How long halt ye between two opinions? If the Lord be God, follow Him; but if Baal, follow him." His fearlessness and fiery zeal inflamed those with whom he came in contact to "fight the battles of the Lord" to the last man. He prevailed even on Ahab to submit to a test of strength between the Lord and Baal. At the king's command the "true" and the "false" prophets were to call to their respective gods in the presence of the people, "the God that answereth by fire, let him be God." The result, according to the Chronicler, was favorable to the God of Israel. After praying in vain to Baal, the fire of the Lord fell, and consumed the burnt-offering, and the wood and the stones, and the dust, and licked up the water that was in the trench, and when all the people saw it, they fell on their faces; and they said: 'The Lord, He is God; the Lord, He is God.'[19]

The situation of those who clung to the God of Israel in those days was dangerous in the extreme. None of those who dared speak out against the Baalim were safe. Most of the Prophets were slain. Many of the Yahvists in the kingdom of Israel had a foretaste of the Marrano-life led by their descendants two thousand years later in the lands of the Inquisition. Hosea left a description of the length to which the Baal priests went in their warfare with the devotees of the God of Israel:

And as troops of robbers wait for a man,
So doth the company of priests;
They murder in the way toward Shechem;
Yea, they commit enormity.[20]

A generation or so after Hosea, Samaria fell before the repeated onslaughts of the Assyrians (721). The kingdom of Israel, which endured for nearly two hundred years, became a howling wilderness. The more cultured and prosperous part of the population was deported to Assyria. There most of them were soon lost among the heathen, thus fulfilling the prediction of the Deuteronomist: "The Lord will bring thee, and thy king whom thou shalt set over thee, unto a nation that thou hast not known, thou nor thy fathers; and there shalt thou serve other gods, wood and stone."

More fiercely than in the Northern Kingdom, the conflict between Yahvism and Baalism raged in Judea, where the sense of nationalism was more strongly developed, and the Yahveh cult more centralized. There the Prophets exerted great influence, and the "holy seed" was tended with the greatest care. With the accession of Asa (915-875 B.C.E.)

Yahvism seemed to take a new lease of life. He put away the "Sodomites," broke the idols, and "even Maachah his mother he removed from being queen, because she had made an abominable image for an Asherah." Probably at the insistence of Azariah, son of Oded, he gathered all the people and, after a solemn sacrifice, pledged them to enter into a covenant "to seek the Lord, the God of their fathers;... and that whosoever would not seek the Lord, the God of Israel, should be put to death, whether small or great, whether man or woman." His son Jehoshaphat (875-51) followed in his footsteps, and sent out missionaries throughout the land to teach the people the Word of God.[21]

But the Baalists would not yield without a struggle. Their chance came when Athaliah, the daughter of Jezebel, married Ahaziah, and after his death seized the throne of Judea. Baal Melkart then became the supreme deity, and those who stood in the way of his worship were ruthlessly destroyed. In desperation, the Yahvists, led by the High Priest Jehoiada who had saved the little prince Joash from the fate suffered by his brothers and relatives, determined to overthrow the government. The conspiracy succeeded. Athaliah was slain in the court of the Temple. Joash, the only survivor of the house of David, was acclaimed king. The shrines of Baal and his images were destroyed, and the king and the populace entered into a new covenant "that they should be the Lord's people."[22]

The internecine war between the Yahvists and the Baalists raged for more than a century, when there arose a reformer of whom it is recorded: "after him there was none like him among all the kings of Judah, nor among them that were before him." Hezekiah (720-692) reopened the Temple which his father had closed, and reinstated the Levites. He also organized the musical service, and rendered it especially attractive and inspiring. Then he made proclamation from Beer-sheba to Dan:

Ye children of Israel, turn back unto the Lord, the God of Abraham, Isaac and Israel.... And be not like your fathers, and like your brethren, who acted treacherously against the Lord.... But yield yourselves, and enter into His sanctuary, which He hath sanctified for ever, and serve the Lord your God, that His fierce anger may turn away from you.

Hezekiah's touching appeal did not meet with the success he anticipated. In Ephraim, Menasseh, and Zebulun, his messengers were generally laughed to scorn. But the neighboring tribes, and all Judah and Benjamin, were enthusiastic. An impressive consecration service was arranged by order of the king for the festival of Passover, and when it was finished,

All Israel that was present went out to the cities of Judah, and broke in pieces the pillars, and hewed down the Asherim, and broke down the high places and the altars out of all Judah and Benjamin, in Ephraim also and Menasseh, until they had destroyed them all.

Hezekiah was thorough in his reforms. He removed even those objects which his predecessors regarded as inoffensive, and demolished the brazen serpent which Moses himself had set up. Of a literary turn of mind, he appointed scribes to copy the proverbs of the wise and compile the ancient Hebrew writings. With him Yahvism begins to assume the form of rabbinic Judaism. No wonder the Rabbis pronounced him a model of the pious Jew, and acclaimed him, as his name indicates, he "who has made firm the bond between Israel and Jehovah." Some even accorded him the title of *Messiah*.[23]

However, Hezekiah's bloodless reformation was of but short duration. With the death of this faithful disciple of Isaiah a reaction set in once more, and wiped away all the reforms inaugurated during his reign. The populace soon forgot the fate of the Assyrians around Jerusalem, but were deeply impressed with the might of the gods who brought about the fall of Samaria. As for the royalty and nobility they had fast become Assyrianized even while still on Palestinian soil.

About a century later, the handful of Yahvists found a powerful ally in Josiah (638-9). With him monotheism and its accompanying iconoclasm came again to the fore. Besides the verbal castigations of the princes and priests by Jeremiah, and the admonitions of a certain woman bearing the un-Hebraic name of Huldah (Weasel), what most influenced his future policy was a book which the High Priest Hilkiah "found" in the Temple while the workingmen were busy restoring it to the condition in which it was before Menasseh allowed it to fall into decay.

The Rabbis claim that the book was the Book of Deuteronomy, that it was hidden in the archives of the Temple during the long reign of Menasseh for fear lest it be thrown into the flames—a fate meted out to other writings of the Yahvists. Modern critics hold that it was a new Book written under the inspiration of the new school of prophets headed by Jeremiah, or perhaps written by Jeremiah himself with whose views it has much in common. Whatever its origin, the Book gives expression to the highest spiritual achievement of the genius of Israel up to that time. In eloquent and moving language, such as a loving teacher would use to instruct his beloved pupils, the Deuteronomist develops his ideas about God and what He expects of Israel. This God is only one, He has no body nor the semblance of a body, and all He requires of Israel is "to walk in all His ways, and to love Him" with all one's heart, and all one's soul, and all one's might. But this love of God must find practical application in love of fellowman. The writer, therefore, pleads with all the emphasis at his command for the broadest justice, mercy, and benevolence not only for an Israelite but also for a stranger, even for one of an enemy-people, such as the Edomite and the Egyptian, even for those who are on the lowest scale of the social ladder, such as the slave. To him every statute and ordinance and commandment, even the Sabbath, was instituted as a reminder of humanitarian obligations, and even circumcision was merely symbolic of God's desire that we "circumcise the foreskin of the heart" and be not stiffnecked.

But loving and merciful as is the Deuteronomist's God to those who worship Him, so implacable is He to those who follow other gods. He is "a devouring fire, a jealous God" and chose Israel to be his own treasure and to proclaim His name to all the peoples that are upon the face of the earth. Israel must therefore avoid whatever may endanger his election, and cause him to forfeit this privilege. He must ruthlessly suppress all idolatrous symbols and all those who hanker after them he must pitilessly exterminate.

> Thou shalt utterly destroy them; thou shalt make no covenant with them, nor show mercy unto them; neither shalt thou make marriages with them; thy daughter thou shalt not give unto his son, nor his daughter shalt thou take unto thy son.... But thus shall ye deal with them: ye shall break down their altars, and dash in pieces their pillars, and hew down their Asherim, and burn their graven images with fire.... and ye shall destroy their name out of that place.... And thou shalt not bring an abomination into thy house, and be accursed like unto it; thou shalt utterly detest it, and thou shalt utterly abhor it; for it is an abominable thing.

Deuteronomy, where both love of God and love of man found their most exalted expression, thus gave sanction to the religious persecutions which have since stained the history of the Synagogue and more especially of the Church. But the Hebraic sanction was to be enforced only against those of Palestine:

> If there arise in the midst of thee a Prophet, or a dreamer of dreams ... saying, 'Let us go after other gods' ... that prophet, or that dreamer of dreams, shall be put to death....
>
> If thy brother, the son of thy mother, or thy son, or thy daughter, or the wife of thy bosom, or thy friend

that is as thy soul, entice thee secretly, saying: 'Let us go and serve other gods'... thou shalt not consent unto him, nor hearken unto him; neither shall thine eye pity him, neither shalt thou spare, neither shalt thou conceal him; but thou shalt surely kill him; thy hand shall be first upon him to put him to death, and afterwards the hand of all the people.... And all Israel shall hear, and fear, and shall do no more any such wickedness as this is in the midst of thee.

If thou shalt hear tell concerning one of thy cities:... 'Certain base fellows have gone out from the midst of thee, and have drawn away the inhabitants of their city, saying: Let us go and serve other gods'... then shalt thou inquire... and behold, if it be the truth... thou shalt surely smite the inhabitants of the city with the edge of the sword, destroying it utterly, and all that is therein and the cattle thereof with the edge of the sword... and it shall be a heap for ever; it shall not be built again.

The terrible comminations of the *Tokahah* (chap. 28) at which section, the Rabbis say, it lay unrolled when discovered, carried the conviction of the Book's inspiration. The Babylonian invasion began to cast its shadows, and the disasters threatened in it seemed to be near fulfillment. Josiah lost no time in executing the demands of the legislator. He convoked all the priests and prophets and the people to Jerusalem and read its contents to them from a platform erected in the court of the Temple. The people were deeply moved, and enthusiastically entered into a new covenant "to walk after the Lord, and to keep His commandments, and His testimonies, and His statutes."[24]

While Josiah was devoting all his energies to enforce the new covenant, he was called upon to rid Palestine of the Scythian hordes which overran the coast country and spread over Samaria. Much against the opposition of Jeremiah, Josiah joined forces with Nechoh II. When Nineveh fell, in fear of the domination of Egypt, he attacked Nechoh II at the battle of Megiddo. The engagement proved disastrous. He was mortally wounded, and the populace crowned Jehoahaz his son in his stead. Palestine was then held for a while by the Egyptians only to be recaptured by Nebuchadnezzar who subdued the Assyrians and drove the Egyptians back to their borders.

The blows which began to fall upon Judea in rapid succession after the battle of Megiddo reacted most unfavorably upon the progress of pure Yahvism. The sophisticated princes, who but recently had upheld the hands of Josiah, soon became skeptical, saying, "The Lord will not do good, neither will He do evil." The pious priests relied on the sacrificial cult, sure that as long as the Temple ritual was maintained their country was safe. Even the Prophets, among them Jeremiah, firmly believed in the inviolability of Jerusalem, hoping that somehow at the last moment God would relent and not let His people suffer destruction. On the other hand, the Baalists became convinced more than ever that the calamities were caused by the irate Baalim. As a consequence, the statues of the gods began to multiply in every city, and "the number of altars in Jerusalem was according to the number of its streets." Those who dared denounce them were put in dungeons or deprived of their lives.[25]

It was a staggering blow and tried the faith and hope of the Prophets, no less than that of the princes, priests, and populace. The old dogma that it was blasphemy even to speak of the destructibility of the Temple was shattered. The majority saw in their degradation a confirmation of the popular, age-old claim that to dishonor the Baalim was to court danger, and that the Queen of Heaven is more potent for good or evil than the Lord of Hosts. It was recalled that with the rise of the reforms under Hezekiah began the decline of Judea's independence. They held that Isaiah was wrong during the reign of Hezekiah; and so seemed to them Jeremiah in the reign of Zedekiah. The Prophet was, therefore, looked upon as the enemy of the people. He was suspected of treason, and those who, against his advice, went to Egypt dragged him along

with them. There they abandoned themselves to every kind
of superstition, sneered at his entreaties and appeals; called
him, according to the Rabbis, son of Rahab the harlot, and
insinuated that his morality was not beyond reproach. The
women were most conspicuous in this attack. Once they defied
him in public and cried:

> As for the word that thou hast spoken to us in the
> name of the Lord, we will not hearken unto thee. But
> we will certainly perform every word that is gone forth
> out of our mouth, to offer unto the Queen of Heaven,
> and to pour out drink-offerings unto her, as we have
> done, we and our fathers, our kings and our princes
> in the cities of Judah, and in the streets of Jerusalem;
> for then we had plenty of food, and were well, and
> saw no evil. But since we left off to offer to the
> Queen of Heaven, and to pour out drink-offerings
> unto her, we have wanted all things, and have been
> consumed by the sword and by the famine.[26]

At last, the rabble, enraged by his reproaches, closed in upon
him and stoned him to death.

He who stood out as "a fortified city, and an iron pillar,
and brazen walls, against the whole land, against the kings
of Judah, against the princes thereof, against the priests thereof,
and against the people of the land,"[27] thus fell a victim to
the fury of his own people. The Baalim appeared victorious
in their battles against the Lord!

CHAPTER IV

EARLY MISSIONARIES
AND CONVERTS

DESPITE the repeated assertion that the Patriarchs builded altars and "called upon the name of the Lord" wherever they went, it does not appear from the Bible that they made a special effort to convert the heathen. Many centuries had to elapse before the Children of Israel became missionary minded, and conceived of themselves as knights-errant in the service of God. It was not in the nature of the ancients to share their special gifts with others. Neither the Egyptians, nor the Greeks, were inclined to impart of their wisdom to outsiders. "It is the business of Jupiter, not mine," was probably at first also the maxim of the early Israelites concerning Jehovah. Thus when Gideon threw down the altar of Baal, his father, himself a Baalist, pleaded, "If he be a God, let him contend for himself," and thus saved his son's life. That a similar view obtained among the Yahvists with regard to their God is shown in the ancient couplet from Micah:

> For let all the people walk each one in
>   the name of its God;
> But we will walk in the name of the Lord,
>   our God, for ever and ever.[1]

Moses was probably the first to proclaim the universal fatherhood of God and the brotherhood of man. His Lord, "merciful and gracious, long-suffering, and abundant in goodness and truth," "loveth the peoples, all His holy ones," and the stranger in particular. He chose Israel to be "a kingdom of priests and a holy people" so as to teach their fellowmen by precept and example. Like Him they were to abhor no one, neither an Edomite, nor even an Egyptian. They are to have the same law for the stranger as for the home-born, and love him as themselves. Whether, as Henry George suggests, the idea of the brotherhood of man gave rise to the belief in the fatherhood of God, or vice versa, Moses insisted on the one as well as on the other. He was a monotheist, he was also a humanitarian.

Besides his profound concern for the well-being of his fellowmen, as indicated in his legislation, Moses was also deeply interested in their spiritual welfare. His constant dread is lest the Gentiles will say that the God of Israel is impotent or indifferent, and thus be confirmed in their idolatry. This fear he transfers even to God Himself, and so sure is he that God would not suffer Israel's enemies to "misdeem" Him, that he resorts to this possibility as a potent plea whenever his people's fate hangs in the balance, and invariably he receives the assurance, "I have pardoned according to thy word."

While Moses indeed nowhere prescribed it as a duty to proselytize, he indicated his anxiety in no uncertain manner that others be converted. He ordained that at the end of every seventh year, during the Feast of Tabernacles, the stranger should be included among those assembled to hear the reading of the Torah, in the hope, as Ibn Ezra comments, that hearing it they might become interested and ultimately accept its teachings as their guide. For the same reason he addressed his parting words not to Israel alone but to the stranger also and to the bondman "from the hewer of wood to the drawer of water." He did not forget even the "stranger without the gates." Among his last injunctions was that huge stones be set up by the Jordan, and plastered with plaster, upon which should be inscribed all the words of the Torah very plainly, so that all the peoples of the earth "may know the hand of the Lord that it is mighty." This command was executed by his loyal servant Joshua.[2]

The mission of Israel began to loom ever larger with the rise of the Prophets of the middle of the eighth century. To these fearless champions of the good life, ethical conduct was far more important than ethnic descent, and to them, all of God's children were equally dear. Because Israel was first-born spiritually, he is obligated to be a guide and mentor of his less mature brothers. He is to teach by precept and example, to be the servant of the Lord, in the accomplishment of His design to establish the kingdom of heaven among the inhabitants of the earth. Intensely patriotic though they were, the Prophets looked upon Zion only as the pulpit out of which would go forth the Torah, and upon Israel as an instrument to spread the word of the Lord. They never, however, advocated that this great consummation should be brought about by force. The Elijah at Mt. Carmel was not their ideal, but the Elijah who would turn the hearts of the children to their fathers. The downfall of Samaria, according to Hosea, would follow the mistaken zeal of those who were guilty of the "blood of Jezreel." Instruction and persuasion were the only weapons of which they approved. Their motto was: "Not by might, nor by strength, but by My Spirit, saith the Lord."

The Prophets necessarily addressed themselves to their countrymen, but many of their "burdens" were direct appeals to the Gentiles. It is not unlikely that they preached to the Gentiles in *Aramaic* which for centuries was the *lingua franca* from Tyre to Carthage, and was understood, if not spoken, in Palestine. Thus Elijah seems to have found no difficulty in conversing with the widow of Zarephath, Phoenicia, and with the King of Damascus; while the captive Hebrew maiden speaks to her mistress, as does Gehazi to her master, without appearing to be handicapped by the language. Jeremiah uses an Aramaic sentence in a communication which he sent to his co-religionists in Babylon. Nor does Jonah plead his ignorance of Aramaic as a reason for his refusal to go to Nineveh. Indeed, the Semitic dialects of those times were so similar that it required but little effort by one who spoke one of them to master another. The language in which Mesha, King of Moab, records the victory of Chemosh over Yahveh on the Moabite Stone discovered at Dibon, is not unlike the lan-

guage in the Bible in which the Israelite Chronicler claims
the victory for Yahveh over Chemosh.[3]

Whatever the language the Prophets used as their medium
in addressing the Gentiles, they displayed the same holy zeal
when they pleaded with those who were at ease in Zion. To
both they denounced the enormity of their vices, and depicted
the blessedness and happiness of those who walked in the ways
of the Lord. Tyre and Zidon, Assyria or Babylonia, Arabia and
Ethiopia, Persia and Syria, Philistia, Ammon, Moab, and Edom
—all nations with whom for better or for worse Palestine came
in contact, or of whom they had any knowledge, were included
in their righteous indignation when they acted sinfully, and
comforted with their divine consolation when they suffered
undeservedly. Amos hears the voice of God roar against
the Arameans, the Philistines, the Ammonites and Moabites,
and pronounces their doom not only because of their brutality to Israel but to the Edomites:

> Thus saith the Lord:
> For three transgressions of Moab,
> Yea, for four, I will not reverse it:
> Because he burned the bones of the king
>   of Edom into lime,
> So will I send a fire upon Moab....
> And will slay all the princes thereof
>   with him,
> Saith the Lord.

Isaiah vents his irrepressible ire, and employs the same heroic
measures to attract the attention and influence the conduct of
both the Ashdodites and his own people. His heart goes out
to the caravans of the Dedonites. He praises the Temanites
who meet the refugees with bread, and appeals to their kinsmen to do likewise:

> Unto him that is thirsty bring ye water. . . .
> For they fled away from the swords, from
>   the drawn sword,

And from the bent bow, and from the
grievousness of war.

He inveighs against Tyre, Philistia, Babylonia, Moab, and
Egypt. But he despairs of none. After seventy years, he
declares, God will remember "the oppressed virgin daughter
of Tyre, and she shall return to her hire, and shall have
commerce with all the kingdoms of the world." He cannot
suppress his pity for the harassed Moabites, Israel's traditional enemy:

My heart crieth out for Moab. . . .
I will weep with the weeping of Jazer
For the vine of Sibmah;
I will water thee with my tears,
O Heshbon and Elealeh;
For on thy summer fruits and upon thy harvest
The battle shout is fallen. . . .

And he beseeches his own people in their behalf:

Give counsel, execute justice;
Make thy shadow as the night in the midst
of the noonday;
Hide the outcasts; betray not the fugitive.
Let mine outcasts dwell with thee;
As for Moab, be thou a covert to him from the
face of the spoiler.

No prophet of the pre-exilic period, however, excelled
Jeremiah (638-9) in his conception of the missionary destiny
of his people, or in the depth of his sympathy with and
hope for the nations of the world. From the very beginning
of his career he dedicated himself to be a "prophet of the
Gentiles," and his great heart ever went out to all the harassed
and underprivileged of mankind. He grieved over the sins
not only of Israel but of Egypt, Philistia, Edom, Moab,
Ammon, Tyre, Zidon, Arabia, Persia, and Babylonia. His
compassion, like Isaiah's, was kindled at the misery of the

Temanites and Dedonites, as if they were his own flesh and
blood, and he sought to solace them with the assurance that
God would not be unmindful of their distress:

> Leave thy fatherless children, I will rear them,
> And let thy widows trust in Me.

It is the same with the Kedarites and Hagarites with whom
he pleads:

> Flee ye, flit far off, dwell deep,
> O ye inhabitants of Hazar, saith the Lord;
> For Nebuchadnezzar king of Babylon hath
>   taken counsel against you.

So did he bemoan the fate of Moab:

> My heart moaneth for Moab like a pipe,
> And my heart moaneth like pipes for Kir Hares;

And so he cried out when he beheld the doom of Philistia:

> O thou sword of the Lord,
> How long will it be ere thou be quiet?
> Put up thyself in thy scabbard,
> Rest and be still.

So also did he rejoice to think that Egypt might yet be restored to her former glory, and that God would yet bring
back the captivity of Elim and of Moab.[4]

Similar expressions may be found in the writings of the
other Prophets who flourished during the two centuries
that elapsed between the time of Isaiah the First and Isaiah
the Second. Their thoughts were with their own people first,
but no less with mankind. The punishments they threatened
and the promises they upheld were for Israel and the other
nations. Israel served them mainly as a text for their preachments. To Israel's exaltation and to his humiliation they
pointed as proof that God rewards the righteous and does
not clear the guilty. Even when they visioned the golden age

when Israel will be "saved by the Lord with an everlasting salvation" they did not forget the other nations. The great Day of the Lord, they said, will purify and redeem the whole human race. People will wander from sea to sea and from the north even to the east "to seek the word of the Lord and shall not find (enough of) it." Joel exclaims in the name of God:

> I will pour out My spirit upon all flesh . . . and
> also upon the servants and upon the handmaids
> In those days will I pour out My spirit.

In the midst of the horrors of the advancing Scythian hordes Zephaniah did not waver in his firm faith in the ultimate victory of Yahvism over paganism. When the Day of the Lord will dawn at last, he foretells,

> Then shall all the isles of the nations worship Him,
> Every one from its place. . . .
> For then will I turn to the peoples a pure language,
> That they may all call upon the name of the Lord,
> To serve Him with one consent.

But the voice that rang out loudest of all was that of Isaiah. No nation was to him beyond the hope of God's redeeming love, no people doomed to grope forever in the darkness of paganism. Tyre will be like a reformed harlot, and will consecrate her ill-gotten gains "for them that dwell before the Lord." Egypt and Assyria shall become a blessing in the midst of the earth, and God will rejoice over them, saying:

> Blessed be Egypt My people, and Assyria the work
> of My hands, and Israel Mine inheritance;

while all over the world:

> Many peoples shall go and say:
> 'Come ye, and let us go up to the mountain
>   of the Lord,

> To the house of the God of Jacob;
> and he will teach us of His ways,
> and we will walk in His paths.'
> For out of Zion shall go forth the Torah,
> and the Word of the Lord from Jerusalem.⁵

The missionary ideal attained its highest peak in Jeremiah. To him the reclamation of the nations was a sacred obligation which no Israelite dared shirk. It was not of his own free will that he became a prophet but by divine compulsion. God had enticed him and overcome him, and his struggle against his destiny was in vain. The same, according to him, is true of Israel. They were divinely commissioned to be missionaries, whether they liked it or not. They might as well accept their fate, and perform their function in God's plan with joy, until

> Nations bless themselves by Him,
> And in Him shall they glory.

Otherwise, he will "pluck them off" from their country, scatter them among the nations until their task will have been performed. If, however, the Gentiles refuse to be converted despite the efforts of Israel, then the Lord will "pluck them off" in their turn and exile them as He did Israel.

> And it shall come to pass, if they will diligently learn the ways of My people to swear by My name: 'As the Lord liveth,' even as they taught My people to swear by Baal; then shall they be built up in the midst of My people. But if they will not hearken, then will I pluck up that nation, plucking up and destroying it, saith the Lord.

Jeremiah entertains no doubt about the conversion of the nations. Like Isaiah he foresees them "built up" in the midst of Israel, and "gathered to the name of the Lord, to Jerusalem," where they shall confess and say: "Our fathers have inherited nought but lies; vanity and things wherein there

is no profit." Then will the ancient covenant between God
and Israel be completed in performance, and Israel's mission
be fulfilled in realization. The teacher will no longer have
to teach, for the pupils will know as much as he. The number of non-Israelitish worshippers of the God of Israel will
be so great that His original devotees will be lost in the multitude. And they shall say no more:

> The ark of the covenant of the Lord; neither shall
> it come to mind; neither shall they make mention
> of it; neither shall they miss it; neither shall it be
> made any more..... And they shall teach no more
> every man his neighbor, and every man his brother,
> saying: 'Know the Lord'; for they shall all know Me,
> from the least of them unto the greatest of them,
> saith the Lord. [6]

These predictions for the dim and distant future were no
doubt suggested by the experiences of the past. There have
been not only reversions among the Israelites, but conversions
of many individuals and even clans and tribes both before
and during the time of the Prophets, some of them voluntarily,
some by coercion. Among the most devoted disciples of the
Prophets themselves there were some who were either of the
Am Haaretz or resident aliens from various races and nations.

The Prophets and the Psalmists were no doubt familiar
with the tradition that Abraham, the founder of his people,
was himself a convert. "God called him when he was but
one, and blessed him and made him many," says Isaiah.
The Deuteronomist required each participant in the festival
of the ripening of the first fruit to profess: "A wandering
Aramean was my father, and he went down into Egypt, and
sojourned there, few in number; and he became there a
nation, great, mighty and populous." Melchizedek is referred
to by a Psalmist as a model priest. And they certainly must
have known about Jethro the father-in-law of Moses, Ruth
the ancestress of David, and others whose offspring became
merged with the rest of the Israelites and were no longer

distinguishable from the rest of "the seed of Abraham." But besides these ancient worthies there were whole groups which accepted the faith of Israel, in more or less modified form, but who preserved their tribal entity. Among the better known of these were the Gibeonites. [7]

These people were Hivites, or Greeks (Achaian) of Indo-Germanic derivation, in whose chief city was a "great high place." When the inhabitants of that place heard what Joshua had done to Jericho and to Ai, they sent envoys to him and beguiled him by false representation into an alliance. After the covenant was ratified Joshua discovered his mistake, but instead of cancelling the covenant, he punished them by making them "hewers of wood and drawers of water for the congregation, and for the altar of the Lord" forever after. Later Saul in one of his fits of melancholy slew many of them, but they avenged themselves under David who at their insistence delivered to them seven of Saul's sons to be hanged "up unto the Lord in Gibeah of Saul, the chosen of the Lord." [8]

This brutal behavior on their part, and perhaps also because their conversion was not of their own free will, segregated them for many generations from the rest of the congregation of Israel, but they remained undisturbed in their sacerdotal functions around the Temple. Their numbers were swelled with other forced converts whom David made of his captive slaves, and whom also he turned over to the Levites for which reason they came to be known as *Nethinim* (devoted or subjected ones). With them also were amalgamated other captives, such as the Arab Meunim and Nefusim. All of them seem to have taken a long time to acquire the rudiments of Hebrew morality, even after they were compelled to abjure idolatry. It is claimed that they supplied most, if not all, of the *Kedeshoth,* or consecrated prostitutes, who infested the Temple court during the supremacy of the Baalim. For this reason, the Rabbis claim, David (or Ezra) interdicted them from marrying pure Jews, and allowed them only to marry proselytes (of the same category), freedmen, illegitimates, and foundlings. It is interesting to note that while in the Syriac version of the Scriptures *Nethinim* is translated by *gayyura* (proselytes), the Septuagint renders the word *Hierodules,* or temple slaves of a certain kind, and this rendition is adopted by Josephus.

With the improvement of their moral conduct the *Nethinim* were gradually assimilated with the rest of the people. They were among those who at the Restoration had separated themselves from the *Am Haaretz,* and cleaving unto "their brethren" entered into a vow and took an oath:

> to walk in God's law .... and to observe and do all the commandments of the Lord our God, and His ordinances and His statutes; and that we should not give our daughters unto the peoples of the land, nor take their daughters for our sons.

Thenceforth they became an integral part of the "seed of Abraham." Even the extremist Ezra granted them the privilege with the other Jews of building the new Temple, and ordained that like upon the legitimate priests and Levites "it shall not be lawful to impose tribute, impost, or toll upon them." [9]

The lot of the Rechabites was a much happier one from the start. Their origin is shrouded in obscurity. As they are connected with the Kenites and Calebites who are identified in the Book of Judges with "Hobab" the father-in-law of Moses, some modern critics claim for them a Midianitish ancestry, among whom the future legislator found the religious conception of his forbears preserved in a higher state of purity than among his own people. According to this it would be Moses and not Hobab-Jethro who became a *Ger,* or convert to Judaism, as the term was later understood. Some claim that the kindred clans of the Kenites, Calebites, and Jerahmeelites, in whose country David took refuge for a while, were Edomites. Whatever their racial origin, they belonged to a people that was hostile to the Israelites. But the Bible and Jewish tradition have nothing but what is good and admirable to say about them, and Jewish genealogists would lead us to believe that if they were not descended from Abraham and Sarah they were the offspring of Abraham and Keturah his concubine.

The Kenites seem to have become attracted to the Israelites soon after the latter departed from Egypt. Unlike Jethro who returned to his native land, they preferred to share the fortunes of the fugitives, and probably acted as their guides and guards in the wilderness. Perhaps it was to them that Balaam referred in his prophecy that they, too, would be carried away by the Assyrians. With the Israelites they entered the Promised Land. It was one of their clan that completed the Israelite victory over Jabin, (one of the kings of Canaan), and inspired Deborah to pen her famous lines:

> Blessed above women shall Jael be,
> The wife of Heber the Kenite.
> Above women in the tent shall she be blessed. [10]

The Israelites in return showed their friendliness to these foreigners on several occasions. When Saul heard that some of the Kenites settled among the Amalekites against whom he waged war, he sent word: "Go, depart, get you down. from the Amalekites, lest I destroy you with them, for ye showed kindness to all the children of Israel, when they came up out of Egypt." David, too, presented them with a share of the spoils which he took from the Amalekites. To judge from their name they must have been originally forgers of cutting instruments of brass and iron. In later times, however, they devoted themselves, like the Jebusites among whom they settled, to the cultivation of the soil. They were also lovers of music, and became noted as scribes. [11]

According to the Chronicler the eponymous ancestor of the Kenites was Jabez who became "more honorable than his brethren." The Chronicler also hints at the probable cause of his conversion. His mother called him Jabez because she bore him with pain. Perhaps he was sickly as a child, and later became healthy and strong, for we are told, that when he grew up he "called on the God of Israel, saying, 'Oh that Thou wouldst bless me indeed, and enlarge my border, and that Thy hand might be with me, and that Thou wouldst work deliverance from evil, that it may not pain me.' And God granted him that which he requested." [12]

For some unknown reason, a Heber of the Kenite clan separated himself from his kin in the early days of the Judges, and his progeny went by the eponym of Rechab. Of these the most distinguished was J(eh)onadab who, as we have seen, participated (c. 842) in the bloody crusade led by Jehu against the house of Ahab and the devotees of the Baalim. Most of them preferred the nomadic life, but some occupied themselves with the making of pottery and the copying of books. They never, however, outgrew the simplicity and freedom of the desert life, and they looked with contempt upon the luxury and indulgence not only of the idolaters but of their Judean co-religionists. They remained loyal to the precept of Jonadab, their patriarch, to drink no wine, nor build houses, nor sow seed, nor have or plant vineyards, but to dwell in tents. They were held in such high esteem that Jeremiah pointed to them as models of faithfulness, and at the Restoration one of their number, Malachiah, was given the honor of setting up one of the gates of the new Jerusalem, and was appointed to be ruler of the district of Beth-cherem. [13]

The Jerahmeelites were another branch of the Rechabites who became attached to the Israelites. Some of them, however, remained hostile despite their supposed conversion. One of them, Ishmael, twenty-four generations removed from the original Jerahmeel, was instrumental in the massacre of Gedaliah and his men. His father, the Rabbis declare, married Atarah, a non-Jewish princess, for the sake of glory and allowed himself to become a tool in the hands of the Ammonite king, in the hope of succeeding to the throne of Judah. Wherefore the saying came into being: "Trust not a proselyte even to the twenty-fourth generation." [14]

Differing both from the Gibeonites who "judaised" from political pressure, and the Kenites or Rechabites who adopted the faith from an inner, spiritual compulsion, were the Samaritans. According to the biblical account they were originally a mixed multitude transplanted into North Palestine by Sargon from Babylonia and other conquered countries (722 B.C.E.). Owing to the depopulation of the country it became in the course of time a haunt for savage beasts, especially lions. The new pagan settlers attributed their harassment to the fact that "they knew not the manner of the god of the land." In their distress they appealed to the king of Assyria. He ordered some of the captive Hebrew priests to go and teach them how to worship the God of Israel. As a result they learned to fear the Lord, but for greater safety, they did not discard their own gods, and even burnt their children to "Adrammelech and Anammelech the gods of Sepharvayim." Josephus maintains that they were mostly Persians. Not unlikely they were Assyrians who were stationed there to check the Scythians whose objective was the invasion of Assyria. [15]

The Prophets exerted themselves to the utmost to instruct them in ethical monotheism, and pleaded with them to relinquish their idolatry. But for centuries their voice was like a voice calling in the wilderness. All that the Samaritans at first learned from their teachers were a few ceremonials and some moral precepts. The higher concepts of God and ethics evaded their spiritual grasp. An unknown Prophet gave expression to his despair:

I gave access to them that asked not of Me,
I was at hand to them that sought Me not;
I said: 'Behold Me, behold Me'
Unto a nation that was not called by My name.

As long, however, as the Temple stood on Mount Zion the Samaritans and the Judeans got along tolerably well. After all, they were not much different religiously: both believed in playing safe by worshiping not only Jehovah but also Baal, and both were impressed with the imposing ritual of the central sanctuary. We have a pathetic picture of these simple and superstitious hybrids who, not having heard of what had taken place in Jerusalem, pilgrimed "from Shechem, from Shiloh, and from Samaria, even fourscore men... with meal offering and frankincense in their hands to bring them to the house of the Lord," only to find that "the god of the land" could not protect His own citadel. Nevertheless they continued to mingle with the Judeans, to learn their customs, and to revere the Torah, or as much as there was then of it, as their very own. [16]

But a schism took place with effects as devastating as those which followed the secession of the Northern Kingdom. The religious zeal of Ezra and Nehemiah and their determination to purge the Jewish people from any foreign admixture, prompted them to pronounce a ban against the Samaritans. When, at the Restoration, the Samaritans who had grown into a numerous people offered their help in the rebuilding of the Temple, they were unceremoniously informed that the sanctuary must be rebuilt by those of undiluted Hebraic blood. To cap the climax, Manasseh, a grandson of the high priest, was disqualified from office because he contracted a marriage with the daughter of Sanballat the ruler of Samaria. Sanballat naturally espoused the cause of his son-in-law. He erected a magnificent temple on the top of Mt. Gerizim, and installed him as its high priest. With a direct lineal descendant of Aaron as its ecclesiastic head, it was but a short step toward making Samaria as independent religiously as it had already become politically. Manasseh had no difficulty in convincing the simple Samaritan peasants that the destruction of the Jerusalem Temple was due to God's displeasure with the manner in which the Judeans worshiped Him; that by the side of it the hallowed shrines of Bethel, Shiloh, and Shechem, (dating back to the days of the Patriarchs), the Solomonic sanctuary was of comparatively recent origin; and that the upstart Zadokites should not be permitted to usurp the place of the tried and trusted Aaronites. To make matters still worse, Ezra dared replace the consecrated Hebrew script with the heathenish Assyrian script. Manasseh insisted that the religion of the Samaritans was true monotheism pure and undefiled; that their Temple on the ancient "Mount of Blessing" was the place where the Patriarchs wor-

shiped; that in their Torah was preserved the alphabet in which
Moses and his servant Joshua wrote; and that they would
be taught by priests who were the direct offspring of Aaron.
In short, they were to be *Shomronim,* defenders and preservers
of the true religion of Israel.[17]

The Samaritans never forgave the Judeans for asserting:
"Ye have no portion, nor memorial, nor right in Jerusalem,"
and grasped every means to hinder the rehabilitation of the
Captivity. Hostile and perhaps unfounded reports have it that
during the persecution of Antiochus they were willing to
dedicate their Temple on Mt. Gerizim to Zeus, and to supply
Apollonius with soldiers to fight their Judean co-religionists.
The Judeans on their part proved themselves no less inimical.
John Hyrcanus destroyed their Temple two hundred years
after its erection, and proclaimed the day of its destruction
(Kislev 21) a religious holiday. They were nicknamed Cuthites
(*Cushim*), and intermarriage with them was strictly prohibited. Ben Sira gave expression to the feeling which pre-
vailed in his time against the Samaritans in his aphorism:

> With two nations is my soul vexed,
> And the third is no nation;
> They that sit upon the mountain of Seir
> (Idumeans), the Philistines,
> And the third is no nation:
> Sichem (Samaritans).[18]

Yet, though they may have been a "foolish people," they
were not an unfaithful one. Whatever of Judaism they did
adopt they clung to with all their might. Even the Rabbis
admitted that "those *mitzvoth* (commandments) which the
Cuthites have accepted they observe more strictly or literally
than the Israelites." They keep the Sabbath most rigorously:
on it they not only kindle no fire but do not leave their
homes, nor have any intercourse with women. They follow
the ancient calendar, and celebrate the Feast of Weeks exactly
fifty days after the Sabbath of Passover, at which they still
sacrifice a Paschal lamb. Except babes in arms, they all fast

on the Day of Atonement. They marry only once. They believe in one God, hold sacred the Pentateuch and the Book of Joshua, and reverence Mount Gerizim, as the *Tura Mabrachta,* or Mount of Blessing. Nor was Jesus the only one who spoke a good word in their behalf. In spite of the ancient enmity, many of the sages of the Talmud were not unkindly inclined toward them, and insisted that they be treated in all respects as Jews. He who robs a Cuthite is as guilty as if he robbed an Israelite, is one of their dicta, and they recommended that their poor be provided for in the same manner as the poor of the Israelites. [19]

There were times when the Samaritans were prosperous and powerful. They rivalled the Judeans as traders, and the term Samaritan, like Canaanite before it, came to mean merchant. They were also enthusiastic proselytizers, seeking to convert the Judeans as well as the pagans to their faith. Their own tradition has it that when they and the Judeans were returning from captivity, led by Sanballat, they stopped at a place called Horan to decide on the locality where the new Temple should be erected. The Judeans insisted on Jerusalem, the Samaritans on Mount Gerizim, and with three hundred thousand *Gerim* repaired to Samaria. But untoward circumstances put a stop both to their material prosperity and their conversionist zeal. After the edict of Constantine the Great (325 C.E.), prohibiting Jews and Samaritans from making proselytes, they retired unto themselves, concentrating their efforts on preserving, as they claimed, the Josephite, or Ephraimite blood, which they regarded as superior to that of the Judeans, and maintained that the promised Messiah would be, like themselves, a son of the house of Joseph. Such a one appeared about the time of Jesus in the person of Dositheus. He made many converts among Jews and Christians, and like Elijah was believed never to have died. [20]

"*Shomronim*" (those who guard) in the truest sense were the Samaritans in that, more than the Judeans, they kept guard over the sacred soil of the Hebrew patriarchs. As if Providence had placed them there to watch over the cradle of Judaism when those who gave birth to it were compelled to leave it, they were never dispossessed even temporarily. For twenty-seven hundred years they stood at the gates of Palestine. Their sword had been blunted, almost broken, but they never let it fall from their hand. With unyielding courage and pride they met Greek and Roman, Arab, Turk, Saracen, Crusader, and "never sought safety in the camp of the real or imaginary enemy." They stubbornly refused to intermarry even with their Judean co-religionists. But by a strange caprice of nature, the number of their male progeny always surpassed their female offspring, and from a numerous tribe they have now become reduced to a handful of about one hundred souls.

CHAPTER V

BIBLE PROSELYTES IN
RABBINIC LORE

THE missionary-mindedness of the Hebrews did not cease with the disappearance of the Prophets and the Psalmists. On the contrary, their sense of obligation to spread their ideals among their neighbors became ever more keen and persistent and brought forth the many legends based on the biblical narratives, which are indicative of the people's

> ...Hunger and thirst of the heart,
> The frenzy and fire of the brain.

In these traditions God is described as the Great Teacher and Propagandist Whose sole object in creating the world was for the sake of the Torah, or, what amounts to the same, for the sake of Israel, the custodian and propagator of the Torah. It was to serve as a laboratory for the development and perfecting of the moral nature. He therefore made man, a being who by his own effort can rise from the animal state to become but a little lower than the angels. Yet He did not leave man entirely to his own resources. He so constructed the world that everything in it should point to His Unity. He arranged that the sun and moon should succeed each other so that nations of the world should not worship them as deities. He contrived that the earth should be irrigated from above so that people should look heavenward. In addition, He endowed certain creatures with a moral instinct, so that as R. Johanan says: "If no Torah had been given us we would have learned modesty from the cat, industry from the ant, continence from the dove, deportment from the rooster."[1]

Had Adam remained in the state of perfection in which he was when still fresh from the hand of the Creator, God would have presented the Torah to him. But the poison of the serpent left its mark on him and his descendants, and as a result the Shekinah withdrew farther and farther from the abode of mortals. At the disobedience of Adam and Eve the Shekinah retired to the seventh, or lowest, heaven; at Cain's murder, to the sixth; at Enoch's idolatry, to the fifth; at the wickedness of the "Generation of the Flood," to the fourth; at the rebelliousness of the "Generation of the Tower," to the third; and as man continued in his evil deeds it finally retreated to the second, and lastly, to the first heaven, or the one furthest removed from the dwelling-place of human beings.[2]

But even while the Shekinah was thus compelled to move away from the mundane sphere, God did not lose His fatherly interest in, or affection for, His children. In His lovingkindness He connived at their conduct, and sought to reclaim them by angels, some of whom were themselves seduced by the vices which they undertook to wipe out. On the other hand, some human beings by studying the work of nature and observing the habits of various creatures around them rose to spiritual heights surpassing those of angels. Among these were Seth, Enosh, Kenan, Mahalalel, Jared, and Enoch. All of them preached the Unity of God, established schools, and left behind them books, which they either wrote or received from the hands of ministering angels, for the instruction of their fellowmen.[3]

Of Seth, Adam's youngest son, tradition has it that he was in the likeness of his father, and one of the thirteen who were born circumcised, thus becoming identified with Judaism even before the rite was accepted by the Hebrews. His name is explained to refer to the fact that it was he who laid the foundation of the spiritual temple of mankind. It was by his own efforts that he managed to perfect himself in the divine wisdom, which he strove to implant in the hearts of his children. The latter, in their turn, dedicated themselves to the uplift of their fellowmen, and their knowledge they inscribed on two pillars, one of brick and one of stone, so that whether the world was destroyed by fire or by water one or the other would remain. According to the Cabbalists the soul of Seth was later incarnated in Moses, and will be reincarnated in the Messiah, or in one of the "Seven Shepherds" who fed the human flock with spiritual food through the ages (Adam, Seth, Methuselah, Abraham, Jacob, and Moses).[4]

It was in the days of Enosh that the "poison of the serpent" began to work and mankind became evermore addicted to the worship of idols and the practice of immorality. However, in the seventh generation from Adam there arose one who, as a missionary and teacher, became, next to Elijah, perhaps the most exalted character of Jewish lore. An humble shoemaker by trade, Enoch, it was claimed, repented of his sins, became a proselyte himself and a most ardent missionary to the whole world. Vast multitudes flocked unto him and proclaimed him their king, and under his reign of three hundred and forty-three years the world enjoyed the greatest peace and happiness. However, lest he, too, become contaminated like his predecessors, God translated him into heaven while yet alive, elevated him to the dignity of Metatron, or Prince of the Presence, gave him the keys to all the gates of wisdom and goodness, and appointed him the guide of the souls of the righteous in the realms of eternal bliss. But Enoch's love for his fellowmen remained as profound in heaven as it was while he was still on earth, and for their sake he composed three hundred and sixty-six books containing all the wisdom he had learned in his celestial abode. These he bequeathed to his children with the injunction that they should read them and pass them on to their children from generation to generation and distribute them among all the nations.[5]

Of Noah, who like Enoch "walked with God," the Bible has so much to say as to leave little room for tradition. Yet the popular fancy would not let even his biography remain without amplifying and embellishing it. He, too, like Adam,

Seth, and Melchizedek, was born "a son of the covenant" (i.e., circumcised), and dedicated himself to the improvement of his fellowmen. He invented the plough, the scythe, the hoe, and other agricultural implements. In the face of ridicule and violent opposition he persisted in building the ark. He purposely prolonged its completion one hundred and twenty years that all might hear of the inevitable doom which awaited them if they continued to lead ungodly and immoral lives. But his most beneficent bequest was a book received by him from God through the angel Raphael. The book contained not alone the precepts which make for the holy life, but also the secrets of wisdom and the art of healing. He also contributed fifty years of his life to the days of Moses, who, he foresaw, would some day present the Torah to Israel. Meanwhile he reaffirmed the code of Adam and, since mankind in his day tended to become carnivorous, added to it a seventh clause—the prohibition of eating "flesh cut from the living animal." Some rabbis point to his name (Hebrew for "pleasant") as indicating that he taught the people to be slow to anger and easy to please, and that he set an example of graciousness by his views, his talk, and even by his walk. Noah was greatly assisted by his wife Naamah, or Amzara, the daughter of Enosh, whose piety equalled that of her husband and her father.[6]

Shem, the third son of the second founder of the human race, continued the work of his father. He, too, was born circumcised and officiated both as priest and prophet. He acted also in the capacity of judge and taught the people how to mete out equal justice to all. His chief claim to fame was the academy which he established within which the Shekinah itself is said to have delighted to rest. It was this school that Jacob attended, and it was to establish a similar one in Goshen that Jacob sent Judah ahead of him when he started on his journey to Egypt.[7]

It was in the tenth generation after Noah that there appeared on the world's horizon one who inaugurated a missionary activity which will cease only when there shall be no more peoples to convert. In Abraham the Jewish fancy found the embodiment of the deepest desires of the people's soul, the exemplification of its divine destiny, and the symbol of the part it was predestined to play in the unfolding of God's plan. His father Terah is described as a fanatical pagan who was not only a priest but also a maker of idols. While merely a child of three and solely by dint of his own reasoning, Abraham arrived at the conviction that there is only One God, and that He is to be worshiped by doing justice and loving mercy. Since the Bible plainly states that he circumcised himself at the age of ninety, tradition could not confer upon him the distinction of having been born with the sign of the Covenant. But this loss was really a gain. It showed how ready he was to make a sacrifice for the religion to the spread of which he dedicated himself from early childhood, and that he stood the test of bodily pain as he stood the ten other tests, which tried his heart and soul, without flinching from his self-imposed duty.

No sooner did Abraham discover the true faith than he betook himself with all the zeal of a neophyte to convince others of its truth. He began by playing pranks upon the idols, thus demonstrating their helplessness. Once, while Terah was away he smashed all of them, except the biggest in whose arms he put the hatchet. Abraham protested his innocence and insisted that it was this idol and not he who had broken the others. His irate father, however, remained unconvinced and reported him to Nimrod, the defender of the faith, who threw him into prison. Seeing that, despite a year's deprivation of the necessities of life, Abraham appeared to be as well as ever, the keeper of the prison himself became converted to the religion of the prisoner and, defying the hangman, exclaimed: "The Eternal He is God, the God of the whole world as well as of the blasphemer Nimrod." Similarly, his deliverance from the fiery furnace so impressed the princes with the power of the God of Abraham that they and their retinues cried out: "The Lord He is God; in the heavens above and on the earth beneath there is none else."

Thereafter, the destruction of idols began to spread, and

people were converted in ever increasing numbers. A woman, whose idol Abraham restored to her after it had been carried off by thieves, broke it and, wending her way through the streets of Ur, called to all within the range of her voice: "Who would save his soul from destruction, and be prosperous in all his doings, let him serve the God of Abraham." Nimrod himself either began to believe or became intimidated and presented Abraham with many costly gifts and with two servants, Eliezer, whom we shall meet anon, and Ogi, or Og, king of Bashan, the last of the biblical giants.[8]

Abraham's departure from Chaldea had no effect on his missionary zeal. In Egypt he sought out the priests and wise men, discussed their beliefs with them. His mastery of the sciences of mathematics and astronomy won their admiration to such an extent that many gave assent to his theological doctrines. He did the same all through his journey to Canaan. Wherever he arrived he set up tents for Sarah and for himself, erected an altar, and proceeded to preach to the passersby. In Haran he won hundreds of souls for his God and thus remade them. Some of his proselytes became highly proficient in the Torah, and many adopted the name Abraham.[9]

It was when Abraham finally settled in Canaan that he entered upon the aggressive campaign which, in the words of the Rabbis, "rendered him a stream of blessings, purifying and regenerating the pagan world." He invaded the market places and sought out the people in their homes. He taught agriculture and astronomy and showed the peasants how to protect their seed from the ravens, and he also exhorted them to serve God with all their heart. In appreciation of his benefactions the crown was offered to him; but he rejected it, insisting that there is but one King, his and theirs—God. He requested that instead of the gifts they made to him, they send their children to him and let him raise them in the fear of God and the love of their fellowmen.

To expand his missionary activity Abraham erected a magnificent mansion amidst the terebinths of Mamre, near where the roads diverge into various directions, and stocked it with all manner of delicious viands. At the doors which were cut on each side he stationed servants whom he himself supervised, and invited all passersby to partake of his hospitality, at the same time reminding them that he was acting only as the steward of the Most High to Whom alone thanks were due. It was not long before his house became known far and wide, and to it flocked not only the poor in need of entertainment, but the great and learned in search of wisdom. According to the statement of the Talmud, on the day of Abraham's death all the notables of the heathens stood in line and mourned, "Alas for the world!"[10]

Abraham's success as a missionary was due not a little to the efforts of Sarah. While her husband took care of the grown, she offered to nurse their infants. Her ability to do so was in itself sufficient to prove to the pagan parents the superiority of her God, and there was something in her nursing that led the children when they grew up to become proselytes. For this reason, Sarah at Abraham's request would suckle the pagan children even in the market place, since the name of God would thus be hallowed among the heathen.

Abraham became the recognized missionary *par excellence* in Christian and Mohammedan lore. Paul acclaimed him as "the father of all of them that believed," and the one through whom "God preached to the heathen before the Gospel." Mohammed held him up as a model Mussulman who proclaimed the belief in Allah alone. To the Jews he was both their father according to the flesh and the father of the whole world according to the spirit, even as Sarah was both a princess of her own people and a princess to all mankind. He was in their estimation greater than Moses, the one whom God thought of when He uttered His divine command "Let there be light," and the "Rock" or foundation of the ever expanding temple of the religion of love and righteousness. With him begins God's kingdom on earth. He was the first *Ger Zedek,* or true proselyte, and the Godfather of all future proselytes, who either assume his name or call themselves his sons. For Judaism does not insist on ethnic descent but on ethical ascent. All are of the "seed of Abraham" or "the disciples of Abraham," who have "a goodly eye, an humble mind, and a lowly spirit," or who exhibit the traits of "kindliness, modesty, and beneficence."[11]

Of the important members of Abraham's household, Hagar was by birth an Egyptian princess. But her father, an Egyptian Pharaoh, was so impressed with the family life of Abraham that he said, "Rather let her be a servant in his household than a mistress elsewhere." The result was that she became one of the nine female converts of the Bible. Because of her holy life and the mortifying treatment she uncomplainingly endured at the hand of Sarah, she obtained special favor from God. To her, God revealed things which He hid from her stern mistress, and "the Holy One Who never before conversed with a woman attached Himself to this beloved, humble and saintly proselyte." Her son Ishmael also repented his sins prior to the death of Abraham.

Eliezer, too, was, according to some tradition, of noble lineage. He was, in fact, no less a personage than the son of Nimrod himself. His father presented him to Abraham to be his body-guard, for he possessed the strength of three hundred and eighteen men but in his admiration for his master he gradually succeeded in completely suppressing his evil inclinations. In the course of time he even surpassed him both in the mastery of the Torah and in the spotlessness of his life, and God found him worthy to be among the nine who were admitted into paradise while yet alive. His two sons, Damesek and Alinus, were commanders of the army which Jacob, on his return home, sent to meet his brother Esau.[12]

Besides Abraham's domestics, most of whom like himself became *Gere Zedek*, or full-fledged proselytes, there were several of his contemporaries who attained a high degree of moral excellence. One of them, strange to say, was Bera, the villainous king of Sodom. After his rescue from death in the slimy pits in which his allies perished, he experienced a change of heart and became a worshiper of the God of Abraham. Another was the Philistine king of Gerar, Abimelech. Far from bearing a grudge against him for his seizure of Sarah, Jewish folk-lore surrounded him with a certain halo and put the blame of the disagreeable incident on Abraham himself. He was credited with possessing the gift of prophecy and was the model of a *Ger Toshab* (semi-proselyte) or "fearer of Heaven." Abraham's three friends, Aner, Eshkol, and Mamre, were also "fearers of the Lord," but Mamre excelled them all. When Abraham consulted them whether he should undergo the rite of circumcision, Mamre urged him to do so, and had himself circumcised in order to encourage him. The Shekinah therefore chose his place as its abode.[13]

Excelling all the pseudo-proselytes of his and later generations was Melchizedek, king of Salem, with whom Abraham concluded an alliance after he rescued his nephew Lot. His charity, like that of Abraham's, we are told, was confined to neither race nor religion. He was lauded as another Elijah, or as a prototype of the Messiah. It was said that had he not committed the error of mentioning the name of Abraham before that of God, the priesthood would have remained forever in his family. The Jews of Alexandria, who were anxious to remove every barrier from the path of those who wished to be admitted into the Jewish fold, held Melchizedek up as an example of one who became an ideal Jew without submitting to the rite of circumcision, while Paul pointed to him as the foreshadower of Christ who "without father, without mother, without descent, having neither beginning of days, nor end of life, but made like unto the son of God, abideth a priest continually." A certain Christian sect, the Melchizedekites, pronounced him "the first-created" of God and superior to Christ.[14]

Abraham's love of humanity and his missionary zeal were inherited by his descendants. Isaac devoted himself to the pursuit of peace, the relief of the poor, and to making proselytes. He gave a tenth of all he possessed to the needy of Gerar, and prevailed upon the Philistines to observe the seven Noahian laws. Through him, the Shekinah descended one heaven nearer the earth.[15]

Jacob, too, like Esau, was a hunter, according to the Rabbis: only he was a hunter of souls, and his weapons were those of a social welfare worker. In Shechem he built public bathhouses, opened markets where people might buy at low cost, and had money coined for the convenience of the traders. Above all, he founded schools for the teaching of the Torah. He delighted in making converts of the captives he took in his wars with the surrounding nations, and counted the days as evil on which he did not gain some proselytes to his religion. Oddly enough, one of his most devoted disciples was Eliphaz who, as a true son of Esau, previously endeavored "to turn men away from God." Eliphaz became one of the three comforters of Job and the ancestor of the prophet Obadiah, who, together with Abraham, Joseph, and Job, constituted, according to some, the quartet of the "great fearers of the Lord."[16]

Job, to whom Ezekiel refers as one of the three who "delivered their souls by their righteousness," though a contemporary of Eliphaz, lived long enough to become a counsellor of the Pharaoh who oppressed the children of Israel in the days of Moses. He was never formally converted to Judaism. But in all his ways he followed in the footsteps of the Patriarchs, and like Enoch and Melchizedek he rose to a level of piety higher even than that of Abraham's. Hence Jacob had no hesitancy in giving him his daughter Dinah to wife. After his death the Canaanitish population buried their corpses in his tomb in the hope that they might be saved by coming in contact with his bones. But he was revered especially among the Rabbis. God loved him, they asserted, despite some of his seeming blasphemous words against Him, since "God condemns no man for what he utters in the hour of his grief." Like Moses, he died by God's kiss, and his name was engraved on one of the seven branches of the golden candelabra. The book attributed to him was prescribed for the inspirational reading of the High Priest on the eve of the Day of Atonement.[17]

As late as the time of Ezra, mention is made of certain Dinaites who, with other non-Jewish elements in Samaria and Trans-Jordania, protested against the permission granted by the king of Persia to rehabilitate the land of Judea. As a rule, however, those who intermarried with the Patriarchs and their descendants were completely fused with the Israelites.

Bilhah, one of the two non-Hebrew wives of Jacob, succeeded Rachel in the affection of her husband, and after his death it was she who was chosen by his other sons to intercede for them with Joseph. Bunah, the wife of Simeon, was noted for her piety as well as for her beauty. Of Tamar, the Canaanitish daughter-in-law and, later, wife of Judah, Philo tells us: "She was reared in the home of idolaters, but became converted to the belief in One God, and by the purity of her life she acquired nobility for her descendants. Because of her extreme modesty, she never removed her veil, so that her husband never saw her features. Though a heavenly voice proclaimed her innocence she was ready to die the death of a martyr rather than cast reflection on the reputation of Judah." Pointing to her as an example, R. Simeon ben Yohai taught: "Sooner let one permit himself to be thrown into a fiery furnace than cause the face of his fellowman to blanch (for shame)." Her one constant prayer was that she might be privileged to become the mother of great men in Israel. It was answered when two of her sons, Perez and Zerah, were sent to spy out the Promised Land. Isaiah the Prophet and David the King of Israel and the progenitor of the Messiah are also claimed by some as her offspring.[18]

Like Hagar, Timnah was a lady of the blood royal who conceived such an admiration for the faith of Abraham that she would rather be "a maid-servant to the dregs of this people, than a princess among my own." For some reason, the Patriarchs refused to accept her as a convert, so she became the concubine of Eliphaz. As a punishment for their intolerance and as a protest against the exclusion of anyone who, from any motive, seeks shelter under the wings of the Shekinah, God, say the Rabbis, permitted Amalek (her descendant) to wreak vengeance on Israel.

There is perhaps no more beautiful character in Jewish folk-lore than Asenath the Egyptian. Notwithstanding the biblical statement that she was the daughter of Potiphar, later legend asserts that she was the love-child of Dinah and Hamor the Shechemite. Fearing that her uncles were resolved to do away with her, so as to remove the remembrance of her mother's disgrace, Jacob secreted her under a thorn-bush with a tin plate suspended from her neck on which he engraved the Holy Name. Thence an angel carried her off to Egypt where Potiphar adopted her as his daughter. In his house she grew up "as slender as Sarah, as beautiful as Rebecca, and as radiant as Rachel," worthy to be the wife of the son of Pharaoh. But the moment she beheld the Hebrew slave whom her father brought into the house, she was captivated by his beauty and despite her maidenly modesty could not resist making advances to him. Joseph also asked God "Who calleth men from darkness to light, from error to truth, and from death to life," to "pour out His spirit upon her, and create in her a new heart that she may become a member of His Chosen People and obtain a portion in the world-to-come." The prayer was effective. Asenath divested herself of her costly robes and ornaments and distributed their price among the poor, destroyed her idols, and for seven days called upon the "jealous God of Joseph, the God Who hates idolaters." On the morning of the eighth day an angel appeared to her and announced that she need no longer do penance. That day she was born anew, and her name was henceforth to be not Asenath but "Manos" (refuge), for through her many Gentiles would take refuge under the wings of the Shekinah. The angel then arrayed her like a bride, made her look more beautiful than ever, and led her to Joseph, who blessed her, saying: "In her God hath laid the foundation of walls, and the children of the living God shall dwell in the city of thy refuge, and the Lord God will be their King forever." The wedding feast was prepared by Pharaoh himself and attended by Asenath's alleged parents and relatives, all of whom rejoiced in her joy and joined with one accord in praising "the Lord Who reviveth the dead."

Thereafter she devoted herself to deeds of loving-kindness, and to the mastery of the secret and revealed Torah, into which she had been initiated by Levi, her brother-in-law. It is said that when she was translated into heaven she was placed in a palace built upon a rock encompassed by a diamond wall.

Joseph was instrumental in converting others besides Asenath. When dispensing corn to the Egyptian peasants he
would plead with them to discard their idols and to give
thanks to Him alone "Who provideth food for every living
being." Some of them were fully converted; others, including Pharaoh, adopted only the rite of circumcision. The only
one whom Joseph rejected was Zulaika, the mother of Asenath,
who, out of love for Joseph, offered to accept Judaism and
to induce her husband and other Egyptian dignitaries to do
likewise. Joseph bluntly told her: "The Lord desireth not
that they who fear Him should walk in impurity, nor hath
He pleasure in an adulterer."[19]

According to a certain tradition Shiphrah and Puah, the
midwives who refused to obey Pharaoh's command to throw
the Hebrew male children into the river, were proselytes. If
this be so, then Moses may have come in contact with converts from the moment of his birth.

Far more explicit is the saga about the Egyptian princess
who adopted him as her son. Thermutis, the daughter of
Pharaoh, was never much devoted to idols. But when she
noticed that the touch of Moses cured her from her leprosy
she rebelled against the religion of her father, assumed the
name Jehudiah, and devoted herself to the amelioration of
the lot of the enslaved Hebrews. She married Caleb, known
also as Mered, because he "rebelled" against the counsel of the
spies who spread an evil report against the Holy Land. Because
she changed from paganism, her name also was changed to
Bithiah ("Daughter of God"), God saying: "Moses was not
thy child, yet thou didst treat him as if he were thy son, I will
call thee My daughter, though thou art not My daughter."
And God so loved this new daughter that He preferred the
name Moses which she gave her adopted child to any other,
and spared her the agony of death by admitting her into
paradise while she was still alive.[20]

Intermarriage, too, played quite an important role in the
life and proselytizing activity of Moses. Zipporah was not
the first non-Israelite whom the future lawgiver married.
During his enforced absence from Egypt he joined the army

of Kikanos in Ethiopia. His personality so impressed itself
upon the people that after the king's death they offered him
the crown, and Tharbis, the king's daughter, or as another
legend has it, Adoniah, the king's widow, offered him her
hand. Moses accepted both. His married life, however, was
not a happy one. After forty years, the queen experienced a
change of heart, blamed him for not worshiping the idols
of the Ethiopians, and sent him back to Egypt, though not
without some costly gifts for his sister Miriam. However,
the generally accepted tradition is that "the Cushite (dark)
woman" was no other than Zipporah, the daughter of the
Midianitish priest Jethro. Her nickname, it was said, was
suggested by her exceeding beauty and noble bearing, which
distinguished her from her contemporaries, as the Cushite
is distinguished from the Caucasian. On the other hand, it
is said that the name of Zipporah (bird) was given her because she "cleansed her father's house from idolatry even
as the sacrificial bird purifies a leper from his impurity."[21]

Though Moses' chief mission was the redemption of the
children of Israel from Egyptian bondage, he was exerting
himself also to free the Egyptians from their spiritual bondage.
His miracles were intended to impress Pharaoh and his princes
with the goodness and greatness of the God of Israel. For
this reason, he smote the Nile and ordered the blood of the
lamb to be smeared on the lintels, as if to say, "Beat the idols,
and the priests will tremble." The Bible also refers to Egyptians
"who feared the word of the Lord," and the large number of
Ereb Rab or *Asafsuf* (mixed multitude) who joined the
Israelites on their departure from Egypt. Most of these proselytes, however, proved disappointing, and the Rabbis blamed
them for all the relapses of the children of Israel. It was
they who made the Golden Calf, and it was men from their
midst who yielded to the seduction of the Moabite women. An
Arab legend, probably of Jewish origin, also has it that the
miracles were witnessed by the twelve chief wizards of Egypt,
each of whom was at the head of twenty chieftains, each of
whom ruled over one thousand lesser wizards, all of whom
(240,252) finally acknowledged the God of Aaron and Moses.[22]

The outstanding proselyte of the Mosaic period is Jethro. According to some rabbinic traditions, he began as a bitter opponent of the religion and the people whom he later joined. In fact, they claim, there was not an idol in the world which he had not worshipped. Like Amalek he, too, urged Pharaoh to throw the male babies of the children of Israel into the Nile and stipulated that Zipporah's first-born son should be brought up in the religion of his grandfather. When he heard what the Lord had done to the children of Israel, his "flesh stung like needles." It took the miraculous crossing of the Red Sea, the crushing defeat of Amalek, and the falling of the manna, to impress Jethro with the power and greatness of the God of Israel and cause him to abjure idolatry. But once converted, he remained faithful to the end. The Midianites divested him of his priesthood and his kingdom and expelled him from their midst. But Jethro was no longer concerned about his worldly honors. He found his greatest delight in the study of the Torah, and the observance of his new religion. His favorite expression, "Blessed be the Lord," (a phrase which no one employed before him) became the formula for beginning various Hebrew benedictions.

As the years advanced, Jethro began to feel that he could serve the God of Israel better by returning to Midian than by following the Israelites. In vain did Moses remonstrate: "Thy refusal to go with us will make the heathen think that the Israelites do not accept proselytes... and will keep them away from the true faith. Come with us; and thy seed shall share with us the Temple, the Torah, as well as the future reward of the pious." Jethro replied: "A candle may glow in the dark, but not when the sun and the moon shed their rays. Thou art the sun, and Aaron the moon; of what avail would my candle-light be? I had, therefore, better return to my home city, that I may make proselytes of its inhabitants, instruct them in the Torah, and lead them under the wings of the Shekinah." And so indeed he did. He converted all his kinsmen and many of his compatriots, and for this was honored by having a *parashah* (section of the Torah) named after him.[23]

Fate has ordained that at every great turn in Israel's history there arose a proselyte of commanding personality. As Abraham appeared at the beginning of Israel's racial entity, and Jethro at the period when it first emerged as "a kingdom of priests and a holy nation," so Rahab loomed on the horizon at the entrance of the Israelites into the Promised Land. At first a harlot, she became in her fiftieth year an ardent convert, a truly "pious one." The Gospel of Matthew has it that she was the ancestress of Boaz and therefore, through David, also of Jesus. Jewish legend, however, conferred upon Rahab honors of its own. When she confessed before the spies that the "Lord your God He is God in heaven above and on earth beneath," the Holy One said: "On earth thou couldst see with thine eyes that there is no other God beside Me; but to acknowledge that I am the only God in heaven needs special faith. I promise thee, therefore, that one of thy descendants shall see what no Prophet before him shall have seen." The reference was to Ezekiel who beheld the *Merkabah* (God's throne of glory). Rahab married Joshua, a descendant of Asenath, and was privileged to number among her offspring eight priests who were also prophets,— the best known of whom are Huldah and Hilkiah, Jeremiah and Baruch b. Neriah.[24]

Though Rahab the former harlot became a favorite rabbinic example of a "proselyte of righteousness," a group of pagan converts were forever deprived of their equal rights with the rest of their new co-religionists. They were the Gibeonites who, by trickery, elicited a covenant of peace from Joshua. Though obtained under false pretenses, the Israelites kept their covenant inviolate, in order to avoid a possible profanation of God's name, and so as not to discourage proselytes. The Gibeonites, however, never became an integral part of the Israelites during the existence of the first Temple, and their revenge for the cruel treatment of Saul on his children proved that they never acquired the quality which characterizes the true Jew.

Concerning Jael, the wife of Heber the Kenite, Jewish lore has it that she was one of the most beautiful women who ever lived, possessed the most charming voice ever heard, and surpassed the matriarchs in her kindliness. That she resorted to a hammer instead of a sword was due to her piety; the Law forbade a woman the use of a weapon of war. Nor did she fail to invoke God's assistance before she committed her heroic deed. Her prayer is quoted as follows:

> O God, strengthen the arm of thy maid-servant this day, for Thy sake, for the sake of thy people, and for the sake of those that hope in Thee.

Rabbinic inventiveness could find little to add to what had already been said about Ruth in the biblical idyl which bears her name. But it could not refrain from filling in some lacunae, and adding some details. According to one story, Ruth and Orpah were the daughters of Eglon, the king of Moab, who oppressed the children of Israel for eighteen years. Another legend has it that they were descended from Balak, king of Moab, who urged Balaam to curse Israel. According to both versions, Ruth and Orpah where thus the offspring of kings of nations which from time immemorial were bitter persecutors of Israel, and whose peoples were excluded from entering "into the assembly of the Lord, even to the tenth generation." Yet both Ruth and Orpah were fascinated by the personality and religion of Naomi; and Ruth, at the age of forty, followed her mother-in-law into Palestine, accepted her faith, and became the progenitor of David and, through him, of the Messiah.

The Rabbis loved to dwell on the manner of Ruth's conversion, and established her practice as a precedent for all future proselytes. In a very dramatic manner they recast the biblical conversation which ensued when Naomi saw that Ruth was determined to follow her. "My child," said she, "it is not proper for a daughter of Israel to attend theaters and circuses." Ruth replied, "Whither thou goest, I will go." Said Naomi, "My daughter, it is not the way of an Israelite to stay in a house which hath no Mezuzah (on its door)." Ruth replied, "Where thou lodgest, I will lodge." Naomi then told her some of the more difficult demands which her new religion would exact of her. Ruth answered, "Thy people shall be my people; and thy God, my God." Seeing her determination, Naomi declared, "My daughter, whatever meritorious deeds thou canst acquire, acquire them in this world; then in the world to come 'naught but death will part thee and me.' "[25]

Gentiles, who, to a greater or lesser degree, were inclined to Yahvism, were conspicuous in the entourage of David. Among his *"Gibborim,"* or body-guard, there were Cretans, Philistines, Iturians, Arameans, and Hittites; some of them, like Ittai and Uriah, proved themselves most dependable in time of trouble, and took part in the coronation of Solomon. It was Ithra the Ishmaelite, presumably a proselyte, who defended David against the contention of Doeg, "the Edomite," that as a descendant of a Moabite woman David was disqualified from being an Israelite, not to say a king of Israel. Ithra's conversion is said to have come about when he entered the School of Jesse and heard him expound the verse (Isa. 45:22): "Look at Me, and be ye saved, all the ends of the earth." Jesse was so pleased with his conduct that he gave him his daughter in marriage.

Proselytes were not only the founders of the Davidic dynasty, they also played an important part in the selection of the site of the sanctuary which became the spiritual center of Israel. The plot selected for the erection of an altar to the God of Israel belonged to the Jebusite Araunah, or Ornan, and the sanctuary erected thereon was due largely to the labor and material supplied by Hiram, king of Tyre. The overseer of the craftsmen was Hiram the Tyrean, who married an Israelitish woman. The former is said to have been such a "fearer of the Lord" that he was privileged to enter paradise while still in the flesh. After a thousand years, however, he like Nebuchadnezzar, conceived himself to be a god and was denounced by Ezekiel for his arrogance.[26]

In the biblical narrative, Solomon is blamed for permitting foreign women "to turn away his heart after their gods." According to the Talmud, however, Solomon's object in

marrying these foreign women was a laudable one. He hoped
thus to "gather them under the wings of the Shekinah." It
was not, however, until after he was shorn of his glory that
his hopes were realized. Reduced by Asmodeus, the prince
of demons, to the position of cook in the court of the king
of Ammon, he attracted the attention of the beautiful princess
Naamah. The outraged king expelled the lovers to a desert,
there to die of starvation. But they managed to reach a city
by the seashore; and there, on cleaning a fish, Naamah found
the magic ring which enabled Solomon to have himself re-
enthroned as king of Israel. The Ammonite king became
reconciled, and his daughter proved to be all that could be
expected of a Hebrew queen. Because of her merits, God took
pity on Solomon and prolonged his reign. Her Ammonitish
birth affected her no more than Ruth was affected by her
Moabitish birth. In fact, both were like "two turtle doves"
with whom God blessed Abraham, and both were predestined
to be the progenitors of the Messiah.[27]

Some rabbis ventured the opinion that no proselytes could
have been admitted into the House of Israel during the days
of David and Solomon, because it might have been suspected
that they were prompted by the prosperity which prevailed
in those reigns. However, the Bible refers to 150,000 craftsmen
who assisted in the building of the Solomonic Temple as
Gerim. Even Ahab was instrumental in converting many to
the Yahvist faith. Hezekiah in particular was the cause of
numerous conversions. After the angel of the Lord smote
the camp of the Assyrians, he found his allies, Pharaoh of
Egypt and Tirhakah of Ethiopia, bound and left to perish
by Sennacherib. Hezekiah at once unbound them and set them
at liberty. In appreciation of his humaneness, they went about
and recounted the miracles and the might of Hezekiah's Lord,
exclaiming, as they bowed toward Jerusalem, "Surely God
is in thee, and there is none else, there is no other God."[28]

Among the prophets who were reputed to be either proselytes or descendants of proselytes, there was no less a personage
than Elijah, the harbinger of the Messiah. More definitely
Obadiah, his contemporary, was an Edomite, of the line of

Eliphaz, son of Esau. Having expended his entire fortune on maintaining the hundred prophets, whom he hid from the vengeance of Jezebel, he continued his benefactions by borrowing money at a usurious rate from Jehoram b. Ahab. Naturally he was especially interested in the salvation of his own countrymen and hence became the apostle to the Edomites. Thus he proved the truth of the saying: "The woods themselves furnish the handle for the ax which is to cut them down." In his love of God, Obadiah was superior, if possible, even to Abraham, and so beloved was he of God that for his sake God would have spared the house of Ahab had it made a little effort to abandon idolatry.[29]

Jonah is said to have been the son of the woman of Zarephath who became a Jewess after Elijah revived her child. When the child grew up he waited upon Elisha and was by him selected from all the "Sons of the Prophets" to go to Ramath-Gilead to anoint Jehu king over Israel. As his prophecies always came true, he was nicknamed *Ben Amittai,* "the son of truth." Fearful lest the conversion of the Gentiles bring disgrace upon the Jews, he refused to go on his mission and fled to Tarshish. But his flight itself effected many conversions. When the kindly sailors noticed that the storm subsided each time he touched the water but would break out anew as soon as they started to withdraw him from it, and that when at last they threw him in, the sea completely calmed down, they not only feared the Lord exceedingly but made a pilgrimage to Jerusalem, had themselves circumcised, and their wives and children converted, and consecrated all their possessions to the God of Jonah. Jonah, like Elijah, never died.[30]

To the list of prophets of supposedly non-Israelitish extraction should be added the names of no less a man than Jeremiah and his amanuensis, Baruk, also regarded by the Rabbis as a prophet and identified with Ebed Melek, who rescued him from the dungeon. Both are assumed to have been descendants of Rahab. Baruk's sobriquet the "Cushite" (Ethiopian), like that of Zipporah, is explained to indicate that compared with the loose morals of the court in which he lived, he was as different from his fellow courtiers as the Ethiopian is differ-

ent from the Caucasian. To him is attributed a late apocalypse
in which is predicted the conversion of the world. Because of
his profound love for the Temple, God spared him the agony
of beholding its destruction by transporting him to another
place. He is also one of the nine who entered paradise alive,
and of the thirteen who never tasted death.[31]

In some instances, it was possibly a feeling of gratitude
to those who treated them kindly that gave rise to legends in
which Gentiles are depicted as Judaizers. Thus Cyrus was
assumed to have been a convert to Judaism. So also Darius,
it is said, became a proselyte after a miraculous recovery from
blindness effected through the intercession of Daniel. He
assigned a tenth of his grain to priests and Levites in Jerusalem,
and sought to convince others of the omnipotence of the God
of Israel. But sometimes a sense of poetic justice prompted
the Jews to make their inveterate enemies ultimately repent
of their cruelty, cast their lot with the very people whom
they were bent on exterminating, and become instrumental in
the spread of the religion which they had despised. Indeed
there is hardly an enemy of Israel on whom the Jewish popular
fancy did not "avenge" itself by turning him or his descendants
into Jews.[32]

Balaam was one of them. Frustrated in his curse, his exclamation, "God is not a man!" resounded from one end of
the earth to the other, and through him Pharaoh, who was
spared when his horsemen and charioteers sank in the Red
Sea, became an avowed monotheist and propagandist of
Judaism. It was Pharaoh who as king of Nineveh decreed the
fast following the warning of Jonah, and proclaimed that
"there is no God beside Him in all the world, all His words
are truth, and all His judgments are true and faithful." This
religious fervor he carried with him into the netherworld,
where he posted himself at the gate of Hell, and whenever
he beheld the kings of the nations enter he exclaimed, "O
ye fools! Why have ye not learned of me? I denied the Lord
God, and he brought ten plagues upon me, sent me to the
bottom of the sea, kept me there for fifty years, released me
then and brought me up!"

Naaman, the captain of the hosts of the king of Aram, and the archer who wounded Ahab king of Israel, after his cure from leprosy became a *Ger Toshab* (i.e., a semi-proselyte). However, in some respects, his firm faith is said to have surpassed that of Jethro, for whereas the latter said, "I know that the Lord is greater than all the gods," thus leaving a loophole for belief in other deities, the former asks God's forgiveness for bowing to the gods even against his will and asserts, "Behold now, I know that there is no God in all the earth but in Israel."

An old tradition recounts that the children's children of Haman taught Torah in B'nai Brak, the children's children of Sisera taught school children in Jerusalem; the children's children of Sennacherib taught Torah in other institutions of learning. Of Nebuchadnezzar, too, it was said that he prayed to be accepted as a convert but was rejected at the protestation of the ministering angels who cried: "Lord of the Universe, wilt Thou accept him who destroyed Thy house under the wings of Thy Shekinah?" Yet even Nebuchadnezzar, "the wicked," is in the apocryphal *Bel and the Dragon,* and the Talmud ultimately reclaimed him. The miraculous deliverances of Daniel and his three companions made a profound impression on the Babylonians, and among the many who became converts was Nebuchadnezzar who is said to have devoted himself to composing hymns of penitence and praise which gave promise to equal, if not to excel, the Psalms of David. In his zeal for his new faith, Nebuchadnezzar ordered the massacre of the Jews who submitted to his former decrees and worshiped the idols. His reverence for the Lord surpassed that of Melchizedek. For, while the latter mentioned God's name after Abraham's, when Nebuchadnezzar learned that his letter to Hezekiah began, "Greetings to king Hezekiah, to the city of Jerusalem, and to the Great God," he ran after the messenger until he overtook him, and ordered him to write the name of God first.[33]

As it was with Sennacherib so was it with some of his leading generals. In the apocryphon of Judith, Holofernes offers to accept the religion of Judith if she would consent to gratify his lust; an offer which Judith rejects with disgust. Achior, "the Ammonite," on the other hand, is drawn to Judaism while he is yet in the service of the pagan king. He is beaten, bound, and thrown into the Jewish camp, but though a fallen enemy, he receives kindly treatment in the home of its leader, and after the sad end of Holofernes "he believed in God exceedingly, circumcised the flesh of his foreskin and was joined into the house of Israel unto this day."

The Talmud has a weird story about the conversion of Nebuzaradan, Nebuchadnezzar's general, who personally participated in the destruction of Israel's independence. When he entered the Temple he saw a pool of blood seething by the side of the altar. The priests assured him that it was the blood of a sacrifice. Not satisfied with the information he put them to torture till they confessed that it was the blood of the prophet Zechariah, who was slain because he constantly reproached them for not mending their ways. To placate his ghost, Nebuzaradan ordered the slaughter of the sages, the Sanhedrin, the scholars and the young priests, and lastly of little children. As many as a million lives were thus sacrificed, but the blood kept on sizzling. Tired of the human holocaust, Nebuzaradan exclaimed, "Zechariah, Zechariah! I have slaughtered the best of them, wouldst thou have me slay them all?" Instantly the blood calmed down, and Nebuzaradan reflected: "If for the killing of one person so many were doomed to lose their lives, how great must be my guilt who have killed so many?" Whereupon he tore off the image of his master from his chariot, wrote his last will and testament, fled to a distant land, where he became a God-fearing Jew. Among his descendants were Shmaya and Abtalion, the two eminent Pharisee sages who served the Jewish people as the President and Vice-President respectively of the Great Sanhedrin.[34]

In the course of time, most of the posterity of these genuine or supposititious proselytes lost their genealogical records, and all traces of their racial origin disappeared. There were, however, some groups which retained or invented a family tree

going back to biblical converts to which they clung for centuries. Among these are the Rechabites and the Falashas.

According to a widespread tradition, the Rechabites and
the Kenites were kinsmen or descendants of Jethro. Jabez,
one of them, was identified as Othniel b. Kenaz, who succeeded Moses as the head of the academy which produced
great scholars and saints. Another, Jonadab b. Rechab was
pointed out by Jeremiah as a model of filial loyalty. From
their midst came members of the Sanhedrin and scribes in
"the chamber of hewn stones" in the Temple court. By marrying into the priesthood some of them officiated at the altar
on a day specially appointed for them. It was believed that
they would be the first to announce the advent of the Messiah
and to bring the first offering to the rebuilt Temple. Of
Jabez, the contemporary of Jeremiah, it was said that he was
admitted into paradise while still alive.[35]

In the Middle Ages, Rechabites were found by the traveler
Benjamin of Tudela (1160) among the B'ne Khaibar whose
abode is "twenty-one days" journey from Babylon through
the desert of Sheba, or Al-Yemen. They are described as independent tribes under the chieftainship of R. Hanan. Their
capital is Tema, and they possess large and fortified cities.
Some, like their allies, the Arabs, lead the life of free-booters;
others are farmers and shepherds. They send a tenth of all
they have for the support of the poor and the learned in
Palestine who dress in black, eat no meat, nor drink any
wine, and fast and pray continually for their welfare. Benjamin
also refers to a brother of R. Hanan, Prince Salmon, who
reigned over Tilmas where there were about one hundred
thousand Rechabites. The two brothers, though Rechabites,
claimed descent from David and fasted forty days a year for
the salvation of their co-religionists in the *Galut* (exile).

About five hundred years later, R. Judah Loew b. Bezaleel
located the Rechabites in China, and applied to them the
prophecy of Isaiah:

> Behold these shall come from afar...
> And these from the land of Sinim (China).

However, in 1828, Dr. Wolff traced them to Arabia near Mecca, and reported that they are strict observers of the Mosaic Law, expert horsemen, and number about sixty thousand.[36]

The most persistent story of proselytism is one in which King Solomon figures as the hero and the Queen of Sheba as the heroine. This royal lady, who in Arabic sources is known as Bilkis, came all the way from Abyssinia to probe the famed Hebrew monarch with hard questions. But Solomon gave her more than answers to questions. He gave her "all she desired" by making her his wife. It was in honor of their wedding that a royal bard composed the epithalamium which concludes with the lines:

> Instead of thy fathers shall be thy sons,
> Whom thou shalt make princes in all the land.

In due time Bilkis bore a son whom she named Menelik (King) or Ibn al-Hakim (son of the wise). Being his firstborn, Solomon himself instructed him and trained him to be his successor to the throne. Out of deference for the opinion of the people, however, Solomon crowned him king of Ethiopia and, bestowing upon him the name of David, sent him to his mother. With him he also sent eminent teachers of the Torah and members of the Davidic dynasty, who were distinguished by their white complexions and red hair, and twelve elders representing the twelve tribes of Israel. They were led by Azariah ben Zadok, the priest, who was entrusted with a replica of the ancient ark. Azariah, however, with the assistance of the archangel Gabriel, managed to exchange the copy of the ark for the original and carried it off to Aksum, Abyssinia's capital, by floating in the air to the height of a cubit above the ground.

Bilkis was succeeded (986 B.C.E.) by Menelik, whose dynasty continued down to and including Haile Selassie, whose coat of arms was a lion passant, proper, upon a field of gules, with the legend: "The Lion of the Race of Solomon and the Tribe of Judah hath overcome." In the course of time, most, if not

all, the people followed the example of their ruler and accepted the religion of Israel. They kept in touch with Palestine as is indicated in the story of the eunuch of Queen
Candace recorded in the Acts of the Apostles. Even after St.
Frumentius won over two sons of the emperor to Christianity
(341), the dynasty continued to be Jewish, and in the ninth
century we still hear of a Jewish emperor who reigned at
Aksum and ruled over Yemen. The Zague dynasty (925-1225)
contains kings by the name of Gideon, the queens called
Esther and Judith. The *Kebra Negest* (the Glory of the Kings),
the most venerated book of the Abyssinians, is an imitation
of the Book of Kings of the Bible. Coptic or Jacobite Christianity, however, steadily gained ground among the populace
and, after the Agaus invasion in the seventh century, many
of the inhabitants accepted Mohammedanism.

Those who continued to cling to the Hebraic faith through
the vicissitudes of centuries are known to this day as *Falashas*
(strangers, reminiscent of the Hebrew *gerim*). They claim
direct descent from the Hebrew patriarchs, and pride themselves on the purity of their blood and are very careful about
bodily cleanliness. They marry and mingle only with their
own, and if compelled to visit an unbeliever they undergo a
thorough lustration and put on a complete change of clothing
before they re-enter their homes or associate with their coreligionists.

They are acquainted with the Bible only through a translation in Gheez. They are strict observers of the Sabbath,
which they personify as an angel who was created before
the heaven and earth were made, was appointed over the
sun and rain, and will precede them on their way to Jerusalem at the advent of the Messiah. Of the months of the
year they know only four Hebrew names: Nisan, Ab, "Lul"
(Elul), and "Teshran" (Tishri). On the tenth day of every
month they observe a fast (in remembrance of Yom Kippur?),
on the twelfth in honor of the Archangel Michael, and on
the fifteenth in memory of Passover and Pentecost. They
slaughter a lamb on the eve of Passover, and eat mazzot
(unleavened bread) also during the Feast of Tabernacles.

The pious fast on the second and fifth day of the week, and during the first nine days of Tammuz in commemoration of the destruction of the first Temple. Circumcision is performed on the eighth day not only on boys but on girls, and the operator is a woman. A first-born may marry only a first-born, and the first-born animal is given to the priest when it is one year old. They also have *nezirim,* or hermits, whom they revere for their wisdom and sanctity, and to whom they confess when about to die. Their *mesgid* (Mikdash?) or synagogue is built on the plan of the Solomonic Temple. It consists of a Holy of Holies, into which only the Cohanim are admitted, and a sanctuary containing a table for the Holy Bible, the priestly vestments, the vessels in which is kept the water of the Red Heifer, and a sacrificial altar.[37]

Many relics of a primitive Judaism have also been retained among the Ethiopian Christians. They observe the Jewish Sabbath as well as the Christian Sunday, abstain from pork and other "unclean" food, fast on Wednesdays and Fridays, practice circumcision, build their mesgids in the style of the Solomonic Temple facing the East, and though they adore ikons are against graven images. The City of Refuge is still a dominant institution among them. One of their leading festivals is called "Hedar Sion" (the glory of Zion), when the people array themselves in their finest garments and celebrate with dancing and floral offerings.

The struggle for survival which was put up by the Falashas was as heroic as that of any other branch of the house of Israel. When forced to accept Christianity, many of them secretly continued to adhere to their Jewish faith, and at the first opportunity took refuge in the mountain gorges where their defection would not easily be detected. On the other hand, the *Tabiban,* or smiths, after their deportation to Shoa, organized themselves into a community under a religious head of their own, and introduced their ancestral faith among the natives on both sides of Equatorial Africa. They are reputed to have been builders of cities, constructors of navigable canals and irrigation dams, and founders of empires, and are spoken of as "the masons of the desert."

When the Falashas were discovered by Professor Joseph
Halevy in 1867, they were said to have numbered about a
quarter of a million of self-reliant farmers, potters, masons,
blacksmiths, tanners, saddlers, etc., who were superior mentally
and morally to their neighbors, and who believed that the
only Beita Israel ("House of Israel") was to be found in their
thatched huts around their *mesgid* with a red earthen pot
on its apex. Since then, persecution and conversion have further
reduced them to about fifty thousand, and many of those who
live in Addis Ababa have become traders. But through the efforts of Dr. Jaques Faitlovitch, a pupil of Professor Halevy, pro-
Falasha Committees have been organized in Europe and
America for the purpose of establishing Jewish schools among
them and for training teachers to instruct them in their ancestral faith. Even Haile Selassie interested himself in the
movement and made large personal gifts towards its further-
ance. It is the first and only mission undertaken by Jews for
the saving of Jews.[38]

CHAPTER VI

BY THE RIVERS OF BABYLON

WHEN the remnant of the Judeans, after the lapse of fifteen centuries, retraced, in an opposite direction, the steps of their first Patriarch, the Chaldeans were no longer in existence. Their successors, the Assyrians, had been vanquished by the Babylonians whose capital became the wealthiest city on the face of the earth. To Babylon, people flocked from all parts of the globe, some to escape boredom in her magnificent palaces and hanging gardens, others as miserable captives scourged into the slave markets. All of them were overwhelmed by the pomp of her princes and fascinated by the sights which continually met their gaze. Her splendor impressed even those who, like Jeremiah and Ezekiel, were repelled by her cruelty and rapacity. At the sight of the great processions as they marched along the Sacred Way with the golden statues of the gods to the temples of Ishtar the warlord, or Ea or Sin the moon-god, of Bel or Shamash the sun-god, to the accompaniment of the horn, pipe, harp, trigon, psaltery and bagpipe, and other instruments and the clashing of cymbals and blaring of trumpets, many even of those who were drawn thither out of curiosity were struck with conviction and joined the multitude of worshipers.[1]

Most of the ten tribes, who had been deported to Assyria in 722 B.C.E., were thus lost to Israel, and the same fate threatened to overtake the Judeans who were led into captivity in 597 and 586. The new immigrants found their former countrymen thoroughly Babylonianized; and if the latter evinced any interest in their newly arrived and bedraggled kinsmen it was to assimilate them as quickly as possible to

130

their own standard of citizenship. Some of them even became "Hebrew pagan" missionaries who "hunted the souls as birds" in the hope that they would thus save their own souls. These, especially the women, Ezekiel tells us, cowed the hearts of the righteous by their divinations and strengthened the hands of the wicked by distributing among them handfuls of barley and crumbs of bread in return for their willingness to admit that they had seen the light of paganism.[2]

It was hard enough to promulgate and maintain Jewish ideals among the masses while Palestine was still an independent state; it seemed almost a hopeless task now that they found themselves in the hotbed of paganism, with every inducement to abandon their ancient heritage. The temptation to follow in the footsteps of their predecessors was well nigh irresistible. The leading families, who even before the exile were more or less Assyrianized, were the first to be absorbed in the Babylonian melting pot. Their lowlier countrymen followed suit. They ceased to celebrate the Sabbath and the festivals, intermarried with the natives, and exchanged the Hebrew for the Aramaic tongue. The descendants of those who vowed never to forget Jerusalem and refused to sing the Lord's song in the land of the stranger forgot, within less than seventy years, both the Lord and Jerusalem, so that when the opportunity presented itself to rehabilitate the land of their fathers and to rebuild the ruined sanctuary, only some forty thousand were willing to take a hand in the great undertaking. They heeded Jeremiah's advice to seek the peace of the city whither they had been exiled; but his constant admonition not to learn the ways of the Gentiles among whom they dwelt, they forgot or ignored.

Yet there were a few, a remnant, who remained steadfast in the face of all allurement and served as religious leaven both among those who became estranged and those who were pagan by birth. Owing to them, the fire kindled by the prophets soon flared forth even brighter than ever just at the moment when it seemed on the point of being extinguished. Indeed it was in Babylonia where the term *ger,* which formerly had a geographic connotation, first assumed a religious significance, and where the Jews who were themselves *gerim,* in the sense of strangers, became convinced of their duty to make *gerim,* in the sense of proselytes, of their non-Jewish countrymen. It was there that Judaism divested itself of the last shred of "blood and soil" and proclaimed that faith alone renders one an alien or a member of the community of Israel. Thus was Israel's very calamity turned into a source of strength, and fitted him for the part which, according to the Prophets, he was destined to play in God's plan for the regeneration of the human race.

These faithful among the Babylonian Jews never became reconciled to the idea that with the *Golah* (exile) their nationhood came to an end. The hope of a speedy restoration never forsook them. Some indeed believed that the captivity was but a momentary means on the part of God in order to reclaim them to Himself, and they hardly had crossed the Babylonian border when they sent a pathetic inquiry to Jeremiah:

Is not the Lord in Zion? Is not her King in her? ...
The harvest is passed, the summer is ended,
And we are not saved.

As the weary years dragged on and no relief came in sight, some of them began to complain: "The days are prolonged, and every sign faileth. Our bones are dried up, and our hope is lost; we are clean cut off." Yet their will-to-live remained as strong as ever. It needed but the encouraging word of some inspiring personality to fan the spark of hope into a flame, or to breathe into the dry bones new life and fresh zeal. This was done by Ezekiel, priest by virtue of his birth, prophet by inner compulsion, who was raised in Palestine but spent the great part of his life with his uprooted brethren in Babylon. [3]

As a priest Ezekiel stressed the importance of ceremonialism, particularly the observance of the Sabbath and the rite of circumcision. While Judea was still bleeding from every pore and writhing in the agony of the Babylonian conquest, he busied himself with preparing plans for the restored Judea, and drew up a model of the reconstructed Temple without which a Jewish state was to him unthinkable. Patriot that he was, yet he would not have his people form merely another nation—"to serve wood and stone." Every Jew was to observe the ceremonials hitherto regarded as incumbent only on the priesthood. "No alien, uncircumcised in heart and uncircumcised in flesh" was to be admitted into the sanctuary.

But Ezekiel's priestly preferences were modified by his prophetic universalism. God, he declares, calls to all to turn from their idols and from all their abominations, and Israel's humiliation as well as his glorious restoration were to sanctify God before the eyes of men, and to bring about humanity's salvation. Far from being prejudiced against the stranger, Ezekiel went so far as to provide in his Great Charter that:

> The land (the new Palestine) be divided by lot for an inheritance unto you and to the strangers that sojourn among you; and they shall be unto you as the homeborn among the children of Israel.[4]

As prophet, too, Ezekiel uttered a number of threatening "dooms" regarding the Ammonites, Moabites, Edomites, Philistines, Tyreans, Sidonians, and Egyptians, and prophesied that a universal conversion would come about in some miraculous way, and the young and tender twig in the mountain of Israel "will bring forth boughs, and bear fruit, and be a stately cedar; and under it shall dwell all fowl of every wing... and the nations that are round about you shall know that I am the Lord."[5]

The first to pave the way for active missionary effort was Jeremiah, to whom the spiritual destiny of his people was more important than even their national independence. From the very beginning of his career he proclaimed himself an appointed prophet to the nations, and he comforted himself with the hope that through the agony of the captivity the nations would be led to a recognition of the God of Israel.

His advice to the exiles was to make Babylon their home: "Build houses and plant gardens, and seek the peace of the city whither God has caused you to be carried away captive, and pray unto the Lord for its peace."

Never before was such advice given by patriot to his vanquished countrymen. But Jeremiah was interested in the fate not only of his own people but also of the nations which were Israel's neighbors, in Egypt, Philistia, Moab, Ammon, Edom, Aram, and Arabia, as fellowmen and prospective proselytes. Nor did he doubt that when backsliding Israel would lead the way and return to God, the nations would follow. They would be impressed by the sanctity and security of the inhabitants of Palestine, "and they shall call Jerusalem the throne of the Lord; and all the nations shall be gathered unto it, to the name of the Lord, to Jerusalem; neither shall they walk any more after the stubbornness of their evil heart." Thus visioning the glorious future, which he was sure awaited mankind, the man of sorrow, who more than any other "saw affliction by the rod of His wrath," was transported with joy, amidst the desolation and disintegration around him and burst forth in a hymn of praise:

> O Lord, my strength, and my stronghold,
> And my refuge in the day of affliction,
> Unto Thee shall the nations come
> From the ends of the earth, and shall say:
> 'Our fathers have inherited nought but lies,
> Vanity and things wherein there is no profit.'[6]

Jeremiah was indefatigable in urging his people to hasten the advent of the great day by teaching and preaching their faith, even as he did, to the nations. From Palestine, and later from Egypt, he kept up communications with the Babylonian captives, in which he spurred them on to take up the offensive in behalf of Israel's God and fight paganism on its own soil. We still have a fragment of what may have been a postscript or part of a long epistle. Since it is written in Aramaic the letter must have been addressed to one who knew not Hebrew, perhaps one of the "lost" of the Ten Tribes. It reads:

> Thus shall ye say unto them: 'The gods that have not made the heavens and the earth, these will perish from the earth, and from under the heavens.'

Not unlikely the prophet must have felt that the native Babylonian Jews, who were assimilated, were better adapted to carry out his plan of personal propaganda than the more recent immigrants. It was the "good figs, very good," of the old but still loyal Babylonian Jewish families who gave tone to the Jewish community, and made Judaism respectable in the eyes of the Gentiles. It was no doubt one of their midst who prevailed upon Evil-Merodach, Nebuchadnezzar's successor, to release Jehoiakim from his dungeon and make him one of his close associates. It was they who could speak and write on Judaism in Aramaic and thus familiarize others with the doctrines of their religion, which was a step forward in the direction of proselytism. [7]

But it was not long ere the Judeans caught up with the older exiles and even surpassed them in their Babylonianization. What it took the Northerners a hundred and fifty years to accomplish, the Southerners compressed into almost one generation. With their orientation came also a sense of self-realization. Those who sat at the feet of Jeremiah or Ezekiel were not afraid to sing the song of the Lord in the land in which they no longer felt themselves to be strangers. Some even did not hesitate to preach their doctrine in the open, and point to the superiority of their religion over that of the Babylonians. Daniel and his associates proclaimed the power of the God of Israel in the august presence of Nebuchadnezzar, Belshazzar, and Darius. And many another zealous Judean declared God's testimonies before the mighty, especially after the era of religious freedom inaugurated by Cyrus and maintained by many of his successors. It was probably by such a missionary, or perhaps even a convert, scorned by those of his own brethren who were at ease and taunted by the crushing remark that the God whom he preaches is a defeated God, that was penned such a lament as:

> I am become a reproach,
> Yea, unto my neighbors exceedingly, and a
>   dread to mine acquaintance;
> They that see me flee from me . . .
> I am become a stranger unto my brethren,
> And an alien unto my mother's children . . .
> They that sit at the gate talk of me;
> And I am the song of the drunkards. [8]

Soon something happened which gave an additional impetus to proselytism in Babylonia. The empire whose ruler once boasted "as one gathered eggs that are forsaken, have I gathered all the earth," was itself gathered in almost without a struggle. The mighty gates of Babylon were flung open by traitors of the "fifth column," and Cyrus the Persian ascended the throne of Nebuchadnezzar. Cyrus was a statesman as well as a general. Probably for political reasons, he showed himself favorable to the Judeans, and not long after he became master of Babylonia, issued a proclamation (537 B.C.E.):

> Thus saith Cyrus king of Persia: All the kingdoms of the earth hath the Lord, the God of heaven, given me; and He hath charged me to build Him a house in Jerusalem, which is in Judah. Whosoever there is among you of all His people—his God be with him—let him go up to Jerusalem, which is in Judah, and build the house of the Lord, the God of Israel, He is God Who is in Jerusalem. And whosoever is left, in any place where he sojourneth, let the men of the place help him with silver and with gold, and with goods, and with beasts, beside the freewill-offering for the house of God which is in Jerusalem. [9]

This unexpected turn in Babylonian affairs caused a tremendous emotional upheaval among the Judeans. It was recalled that Isaiah predicted the fall of Babylonia; it was therefore believed that his other predictions would also come true and that:

> The Lord will have compassion on Jacob, and will yet choose Israel, and set them in their own land; and the stranger shall join himself with them, and they shall cleave to the house of Jacob. And the peoples shall take them, and bring them to their place; and the house of Israel shall possess them in the land of the Lord for servants and for handmaids, and they shall take them captive whose captives they were; and they shall rule over their oppressors.

The strain was taken up by the later prophets. Haggai was certain that the day which would witness the laying of the foundation of the Temple would mark the beginning of the realization of God's plan, and that in a little while thereafter He "will shake the heavens and the earth, and the sea and the dry land; and the choicest things of all nations shall come and fill this house with glory." Zechariah, a priestly prophet, announced that he had been sent "after glory to the nations which spoiled" Israel, and that

> It shall come yet to pass, that there shall come many peoples, and the inhabitants of many cities; and the inhabitants of one city shall go to another, saying: 'Let us go speedily to entreat the favor of the Lord, and to seek the Lord of hosts; I will go also.' Yea, many peoples and mighty nations shall come to seek the Lord of hosts in Jerusalem, and to entreat the favor of the Lord. Thus saith the Lord: In those days it shall come to pass, that ten men shall take out of the languages of the nations, shall even take hold of the skirt of him that is a Jew, saying: 'We will go with you, for we have heard that God is with you.' [10]

In this universal conversion, not only will Hadrach, Damascus, and Hamath, Tyre, Zidon, Ashkelon, and Gaza be refined as silver and purified as gold, but also they that are far off shall come and "join themselves to the Lord," and perform their annual pilgrimage on the Feast of Tabernacles. God's plan will at last be accomplished. Jerusalem will become a reservoir of spiritual strength, the religious clearing house of mankind.

And the Lord shall be king over all the earth;
In that day the Lord shall be One, and His name One.[11]

Surpassing Zechariah in his glowing Messianic expectations and missionary fervor was a contemporary who is generally referred to as Isaiah the Second. This great unknown seer, in whose inspired prophetic fragments Jewish universalism takes its highest flight, was the embodiment of the missionary conscience of his people. For him, Israel's *raison d'etre* is to be "the servant of the Lord." Nothing else matters. Unlike Haggai and Zechariah, he regards the Temple as of secondary importance:

The heaven is My throne,
And the earth is My footstool;
Where is the house that ye may build unto Me?
And where is the place that may be My resting-place?

And he exclaims in the name of God:

This people I have formed for Myself,
That they might tell My praise!

And addressing himself directly to his fellow-captives he exclaims:

I the Lord have called thee in righteousness,
And have taken hold of thy hand.
And kept thee, and set thee for a covenant
of the people,
For a light of the nations;

To open the blind eyes,
To bring out the prisoners from the dungeon,
And them that sit in darkness out of the
prisonhouse. [12]

Contemporary events also contributed not a little to confirm the prophet's faith in the speedy conversion of mankind.
The conquerors of Babylonia were no ordinary pagans. They
professed a religion in some respects similar to Judaism. In
the first place, they tolerated no images and observed the
Noahian commandments. They also practiced many rites
of purification and were tolerant towards the religion of
Israel. The invaders did not hesitate to visit the synagogue,
nor were they averse to learn about, or from, the Judeans.
In the court of the king there were eunuchs and high officials
who observed the Sabbath. Some even submitted to the rite
of circumcision. Verily, it seemed that at last:

The Lord hath made bare His holy arm
In the sight of all the nations;
And all the ends of the earth shall see
The salvation of our God. [13]

Encouraged by these propitious signs, the prophet's confidence in the success of Israel's mission was greatly enhanced,
and he called on his people to redouble their efforts to share
their spiritual possession with the rest of their fellowmen.
Surely the day would come when the nations will recognize
that Israel suffered not because of God's hatred for him but
because of His love of all mankind, and will acknowledge
that:

He was wounded because of our transgressions,
He was crushed because of our iniquities:
The chastisement of our welfare was upon him,
And with his stripes were we healed...
Yet it pleased the Lord to crush him by disease;
To see if his soul would offer itself in restitution,

That he might see his seed, prolong his days,
And the purpose of the Lord might prosper by
his hand.

This became an *idee fixe* with our prophet. The world must
and will be converted, if only Israel will remain true to his
task as God's witness. He must remember that as a Servant
of the Lord:

It is too light a thing...
To raise up the tribes of Jacob
And to restore the offspring of Israel,
I will also give thee for a light of the nations,
That My salvation may be unto the end of the earth.

And Isaiah himself set the example and devoted himself
with every fibre of his being to enlighten them that walked
in darkness. With the same trumpet voice which declared
unto the house of Jacob their sins, he called also upon
the peoples to abandon their idols. He resorted to every ex-
pedient. He reasoned sweetly, he asserted defiantly, he pleaded,
he threatened. We can almost see him calling like Wisdom
personified "in the top of high places... beside the gates
... at the coming in at the doors":

Ho, everyone that thirsteth, come ye for water,
And he that hath no money;
Come ye, buy and eat;
Yea, come, buy wine and milk
Without money and without price.

To him nobody is too exalted or too humble. He does not
hesitate to appeal to Cyrus himself. He assures him that
though a Zoroastrian he is "God's anointed," and that
without being aware of it he is performing God's pleasure
in Babylon. He should therefore take one more step and

join the Judeans in their monotheistic creed, and in their effort to propagate it:

> For the sake of Jacob My servant,
> And Israel Mine elect,
> I have called thee by thy name,
> I have surnamed thee, though thou hast not known Me.
> That they may know from the rising of the sun, and from the west,
> That there is none beside Me;
> I am the Lord, and there is none else;
> I form the light, and create darkness;
> I make peace and create evil;
> I am the Lord, that doeth all these things.

And again:

> Bel boweth down, Nebo stoopeth;
> Their idols are upon the beasts, and upon the cattle;
> The things that ye carried about are made a load,
> A burden to the weary beast.
> They stoop, they bow down together,
> They could not deliver the burden;
> And themselves are gone into captivity. [14]

But Isaiah did not always ridicule or contend. Frequently he drew his listeners with the cords of love and painted to them a picture of the bliss and peace which would follow their regeneration. That they are not of the seed of Abraham need not give them any concern. God's love is free to all. They can feel perfectly at home in His house and His walls:

> Thus saith the Lord:
> 'Keep ye justice, and do righteousness;
> For my salvation is near to come,
> And My favor to be revealed...'
> Neither let the alien,

That hath joined himself to the Lord speak, saying:
'The Lord will surely separate me from His people':
Neither let the eunuch say:
'Behold, I am a dry tree.'
For thus saith the Lord
Concerning the eunuchs that keep My Sabbaths,
And choose the things that please Me,
And hold fast by My covenant:
Even unto them will I give in My house
And within My walls a monument and a memorial
Better than sons and daughters;
I will give them an everlasting memorial,
That shall not be cut off.
Also the aliens, that join themselves to the Lord,
    to minister unto Him,
And to love the name of the Lord,
To be His servants,
Everyone that keepeth the Sabbath from profaning it,
And holdeth fast by My covenant:
Even them will I bring to My holy mountain,
And make them joyful in My house of prayer;
Their burnt-offerings and their sacrifices
Shall be acceptable upon Mine altar;
For My house shall be called
A house of prayer for all peoples. [15]

Isaiah's was the first, direct, and official welcome extended to
non-Jews into the household of Israel. But Isaiah had a word
of encouragement for those also who, for some reason, "joined
themselves to the Lord" but did not assume the full burden
of Judaism. Those who are the *Yire Adonai* (fearers of the
Lord), and keep justice and righteousness, are equally dear
to God by whatever name they choose to call Him or themselves, and He will gather them also "beside those of him
that are gathered":

Who is among you that feareth the Lord,
That obeyeth the voice of His servant?
Though he walketh in darkness, and hath no light,

Let him trust in the name of the Lord,
And stay upon his God.

If the prophecies we possess of the Babylonian Isaiah are
arranged in chronological order, it is pleasant to think that
his sanguine hopes did not forsake him to the last. In fact,
the further we proceed the more glowing becomes the vision.
The last six chapters constitute a rhapsody of Zion, and through
Zion the whole world, redeemed. It begins with a call to duty:

Arise, shine, for thy light is come
And the glory of the Lord is risen upon thee,

And culminates with the blessed assurance that

Nations shall walk in thy light,
And kings at the brightness of thy rising...
And they shall call thee the city of the Lord
The Zion of the Holy One of Israel. [16]

The Prophet then proceeds with a vision which the Palestinian
Isaiah had put off to the "last of days." Jerusalem is become
the spiritual home of humanity. To it the sons of those who
afflicted Israel flock and deem it a privilege to be accepted as
priests and Levites. Among them are princes and peasants,
sovereigns and slaves; they come from Egypt and Ethiopia,
from Midian and Ephah, from Tarshish, Pul and Lud, from
Sheba and Kedar and Nabaioth and the land of the Sinim,
with offerings of frankincense, and

He who blesses himself in the earth
Shall bless himself by the God of truth;
And he that sweareth in the earth
Shall swear by the God of truth...
And it shall come to pass,
That from one new moon to another,
And from one Sabbath to another,
Shall all flesh come to worship before Me,
Saith the Lord. [17]

This vision was partly realized by those who started on their way back from Babylon to Jerusalem in 537 B.C.E. Besides the Judeans, including the Benjaminites, who constituted the majority, and probably also numerous offspring of the ten Lost Tribes, there were not a few who had separated themselves "from the filthiness of the peoples of the land, to seek the Lord, the God of Israel." Some of them were, as a psalmist describes them, of "the princes of the peoples," others were of the descendants of those who a generation or two before had "given the dead bodies of God's servants for food unto the fowls of heaven," or had themselves "burned up all the meeting-places of God in the land." The last named had since experienced a change of heart. Cyrus' proclamation convinced them of the power of Israel's God even more than the reasoning, the reproach, the pleadings, and the irony of the prophets.

The Restoration caused a sensation among the nations. Everywhere they spoke of the great things which the Lord had done to the captives of Zion. As they were met while on their way with gifts from the people, it appeared to a psalmist that already

> From the rising of the sun unto the going down thereof
> The Lord's Name is praised.

and an enraptured prophet by the name, or pseudonym, of Malachi (c. 430) proclaimed:

> From the rising of the sun unto the going down
>   of the same
> My Name is great among the nations,
> And in every place offerings are presented unto
>   My Name,
> Even pure obligations,
> For My name is great among the nations,
> Saith the Lord of hosts.

As for the aliens who joined themselves unto the Lord, "the former things were not remembered, nor came into

mind." Though not of the seed of Abraham, they were welcomed as brothers. When the new altar was erected the dedi-
catory exercises were participated in not only by priests, Levites,
and laymen, not only by full-fledged converts, but also by
"fearers of the Lord" and those who hung on the outer fringe
of Judaism. Even the nationals who had no connection with
the faith of Israel were invited to join in thanking God for
His goodness:

> O let Israel now say:
> 'For His mercy endureth for ever.'
> O let the house of Aaron now say:
> 'For His mercy endureth for ever.'
> O let the *Yire Adonai* now say:
> 'For His mercy endureth for ever...'
> O praise the Lord, all ye nations;
> Laud Him, all ye peoples...[18]

There was an element, however, to whom this throwing of
the gates of Judaism wide open was distasteful. This group,
known as the "Mourners of Zion," or *Haredim,* because "they
trembled at the words of the God of Israel," were the opposite
of the "lost" Ten Tribes. The Captivity evoked all the con-
servatism of which they were capable. They were in constant
dread lest the people relapse into idolatry and expected the
conversion of the world and the rebuilding of the Temple
by a sudden and miraculous interposition of God. They insisted
on the continuance of the fast days which commemorated the
tragic events which led to the assassination of Gedaliah. They
imposed upon the laymen the dietary regulations which were
formerly practiced only by the priests; and circumcision to
which neither Jethro, nor the Kenites, nor the Gibeonites
were required to submit, they required as a *sine qua non* a
"sign of admission into the Covenant of Abraham." [19]

It goes without saying that intermarriage went under the
ban. Hitherto, though marrying outside of the faith was not
encouraged, it was not forbidden. Certainly there was no
discrimination against anyone because of his being the child
of a non-Jewish parent. Even the priestly code limited the

prohibition to the "seven nations" of Canaan. But the "Mourners of Zion" in their anxiety for the integrity of Judaism set themselves against any foreign infiltration, and excluded from their midst not only those who were themselves guilty of the offense but also their children and children's children.

This movement, of which Ezekiel was partly the protagonist, reached its climax under Ezra, the priestly scribe, who obtained a royal firman to lead the second *Aliyah* (immigration) under Artaxerxes (458). The Rabbis claim that the reason why he did not join the first *Aliyah* under Cyrus was because he then regarded the study of the Torah as more important than the rebuilding of the Temple. Possibly he was one of those pietists who, in their firm faith in a miraculous deliverance, did not encourage the rehabilitation of Palestine in the prosaic manner of a political adventure, and believed "the time is not come, the time that the Lord's house should be rebuilt." Swept away at last by the fervor of the "Zionists," of those days Palestine was to him still mainly a place where the Judeans would be able to maintain their faith in its pristine purity, and, chastened by their sufferings, would become indeed a "kingdom of priests, and a holy nation."

Ezra's first official act on his arrival in Palestine was to take a census of the Judeans who were racially pure. He was appalled at the extent to which not only the laymen but the priests and the Levites "have not separated themselves from the people of the land ... so that the holy seed have mingled themselves with the people of the land." It was enough to make him rend his garments, and pluck off the hair of his head and beard. So he made the people enter into a covenant "to put away all the (foreign) wives, and such as are born of them." In this he was assisted by his disciple Nehemiah who with another group arrived in 445. Unlike Zerubbabel, his predecessor, Nehemiah, too, espoused the cause of the *Haredim,* (those in fear of the commandments of the Lord) and at a great assembly the Judeans resolved on strict observance of the Sabbath and the holidays and the year of Jubilee, and to exclude all who were guilty of intermarriage. Even the Gibeonites, whose Hebrew ancestry went back to the days of Joshua, were dropped from the congregation, and the Nethinim, who were reputed to be kin or descendants of Jethro, and whose connection with the sanctuary dated from the time of Solomon, were reduced in rank beneath that of bastard. As for the bastards, the Rabbis claimed that Ezra prayed that they die young, so that their blood might not pollute the blood of others. [20]

These drastic measures to stem the tide of intermarriage stirred up much bitterness and defiance both in Palestine and Babylonia. As a consequence, Ezra and Nehemiah found themselves compelled to connive. The tainted Hakkoz family was reinstated in the priesthood, and Meshulam and Sabbathai and others, whose Levitic lineage was defective, were allowed to perform their sacerdotal functions. Of those who were excluded, many emigrated to Samaria and other neighboring nations, where they made converts from the local religions. Among these were Sanballat and Tobias, who were instrumental in building the temple on Mt. Gerizim. Samaritan sources have it that three hundred thousand *gerim* joined Sanballat in his reclamation of the ancient Israelitish capital. [21] But notwithstanding their ostracism in Judea, most *gerim* refused to leave the Holy Land or to renounce their new faith. A complaint, or rather plaint, of one of them is, however, included in the Isaiahnic anthology:

> Look down from heaven and see,
> Even from Thy holy and glorious habitation...
> For Thou art our Father;
> For Abraham knoweth us not,
> And Israel doth not acknowledge us;
> Thou, O Lord, art our Father,
> Our Redeemer from everlasting is Thy name.

And a psalmist has preserved for us the supplication of another:

> Hear my prayer, O Lord, and give ear unto my cry;
> Keep not silence at my tears;
> For I am a *Ger* with Thee,
> A *Toshab,* as all my fathers were.

> Look (not) away from me, that I may take comfort,
> Before I go hence, and be no more. [22]

One of the champions of the rights of the discriminated groups was the above mentioned Malachi, who is said to have been the last upon whom rested the Holy Spirit. In words which rang high above the clash of parties, he gave utterance to his outraged feelings at the unjust treatment of the proselytes and especially the "foreign" women who were married to Judean husbands. He reminded his hearers that God never condemns anyone except on the ground of conduct, that He rejected Esau, though a brother of Jacob, and will reject the priests, though sons of Aaron, who do not follow the covenant of life and peace, of truth and the turning of many away from iniquity, which was observed by Aaron. They who severed marital ties because of racial origin committed a crime more flagrant even than marrying out of the faith, for

> Have we not all one father?
> Hath not one God created us?

And his righteous indignation rising to its highest pitch, he curses those who sent them away:

> May the Lord cut off to the man that doeth this,
> Him that calleth and him that answereth out of
>   the tents of Jacob...
> Because the Lord hath been witness
> Between thee and the wife of thy youth,
> Against whom thou hast dealt treacherously,
> Though she is thy companion,
> And the wife of thy covenant...
> For I hate putting away,
> Saith the Lord, the God of Israel,
> And him that covereth his garment with violence,
> Saith the Lord of hosts.

God will also be a swift witness "against those who turn the *ger* aside from his right," and will gather in those who are excluded, even if they be not of the stock of Abraham. Their names are written down in His book of remembrance:

> And they shall be Mine, saith the Lord of hosts,
> In the day that I do make, even Mine own treasure;
> And I will spare them, as a man spareth
> His own son that serveth him...
> And unto you that fear My name
> Shall the sun of righteousness arise with healing
>   in its wings...

There is a tradition that Malachi was identical with Mordecai, whose niece Esther married the king of Persia. This perhaps explains the intensity of feeling which the prophet displayed in his defense of those who, though married out of the faith, remained loyal to their religion. [23]

Malachi, however, was not the only one who espoused the cause of intermarriage, or of the *gerim*. Stories became current of eminent Judeans who married daughters of other gods. Later these stories were put in literary form by chroniclers and scribes. In one of these, the fascinating Book of Ruth, the heroine belongs to the nation which was believed to have had an incestuous origin, and which always sought the destruction of Israel. Despite all this, she is depicted as a model of modesty and as the ancestress of the founder of the Davidic dynasty. What a stern rebuke to the *Haredim* is the relation of Naomi and Boaz to this Moabitish maiden who gave up her people and her god and came to take refuge under the wings of the God of Israel, and who gave voice to the inarticulate thoughts of the numerous proselytes of all ages in the sublime words:

> Entreat me not to leave thee, and to return from following after thee; for whither thou goest, I will go; and where thou lodgest, I will lodge; thy people shall be my people, and thy God, my God; where thou diest, I will die, and there will I be buried; the Lord do so to me, and more also, if aught but death part thee and me. [24]

Another tale of intermarriage and conversion which appeared in those days is the Book of Esther. In it, it is the Jewess who marries the heathen without protest either on her part or that of her uncle Mordecai, and the author seems to take special pains to tell us that "many from among the people of the land became Jews" (Mityahadim). Josephus indeed explains that they not only passed as Jews, as the term *Mityahadim* might suggest, but submitted to the rite of circumcision. But it also indicates that conversions were not infrequent before the Book of Esther was written, since the Hebrew vocabulary had already a word for what it formerly expressed by the improvised or secondary meaning of *ger*. [25]

In the Book of Jonah we are given a picture of the discomfiture of a Jew who is indifferent to the fate of the Gentiles. The scene is Nineveh, the great, "filthy, polluted and oppressive city" whose doom, predicted by Nahum and Zephaniah, is now at hand. Jonah receives the command to warn and save the city. But the prophet refuses to perform his duty. The Ninevites were not only non-Jewish, but were more than once the cause of Israel's suffering and humiliation, and he thinks these Gentiles are most likely incorrigible. He therefore seeks to shirk his duty by boarding a ship going to Tarshish. But God throws a storm on the sea, and the boat is about to capsize. In vain the mariners cry every one to his god, the storm does not cease. As a last resort they draw lots to find the guilty one and the lot falls upon Jonah. Jonah thereupon recognizes and admits his guilt, and much against their will the mariners cast him into the sea. There he is swallowed by a great fish, in whose belly he is confined for three days, during which he cries to God, and God orders the fish to spew him out. Jonah then reluctantly goes to Nineveh, warns the inhabitants of their doom, and they repent and are saved.

The whole narrative is suffused with the sunshine of sympathy and good will to all. The heathen mariners treat the prophet with utmost consideration, and even after he acknowledges his guilt they still row hard to bring the vessel to land in the hope of saving him. They are loath to shed what may prove to be innocent blood. The Ninevites, too, react to the prophet's preaching with a readiness and sincerity which might put the Jews themselves to shame. Verily none is beyond the scope of salvation, and Israel can bring about the conversion of the world only if he will be true to his mission to be a light unto the nations. [26]

Besides these and probably similar works which we no longer possess which were intended to remove prejudice against intermarriage, books were also produced with the object to teach non-Jews as well as Jews by means of anecdotes and aphorisms that:

> The fear of the Lord, that is wisdom;
> And to depart from evil is understanding.

The aim of the authors of the Books of Wisdom is not so much to make of the pagans proselytes of righteousness as to inculcate in them the basic virtues of justice, truthfulness, purity, and diligence and to lead them at least to become Noahides, or "fearers of the Lord". Neither in the Book of Proverbs nor in the Book of Job are there any references to the Law, to the Temple, or to any outstanding event in the history of Israel. The "strange woman" against whom Proverbs warns has nothing to do with the one whom Ezra condemned. It has nothing to do with intermarriage. Job is not even claimed as a Jew, nor is his habitat in Palestine. But he was "wholehearted, and upright, and one that feared God, and shunned evil," and having been tested and found true, God accepted him as His servant and blessed him.

Even more appealing and inspiring are the psalmists whose compositions go back to the early days of the Captivity. They address all nations in the name of Him Who "is good to all, and Whose tender mercies are over all His works." Their God rendereth to every man according to his work, but like a father has compassion upon all them that fear Him. Their one irrepressible yearning is to "declare His glory among the nations," to proclaim among the nations that "the Lord reigneth". They call upon all the inhabitants of the world

"both low and high, rich and poor together" to bless the God
of Israel and admonish kings and judges to

> Serve the Lord with fear
> And rejoice with trembling.

Above all they hurl the shafts of their sarcasm at the heathen:

> Their idols are silver and gold.
> The work of man's hands.
> They have mouths, but they speak not;
> Eyes they have, but they see not;
> They have ears, but they hear not;
> Noses they have, but they smell not;
> They have hands, but they handle not;
> Feet have they, but they walk not;
> Neither speak they with their throat.
> They that make them shall be like unto
>   them;
> Yea, every one that trusteth in them. [27]

The psalmists' hopes were heightened by the Restoration.
The sight of the scattering of God's enemies, they were confident, would quicken the process of conversion. "The wild
beasts of the reeds, the multitude of the bulls, with the calves
of the peoples" will be rebuked, and will submit themselves
to the Lord of Israel. Rahab and Babylon will know Him;
Philistia and Tyre will acknowledge Him, and all their
thoughts will be in Zion,

> Nobles shall come out of Egypt,
> Ethiopia shall hasten to stretch out her hands
>   unto God.

So sure were the psalmists at the Restoration of the realization of this expectation, and so little regard had they for Ezra's
racism that one of them composed an epithalamium for an

anticipated marriage of a Tyrean princess to a Judean king, part of which reads:

> Hearken, O daughter, and consider, and incline
>   thine ear;
> Forget also thine own people, and thy father's house;
> So shall the king desire thy beauty;
> For he is thy lord; and do homage unto him...
> Instead of thy fathers shall be thy sons,
> Whom thou shalt make princes in all the lands. [28]

CHAPTER VII

THE RISING TIDE OF PROSELYTISM

THE HIGH HOPES entertained by the post-exilic prophets were not realized for many a day. "The glory of the latter house" which, Haggai predicted, "shall be greater than that of the former," proved a bitter disappointment. The new Temple presented a poor imitation of its hallowed predecessor. It lacked all the accessories which haloed the ancient Solomonic sanctuary. It was devoid of the "ark, the sacred fire, the Urim and Thummim" and, the Rabbis add, "the Shekinah and the Holy Spirit." Indeed, Palestine itself never ceased to be a satrapy of Persia, and instead of having a king of the house of David, was ruled by High Priests who claimed descent from the house of Zadok. [1]

The priests whom already Malachi had denounced as they "who despise God's Name," became puffed up with power and wealth and constituted themselves a worldly-minded aristocracy. They were among the first to become Hellenized, but were opposed to the innovations of the Pharisees who by their biblical explications kept Judaism a living, progressive religion. The priestly class refused to recognize as Jewish the novel doctrines which came into being since the Captivity, such as the coming of the Messiah, the resurrection of the body, and the immortality of the soul. They also insisted on the literal execution of the Mosaic *lex talionis,* and, in general, adhered to the strict letter of the Law.

In the course of time they and their followers came to be known as Sadducees, either because they boasted of their descent from Zadok the High Priest of David or perhaps as *Zaddikim* (the righteous, or saints). They distinguished them-

selves from the progressive Pharisees (Separatists) who, as
they were later denounced by Jesus, "made the word of God
of none effect" by their traditions. The Pharisees on their side
regarded the Sadducees as those "who do wickedly against
the Covenant" of whom Daniel wrote, and used their name
as synonymous with Epicurean, hypocrite, heretic, and even
idolater. The Talmud attributed their disaffection to the teaching of Antigonus of Soko, who taught his disciples in the
name of Simon the Just: "Be not like servants who wait on
their master with a view to receive recompense. Be ye rather
like servants who wait on their master without a view to receive recompense, and let the fear of heaven be upon you."
There were two pupils who said: "Is it likely that our ancestors taught a doctrine such as this? Could they have expected
one to labor all day without looking forward to a wage in the
evening?" They rose and departed and founded two sects, one
named after Zadok, the other after Baithus, and used vessels of
silver and vessels of gold, not because they were proud but
because they scoffed at the Pharisees who mortified themselves
in this world and had nothing in the world to come.[2]

Whatever the origin of this sect, or school, Judea became,
shortly after Simon the Just, a prey to these worldly-minded
leaders. Hellenizing Sadducees were at the helm, and when
Antiochus Epiphanes came in control of Judea (168) he found
many among them ready to do his bidding. The Temple on
Mt. Zion was converted into a shrine of Jupiter the Olympian,
heathen altars were erected, and sacrifices were offered to idols
all over the land. Torah scrolls were torn and burned. Men
and women were tortured and murdered for refusing to eat
swine's flesh, for observing the Sabbath, or for circumcising
their children. The number of apostates increased by leaps
and bounds, and the rift between the Sadducees and the Pharisees became wider and wider.

The victory of the Maccabeans over the Syrians was a triumph of Pharisaism over Sadduceeism. The first Hasmoneans
were country priests who were not ambitious for power. They
loved their Temple and Torah and maintained the priestly
tradition established by Aaron of old. For a short while Hel-

lenism dwindled away, and apostasy almost ceased. But this was only the lull before the storm. Their descendants concentrated more on the expansion of Judea than on the promulgation of Judaism and showed decided leanings to Sadduceeism. Simon, son of John Hyrcanus, not content with the crown of the priesthood, coveted and assumed also the crown of royalty. Alexander Jannai, dissatisfied with the extent of Judea which now reached to the boundaries of the Solomonic kingdom, waged incessant wars against his neighboring nations. Their successors followed in their footsteps, and civil wars became of frequent occurrence. At last Rome, which had been biding her time to collect her due for the honor of admitting Judea into the Roman Confederacy, was invited by Aristobulus and Hyrcanus II, the last scions of the Hasmoneans, to decide as to who was entitled to the crown. Rome decided in her usual manner. Having taken all she could get from the former, she declared for another price, in favor of the latter, and on the Day of Atonement (63 B.C.E.) Pompey stormed the Temple and mingled the blood of the priests with that of their sacrifices.

Very likely both the Sadducees and the Pharisees exaggerated and distorted each other's beliefs and heresies. Nor did either of them have a monopoly of saints or sinners. Alexander Jannai, who repented before his death his persecution of the Pharisees, came nearer the truth when he bade his queen to fear neither the one nor the other but only the hypocrites "who do the deeds of Zimri and seek to be rewarded like Phinehas" (Num. 25:6-14). It is reasonable, however, to surmise that the missionary ideal which was irrefragably linked with Messianism had its most zealous supporters among the Pharisees. It was they who, while the Sadduceans were bent on conquest of territory, continued to foster the teaching of the Torah and remained indifferent and even hostile to the victories of the Maccabeans. They were also the party of peace. They were not interested in a temporal kingdom in Palestine but in the Kingdom of God on earth. It was one of them, Onias by name, who on being asked by the soldiers of Hyrcanus to pray for the defeat of those of Aristobulus, implored: "O God, King of the

Universe, since both those within and those without are Thy people, accept Thou the prayers of neither."

The missionary efforts under the regime of the Maccabeans were facilitated on the one hand by the influx of many Gentiles into Judea and on the other by the wide distribution of the Jews in the lands outside of Palestine. Jerusalem during the Second Commonwealth became one of the most cosmopolitan centers of the world, and many colonies of Gentiles were founded in the midst of the Land of Israel. At the same time Judeans flowed in a steady stream into the other countries. We may judge of the far flung extent of the Diaspora from King Agrippa's letter to Caligula two centuries after the Maccabean Restoration:

> Concerning the holy city I must now say what is necessary: It, as I have already stated, is my native country, and the metropolis not only of one country of Judea, but also of many, by reason of the colonies which it has sent out from time to time into the bordering districts of Egypt, Phoenicia, Syria in general and especially that part of it which is called Coelo-Syria, and also into those more distant regions of Pamphylia, Cilicia, the great part of Asia Minor, as far as Bithynia, and the furthermost corners of Pontus, and in the same manner into Europe, into Thessaly and Boeotia, and Macedonia, and Aetolia, and Attica, and Argoes, and Corinth, and all the most fertile and wealthiest districts of Peloponnesus, and not only are the continents full of Jewish colonies, but also all the most celebrated islands are so, too; such as Euboea, and Cyprus and Crete.
>
> I say nothing of the countries beyond the Euphrates, for all of them except a very small portion, and all the satrapies around which have any advantages whatever of soil or climate, have Jews settled in them. So that if my native land is, as it reasonably may be, looked upon as entitled to a share in your favor, it is not one city only that would be benefited by you but ten

thousand of them in every region of the habitable world; in Europe, in Asia, in Africa, on the Continent, in the islands, on the coast and in the inland parts.[3]

The declaration which the Judean king makes to the Roman emperor in the hope of winning his favor he reiterates in his warning to his own people against incurring Caesar's displeasure. "There is no people in the habitable earth which have not some portion of you among them, whom your enemies will slay in case you go to war." The letters which the Roman Consul wrote to the Latin allies informing them of the treaty with Simon Maccabeus were sent to Syria, Pergamus, Cappadocia, Parthia, Sparta, Delos, Myndos, Sicyon, Caria, Samos, Pamphylia, Lycia, Halicarnassus, Rhodes, Phasalis, Cos, Side, Gortina, Cnidus, Cyprus, and Cyrene. In all these places the Judean military, industrial, or agricultural colonies were protected in their right to worship their God and were privileged to spread their faith among the Gentiles. "Every land is full of thee, and every sea," sings the Jewish Sibyl; while the Rabbis assert that no Jew can be an *Aksanai* (stranger) anywhere since everywhere he went he would meet someone of his race or religion. [4]

This multitude of Jews all over the world on the eve of the Roman invasion of Palestine was not the result of an abnormal fecundity. A very large proportion of them were converted Gentiles. As formerly, according to Deuteronomy, they

> Called people unto the mountain
> Where they shall offer sacrifices of righteousness;

and, as during the Captivity, they were exhorted in the Book of Tobit:

> Give thanks unto Him before the Gentiles...
> For He hath scattered us among them
> There to declare His greatness,
> And extol Him among the living;— [5]

So now, with even greater zeal they launched out upon a crusade of converting the heathen "not by power, nor by might but by the spirit" of peaceful persuasion. The urge to bring people "nigh unto the Torah" or "under the wings of the Shekinah" became the dominant passion of every Pharisee. Funds were collected not only for the support of widows and orphans but of converts as well. Some did not hesitate to "compass sea and land" to make even one proselyte. [6]

Rumors of great multitudes of proselytes all over the world corroborated by many pilgrims to Jerusalem, and the generous contributions of foreign *gerim* and semi-*gerim* to the sacred treasury of the Temple, fed the flame of the conversionist zeal of the Pharisees. The Messiah, they were sure, must be near at hand. All that was necessary was to redouble their efforts, to resort to every form of persuasion to make clear the way before him, who, as the last prophet Malachi predicted, "will suddenly come to His Temple." What they had been anticipating for hundreds of years seemed about to come to pass. The yoke of the heathen was at last removed. Israel, under Simon Maccabeus, sat again "every man under his vine and under his fig-tree." The Romans, on their own initiative, renewed their friendship with the Judeans. The Spartans did likewise, and mourned and grieved when they heard that Jonathan was dead. The old dream was soon to come true. Simon, it was believed, would in all probability be the last leader of the pre-Messianic period, and as an expression of their faith as well as gratitude the Judeans appointed him their High Priest "until there should arise the faithful Prophet."

Spurred on by the signs of the times, Simon sent ambassadors to Rome, ostensibly to renew the treaty made by his brother; but, according to the report of the Praetors for foreigners (139 B.C.E.), the ambassadors engaged in religious propaganda as well as political conversation, and were sent back to Jerusalem. Nothing daunted, Jonathan the High Priest and Aristobulus entered into communication with the Lacidemonians, the Ithureans, the Pergameans, and others, claiming for them a common kinship as the seed of Abraham and suggesting that they might as well cement that kinship by accepting the religion of Abraham.

The missionary activity which marked the Maccabean period

is reflected in the Apocrypha and Pseudepigrapha which were then produced either in Greek or translated from the Hebrew into that language. In them the Jews are represented as apostles of truth, and the possessors of a religion which all who are brave and wise eagerly accept once they learn to know its teachings. In First Esdras, Zerubbabel is depicted as one of three court pages charged with the task of providing entertainment for King Darius at one of his great feasts. By a preconcerted plan, each of the three writes his opinions as to what is the strongest thing in the world, and puts it under the king's pillow. When the king awakes and reads the answers, he sends for his grandees and subjects to come to hear them. The first answers—wine, since it renders the mind of the king like unto that of the fatherless child, and makes the bondman as happy as the freeman. The second answers— the king, since all must obey him. Zerubbabel, in his answer cleverly begins with stating that woman is stronger than either wine or the king, for the king himself helplessly submits to the whims and humors of Apame his concubine. But Zerubbabel does not stop here. He knows what is stronger even than woman: it is Truth:

> All the earth calleth upon Truth, and the heaven blesseth her... wine is unrighteous, the king is unrighteous, women are unrighteous, all the children of man are unrighteous. . . . But Truth abideth, and is strong for ever; she liveth and conquereth for evermore. . . . She is the strength, and the kingdom, and the majesty, and the power, of all ages. Blessed be the God of truth. And all the people then shouted: 'Great is Truth, and strong above all things.' [7]

Propaganda of another kind is furnished in the Second Maccabees. Heliodorus, chancellor of Seleuchus IV, was sent by his king to Jerusalem to seize the treasures of the Temple. The people protested against this high-handed act. The High Priest pleaded that the money was reserved for widows and orphans, but all in vain. Heliodorus entered the sanctuary and was about to help himself to the sacred treasure. But suddenly the "Sovereign of Spirits" sent down a terrible horseman in a complete armor of gold who, together with two powerful youths, "scourges him unceasingly, inflicting upon him many sore stripes." Heliodorus thereafter recognized the power of God, vowed great vows, and on his return "testifies to all men the works of the great God which he had beheld with his own eyes."

A somewhat similar story is told of Nicanor, the general of Antiochus Epiphanes. Anticipating an easy victory, he carried with him one thousand slave-dealers to buy the Judean captives. But he was routed, "and he, that had taken upon him to make tribute sure for the Romans by the captivity of the men of Jerusalem," published abroad that the Jews have One who fights for them, and that "they are invulnerable so long as they follow the laws ordained by Him." Antiochus himself, smitten with a dire disease, offered not only to make amends for the evil he had done to Israel but to become a Jew, and to "visit every inhabited place, proclaiming the might of God." His death-bed repentance, however, was of no avail. "The murderer and blasphemer, having endured the sorest sufferings, even as he had dealt with other men, ended his life among the mountains by a most piteous fate in a strange land."

Characteristic of the age was a book entitled "The Wisdom of Jesus the Son of Sira," or *Ecclesiasticus*. It is aglow with patriotism, genuine piety, pride of race, and the hope of winning over the Gentiles. The author, Ben Sira, describes rapturously the glorious history of "the Congregation of the Most High," whose days are innumerable. He rises to poetic heights when he refers to Simon the High Priest:

> How glorious was he when the people gathered round
> him
> At his coming forth out of the sanctuary!
> As the morning star in the midst of a cloud,
> As the moon at the full:
> As the sun shining forth upon the Temple of the
> Most High,
> And as the rainbow giving light in clouds of glory:

> As the flower of roses in the days of new fruits,
> As lilies at the waterspring,
> As the shoot of the frankincense tree in the time of
>   summer:
> As fire and incense in the censer,
> As a vessel of beaten gold,
> Adorned with all manner of precious stones;
> As an olive tree budding forth fruits,
> And as a cypress growing high among the clouds...

He lays the greatest emphasis on the spiritual mission of his people. In polished aphorism, replete with beautiful similes drawn from nature, he marshals the moral maxims based upon the teachings of Judaism, especially those which are universally human. Israel is the repository of God's truth and must disseminate it both for his own sake and for the sake of mankind. He calls upon him to

> Bud forth as a rose growing by a brook of water;
> And give ye a sweet savor of frankincense,
> And put forth flowers as a lily,
> Spread abroad a sweet smell, and sing a song of praise...

Finally Ben Sira himself pours out his soul in a prayer for the world's conversion:

> Have mercy upon us, O Lord the God of all, and behold
> And send Thy fear upon all the nations;
> Lift up Thy hand against the strange nations,
> And let them see Thy mighty power.
> As thou wast sanctified in us before them,
> So be Thou magnified in Them before us;
> And let them know Thee, as also we have known Thee,
> That there is no God but only Thou, O God...
> Give testimony unto those that were Thy creatures
>   in the beginning,
> And raise up the prophecies that have been in Thy name.
> Give reward unto them that wait for Thee;
> And men shall put their trust in Thy Prophets.

Hearken, O Lord, to the prayer of Thy suppliants,
According to the blessing of Aaron concerning Thy people;
And all they that are on earth shall know
That Thou art the Lord, the eternal God.

Ecclesiasticus enjoyed great popularity both among Jews and
Gentiles. It was cited in other Apocryphal works, in the Talmud
and Midrash, was translated into Aramaic and Greek, and
traces of it are also found in the New Testament. It was a great
favorite with many of the Church Fathers and used as a textbook for those who were preparing for the priesthood. It was
finally declared canonical by the Catholic Church at the
Council of Trent. [8]

More effective than the written propaganda were the contacts which Gentiles made with Jews and which grew ever
closer and more frequent with the advent of the Maccabeans.
Both in Judea and the countries outside, the Sabbath and the
manner of its observance was probably the most conspicuous
sign that drew to the Judeans the attention of their Gentile
neighbors. To the heathen, a weekly day of rest was something
they never had heard of, and when they saw men, women,
and children suddenly cease from their labors and retire to
their homes, their curiosity was aroused and started them to
thinking and inquiring about the religion of these peculiar
people. This not infrequently led to attendance at their service
in the synagogues, which were founded during the days of
Ezra, if not earlier, in every Judean settlement. There they
heard "them that preach him" (Moses) interpret or translate
the weekly selections from the Torah. Perhaps they would
find an entire copy of the Scriptures in the vernacular. The
Talmud refers not only to the Aramaic *Targum* (translation),
which is attributed to Ezra, not only to the Greek Septuagint
and the translation of Akilas (Onkelos or Aquila), but also
to renditions in Coptic, Median, Iberian, Elamian, Assyrian,
Armenian, Arabic, and Persian or Pahlavi. There was also
the *Peshitta* in Syriac, attributed by some to a proselyte but
ascribed by others to the days of Solomon. Whether they heard
it or read it they must have become deeply impressed with

the Judeans' claim that they were in possession of a book containing an explanation of the riddle of the universe and the information whereby one was assured of happiness in this world and even greater happiness in the world to come. What is more, this book was not held in the exclusive custody of the priests or initiates, as were the sacred books of other peoples, but used as a textbook for the instruction of the young, made obligatory for reading by the old, and placed at the disposal of all who cared to become familiar with its contents.

The reading of the Scriptures, but more especially attendance at the synagogue, and subsequent conversations or disputation with the Jews, whom they thus came to know, led not infrequently to conversions, or at least to the adoption of some Jewish customs and beliefs. Philo reports that in Egypt many heathens embraced Judaism and became conspicuous for their moderation, gentleness, and humaneness. Josephus states that:

> There is not a city of the Grecians, nor any of the barbarians, nor any nation whatsoever, whither our custom of resting on the seventh day hath not come, and by which our fasts and lighting up lamps, and many of our prohibitions as to food, are not observed: they also endeavor to imitate our mutual concord with one another, and the charitable distribution of our goods, and our diligence on our trades, and our fortitude in undergoing the distresses we are in, on account of our laws.

On the other hand, the inimical Strabo complains:

> They (the Jews) have now got into every city, and it is hard to find a spot on earth which has not admitted this tribe and has not come under its control.

And the embittered Seneca exclaims:

> The customs of this most accursed race have prevailed to such an extent that they are everywhere received.

The conquered have imposed their laws on the conquerors. (*Victi victoribus leges dederunt!*)

The novitiates, as could be expected, were not always conversant with the Torah. But what they lacked in knowledge they sought to make up in piety. As a rule they clung tenaciously to the customs of Israel, even those which were discarded by the "true" Jews or were regarded by these as not valid in the lands outside of Palestine. Wherever there was a sufficient number of them they organized themselves into a distinct *Kahal,* or community, and sometimes went to the extent of continuing the Palestinian sacrificial cult. This cult became so inrooted among the proselytes that those in Mesopotamia adhered to it even after they had been converted to Christianity. In Alexandria and Sardis they sacrificed not only on the stated occasions but also at weddings. In Damascus, which became a center of proselytes, they joined some Judeans who rejected Jerusalem, entered into a "New" Covenant, and as "the Saints of the Most High," built a Temple in a place which they called "the Most Holy City." [9] Most proselytes were fond of making pilgrimages to Jerusalem. There they usually grouped themselves according to the place whence they came and the language which they spoke. They were faithful worshipers at the Temple, and students at some of the four hundred and eighty synagogues which were said to have existed there at the time of Jesus. A description of one of the multilingual services at the Sanctuary on Pentecost is given by St. Peter in the following:

And when the day of Pentecost was fully come, they were all with one accord in one place. . . . And they were all filled with the Holy Ghost, and began to speak with other tongues, as the Spirit gave them utterance. . . . Parthians, and Medes, and Elamites, and the dwellers in Mesopotamia, and in Judea, and Cappadocia, in Pontus, and Asia, Phrygia and Pamphylia, in Egypt, and in the parts of Libya about Cyrene, and strangers of Rome, Jews and proselytes, Cretes and Arabians.

Foreign merchants were drawn to Palestine, especially during the more prosperous Hasmonean period, in the interest of their business trips. In some places the non-Jewish element even predominated over the Jewish contingent. In Galilee there was a mixture of all races. In Acco, or Ptolomais, and Haifa, to the North; in Dora, Stratanos, Apollonia, Anthedon, Skythapolis, Hippos, Pella, Philotheria, Sylikia and other cities to the South, the majority of the population was Greek. There were also slaves either imported as merchandise or brought as captives of war.

This conglomerate mass came in constant contact with the Jewish populace, and their reactions naturally varied. Some of them looked upon the Judeans with loathing and hate, or as barbarians, while others sought to become identified with them even to the extent of accepting their religion. Slaves, of course, could be converted against their will. But the Judeans would not buy them unless they were reasonably sure there would be no need to resort to force. Once a cargo of slaves was landed at a Palestinian port and was bought by the Jews. After they persistently refused to submit to circumcision they were resold to the heathen. This, however, must have been a rare exception. As a rule they yielded, for otherwise they would not be trusted with wine and meat, and if the master was a priest, could not partake of the consecrated food. There was still less difficulty with women slaves. They had merely to be baptized, to be qualified to marry into the best families of Judea. [10]

The ranks of the proselytes were sometimes swelled with those who were originally excluded from "the assembly of the Lord even to the tenth generation", the mamzerim ("bastards") and asufi or shetuki (foundlings). The former were not "bastards" as understood in western countries, but were the offspring of the prohibited degree of propinquity or of a pagan parent. The sentiment against this class was so deep-rooted that even in the anarchic times of the Judges the children of Gilead drove Jephtha out because he was "the son of another woman". With the influx of many pagans after the Restoration, and the consequent increase in children born of mixed marriages, steps were taken to mitigate the rigor of the biblical injunction. As in the case of the Ammonites and Moabites, the law was at first interpreted to apply only to the males. Then it was declared that the child of a Gentile father or of an incestual marriage by his heathen parents who embraced Judaism, was not included in the category of *mamzer*. The Rabbis in particular revolted against enforcing the letter of the Deuteronomic and Ezranic law against these innocent offenders. "Their fathers have sinned," exclaims one of them, "but what have these unfortunates done?" Tho they retained the prohibition with regard to a Jew, they found a loophole of escape concerning a convert. A *ger*, they decided, may marry a *mamzer*, and a *mamzer* a slave, whose child on being emancipated may marry a freeman. Cases are on record of priests who married *mamzerot*. But even while the taint still clung to them they were given every encouragement to enter into the Jewish fold. When R. Simlai found that the proprietor of the inn in which he stopped was a *mamzer*, he expressed his regrets that he had not known him before he was married, for he would have taught him how to remove his disability. *Mamzerim* were included in the distribution of charity and were accorded due honor and praise for wisdom and integrity. R. Jose taught that *mamzerim* and Nethinim would be "made pure" in the future. An ancient *Mishnah* fixed their social status as follows:

> A Cohen is to be given precedence over a Levite, A Levite over a (lay) Israelite, a (lay) Israelite over a *mamzer;* a *mamzer* over a *nethin;* a *nethin* over a *ger;* a *ger* over an emancipated slave. This order holds good when they are all alike. But if the *mamzer* is a disciple of the wise he should be given preference over a High Priest, as it is written: 'She (the Torah) is more precious than rubies.'

The *Asufi*, or *Shetuki* were deserted children whose parents were unknown. Such waifs were not uncommon among the

pagans who had no compunction for exposing their babies
in the woods or abandoning them in the streets. Ezekiel refers
to what must have been in his day quite a familiar sight:

> In the day thou wast born thy navel was not cut,
> neither wast thou washed in water for cleansing; thou
> wast not salted at all, nor swaddled at all. No eye pitied
> thee, to do any of these unto thee, to have compassion
> upon thee; but thou wast cast out in the open field
> in the loathsomeness of thy person, in the day that
> thou wast born.[11]

Among the Jews, with their high regard for the sanctity
of life, such sights aroused sympathy and the tenderest
pity. However, besides their aversion to illegitimacy there
was also the fear lest the foundling, if of Jewish descent,
might later marry a Jew within the prohibited degrees of
consanguinity. Every effort was, therefore, made to ascertain the
child's ancestry. When this failed, the child was regarded as
non-Jewish and was converted by the court. There must have
been many of the heathen *Asufi* and *Shetuki* who thus became
an integral part of the Jewish population.[12]

The most usual way of gaining converts was by intermarriage. The proclivity of the Judeans for "the daughters
of strange gods" was strengthened after the Restoration by
the increasing contacts with their Gentile visitors and neighbors. Ezra's efforts, it appears, proved futile. The genealogies
which he instituted, at least for the priesthood, were disregarded even before they were destroyed by Herod I. Neither
the priests nor even the nobility were proof against intermarriage. Some of those who fled to Samaria intermixed with
the Cuthites. The two powerful families of Beth Zebuim and
Beth Kufai were, according to R. Joshua, not free from "blem-
ishes". So it was with the Beth Zerifa on the other side of
the Jordan, and with those who claimed descent from no
less an ancestry than that of the Maccabeans. "Whoever
saith I am of the family of the royal Hasmonean is no other
than a slave," was the bold statement of Mar Samuel. Some
family trees were evidently regarded as spurious.

Not until Christianity began to make inroads among proselytes to Judaism was there any serious objection raised against
intermarrying with *gerim* or *giyurot*. Simon the High Priest's
daughter was married to Ptolemy of Jericho, who apparently
was of non-Jewish origin. Herod I, though of Edomite lineage,
always protested his attachment to Judaism, and married out of
the faith. His son, Alexander, took unto himself Glaphyra, the
daughter of Archelaus, King of Cappadocia. When the Arab
Sylleus refused to become converted, Herod annulled his marriage to his sister Drusilla and gave her to the Idumean Canto-
barus, who complied with his demands. His great-grandson
Agrippa II objected to Epiphanes, king of Antioch as a son-in-
law because he had refused to fulfill his promise to accept the
Jewish religion, and chose instead the convert Azizus King of
Emesa. Bernice, another daughter, married Polemo, king of
Cilicia, a converted heathen who later repented of the bargain
and relapsed into idolatry. Indeed, much of the marital troubles
of the Herodians, as well as the disastrous condition of the
people, may be attributed to the royal family connections with
heathens who were induced to accept Judaism. [13]

What took place among the upper classes occurred also in
the other strata of society. Jewish men attracted pagan women
because they had a reputation for chastity surpassing that of
any other people. Even Tacitus, who on the one hand branded
Jews as "haters of the human race" as well as "the lewdest
nation upon the earth," admitted that, among themselves,
"there is unalterable fidelity and kindness always ready at
hand," and that they "will not corrupt foreign women". Needless to say that the children of mixed marriages were, with
scarcely an exception, raised in the Jewish faith.

Gerim, according to the Rabbis, frequently hailed from the
ranks of merchants who passed through Judea in pursuit of
their business. Compared to the conditions which everywhere
obtained in their homelands, the greed and insolence of the
office holders, from royalty down to the lowliest underling,
the misery and frequent massacres of the slaves, the dishonesty
and immorality both of the men and the women, Palestine

presented to them a veritable Utopia. The Midrash draws a picture of what "the nations" found who went thither "to see what kind of goods these Jews have." When they reached Jerusalem they beheld that all worshiped the same God, ate the same sort of food (among the idolaters the god of one is not like the god of the other, nor is the diet of the one similar to the diet of the other). Then said they, "What can be better than to unite ourselves with this nation?" And they did not depart from there until they were converted, and came and offered sacrifices and holocausts. [14]

The high standard of Jewish business ethics was indeed a source of wonder amòng the Gentiles. In their own lands the stranger or barbarian could be fleeced with impunity. He had no rights which he could claim as his own, no friends in court to defend him. Among the Jews it was just the contrary. The hope of *Kiddush Hashem* (the sanctification of the Name of God) and the fear of causing the *Hillul Hashem* (profanation of the Name of God) long had become deeply rooted in their conscience. They were even more careful in their dealings with pagans than with their own people. This not infrequently spoke more eloquently in favor of their faith than any argument or persuasion.

The Talmud mentions several conversions which were the result of honest dealing with Gentiles. Once a Jew bought a sack of wheat from a pagan and, when he opened it and found therein a purse of gold, he hasted and returned it to the merchant. Amazed at such unexpected conduct, the Gentile exclaimed: "Blessed be the God òf the Jews." Of Simeon b. Shetah, brother of Queen Alexandra (Salome), it is told that, despite his connection with royalty, he eked out a livelihood by conducting a small business in linen goods. Once his pupils presented him with an ass purchased from an Arab. Upon scrutinizing the animal they discovered a precious jewel suspended from its neck. The pupils were delighted, hoping their master would from now on live in comfort. But Simeon would have none of it. "The Arab," he insisted "sold the ass, not the jewel, and it should be returned to him." On receiving it, the Arab exclaimed: "Praised be the God of Simeon b. Shetah." [15]

The Hasmoneans, however, grew impatient with the slow progress of proselytism necessarily resulting from the peaceful method insisted upon by the Pharisees. Not that their "passion for soul" was greater but for political expediency. They were infected by the virus of "totalitarianism," and would brook no differences in their domain. Simon the High Priest (Maccabeus) may be regarded as the father of the Synagogue Militant. He forced the Gentiles of Jaffa and Gezer either to convert or quit the country. John Hyrcanus (135-104 B.C.E.) demolished the Temple of the Samaritans and gave the Idumeans the alternative of conversion or extermination. His son Aristobulus compelled the Itureans who settled in the district of Lebanon to submit to circumcision. The same policy was pursued by Alexander Jannai (103-76). All the places in Phoenicia, Syria, Philistia, Samaria, Jaulan, and Moab, which yielded to the Hasmoneans, were forcibly Judaized. Pella, which stubbornly resisted, was razed to the ground. The descendants of those who shed their blood in opposing the intolerance of Antiochus themselves paid no heed to Zechariah's admonition: "Not by power, nor by might, but by My spirit!"

The Judeans, however, reaped little benefit from these forced proselytes to Judaism. The Itureans became even more hostile after their conversion than before, and Bethshan grasped the first opportunity to wreak bloody vengeance on the Judeans in its midst. Those who appeared to profess Judaism were often only heathen "Marranos," prototypes of the Jewish Marranos of medieval Spain and Portugal, and were ever on the alert to throw off the yoke of their oppressors together with their religion. It remained for those who seemingly were loyal to their new faith to bring about the catastrophe which devastated Judea and made the Jews the martyr people of mankind. [16]

Among the craftiest Roman henchmen was Antipas, governor of Idumea, who had been converted to Judaism under

Alexander Jannai. His son Antipater, who succeeded him, was appointed procurator of Judea and soon became all-powerful. One of his sons, Phasael, was made governor of Jerusalem; another, Herod (73-4 B.C.E.), prefect of Galilee. It was not long before Herod usurped the reins of government and became king of Judea (37 B.C.E.).

A most cruel despot, whose hands were steeped in the blood of his own wife and children and other relatives, no less than in that of thousands whom he disliked or had cause to suspect of disloyalty, this "Idumaean slave," as his subjects called him, remained an enemy of the Jews despite his opposition to intermarriage and the treasures he lavished upon the Temple. The Jews, says Josephus, "had borne more calamities from Herod in a few years than during all the interval of time which had passed since they had come out of Babylon and returned home in the reign of Xerxes." [17]

CHAPTER VIII

AT THE CRADLE OF CHRISTIANITY

Herod's subserviency to Rome was well rewarded. He received numerous gifts and honors from Antony and Octavianus, and rejoiced in the possession of the bodyguard of four hundred Gauls formerly in the service of Cleopatra. The boundaries of Judea were extended, and new and beautiful cities rose on all sides. Caesarea became another, a smaller, Rome. Samaria, now a part of Judea, was rebuilt, enlarged, and renamed Sebaste. Jerusalem now enjoyed a theater and a hippodrome, but to show that he was not indifferent to his own religion, Herod took more than eight years in renovating and expanding the antiquated Temple of Zerubbabel and rendering it so magnificent that, it was said, he who has not seen it had never seen a beautiful building in his life. Even here, however, Herod did not forget to fawn upon the Romans. He placed a golden eagle over the main entrance and offered sacrifices in honor of Augustus.

But there was little joy in Judea. Herod and his henchmen were eating away at the heart of Judaism. The priesthood was shorn of its prestige. The office of the High Priest was no longer hereditary, but bartered away to the highest bidder, or to the one who ingratiated himself in the favor of Rome. Uncertain of their tenure, these High Priests, mostly Sadducees, sought, like their Roman superiors, to feather their nests while they could, and resorted to all sorts of extortion to maintain their station after they were deposed. Those who could, fled to other lands. In time, forebodings of an impending calamity began to spread among the people, and omens that God was about to destroy His sanctuary were reported to have been made manifest. It was said that voices emanating from the Temple-court were heard crying:

> Go forth hence sons of Eli. . . . Go forth hence Issachar of Kfar Barkai. . . . Lift up your heads, O ye gates, and let Johanan b. Narbai enter and fill his belly with things consecrated to heaven.

It was rumored that once, just before sunset, chariots and soldiers clad in armor were seen among the clouds, the earth shook, and sounds were heard whispering, "Let us hasten hence"; that the scarlet cord did not turn white on the Day of Atonement, the fire on the altar burned low, and the Perpetual Lamp was extinguished. A resplendent light was said to have appeared one Passover night over the Temple, and the eastern gate, which usually required twenty stalwart men to move, opened wide of itself. The people fled in trepidation, except R. Johanan b. Zakkai who exclaimed: "Temple, Temple, do not terrify us! I know that thou art in the end to be destroyed; for long ago did Zechariah B. Iddo prophesy concerning thee:

> 'Open thy doors, O Lebanon,
> That the fire may devour thy cedars.'

The gloom, despondency, and resentment of the Judeans is also reflected in the Apocrypha which were composed after the brief heyday of the early Hasmoneans came to an inglorious end. In them we look in vain for the idyllic picture of Jewish piety and domestic devotion which shoot through the tale of Tobit, or the sweet reasonableness which characterizes the Wisdom of Jesus b. Sira. They are mostly Apocalypses that are overcast with a pall of gloom. They concern themselves either with the world-to-come beyond the grave, or the world-to-come after this sublunar sphere will have met its inevitable doom. In some of them indeed these two worlds are indistinguishable one from the other. They all foresee that the vale of tears, of hate and violence which they knew, must pass away also by violent means; and that those who persistently rebelled against God, will be given no chance to reform. They are filled with threats of a hell of brimstone and fire. Their favorite theme seems to be the fate of the wicked, as depicted by Isaiah:

> ... Their worm shall not die,
> Neither shall their fire be quenched;
> And they shall be an abhorring unto all flesh.

Thus to the questions of the author of the second Esdras how the misery of Israel can be reconciled with God's justice; and when will Israel's religion pervade the world, the answer given him by the angel Uriel is that the Resurrection is soon to come, when "there will be woe unto them that shall be left in those days, and much more woe unto them that are not left," after which

> The Most High shall be revealed upon the seat of judgment, and compassion shall pass away, and long suffering shall be withdrawn; but judgment only shall remain, truth shall stand, and faith shall wax strong.... And the pit of torment shall appear, and over against it shall be the place of rest; and the furnace of hell shall be shewed, and over against it the Paradise of delight. And then shall the Most High say to the nations that are raised from the dead, See ye and understand Whom ye have denied, or Whom ye have not served, or Whose commandments ye have despised. Look on this side and on that: here is delight and rest, and there fire and torments! ... And it shall be that whosoever remaineth after all these things that I have told thee of, he shall be saved, and shall see My salvation, and the end of My world.... For evil shall be blotted out, and deceit shall be quenched; and faith shall flourish, and corruption shall be overcome, and the truth which has been so long without fruit, shall be declared. [1]

The condemnation of the nations becomes even more vehement in the Apocalypses of Enoch, wherein the angel Gabriel (the Prince over Israel) is commissioned by God:

> Go to the biters, to the reprobates, to the children of fornication; and destroy the children of fornication, the offspring of the Watchers, from among men; bring them forth and excite them one against another. Let them perish by mutual slaughter; for length of days shall not be theirs....
>
> Then shall they be taken away into the lowest depths of the fire in torment; and in confinement shall they be shut up forever....
>
> Purify the earth from all oppression, from all injustice, from all crime, from all impiety, and from all the pollution that is committed upon it. Exterminate them from the earth....
>
> Then shall all the children of men be righteous, and all nations shall pay me divine honors, and bless Me; all shall adore Me.
>
> The earth shall be cleansed from all corruption, from every crime, from all punishment, from all suffering.

In the Book of Jubilees, claimed to be a revelation to Moses through the Angel of God's Presence, the Gentiles are condemned as hopelessly degraded and incapable of regeneration. "All their ways are unclean, and they will be destroyed from the earth, nor will they be saved in the Day of Judgment." Any hope that they will ever accept Judaism, or cultivate a friendly feeling toward the Jews, is an illusion. The leopard will not change his spots. Esau will never be reformed. His hatred for Jacob is eternal. In a dramatic scene where Jacob discovers that instead of coming to console him on the death of his mother Rachel, Esau intends to fight him, the former reminds him of the oath he swore to their father and mother that he would devise no evil all his days against his brother. To this Esau makes reply:

Neither the children of men nor the beasts of the
earth have any oath of righteousness which holds valid
forever; but every day they devise evil one against
another, and each may slay his adversary and foe.
And thou dost hate me and my children forever. And
there is no observing the tie of brotherhood with thee.
Hear these words which I declare unto thee:

'If the bear can change its skin and make its bristles
    as soft as wool,
Or if it can cause horns to sprout forth on its
    head like the horns of a sheep or a stag,
Then will I observe the ties of brotherhood
    with thee. . . .
Thou shalt be rooted out,
And thy sons shall be rooted out,
And there shall be no peace for thee.'

But the more the Judeans desponded of the regeneration
of the Gentiles the more intense grew their belief in the
momentary arrival of a deliverer. The old messianic expectation blazed fiercer and stronger than ever. It was no longer
postponed to the last of days; it was felt that it was due
immediately, and that the "birth pangs of the Messiah" had
already begun. So firm became this conviction that the people
fell an easy prey to any impostor who passed himself off as
a scion of the house of David or a survivor of the Hasmonean
dynasty. It became sufficient merely to have a name like Joshua
(God saves) or Johanan (God is gracious) or Menahem (con-
soler), to qualify one for the Messiahship. And the demand
produced a supply. A certain young man who claimed to be
the Hasmonean Alexander who escaped Herod's massacres,
became a popular hero, attracted great multitudes and was
accorded royal honors in Crete and Melos. Judah b. Ezekiel,
a robber chief, Simon, a slave of Herod, and Athronges, a
shepherd, "because he was a tall man, and excelled others in
the strength of his hands," were in turn acclaimed as "new
Prophets" or Messiahs by frenzied multitudes. Theudas, or
Judah, obtained a large following merely on the promise that

he would divide the Jordan. They were decimated at the riverside by the Roman governor and their leader was decapitated. An Egyptian pretender drew a crowd of thirty thousand on the assurance that he would cause the walls of Jerusalem to fall on the heads of the Roman garrison merely with the breath of his mouth. As he managed to escape from the vigilant authorities, he was said to have been endowed with special divine power. [2]

Among these numerous claimants to Messiahship stands foremost the man who made Judaism accessible to a large portion of the human race, but on account of whom the Jews have become a maligned and martyred people—Jesus of Nazareth, or as he was probably known among his own people, Joshua ben Joseph.

Jesus was born in the year when Herod, whose day of death the Pharisees declared a holiday, died, or four years before the commonly accepted date. Jewish history of the time has nothing to say about him, or says it in a manner far from clear. The only unmistakable reference to him, by Josephus, reads:

> There was about that time Jesus, a wise man; if it be lawful to call him a man, for he was a doer of wonderful works, and a teacher of such men as receive the truth with pleasure. He drew over to him both many of the Jews, and many of the Gentiles. He was the Christ. And when Pilate, at the suggestion of the principal men among us, had condemned him to the cross, those that loved him at first did not forsake him; for he appeared to them alive again, the third day, as the divine Prophets had foretold these and ten thousand other wonderful things concerning him. And the tribe of Christians, so named from him, is not extinct to this day.

Whether this paragraph is authentic or, as most scholars agree, it is the interpolation of a zealous Christian scribe, there is no doubt that when Jesus first started on his messianic career he attracted little, if any special attention.

Nor was there any reason, comparing his recorded teachings with those of the Pharisees, why he should have later aroused any opposition. There was nothing in what he said which would be in the remotest manner new or offensive to, or not approved by, other Pharisees though some might have held divergent views. He was a strict observer of the ceremonial law. He wore the consecrated *zizith* (fringes). On the occasion of the Passover he made a pilgrimage to Jerusalem where he celebrated the event of the Exodus by eating the unleavened bread, drinking the cups of wine, singing the *Hallel,* etc. He did not, like the prophets, denounce the sacrificial cult or insist with Samuel that "to obey is better than sacrifice," or repeat the admonition that "to do righteous and justice is more acceptable to the Lord than sacrifice." His principle was, "These ought ye to have done, and not to leave the other undone"—even as taught the Jewish sages of all times, and he would undoubtedly have agreed with R. Simeon b. Azzai that "whether the *mizvah* be great or small matters little, provided only one directs his heart to heaven." He exhorted that "the scribes and the Pharisees sit in Moses' seat; all therefore whatsoever they bid you observe, that observe and do." His answer to the scribe's question as to which is the great commandment of the Torah sounds almost as if he quoted it from Hillel, "The first of all the commandments is 'Hear, O Israel: the Lord our God is one Lord' ... And the second is like unto it, 'Thou shalt love thy neighbor as thyself,' except that Hillel showed himself more liberal by mentioning only the second. Jesus assured his hearers:

Think not that I am come to destroy the Torah, or the Prophets: I am not come to destroy, but to fulfill. For verily I say unto you, Till heaven and earth pass, one jot or one tittle shall in no wise pass from the Torah, till all be fulfilled. Whosoever therefore shall break one of these least commandments, and shall teach men so, he shall be called the least in the kingdom of Heaven; but whosoever shall do and teach them, the same shall be called great in the kingdom of Heaven.

But even had he disagreed with some Pharisaic constructions of the text or recommendations of ceremonies he would still not have been regarded as a heretic. Though the rabbis differed in their interpretation of the Torah, and their contention sometimes became very bitter, they permitted and even encouraged the search for truth regardless of where it led. "Would they had forsaken Me, but kept My Torah," is the interpretation given by one of them to Jeremiah 16:11, while another makes bold to strike at the root of such an all-important and precious belief as the advent of the Messiah by declaring "Israel hath no Messiah, for he hath long been used up (consumed) in the days of Hezekiah." Academic freedom was a perpetuated mind habit among the Jews, and the contending parties always recognized that "these as well as those are the words of the living God." When R. Eliezer b. Hyrcanus was greatly pleased with the rendition of a biblical verse given by a Christian, he neither hesitated to say so nor was he reprimanded when he admitted it.

Certainly Jesus would not have condemned the Pharisees as a class, for he was himself one of them. Like them he insisted on the unity and Fatherhood of God. Like them he believed in the immortality of the soul, and the perpetuity of the whole Torah. Neither was he more severe on those who were hypocritical than were some of the sages. More than a century before, Alexander Jannai declared on his death-bed (what was probably a commonplace among the Jews): "Fear thou neither the Pharisees nor those who are not Pharisees, but the dyed ones (hypocrites) who look like Pharisees: who do deeds like unto those of Zimri, and expect the reward of Phineas." Hypocrites were looked upon with such detestation that they were said to be "doomed to inherit two hells" (one in this world, the other in the world to come), and R. Gamaliel II warned: "Let no scholar whose inside is unlike his outside enter into the house of study".

They were held up to ridicule and execration in both the Palestinian and the Babylonian Talmuds.

> The Rabbis taught: There are seven varieties of (undesirable) Pharisees: the Shoulder Pharisee (who puts his good deeds on his shoulder, as it were, so that all might see them); the Stubbing Pharisee (who assumes such humility that he stubs his toes every time he walks); the Butting Pharisee (who shuts his eyes lest he look at a woman, so that he sometimes butts his head against a wall); the Hammer-shaped Pharisee (who bends his shoulders and head like a hammer); the What-else-is-my-Duty-and-I'll-do-it (insinuating that he has already done all that was required of him); the Wait-a-bit Pharisee (who tells one to wait a while till he will perform some good deed); the Calculating Pharisee (who keeps account of his good deeds so as to balance his evil ones); and the Show-me-my-fault Pharisee.

On the other hand, the teaching that "God is love" was stressed by the Rabbis no less than by Jesus. With all their dislike of the *Am Haarez* (the ignoramus), they never doubted that the Father in Heaven loves his untutored child as deeply as He does him who is versed in the whole Torah. It is said that R. Berokhah of Khuza once asked Elijah the Prophet in the market place if there was anyone in the multitude who would have a share in the world to come. Elijah pointed to an ignorant prison warden in black shoes (proscribed at that time by the Jews), who, moreover, had no *zizith* on his garments, whose merit consisted in that he protected the women prisoners against the attacks of the guards even at the risk of his life. There were also two brothers whose only claim to a share in the world to come was that they made people merry and promoted peace among their fellows. [3]

In many respects the attitude of Jesus was rather that of the author of the Book of Jubilees, or of the rigorous and isolationist Shammaites, than that of the liberal and universalist

Hillelites. He warned his disciples against going in "the way of the Gentiles". He did not teach that one should do good for its own sake. He constantly promised rewards and threatened punishment. He repeatedly expressed a predilection for the sons and daughters of Abraham. He insisted that he was sent only "to the lost sheep of Israel" and forbade his followers to enter any city of the Samaritans. To the pitiful appeal of a Canaanitish woman to exorcise a demon from her daughter, he made the uncalled for and insulting reply, "It is not meet to take the children's bread, and to cast it to dogs." [4]

Jesus certainly knew nothing of the Trinity. Nor is there any evidence that he used the expressions "son of man" or "son of God" in any other sense than that in which they were understood by the prophets, the psalmists, and the Pharisees, which is, as the Wisdom of Solomon states explicitly, that "the righteous man is God's son." He rebuked the young man who called him "Good Master," saying, "There is none good but One, that is God," and far from regarding miracles as an evidence of Messiahship he warned:

> If any man shall say unto you, Lo, here is Christ, or there; believe it not. For there shall arise false Christs, and false Prophets, and shall show great signs and wonders: insomuch that, if it were possible, they shall deceive the very elect.

Jesus never pretended, at least at the beginning of his career, to be the predicted Messiah, nor was he so taken to be by those who knew him or heard of him. It was Simon Bar-Jonah (Peter) who is said to have acclaimed him as "the Christ, the Son of the living God," but Peter later denied it with an oath. By some he was regarded as a Samaritan or possessed of the devil, or one of the numerous "New Prophets" with whom that time was so prolific, and within a generation after his crucifixion he, like most of the other aspirants to messianic honors, was also forgotten. Festus, the Roman governor of Judea, spoke vaguely of "one Jesus, which was dead, whom Paul affirmed to be alive," while Josephus, if he had really been the author of the above quoted paragraph, strangely indeed was never curious enough even temporarily to cast his lot with the "tribe of the Christians" though he joined every other Jewish sect in turn. The saintly John the Baptist, whom some regarded as himself the Messiah's forerunner, wondered and doubted whether Jesus was indeed the Messiah "or should we look for another".

The parents of Jesus seem to have had no inkling of his Messiahship and never joined his followers. James the Just, who did become one of the pillars of the Judeo-Christian community in Jerusalem, was, unlike Jesus, an ascetic, or Nazarite. He drank no wine, ate no animal food, and his head was never touched by a razor. He went daily to the Temple, where he knelt continually, beseeching God for the forgiveness of the people, until the skin of his knees grew thick like that of a camel. As for the other members of the family, Hegesippus of the second century tells that Domitian summoned before him two peasants who were said to be grandsons of "that Judas who was called the brother of the Lord according to the flesh." He feared that they might possibly be claimants to the throne of Judea, but when he saw their poor estate and their horny hands knotted with toil, he let them go.

It was more or less the same with the other Apostles. Of Peter, both the Acts of the Apostles and Jewish lore testify that he was an observant Pharisee. He refused to take a meal with Cornelius, the centurion of the Italian band, because, though "a devout man and one that feared God with all his house, which gave much alms to the people, and prayed to God always," he was not a proselyte of righteousness, that is, circumcised. It was as a result of a special revelation that he permitted himself to eat with Gentiles, probably in the hope of converting them (on the Pharisaic principle that it is permissible to commit a small sin in order to effect a great good). Peter, in addition to the belief in the Unity, also insisted that Gentile proselytes must observe circumcision and at least four cardinal laws: abstention from meats offered to idols, or containing blood, or of strangled animals, and from fornication. Yet, he was the favorite disciple of Jesus, and the Jews held him in such esteem that his audience is said to have numbered about five thousand. [5]

It was neither James, the brother of Jesus, nor Peter, his beloved Apostle, nor Philip, whom he called to the Apostolate the day after Peter's appointment, nor the others who knew Jesus in the flesh, who broke away from Jews and Judaism. They and most of their followers were all, like Jesus himself, orthodox Pharisees. They would have been the last to deny the validity of the Torah, or to disregard any of the ceremonies of Judaism.

Had it rested with the immediate disciples of Jesus, Christianity would very likely have remained a Jewish sect. Even the assumption that Jesus was the Messiah was not considered so heretical that those who professed it should be read out of the synagogue. To be sure, there would have been some bitterness and bickering, but after a while the shouting and the tumult would have subsided, even as they did between the Hillelites and the Shammaites, the Sadducees and the Pharisees, the Rabbanites and the Karaites, the Maimonideans and the anti-Maimonideans, the Hasidim and Mithnagdim, the Maskilim and the anti-Maskilim, the Orthodox and the Reformists. It was the eminent Rabban Gamaliel who stood up against the High Priest and the captain of the Temple—all Sadducees and creatures of Rome—and pleaded for leniency to Peter and his men. [6]

The one who was responsible for the schism between those who regarded Jesus as the Messiah and their opponents was Saul of Tarsus (c. 10-64). According to his own testimony, he not only spoke Greek but was well acquainted with the "wisdom of the Gentiles." He asserted that as a pupil of Rabban Gamaliel he outstripped his generation in the knowledge of "the perfect manner of the Torah of the fathers." He was, however, little influenced by his master's liberality. While in Jerusalem he identified himself with the zealots, and he tells

us, "after the most straitest sect of our religion I lived a Pharisee," and was "more exceedingly zealous of the traditions of
my fathers than many of my equals in mine own nation."
As a young man of about nineteen he instigated a mob to seize
Stephen, the first Christian martyr, and stone him to death
because he said that Jesus would destroy the Temple and
change the customs instituted by Moses. Not content with
being a heresy-hunter in Jerusalem, he applied to the High
Priest for letters of introduction to the synagogue in Damascus
where laxity was probably more rife, in the hope of eradicating
the heretics from among them also, "whether they were men
or women". [7]

Whether it was the result of a fit of epilepsy to which it
is said he was subject, or of a remorseful conscience, something happened to him as he came near to Damascus. He believed he saw a light from heaven, and as he fell to the ground
he heard a voice saying, "Saul, Saul, why persecutest thou
me?" The "me" he interpreted to be no other than Jesus.
Jesus, therefore, must be the Messiah, and thereafter Saul
became an ardent advocate of "Christ and him crucified,"
who, however, will

> reign, till he hath put all enemies under his feet...
> and when all things shall be subdued unto him,
> then shall the Son also himself be subject unto Him
> that put all things under him, that God may be all
> in all.

Saul thus still taught that Jesus, like Elijah in Jewish tradition, was sent temporarily to prepare the way for the acceptance of the God of Israel. He also, even when he preached
that in Christ there is "neither Greek nor Jew, circumcision
nor uncircumcision, Barbarian, Scythian, bond or free," nevertheless proclaimed that Jews are the first fruit, which is holy,
and that Jews are virtuous by nature, and not sinners like
the Gentiles, and while he did not, like Jesus, limit himself
exclusively to the Jews, he gave them the preference: "To

the Jew first, and also to the Greek." For a long time his love
for them knew no diminution:

> For I wish that myself were accursed from Christ for
> my brethren, my kinsmen according to the flesh; who
> are Israelites; to whom appertaineth the adoption, and
> the glory, and the covenants, and the giving of the
> Torah, and the service of God, and the promises;
> whose are the fathers, and of whom as concerning
> the flesh Christ came, who is over all, God-blessed
> for ever. Amen.

Nor would he, any more than James and Peter, have aroused
any antagonism had he confined his conversionist efforts to
the Gentiles. It is just what the most devout Judeans had
always tried to do. He was at first almost always welcomed
to their homes and invited to occupy the pulpits of the synagogues. It was only later, when he began to foist his personal
views on the Pharisees with the same fanatic zeal that he
formerly used upon the Judeo-Christians, that he himself became an object of persecution. Convinced that the Messiah
had already appeared in the person of Jesus, Saul preached
to the Jews not only to accept him but to show the sincerity
of their faith in him by discarding the Law which, in accordance with tradition, was, with the advent of the Messiah,
no longer binding. Moreover, by a peculiar mode of reasoning he endeavored to prove that the Law and sin were synonymous, hoping that by thus removing the "yoke of the Torah,"
he would the more easily win over not only the Gentiles but
the Jews who were lax in observing its commandments. In
the pursuit of this goal he was not very particular about
the means. His motto was: "So run, that he might obtain."
He admits:

> I made myself servant unto all that I might gain
> more; and unto the Jews I become as a Jew, that I
> might gain the Jews; to them that are under the Law,
> as under the Law, that I might gain them that are

under the Law; to them that are without the Law, as without the Law that I might gain them that are without the Law. To the weak became I as weak, that I might gain the weak; I am made all things unto all men, that I might by all means save some.

In Damascus, his first field of activity, Saul stayed three years and, though aided by a certain Ananias, a Hellenized Jew who accepted Jesus as the Messiah, he made but little headway either among the Jews or their many proselytes. Thinking that he would meet with greater success if he could obtain authorization as an Apostle, he returned to Jerusalem. But the Jerusalem Council was reluctant to admit him into the circle of the elect, perhaps because he never came in touch with Jesus during his lifetime. They may also have recalled the part he played in the stoning of Stephen, but above all, they opposed his antinomian preaching to uncircumcised Gentiles. Peter and James with difficulty permitted him to work among the Jews, and disappointed but not discouraged, Saul left for Tarsus.

While marking time in his native city there came to him Joseph Barnabas (supposed to be the Grecianized form of Bar Nahamah, or Bar Nebuah—son of consolation, or son of exhortation), a Levite, and a native of Cyprus and therefore, like Saul, a Jew of the Dispersion. Because of his eloquence he was sent by the Apostles to Antioch to preach Christ to the Jews. Here Barnabas envisioned an opportunity to spread Christianity among the many proselytes who were naturally rather weak in their faith and invited Saul to help him. In Antioch the two worked together for about a year with considerable success. Not only individuals but whole families accepted the new faith, and for the first time they proudly assumed, or were contemptuously given, the name "Christians." They asked, however, for nothing more than the belief in Jesus as the Messiah.

Gratified with their achievement, Saul and Barnabas set out to make a report to the Apostolic Council in Jerusalem, presided over by James the brother of Jesus. They also carried with them the money which Jews everywhere contributed for the relief of converts, this time to be distributed among "their brethren in Christ". Saul then appealed to each Apostle separately to accede to the abrogation of the rite of circumcision, and Peter, who, contrary to his name, was soft and vacillating, yielded. But James, the brother of Jesus, remained stubbornly opposed to this innovation. At last an agreement was reached: Simon, the orthodox Palestinian was chosen to spread the "Gospel of circumcision," while Saul the antinomian, who spoke Greek and was a Roman citizen, was appointed to be the "Apostle to the Gentiles". It was a happy choice, and had Saul lived up to the agreement he would probably have retained the affection of all Jews, as did James, the brother of Jesus. Saul, however, seems to have consented only in order to be appointed an Apostle, and, once accredited, he ignored the fact that it was merely by sufferance, and declared, "I am nothing but I yield in nothing to the chiefest Apostle."

On his return to Antioch with Barnabas and his cousin Johanan (or John Mark), he, as his manner was, sought out the Jews and preached to them as well as to the proselytes and the Gentiles. But being invited by the "rulers of the synagogue" to deliver the Sabbath sermon, Saul, contrary to the Jewish custom not to single out the *gerim* in the congregation, began his discourse: "Men of Israel, and ye that fear God, give audience. . . . Men and brethren, children of the seed of Abraham, and whosoever among you feareth God, to you is the word of salvation." His doctrines outraged not only the Jews but the converts to Judaism, and many "devoted and honorable women, and chief men of the city" united with their new coreligionists to drive him out of Antioch. Even Barnabas and John Mark were greatly incensed, and soon parted company with him. Saul then selected as his associate one Silas, who, like himself, was a Jew of the Dispersion and a Roman citizen.

The departure of Barnabas and Mark removed the last restraint from Saul. Thereafter he moved ever further away from the old moorings, finally pronouncing the Torah accursed and those who adhered to it as cursed. Already he assumed the name of Paul, either as an indication that he was more interested in Gentiles than in Jews or in honor of a noble convert, the Roman pro-consul of Cyprus, Sergius Paulus. This conversion enhanced Paul's confidence in himself and he redoubled his efforts, especially among the women who were more readily impressed by his indomitable personality. Yet he still sought out the Jews wherever he went, and accepted their hospitality and invitations to address them in their synagogues. In places such as Pisidea, Cilicia, Lycaonia, Phrygia and Macedonia where there were no synagogues and where the Jews would assemble on the Sabbath by the riverside, he preached to them in the open. In Thessalonica and Athens, he "reasoned with them out of the Scriptures" for three successive Sabbaths. In Corinth he first stayed with a Jew named Aquila, who fled from Rome because of the Claudian persecutions, and later with a fearer of the Lord whose house adjoined the synagogue, and for eighteen months, "reasoned in the synagogue every Sabbath". There, among others, he "persuaded" Crispus, the *archisynagogus*.

Paul's claim to have been a disciple to Rabban Gamaliel, coupled with his fiery eloquence and the fact that he was a Roman citizen which he everywhere proclaimed, drew large audiences to him. But somehow sooner or later he repelled them even as he did the Apostles in Palestine, and sometimes drove them to rioting. The tempest which broke out against him in Antioch broke out afresh in almost every place which he visited during the last decade of his missionary activity.

Paul could stand opposition, and even persecution, and difficulties only prodded him on to proceed with the prosecution of his plans. The only thing he could not stand was ridicule. And this was his experience in Athens. The fame of that ancient seat of learning spread as far as Palestine. Stories about the *Sabe d'be Atuna* (the sages of Athens), and how Jews sometimes outwitted them, passed from mouth to mouth, and helped to while away the intervals between the Talmud lectures in the Bate Hammidrash. Athens possessed a synagogue, and, as everywhere in the diaspora, pagans were attracted to it, and a number became "devout persons" or "fearers of the Lord". Paul expected that surely the Greeks would be con-

vinced by his "reasoning". The fact that after his usual discourse
at the synagogue neither the Jews nor the Gentiles evinced any
signs of hostility toward him confirmed him in this belief. He
was further encouraged by an invitation to appear at the
Areopagus to expound his doctrines before its distinguished
philosophers and aristocrats, who exercised a tremendous influence on the educational, religious, and social life of Athens
if not of Greece. But as he faced his audience his courage forsook him. He heard some mocking his accent, calling him
"a babbler," and ridiculing his "reasoning" as merely a matter
of "words and names". To remedy the situation Paul modified his preaching. In his great speech on Mars' Hill there
is no mention of Christ, but of the Unknown God, to whom he
found an inscription on one of the altars, and of the resurrection
of all men who worship Him. It was a discourse, if it could
have impressed the cultivated pagan mind, fit to make one
a "fearer of the Lord," but not a Christian. [8]

The news of the teachings of Paul greatly astonished and
embittered the little Judeo-Christian circle in Jerusalem whose
emissaries followed the Apostle to the Gentiles. When Paul's
adherents got wind of this, they tried to dissuade him both
from preaching his doctrines and from returning to Jerusalem.
A "Prophet" by the name of Agabus, whom Paul had met at
Antioch some fourteen years before, imitated the mannerism of
some of the prophets, and taking off the Apostle's girdle and
binding it around himself declared: "Thus saith the Holy
Ghost, so shall the Jews of Jerusalem bind him that owneth it
and deliver him into the hands of the Gentiles." But Paul was
not a man to be intimidated. He was confident he would be
able to exonerate himself again as he did before, especially
since he was carrying with him from the places he had visited
a goodly amount of the alms collected for the converts.

His reception in Jerusalem this time justified the worst fears
of his friends. Judeo-Christians as well as Jews united in
accusing him as one who, like the notorious Jeroboam ben
Nebat, "sinned and caused others to sin". He was denounced
as an apostate, and a dangerous enemy of Jews and Judaism.

He and his followers were spoken of as the "Nicolaites" (pagans), or "Balaamites" who pretended to bless while they intended to curse. They were accused of leading lives "of unrestrained indulgence," and their synagogues were dubbed "the Synagogues of Satan". A legend soon grew up that Paul was himself not a Jew by birth, but a "proselyte of love—of a woman," and that in order to marry the daughter of the High Priest he had himself circumcised. On being rejected Paul avenged himself by declaiming against circumcision, the Sabbath, the dietary laws, and so on. Instead of coming out to welcome him, James summoned him to appear before the Council of the Apostles which met at his house. There he was formally indicted as teaching "all the Jews that are among the Gentiles to forsake Moses, saying that they ought not to circumcise their children, neither to walk after the customs" (of Israel).

It must have been a cruel blow to Paul's self-esteem, but, in accordance with his principle to be "all things to all men" he swallowed his pride and consented to do penance, to purify himself from all pollutions and together with four raggedy Nazarites, whose expenses he was to pay, to shave his head and offer a sacrifice after the expiration of a seven-day retreat at the Temple. But when the Jews, from the countries outside Palestine, recognized him and recalled his preachments against the Law, his assumed penitence added fuel to the flame of hate. Soon it was bruited abroad that he spitefully concealed an uncircumcised Greek in the Temple. Paul was dragged out of the Temple, and would possibly have been killed but for the timely intervention of a Roman tribune who placed him in the tower for safe-keeping. Again he resorted to the subterfuge of "being all things to all men," and claimed that he never said or did anything not in keeping with the Law and the Prophets. He was carried to Caesarea where he made a very favorable impression not only on the Roman procurator, but on Agrippa II and his sister Berenice. They marvelled at his cleverness, were amused by his reasoning, and enjoyed his repartee. When King Agrippa told Paul, "Almost thou persuadest me to be a Christian," Paul replied: "I would to God, that not only thou, but also all that hear me this day were both almost and altogether such as I am, except these bonds."

King Agrippa was for giving Paul his liberty. But Paul, as a Roman citizen, would not accept a favor from a Jewish King and demanded his right to appeal to Caesar. Besides, he claimed he had another vision in which Jesus stood by him, and said, "Be of good cheer, Paul: for as thou hast testified of me in Jerusalem, so must thou bear witness also at Rome." Probably he heard that many noble pagans of the city of the Caesars were turning to Judaism, and felt sure that they would so much the more be attracted to Christianity. He arrived in Rome a prisoner, in the care of the not unkindly centurion Julius, who permitted him to preach his new faith without molestation.

His experience in Jerusalem embittered Paul more than ever against the Jews and the Judeo-Christians. He accused Peter of hypocrisy, as one who himself a Jew lived after the manner of the Gentiles, but expected the Gentiles to live as Jews do. At Corinth he shook his raiment and, pronouncing a curse, exclaimed: "From henceforth I will go unto the Gentiles!" Thereafter his hate of Jews was as bitter as was formerly his hate of Christians. All of them, even Judeo-Christians, were to him false brethren, a pack of dogs, and a band of evil doers. The Epistles which he henceforth sent out concluded with the significant sentence still retained at the end of First Corinthians:

> If any man love not the Lord Jesus Christ, let him be Anathema: *Maran atha.*

Again, despite his resolution to have nothing more to do with the Jews, the first thing he did on his arrival in Rome (62 C.E.) was to call them together to hear him preach. They came, and he expounded "concerning Jesus, both out of the Law and the Prophets, from morning till evening." But they came no more. This exasperated Paul still further and completed the rupture between him and the Jews. In disregard of the Apostles and the Judeo-Christians (and himself as well), he pronounced them to be totally incapable of salvation.

> Well spake the Holy Ghost by Esaias the Prophet unto our fathers, Saying, God unto this people and say, Hearing ye shall hear and shall not understand; and seeing, ye shall see and not perceive: For the heart of the people is waxed gross, and their ears are dull of hearing, and their eyes have they closed; lest they should see with their eyes, and understand with their heart, and should be converted, and I should heal them. 'Be it known, therefore, unto you that the salvation of God is sent unto the Gentiles, and that they will hear it.'[9]

In reading the Epistles of Paul and the Acts of the Apostles, one would imagine that Paul's missionary activities resulted in conversions *en masse*. In reality, the number of Pauline proselytes must have been rather small. At the most, Renan estimates, all of them taken together did not much exceed a thousand. Many of his converts, too, relapsed into Judaism or paganism during his lifetime, and he was disheartened to find quite a number of those who concerning the faith "have made shipwreck." "All they which are in Asia," he complains, "be turned away from me." His only consolation was the thought that "they went out from us, because they were not of us; for if they had been of us, they would no doubt have continued with us." This disavowal of the Apostle to the Gentiles by the Gentiles continued until the Reformation, and his writings remained apocryphal for many generations.

One of the obstacles to the propagation of Pauline Christianity was the counter-mission organized by James, the brother of the Lord, and the rumors the emissaries from Jerusalem spread about Paul. But Paul himself unknowingly contributed much to the reaction which set in against his theology. Paul was a poor psychologist, despite his skillful "reasoning". His boastfulness of his Roman citizenship embittered the Jews, his renunciation of the Law spoiled the Gentiles. He judged the Graeco-Roman mind by the Palestinian-Hebraic. To the Judeo-Christians the acceptance of Jesus as the Messiah gave an additional impetus to leading a life of sanctity and resignation. Their righteousness was to exceed the righteousness of the Scribes and the Pharisees. It was not so with pagans and Hellenized Jews. His doctrine that faith in Christ is all in all, opened the door for many "false brethren" to self-indulgence and immorality. What the Rabbis said of the Jews who worshiped idols could be applied to those who now embraced Christianity: "They knew that it had no substance, but they affected idolatry to justify their immorality." Many naive pagans who sincerely accepted Paul's theology continued in their uncleanness, lasciviousness, covetousness, and drunkenness, "bitterness, and wrath, and anger, and evil speaking." Sometimes intemperance penetrated even into the celebration of the *Agape,* or love feast, which was instituted to commemorate the Eucharist, or last supper of Jesus. Before long, according to Renan,

> ... the scenes of rioting which followed the pagan sacrifices, were there reproduced.... The poor were covered with shame; the rich seemed by their abundance to insult those who had nothing. The remembrance of Jesus, and of the high significance he had given to this repast, appeared forgotten.[10]

There was also another, perhaps more potent, factor in the alienation of the more conscientious Christians from Paul's sect. Paul never failed to assert, both in preaching and in writing, *Maran atha*—the Lord cometh. After an entire generation passed away since the crucifixion and the old order remained as before, and Jesus failed to make his reappearance, and the promised resurrection of the dead did not materialize, even the faithful began to doubt. "Since the fathers fell asleep," they complained, "all things continue as they were from the beginning of creation. Where is the promise of his coming?"

Yet, as Paul asserted before he became embittered, Christians owe a debt of gratitude to Paul for introducing Christianity or its code of ethics, to the Gentiles. As he almost always utilized the Synagogue to disseminate Christianity among Jews, so did Christianity propagate the Jewish standard of morality among Gentiles. Through him, mother and daughter became mutually helpful. The former led the way. She inspired her daughter with missionary zeal, put at her disposal her sacred places of study and worship, and taught her the technique of missionary *modus operandi*. Christianity, in her turn, made the moral content of Judaism known to mankind much more rapidly than could Judaism with its strict monotheism, if left to its own unaided efforts. In later years, as we shall see, the Church was to become a training school for many proselytes not only "of the Gate" but even "of Righteousness," and multitudes of Gentiles retraced the steps of Paul, and, as it were, journeyed back from Rome to Jerusalem. The Jewish Apostle to the Gentiles opened the door of the unknown sanctuary and by preaching "Jesus Christ and him crucified," did more than anyone to clear

> In the wilderness the way of the Lord,
> Make plain in the desert
> A highway for our God.[11]

Paul, the Apostle to the Gentiles, died a martyr's death in Rome, as Jesus had died in Jerusalem. To the Romans, both were Jews, though the one hated them and the Law and prided himself on his Roman citizenship, and the other loved them and the Torah and had little use for the Gentiles. They were not, however, the only Jews, loyal and disloyal, who were victims of Roman rapacity and brutality. Ever since the Caesars gained a foothold in Judea, their path was marked with fire and blood. Had Jeremiah been alive during the days preceding the destruction of the Second Temple he might well have repeated his lament: "Abroad the sword bereaveth, at home there is the like of death!"

With the deepening despair of the Judeans, there developed among them groups of *Kanaim* (super-zealots), some of whom objected to receiving non-Jews into the faith or even their gifts or sacrifices for the Temple, and others who would force them to adopt the Jewish religion. Metelus, the defeated Roman general, was given the alternative between circumcision or death, and it was with great difficulty that Josephus prevailed upon the mob not to constrain two of his prominent Gentile friends to become converts to Judaism. Luckily, the counsel of the sages prevailed. They were opposed to coercion no less than to rejection. They were still happy to welcome everyone who voluntarily sought admission into the house of Israel, they still hoped to become "a light unto the nations," even when the sun of their own nationhood was beginning to set. They hated the Greeks and the Romans, as they did their Jewish henchmen, but only as long as they were enemies, not because they were Gentiles. For those of them who cared to join themselves to the Lord, the gates of Judaism were as wide open as before, and their burnt offerings and their sacrifices were acceptable on God's altar almost to the very last. Nor would they visit the sins of the fathers upon their children. When Agrippa I burst into tears at the reading of the verse, "Thou mayest not put a foreigner over thee, who is not thy brother," the people forgot his Herodian descent, and in an overflow of affection exclaimed: "Fear not, Agrippa, thou art our brother!" [12]

A frequently repeated midrashic homily of that time gives us an insight into the Judean soul perhaps better than any fact. It is based on the verse, "The Lord preserveth the strangers (gerim)". This interpretation may have been the original of Jesus' parable of the lost sheep, with this difference, however, that while in the latter the sheep is Jewish and strays into the pagan fold, in the former the gazelle is pagan and comes into the Jewish fold:

> Once there was a king who had a herd which went every day to the pasture and returned every evening to the enclosure. One day a gazelle accompanied the sheep, foraged with them all day, returned with them toward eventide, and went back with them the next morning into the commons. The king was told: 'This

gazelle has joined herself to thy flock, forages with them all day, and returns with them toward eventide.' Thereafter the king commanded every morning: 'Let the gazelle feed wherever it liketh her best. Let no one strike her. Let everyone take care of her.' Likewise every evening on her return he would command: 'Give her all she wants to drink.' Said his servants: 'Sire, thou hast so many rams, so many lambs, so many goats, yet thou never didst command us concerning them, but concerning this gazelle thou commandest us day after day!' Replied the king: 'A sheep whether she wants it or not is prompted by her very nature to go every morning into the pasture, and to return every evening to the enclosure. The gazelles are children of the open spaces. It is not their nature to come to dwell with the children of man. Should we not appreciate it that this one left the wide, wide wilderness, where all of their kind love to roam, and comes to stay in an enclosure?' 'Thus also the *ger*. He left his family and his father's house, his own nation and all the nations of the world, and came of his own accord unto us. Take therefore special care of him, and be exceeding careful to do him naught harmful. As it is written, "Ye shall love the stranger (ger)"; and "a stranger (*ger*)" shalt thou not wrong.' [13]

That many Gentile "gazelles" joined the Jewish flock the Gospels bear ample evidence. That, as a rule, they received a cordial welcome we can judge from the story of the family of Antibla (or Agathobulos, also Nablata), of the first century B.C.E., who traced their ancestry to Araunah the Jebusite. When it was learned in Jerusalem that this family of *gerim* was contemplating leaving the holy city because it could not maintain its standard of living in the metropolis, a collection of six hundred talents was made to induce them to stay.

A further evidence of the affectionate regard in which some *gerim,* or their descendants, were held is contained in a tradition concerning Shmaya and Abtalyon. Though both of them were reputed to have derived from the stock of Senna-cherib, or Haman, they rose to the highest position of honor among the Judeans. Shmaya was appointed President and Abtalyon Vice-President of the Sanhedrin and were principals of the academy of Jerusalem. Once, in the heat of a legal argument, a derogatory reference was made to their birth by no less a personage than Akabia b. Mahalalel. Thereupon Akabia was excommunicated, and his opinion was rejected. One Day of Atonement when the people rushed to greet the High Priest, as was their wont, they noticed Shmaya and Abtalyon. Immediately all turned towards them and left the High Priest to himself. The latter, chagrined, re-marked: "Peace to the children of the nations," alluding to their descent. To this, Shmaya and Abtalyon replied: "More be the peace of the children of the nations who do the deeds of Aaron, than to a son of Aaron who fails to do the deeds of Aaron." To Abtalyon is attributed the saying which may have been intended for Jewish missionaries: "Ye sages, be heedful of your words, lest ye incur the penalty of exile, and be exiled to a place of evil waters, and the disciples who come after you drink thereof and die, and the Heavenly Name be profaned." [14]

The most zealous missionary of Judaism was Hillel, a contemporary of Herod, who, according to Renan, stood in the same relation to Jesus as Rabban Gamaliel did to Paul, and whom the Rabbis put by the side of Moses and Ezra. His maxim was: "Be of the disciples of Aaron, loving peace and pursuing it, loving all creatures, and drawing them nigh to the Torah." Around his luminous personality cluster many legends, several of which have proselytes for their subject. One is about a Roman official who, probably in a bantering mood, approached Shammai, Hillel's great antagonist in the interpretation of the Torah, and asked him how many Torahs the Jews had. "Two," said Shammai, "One the Torah that is in writing, the other that is transmitted by the word of mouth." "I will become a convert on condition that you teach me only the Written Torah," suggested the Roman. The rigor-ous and impatient Shammai ordered him to leave. Hillel, however, received him cordially and began to teach him the Written Torah. The first day he taught him Alef, Bet, Gimmel, Dalet. The next day he turned the names around and said Dalet, Gimmel, Bet, Alef. When the Roman reminded him that the day before he had taught him differently, Hillel replied: "Just as we would not know the names of the letters of the Torah unless we followed our tradition, so would we not know the meaning of the teachings of the Torah had it not been for the explications of the Unwritten Torah."

Once a Roman told Shammai that he would like to become a Jew if he could learn the whole Torah while standing on one foot. Shammai seized a rod and drove him away. Hillel, to whom the Roman made the same proposition, was happy to comply with his request. "What thou hatest, do not unto thy neighbor," said he, while the heathen was standing on one foot; "this is the fundamental principle of our Torah. The rest is commentary upon it. Study it and thou wilt see for thyself."

On another occasion a heathen stepped into a school and heard the children studying from the Book of Exodus concerning the vestments which the High Priest wore while performing his sacred functions. The heathen became greatly interested and informed Shammai that he would consent to become a Jew if he were to be made a High Priest. Shammai angrily ordered him away. Hillel calmly listened to his offer and said: "My son, sit down, and hearken to my words. When one wishes to receive a king of flesh and blood, does he not have to study how to appear before him and how to depart from him? ... Thou desirest to stand in the presence of the King of Kings, the Holy One, praised be He, shouldst thou not learn first how to enter into the Holy of Holies, how to kindle the lights, how to approach the altar, etc., etc.?" The pagan agreed. So Hillel began to instruct him in the alphabet, then in the Torah of the priesthood (Leviticus). When they reached the verse, "And the common man that draweth nigh shall be put to death," the (prospective) ger began to revolve in his mind: "If such is the law concerning the Israelites who are called 'sons unto the Lord,' and 'a kingdom of priests and a holy nation,' how should I, an humble stranger who hath only a knapsack and a staff, aspire to such honors?" Thereupon the heathen, embracing Hillel, exclaimed: "May all the blessings of the Torah rest upon thy head. Hadst thou been like unto Shammai the Elder, I might never have sought to be integrated in Israel. The severity of Shammai would have caused me to lose this world and the world to come, thy patience made me gain the bliss of this and the other world." It is said that to this proselyte there were born two sons, one of whom he named Hillel and the other Gamaliel, after Hillel's son. Some time later he and the other *gerim* recounted to one another their experiences with the two sages, and with one accord repeated: "The severity of Shammai nearly caused us to lose the bliss of the world to come, the patience of Hillel brought us nigh under the wings of the Shekinah." [15]

At least two of the *Gerim shel Hillel,* as the proselytes were called who had been converted either by Hillel or by those who adopted his method of winning souls, attained fame as great scholars. They were Ben Bag-bag and Ben He-he, presumably so nicknamed because they had to start with the alphabet. In the sayings of the fathers they are credited with the following moral maxims: Ben Bag-bag used to say: "Turn it (the Torah), and again turn it, for everything is in it, therein meditate, therein grow gray and old, and from it do not stir. Thou canst form no better habit than this." Ben He-he used to say: "One's recompense is in keeping with one's effort." Of a certain R. Johanan b. Bag-bag it was testified that he was "at home in all the chambers of the Torah." [16]

The frequency of conversions is evidenced by the manuals containing the basic requirements of Judaism with special regard to proselytes. One of these was adopted, with numerous modifications and interpolations, by the early fathers as a Christian catechism. It was called The Way, or *Didache,* and was intended to teach the neophite "the Way of Life and the Way of Death." Its contents may be judged from the following:

The Way of Life is this: First, thou shalt love the Lord that made thee, and all things that thou wouldst not should happen unto thee do not unto another. Secondly, love thy neighbor as thyself. Thou shalt not kill. Thou shalt not commit adultery; thou shalt not seduce boys; thou shalt not commit fornication. Thou shalt not steal. Thou shalt not use magic; thou shalt not use sorcery. Thou shalt not kill a child by abortion, nor what is born shalt thou put to death. Thou shalt not covet things that are thy neighbor's. Thou shalt not forswear thyself. Thou shalt not bear false witness; thou shalt not speak evil. Thou shalt not bear a grudge; thou shalt not be doubleminded or doubletongued, for a snare of death is a double-tongue. Thy speech shall not be false, nor empty, but fulfilled by deed. Thou shalt not be covetous, nor rapacious, nor a hypocrite, nor malicious, nor haughty. Thou shalt not take evil counsel against thy neighbor. Thou shalt not hate any man, but some shalt thou reprove, for some shalt thou pray, and some shalt thou love above thy life. . . .

My child, flee from everything evil, and from whatsoever is like unto it. . . . Of him that speaketh the word of the Lord shalt thou be mindful night and day; thou shalt honor him as the Lord. . . .

Thou shalt not hesitate to give, nor, giving, shalt thou murmur. . . . Thou shalt not command in thy bitterness thy servant or handmaid who hopes in the same God, lest haply they shall not fear the God Who is over both. . . . Thou shalt in no wise forsake the Lord's commandments, but thou shalt observe the things thou didst receive, neither adding nor taking away. . . . . This is the way of life.[17]

Neophytes who wished to proceed further had, after due instruction, to undergo the ceremony of initiation. A male had to submit first to circumcision and then to baptism, a female only to baptism. This was followed, while the Temple was in existence, by a burnt offering of a dove or pigeon which removed from the neophyte the last vestige of the "dust of idolatry" and rendered him or her a full-fledged Jew or Jewess, a son or daughter "of the Covenant," as much as if he or she had been of the "seed of Abraham." If he later relapsed, he was no longer in the category of a heathen but of an apostate Jew. [18]

While it is impossible to estimate the number of Proselytes of Righteousness on the eve of the *Hurban,* it was indisputably very large. They came mostly as individuals not infrequently as families, and sometimes even in groups. They came principally from Antioch, from Damascus, from Alexandria, from Rome. Where they were but few, they were quickly assimilated with the Jewish community; where they were numerous, they sometimes established a *Kahal* (congregation) of their own, but worked for the common cause. They most likely constituted an uneducated element, but some of them attained proficiency in the Torah, and many more were noted for their piety. Among them was Abba Saul b. Batnit, said to have been the son of a Batanian proselyte, a severe critic of the Sadducean priesthood. Tiberias, which was settled mainly by foreigners and slaves, became a center of Talmudists and later disputed its prestige with Jerusalem and Yamnia.

When, finally, the last hour of Judea's independence sounded, among those who fought most valiantly on the side of the Jews were either *gerim* or descendants of *gerim.* From Galilee came some of the most zealous and self-sacrificing patriots. In Damascus the enemy's designs were frequently put to naught by the women who embraced Judaism. In Caesarea proselytes defended their new coreligionists against their own countrymen. Idumeans mingled their blood with that of Judeans in defense of the Temple. Among the hostages whom Titus carried off to Rome to ensure the submission of the Jews were Monobaz and Kenedius, members of the converted royal family of Adiabene. Perhaps the most conspicuous of the heroes who participated in this most bravely fought war in history was Simon bar-Gurion (or Bar Giora), who led the dauntless *Sicarii.* Him Titus reserved for his triumphal march through Rome, and afterwards had him hurled from the Tarpian Rock. His death was then proclaimed by Titus, Vespasian, and Domitian in front of the Temple of Jupiter Capitolinus, while holocausts were sacrificed to the gods for their favoring the Romans. Judea's national existence expired with the last breath of one of her adopted sons. [19]

CHAPTER IX

IN THE SHADOW OF DEFEAT

JEWS were the first to salute the founder of the Flavian line with the title of Caesar. When, on the eve of the *Hurban,* R. Johanan b. Zakkai was brought before Vespasian, (then the commanding general of the Roman legions,) he quoted Isaiah's prediction, "and Lebanon shall fall by a mighty one," as indicating that the conqueror of Palestine would be an Imperator. Josephus, too, predicted that Vespasian and his son would be Caesars and Emperors. Perhaps this, and the love for the Judean princess Berenice, which Titus continued to cherish, may account for the relative leniency which the Roman rulers showed toward the vanquished Judeans. The Jews also, either out of sheer exhaustion or because they realized the futility of resisting the powerful Romans, seemingly became resigned to their lot and devoted themselves with increased fervor to the study of the Torah and the practice of their religion.

The peaceful reconstruction of Jewish life in Palestine was rudely interrupted under Trajan, the second of Rome's "five good Emperors," when the Jews in the surrounding countries joined the ranks of the nations who were driven into open rebellion. Trajan's design to stamp out the Jews and Judaism once and for all, however, was frustrated by his death in 117, and Hadrian, his successor, resorted to the conciliatory policies of Vespasian and Titus. He recalled the brutal governor Quietus and subsequently had him executed. He even pardoned Julianus and Papus after they had been condemned to death for trying to raise an insurrection among the Palestinian Jews. To win the good will of the Jews yet further,

Hadrian promised to rebuild Jerusalem and there to erect another Temple in place of the one destroyed by his predecessors, but it was to be a pagan temple. He believed that all the Jews wished was to have a sanctuary, regardless of whether it was dedicated to the worship of Jehovah or of Jupiter.[1]

When the Jews discovered the Emperor's intentions, their disappointment exceeded all bounds. In their deep resentment they lost all sense of prudence. Led by Bar Kokba, two hundred thousand stalwart men plunged headlong into a war with their perfidious enemy. With them, according to the historian, Dion Cassius, were many of other races. For once, the Samaritans, too, forgot their traditional hatred and made common cause with the Jews. So confident was Bar Kokba of his success that he is said to have uttered: "Lord, if Thou carest not to help us, do not at least help our foes, and we shall not be defeated." It looked for a while as if, after all, the Judean lad would with his pebble strike down the Roman Goliath.

But the inevitable came to pass. After three years of deeds of unsurpassed valor on the part of Bar Kokba and his followers, the impregnable stronghold of Bethar was captured by the Romans through the defection of a traitor (135 C.E.). The most horrible massacre in the history of ancient warfare ensued. Hadrian would not taste food until thousands of those who gave themselves up on the promise of mercy were butchered. Women and children were sold into slavery. Upon the site of old Jerusalem a new city, Aelia Capitolina, was founded, built in Grecian style and populated exclusively by pagans. On the Temple Mount a column was raised in honor of Hadrian, and a temple was dedicated to Jupiter Capitolinus. A shrine also was erected on Mt. Gerizim, and statues were set up to Venus and Adonis on Mt. Golgotha and in Bethlehem. The gates leading from Jerusalem to these holy places were decorated with the head of swine. It was indeed such a dearly bought victory that Hadrian could only report, "I and my army are well," and the Senate refrained from celebrating it with the usual triumph. But Jupiter seemed again to have vanquished Jehovah, and Titus' coins commemorating *Judaea*

Devicta were now supplemented with others bearing the inscriptions *Exercitus Judaicus* and *Adventi Augusti Judaeae* and the image of a woman, representing Judea, in the act of sacrificing to the victorious gods of Rome.

Having destroyed every vestige of Judean independence, Hadrian now betook himself to the extirpation of Judaism. Jewish scholars who dared teach the Jewish religion or ordain a rabbi were sentenced to death, and the town in which this "crime" was committed was doomed to destruction. Circumcision was strictly prohibited. A Jew who was caught nailing a *mezuzah* to his door was fined a thousand denarii; one who was seen with phylacteries upon his forehead was in danger of having his skull crushed. *Delatores* (informers) were constantly on the lookout for any sign which would indicate that a Jewish rite was being performed. Any ceremonial which bore the least tinge of a religious nature was likely to expose one to severest punishment. The sound of mortar they learned meant that a child was about to be circumcised (powder being prepared for the operation). The sight of more than ordinary illumination in a house was proof that a wedding was taking place, in which event the bride would be snatched away and carried to the home of the Roman official. A dialogue in the Talmud describes the state of the Jews after the fall of Bethar as follows:

> 'Why art thou dragged to be stoned?' 'Because I circumcised my son.' 'Why art thou dragged to be burnt?' 'Because I observed the Sabbath, or read the Torah.' 'Why art thou dragged to be crucified?' 'Because I ate Matzot.' 'Why art thou beaten with a club?' 'Because I built a sukkah, or shook a lulab, or wore tefilin, or put on a tallith, or have done the will of the Father in Heaven.' [2]

It was the teaching of the Torah to the Gentiles that led to the martyrdom of "the Ten who were murdered by the government (*Asarah haruge malkut*)." A certain Roman emperor, we are told, while reading the Torah came across the verse, "And he that stealeth a man, and selleth him, or if

he be found in his hand, he shall surely be put to death."
Seeking for a pretext to wreak vengeance on the Jews, he
summoned the ten most scholarly and saintly of them and
demanded what, in accordance with their Torah, was the
penalty prescribed for a kidnapper. They answered, "Death."
"Then," exclaimed he, "prepare yourselves to die, for your
ancestors committed such a crime (by stealing Joseph and
selling him); and as representatives of the Jewish nation you
must expiate for their crime." Whereupon the ten sages were
done to death in a most horrible manner.[3]

It was only natural that such savage persecution should
kindle Jewish animosity to the heathens. Who can blame R.
Simeon b. Yohai, an eye-witness and victim of pagan fiendishness, for declaring: "Jews alone deserve to be called human beings," but no heathens deserve to be called human beings and "The best of the Gentiles, kill; the best of
serpents, crush its brains." True, the leading authorities agree
that the latter saying was qualified by the phrase "in times
of war." But even if it was not, who will fail to understand
the rabbinic advice: "No man should be condemned for
words uttered while his soul is in anguish"?[4]

Thereafter Rome became identified in the Jewish mind with
the "wild beast of the reeds," and the "boar out of the woods,"
against whom the Psalmist invoked the vengeance of God.
To the Jews of Rome she was the swine of mankind: "As
the swine stretches out its hoofs to show that they are cloven
(like those of clean beasts), so Rome robs and steals and
boasts of her culture." She represented the embodiment of
all that was abhorrent and revolting to the Jewish highly
developed sense of morality. Brutality was her heritage, even
as the Torah was the heritage of the House of Israel. "Five
things did Canaan command his children (before his death)"
runs a saying of the Rabbis: " 'Love ye one another, love robbery, love fornication, hate your superiors, and never speak
the truth.' " In comparison with Rome the Babylonians were
merciful, and for her the gates of repentance would be forever closed. According to some rabbis, in the days of the
Messiah God will gladly accept the offerings brought by all

the other nations. But Rome's gifts he will reject with loathing. Concerning her He will command the Messiah: " 'Roar at this monster that devoured peoples, that permitted everything for the sake of lucre, that kept Israel back from the study of the Torah, and compelled them to commit acts of Satan!' " [5]

To save their people from total annihilation, the Sages resolved to surround them with an impregnable wall of ceremonial observances, and pronounced the study of the Torah as the highest mode of worship. But they realized that still more substantial protection was necessary. The sheep must not only have a shelter but must be protected from coming within reach of the wolf. The Jews were henceforth to separate themselves, to become "a people that dwelleth apart."

And so at the very time when the Romans were besieging Jerusalem, a clandestine meeting was held in the attic of one (Eleazar b.) Hananiah b. Hezekiah, at which "Eighteen Points" were proposed whereby every link between the Jews and the pagans was at last to be broken. On "that Day," (as the occasion came to be known) it was prohibited to buy bread, wine, oil, or any edibles handled by heathen, also to accept their testimony or their offerings, or even to study their languages, and, of course, to intermarry with them.[6] But some leaders did not stop with drawing the line at social intercourse. They would prohibit Gentiles the benefit of the study of the Torah. Since, however, the Scriptures had already been translated into the Greek and since converts to Christianity arrogated to themselves the claim that they were the true Israelites, the Rabbis forbade the teaching of the Talmud to any non-Jew. Says R. Judah b. Shalom: "God wanted to make His secret known only to those who fear Him (or to distinguish between those who truly know Him and those who do not), so He gave them the *Mishnah* (Oral Law)."

More than this, there began to develop a sentiment among some of the Sages adverse to proselytes. "Evil after evil," declared R. Isaac, "comes on those who accept proselytes." Proselytes, it was said, delay the coming of the Messiah. They thought so perhaps because it was believed that it requires twenty-four generations to eradicate the penchant for idolatry,

or because it was believed that they accept the Torah out of
fear instead of love, as Jews were supposed to do. It was
argued that despite their conversion, the standards of morality of the proselytes were necessarily lower than those of
a born Jew, and that they continued to be prejudiced against
those whom they grew up to regard as their enemies. R. Helbo,
of the fourth century, remarked that proselytes are as much
a source of trouble to Israel as the itch.[7]

It is significant that though the Jews had every reason to
recoil from the thought of admitting pagans, and notably
Romans, into the household of Israel, the anti-conversionists
remained an insignificant minority. According to a recent authority, "We can find only four passages in the entire literature (of the Talmud) which are unfavorable (to *gerim*)
without reservation. Two of them are Tannaitic, two later."
And even these have been so construed by the other rabbis
as to render them inoffensive. The vast majority refused to repudiate their self-imposed task to be "a light unto the nations,"
and still clung to their abiding faith in the ultimate reclamation and regeneration of the Gentiles. Not even of Rome did
they despair, and like R. Judah b. Ilai, they found good even
in their enemies. R. Simeon b. Lakish (Resh Lakish) applied
to Rome the passage, "And God saw everything that He hath
made, and, behold, it was very good, because it will yet right
the wrongs of the people." In the very name *hazir* (swine),
which some applied to Rome, Rabbi Meir saw a prophecy
that some day Rome would restore (*hozeret*) "the crown
to whom it belongs." In fact, according to R. Joshua b. Levi,
the Messiah would come from Rome, and R. Jose bar Haninah
predicted that "the princes of Judah will yet publicly teach
the Torah in the circuses and theaters of Edom."[8]

To these missionary-minded men, "The Day" on which
the "Eighteen Points" were passed "was as grievous as the
day on which was fashioned the Golden Calf," and they
condemned the act as subversive of the noblest ideals of their
people. It was like pouring water into the oil of Judaism,
said R. Joshua. Not only did they not tolerate any restrictions,
they even connived at some lapses for the sake of maintain-

ing peace and good will with Gentiles, in the hope of drawing them nigh to the Torah. Said R. Johanan, "The rigor of R. Zechariah" (b. Abkulos), who rejected a Roman offering because it was legally unfit, "destroyed our house, burned down our sanctuary and caused us to be exiled from our land." For a Jew, they claimed, it was not sufficient to sacrifice himself for the sanctification of God's Name, he must bring non-Jews under the wings of the Shekinah. Far from withholding the knowledge of Judaism from the Gentiles, they encouraged the study of the Torah among those who wished to know it, or to follow its precepts. "Whence do we know," asks R. Meir, a pupil of the martyred R. Akiba and a survivor of the Hadrianic persecutions, that a

> . . . heathen who studies (or does what is enjoined in) the Torah is the equal of a High Priest? It says: 'Ye shall therefore keep My statutes, and Mine ordinances, which if a *man* do, he shall live by them.' It does not say 'Priests, Levites or Israelites,' to teach thee that even a heathen who studies the Torah is the equal of a High Priest.

Most of the "Eighteen Points" were indeed neither enforced nor observed. The educated classes studied Greek and other languages. In fact, it was said that a member of the Sanhedrin had to master all the "seventy languages." Intermarriage with pagans who embraced Judaism continued as heretofore. Abstention from the wine and meat of the heathen was indeed observed more or less completely (as it was by the Christians) because of their relation to the practice of idolatry, but frequent and even friendly contacts between Jews and Gentiles were not unusual. It was during the bitterest persecutions that the Rabbis taught:

> The Gentile poor should be maintained like the poor Israelites; the Gentile sick should be visited like the Jewish sick; the Gentile dead should be buried and eulogized like the Jewish dead; and Gentile mourners should be visited and comforted like Jewish mourners.[9]

This opinion the Sages, as legalists, based upon the Torah as a code of laws. As preachers and moralists (*agadists*), they founded the same upon the interpretation of the Bible from an exegetical viewpoint and from the sayings of the wise. Hence we find not infrequently that the same rabbi who is strict as a *hakalist* (legalist) is very lenient as an *agadist* (moralist), and sometimes the very word which one interpreted against accepting *gerim* was used by another to show just the opposite. Thus *v'nisp'hu,* which R. Helbo derives from leprosy (*sappahat*), R. Berekiah gives the sense of "joining" (*sfaheni*) and concludes that converts will in the future, officiate as priests in the Holy of Holies.[10]

Of the several tales which the agadists used to point a moral, the following may serve as an example. It is based on the verse, "Cast thy bread upon the water," and is in some respects reminiscent of the story of the Good Samaritan, except that it may have had a basis in fact. At all events, it shows how the Rabbis insisted on kindness and good will, even to such as had forfeited any claim upon the consideration of the Jews. A shipwrecked Roman officer, upon seeing a number of Jews on their way to Jerusalem, appealed to them: "I am of the children of Esau, your brother; give me a garment to cover my nakedness." The people answered: "Would that thy entire nation were in thy plight," and passed on. Not so R. Eleazar b. Shamua. He gave him one of his robes, took him to his house, where he set before him meat and drink and, after presenting him with two hundred denarii, escorted him fourteen parasangs to show him the way. Some time later, a wicked emperor decreed that all the Jewish men should be murdered and all their women sold as slaves. The Jews delegated R. Eleazar to go to Rome to plead in their behalf and gave him four thousand denarii to use as a gift. It turned out that the wicked emperor was no other than the castaway. When told by the rabbi of his mission, the emperor rose and exclaimed: "Is it not written in your Torah, 'An Ammonite and a Moabite shall not be admitted into the assembly of the Lord because they did not meet you with bread and water?' Is it not also written, 'Thou shalt not despise an Edomite, for he is thy brother?' I am a son of Esau, your brother, and since your people have transgressed the commands of the Torah they, by their own laws, deserve to die." R. Eleazar appealed to his mercy, but the emperor, who seems to have been conversant not only with the Torah but with the sayings current among the Jews about the Romans, quoted: "Knowest thou not our Government does 'nothing for nothing'?" The rabbi offered him the treasure he brought with him as a gift. But to his amazement the emperor refused to accept it, saying: "These four thousand denarii be thine instead of the two hundred thou gavest me in my hour of need, and select thee out of my wardrobe seventy of my robes in lieu of the garment thou gavest me when I was naked, and go thou in peace to thy people whom I have forgiven because of thee." [11]

But the Sages were not concerned merely with promoting the peace and good will of the Gentiles. They were even more anxious to rescue them from their spiritual degradation. To save a human soul was to them "to do a deed of pleasantness to the Creator" Who was Himself the Great Teacher and the Supreme Missionary, and Who yearns for all "to return to repentance." The Sages affirm almost unanimously, that God rejoices over proselytes more than if they were of the seed of Abraham. More precious are their names to Him than the wine poured on the altar; dearer are their souls to Him than those which stood before Him on Mt. Sinai. In fact, in His sight they are Israelites from the moment they decide to abjure idolatry. He blesses them with the same benediction as He does Israelites as soon as they accept Judaism. [12]

One of the most beautiful of rabbinic folk tales is their saga concerning the presentation of the Torah to mankind. Ever since men began to pervert their way of life, it claims, He sent messenger after messenger to reform them. The revelation on Mt. Sinai was not the first. After the dispersion which followed the building of the Tower (of Babel), and the variation in languages which succeeded it, He sent the angel Michael to each of the "Seventy" Nations to induce them to live in accordance with the teachings of the Torah. Though the ancestors of the children of Israel proved themselves from the beginning worthy to possess the Torah, God would not withhold His Torah from any who would promise to honor and obey her. Indeed, 'there was not a door of the "Seventy Nations" at which He did not knock,' and offer her in marriage. He finally betrothed her to Israel because none would have her save Israel. Israel, alone of all nations, was anxious "to ascend on high and lead the fair celestial maiden captive."

Yet even while the nuptials between Israel and the Torah-Bride were being consecrated on Mt. Sinai, God proclaimed to the world that she was not to remain in the exclusive possession of her husband. Her "wedding day" was purposely set for the month of Sivan, whose sign of the zodiac is Twins, to indicate that she was to belong to Esau as well as to his twin brother Jacob. As the locale of the marriage He chose the desert, the common property of all. And the wedding ceremony was performed in all the "Seventy Languages" spoken by men, and in the presence of all the souls who in all ages will come to join themselves to the house of Israel. "As the hammer that breaketh the rock," says a rabbi, "produces innumerable sparks, so every word uttered by God at the Revelation struck seventy different sounds," suitable for all who heard it. [13]

Four more Revelations, said the Rabbis, will be necessary ere the world will forever be established under the Kingdom of the Almighty. Meanwhile, God teaches the Gentiles by precept and example through the Jews. Every important event in their history was designed to attract the heathen to Judaism. All the miracles that were performed in Egypt and in Babylon were for the purpose of gaining proselytes. And the main object of the long and bitter exile was to bring about the great event for which the world was created—the acceptance of the God of Israel as the sole God of all men. The Dispersion, according to R. Eleazar, R. Johanan, and R. Oshayah, was not a punishment but a privilege: "God did loving kindness with

Israel in scattering them among the nations; for thus will be
added *gerim* unto them." [14]

The Rabbis scanned the Scriptures for the word *ger* and
almost always construed it to refer to a proselyte. From this
study, together with the incidents in the lives of the biblical
converts, they constructed many a homily as well as a system
of jurisprudence pertaining especially to proselytes. One section of the Pentateuch, which they named *Parashat Hagger*
(Numbers, Chapter V), forms the basis of a dissertation attributed to R. Abbahu (279-320). It must have been a great
favorite, since it is repeated in many Midrashim as well as in
the Talmud:

> R. Abbahu saith: 'They that dwell under His shadow
> shall again make corn to grow (Hos. 14:8),' these are
> the *gerim* who come and seek refuge under the shadow
> of the Holy One, praised be He. 'They shall make corn
> to grow,' that is, they shall become an essential part
> (*ikkar*) like Israel. Another explanation, 'They shall
> make corn to grow,' that is, the Talmud; 'and shall
> blossom as the vine,' that is the *aggadah*. 'The scent
> thereof shall be as the wine of Lebanon': the Holy
> One, praised be He, saith, 'Beloved to Me are the
> names of *gerim* like libation wine which is poured
> upon the altar (which maketh white the red sins of
> Israel)'....
>
> Thus it is that just as there is a section in the Torah
> concerning the dealings of one Israelite with his fel-
> low Israelite ... so also did the Holy One, praised be
> He, insert a section in the Torah with regard to the
> treatment of *gerim* by Israelites. For the Israelite who
> robs a proselyte is as guilty as if he robs another
> Israelite. [15]

The idea that one who accepts Judaism becomes *ipso facto*
an integral part of the Jewish people (*naaseh ikkar k'Yisrael*)
is stressed everywhere in rabbinic hermeneutics. Thus one

aggadist applies "And they go from a holy place" to *gerim*: i.e., "from the same place whence Israel goeth, for Israel is called holy." Taking Psalm 128 as a text, another aggadist continues:

It doth not say, 'Happy is Israel,' 'Happy are the priests,' 'Happy are the Levites,' but 'Happy is everyone that feareth the Lord,' because it refers to *gerim,* for all that fear the Lord are happy even as Israel is happy. But the *ger* to whom it refers is the *Ger Zedek* not the Cuthites, concerning whom it stated, 'They feared the Lord, and served their graven images.'...
'When thou eatest the labor of thy hand,' this also refers to the *ger,* who cannot depend on the merit of his fathers. Peradventure he will say, 'Since I cannot rely on the merits of the fathers, I can expect a reward for my good deeds only in this world, therefore does Holy Writ announce that by his own labor the *ger* may acquire the bliss of this world and also of the world to come....

'Thy children (shall be) like olive plants': even as the olive tree produces olives for immediate food, olives for preserving, and olives for illumination, and the light thereof is brighter than that produced by any other oil, so will there come forth from the sons of *gerim* masters of the Scriptures, masters of the Mishnah, masters of social relations, and some of them will be scholars, and some sages, and some sagacious, and their children will endure forever. . . .

'Round about thy table': for because of them thy children's merit will be enhanced, and they will obtain great excellencies.... 'Behold, surely thus shall the man be blessed that feareth the Lord': this is illustrated by Abraham and Sarah, both of whom were *gerim.* Because Abraham was a Fearer of the Lord, he obtained a blessing, so will all the *gerim* who conduct themselves as they did....

'And see thy children's children. Peace be upon
Israel': How will there be peace upon Israel merely
because the *ger* will see his children's children? It refers to a *ger zedek* who may marry his daughter to
a priest, whose descendants will therefore themselves
be priests, who will bless Israel and say: 'May the
Lord bless thee ... and give thee peace.' Thus we find
that Rahab, the harlot, for having sheltered the spies
and helped them to escape, the Holy One, praised
be He, considered it as if she helped Him and gave
her her reward.... And what was her reward? Her
daughters were married into the priesthood, and their
sons officiated at the altar and entered into the sanctuary and blessed Israel with the Ineffable Name. [16]

The Rabbis dwell affectionately upon God's singular love
for proselytes. They say that God, knowing how hard it is to
break away from old habits, makes allowances for their
lapses which He would not tolerate in those to the manner
born. Commenting upon the doom of the descendants of
Saul, who killed the Gibeonites, the Midrash proceeds:

'For them that honor Me will I honor, and they that
despise Me shall be lightly esteemed,' this speaks concerning *gerim*. They honor the Holy One, praised be
He, by abandoning their evil deeds, and coming to
seek shelter under the wings of the Shekinah, therefore the Holy One, praised be He, honors them....
And what honor did the Holy One, praised be He,
show unto *gerim*? He placed the section with regard
to *gerim* immediately after the one which treats of the
exclusion of the unclean. This is intended to teach
thee that He removeth afar the sinners who are of
Israel and draweth nigh the *gerim* who come to His
Name. He, therefore, that robs them of their rights
is as guilty as if he did so to an Israelite.

The aggadists loved particularly to dwell on the story of the Gibeonites. One of them thus represents God as making a direct appeal to converts:

> Are you afraid because I disqualified you concerning the paschal lamb (Ex. 12:43)? Inquire of the Gibeonites, what favors I showed them.... If I did this for the Gibeonites who were Amorites, and came out of fear, and practiced guile on Israel ... shall I not receive and exalt converts who come out of love of My name?

The approval of proselyting by the sages is perhaps best expressed in the following amplifications of passages from the Bible:

> Precious (in the sight of God) are *gerim,* for in every instance He speaks of them as if they were Israelites: Israelites are called servants, as it is said (Lev. 25:55), 'For unto Me are the children of Israel servants,' so are *gerim,* as it is said (Isa. 56:6), 'Also the aliens that join themselves to the Lord, to minister unto Him, and to love the name of the Lord, to be His servants.'
> Israelites are called friends, as it is said (Isa. 41:8), 'The seed of Abraham My friend,' so are *gerim,* as it is said (Dt. 10:18), 'He loveth the *gerim.*'[17]

Similar remarks can be quoted from the leading sages of the Talmud. According to R. Simeon b. Lakish, "The proselyte is dearer to God than Israel when they assembled at the foot of Mt. Sinai. For Israel would not have accepted the Torah without seeing the thunders and the lightning and the quaking mountain and the sound of the shofar, whereas the proselyte, without a single miracle, consecrates himself to the Holy One, praised be He, and puts upon himself the yoke of the Kingdom of Heaven. Can anyone be more worthy of God's love?" Especially interesting is the statement of R. Simeon b. Yohai, he whose suffering wrung from him the bitter condemnation of Gentiles in general and the Romans in particular. Referring to the verse (Jud. 5:31): "But they that love Him shall be as the sun when he goeth forth in his might," he asks: "Who is greater, he who loves the King, or he who is beloved by the King? Is it not he who is beloved by the King?" Such is the proselyte as it is written (Dt. 10:18), "And He loveth the ger." For when a Gentile becomes a ger, says R. Eliezer, he confers a favor on all Israel. God Himself is, as it were, obligated to Abraham, Isaac, and Jacob for proclaiming His Name among the nations. Gerim contribute to the peace of Israel. They are like the poppy-seed which, when stuffed with nuts in a barrel, keeps the nuts from rubbing against one another. Hence God delights to show gerim honor. Moses had several names, but God preferred to call him by the one given him by Bithiah, the daughter of Pharoah. He also added an extra letter (as he did to Abraham) to Jethro, the Priest of Midian.[18]

The conversion of the Gentiles to Judaism, say the Rabbis, is also a manifestation that God takes pleasure in Israel. It is like unto a king who has presented his son with a vineyard. When the prince does his father's will, the king searches all over the world and wherever he finds a pretty plant he transplants it into his son's vineyard. . . . Thus also when Israel does the will of the Father, He sees wherever there is a righteous one among the nations of the world, such as Jethro and Rahab, and brings him and adds him to Israel. So also whenever Israel enjoys the favor of God, His Name becomes exalted among the nations. Hence, says R. Berakiah, Israel pleaded with the Holy One, praised be He, "Lord of the Universe, send us the light of the Redemption; for whenever Thou sendest us that light, many strangers come and join themselves unto us."

Furthermore, to convert a Gentile is to perform an act of imitatio Dei in the highest sense, according to the Sages. The missionary assumes the character of the Creator, for "he who brings a creature under the wings of the Shekinah is as if he created him, formed him, and wrought him." To cause others to love the Lord is greater than merely to love Him oneself, and the only way Israel can show his appreciation of the precious gift of the Torah is to pass it on to those who are ignorant of it. God's injunction is that Israel should make the Name of Heaven revered by others. His eternal admonition is:

> Enlighten My world for Me, as I have enlightened it for you. . . . Cleanse it for Me, even as the pool purifies those who are defiled. . . . Bring those who are infected with idolatry under the sheltering wings of the Shekinah! . . . If you separate the nations of the world from yourselves, not only they but you also will not endure.[19]

In their missionary zeal, some rabbis censured even Abraham for sometimes being remiss, as they thought, in his duty toward the cause of conversion, as, for instance, when he compromised with the King of Sodom about the surrender of the captives, thereby preventing them from entering 'neath the wings of the Shekinah. It was this, they said, that caused him to suffer the tribulations which befell him, and that brought upon his descendants the bondage of Egypt. They also blamed Isaac and Jacob for not giving a more encouraging reception to Timnah, the sister of Lotan, and attributed to it Israel's suffering at the hands of her son Amalek. Jacob, they taught, was particularly aroused against Simeon and Levi because, by avenging their sister's rape, they gave cause to the Gentiles to refuse to accept Judaism. The priestly benediction which is prefaced by "thus shall ye bless the Children of Israel," the Rabbis interpreted to include those who would join the house of Israel by conversion. They also declared that *gerim* may, without mental reservation, recite "God of our Fathers" and "the land which Thou has sworn to our fathers," since Abraham was the ancestor of all who accepted his religion. [20]

Dating back probably to the first century B.C.E., special

prayers began to be offered in behalf of proselytes. One of these, perhaps the oldest, reads:

> Towards the righteous and the pious, towards the elders of Thy people the house of Israel, towards the remnant of their Scribes, towards the proselytes of righteousness, and towards us also, may Thy tender mercies be stirred, O Lord our God; and grant a good reward unto all who faithfully trust in Thy name.

Invocations were also made for God's assistance in the conversion of the world. A series of verses, culled from the Scriptures, were joined into supplications in which God is reminded of his promise to "perfect the world in the Kingdom of the Almighty, and to abolish the abominations from the earth." To these supplications, originally recited on the New Year, was added the *Alenu*. Prayers also, such as the following, were suggested for the private devotion:

> The Rabbis have taught: He who sees (a temple, or statue of) Mercury should say, 'Blessed be He who prolongeth His wrath to those who transgress His will.' He who sees a place from which idolatry has been uprooted should say, 'Praised be He Who hath uprooted idolatry from our land; and as it has been uprooted from this place, so may it be uprooted from every other place where Israel dwelleth, and mayest Thou turn the heart of those that worship them to worship Thee.' But in the lands outside of Palestine he need not say 'to worship Thee,' for they are mostly Samaritans. R. Simeon b. Eliezer, however, is of the opinion that in the lands outside of Palestine, too, he should say it, for they will ultimately become proselytes. [21]

These prayers were embodied in the ritual. One of them, dealing with proselytes and inserted in the middle of the Eighteen Benedictions, and the other, Alenu, at the conclusion of the regular services were to be recited at the regular services three times every day of the week. When, under the Romans it became dangerous to be a convert or a missionary, an imprecation was added against *delatores* and apostates (who played into their hands):

> And for the slanderers let there be no hope, and let all wickedness perish in a moment; let all Thine enemies be speedily cut off, and the dominion of arrogance do Thou uproot and crush, cast down and humble, speedily in our days. Blessed be Thou, O Lord who breakest the enemies and humblest the arrogant.[22]

Among the seven ordinances passed upon by the Sanhedrin after its firm establishment at Yamnia was one that when a gentile brings an offering unaccompanied by the required libations, the libations should be supplied from the public treasury. At that famous session, at which the traditional law was reformulated, the problem of proselytism was taken up also. In the midst of the discussion, as if by prearrangement, Judah, an Ammonite convert, rose and demanded a decision as to whether he was permitted to enter the assembly of the Lord. Rabban Gamaliel replied, "It is written in the Torah (Dt. 23:4): 'An Ammonite or a Moabite shall not enter into the assembly of the Lord.' " Said to him R. Joshua b. Hananiah: "Do the Ammonites and Moabites still dwell in their places? Did not Sennacherib, king of Assyria, intermix all the nations, as it is said (Isa. 10:13): 'I have removed the bounds of the peoples'?" Answered Rabban Gamaliel, "Was it not also said (Jer. 49:6): 'But afterward I will bring back the captivity of the children of Ammon'? Hence they must have returned." Said to him R. Joshua b. Hananiah, "Was it not also long ago said (Amos 9:14): 'And I will turn the captivity of My people Israel,' and yet they have not returned? As in this case, it is a prediction for the future, so, too, in the former instance it is a prophecy for the times to come." R. Joshua carried the day. [23]

Once before R. Joshua, who had witnessed the glory of the sanctuary as well as its destruction by the Romans, counselled

his people not to grieve too much over its loss nor to bear
hatred toward their oppressor. Once before, when they heard
of Hadrian's change of plans with regard to the rebuilding
of the Temple, R. Joshua soothed them with the fable of the
lion and the crane, and urged them to be grateful that they
escaped with their lives. It was he, by the way, who made the
famous statement, "The righteous of the nations of the world
have a portion in the world to come." That R. Joshua's opinion
prevailed must ever redound, not only to the glory of the
humble scholar, who eked out a livelihood by making needles
or peddling coal, but to that of the other Sages. On that day,
Judaism declared officially that the "seed of Abraham" does
not depend on blood and soil, but that Israel transcends the
bounds of racialism and nationalism, and that whoever is
hungry for the bread of life may come and eat, regardless of
his ancestry's treatment of the Jews.[24]

In reading these discussions, however, one must bear in
mind that the scholars who expressed themselves as adverse
to proselytism were not necessarily personally opposed to converts. They were merely discussing the legal aspect of the *ger*
according to their interpretation of the Torah. We have already
noticed the instance of R. Simeon b. Yohai. To cite another
example, R. Isaac, who declared that "Evil after Evil pursueth
those who make proselytes," also expresses his disappointment
that converts are not more welcome than they are.

There were some, however, who reasoned that in order to
become a full-fledged, bona fide convert, a gentile must pass
through the same processes as the children of Israel did prior
to their becoming a "kingdom of priests, and a holy nation."
As they were circumcised on leaving Egypt (Joshua 5:2f.) and
baptized while in the Wilderness (Exodus 19:10), so must the
Gentile be. But there were not lacking, also, those who asserted
that baptism alone was sufficient, and others who would require no ceremony at all. We have already noticed R. Johanan's
dictum, "anyone who rejects idolatry is a Jew." R. Joshua b.
Hananiah and R. Meir pointed out that Ruth and Orpah were
not required to submit to any ceremony. It was also argued
that were circumcision important, Adam would have been

enjoined to observe it, and a tradition was repeated that Abraham himself was afraid lest the rite might interfere with the conversion of the Gentiles. [25]

Similar controversies were carried on concerning the refusal of a proselyte to subscribe to any one ceremonial law. Some insisted that his surrender to Judaism must be unconditional. He cannot enter the household of Israel any more than the children of Israel could enter the Promised Land, unless he be willing not only to proclaim God's Unity, but to accept all the other laws and customs of Israel. R. Jose b. Judah and those of the Shammaite School maintained that "even if he takes upon himself to obey all the words of the Torah, save one word, he should be rejected." The opinion, however, prevailed that Jews should accept all who come, even if "not for the sake of Heaven," and none should be rejected. In general, it was held that, in accordance with the verse:

> 'The stranger (*ger*) did not lodge in the street,
> My doors I opened to the roadside':
> Always let thy left hand hold back and thy right
>   hand draw nigh (him who seeks to be
>   converted);
> be not like Elisha who thrust Gehazi away with
>   both hands, nor like Joshua b. Perahiah who
> thrust away Jesus of Nazareth with both hands. [26]

Rigorous though the Rabbis were regarding personal purity, they would not exclude even such as were guilty of any breach of the sexual relations provided they sincerely repented of their past indiscretions. A prospective convert once came to R. Eliezer b. Hyrkanos who admitted that "her younger son was the son of her older son" and that this was "the lightest of the lightest" of which she was guilty. He dismissed her in disgust. R. Joshua b. Hananiah, however, accepted her. When his disciples called his attention to R. Eliezer's treatment of her, R. Joshua remarked: "Since she has made up her mind to become converted she is no longer alive to the old self (and is therefore to be treated as if she were born anew)." [27]

The Rabbis were not unaware of the risk they were running.

They granted that among the Gentiles who sought entry into the household of Israel there were hypocrites. Some, they said, instead of joining the Lord out of love were motivated by a desire to marry a Jewish man or woman. These they sarcastically called *"gerim* of love." Others they styled *"gerim* of the king's table," because they expected to gain some material benefits; or "lion *gerim,"* because, like the Samaritans of old, they were converted out of fear; or "dream *gerim,"* because they were induced to take the step by some dream or vision; or "revenge *gerim,"* because, as in the days of Mordecai and Esther, they "Judaized" in order to avoid possible retaliation; and "tramp *gerim,"* (*gerim gerurim*), because like the mixed multitude at the time of the Exodus they were merely following the crowd. This, however, did not deter them from taking the risk. They required, indeed, that the candidate for conversion be investigated as to whether he was motivated by "money, position, marriage, or fear," but laid down the law that if one sought admission more than three times he should be accepted. They felt that in those perilous times, when Israel became the suffering Servant of God and many born Jews apostatized to escape the persecutions, those who were willing to embrace the religion of the scorned and spurned must, as a rule, be actuated by the best of motives. They interpreted the verse in Isaiah (54:15), in which the term *ger* occurs in three different forms,

> Behold, they may gather together, but not by Me; Whosoever shall gather together against thee, shall fall because (of thee)[28]

to suggest that "he who joins thee in thine adversity should be given the opportunity to be one of thee in thy prosperity." God himself does not discriminate and allows the unworthy to join because of the worthy.

Thereafter he is regarded as an Israelite in all respects.

As for the unworthy proselytes, they said they will, of course, pay the penalty they deserve. On Judgment Day, God will unmask the pretenders who proclaimed themselves Jews with their lips but hankered after idolatry in their hearts. He will also demand an accounting of the gentiles as to why they did not come nigh unto Him. If the latter will answer, "I was too miserable a sinner," God will say: "Wert thou more wicked than Rahab, whose house was by the side of the wall where she received robbers and entertained them? Yet, when she came nigh did I not accept her, and make her mother of prophets and saints? Was not Jethro a priest to idols? Yet when he came to Me did I not accept him and make him father of prophets and saints? Did I not accept Ruth the Moabite when she came unto Me, and produce from her kings?" Then will He say: "Hitherto it was through the labor of the righteous (Jews) that gentiles became proselytes, but henceforth I (Myself) will draw the righteous (Gentiles) near, and bring them under the wings of the Shekinah," as it is written (Zeph. 3:9):

> For then will I turn to the peoples
> A pure language,
> That they may all call upon the Name of the Lord,
> To serve Him with one consent.

Thereafter all the heathen will accept Judaism with a willing heart, and the Jews will welcome them with joy supreme, "and even as the Shekinah once rested between the Temple and Jerusalem, so will it henceforth expand till it will include the whole earth, and Egypt will send gifts to the Messiah, and into Jerusalem will flock all the nations and all the kingdoms, for it will become the spiritual metropolis of all lands." [29]

On one thing the Rabbis agreed: the prospective proselyte must seek admittance of his own free will and accord. No coercion or inducement was permissible. A slave could not be compelled to submit to circumcision, but if he refused for a period of twelve months, his new master was to return him to his former Gentile owner. The same applied to a female slave. It is recorded that in a certain city in Palestine, the pagan slaves persistently refused to undergo the rite. They negotiated with them for twelve months, and then sold them to the heathen. However, the hope was always entertained that slaves would, for their own sake, be glad to be converted. To the question whether it was permissible to buy pagan slaves during the semi-holidays (*Hol Hammoed*), Resh Lakish replied that it was permissible to do so even on the Sabbath "because they may come under the wings of the Shekinah." [30]

So highly meritorious was the act of conversion esteemed that the rite of circumcision was permitted to be performed on the Day of Atonement. It was also held to be an occasion worthy of special celebration. The conversion of a woman of Laodicea was once graced with the presence of R. Judah Hannasi and R. Joshua b. Levi. [31]

The child of a woman converted during her pregnancy was regarded as the child of a Jewess, and baptism was not necessary. A minor could be converted by his father. If he had no father, the court could act *in loco parentis* with the consent of his mother. The child, on attaining majority, could cancel his conversion and was not held in the category of an apostate; but if he continued for some time after attaining his majority to pass himself as a Jew, he was in all respects treated as a renegade after his apostasy.

The ceremony of admission as it was practiced in Palestine in post-Hadrianic time is given in detail in the Talmud:

> The Rabbis have taught: When one comes in these days and seeks to be converted, they do not receive him at once; but they say unto him: 'Wherefore dost thou seek to be converted? Seest thou not that the members of this nation are down-trodden and afflicted more than any other, that they are subjected to many ills and all manner of affliction; that they bury their children and grand-children, and themselves suffer death because they observe the rites of circumcision, baptism, and all other commandments, and may not appear in public as all the other nations do?' If he says, 'I am unworthy to put my neck in the yoke of Him Who spake and the world came into being, praised be He,' they receive him at once; if not, he departs and goeth away.
>
> Should he accept, they take him to the immersion house, and cover him with water as far as his hips.

They then tell him some of the lighter and some of
the weightier commandments, and they instruct him
concerning the sin one may commit in the matter of
leḳet, Shiḳhah, peah (gleaning, picking up, and reap-
ing the corner of the field) and the Second Tithe.
They then inform him regarding the penalties consequent upon the breaking of the (weightier) commandments. They say unto him: 'Know that until thou hast
attained to this degree if thou atest fat thou wert not
penalized with excision, if thou profanest the Sabbath
thou wert not liable to stoning.' And as they reveal
to him the penalties attached to the violation of the
commandments, so they reveal to him the rewards
of keeping them, saying to him: 'Know that the world
to come is intended only for the righteous, and the
Israelites at this time are incapable of enduring either
too much good or too much suffering.' Should he still
wish to proceed, they circumcise him forthwith and
when he is healed they baptize him at once while two
learned men stand by him and rehearse to him
some (more) of the lighter and weightier commandments. . . .

After he was immersed and came up, they speak
to him kindly words, welcoming words: 'To whom
dost thou now cleave, thou happy one? To Him Who
spake and the world came into being, praised be He.
For the world was not created save for the sake of
Israel, and none is called a child of God but Israel, and
none is beloved of God except Israel, and all the things
we have told thee, we told only in order to increase
thy reward." . . . Thereafter he is regarded as an
Israelite in all respects.

A woman was placed in water up to her neck in the presence
of other women, while two learned men stood without and
rehearsed some of the lighter and some of the weightier commandments, laying special emphasis on those observances re-
lating to women, such as menstruation (*niddah*), the dough

offering (*hallah*), and the lighting of candles (*hadlakat hanner*). The bath had to contain at least two hogsheads (40 *seah*) of pure, flowing water which had to come in direct contact with the body.

In Palestine, the mere declaration that one was a *ger* was sufficient for him to be accepted as such. Outside of Palestine, he was required to produce witnesses in case he intended to marry a Jewess. In general, the legal and ritual requirements concerning converts were construed very liberally and always in favor of declaring one a proselyte. His testimony in his own behalf was inadmissible if it would affect unfavorably the status of his children. "Thou mayest disqualify thyself; thou art not competent to disqualify thy children (by testifying that they are not Jews by birth)," said R. Judah to one who claimed that he became a convert without due formality. Though the circumcision and the baptism had to be in the presence of three competent witnesses and performed neither on the Sabbath nor on a holiday, nor at night, if, for any reason, these requirements were disregarded, he was not rejected; and if he married an Israelite, his child was looked upon as a Jew by birth. A child born of a pagan father and a Jewish mother was accepted as a Jew without the formality of conversion. [32]

From the rabbinic viewpoint, a proselyte was looked upon as "a newly born (Jewish) child" or "as if born today." His admission into the new faith rendered him, in the phraseology made familiar through the Gospels, "born again." He was reborn not only spiritually but ethnologically, one of "the seed of Abraham" in the physical as well as in the spiritual sense. As such, every tie which held him to his pagan past was broken. All his prior sins were pardoned. His blood-relations were no longer his relatives, so that legally he might marry within the prohibited degrees of consanguinity. Such marriages, however, were not permitted so that converts might not say, "We came down from a higher degree of holiness to a lower degree of holiness." But if the marriage took place before conversion, the contracting parties were not required to be separated. If husband and wife were converted at the same time, they had to live apart for a period of at least three months.[33]

Despite all their anxiety to integrate the convert into the community of Israel, the Sages realized that it must take some time for a non-Jew to become a Jew in every respect. Some rabbis estimated that it required twenty generations before a neophyte could entirely rid himself of the stain of paganism, and ten generations before he felt at home in his new environment. Hence they saw nothing improper in the Mosaic injunction (Dt. 17:15), "One from among thy brethren shalt thou set king over thee." For the same reason they decided that a *ger* cannot be a member of a criminal court. There were also some discriminatory enactments which were prompted not by the belief in the superior purity of Jewish blood from a biological point of view but from a moral one. The Jewish sense of morality revolted against the laxity of the marital relations which then prevailed among the Gentiles. Against this, even the doctrine of the "rebirth" was of but little avail. This was especially the case as regards a priest whose purity was to be beyond suspicion. No priest, therefore, was theoretically permitted to marry a *gioret* though a *ger* might marry a *mamzeret,* which a born Jew was prohibited to do. With these exceptions, it may be affirmed that all the rabbinic enactments give evidence of profound sympathy for the *ger* and were intended to give him no cause to regret his change of faith. He could use wine which he had before his conversion, provided it was not specifically devoted to idolatrous purposes. He was exempt from the priestly dues levied upon the first-born of Jewish fathers, or on his cow which had borne a calf or had been slaughtered before his conversion. On the principle that he was newly born, he had no legal heirs except those who were born to him after his conversion. If he loaned money to an Israelite on interest he might, after his conversion, exact the payment of the principal and interest (which as a Jew he was not allowed to do). However, if he borrowed money from an Israelite on interest, he had to pay both the principal and interest even after his conversion, lest "they suspect that he became converted for the sake of his money." On the other hand, though he could no longer claim sonship to his pagan father, the Rabbis allowed him to obtain his inheritance, "for fear that he might relapse to his abomination." They also freed him from the obligation of submitting to martyrdom "for the sanctification of the Name."

A slave who preceded his heathen master into the fold *ipso facto* became free. It happened that some of the slaves of Beluria, or Barzila, took the bath of baptism before their mistress, and some after her. The Sages decided that the former should be emancipated and the latter remain slaves. The widow and creditors of a *ger* might collect from his estate what became their due only after his conversion unless they were first to seize it. It was, however, expected that at least part of such property would be devoted to some charitable or religious use. [34]

The disabilities to which the convert was subject terminated with his life. His descendants could aspire to the highest offices to which any Jew could attain. Whatever the discussion may have been regarding the marriage of a priest and a proselyte, the opinion prevailed that the daughter of a convert might become the wife of a priest. The Rabbis removed the last bars which discriminated against any nationality. From R. Johanan b. Zakkai onward, some of the leading Talmudists took up the cause of the Ammonites, the Moabites, and the Egyptians, and encouraged them to penetrate into the most exclusive Jewish circle, the priesthood. Thus, when Miniamin, an Egyptian proselyte who married a proselyte and whose son also had a proselyte wife, expressed his disappointment that, in accordance with the biblical injunction, his son's child would have to wait three generations in order to be regarded a full-fledged Jew, R. Akiba, his master replied: "Miniamin, thou art mistaken. Since the conquests of Sennacherib the world is mixed, and there are no longer Ammonites or Moabites, Egyptians or Edomites." A girl who had been converted before she was three years and a day old could marry a priest, and thus become the mother of a priest during the first generation.

Though the Sages were convinced that God loved the *gerim,* they were sometimes puzzled, "Why then does He permit them to suffer?" In answer to this, R. Hananiah b. Gamaliel ventured the opinion that proselytes are afflicted because they postponed their conversion: "They consider 'Let a year pass, let two years pass, meanwhile I will collect what is due me, and indulge in what pleases me.'" But, asked R. Jose, "Why are they permitted thus to suffer for their preconversionary sins since on their conversion they are as newly born babes?" The other answers that were suggested could hardly have been more satisfactory, such as: that while in heathendom they failed to observe the Seven Noahian commandments, or that because of their ignorance they knew not how to perform their religious duties as they should. The most acceptable answer probably was the one given by R. Eleazar. "They are afflicted," he said, "because they, as a rule, do not serve the Lord out of love but out of fear." [35]

Perhaps the most besetting sin of the converts was the practice of, or belief in, divination. That Jews, too, were addicted to this means of discovering the events of the future we may judge by the numerous warnings in the Talmud against it, and the assertion that "a person who refrains from practicing divination is assigned a place in Heaven which even the ministering angels cannot penetrate." R. Simeon b. Shetak is said to have hanged eighty witches in one day. But this superstition was specially prevalent among the Gentiles, as is indicated in the following anecdote: A pagan astrologer who embraced Judaism wished to set out on a journey. Prompted to consult the stars he refrained from so doing, saying: "Did I not attach myself to this holy people and vow to separate myself from all superstition? I will rely only on the Creator." On the way he was seized by a tax gatherer who deprived him of his ass but permitted him to go. Why was he penalized? Because he still thought of omens. What caused him to be saved? The fact that after all he trusted in his Creator. [36]

While the Rabbis themselves were not free from superstition, they were sure that charity is a prophylactic against the evil decrees of the stars, and some even maintained that "the planets have no influence over Israel."

Whether the Rabbis succeeded in eradicating superstition from the converts or not, they took the *ger* under their protection and insisted that he should be treated with utmost consideration. "Whoever", they maintained, "deprives a convert of his just due is as if he deprived God Himself of what is His due" and "Whoever causes an injury to a convert is as guilty as he who worships an idol." They pointed out that the Torah cautions us no less than thirty-six (or forty-eight) times against hurting a *ger* in any way.

> 'And ye shall not wrong one another' (Lev. 25:14, 17) refers also to wronging him with words.... If he is the son of a *ger* say not to him 'remember the deeds of thine ancestors.' If he was himself a *ger* and desired to study the Torah, say not unto him: 'The mouth that hath eaten all kinds of abominable, prohibited food should it now study the Torah that came forth from the mouth of the Almighty?'...
> Say not to him, 'Last night thou didst worship Bel and Nebo, and thou still hast swine-flesh between thy teeth, and dost thou seek to associate with me?' ...
> 'For ye were *gerim* in the land of Egypt' (Ex 22:20): Unto the tenth generation do not put to shame an Aramean in the presence of a *ger*....
> Wherefore was the Torah given in the Wilderness? To teach thee that even as the Wilderness is open to all men, so are the words of the Torah accessible to all. Let, therefore, no man say: 'I am learned and the Torah was given to me and my ancestors; not so thou and thy ancestors, who were *gerim*. It is written (Dt. 33:4): 'An inheritance of the congregation of Jacob,' that is, the Torah is for whosoever is acceptable among the children of Jacob....
> And what is more, the *gerim* who study the Torah are as great as the High Priest.... See what is said concerning the descendants of Jethro.... They sat in Hewn Chamber.... All Israelites came to listen to the

halakah they propounded.... And they were replete with the Holy Spirit.... So it was with Shemayah and Abtalion, the children's children of Sisera, who taught the Torah in public as members of the Great Assembly.

With all these warnings, it must have been difficult for a faithful Jew to be thrown into contact with a proselyte. One had to be constantly on his guard lest he hurt the feelings of the neophyte. While many proselytes, according to the Rabbis, were more punctilious in their observances than were born Jews, most of them were ignorant, and some of them continued to hanker after the liberties which they had to abandon on conversion. R. Simeon b. Eleazar depicts perhaps as a parable, a scene not infrequently witnessed in homes where the wife was a convert. "To whom was Adam like?" he asks, and answers: "To one who married a proselyte whom he was instructing." Said he to her: "My daughter, do not eat bread when thy hands are unwashed, do not taste fruit of which a tithe hath not been given, do not desecrate the Sabbath, do not break any of the fences (of decency), and do not go out with other men. If thou doest thus thou wilt not die." But what did the man himself do? In her presence he ate bread with unwashed hands, tasted fruit of which the tithe was not given, broke "the fences" and desecrated the Sabbath. Then he divorced her for not observing her religion: What did the proselyte think? Verily all that my husband taught me are falsehoods, and so she violated all his commandments.

However, Jews, even Kohanim, did not refrain from marrying proselytes, and the prospect of marrying may also account for the many women who were converted to Judaism. That they were not disappointed in their expectation can be deduced from the fact that the disciples of R. Eleazar b. Zadok discussed the question, "Why is everyone bent on marrying a *gioret* (female proselyte), but not a freed woman?" The master's answer was, that it was either because the latter was included in the curse (which Noah put upon Canaan), while the former was not included in the curse; or because the freed woman, as a slave, could not, even if she would, protect her honor, while the proselyte, as indicated by her high resolve, must have insisted on her chastity even while a pagan. [37]

Despite the danger that lurked in the attempt, the Jews continued their propaganda for Judaism after the destruction of the Temple almost as much as they did while they were still a nation on their own land. One of the methods to which one of them resorted was to carry a peddler's pack and cry: "Who is the man that desireth life?" As the villagers flocked to buy his elixir, he would recite to them the rest of the Psalm: "Keep thy tongue from evil, and thy lips from speaking guile," etc. When he was in the neighborhood of Caesarea, R. Yannai sent to him to come and show him his wares. At this the peddler pointed to his Book of Psalms and said, "Neither thou nor those like thee need them." The same anecdote is related of a R. Alexandri of whom little else is known. His cry is given in Aramaic. [38]

The Rabbis warned their disciples to be prepared so as to know what to answer an *apikoros,* i.e., a scoffer or unbeliever, who may have been a renegade Jew or a more or less interested Gentile. That Gentiles would invite discussion or ask for explanations, or heckle the Rabbis on some weak points, is repeatedly mentioned in talmudic literature. "Once," runs the story in *Tanna D' be Elijahu,* "as I was passing from place to place, I was searched out by an old man who asked me how the nations of the world would fare in the days of the Messiah? I said to him: 'My son, every nation and every kingdom which has oppressed Israel will behold Israel's happiness and then return to their graves ... and every nation and kingdom which has not oppressed Israel will remain in life and rejoice in the bliss of the Messiah.' " Rabban Simeon b. Gamaliel narrates another story: "While on my way, a man approached me in great anger and demanded: 'Do you teach that the nations of the world will all descend into Gehenna?' I answered, 'Yes.' 'But what about those to whom the Torah was not given, and whom the Prophets have not yet admonished?' Said I to him: 'My son, thus teach the Sages in the *Mishnah:* "A stranger who comes for the purpose of being converted should be extended the hand of welcome and brought under the wings of the Shekinah." To this, the proselytes of the past bear ample witness. Those, therefore, who remained pagans have none but themselves to blame for their lot in the world to come.'[39]

It is noteworthy that, unlike the disciples of Jesus and the Apostles, Jewish missionaries seldom resorted to miracle-mongering in their efforts at the conversion of gentiles. Not that they did not believe in miracles, or in the power of some saint to change the laws of nature for some great, or even trivial, purpose. There were not a few among the scholars who were reputed to be *melumadim benisim* (adepts in miracles). R. Simeon b. Yohai was said to have exorcised a demon from the daughter of Marcus Aurelius. But Jewish missionaries seldom if ever sought to attract Gentiles by reciting the marvels performed in the name of their God. The Rabbis, in fact, had an aversion to the display of the miraculous. Thus Simon b. Shetak, allegedly no mean performer of miracles, threatened the saintly Honi Hameaggel with excommunication for trying to bring down rain by means of prayer. Later rabbis cautioned their hearers not to rely on miracles for, they explained, since people no longer sacrifice themselves for the sanctification of God's Name, miracles are not likely to happen any more. [40]

Some Gentiles, however, are said to have been converted through the instrumentality of miracles. One of them was R. Johanan b. Torta, a contemporary of R. Akiba. While still a heathen he bought a cow from a poor Jew. When the Sabbath arrived he found to his amazement that the animal stubbornly refused to do any manner of work. Finally he sent for the Jew. The Jew at once guessed the reason. So he whispered in her ear: "Cow, cow! Thou knowest that as long as thou wert with me thou didst rest on the Sabbath. Now, for my sins, I was forced to sell thee to a heathen. I beg of thee, for my sake, arise and plow." The cow immediately arose and pulled the plow. At the heathen's insistence to know what he had whispered to the cow, the Jew replied: "I am neither a magician nor a wizard, I have merely whispered to her thus and thus." At this, the heathen exclaimed: "If a cow which can neither talk nor understand recognizes her Creator, I whom the Creator hath made in His own image and endowed with understanding, should I not acknowledge Him?" He became a *ger* and betook himself to the study of the Torah. Hence they called him Johanan b. Torta (i.e., son of the cow). [41]

R. Phineas bar Hama, of the fourth century, tells of the miraculous conversion of Abba Gulyash, a priest in a temple in Damascus. Finding no relief from illness after many days of supplicating the idols, he invoked the God of Israel. His prayer was answered and, in gratitude, Abba Gulyash went to Tiberias and became a Jew. Because of his piety and probity they appointed him treasurer of the funds for the poor. But not long after his conversion he turned stone blind. The elated pagans began to sneer at him and taunt him: "Abba Gulyash, the idols are kind, and are less exacting than the God of Israel" or "It serves thee well for having forsaken the true religion." When at last he prevailed on his wife to lead him back to Damascus, the rumor spread that he wanted to appease the idols from the pulpit which he had formerly occupied. But it was thus that he addressed the vast multitude that came to hear him:

> My brethren, and men of Damascus! When I was a priest and served this idol, people would entrust me with their possessions, and though I did not always account for them the idol did not punish me, because he has neither eyes to see nor ears to hear. Since I went after Him Whose eyes 'run to and fro throughout all the earth,' and who knows all our thoughts, I could not escape an accounting, and have, therefore, been stricken with blindness.

After Abba Gulyash made that public confession, it is said that the light returned to his eyes and he could see far better than before; and many thousands of the nations of the world were converted through him to the faith of Israel.

With due allowance for the legendary element in these and similar stories, it is not unlikely that some Gentiles embraced

Judaism in consequence of an unusual experience they had heard or had had in their contact with Jews or Jewish practices. Others, again, found the cruelty and obscenity which constituted part of the pagan cults revolting and became attracted by the moral beauty, if not the lofty ideals, of Judaism. Thus we are told of a gentile woman who vowed that if the gods would cure her of her ailment she would worship them all. On her recovery she started to fulfill her vow by visiting a temple of Baal Peor. But she recoiled with loathing at what she heard and saw there and vowed never again to enter such a place even if she were to be an invalid for the rest of her life. [42]

Among the numerous *gerim,* or their descendants during the Hadrianic period are several who have attained the highest rank in the mastery of the Torah, and have become shining lights in Israel. One of them, R. Akiba b. Joseph, is reputed to have been of the progeny of Sisera, and of Jael the wife of Heber the Kenite. His romantic story as a shepherd boy who married the heiress of the wealthiest man in Jerusalem and devoted himself to the study of the Torah at the age of about forty, his fame as a Talmudist which attracted to his academy thousands of students from all parts of the Diaspora, his espousal of the cause of Bar Kokba and, crowning it all, his martyrdom during the reign of Hadrian, rendered him one of the most admired and beloved characters in Jewish history. He is regarded by some as the founder of Rabbinic Judaism, and legend has it that at his death Elijah, together with many bands of angels, carried off his charred remains.

Akiba was a zealous proselytizer and very lenient in the interpretation of the regulations concerning converts. We have seen how he encouraged his disciple, Minjamin, the Egyptian *ger.* He did the same on his numerous and extensive trips abroad. "When I went to the cities by the sea," testified a certain Bar Yasyan, "I met a proselyte who married the widow of his brother on his mother's side. Said I to him, 'My son, who gave you permission to do so?' Said he, 'Seest thou that woman and her seven sons? On this bench sat R. Akiba when he granted permission for the convert husband to marry her.'" This view was adopted as decisive in a similar case. [43]

It is interesting to note that R. Simeon b. Yohai, himself a martyr and the pupil of R. Akiba, was also the teacher and colleague of several converts, among them the already mentioned R. Judah. Because both of his parents were proselytes, he came to be known as ben Gerim, or in the Aramaic, bar Giyura. [44]

In the *Zohar*, R. Simeon b. Yohai tells of a "Philosopher of the nations of the world" who came to him with the query:

> You claim that your God is so exalted above all, for you say (Jer.10:7): 'Among all the wise men of the nations, and in all their royalty, there is none like thee.' Again, your Torah states (Dt. 34:10): 'There hath not arisen a Prophet since in Israel, whom the Lord knew face to face,' from which you conclude that 'among the nations there hath arisen.' Reasoning the same way, you should also conclude that if there is none like God among the wise of the nations there is one like him among the wise of Israel. R. Simeon's reply was: 'Thou speakest correctly. God reviveth the dead so did Elijah and Elisha; He causes the rain to fall as did Elijah; He made heaven and earth, but they endure for the merits of Abraham; He causes the sun to go forth, Joshua came and caused it to stand still; He decrees evil decrees and the Saints of Israel avert them. What is more, He commands us to walk in His ways, and to be in every way like unto Him.'
>
> That Philosopher went and became a proselyte in the village of Shahlin, and assumed the name Josi Katinaah, and became one of the great scholars and one of the saintliest and wisest of the men of that place. [45]

R. Meir was thoroughly at home in the "wisdom of the Gentiles," and is reputed to have mastered three hundred Aesopean fables. But he treasured the Torah above everything else, and to spread a knowledge of it among all men was the great passion of his life. Not in vain was he called, as his name signified, "the enlightener." He hated ignorance. "A heathen," he used to say, "who studies or does (the commands of) the Torah is as great as a High Priest." He pointed out that the Prophet Obadiah was himself of Idumean birth. God loves all mankind as a father loves his children; but He gave the Torah to Israel because Israel is morally stronger than the other nations. Liberal as he was in the observance of Jewish ceremonials, he was very rigorous in matters concerning "pagan practices" and vehemently inveighed against the theaters and circuses of the Gentiles where men were maimed and killed for the amusement of the populace.

But his dislike of the pagan practices did not prevent R. Meir from being on friendly and even intimate terms with many of the Gentiles in the hope of bringing them nearer to the Torah. As a controversialist he was much sought after by the Gentiles. The following are some of the topics which he discussed with them. Once he was asked: "How can He Who said (Jer. 23:23): 'Do not I fill the heaven and the earth,' have spoken to Moses from between the staves of the Ark?" R. Meir answered by asking his interlocutor to look into a big mirror and then into a small mirror, and to tell him what he saw. The same face, was the reply, save that it appeared larger in one and smaller in the other. "Since then," said R. Meir, "thou who art but flesh and blood canst make thyself seem larger or smaller and still be the same, how much the more He spoke and the world became!"

At another time, a Gentile friend told him: "A slave whom the master drove out of his house would try to please another master. Your master has driven you out of your country. Now you are among us, why do you not try to please us?" said R. Meir: "I have one son whom I love dearly, but who, being pampered, became a libertine. At last I found myself compelled to drive him out of my house, but have told him that whenever he will mend his ways I will welcome him back. We, too, are God's children. We rebelled against Him and He became wroth with us, and drove us out of our country. Whenever we repent He will relent, and take us back to our land; but as long as we adopt your habits He will not permit us to return to our home." . . . Thereupon the "Hegemon" exclaimed: "Verily, thou hast conquered. Thou art right, and thy Torah is true."

R. Meir's best known friend was Euonymous of Gedara, a heathen, "than whom there arose no greater (thinker) among the nations." To him is ascribed the remark that as long as Jewish children are brought up in their synagogues and schools, all efforts to exterminate Judaism will be in vain. It is not stated whether Euonymous embraced Judaism. But he was certainly conversant with the teachings of the Rabbis and observed some Jewish customs. When R. Meir called on him to express sympathy at the death of his mother, he found him in mourning; while at the death of his father, he saw him pursue his business as usual. Euonymous explained that a pagan mother always remains a true mother, but no filial duties are due from a convert to a pagan father.

It is hinted in one tradition that R. Meir finally succeeded in reclaiming his skeptic teacher Elisha b. Abuya to the faith of his fathers. While visiting him during his last illness, R. Meir urged him to repent. "Will I be accepted?" asked the dying philosopher. "Certainly," replied R. Meir, "is it not written (Ps. 90:3): 'Thou turnest man to contrition and sayest: Return ye children of men'?" Whereupon Elisha burst into tears and died. After his burial, R. Meir spread his robe over the grave and, taking his text from Ruth (3:13), he exclaimed: "Thou didst tarry for a while in this world which is like unto night, but in the world to come where dawneth the light, if the Holy One, who is all good, will redeem thee, it is well; if not, will I redeem thee." Asked whom he would like to meet in the world to come, R. Meir replied: "First my master (Elisha b. Abuya), then my father." [46]

Other eminent Talmudists who traced their descent to *gerim* were R. Halafta and his even more famous son, Jose (c. 97-180). The roots of their genealogical tree extended back to Jonadab b. Rechab, and their love for the simple life lends color to that claim.

R. Jose insisted that it is not the place or the position but rather the disposition of a person that matters, and he ridiculed the Palestinians who considered themselves superior to the Babylonians. He believed that the *Sarim* (celestial princes) of the nations of the world were present at the Revelation on Mt. Sinai and that "in the world to come the nations of the world would be converted of their own free will," and God would readily accept them.[47]

It was R. Jose who wondered why God permitted *gerim* to suffer, and had a good word to say in behalf of the Gibeonites, and even in behalf of *mamzerim*—those born out of traditionally prohibited unions. According to him, "In the world to come, the *Nethinim* and *mamzerim* will be relieved of their disabilities, for it is written (Ezek. 36:25): 'And I will sprinkle clean water upon you, and ye shall be clean; from all your uncleanness and from all your idols will I cleanse you.'"

R. Jose was in great demand among the Gentiles who were interested to know what Judaism teaches about the creation, free will, the life beyond, and the destiny of the Gentiles. Sixteen such dialogues between him and a prominent matron of Sepphoris are found in the Talmud, among them the following: Once she asked him in how many days did God create the world? His reply was, "in one day." "How canst thou prove it?" "Well," said he, "didst thou ever prepare a banquet?" "Yes." " How many courses didst thou have?" "Ever so many." "Didst thou serve them all at one time?" "No," answered she, "I cooked them all at one time but served them one after the other." "Even so did God."

Like R. Meir, R. Jose did not shun the company of infidels and never despaired of bringing them to the light of Judaism. Once he called on an unbeliever to console him on the death of his son. But instead of looking sad, the rabbi's face was wreathed in smiles. The unbeliever asked, "Why this smiling countenance?" "Because," answered he, "we trust in the Lord of heaven to meet again in the world to come." "Is not my sorrow great enough that thou comest to add to it?" protested the unbeliever. "Can shards be reunited once the vase is broken?" . . . said R. Jose, "A vessel of clay, made with water and finished by fire, cannot indeed be mended; but a vessel of fine glass produced by fire can be mended. If this is so with a vessel into which mere flesh and blood has blown, how much the more with the vessel of which it is said that God blew into it the spirit of life!" [48]

Last, but by no means least, of the Talmudic *gerim* of Palestine, mention should be made of Rab Samuel bar Shilat, whose forbear is said to have been the most notorious of Jew-baiters, no less than Haman the Aggagite. Samuel was noted as a pedagogue and his school at B'nai B'rak came to be known as a model of its kind. Abba Arika (Rab) once saw him working in his garden. "Hast thou become a slacker in thy work (as teacher)?" teased the Babylonian sage. "By no means," replied Samuel, "even now my mind is on my school children." Thereupon Abba Arika applied to him the verse (Dan. 12:3): "And they that turn many to righteousness (shall shine) as the stars for ever and ever." [49]

A family of proselytes which produced several scholars of note was known as the House of Bar Ashtor, or Ashtin, and lived in Emesa during the post-Hadrianic period. Though removed from the center of Jewish learning, they kept abreast with the rabbinic interpretations of the Torah. Their eagerness for knowledge is attested by their inquiries from the sages who happened to visit their country. In their zeal for the observance of their religion, they gave tithes for crops which were raised by Gentiles to whom they leased their estates. [50]

The instances which the Talmudists cite were intended merely as episodes in the lives of some noted sages, or apropos of some necessary elucidation of a legal or moral problem. But they are sufficiently numerous to show that all through the period under consideration, the ranks of Judaism were constantly being replenished with proselytes. Circumcision did not deter them, nor did persecution prevent them. Where they were numerous they settled in a community of their own, a *Kahal Gerim*. There must have been a great deal of mutual good will and helpfulness among these transplanted vines in the vineyard of Israel, judging by the talmudic proverb: "These three love one another: the proselytes, the slaves, and the ravens." [51]

There can be little doubt that the Judaism of these proselytes was crude and sometimes bordering on idolatry, though, as the sages said of the Cuthites, many of them were more punctilious in the observance of the ceremonies than the native Israelites. Some *gerim,* however, as we have seen, attained eminence as Talmudists and some gladly gave their lives for their adopted faith, even though the Rabbis absolved them from martyrdom.

CHAPTER X

FROM IRAQ TO IRAN

AN OLD TRADITION recounts that when the Temple was destroyed by Nebuchadnezzar, the sacred fire which burned continually on its altar was carried off to Babylon and there hidden in a cave. This tradition contains a germ of truth if the sacred fire symbolizes the Scriptures and the cave the synagogues. These *Moade El*, or "little sanctuaries," created by necessity because of the lack of a central sanctuary, became foster homes for the genius of Judaism and, erected in every town and hamlet, made Babylonia, for more than a thousand years, the greatest seat of Jewish learning and achievement.

In point of fact, the Jews of Babylonia never yielded to the assumptions of superiority by the Jews of Palestine. Like the orthodox anti-Zionists of our time, they did not approve of the Restoration in the prosaic way which it was effected under Zerubbabel and Ezra. They insisted on a prince of the House of David and on a High Priest of the House of Aaron. They boasted the possession of a synagogue built by Jehoiakin, the last independent king of Judah.... This he built while a prisoner in Babylon, with soil and with the stone which he brought from Palestine. The name which they gave to that synagogue —*Shaf Veyatib*—implied the belief that the Divine Majesty went with Israel into the Babylonian exile. At one time they even were on the point of establishing a High Priesthood of their own. Nor did "the sceptre depart from them"; their *Reshe Galuta* (exilarchs) claimed to be of the blood royal. In some districts they were autonomous. At Mosul, in the sight of Nineveh, they had their own fort, *Hisna Ebrays*. Many of them ceased to regard themselves as exiles and became attached to their new native land with a devotion which rivalled their romantic love for Palestine. To live in Babylonia, they maintained, is as meritorious as to live in the Land of Israel, and to emigrate thence is as sinful as to emigrate from Palestine. If Palestine was their fatherland, Babylonia was their motherland.

The Jews of Babylonia were very fond of their adopted tongue, the Aramaic. It was a Hebraic dialect, and in it was made the first translation of the Torah, which Abba Arika, their leading sage, traced to Ezra himself. In fact, according to him, Adam, the first man, spoke Aramaic, and thus it is therefore even more ancient than Hebrew. This *Targum* became. an integral part of the Bible, and even in Palestine it was required to be read together with the weekly portion of the Pentateuch. Even the Palestinian R. Johanan, who cautioned against praying in that language "because the ministering angels are not familiar with it," asserted: "Let not Aramaic be held lightly by thee, for in all the three parts of the Bible this language is employed." In the course of time Aramaic became a second sacred language, the *Leshon Galut* of the Jewish people, and they clung to it even when Persian became the vernacular of the rest of the population. In it were composed some of the most appealing hymns and prayers (such as the *Kaddish* and *Yekum Purkan*) as well as the Talmuds and the responsa literature. It was adopted as their medium by the Kabbalists and in it was written the Holy Bible of all mystical speculation, the *Zohar*.[1]

Babylonian Jews were especially proud of their great *yeshibot* (academies), said to have been established by Jehoiakin, the fame of which spread far and wide. No less a Palestinian sage than R. Simeon b. Lakish (Resh Lakish) declared: "When the Torah was forgotten in (the Land of) Israel, Ezra came up from Babylon and re-established it; when it was again forgotten, Hillel the Babylonian came up and re-established it when it was again forgotten, R. Hiyya and his sons came up and re-established it." The final redemption of Israel, it was believed, will begin from the two *yeshiboth* "which have never been destroyed, nor robbed, nor exiled, and over which neither the Greeks nor the Romans ever held sway."

Besides their *yeshibot,* the Babylonian Jews vaunted of the purity of their race. Contrary to the dictum of the Palestinians, they maintained that before Ezra left for Judea he made his native land as pure as the "finest of flour," while Palestine was merely "mixed dough." Mar Samuel laid down the rule that the racial integrity of Jews outside of Palestine should be regarded with suspicion unless it could be proved beyond the shadow of a doubt; that of the Palestinians should be determined according to evidence, but that of the Babylonians should always be taken for granted. When Rab Judah b. Ezekiel of Pumbedita hesitated about taking a wife for his son from Babylonia, Ulla quoted the verse: "They have ravished the women in Zion" (Lam. 5:11) as a reminder that the boasted racial purity of the Palestinians was far from being a fact. [2]

The milieu in which the Persian Jews found themselves since the invasion of Babylonia by Cyrus was far more ethical than that of any other land. Its prophet Zoroaster preached a religion of a high standard of ethics and self-improvement. According to him, there are two Powers ceaselessly contending for the hegemony of this world, the Spirit of Good and the Spirit of Evil, the first being represented by Ahura Mazda and the other by Ahriman. Man, however, can vanquish the evil Power by striving for spiritual and physical perfection, and can govern himself by "good thoughts, good words, and good deeds." And so man will do. At the end of days, or after a period of three thousand years since the advent of Zoroaster, the Good Kingdom will be established, and Mazda the God of Light will be the sole ruler over all.

The Rabbis maintain that the names of the months and the belief in good and evil spirits were adopted by the Jews from the Persians. They might have added that not only in their angelology and demonology, but also in their eschatology, their doctrines about reward and punishment after death, and the resurrection of the body which will take place at the end of the present cycle, bear resemblance to those of the Zoroastrians, or Mazdeans. Both, however, have modified their views in the course of time to suit their own genius. Among the Persians, the fire which to Zoroaster was a symbol of the God of Light came to be worshiped as a deity, while among the Jews, Satan or Ashmedai was reduced to a subservient power, or God's instrument to test the goodness and sincerity of mankind.

If, however, the Jews received their angelology and demonology from the Persians, they also contributed some of their moral and religious concepts to the Zoroastrians. Their long residence in the land and their use of Aramaic facilitated their assimilation and brought about the intimate intercourse which is depicted in the Book of Esther and the Book of Tobit,—the still existing product of Persian Jewry during the Achaemenian period. James Darmesteter and Alexander Kohut may have exaggerated the effect of the Jewish influence on the Avesta, but no one can deny that there are in it ineluctable traces in form and content of the Bible and the Talmud.

This friendly, mutual reaction was interrupted at the beginning of the present era by a group which sought to fuse Hebrew theology with Iranic mythology, a group variously known as Mandaeans, Sabeans, or Nasoreans, as well as Christians of St. John the Baptist. According to them, all religions and their professors were called into being by planetary spirits, Judaism by Shemesh (sun) "whom people call *Adonai.*" But the *Mshika* (Christ), called Yishu, was a false Messiah of the Jews, and the son of a devil. He had himself baptized by Yahyab Zacharia who was the incarnation of Hibil, the reincarnation of *Manda d'Hayye* (the word of life), for which Anosh Uthra, Hibil's brother, caused his crucifixion. This picturesque distorted account of Christianity found wide acceptance in and outside of Persia for several centuries.[3]

Somewhat friendlier to orthodox Christianity but equally full of a jumble of Jewish and Christian theology and phraseology were the doctrines of the Manichaeans. Their founder, who went by the name of Mani, was raised as a Mandaean. But at the age of twelve he was bidden by an angel to give up his father's faith; and after some twelve years more of preparation and meditation, he proclaimed himself on the coronation day of Shapur I "The Apostle of the true God." While he admitted that there were some truths in the doctrines of Zoroaster, Moses, and Jesus, he maintained that Judaism and orthodox Christianity were religions of the devil. Adam was engendered by Satan and stood under the dominion of the demons. But the spirits of light sought to save him and his progeny by sending down prophets of morality such as Seth, Noah, Abraham, and Jesus. This Jesus, however, was not the "devilish Messiah of the Jews" but his contemporary phantom who neither suffered nor was crucified. Him he proclaimed as "the friend in the love of the Father." Mani's mystic cosmogony and ascetic morality spread with great rapidity over Asia, Africa, and Europe, and supplied fertile seed for the many heresies which plagued Catholicism for a thousand years. [4]

Meanwhile, the Persian caste of the Magi, which constituted themselves the guardians of the religion of Zoroaster, undertook to purge their country of its heresies and demanded a return to the teachings of the master, with all the expansions and accretions which developed during the centuries. At last the Iranian element found a champion in Ardashir (226-240), of pure Persian blood, whose ambition it was to make Persia again a world power, and to foist Zoroastrianism on all his subjects and vassal states. After overthrowing the Parthian ruler, Ardashir proclaimed himself the king of the kings of Iran, and betook himself to spread his faith with the utmost vigor. Under him the Mandaeans were almost exterminated, and Bahram I, soon after his succession, had Mani crucified and flayed and his stuffed skin hung up at the city gate as a warning to his followers.

There is a tradition that Peter and Thomas preached the Gospel in Persia, and references are made to missionaries with such Jewish names as Abraham, Jacob, and Addai. They succeeded so well that by the beginning of the third century, one of their kings is said to have been converted to the faith, and three hundred and sixty churches were scattered all over the Empire. With the rise of the Sassanids, and especially since the adoption of Christianity by the Romans, the Christians in Zoroastrian Persia were reduced to the same level as their coreligionists in pagan Rome. Under Shapur II (310-380), there took place the first great persecution in the history of Christianity in Persia. This was followed with renewed violence under Bahram V (420-438), and repeated under Yezdegerd II (438-457), Chosroes I (531-579), and Chosroes II (590-628). Bishops and priests were massacred. Churches were demolished. Christians were compelled to pay a double tax to maintain the wars in which they could not serve as soldiers, and their testimony was not accepted in a court of law. They were forbidden to ring bells on Sundays or to display their crosses in public, or even to lament for their dead. They had to wear a distinctive garb or a patch of identification. In a word, all the discriminatory laws which were later introduced by Moslems against Christians and by Christians against Jews had their prototype in Persia during the dynasty of the Sassanids. [5]

One of the first acts of Ardashir was to resume the collection of the sacred writings in Pahlavi begun by Volosges III, and to complete the Bible of the Parsees, the Avesta. The revival of Magi orthodoxy brought with it an ever increasing hostility to all other religious denominations of Persia, and particularly to Judaism. In the Dinkart, we are told that the Bible had a diabolic origin, and that all the evil of the world derived from the Yahudi religion. It claims that the Hebrew Scriptures were composed by Zohak, a Babylonian dragon who deposited them in the fortress of Jerusalem. As a specimen of this religion, which another writer describes as "full of delusion and of every iniquity and demonism," there are given the ten "universally noxious precepts" propagated by Abraham and Moses:

1. The Almighty is the injurer of the universe.

2. Devs (demons) are to be worshiped as the source of all earthly prosperity.

3. Men should practice injustice rather than justice.

4. Men should act unrighteously and disgracefully in every matter.

5. Men should lead greedy and selfish lives.

6. Children should not be trained for noble fatherhood.

7. The poor should receive no protection.

8. Goats should be killed before reaching maturity.

9. Good men should be sacrificed to the devs.

10. Men should be cruel, revengeful, and murderous. [6]

This intolerance of the Zoroastrians was fraught with even greater misery for the Jews than for the pagans. In keeping with their Magi teaching that corpses pollute the earth in which they are buried, Jewish dead were exhumed and thrown out to be devoured by birds and beasts of prey. On the days dedicated to the adoration of light, no fire was allowed to be kindled in Jewish homes even for the sick. So unbearable became the Jewish position in Persia that Rabbah bar bar Hana prayed: "All merciful, if not beneath Thy shadow, grant us to live under the shadow of Esau (Rome)," while R. Johanan bar Napaha could find the only consolation to offer his Babylonian coreligionists in the fact that Persians were amenable to bribery.

These persecutions were resumed with greater intensity under Bahram V, the son of the liberal Yezdegerd I, who was nicknamed *Gor* (wild ass). His son Yezdegerd II even forbade Jews to observe the Sabbath, or to recite the *Shema* because of its declaration of God's Unity. Peroz earned a place among the tyrants whom the Jews dubbed *rashia* (the wicked). Under him, the famous *yeshibot* were closed, the Exilarch and many of the notables were executed, half of the Jewish population of Ispahan was exterminated, and their children were raised in the religion of the Magians. Finally, under Kavadh I (488-531), the Jews were driven into open resistance. Kavadh, in his struggle against the powerful nobles, favored the teachings of the new prophet Mazdak, who proclaimed that in order to bring about the victory of light over darkness, all wealth should be distributed equally among the people, and everything, including wives, should be held in common. The Jews were determined to defend the sanctity of their homes to the last drop of their blood. Armed with little else than the courage of despair, Mar Zutra II, at the head of four hundred men, expelled the Mazdakites from the Jewish settlements and established Mahoza as the capital of a little Jewish state. But after resisting the superior forces of Kavadh for seven years Mar Zutra was overpowered and crucified, and his followers were dispersed.

With this exception, however, the Jews of Persia bore their burdens with stoic resignation. Whenever their morality or religious scruples were not involved, they drew no line of demarkation between themselves and their Zoroastrian countrymen. They formed partnerships with them, bought from and sold to them, visited them and exchanged gifts with them on their holidays and birthdays, and also dined with them at their wedding feasts. To the Jews the Persians were a superior race, one which appropriated nine of the ten measures of strength and grace that the world possesses, and whose warriors were like the warriors of King David. Mar Samuel laid down the legal maxim that the law of the land is to be considered law also in Jewish jurisprudence, and carried his devotion to his country to the extent that he displayed no sign of grief when the Persians, in capturing Mazaca, in Cappadocia, slew thousands of his fellow Jews. It is reported that he had more confidence in the assurance of a Persian widow as regards ritual cleanliness than in that of a Jewess. Some rabbis even refused to include the Persians in the category of idolaters. The kings of Modai, says R. Hiyya bar Abba, are righteous kings; they hold on to their religion merely because they inherited it from their ancestors. They are called *Modai* (Heb., acknowledgers) because they ultimately will acknowledge the Holy One, praised be He.

This was true at least of some of the Modai. There were

always a few among all classes who were favorably inclined to Judaism and refrained from hurting the religious sensibilities of their Jewish compatriots. There was, for instance, Ablat the philosopher, who frequently exchanged visits with Mar Samuel, whom he regarded as "wisest of the Jews." Knowing that as a Jew he would not drink wine which was handled by a pagan, Ablat on one occasion waited for Mar Samuel to drink first. Mar Samuel, however, explained to him that what he was serving, mullet, did not come under the taboo. Rab (Abba Arika), the foremost of the rabbis of Babylonia, also enjoyed the friendship of Artabanus IV, the last of the Arsacid dynasty. The two frequently discussed not only politics but religion. Once Artabanus made a gift of a precious jewel to Rab. The latter reciprocated by giving him a *mezuza*. When Rab received the news of the fall of his royal friend, he rent his garments and lamented, "Alas, the tie is severed!"

Perhaps the brightest chapter in the history of the Jews of Persia was written during the reign of Shapur I (240-271). He loved to be entertained by Mar Samuel's performances of sleight of hand and his ready repartee, and also displayed an interest in his views on more serious topics. Once he asked the rabbi why Jews should expect their Messiah to come riding on an ass when he himself would be glad to provide a handsome horse for him. Samuel replied that if it were a matter of pomp, the Persian king himself could not find a stallion befitting the honor of God's anointed. On another occasion he asked Samuel to tell him what he would dream about that night. Samuel who, as a scientist, knew the effect of suggestion, answered that he would dream that he was captured by the Romans. And so he did. It is said that Shapur always spared Jewish lives save, as at Mazaca, when they fought in the armies of the enemy. His reputation among the Jews was such that they believed the taxes he imposed upon them he intended to distribute among their own poor and hoped that, like Cyrus, he would ultimately rebuild the Temple and restore their national independence. Glorying in the honor shown him by their king, the Jews nicknamed their beloved sage Shabur Malka and Aryoch (King Shapur and Aryan). [7]

The following episode throws a sidelight on Shapur's knowledge of Judaism and his thoughtfulness concerning its adherents. Batti bar Tobi, evidently a highly cultured slave, became a *ger*. This led to his emancipation in accordance with the law; and by dint of his cleverness, he became the associate of leading personages among Jews and Persians. Once he and Mar Judah were invited to dine with the king. On reaching the dessert, Shapur peeled two oranges, one for himself and one for Batti. Then, according to a local Jewish custom, he stuck the knife ten times into the ground and then with it, peeled one for Mar Judah. Batti felt somewhat discriminated against and asked: "Am I not also a son of Israel?" "Yes," replied His Majesty, "but your conduct is not yet like that of a son of Israel"—referring to the fact that the night before, when he sent women to entertain his guests, Mar Judah avoided them while Batti took full advantage of this form of royal hospitality. [8]

It was during the reign of Shapur I that the Persian hegemony of the East was seriously threatened by the insurrection of Palmyra (Tadmor), once a flourishing commercial principality of the Empire. These Palmyrians, by the way, traced their descent to the Gentile slaves of Solomon who married Jewish women "for their wealth" or to those daughters of Zion whom they carried off at the sack of Jerusalem, in which they participated. Their King Odenatus waged war against Shapur and pursued him twice to the gates of Ctesiphon, destroyed the great seat of Jewish learning in Nehardea, and inaugurated an era of persecution in which many of the Sages were put to death. Some rabbis, therefore, declared that no Palmyrians should be admitted into the congregation of the Lord. "Happy he," said R. Johanan b. Zakkai, "who will see the downfall of Tadmor," and Rab Judah, the pupil of Mar Samuel, declared: "the day on which Tadmor is destroyed will be made a holiday." To the honor of the Sages be it said that despite their personal feeling, they decided that Tadmorites should not be excluded. [9]

When Odenatus died (260), supposedly at the hand of an assassin, Zenobia, famed as "Shemiramith the Second" and

Queen of the East, took over the regency during the minority of her two sons. Under her, Palmyra reached the peak of its prosperity. She encouraged the pursuit of knowledge and invited philosophers from all parts of the world to stay at her marvelous palace. But in her relation to the Jews, she adhered to the policy of her husband. This hatred was intensified by a rumor that the Jews were in league with the Persians and were plotting against her sons. When a certain Zeira bar Hanina was accused of being one of the conspirators and Rab Ami and Rab Samuel interceded in his behalf, she exclaimed, "Do you think that because your God is said to have worked many miracles for your nation, you can do anything you please with impunity?"

But the God Who worked so many miracles before seemed now to work another miracle. Just as Zeira was about to be removed from the queen's presence, a Saracene rushed in and, exhibiting a dagger, exclaimed, "With this sword Bar-Nazar killed this man's brother." The wise queen at once realized that the accused was the victim of a frame-up. She ordered the release of Zeira and thereafter thought more kindly of the Jews. The Talmud has nothing to say about her conversion, but Christian chroniclers hint that she was either born or became a Jewess. She certainly did not accept, as some would have it, the form of Christianity which was then being spread in the Roman Empire. She opened wide her court to all who were persecuted for their beliefs. Her hospitality was extended to Longinus who, though a pagan, expressed his admiration for the Books of Moses, and also to Paul of Samosata, the Bishop of Antioch, who refused to admit the divinity of Jesus, and insisted that Christians should adhere to Jewish custom and observe even the rite of circumcision.

After a valiant struggle against the Romans, in which she proved herself the "Joan of Arc" of her day and defended her country against the armies of Gallienus and Claudius, Zenobia's reign came to an end (273), and she was carried in golden fetters to Rome to grace the triumph of Marcus Aurelius. The Roman Emperor then presented her with an elegant villa on the Tiber, where she spent her remaining days "in reading

only Jewish books, and in contemplating the hopes and in-
spirations of her new Jewish faith." As late as the fifth century
her descendants were still sought after by the best social element of the Eternal City.[10]

Of the Queen Mother of Shapur II, the Talmud tells us that
she was close to becoming a convert (*krobah l'hitgayer*), but
whether she took the final step is not recorded. Her treatment
of the Jews, however, while she was regent during the infancy
of her son, and the favors she showed to the heads of the
academy of Pumbedita, amply prove that she took a great interest in Jews and Judaism. It was her belief that "the God of
the Jews does whatever His people ask of Him." When Rab
Joseph the Blind was called to the presidency of the academy,
she presented him with a valuable gift. When Raba's life was
threatened because he administered a severe punishment to
a Jew who was accused of illicit relations with a Persian
woman, she interceded in his behalf. She also asked him to
offer sacrifices for the salvation of her soul and donated four
hundred denarii for distribution among the Jewish poor.

Jewish chroniclers are not clear as to whether Shapur II, who
surrounded himself with Jewish physicians and counsellors,
followed in the footsteps of his mother; but since Christian
writers claim that it was the Jews who instigated him to slaughter twenty-two bishops, we may surmise that he, too, was friendly to them. An anecdote in the Talmud indicates that he was
favorably inclined to Judaism, or sufficiently interested in it
to seek information from Jewish sages. He consulted Rab
Hama, the head of the Pumbedita academy, about what the
Torah had to say on the matter of burying the dead, which
to the Magians was an act of desecration. Rab Hama could
think of no passage in the Bible to justify the Jewish custom.
When Rab Aka bar Jacob heard of it, he was greatly incensed
and exclaimed: "Verily the world is ruled by ignoramuses.
He should have referred to the passage: 'And thou shalt bury
him on the same day.' " [11]

With the accession of Yezdegerd I (399-420), who was nicknamed Al Hatim (the sinner), the position of the Jews brightened considerably. Intelligent and liberal, he was determined

to rid his kingdom of the oppression of the magnates and the domination of the Magian priests. He stopped the persecution of the Christians and was especially well disposed toward the Jews. He invited into his courts the heads of the Jewish academies of Sura, Nehardea, and Pumbedita, and took to wife the daughter of one of the Exilarchs, who became the mother of Bahram V and established Jewish colonies at Shushan, Shuster, and Ispahan. He is said to have himself adjusted the girdle of the Exilarch Huna bar Nathan "in a manner befitting the son of the people who were the priests of the Most High." This act, according to Amemar, was in fulfillment of the Isaiahnic prophecy (49:23): "And kings shall be thy foster fathers."

The longing for the coming of the Messiah, though never absent, was for a while rather weak in Babylonia. It was there that Samuel declared that the only difference between this world and the Messianic era would be the cessation of persecution, and it was there that a certain Rabbi Hillel sounded the only solitary doubtful note about the coming of the Messiah to be found in the Talmud, and that Ulla and Raba expressed the wish that he would not come in their lifetime. But the decline of the Parthians and the ever-increasing suffering under the Sassanids made the hope more and more fervent, and the Bible was searched for definite signs and dates of the Messiah's arrival. These dates naturally changed from time to time. Rab Ashi, though he discouraged metaphysical speculations about "the End," believed that it would begin at the conclusion of "the eighty-fifth Jubilee" (between 440 and 490). R. Hanan b. Tahlifa saw in a scroll (written in Assyrian and Hebrew script) which a mercenary had found in Persian archives, "After 4291 years from the Creation (531) the world will be destroyed by sea-monsters and by the wars of Gog and Magog, and thereafter will follow the days of the Messiah." When these predictions failed to materialize, Messianic expectations nevertheless continued to glow, and it needed but some change, for better or for worse, in the fortunes of the Jews for the millennial flame to flare up anew. This happened in the reign of Chosroes II (590-628). The rapid tide of his successes over the Romans, which earned for him the title of

Parvez (the Conqueror) and his granting to the *Yeshibot* permission to remain open won the Jews over to his side. Twenty-six thousand of them enlisted in the army led by the redoubtable general Shahr-Barz; and, due not a little to their bravery, Galilee was reduced, Syria was conquered, and in the fateful month of Tammuz, the month when Nebuchadnezzar first made a breach in Jerusalem, the holy city was captured by his remote successor, Chosroes II (614). [12]

Those, however, who believed with Rab that when the Persians would rule the world (i.e., conquer the Romans), the son of David would appear, were doomed to disappointment. In the midst of his enjoyment of the fruit of his victories, Chosroes is said to have received an epistle from Mecca inviting him to acknowledge Mohammed as the Apostle of God. When Mohammed heard that the king tore the epistle into shreds, he exclaimed: "Thus will God tear the kingdom and reject the supplications of Chosroes." And so it came to pass. In the same year that Chosroes' son, Yezdegerd III (633), mounted the throne the Arabs penetrated into Persian territory and before long replaced Zoroastrianism and Christianity by Mohammedanism.

But the mode of Jewish life and their system of self-government must have already made their impress on many a Persian. The splendor which for many generations surrounded the office of the *Resh Galuta* (exilarch), the thousands of students and their teachers, dressed in their immaculate scholars' robes, who filled the great *yeshiboth,* and the gatherings of the *kalla* (semi-annual conventions of scholars) could not but profoundly affect the populace. "The scholars of Babylon are like ministering angels," declares R. Levi. In the simple and impressionable Persians they stirred feelings of awe or reverence or aroused a desire to become associated with them. Rab Joseph expresses surprise that the Gobeans "who see the splendor of the Torah twice every year yet produce no *gerim!*" So does Rab Ashi at the inhabitants of Mata Mehasia. The number of proselytes in some places must, however, have been considerable. "Big measures and little measures of proselytes," runs a talmudic proverb, "mingle and flow to Sheol (Babylonia), from Sheol to Tadmor (Palmyra), from Tadmor to Meshan (Mesene), and from Meshan to Harpania." R. Hiyya bar Abba found in Gabala many Jewish women who married those who were circumcised, but failed to be baptised by immersion. Instances are recorded of men who claimed that they had been fully converted but could not produce witnesses or certificates to substantiate the fact. No rabbi, while addressing a congregation, could tell whether his audience consisted entirely of "pure" Jews or converts. Rab Zeira II, as late as the fifth century, once delivered a discourse in Mahoza. Desirous to please his audience, composed mostly of *gerim*, the rabbi declared that a *ger* might marry a bastard. His hearers, however, felt that this supposed privilege was in reality a reflection on their status as Jews; and, as it was the Feast of Tabernacles, they rushed at him with their palm branches. Thereafter, he studiously refrained from referring to this permission and was careful to stress the point that a proselyte may marry even the daughter of a priest. [13]

There were of course in Persia, as in Palestine, some who opposed the admission of Gentiles into the household of Israel and looked upon *gerim* with ill-concealed distrust. To this, the behavior of converts who experienced no change of heart even after they changed their faith contributed not a little. The Mahozans, we are told, remained as they were before, "children of hell," indulging in drunkenness and various unethical practices. Some Nehardeans persisted in following in the footsteps of the notorious robber brothers Anilai and Asinai, who defied the Parthians for more than fifteen years. In Pumbedita not a few of the swindlers were either converts or their descendants. Some of these who "saw the light" of Judaism were merely lured on by the prospect of marrying into prominent or prosperous families. There were Persians who learned to master the dialect of the Jews and, without having become converts, passed as such. It was hard to distinguish between the sincere and the charlatans. Nor could one be sure that the *ger* would not at any time regret her conversion and relapse into idolatry. Hence Raba forbade anyone to marry a proselyte. The Jews of North Apamea went to the extent of refusing a spark to light the fires of the inhabitants of South Apamea, for fear that as former fire-worshipers the latter might use it in the service of idols. Playing upon the names of the communities, in which proselytes predominated, some rabbis declared "Mesene (Heb. *mitha*) is dead, Media (Heb. *madve*) is diseased." [14]

But, even as it was in more conservative Palestine, the spirit of liberalism dominated the leading exponents of Babylonian Judaism. After all, Babylonia which produced an Ezra produced also a Hillel, whose motto it was: "Love thy fellow creatures and draw them nigh to the Torah," and a R. Hiyya bar Abba, who warned his colleagues "not to make the fence too high, lest it fall and destroy the plants." It was in Babylonia, too, that Rab, the head of the Sura academy, taught: "Whosoever seeks to be converted should be accepted.... Do not impugn the motives of *gerim*; perhaps they come for the sake of Heaven." His no less renowned contemporary, Samuel of Nehardea, was sure that "Before the throne of the Creator there is no distinction between Jew and Gentile." It was the Babylonian R. Ishmael bar Nahman who explained the verse, "All ye the seed of Jacob, glorify Him," as expressly referring to proselytes of righteousness; and Raba bar Ulla applied the Psalmist's "people of the God of Abraham" to those who, not being Jews by birth, were the spiritual children of the first of all *gerim*. These scholars and their colleagues would not permit all neophytes to be rejected because they might harbor some unworthy ones among them. They expected that there would be among them those who resembled Hamor, who submitted to circumcision because of Dinah; but, they held, there would also be those who, like Abraham, would be willing to sacrifice their all on the altar of their new religion. [15]

And indeed, many of the *gerim* proved themselves worthy of the confidence of even the most exacting. They observed their new faith with a zeal sometimes surpassing that of born Jews. In their anxiety to live up to all the requirements of their religion, some nailed *mezuzas* to the gates of the towns in which they resided or kept even the obsolete restrictions of the Shemitah year. Some became Nazarites. They contributed generously to the maintenance of the institution of learning. When the academy of Sura became overcrowded, the bequest of a *ger* made possible its expansion.

Some of the stories concerning the attitude of Rab and Samuel, the leading rabbis of Babylonia, to *gerim* are so slightly different from those current in Palestine with regard to the attitudes of Shammai and Hillel that it is difficult to decide where they originated or whether they are mere repetitions of the same episodes. Once a Persian approached Rab with the request to teach him the Torah. As he knew no Hebrew, Rab advised him to begin with the study of the alphabet. The Persian proved a recalcitrant pupil and, when told the name of a letter, would demand to know why it might not have had another name. Rab at last lost patience and drove him from his presence. He then went to Samuel and repeated the performance. Samuel, instead of driving him away, gave him a box on the ear. "My ear, my ear," screamed the Persian. "But how do you know it is your ear?" asked Samuel. "Why," answered the Persian, "everyone knows that." "And everyone knows," replied Samuel, "that this is Aleph, this Bet, and so on." The Persian ultimately became an adept in the Torah, and the Rabbis used the incident to illustrate the truth of the saying in Ecclesiastes: "It is better to be patient in spirit (like Samuel) than to be proud in spirit (like Rab)." [16]

In many instances the Babylonian Sages, like their Palestinian colleagues, went out of their way to protect the *ger* and even to favor him. Thus, in accordance with the legal maxim: "A *ger* is like a newly born child," all his past transactions were wiped out. However, they applied this principle only to debts owed by him. Debts due him were not to be canceled by his conversion and, what is more, he might collect both principal and interest, which a Jew by birth was not permitted to do. Raba disapproved of this decision for the reason that it might be said that one became a convert in order to escape his financial obligations. Rabbah bar Abahu advised a prospective proselyte, who came to consult him about the gold and silver idols in his possession, to dispose of them first and be converted afterward. The Rabbis also did their utmost to eradicate prejudice against *gerim* wherever it still prevailed. Once a neophyte inn-keeper ran for the office of mayor of the Jewish community. His opponent was the very prominent Rab Bebai and was backed by R. Joseph on the ground of the Deuteronomic injunction: "Thou mayest not put a foreigner over thee." The saintly Adda bar Ahaba, who happened at the time to be staying at the hostelry, took up for his host and effected a compromise. Rab Bebai, the scholar, was appointed to attend to the religious needs of the place, while the proselyte inn-keeper was honored with the office of supervising its civic affairs. When the information reached Abbaye he jokingly remarked: "Let an inn-keeper admit into his hostelry only guests of the type of Adda bar Ahaba, lest he will get into difficulties and need someone to take up his cause." [17]

The crowning glory of Babylonian Judaism was the conversion of the entire royal family of Adiabene, an independent state on the Tigris, north of Mesopotamia. King Monobaz and his Queen Helena were especially fond of their younger son Izates (1-55 C.E.) and, fearing the jealousy of the other members of the family, sent him away to the neighboring court of King Abinerglus at Charax. The king became much attached to his princely ward and later gave him his daughter Samacha to wife. A merchant by the name of Ananias (supposedly himself a convert) visited the court to sell his wares and, while on business, recommended also things spiritual. Gradually the princess became persuaded and adopted the religion of Israel. Similar missionary endeavors were made at Adiabene; and before long, Queen Helena and many of her kin also adopted Judaism. Wife and mother now concentrated their efforts on Izates, and he, too, became a convert. He did not, however, submit to circumcision since his physician, a Hellenized Jew, assured him that it was not necessary, and his mother feared the consequences of the operation. [18]

Through the influence of Helena, Izates, after the death of Monobaz, was elevated to the throne. Helena showed the effect of her conversion; and instead of condemning his brothers to death, as was then customary, in order to eliminate any possible opposition, she only put them under guard. Izates, however, removed the guard altogether and sent them as hostages to Rome and Persia.

Shortly after his accession, one Eleazar, a Galilean Jew, while visiting at court found Monobaz and Izates reading Genesis 17:11. In the discussion which followed, Eleazar convinced them that to become a full-fledged Jew one must undergo the rite of circumcision. Thereupon Izates, his older brother Monobaz II, as well as others of his relatives, submitted to the operation. When the news of Izates' conversion became known among the nobility, they formed a conspiracy and induced Abia, an Arabian chief, to help them dethrone him. The nobles then appealed to Vologeses, king of Parthia, but he, too, was vanquished (for Izates appealed to God for help), and Izates remained in the undisputed possession of his throne. His descendants continued to reign for several generations. The kinsmen of Monobaz fought bravely against the Romans in defense of the independence of Palestine, and some of them together with other Palestinian Jews were led by Titus to Rome to add to the impressiveness of his triumphal return. In 115, Trajan crossed the Tigris, conquered and annexed Adiabene, and the royal house of Monobaz ceased to exist.

From their conversion to the end of their career, this princely family evinced an ardent attachment to the faith of Israel. Helena visited Jerusalem (43), for fourteen years she took upon herself the Nazarite's vow, became proficient in the Torah, and made her home a rendezvous of the sages. She enriched the Temple with golden portals. During the famine of 48, she imported from Alexandria and Cyprus shiploads of wheat and figs for distribution among the poor. She died at Adiabene. At her request, she was buried in Jerusalem, together with Izates, who preceded her a little before. Pausanias, the Greek traveler, narrates that her tomb was so contrived that the door leading to it would open and shut itself once a year at a certain hour. The Moslem Orphanage in the old quarters of Jerusalem is said to stand on the spot of her imposing palace, and the nearby street is still called by the Arabs *Akabat al-Sit,* "the ascent of the Lady," or more explicitly *Akabat al-melikat Helani,* "The ascent of the Queen Helena."

Helena's children were no less devout than their Queen Mother. They observed strictly all the minutiae of the Jewish religion; and when they were on a journey, they carried with them a staff on which was affixed a *mezuza,* and set it up in front of the inn in which they lodged. A disciple of R. Akiba, who was called Monobaz, may have been one of their descendants. Like his mother, Monobaz II, who succeeded Izates, lavished his fortune on beautifying the Temple and in relief of the indigent. When his kinsmen remonstrated with him for squandering the wealth of their family, he is reported to have replied:

> My fathers have laid up treasure here below, I have laid up treasures here above, as it is said:
>
>> 'Truth springeth out of the earth;
>> And righteousness looketh down from heaven.'
>
> My fathers have hidden (their treasure) where the hand can prevail over it, I have hidden mine where no hand can prevail over it, as it is said:
>
>> 'Righteousness and justice are the foundation
>> of Thy throne.'
>
> My fathers have hidden something which produces no fruit, I have hidden something which produces fruit, as it is said:
>
>> 'Say ye of the righteous, that it shall be well
>> with them;
>> For they shall eat the fruit of their doings.'
>
> My fathers have hidden (treasures) of money, I have hidden treasures of souls, as it is said:
>
>> 'The fruit of the righteous is a tree of life,
>> And he that is wise winneth souls.'

My fathers have hidden for others, I have hidden for myself, as it is said:

'And it shall be righteousness unto thee.'

My fathers have hidden for this world, I have hidden for the world to come, as it is said:

'And thy righteousness shall go before thee,
The glory of the Lord shall gather thee in.' [19]

CHAPTER XI

JEWISH ENLIGHTENMENT
IN EGYPT

THE earliest contact of Semites with Africa probably goes back to the invasion of Egypt by the Hyksos, or "princes" of the desert," who overthrew the pyramid-building Pharaohs and introduced the worship of a Supreme God, Aton or Adon. Under these dynasties the Hebrews were always sure of a friendly reception as allies and kinsmen, until the "new king who knew not Joseph" reintroduced the old gods and reduced the status of the Hebrews to that of serfs. Their bondage, however, was an economic bondage. They were not hindered in the free exercise of their religion. They were not treated like human chattel. Their families were not broken up; their communal organizations were left intact. They had their own overseers who were responsible to the government for the "tale of the bricks" which they were to supply. Many Egyptians, for one reason or another, cast their lot among them and became assimilated with them; and Egyptian waifs and strays were picked up and adopted by the members of the various Hebrew clans. At the Exodus, these "fearers of the Lord" and the *Asafsuf* or *Erev Rav* (mixed multitude) constituted an important part of the host which left the land of bondage under the leadership of Moses.

That the Hebrews during the age of bondage did not find it necessary or advisable to hide or give up their religion is proved by one of the recently discovered Egyptian tablets of a chief of cavalry under Rameses II. On it are seen Egyptians in adoration of the various gods of the country, and on the blank edges are inscribed the names of the servants of the household, headed by the "scribe engraver" Yehu-naam (Jehovah speaks), which, according to Flinders Petrie, "seems unmistakably to refer to a worshiper of Yehu or Yahveh, and hence an Israelite." It shows, too, that not all Hebrews were then brick-makers or brick-layers, but that some were among the highly skilled artists employed to draw and engrave hieroglyphics and the figures of the gods and that, like the Babylonian Psalmist, at least some of them could say:

> I will also speak of Thy testimonies before kings,
> And I will not be ashamed. [1]

It is not unlikely that many of these privileged Jews remained in Egypt after the Exodus, even as did the more prosperous Jews of Babylonia after the Ezranic return. Far removed from a Hebrew center, they did, what their co-religionists usually did where they were few in numbers, they intermarried with the daughters of the land and brought up their children in their ancestral faith. Thus there was hardly a time when there was no Israelitish contingent in the land of the Pharaohs. Their numbers must have increased considerably with the resumption of friendly relationships under Solomon, who married an Egyptian princess and whose extensive horse-trading led to the establishment of mercantile colonies from the valley of the Nile to the plains of Central Africa. To these were added those who were sent to Egypt either as soldiers, as captives of war, or as slaves after Shishak invaded Judea. Psamtik I, Psamtik II, and Hophra also established Judean military colonies in Nubia, Libya, Cyrene, and other places, where the colonists won over many of the natives to their religious belief. Isaiah even predicted that some day "There shall be five (i.e., many) cities in the land of Egypt that shall speak the language of Canaan and swear to the Lord of hosts," that there shall be "an altar to the Lord in the midst of the land of Egypt, and a pillar at the border thereof to the Lord," and that like Jerusalem (the city of peace) one of its cities will be called *Ir Hazzedek* (the city of righteousness). The following hieroglyphic in-

scription on a tomb at Hermopolis may have been intended
as a bit of propaganda by one of these proselytes:

> Good is the way of the man who obeys God; hap-
> py is he whose heart strives to follow Him.... I will
> have you informed of the will of God; I will have
> you advance in the knowledge of His spirit. All the
> night the spirit of God is in my soul, and I rise in the
> morning to do what He loves.... I have not agreed
> with those who know not the spirit of God, but I
> lean on those who act according to His will.... Happy
> is he who loves God and comes to his grave without
> sin. [2]

That Isaiah's prediction came very near fulfillment is evidenced by the Elephantine papyri which date from 494 to
400 B.C.E. In that region the Jewish military colony erected
a sanctuary of its own at Yeb, on an island in the Nile near
the Cataract, consisting of stone columns, five gates with
bronze fittings and a roof of cedar, and containing vessels of
gold and silver. This Temple became widely known as "the
House of Yahu Who is in Yeb," or the "House of sacrifices
of the God of the Heavens." It was spared by Cambyses
when he demolished the Temples of Egypt, but was destroyed
in a raid made by the Egyptian priests of Khnum, with the
connivance of the Persian governor.[3]

The reason for the enmity of the priests of Khnum is
indicated by the names and description of many of the members of this garrison colony. Most of them are Assyrian, Babylonian, Persian, and theophorous Egyptian. As-Hor (Servant of Horus) married Mibtah-Yah (Trust in the Lord),
daughter of Mahse-Yah (Shield of the Lord), son of Yedan-
Yah (Let the Lord Judge). He was an Egyptian and a royal
architect, but in order to marry a Jewess he changed his name
to Nathan; and like a good Jew, he obligated himself in a
ketubah (marriage document) to forfeit twenty *kebhes* of silver
should he ever drive Mibtah-Yah out of his house. There are
such names as Anath-Yahu and Anath-Bethel. Hoshea claimed

to be the son of the Egyptian Pedukhnum, while Yathom and Melkiel were respectively the sons and grandsons of the Babylonian Hadadnuri. There must have been some Greeks, too, among these worshipers of Yahu, for the word used for the court of the Temple built by the contributions of "all the Jews, citizens of Yeb the fortress" is the Greek *agora.*

What took place at Yeb probably occurred also in other parts of Egypt, and some day we may yet hear of other cities that "called on the name of Jehovah." But the more authentic history of the Jews in Egypt begins with the reign of Alexander the Great, the son of a "barbarian" who became the leading champion of the culture of the Greeks.

Alexander "the Macedonian" (356-23 B.C.E.) possessed all the virtues and few of the vices of the Greeks. His teacher Aristotle imbued him with a passion for truth. After completing the work begun by his father, of subjugating and unifying the over-contending city-states of Greece, he crossed the Hellespont and began his triumphal march thru Asia Minor. On his way he stopped in Egypt and was welcomed by the Judeans as a deliverer both from the foreign Persian and the native Egyptian oppressors. The Jews also aided him materially in laying the foundation of the port city of Alexandria, which soon became the greatest trading post in the East and the cultural center of the Grecian world. In appreciation of their assistance, Alexander granted them equal rights with the Greeks and, as a mark of his singular favor, the privilege of calling themselves Macedonians.

The liberal policy of Alexander was followed by the Ptolemies. Ptolemy I regarded the Jews as the most trustworthy of the conglomerate elements which composed his empire, and at one time had as many as thirty thousand Judean soldiers entrusted with the guardianship of the forts. Ptolemy II showed his especial esteem for the Judeans by sending his thank-offering for the conquest of Syria to the Temple at Jerusalem, together with many gifts for the priesthood. Ptolemy Philometor had as his teacher Aristobulus of Paneas, a Jewish philosopher "of the stock of anointed priests," and as the commanders-in-chief of his army Dositheos and Onias, the sons of the High Priest of Alexandria. Among the invited wedding guests at the marriage of his daughter Cleopatra to Alexander Balos was Jonathan the High Priest of Judea. As a result of this liberal attitude, the Jewish community kept on steadily increasing. At the time of Philo there were more than a million Jews in Egypt having the "entire custody of the Nile on all occasions," and Josephus reports that many Jews continued to flock thither "of their own accord as invited by the goodness of the soil and the liberality of Ptolemy." [4]

The Ptolemies were great patrons of learning. Ptolemy I laid the foundation for the famous library which ultimately numbered over two hundred thousand volumes. He also organized the Museum Society whose associates, maintained at public expense, devoted themselves to the pursuit of science, philosophy, and literature. The palace of Ptolemy Philadelphus became an asylum for the sages of all the nations. In his fondness for books, Ptolemy Evergetes paid fifteen talents to the Athenians for permission to copy the manuscripts of Aeschylus, Euripides, and Sophocles. Even the least worthy of the Ptolemies, Evergetes—"Kakergetes" (the evildoer) was a bibliophile and an author in his own right. His commentary on Homer and his history of the world were much admired and frequently quoted for their elegance of style and display of erudition.

Among the Jews of Egypt, Alexander became another Cyrus. Some indeed believed that he was a convert to Judaism, and others acclaimed him even as the Messiah. The fact that on his expedition into Asia he left the Judeans unmolested and even exempted them from the payment of tribute could not be explained otherwise than by a miracle. It was said that when Alexander was about to invest Jerusalem, the High Priest, Jaddua, having been warned in a dream of Alexander's intention, arrayed himself in the regalia of his office and together with a coterie of priests, all clad in fine linen, set out to meet him. Alexander was so impressed by the sight of the venerable man that he advanced toward him and worshiped him. On noticing the surprise of the kings who were with him, he explained: "I did not adore him, but the God Who hath honored him with the High Priesthood. I saw this very person in a dream, in this very habit, when I was at Dios, in Macedonia, and heard him, when I was considering how I might obtain the dominion of Asia, exhort me to make no delay, but boldly to pass over the sea thither, and he would conduct my army and would give me dominion over the Persians." Alexander then went to the Temple and offered sacrifices unto God "according to the High Priest's direction" and magnificently treated both the High Priest and the (lesser) priests; and when the Book of Daniel was shown him, wherein Daniel declared that one of the Greeks should destroy the empire of the Persians, he supposed that he himself was the person intended. Daniel's prediction that those "who shall stand up against the king of the south" will "stumble by the sword and the flame" was interpreted as a warning against disloyalty to the Macedonian dynasty.

In appreciation of Alexander's favors, the Judeans named the boys born during the year following his visit to Jerusalem after him, and the name Alexander thus became rooted in Jewish nomenclature. [5]

Local patriotism among the Jews of Egypt reached even a higher peak than among those of Babylonia. Their ancestors came thither not as captives but either as soldiers or selected immigrants upon whom were conferred privileges denied to the native-born Gentiles. Of course they still remembered Zion, but not with that passionate love of the Judeans of the *Golah* (Dispersion). Egypt was their Palestine, the Ptolemies their princes, and they were ready to fight their own coreligionists in behalf of their king and country. We may judge of the fervor of their patriotism by the fact that in the war which broke out under Cleopatra III two Jewish generals, Helkias and Ananias, and many Jewish soldiers fought against Lathyrus and his ally, the Judean king Alexander Jannai. An inscription, recently discovered in Sheida, Lower Egypt, states that the synagogue there had been built "in honor of king Ptolemy and Queen Berenice, his sister and wife, and their children." [6]

The arrival of Onias IV, the heir to the High Priesthood, gave an additional impetus to the sanguine expectations of the Judeans in Egypt. Onias was at once made commander-in-chief of the king's army, and his retinue were allotted tracts of land between Memphis and Pelusium and were granted permission by Ptolemy VII to erect a Temple at Leontopolis, not far from ancient Goshen (c., 154 B.C.E.). The site on which it was built was probably that of a pagan shrine, and the material was likely taken from the ruins of the palace of Rameses III and the fortifications of the Hyksos kings; but its architecture was modeled after the sanctuary in Jerusalem. It had seventy-one golden chairs, in allusion to the number of the members of the Palestinian Sanhedrin, and it was so large that the *hazan* (reader) had to make use of a handkerchief as a signal for the congregation to respond with "Amen." With its completion, the Egyptian Jews felt that at last Isaiah's prediction came true: there was now "an altar to the Lord in the midst of the land of Egypt, and a pillar at the border thereof to the Lord."[7]

But the Judeans were not content with merely maintaining their religious integrity; they were ambitious to make themselves a "blessing in the land." In this, their efforts were greatly facilitated by their thorough assimilation with the Greek civilization. They were, as Clearchus says, "Greek not only in language but also in soul." They were familiar with Homer and the other poets, with Plato and the other philosophers, with the tragedians, comedians, and the whole gamut of Greek mythology. They could dress up their ideas in the finery suitable to the Grecian taste and reinforce them with the authority of the greatest Greek luminaries.

Now, from remote times some glimmerings of Jewish concepts of God and morality had been caught by the Greeks. Pythagoras (c. 582-500 B.C.E.) is said to have declared that he had seen Hesiod tied to a brazen pillar in hell, and Homer hung upon a tree surrounded by serpents, because of the fables they had invented about the gods; and the precepts of Pythagoras on obedience, abstinence, simplicity, and frequent self-examination are suggestive of the Jewish counsels of moral perfection. Stilpo ridiculed the religious ceremonials of the heathen and denied that the Athene of Phidias was a goddess. Xenophanes, founder of the Eclectic School (c. 535 B.C.E.) affirmed à la Voltaire, that every people makes its god to conform with its own likeness: to the Ethiopians, the gods appear with black skins; to the Thracians, with red hair and blue eyes; and if horses could express their ideas, they would represent their gods in the semblance of horses. Of him it is reported that "He looked up to the whole heaven and declared: 'God is One.'" Socrates indicated what he thought of the gods by sacrificing a louse to them before the hemlock took effect. Plato taught that "God is a Being of perfect simplicity and truth, both in deed and in word, and neither changes in Himself, nor imposes upon others either by apparition or by words, or by the sending of signs, whether in dreams or in waking moments." To Aristotle God "is a living Being, eternal, very good, the essence of all intelligence, unconjoined with matter, different both from nature and men, the final good of the whole universe." It was probably from him that his royal pupil Alexander learned his credo which was, according to Plutarch, that God was the Father of all men and that it was his mission to pacify the whole human race.

The Jews of Egypt took advantage of these and similar statements and maintained that many of the most illustrious Greeks, such as Pythagoras, were converts to Judaism, and that Plato, while in Egypt, was a pupil of Moses. Aristotle in particular became the favorite heathen who was drafted in the service of Judaism. It was claimed that when he accompanied Alexander to Jerusalem, he was deeply impressed with the views of Simon the High Priest, and that after reading a copy of the writings of Solomon he acknowledged that the Jews had the first and greatest philosophers. He was alleged even to have embraced Judaism. This legend persisted among some Jews down to the nineteenth century. R. Joseph b. Shem-Tob (d. 1480) claims that he saw in an ancient volume that the great philosopher, who had to flee Athens to avoid the fate of Socrates, found peace and shelter under the wings of the Shekinah. [8]

A further rapprochement between Judaism and paganism was made through Stoicism. The Stoics were among the first Gentiles who groped their way to ethical monotheism, and Josephus pronounces their teachings to be almost identical with Pharisaism. Some of them taught the Unity of God, the resurrection of the body, and the coming of a Day of Judgment, and decried the worship of images. Only the good, they insisted, are wise, and only the moral are free and happy. Philosophy they defined as zeal for virtue, and temperance as the goal thereof. Jupiter they regarded as a Providence who takes an interest in the affairs of men and metes out reward and punishment. Cleanthes, the successor to Zeno, addresses the Deity in a hymn which is almost Hebraic:

> O Divine Being, no action takes place
> without thee on earth,
> Nor in the divine ethereal heaven, nor
> on the sea,
> Except what the wicked accomplish by
> their senselessness.
> Thou ornamentest what is rude, and
> unlovely things are lovely to thee;
> For thus thou hast fitted all things into
> a whole, good things and evil ones.

These teachings of the philosophers were reiterated by the tragedians and comedians. "The language in which the first Greek dramatists asserted the supreme authority and universal providence of Zeus," says Lecky, "was so emphatic that the Christian Fathers (and the Jewish sages) commonly attributed it either to direct inspiration or to a knowledge of the Jewish writings." In Aeschylus we hear an echo of Jewish ideals of truth, justice, mercy, repentance, reward, and punishment. In Euripides the Greek world received "the first great revelation of the supreme beauty of the gentler virtues." In the plays of Sophocles there runs a devastating sarcasm about the gods, worthy of the prophets and the psalmists. These Greeks proved the truth of the rabbinic assertions that God sent Prophets to the Gentiles as well as to the Jews, and that even without the Torah man would learn the essentials of morality by meditating upon nature. But not only were they on the road to Hebraic ethics, they were tending in the direction of Hebraic monotheism. Among the many altars in Athens there was one which was revered beyond all others. It had no symbol and no image of a god. It was so old that it was said to have been erected by the descendants of Hercules. It was dedicated to Mercy, or the Merciful One. [9]

To be sure, these higher glimpses were not shared by the populace and the politicians. These were very jealous for the gods, and those who dared doubt or deny their existence were as unsafe among their countrymen as were infidels and heretics among Christians and Mohammedans of a later day. The Amphictyonic war was a holy war. Heraclitus was persecuted by the Ephesians for impiety. Enlightened Athens exacted from her citizens a solemn vow to conform and to defend the established religion. Protagoras, Diogenes, Alcibiades, Anaxagoras, even Pericles who rendered such eminent services to his country, were at one time or another in peril of their lives. Stilpo and Aeschylus were compelled to flee for safety, while Socrates was condemned to drink the hemlock, because they were suspected of unorthodox views concerning the gods. Even the more liberal Greeks confined their tolerance to their own narrow circle. [10]

The Macedonian rulers of Egypt, however, were broad minded, and as long as heretics and infidels lived within the law and paid their taxes, they were left unmolested in their preachments or practices. The obstacles which the Jewish advocates of monotheism and morality encountered were not material but mental. The Alexandrian Jews found it an almost insurmountable difficulty to convey to their Gentile neighbors the idea of an only One, invisible yet Invincible God, as there is no term either in the Greek or in the Latin that would express it. "God" was a common noun, and to speak of God would mean no more than to speak of man, that is, one of many. Both languages lacked even the word for conscience—the Latin *conscientia* originally referred to an "awareness or cognizance of anything whatever."[11]

The difficulty of converting the Greeks is well illustrated in the experience of Paul and Barnabas. When the Lycaonians saw them heal the cripple, instead of accepting the miracle as proof that their teachings are of God, they exclaimed: "The gods are come down to us in the likeness of men." They called Barnabas Jupiter and Paul Mercury, and were preparing to offer sacrifices unto them. To Sergius Paulus, of Cyprus, Paul's thaumaturgy was a sign that Paul was either a god or merely a performer of sleight-of-hand. It was the same with Cornelius, the centurion at Caesarea. [12]

Yet this did not deter the Jews from preaching their religion to the Gentiles. The consciousness of their mission "to say to the prisoners, go forth," urged them on regardless of the consequences. They would stop people and engage them in religious conversation. They would reason with them about the Unity of God. They would point from nature to nature's God, from the visible world to the invisible. Aristeas informs us that "Jews eagerly sought intercourse with other nations, and they paid special care to this, and emulated each other therein." Hecateus tells of a Jewish cavalryman, named Mossolam, who was "admitted by all to be the most skillful archer that was either among the Greeks or the barbarians." When he heard an augur command the soldiers to halt because a bird suddenly stopped in its flight, he drew his bow and killed it, exclaiming: "How can you believe that the bird could give us information about our march when he could not foresee how to save himself? Had he been able to know what will happen he would not have come to this place to be killed by Mossolam the Jew!" [13]

On the other hand, the wisdom-loving Greeks looked upon the Judeans as a nation of thinkers. According to Clearchus, the disciple of Aristotle, his master believed that "Jews are derived from Indian philosophers; they are called by the Indians Calami, and by the Syrians Judaei, and took their name from the country they inhabit, which is called Judea, but for the name of their city it is a very awkward one, for they call it Jerusalem." Clement of Alexandria quotes Megathenes the historian (c. 300 B.C.E.) to the effect that "all matters of natural science spoken of among the ancients are also taught by the philosophers outside of Greece, namely among the Hindoos by the Brahmins, and in Syria by those called Jews." The Talmud states that "whenever the children of Jerusalem went to the lands outside of Palestine, the natives would seat them upon thrones and flock around them to hear their wisdom." It also narrates many clever repartees wherein the Jerusalemites worsted "the wise men of Athens." Allowing for exaggerations, the fame of the wisdom of the Judeans was nonetheless great among the Greeks, and their views were eagerly sought by their sages. Aristotle himself did not disdain listening to a Jew whom he met on his travels in Asia and who is described by his disciples as one "who had converse with learned men." "He conversed with us," says Clearchus, "and with other philosophical persons, and made a trial of our skill in philosophy; and as he had lived with many learned men, he communicated to us more information than he received from us." [14]

Besides the propaganda by word of mouth, the Jews early resorted to writing books in the Greek tongue and though primarily intended for Jews themselves, they served also to acquaint the pagan Greeks with Jewish traditions and ideals. Fragments are extant of the work of Demetrius, who chronicled the leading events in Jewish history down to his time. Eupolemus, possibly he whom Judas Maccabeus sent on a mission to Rome, wrote a history of the kings of Judea in which he inserted many details for the greater glory of his people. He tells, for instance, that Moses originated the art of writing among the Jews, from whom it passed on to the Phoenicians and through them to the Greeks. Solomon was assisted in the building of the Temple by Vaphres, king of Egypt, who sent him eighty thousand artisans and rejoiced "that so worthy a man enjoys the favor of so mighty a God." Artapanos went farther still in his glorification of Jews and Judaism. He made Moses the teacher of Orpheus, the inventor of the hieroglyphics, the Hermes Trismegistus, or messenger and herald of the gods who founded the Egyptian religion. Theodotus composed an epic poem on Shechem, in which he claimed that the sacred city of the Samaritans was built by Sicimos, a son of the god Hermes, and another poet painted with glowing colors the unsurpassed beauty of Jerusalem. Miracle and moral plays dramatized the story of the Exodus.[15]

These writings exalting the Jews were supplemented with books on the doctrines and practices of Judaism, explaining them in a way consonant with Greek ideology. Aristobulus of Paneas wrote a treatise on the laws of Moses which he dedicated to his royal pupil Philomater. Some time during the reign of Ptolemy VII, the grandson of Joshua b. Sira translated his grandfather's classic Sefer Ben Sira (*Ecclesiasticus*) into Greek so that "those who are desirous to learn may fashion their manners beforehand and know how to live according to the Torah." An anonymous writer put into the mouth of the poet Phocylides doctrines which are almost in verbal agreement with passages of the Bible. This didactic poem, by the way, served until the Reformation as the most popular manual for instruction in the epic style. [16]

In these and other writings, great stress was laid on Judaism as a religion based on pure reason, and in harmony with the teachings of the great sages of the Greeks themselves. Even the dietary laws of Judaism, Aristeas assures his readers, have a profound reason for their observance:

> The winged creatures of which we may partake, such as doves, geese and the like, are tame and distinguished by cleanly habits, using wheat and pulse for their sustenance. On the other hand, those that are forbidden to us are wild and carnivorous, and use their power to oppress the remainder of their kind. Hence the Lawgiver signified that those for whom the laws are ordained must be outwardly righteous and oppress none through confidence in their strength, but must direct their lives by righteous motives.

So also the parting of the hoofs, and the chewing of the cud,

> ... symbolize discrimination in directing every action to a good end; for the strength of the whole body, in order to display itself in action, is dependent on the arms and legs. Again, the chewing of the cud to thoughtful minds clearly indicates memory; for it is nothing else but a calling to mind of one's life and experience.

Judaism was thus depicted as an emanation of God-directed reason, so dear to the Greeks, a sacred philosophy. Its aim is to implant in the human heart the supreme virtues of temperance and forbearance, justice and fortitude, advocated by Zeno and his Stoic disciples. "Our philosophy teaches us temperance," says the author of the Fourth Maccabees, "so that we master our pleasures and desires, and it exercises us in fortitude so that we willingly undergo every toil, and it instructs us in justice, so that in all our behavior we give what is due; and it teaches us to be pious, so that we worship the only living God in a manner becoming His greatness." [17]

One of the finest productions of Graeco-Judean literature is the Wisdom of Solomon. Here we see a direct attempt at propaganda. The author dwells on the universalism of Judaism, makes no mention of the sacrifices, and refers only once to the Temple. But in contrast with the sweet reasonableness of the religion of Israel, he points to the absurdity of paganism. Like another Isaiah, he hurls the shafts of his sarcasm at the believer in idols:

> When he maketh his prayer concerning goods
> and his marriage and children,
> When he is not ashamed to speak to that
> which hath no life;
> Yea, for health he calleth upon that which
> is weak,

And for life he beseecheth that which is
dead,
And for aid he supplicateth that which
hath least experience,
And for a good journey that which cannot
so much as move a step,
And for gaining and getting and good
success of his hand
He asketh ability of that which with his
hands is most unable...
And about to journey over raging waves
Calleth upon a piece of wood more rotten
than the vessel that carrieth him.

The trouble with the Greeks, the author maintains, is their
reliance upon human reason. They forget that the profane
wisdom of the philosophers is likely to be fallible.

For a corruptible body weigheth down the soul,
And the earthly frame lieth heavy on a
mind that museth upon many things.
And hardly do we divine the things that
are on earth.
And the things that are close at hand we find
with labor.

He accounts for the idolatry of the Greeks by their love
of works of art. A king, he says, who lost a beloved son
sought to soothe his grief by having an artist reproduce his
likeness in stone or wood, and

The multitude allured by reason of the grace of
his handiwork,
Now accounted as an object of devotion him that
a little before was honored as a man.

But the evil, once started, did not stop with the worship of
statues. It led to the worship of human beings, the corrup-

tion of morals, and even the slaughtering of children in
solemn rites:

> Blood and murder, theft and deceit,
> Corruption, faithlessness, tumult, perjury,
>   turmoil,
> Ingratitude for benefits received,
> Defiling of souls, confusion of sex,
> Disorder in marriage, adultery and wantonness.
> For the worship of those unmentionable idols,
> Is a beginning and cause and end of every evil.

How different in every way is the divine wisdom which
inspired the teachings of Israel. It is motivated by a "spirit
that loveth man." Its God is one who is

> Quick of understanding, holy, alone in kind,
>   manifold, . . .
> Loving what is good, keen, unhindered,
> Beneficent, loving toward man,
> Steadfast, sure, free from care, all-powerful,
>   all-surveying,
> And penetrating through all spirits
> That are quick of understanding, pure, most
>   subtle.

This God abhors nothing that He has made. He waits
for all to return unto Him, but never clears the guilty, as is
proven by the downfall of Egypt and Canaan, and the destruction of Sodom and Gomorrah:

> To those wickedness a smoking waste still
>   witnesseth,
> And plants bearing fair fruit that cometh not to
>   ripeness.
> And a disbelieving soul hath a memorial in a
>   pillar of salt still standing.

Solomon, or the author, therefore appeals to the kings of
the earth to turn from human wisdom and man-made beauty

to the Source of all wisdom and all beauty, Who "guarded
to the end the first holy father of the world," and Who exacts
of His children,

> Soberness and understanding, righteousness and
> courage,
> Than which there is nothing for man in life more
> profitable. [18]

The boldest and most direct step taken by the Egyptian
Jews in their desire to reach the mind and heart of the heathen
was when they put under contribution the most venerated
and dreaded of pagan prophetesses, the frenzied Sibyl, who,
it was universally believed, uttered her oracles long before
the Trojan war, and inspired Homer by her vaticinations.
According to the Alexandrian Jews, the true Sibyl was a
Jewess or a convert to Judaism. Some asserted that she was
the daughter-in-law of Noah, others that she was the daughter
of Berosus, Chaldean historiographer and priest of Bel, who
later saw the light. At all events, she was not "the shameless
one of Erythrea," or the offshoot of Circe and Gnostos, who
was distraught and deceived others. The original, Jewish
Sibyl was a prophetess of "the High God," "sent in frenzy as
a fire into Hellas, foretelling to all mortals the manifold
wrath of God." She would fain have refrained from prophecy-
ing. She constantly prayed "the Heavenly blessed One" to
give her a respite from her task. But her spirit would be
smitten as with a scourge, and against her will a voice from
within her would proclaim the things at which God is indignant. [19]

True to Jewish traditions, the Sibyl announces that at
first all mankind was monotheistic. The polytheism of the
Greeks was due to a deceitful old author (Homer), false to
his country as well as to his God, who unrolled and plag-
iarized her books, and wrote "all manner of lies for empty-
headed mortals" in her style and meter. Now she is come
again to reclaim them to their own. She would have them

imitate the example of that people which retained the pristine purity of ethical monotheism:

> There is a city, Chaldean Ur,
> Whence come the race of most upright men,
> Who are ever right-minded and their works
> good.
> They are neither concerned for the sun's course,
> Nor the moon's, nor for monstrosities on earth,
> Nor for satisfaction from ocean's depths,
> Nor for signs of sneezing and the augury from
> birds;
> Nor for soothsaying, nor sorcery, nor incantations;
> Nor for deceitful follies of ventriloquists.
> They do not, Chaldean fashion, astrologize,
> Nor watch the stars....
> But they are concerned about rightness and virtue.
> Their measures are just both in field and in city.
> They do not steal from each other by night,
> Nor drive off herds of oxen and sheep and goats.
> Nor does neighbor remove his neighbor's landmarks.
> Nor does the wealthy man vex the poor one,
> Nor oppress widows, but such rather assists them,
> Providing them always with grain, wine, and oil;
> Always a blessing to those in want among them
> He gives back part of his harvest to the needy
> people,
> For 'The Heavenly' made the earth common to
> all.[20]

To obviate the danger of anthropomorphism, the Sibyl always refers not to God Himself but to God's attributes. He is "The Heavenly," the "Great," the "True," the "Highest," the "Unborn or Self-born," the "Invisible," "Imperishable," "Indestructible," "Fore-Father," "All-Ruler," "Ineffable," "Guardian-of-all-Things," "Who Himself alone seeth all

things," "Who is and was and ever will be." As his mouth-
piece, she cries:

> Why, mortals, do ye wander? Stop, heedless
>   ones,
> And leave the darkness of night.
>   Accept the light....
> Come, do not forever seek darkness and
>   the netherworld.
> See how cheering are the beams of the sun.
> Place wisdom in your hearts, and know
> There is One God Who sends rain, winds
>   and earthquakes,
> Lightnings, famines, plagues, and bitter
>   sorrow,
> Snow-storms and hail. Shall I say it in one
>   word?
> He guides heaven and governs earth. He is
>   *The* Ruler. [21]

But merely to believe in Him is not enough. Hellas and
the other nations must reform, must "wash from head to
foot," to obtain favor in the sight of Him Who inhabiteth
the skies. Otherwise His judgment is sure to come, and the
world will be consumed by a conflagration, and the earth
will cover all "in the dark spaces of Tartarus and the Sty-
gian recesses of Gehenna," where they will be made to pass
through a flaming river of unquenchable fire; she therefore
implores:

> Flee lawless robbery, serve the living God,
> Keep yourselves from adultery and unnatural lust.
> Nurture your own children: do not murder
>   them;
> For the Immortal is angry at whoever sins
>   thus. [22]

While in her eschatology the Sibyl is more heathenish
than Hebraic, she is Isaiahnic in her presentation of the

golden age which will dawn in the last days. "The city which God loved will shine more bright than the sun, moon and stars." There will be "no adultery, no lawless lust for boys, no murder nor noise of war, no contentions save in righteousness." Isis will be left to perish, wretched and solitary, by the Nile's water, while the Jews will be revered as "the guides of life to all mankind, and the bearers of great joy to all mortals." [23]

Even more far-reaching in its effect on the pagans was the translation of the Bible into the Greek. Strangely enough the one who was instrumental in its production was himself an ardent Hellenist, Ptolemy Philadelphus (285-47 B.C.E.).

The story goes that at the suggestion of Demetrius of Phalerum, chief of the famous library of Alexandria, Philadelphus sent an embassy to Jerusalem with rich gifts and a letter to the High Priest requesting a scroll of the Pentateuch and a number of scholars able to translate it into Greek. After the envoys were instructed by the High Priest in the Torah, they returned with an artistic copy of it executed in letters of gold. With them went seventy-two scholars, six for each tribe of Israel, all masters of Hebrew and Greek. They were accorded a royal welcome. A banquet, which lasted seven days, was graced by the presence of the king and enlivened by his searching questions pertaining to Judaism. They were then put up in a palace containing seventy-two compartments, on the Island of Pharos, opposite Alexandria, where, without any consultation among themselves, they labored at their task for seventy-two sessions. When the various translations were examined, they were found to be exactly alike in every respect, and the king was convinced that the translation was correct.

Little did the king dream that he had thus himself dealt a staggering blow to paganism. It was through the medium of this translation, the *Septuagint* as it came to be known, that many Jews, who had drifted into the worship of idols, were reclaimed to the Jewish fold; and it was especially through it that Judaism, or at least its ethical content, ultimately became the possession of a very important part of mankind. In the words of Professor Graetz:

> The Greek translation was the first apostle Judaism sent forth to the heathen world to heal it of its perversity and godlessness. Through its means the two opposing systems—the Judean and the Greek—were drawn nearer together. Owing to their subsequent circulation through the world by means of the second apostle, Christianity, the tenets of Judaism were fused into the thought and language of various nations, and at present there is no civilized language which has not, by means of this Greek translation, taken words and ideas from Judean literature. Thus Judaism was introduced into the literature of the world and its doctrines were popularized. [24]

But while the pagan Philadelphus thus unlocked the doors of their "unknown sanctuary" to the heathen, the Jews themselves exposed it to the danger of desecration by idols. The pagan mind, lacking the monotheistic sensitiveness of the Hebrews, sought and found in the *Septuagint* authority and justification for theories which were alien to Judaism in its purity. The result was the synthesis of Judaism and paganism which fashioned the theology of Christianity and the prejudice and hatred which followed upon the heels of that theology. As some rabbis put it, a thick fog began to spread over Judea while the translation was being made, and "the day when it was completed was as hard for Israel as the day of the Golden Calf." At this period, however, the Jews hailed it as another, a spiritual sanctuary out of which would radiate a knowledge of the God of Israel in the land of Egypt, and, like the Babylonian Aramaic, the very language of the Greeks assumed a quasi-sacred character because of its association with the Bible. Even in Palestine, Rabban Simon b. Gamaliel saw in the *Septuagint* the fulfillment of Noah's blessing:

> God enlarge Japhet (Greece)
> And he shall dwell in the tents of Shem.

In Egypt the Septuagint was exalted almost to the rank of
the original. The translators were declared to have been inspired, and a curse was pronounced on anyone who would
alter anything in its text. The day on which the first copy was
presented to the king was celebrated for many years as a
holiday, upon which Jews would invite their heathen friends,
repair to the Island of Pharos, and there hold a feast and offer
prayers of praise and thanksgiving.[25]

That those who participated in the Greek translation had
an eye also to the propagation of Judaism among the Gentiles
is indicated by the variations and interpolations which they
introduced into the version. The Talmud enumerates thirteen
modifications intended either to guard against anthropomorphism or for the glory or safety of Israel. Thus, instead of
translating "In the beginning God created," the *Septuagint*
had it "God created in the beginning," for fear lest "beginning" become identified with Chronos. Where the Hebrew
has "Let *us* make man in *Our* image, after *Our* likeness,"
the *Septuagint* took care to render it: "I will make man in
an image and likeness." Instead of Moses seeing God face
to face, he is said to have beheld the place of His abode;
instead of God's speaking to Moses, He appears to him in a
vision. To the verse "When thou seest the sun and the moon
and the stars ... which the Lord thy God hath allotted unto
all the peoples under the whole heavens," they added "to
lighten unto them." In the list of names of unclean animals,
they omitted to mention the hare because, the rabbis surmise, it might have given offense to Ptolemy who called his
wife Hare. [26]

It was not long before Egyptian Jewry became a center
of lively missionary activity. In their synagogues, eloquent
preachers sought to harmonize Hellenism with Judaism, and
to prove that the finest teachings of the Greek philosophers
and moralists are surpassed by the teachings of the Torah.
As some of the Greek thinkers explained the myths of heathenism as similitudes of nature, so did they interpret the biblical stories as allegories, "manifest symbols of things invisible,
and hints of things inexpressible." Abraham, for example, was

made to represent virtuous thoughts; Sarah, virtuous deeds; Jacob's ladder signified divine Providence, and the ceremonial laws were project lessons in mercy and justice. In the Bible, they claimed, was to be found more wisdom and knowledge than the Greek philosophers had attained by the instrumentality of their reason. [27]

The most illustrious of this group of Jews was Philo Judaeus (c. 20 B.C.E.-40 C.E.). A scion of a noble family, saturated with the literature of the Greeks, he never ceased to feast, as he tells us, "with the truly blessed Mind which is the object of all desire, communing continually in joy with the Divine Word and Doctrine." He loved Plato, "the philosopher of truth," but he loved Judaism still more, and devoted all his life to bring the truth of Judaism to both disaffected Jews and truth-seeking pagans. Like Hillel, he loved all mankind; and like Hillel, he was the finest type of Jewish missionary. His heart went out to all who were in physical or spiritual bondage. He devoted a special discourse to the slaves, and comforted them with the assurance that even in their abject state they could still be freemen if they retained their moral stamina. But his greatest concern was for those who were in bondage of the soul and whom, as an older brother, he felt it his duty to "turn to goodness." "Kinship and greatness," he would say, "are not measured by blood when truth is the judge, but by likeness of conduct, and the pursuit of the same objects." Cain, Ham, and Esau were of noble birth, yet God rejected them because they failed to pass the test of goodness. Abraham was of a family of idolaters, but God accorded him the patent of nobility. Like Ezekiel, Philo stressed individual responsibility. "I know not," says he, "if there could be a more pernicious doctrine than this; that there is no punishment for the wicked offspring of good parents, and no reward for the good offspring of evil parents. The Torah judges each man upon his own merit, and does not assign praise or blame according to the virtues of the forefathers." [28]

In the laws of Moses, Philo finds reflections of his inner virtues. They are superior to all laws, because Moses was superior to all men. They are, as it were, stamped "with the seal of nature herself." He teaches that God loves with a special tenderness the man who turns from idolatry to the true faith, and includes him "in the class of the weak and humble together with the widow and the orphan."

Philo proceeds to explain the elementary teachings of Judaism which "can surely never be looked upon by us in any other light than as objects of all admiration, and beyond all powers of description in respect to their excellence." He does not, however, insist that one must be integrated in the Jewish people in order to reap the benefits of their religion. Israel means "the man who sees God." Anyone, or any nation, who attains the beatific vision and lives in accordance with the humane laws of Judaism, is as much an Israelite as one who is of "the seed of Abraham," and is one of those whom Moses had in mind when he said: "Ye are the sons of the Lord God." Moses' object was not to make all mankind Jews, but to ennoble them and to make them happy by making them virtuous:

> This is the supreme aim of the inspired Prophet throughout his legislation, to ensure concord and good understanding and the harmony of different characters, so that families and entire nations and countries, and indeed the whole race of mankind, might advance to perfect happiness. Up to the present time, indeed, this is only a hope, but that it will come to pass I am firmly convinced, and facts show irrefutably that God increases the harvest of virtue year by year. [29]

The translation of the Bible, the numerous Apocrypha and Pseudepigrapha, the vehement eloquence of the Sibyls, and the learned discourses of the Philonians had their effect. Many of the Greeks began to tire of the contradictions of the philosophers, each of whom claimed to speak in the name of pure reason. They were anxiously looking for some authority which would resolve their doubts. Some became satiated with self-indulgence and yearned for a life of simplicity and temperance. Asceticism began to spread and sects like the Therapeutae and Essenes came into favor. The books of the Jews, written in popular Greek, found their way into the homes of the populace as well as of the philosophers. The synagogues, wherein the services were recited in Greek and the Torah was translated and interpreted as a synthesis of Hellenism and Judaism, came to be known, as Philo tells us, as schools where were taught "temperance, bravery, prudence, justice, piety, holiness and, in short, all the virtues by which things human and divine are well ordered." Crowds who eagerly listened to the harangues of sophists and who would drop in on a Sabbath, perhaps to scoff or contradict, not infrequently went home disarmed and penitent.

The result was a steady stream of converts to Judaism, either as proselytes of righteousness, as "fearers of the Lord," or merely as practicing some Jewish ceremonials without comprehending their significance. In many Greek-speaking provinces in Asia Minor whole communities adopted Jewish observances though not always abandoning their pagan worship. In Phrygia, the Porphyrabaphsi introduced the feasts of Passover and Pentecost among their holidays, and the Hypsistarians accepted the belief in a Most High and Almighty Being, kept the Sabbath, and observed some dietary laws. So did the Euchomenoi and the Euphemitai (God worshipers). There were numerous pagan Sabbatarians in Cilicia, and the pagan High Priestess Julia Severa of Alemonia became a benefactress of the synagogue. While the Cyrene women would eat pork but no cow's flesh, out of reverence for Hat-Hor, the Egyptian divinity, the Barca women would eat no pork because it is tabooed by the Jews. In Cyprus, proselytes became sufficiently numerous in the first century B.C.E. to render valuable assistance to Ptolemy Lathyrus in his war against his mother, Cleopatra. According to Philo, who must have had some authority for his statement,

> Not only the Jews but all the other peoples who care for righteousness adopt them (the Jewish laws) ... The Jewish Law attracts and links together all peoples, barbarians and Greeks, those who live on

the mainland, and those who live on the Islands. . . .
And it both came to pass that Egypt and Cyrene, as
having the same government, and a great number of
other nations imitate their way of living, and maintain great bodies of these Jews in a peculiar manner,
and grow up to great prosperity with them, and make
use of the same laws with that nation.

Philo also tells us that those who were converted "changed
not only their faith but their mode of living, becoming conspicuous for their moderation, gentleness, and humaneness,"
and concludes that if all men would follow their example
"the age of universal peace will come about, and the Kingdom
of God on earth will be established." [30]

The Egyptian Jews, however, had to pay a price for the
success of their propaganda. Their conversionist activity, added
to their economic prosperity, aroused the dormant hatred of
the Greeks, whose animosity increased with the advent of
the Romans who, in appreciation of the assistance of the Jews
in the conquest of Egypt, confirmed them in their ancient
privileges and deprived the unfriendly Greeks of some of
their rights. The Stoics, in particular, whose sect or school
was nearest to Judaism both in its ethics and in the method
it employed to gain adherents, saw in Judaism a dangerous
rival; and, being as a rule more educated than the rest, they
were also more articulate. Manetho, one of the early Graeco-
Egyptian historians, was given credit for the statement that
the Jews were the offspring of Egyptian outcasts, and that
Moses, or Osarsiph, forbade them "to have any dealings with
anyone whatsoever except their confederates." Other Stoic
contemporaries of Philo maintained that Jews offer human
sacrifices to the head of an ass which they worship as a deity,
that they are the most credulous and at the same time the
most atheistic of people and haters of the human race. [31]
At last the Romans did to the Jewish new Jerusalem what
they had done to their old Jerusalem. The Temple of Onias,
like its predecessor the Temple of Yaho, was closed, and
the Jews of Egypt ceased to be articulate. Some, like Ti-

berius Alexander, nephew of Philo, even adopted paganism. Others, ignorant of the original Hebrews and deriving their knowledge of Judaism from the Jewish Sibyl and the Philonic allegorists, became, like Stephan "the martyr" and Apollos of Alexandria, ardent Christians. Among the earliest to organize themselves into a Christian sect were Jews, or converted Jews, from Cyprus and Cyrene. Yet the work of the Egyptian Jews was by no means a failure. It did not bring over the world to pure Judaism, but it helped undermine the grosser form of paganism and introduced Hebraic ideas into the culture of the most civilized nations, and thus "conditioned" them for the ultimate establishment of the Kingdom of God. [32]

CHAPTER XII

THE CONQUERED GIVE LAWS
TO THE CONQUERORS

JEWISH missionary activity among the Romans was almost coincident with the first visit of the Jews to Rome. Already in 139 B.C. their efforts attracted the attention of the government and the Praetor for Foreigners "sent to their homes those who by a pretended worship of Sabazian Jove (Jehovah *Zbaoth*?) endeavored to corrupt Roman customs." Those, however, who followed and formed the nucleus of the Jewish settlement in the Eternal City, continued to spread ethical monotheism in their adopted land. St. Paul, who was himself by no means averse to resort to all means in order to win souls to Christianity, depicts his former coreligionists who "creep into houses, and lead captive silly women laden with sins, led away with diverse lusts, ever learning and never able to come to the knowledge of truth." Pliny the Elder describes the Jews as *Gens contumelia numinum insignis,* "a race notorious for its insults to the gods." Horace jocosely threatens his patron: that if he refuses to comply with his request, "a tremendous band of poets shall come to my aid ... and like the Jews, we will compel thee to give in to our crowd." From all sides complaints were heard: "These men being Jews, do exceedingly trouble our city, and teach customs which are not lawful for us to receive, neither to observe, being Romans." [1]

Through these ardent missionaries Judaism filtered into all strata of Roman society, from the lowliest to the loftiest. We must not forget that despite the intense prejudice fostered by the Senecas and Ciceros, the Apions and the Tacituses, there was hardly a time when Jews could not have said, "Some of my best friends are Romans." Herod Agrippa, the grandson of Herod the Great, was the favorite of Tiberius, the companion of Caligula, the confidant of Claudius. It was perhaps through his influence that Asinius Pollio, with whom he and his brother stayed while in Rome, evinced an inclination to monotheism, and that Augustus moderated the brutal public games so revolting to Jewish humanitarianism. It was also probably because of the expressed views of Apollonius, who after the death of Caesar completed the organization of the Roman public library, that Horace addressed to him his almost Jewishly Messianic Fourth Eclogue. Asinius' son, Gallus, too, was a well known opponent of the reactionaries in the reign of Tiberius. Antonia, daughter of Marc Anthony, sister of Augustus and sister-in-law of Tiberius, and celebrated for her beauty, virtue, and chastity had as her most intimate friend a Jewess, and as her business agent the brother of Philo Judaeus. Nero, as we have seen, was very fond of the Jewish actor Alityrus, and Livia his wife had a Jewess as her most trusted companion. Caracalla is said to have had a Jewish lad as his playmate. Quintus, the brother of Cicero, who succeeded Flaccus to the governorship of Syria, did not conceal his sympathy for Jews and his predilection for monotheism. The Roman proconsul of Caesarea was so impressed with the saintliness of R. Hanina bar Hama and R. Joshua b. Levi that he immediately arose in their presence and paid them homage. [2]

The most frequent contacts between Jews and Romans, however, were made among the lower classes. Especially was this the case after the *Hurban* (Destruction of the Temple) which brought into Rome and its provinces an influx of voluntary and involuntary Jewish immigrants. It was not only those who were learned and Romanized, like R. Reuben b. Strobilus and his son Eutolemus, who propagated among the masses the ideals of Judaism. Every Jew constituted himself a self-appointed missionary. Renan's description of the Jewish proselytizing activity is not without foundation. The destitute Jew, he tells us:

> when begging, found the opportunity, in a trembling voice, to whisper into the ear of the grand Roman dame a few sentences of the Torah, and often gained over the matron who had given him a handful of small change. The captives carried with them their sacred books, and read them to their fellow-slaves. The prisoners would recite aloud from memory what they remembered of their Torah, as did the future martyr R. Akiba and, as a mere lad, R. Ishmael B. Elisha. [3]

But even without active propaganda some Romans were attracted to Judaism by sheer curiosity. There was something about the denizens of the quarters adjacent to the Trastevere which, while it impressed some as barbarous or ridiculous, inspired others with fear, respect, and sometimes admiration. These lowly dwellers of the slums, belonging to a people that had been subjugated, did not act as if they had been conquered. Their Ghetto, despite its poverty and misery, was a happy little world, almost a Utopia, in comparison with the sections inhabited by the Roman poor. The slave in the ghetto received nothing but sympathy. Huge sums were spent for his redemption if he were a Jew, and, if a pagan, he was admitted into the community and treated as an equal the moment he embraced Judaism, and his master gave him his freedom. His former condition of servitude did not taint his blood; and if he was learned or pious, he would be called rabbi and revered as a saint. They were also struck by some of the traits which seemed to characterize the Jews. Instead of exposing their infants to test their power of endurance, and letting the sick and the aged perish because they could no more defend the state, these were given the utmost consideration. Charity, or *Gemilat hasadim* (deeds of kindness) which among the Romans was hardly known, was among the Jews preached and practiced as the noblest virtue. Among the Romans, education of the masses was unthought of, the religious mysteries were exclusively in the province of the priesthood, and the gods themselves were believed to have no use for the slave and artisan; among the Jews it was held that "he who eateth of the toil of his hands it shall be well with him in this world and in the world to come"; that "God is near to all who call upon him in truth"; that it was everyone's sacred duty to meditate on the Torah day and night, and have his children taught diligently therein. [4]

Another thing noticed by the Roman observer was that these people, despite their unaccountable taboos and superstitions, possessed many virtues which the heathen lacked— even those who proclaimed themselves Stoics. They were seldom, if ever, guilty of illicit relations with women, no matter how attractive they happened to be and how easily their favor could be obtained. The conduct of Joseph in Egypt was characteristic of many a Hebrew slave in Rome. There is the story about R. Zadok who, in the prime of his life, was sold as a slave into a patrician house. The matron, desiring to breed handsome slaves, locked him up in a room with one of her most beautiful maid-servants. But R. Zadok sat up all night studying the Torah, without turning once to look at his female companion. Next day the maid complained to her mistress of his "ungentlemanly" behavior. When taken to account, R. Zadok retorted that though he was now a Roman slave, he was still a Jew, and it was against his convictions to "multiply bastards in Israel." [5]

A trait which led some pagans to modify their judgments concerning Jews and Judaism was the probity of the Jews. They were especially careful in their dealing with the Gentiles, since any unethical behavior toward the latter would involve not only a breach of the moral law but also the heinous crime of *Hillul Hashem* (profaning the Name of God), for which, as they were taught, neither repentance, nor prayer, nor penance, but death alone can atone. The effect of their scrupulous honesty is related in various anecdotes.

A certain *hasid,* or one noted for his piety, once found a box full of denarii. He returned it to the owner, who happened to be a matron of rank. Since the box was encrusted with gold, she was sure he was aware of its valuable contents, so when she took it she remarked: "I hope thou art the only one of thy nation, for if there be but one other like thee we (Gentiles) would be doomed (by God) to die." The *hasid* thereafter became one of the privileged frequenters of her palace.

Abba Hoshaya was a wool-washer and struggled hard for a livelihood. Once he found some gems which belonged to a Roman princess and hastened to return them; but the princess, out of the goodness of her heart, refused to accept them, saying that since they were unclaimed they were his. Abba Hoshaya, however, would have none of it and insisted that according to the Torah a lost article must be restored. Whereupon the princess exclaimed: "Praised be the God of the Jews." It was this act of *Kiddush Hashem* (sanctification of the Name of God) that preserved Abba Hoshaya's name in the Talmud and earned for him a eulogy based on the text (which the Rabbis interpreted as referring to the love of God):

> (Many waters cannot quench love,
> Neither can the floods drown it;)
> If a man would give all the substance of his house
> for love
> It would utterly be condemned. [6]

The story of R. Johanan is of a different sort but with the same moral. The rabbi was wont to visit the daughter of a Roman official to be relieved of a tooth-ache. As he was loath to violate the Sabbath, she gave him the recipe so that in case of emergency he might concoct the medicine at home, on his promise that he would reveal the secret to no one. R. Johanan did not keep his promise, because, as he explained, the withholding of any information which might benefit the rest of the population is worse than the violation of a promise. On hearing this, the lady exclaimed: "A religion which teaches such concern for the public weal is worthy to adopt as one's own," and she became converted to Judaism. [7]

The Jewish tenacity in their "superstition" also deeply impressed the Romans. The legions which were stationed in

Palestine saw them pull down the golden eagle which their own king, Herod, had set up over the great gate of the Temple. They observed that when Pontius Pilate ordered them to bow to Caesar's effigies they laid their necks bare, and were resolved to "take death very willingly rather than that the wisdom of their laws should be transgressed," and that on other occasions, to quote Josephus, they were ready to endure "racks and deaths of all kinds without a murmur, yet could they not be dissuaded from acting but as they thought best; and when they were stripped and had torments inflicted upon them, and brought to the most terrible kinds of death, they met these after an extraordinary manner, beyond all other people, and would not renounce the religion of their forefathers." Such martyrdom was beyond the grasp of pagan psychology. Horace and other poets sang *Dulce et decorum est pro patria mori*. ("It is sweet and seemly to die for the fatherland"). They knew what it was to die *Rei publicae causa,* but not *religionis causa.* Especially could they not understand how a people could remain loyal to a god who by his treatment of them repeatedly demonstrated that he was either impotent or hated them. Cicero gave expression to what many of his countrymen must have thought when he ridiculed the Jews' claim to God's special favor by pointing out that they are conquered, scattered, and enslaved. [8]

But while there were those to whom this inexplicable stubbornness of the Jews was proof of their perversity, there were others who, like Hecateus, felt that "such men deserve to be admired on that account." The very catastrophe which led some to the conclusion that the God of Israel is impotent, caused others to see in it the dire consequences of provoking Him. There are many facts to substantiate this statement. The Rabbis report that there were (Roman) soldiers guarding the (Temple) gates in Jerusalem who took ritual baths (on Passover eve) so that they might partake of the Paschal sacrifice in the evening. These Romans would not have been permitted to do it unless they had previously been won over to Judaism. On the other hand, Dion Cassius relates that during the siege of Jerusalem many Roman soldiers went over to the side of the heroic defenders of their State, and that they stood in such awe of the Temple that for a long time they would not enter its precinct. Under Tiberius, four thousand freedmen were condemned to be deported to Sardinia for being "infected with the Jewish superstition."[9]

A similar effect was produced by the sight of those who died "for the sanctification of the name." The blood of the martyrs was the seed of the Synagogue no less than of the Church. Among the many legends related to the *Asarah haruge malkut* (the ten who were murdered by the Government) under Hadrian, several relate that a number of those who acted as executioners, or watched the martyrdoms, themselves became martyrs to the Jewish religion. When R. Hananiah b. Tradyon was wrapped in a scroll of the Torah and placed on the pyre with wet wool on his chest to prolong his agony, the executioner said to him: "Rabbi, if I remove these woolen lumps from thy chest so that thou wilt die sooner, wilt thou vouchsafe to me a portion in the world to come?" Said he, "Yes." "Wilt thou swear to me?" He swore to him. As soon as he swore, the executioner removed the wet lumps, increased the fire, and threw himself into the flame. Whereupon was heard a *Bat Kol* (mystical echo): "R. Hananiah b. Tradyon and the executioner both are destined for life in the world to come." On hearing this, Rabbi Judah Hannasi wept and said: "There is one who earns the world to come in a moment, such as the executioner, and there is one who serves the Lord all the days of his life and forfeits his future reward in one moment, as did Johanan the High Priest, who served in the High Priesthood eighty years and toward the end became a Sadducee."

Concerning another of the Ten Martyrs, R. Huzpit the Interpreter, who was still surpassingly handsome when a hundred and thirty years of age, we are told:

> They came and pleaded with the Emperor to pity his age and respect his appearance. The Emperor asked him how old he was, and when he gave his age he said to him, 'What difference does it make to thee whether thou diest today or tomorrow?' Said he, 'Be-

cause I wish to perform two more Commandments:
To recite the *Shema* in the evening and the morning,
and to proclaim the Kingdom of the Only Name of
the Great and Awful One.' Said the Emperor: 'O thou
brazen-faced and stiff-necked! How long wilt thou
trust in thy God Who is unable to save thee from
my hand. Behold, my ancestors have destroyed His
Temple, and have thrown the carcasses of His worshippers round about Jerusalem. Surely, thy God
must have grown old by now, and can no longer
save thee. Were it otherwise He would have avenged
Himself and His people and His house, as He did of
Pharaoh, and Sisera, and all the kings of Canaan.'
Hearing this, R. Huzpit burst out in a bitter cry and
took hold of his raiments and tore them because
of the blasphemy of the Name of the Blessed One,
and he said to the Emperor: 'Woe to thee, Caesar!
What wilt thou do when on the last days the Name,
praised be He, will visit His wrath upon Rome and
upon thy gods?' Thereupon the Emperor exclaimed:
'I will argue with him no longer,' and ordered him
to be stoned and crucified. But the patricians and
philosophers, who took pity on the aged sage, prevailed on him and he allowed him to be buried.[10]

Indeed there were not a few in Rome itself who sympathized
with the unfortunate Jews and did what they could to lighten
their burdens. There is the story of the young Jewess whom
her owner emancipated when she heard from other captives
that her mother was once herself the mistress of five hundred
slaves. Of another captive we are told that the "Lord of
Dreams" appeared to her master who was about to maltreat
her and warned him to send her away, and when the poor
maiden was bitten by a snake when she stopped at a spring
to refresh herself, gave her a decent burial, saying to his wife:
"Thou beholdest (one of) the people with whom their Father
in Heaven is wroth." [11]
This pity and commiseration sometimes opened up hidden

springs of repentance, and resulted in Romans sacrificing their lives for the sake of Jews and Judaism. Thus, when Rabban Gamaliel II was condemned to die, there appeared a certain *hegemon* (officer) at the academy where he was teaching and called out: "The nosey one is sought! The nosey one is sought!" The Rabbi understood what it means (i.e., "the well-known person") and fled and hid himself. But the *hegemon* did not rest until he found him and, having made certain about his share in the world to come, jumped from the roof and died. He committed suicide, the Rabbis explained, because according to a Roman rule, if a messenger who announces a death sentence dies before the execution thereof, the sentence is voided. They also add that a *Bat Kol* was heard proclaiming: "This *hegemon* is assured of the life of the world to come!" [12]

The miserable end of many of the persecuting Roman Emperors also inclined some of the pagans to see in it "the hand of the God of the Jews." After Hadrian succumbed to a dire disease, it was a Roman matron "with whom all the patricians were proud to associate" who counseled R. Judah b. Shamua (or R. Eleazar) and his colleagues to appeal to the Roman governor. Accordingly, they assembled at night in front of his residence and in a loud voice they lamented: "O, Heaven! Are we not your brethren? Are we not the sons of the same father and the same mother (Isaac and Rebecca)? Wherein do we differ from all other nations and tongues that you issue such cruel edicts against us?" The heart-rending plea produced some effect. Many of the Hadrianic cruel measures were revoked, and the dead were permitted to be buried. The Rabbis declared the day a holiday and ordered a thanksgiving prayer to be recited in memory of the event. [13]

Even the oft-maligned and ridiculed Sabbath and holidays sometimes became factors in bringing some Romans under "the wings of the Shekinah." To many a heathen, as we have seen, this stubborn observance of a day of rest was proof of the incorrigible laziness of the Jews. The Rabbis, who frequently attribute to former generations the events current in their own times, put into the mouth of Haman the accusation that Jews seek to evade their duties by constantly protesting *Sh'hi, P'hi* ("today is Sabbath," "today is Passover"). But there were also Romans who found that these peculiar people were usually rather industrious and diligent. Upon these Romans, observance of the Sabbath produced a strange effect. The refusal of the poor artisans to ply their trades, and even of the starving beggars to accept a dole, or to receive the corn distributed by the Government, and of the slave to obey his master despite the punishment that awaited him, could not but challenge their attention and fill them with awe. They could not classify the Sabbath either as *Fastus* or as *Nefastus*. Some, therefore, came to regard it either as a lucky or unlucky day, and would even repair to the synagogue to assure the one or avert the other. Ovid humorously pleads with his young friend to start his courting on the day "which the Syrian from Palestine celebrates," as the day is most auspicious, yet not to permit the sanctity of the day to interfere with his other plans, and on general principles he warns him not to pass the place "where the Syrian Jew performs his rites every seventh day." Horace, in one of his Satires, describes a conversation between him and his friend Fuscus Aristius. "Did you not say you had something you wanted to speak to me about in private?" asked the poet as a preliminary to a pleasant chat. "I certainly did," answers Fuscus, "but I will speak to you at a more suitable time. Today's the thirtieth (?) Sabbath. Would you dare offend the circumcised Jews?" "I can't say I have any scruples on that score," answers Horace. "But I do," replies Fuscus. "I am weaker than you; just one of the many. You must pardon me. I'll talk the matter over with you some other time." Persius more seriously pokes fun at those of his countrymen who seem to be affected by the sight of the lighted candles, the flowers, and the stuffed fish with which the Jews celebrate "Herod's Day":

> When every room is decked in meet array,
> And lamps along the greasy windows spread,
> Profuse flowers, gross, oily vapors shed;

> When the vast tunny's tail in pickle swims
> And the crude must foams o'er the pitcher's brims;
> You mutter secret prayers, by fear devised,
> And dread the Sabbath of the circumcised.[14]

The widespread belief that Jews were adepts in the black
arts prompted many Romans to seek out Jews in order to
learn what the future held in store for them, whether concerning the constancy of a paramour or the stability of the
Empire. Juvenal paints a picture of what may have been not
an unusual scene in his day. As soon as a Roman matron
leaves the priest who impersonates Anubis and supplicates
Osiris:

> Without her badge, a Jewess now draws near,
> And, trembling, begs, a trifle in her ear.
> No common personage! She knows full well
> The laws of Solyma, and she can tell
> The dark decrees of heaven; a priestess she,
> And hierarch of the consecrated tree!
> Moved by these claims thus modestly set forth,
> She gives her a few coins of little worth;
> For Jews are moderate, and, for farthing fees,
> Will tell what fortune, or what dreams you please.

Such practices were of course censured by those who would
guard the honor of Judaism and who regarded them as a "profanation of the Name." But it seems that despite the small
fee, the profession must have been a lucrative one and some
pagans pretended to be Hebrews so as to reap the benefit.
A Sibylline Oracle condemns both the soothsayers and their
dupes:

> They shall intensely suffer..., who for gain
> Shall basely turn soothsayers, prolonging (this)
>   evil time;
> Who clothing themselves with the thick wooly
>   skins of sheep

Pretend to be Hebrews, a race whose interpreters
      they are not,
But prating talkers, gain makers amid (our)
      suffering,
They change their course of life, yet shall they
      not persuade the Just
Who propitiate the All-Illustrious God in their
      hearts.[15]

That necromancy and divination sometimes led to conversion we may judge from the inclusion by the Rabbis of certain proselytes in the category of "Dream Proselytes."

There were, of course, always those who, despite or just because of, the general prejudice were curious to know what constitutes Judaism, and either discussed its doctrines with Jews or read them in their sacred books. The Talmud may have exaggerated in describing the familiarity of some pagans with the teachings of the Torah. Many of the passages from the Scriptures which they put into their mouths may have been merely what, according to the Rabbis, they themselves might have said on such occasions. Yet it would be a fallacy to think that all the Romans were ignorant of the Torah, even before the Bible was translated into Latin. Quite a number of them were bilingual. The slaves, the artists, the merchants, as well as the philosophers mostly hailed from Greek-speaking countries. What reading the patricians did was mostly in Greek. The *Septuagint,* therefore, was accessible to all who either out of a wholesome curiosity wished to learn the real belief of the Jews, or in order to collect material for tormenting and ridiculing them. So were the other writings of the Greek-speaking Jews.[16]

The Rabbis of the Talmud love to expatiate on the discussions between their notables and Roman patricians and philosophers concerning God, the creation of the world, the future life, and Judaism in general. Many of these may have been improvisations, but some may also have been factual. Such controversies, carried on in a more or less serious mood, are recorded of R. Johanan b. Zakkai, who, like his master Hillel, was a lover of all men, a linguist, and a philosopher; of his disciples, Rabban Gamaliel II and R. Jose Hakkohen; and of their disciples, R. Eleazar b. Azariah, R. Akiba, R. Joshua b. Hananiah, and R. Meir, to mention a few of the more prominent ones. That some of these dialogues were not without a flavor of ingenious repartee will be seen in the following specimens:

> A Roman lady once asked R. Gamaliel: It is stated in your Torah, 'The Lord your God ... regardeth not persons,' but it is also stated, 'The Lord will lift up his countenance upon thee.' How can these contradictions be reconciled? R. Jose, who overheard her query, craved permission to answer her, and replied by telling a parable:
>
> To what is this like? To one who owed a debt and swore by the name of the king that he would pay it. When the time expired instead of paying he went to the king and begged his pardon for swearing by his name. Said the king, 'My humiliation is forgiven thee, but thou must go and make up with thy neighbor.' Thus also, the Lord will lift up His Countenance upon those who sinned against Him, but He regardeth not the persons of those who transgressed against their fellowmen.[17]

The four rabbis who visited Rome had frequent questions propounded to them by philosophers and rhetoricians, and had many a battle of wits even with Hadrian. One of these philosophers asked Rabban Gamaliel:

> It is written in your Torah: 'For the Lord thy God is a devouring fire, a jealous God.' Now a wise man is jealous only of another wise man, a mighty man of another mighty man, and a wealthy man of another wealthy man, why is God jealous of insignificant idols? Said Gamaliel I will tell thee a parable. To what is this like? To one who married another woman

in addition to his first wife. The first wife who truly
loves him would not be jealous if the second one is
an improvement, but not so if she is inferior to her.

With another philosopher who asked the same question
R. Gamaliel had the following discussion:

(R. G.) — I will tell thee a parable: to what is this
thing like? To a king of flesh and blood who had an
only son. This son raised a pet dog to whom he gave
his father's name, and by whose name he swore. With
whom is the father wroth, with the son or with the
dog? Surely he is wroth with the son.

Roman: Once a fire broke out in our town. The
whole town was destroyed, but the place of the idol
remained unscorched.

(R. G.) — I will tell thee a parable: To what is this
thing like? To a king against whom a certain district
rebelled. When he comes to wage war against it, does
he battle with the living or with the dead?

Roman: Thou callest it (the idol) dog, thou callest
it a corpse, why then doth He not destroy it from
the world?

(R. G.) — If the heathen would worship those things
which the world hath no need of, He would probably
remove them, but they adore the sun, the moon, the
stars, the planets, the valleys, and mountains—should
God destroy His world because it has fools in it? The
world must continue to run its wonted course, but the
fools will some day have to pay the penalty. [18]

Sometimes women, too, joined in the conversation. Once
an unbeliever (Roman) told Gamaliel: "Your God is a thief,
for he stole a rib from Adam while the latter was asleep."
Whereupon the daughter of R. Gamaliel asked permission
to answer him. Said she to him: "What thinkest thou of a

burglar who breaks into our house, steals a silver pitcher, and leaves us a golden one?" Said he to her: "Would that such burglars would break into my house every night of the year." Said she to him: "Is not this what the Lord did to Adam? He robbed him of a superfluous rib and left him a useful handmaiden." "But," retorted the unbeliever, "why did He not do it in the open?" Thereupon she took a slice of raw meat and invited him to eat it. When he refused she told him that had Adam witnessed the fashioning of Eve, she probably would have been equally repellent.

Notwithstanding his dislike for Jews, Hadrian, the *curiositatum omnium explorator,* found the very plain looking but witty R. Joshua b. Hananiah such a delightful controversialist that when he visited Palestine (130 C. E.) he ordered him to travel with him to Egypt. The folk-tales concerning their relationship are not unlike that which obtained between Frederick the Great and Moses Mendelssohn in the eighteenth century. The Jew of fiction gets the best of the Emperor while saying many a thing which the Jew of fact would wish to have said:

> One day Caesar said to R. Joshua b. Hananiah, 'I wish to see your God.' R. Joshua said, 'Thou canst not see Him.' As Hadrian insisted, he asked him to look at the sun. Said he, 'I cannot.' Upon which R. Joshua replied, 'If thou canst not look at the sun, which is only one of the servants of the Holy One, blessed be He, how canst thou expect to behold the Shekinah?'

> One day Caesar said to R. Joshua b. Hananiah, 'I wish to prepare a banquet for your God.' Said he to him, 'Thou canst not.' 'Why?' 'He has very many attendants.' 'But I wish it.' 'Then set it out by the sea shore, where there is much room.' Caesar set it out during the six months of summer, but each time a wind would blow it into the sea. He set it again during the six months of winter, but each time a rain descended and swept it into the sea. Said he, 'Where-

fore is this?' Said he, 'These are His little servants who precede Him to settle the dust; and helped themselves to the banquet.'

One day, as Caesar read (Amos 3:8):

'The lion hath roared, who will not fear, The Lord God hath spoken, who will not prophesy,' he remarked, 'This likens your God to a lion. Is it such a distinction? A bowman can kill a lion.' Said R. Joshua b. Hananiah: 'He means not the common lion, but the superior lion.' Then, said Caesar, 'Show him to me.' Said he, 'Thou canst not see him.' Said he, 'I must see him.' R. Joshua b. Hananiah prayed, and as he prayed the lion arose from his lair. At his growl at a distance of four hundred miles, all the bridges and forts of Rome began to totter; at the distance of three hundred miles the teeth of the people began to rattle, and Caesar himself fell off his throne. Said he, 'Pray intercede for me that the lion may return to his lair.' R. Joshua prayed and the lion returned to his place.

In this story, Jews probably expressed their confidence that Hadrian with all his pomp was insignificant in comparison with the God whom he defied. In another tale, R. Joshua is made the mouth-piece of the contempt and derision in which the great Caesar was held by his Jewish subjects:

Hadrian, may his bones be crushed, once told R. Joshua: 'Your God has shown great respect for the nations of the world, for in the first five Commandments which were intended exclusively for Jews He included His name and threatened punishments, but in the last five commandments His name is not included because, as they were intended also for the nations of the world, He felt that threats were unnecessary.' Said he, 'Come, let us stroll through the provinces.' Wherever they arrived they found a statue

erected to the Emperor. Said R. Joshua, 'What is this?'
Caesar answered, 'This is my likeness.' He then took
him to the draught-houses and said: 'My Lord the
king, it seems that everywhere thou reignest but not
in this place' (there being no statue of his). Said he
to him: 'Art thou indeed a Jewish sage! Would it
be to the glory of the Emperor to set up a statue for
him in a dirty, despicable, privy place?' Said he to
him: 'Now let thine ears hear what thy mouth speaks:
Would it be for the glory of the Holy One, praised
be He, to mix in His name with murderers, adulterers,
and thieves?'

Once, in reading Ecclesiastes (9:4), Hadrian came across
the verse, "For a living dog is better than a dead lion." Thereupon he remarked to R. Joshua, "Am I not better than Moses
your teacher, for he is dead and I am alive?"

Said he to him, 'Canst thou decree that no one
should light a fire in his house for three days in succession?' Said he, 'Of course.' At eventide the Roman
Caesar and the Jewish sage went up to the roof of the
palace and saw smoke come up from a house. Said
R. Joshua, 'Look at this!' Said Hadrian, 'It is the
house of one of my lords, who caught a cold, and
was ordered by the physician to drink hot beverages
in order to get well.' Said he, 'May that man exhale
his soul. Thy decree has been ignored while thou art
yet alive, but never since Moses our teacher has enjoined us, "Ye shall not kindle a fire on the Sabbath
in all your habitations" to this very day has a Jew
lighted a fire on the Sabbath.'

In an apocryphal story, a king (probably Hadrian) is said
to have asked R. Joshua: "Is it not written in your Torah,
'All His ways are just (Dt. 32:4)?' How will you account
for the many who have never sinned and yet are afflicted
in one way or another, such as those who are born blind,

or lame or crippled or deaf or dumb?" R. Joshua answered: "The wicked among them were punished before their birth because God knew that they would sin while on this earth; however the virtuous among these will receive a greater reward in the world to come." R. Joshua then proved that some men are restrained from committing crimes only by reason of their affliction. Thereupon the Emperor exclaimed: "It is true and established that your God is just, and His judgment is correct, and there is no evil in all his ways. He is One, and there is no other like unto Him." [19]

Unsurpassed in his hatred of the Jews was Turnus Rufus, the Governor of Judea during the Bar Kokba rebellion. Most of the cruel decrees of the Emperor may be laid to his charge. But not content with torturing them physically, he delighted in tormenting them mentally. He is reputed to have been an adept in the Torah and picked out the saintly R. Akiba as the special butt for his sarcasm. In one of their numerous dialogues:

> Turnus Rufus the wicked asked of R. Akiba: 'Whose works are better, the Holy One's, praised be He, or a human being's?' Said he (R. Akiba) to him, 'A human being's are better.' Said to him Turnus Rufus, 'Behold the heaven and the earth, can a human being make anything like them?' Said to him R. Akiba, 'Tell me not about things over which people have no control, but about those things with which men come in contact.' Then said he to him, 'Wherefore do you undergo the rite of circumcision?' Said he (R. Akiba) to him, 'I knew what you were driving at, that is why I said that the works of a human being are better than those of the Holy One, praised be He.' Thereupon he brought him grain and rolls, and said, 'Here is the work of the Holy One, praised be He, and here the work of the hands of man; is not this better than that?' Said to him Turnus Rufus, 'If He desires circumcision, why is not the child born circumcised?' Said to him R. Akiba, 'And why did

He make the child attached to his mother by his navel and the mother has to cut it apart? Besides, God has given the Commandments to Israel so as to discipline them, even as it is said: "The word of the Lord is tried (i.e., intended to try out, Ps. 18:31)." '

Once Turnus Rufus remarked to R. Akiba: "If, as you maintain, your God loveth the poor, why does He not provide for them?" Said R. Akiba, "Because He wants the rich to escape the torments of hell by helping the poor." The former, however, protested:

'On the contrary, your giving charity to the poor should be the cause of your going to hell. Let me illustrate this with a story. To what is it like? To a king of flesh and blood who is wroth with his servant, and claps him into jail, and a certain man comes and gives him to eat and to drink, would not the king be angry if he heard of it? Now you are called servants, for it is said: "For unto Me the children of Israel are servants" (Lev. 25:55).' Said to him R. Akiba: 'I, too, will tell thee a story. To what is it like? To a king of flesh and blood who is wroth with his son and orders him to be sent to jail, and commands that they should give him neither meat nor drink. Comes a certain man and gives him to eat and to drink. Will not the king, on hearing of it, send him a gift? Now we are called sons, for it is written: "Ye are the sons of the Lord your God (Dt. 14:1)." '

If in the above R. Akiba proves himself a doughty defender of his faith, he shows himself in the following a valiant fighter in the battle with paganism:

Once he (Turnus Rufus) asked R. Akiba: 'Why does the Holy One, blessed be He, hate us, as it is said: "But Esau I hate" (Mal. 1:3)?' Said he to him, 'I will answer thee tomorrow.' The next day Turnus Rufus asked him: 'What hast thou dreamed last night?

and what hast thou seen?' Said he to him: 'I dreamed
I had two dogs, the name of the one of which was
Rufus, and of the other Rufina.' Turnus Rufus became furious and cried: 'Thou hast called thy dogs
after me and my wife? Thou deservest to die.' Said
to him R. Akiba: 'And wherein dost thou differ from
them? Thou eatest and drinkest and they eat and
drink; thou increasest and multipliest, and they increase and multiply; thou wilt die, and they will die.
Yet art thou angry because I called them by thy name.
The Holy One, praised be He, Who spread out the
heavens and established the earth, Who killeth and
quickeneth—should not He hate them who take a dog
and call it by His name?'[20]

Sometimes the Government itself deemed it advisable to
learn at first hand what Judaism teaches. Once, the Talmud
states, "the wicked Government sent two of its representatives
to the sages of Israel with instructions that they be taught
the Torah. They were taught it once, they were taught it
twice, they were taught it thrice, until they mastered the
Bible, the *Mishnah,* and the *Gemara.* On their departure, they
declared: "We have scrutinized your entire Torah, and found
it acceptable in every way, save in that it teaches that the
Israelite whose ox gored the ox of an idolater is not held
to be responsible, while the heathen whose ox gored the ox
of an Israelite is to pay damages.... However, we will not
report this to the authorities." To this the Sifre adds that
so favorably impressed were the Roman officials with the Torah
that they ultimately became converts to Judaism.[21]

Some time later, during the brighter but too brief reign
of Nerva, the Government again sent a request for a Jewish
sage to expound Judaism to the Romans. For some reason
the request was couched in veiled language: "Send us," it
read, "one of your lanterns." Said the sages: "They have
hundreds of lanterns, numberless precious stones and jewels;
why do they ask us for one of our lanterns?" So they sent
them R. Meir, whose name signifies the "luminary." The

Romans set before him numerous questions, all of which he answered to their complete satisfaction. Toward the end they asked him: "Why do your people call our nation 'Swine' (*hazir*)?" "Because," answered the rabbi, *"hazir* in Hebrew means also 'return,' and it is our belief that your nation will ultimately turn over the Kingdom to Him to Whom it belongs." [22]

A very important role in the undermining of Roman paganism was played by prophecies attributed to the Sibyl, who held sway over the minds of the Romans no less than over those of the Greeks. Among her many predictions was that of the coming of a king from the East, that is from Palestine, who would subdue the oppressors of the Jews and rule over all mankind. This belief, we have seen, was widespread and deep-seated among the Jews. There are indications that Herod himself entertained a hope of some day becoming ruler of the world as well as of Palestine. Among the Romans, some applied this prediction to one of their own. Suetonius tells us that a few months before Augustus was born, there was witnessed in Rome a public prodigy which was interpreted as an omen that Rome was about to bring forth the great king, and that the frightened senate enacted a law that no one born that year should be raised to maturity: an enactment which probably led to the "Slaughter of the Innocents" attributed to Herod.

But the Jewish Sibyl, whose verses were said to have been imported from Erythrea in 73 B.C.E. and carefully guarded in the Capitol, left no doubt that the looked-for universal ruler was to be neither an Idumean proselyte nor a Roman pagan. Rome herself was to suffer the fate of Palestine, but without her recompense:

> Egypt's destructive race is near destruction....
> Whatsoever Rome has received from tribute-paying
>   Asia,
> Thrice so much riches shall Asia receive again
> From Rome, and shall repay deadly insult upon her.

As many as from Asia have waited upon Italian
    homes,
Twenty times so many shall be hirelings in Asia,
Italians (who) shall serve in deepest poverty,
O tender, wealthy virgin, offspring of Latin Rome,
Often intoxicated by being much sought for in
    nuptials,
A Servant! Thou shalt not wed in the world,
And often thy mistress shall shear thy luxuriant
    hair....
Samos shall be a sand heap, Delos shall be invisible,
Rome shall be a ruin, and all heathen oracles
    come to an end.[23]

Such admonitions and prognostications a Sibyl was made
to reiterate after almost every occurrence which disturbed
Roman political and economic life, and after every unusual
natural phenomenon. The earthquakes and famines which
followed Pompey's invasion (63 B.C.E.) and Caligula's attempt to place his effigy in the Temple (52 B.C.E.), the conflagration which nearly destroyed Rome (64 C.E.), the murder
of Galba and Otho a few months after they had assumed
the purple (68 C.E., 69 C.E.), the great plague which killed
ten thousand Romans in one day (77 C.E.), and the eruption
of Vesuvius which destroyed Herculaneum and Pompeii as
Titus became Emperor (79 C.E.), the civil wars and the revolt
of the slaves,—all these were pointed at as admonitions of
God's anger and the sound of the feet of His messenger to
reclaim mankind. Even the Roman triumphs were regarded
as indicating Rome's approaching dissolution. The Triumvirate and the reduction of Egypt (c. 30 B.C.E.), inspired the
Sibyl to predict that

....When Rome shall rule over Egypt also,
Uniting it to its empire, then shall the mightiest
    kingdom
Of the immortal King appear among men,

And a Sacred Prince shall come to hold the sceptre
    of the whole earth,
To all ages of the time which approaches.
Then inexorable anger for Latin men,
A Triumvirate shall destroy Rome by miserable fate,
But all men shall be destroyed in their own chambers
When the fiery cataract shall stream from heaven....
But at present go on building, O cities! Ornament
    yourselves
With temples and stadiums, market-places and
    gold images,
With silver and stone ones, that you may come
    to the bitter days....
O self-confident Rome! After the Macedonian
    phalanx
Thou wilt shine to Olympus; but God will make thee
Totally unheard of. When thou seemest to the eye
To sit firmest, then I will cry these things in
    thine ear;
'Destroyed, thou shalt bewail thy brilliancy and
    marble.'

The Sibyl then calls upon the Romans to "return in repentance" ere it be too late, before

The all-producing earth shall be shaken in those days
By the Immortal Hand, and the fish in the deep
And all the wild beasts of the earth and countless
    tribes of birds
And all souls of men and the whole sea
Shall shudder under the Immortal Look....
All the well-made walls of evil-minded men
Shall fall to the ground, because they recognized
    not the Law
Nor the Judgment of the great God.... There shall be
Sulphur from heaven, stones and hail,
Frequent and destructive, and quadrupeds shall
    perish.

And then they shall recognize the Imperishable
   God, whose judgments these are....
Then shall ye know the face of the Great God,
And all souls of men, deeply wailing,
Holding up their hands to broad heaven,
Shall begin to call upon the great King
As their Helper, and to seek who shall save them
From the great wrath.[24]

The symbolism of numbers was also a factor in alarming
the Romans. From early times there was a tradition among
the Jews that numbers seven and ten, or any multiple of them,
had a sacred and prophetic significance. The Sages pointed
out that the two great villains of the Bible, the Serpent who
hated the human race and Haman the enemy of all the Jews,
had their sentence pronounced at the end of the seventieth
verse from the beginning of their story; that the Flood came
in the tenth generation after Adam, and that Abraham appeared in the tenth generation after Noah. To the Jews, the
time when Rome rounded out the seventh centennial since
her foundation and "The ninth age was running its course"
was the time when she was destined to meet her inevitable
doom, and the Messiah would then appear and establish in
the world the Kingdom of the Almighty. This belief the
Sibyl capitalized and used as a signal of distress and a war-
cry against Roman idolatry:

But when on earth are earthquakes and violent
   thunderbolts.
Thunder and lightning and mildewed land....
And fruits shall fail, and freemen be sold as slaves
Among most mortals, and temples be robbed:
Then after these things shall the Tenth Generation
   appear
When the Sender of earthquakes and lightnings
Shall break the zeal for idols, and agitate the people
   of seven-hilled Rome, and great wealth shall perish,
Consumed in a vast conflagration by Vulcan's
   flame....

And the whole world of countless men
Having gone mad shall destroy each other...
Then once more shall the great God Who dwells
      in heaven
Be everywhere the Preserver of the righteous.
And thereafter shall be deep peace and (good)
      understanding,
And the fruitful earth shall again bear various fruits,
Not being divided (by hostile factions) nor enslaved;
But every harbor and roadstead shall be free to men,
As it originally was, and shamelessness shall be
      destroyed.[25]

Similar forebodings and denunciations were repeated also
after every persecution. In the following, the Sibyl plays upon
the name Hadrian which reminds her of the "neighboring
sea" (the Adriatic) and Alion which sounds like the Greek
for wretched:

But when thou hast had thrice five luxurious kings
Enslaving the world from the East to the West....
Thenceforward a wretched time when the wretched
      one shall perish
And the populace will say 'Thy power, O city,
      will fall....'
And then shall they wail together, foreseeing thy
Most wretched fate, both fathers and young children.
They shall wail, 'Alas, alas, by the sorrowful banks
      of the Tiber.'
After him three shall reign, occupying the very
      last time,
Filling out the Name of the Heavenly God,
Whose power is now and shall always be....
Mars shall destroy the boasting Roman threats.
The once flourishing government of Rome is
      destroyed,
Of Rome, the former queen over neighboring cities.
No longer shall the army of luxurious Rome be
      victorious,

> When the conqueror from Asia shall come with
>   his host,
> And shutting in these (forces), shall enter the city.
> Thrice three hundred and forty-eight years
> Shalt thou fulfill, when there shall come on thee,
> Evil fate, overpowering thee, and fulfilling
>   thy name. . . .
> And then a holy Prince shall hold the sceptre of
>   the whole earth,
> To all ages, having wakened the departed.[26]

The writings of Josephus may also have had a share in moulding the opinions of some Romans. This Judean patriot who, like R. Johanan b. Zakkai, preferred at the risk of his reputation, to save something rather than lose everything, dedicated himself, after the *Hurban,* to the task of propagating Judaism among the Romans even as R. Johanan did to preserve it among the Jews. He rewrote Jewish history and reinterpreted the Jewish religion in a manner most appealing to Roman psychology. He showed, what with the Romans carried great weight, that Jewish history dates back to the hoariest antiquity, and that the Jews ever proved themselves intrepid warriors and chivalrous enemies. But unlike the Romans, Jews never fought save in self-defense, and never imposed heavy burdens upon those whom they had vanquished. They even respected the religion of the Romans for "our legislator has expressly forbidden us to laugh at and revile those that are esteemed gods by other people, on account of the very name (god) ascribed to them." With this background, Josephus in a masterly manner summed up the teachings of Judaism and showed that all its precepts and practices have only one object—to make one prefer the common good before his own:

> They do not make men hate one another, but encourage people to communicate what they have to another freely; they are enemies to injustice; they take care of righteousness; they banish idleness and expensive living, and instruct men to be content with

what they have, and to be laborious in their calling; they forbid men to make war from a desire of getting more, but make men courageous in defending the laws; they are inexorable in punishing malefactors; they admit no sophistry of words, but are always established by actions themselves, which actions we propose as surer demonstrations than what is contained in writing only; on which account, I am bold to say, that we are become the teachers of other men in the greatest number of things, and those of the most excellent natures only.... If these precepts had either been written at first, or more exactly kept, by any others before us, we should have owed them thanks as disciples owe their masters.

In conclusion, Josephus assures the Romans that should they but wish to join this religion of truth and justice and goodwill, they would be most welcome. "Our legislator," says he, "admits all those that have a mind to observe our laws so to do, and this after a friendly manner, as esteeming that true union which not only extends to our own stock but to those that would live after the same manner with us." [27]

Judaism, like Solomon's wisdom, was thus calling to the Romans "from the top of high places by the way... beside the gates, at the entry of the city, at the coming in at the doors." Nor was hers always a voice calling in the wilderness. To be sure, not all those who responded were motivated by the high ideals it proclaimed. Some still associated the God of Israel with some foreign but exacting deity whom, whether they wanted to or not, it would be safer to please or placate. But there were always some who hungered for the spiritual bread of Judaism and knocked for admittance into its unknown sanctuary. These came from all walks of Roman life. The names of patricians as well as slaves are found on Jewish tomb-stones dating to the days of Augustus. Cicero very dramatically, but probably not without some foundation, in his defense of Flaccus referred to Roman sympathizers with Jews and Judaism: "I shall speak in low tones," says he, "just loud enough for the jury to hear. There is no lack of men, as you well know, to stir these fellows up against me, and every patriotic citizen." Josephus dedicated his book *Against Apion* to Epaphroditus whom he describes as a "great lover of truth" and, through him, "to those who have been in like manner desirous to be acquainted with the affairs of our nation." He also states that much of the wealth of the Temple treasury came from the contributions of those in Asia and Europe whose lives had been transformed by the religion of Israel. That Titus, the conqueror of Jerusalem, a city which according to an inscription on the arch erected to him, "all kings, commanders and nations before him have either attacked in vain, or left wholly unassailed," did not assume the title "Judaicus," is evidence of the fear that the word might have been understood as referring to his religion instead of his generalship. Indeed, according to Leroy-Beaulieu, toward the end of the first Christian century:

> The prediction of the Prophets seemed for a moment on the point of being realized; it appeared as though the nations were about to set out for Jerusalem in order to worship there. The Sibyl had not been mistaken. Isis, Serapis, Zeus, and all the other gods had to succumb to the God of Israel. Had not the world become Christian it might, perhaps, have become Jewish.[28]

This Roman drift toward Judaism aroused the indignation of many of the poets and statesmen. Tacitus, like Cicero, inveighs against the "vile fellows" who pay homage to the Jews and teach their children to despise the gods and to hold the pagans in utmost contempt. Juvenal, in his tirade against women, has much to say about the mistress who is content with nothing less than

> That far-famed gem which Berenice wore,
> The hire on incest and hence valued more;
> A brother's present, in that barbarous State,
> Where kings the Sabbath, barefoot, celebrate;

> And old indulgence grants a length of life
> To hogs, that fatten fearless of the knife.

But Juvenal reserves his sovereign scorn for the men who,
starting with the observance of the Sabbath, end up with
adopting Jewish ideas and go to the extent of circumcising
either themselves or at least their children and rearing them
in the Jewish faith:

> Some sprung from a father who reveres the Sabbath,
> Adore nothing but clouds and the divinity of heaven,
> Nor think less of swine flesh than that of human,
> And soon they even become circumcised.
> Trained to despise the laws of the Romans,
> They maintain and revere the laws of the Jews,
> Which Moses has transmitted in his mystic tome:
> Not to show the way but to those of their own faith,
> To guide to a spring only those who are circumcised.
> Blame the father, to whom each seventh day
> Is idle, and disconnected from the duties of life.[29]

One of the more prominent patricians who was attracted
to Judaism was Clemens Romanus, presumably a freedman
of T. Flavius Clemens who later, like many other Roman
proselytes, embraced Christianity and became Bishop of Rome
(c. 96). He is of interest to us mainly because he managed
to cause the discomfiture of Apion. Feigning illness, he sent
for the arch-enemy of the Jews, who boasted of his thera-
peutic skill, and told him that he was suffering from unrequited love. Apion promised to put him in possession of the
lady of his desire within six days by means of his magic,
and wrote a philter in which he adjured her by the amatory
examples of Zeus and the other gods to yield. When Apion
came to visit him again, Clemens informed him that the
lady censured and abused the gods for their lustfulness. Influenced by a Jew that the true God despises adulterers, she
urged him to pray to that God to help him in his effort to
be chaste. Apion flew into a rage and exclaimed: "Have

I not reason to hate the Jews? Behold some Jew has converted her and persuaded her to chastity, and she is no longer responsive to my charms. For these fellows, setting God before them as the universal Inspector of man's actions, are extremely persistent in chastity, holding that the opposite cannot be concealed from Him." Then, when Clemens confessed that he was not at all infatuated with any woman, but that it was himself who had learned from a Jewish linen merchant about God and morality, Apion, "with the unreasonable hatred of the Jews, neither knowing nor wishing to know what their faith was, forthwith quitted Rome in silence."[30]

A converted freedman who attained eminence in literature was Caecilius of Calacte, of Sicilian or Syrian origin. Soon after his emancipation he went to Rome and studied rhetoric under Apollodorus and Dionysius, and became the representative of the Attic style of oratory. He was also regarded as an authority on the Greek classic orators, such as Demosthenes and Aeschines, and was noted for his works on aesthetics, history, and philosophy. He made a specialty of the writings of Cicero and was among the first students of Latin literature at a time when it was fashionable to look upon it with contempt.[31]

Another distinguished proselyte was Pomponius, a relative of Tiberius, and a friend of the Elder Pliny who wrote his life. Charged with "atheism," he was thrown into jail, where he was confined for seven years, but was set at liberty by Caligula and made supervisor of the Imperial entertainments. During the Emperor's absence in Gaul, however, he was re-arrested, and together with Quintilia, a freed woman of great beauty, was tortured to elicit a confession. Both were released on Caligula's return and provided for in his own house. As a result of the torture he suffered while in prison, Pomponius became crippled for life, and, at the banquet which Caligula tendered in his honor, the Emperor's foot served him for a pillow. On the assassination of Caligula, Pomponius and his woman companion perished from want.

Seventeen years later, Pomponia, a sister or daughter of

Pomponius, was also suspected of adherence to the "foreign superstition," because she·put on mourning for her best friend Livia, a grand-daughter of Tiberius, who was banished and murdered. Fortunately, through her husband's influence, the charge against her was quashed.[32]

It was under Tiberius that an incident occurred which brought about the temporary expulsion of Jews from Rome. Fulvia, a woman of great dignity and the wife of a senator, adopted the Jewish religion and sent for a Jew to "instruct her in the wisdom of the laws of Moses." The fellow, who had been driven out of his own country as a robber and thief, absconded with the treasures which Fulvia sent through him and his confederates as a gift to the Temple in Jerusalem. Fulvia's husband, Saturninus, reported it to the Emperor, and all the Jews of Rome were made to suffer in consequence.[33]

Somewhat later, a youth of fifteen years, of high rank, confessed before his death to have been a convert to Judaism. Also, a Latin epitaph on the tomb of one Paulina Beturia (c. 50) states that during the last sixteen years of her eighty-six years and six months she went by the name of Sarah, lived as a Jewess, and was honored as *Mater Synagogarum* by the Compesian and Volumnian Synagogues. By some she is identified with the learned Beluria, Beruria, Belurit, or Beruzia of the Talmud whose slaves insisted on serving her even after, at her persuasion, they became proselytes and were thereby made free.[34]

Reference has already been made to a Jewish tradition that after the great fire, Nero fled to Palestine and became a convert to Judaism. The legend probably originated in his mild treatment of the Jews, and because he blamed only the Christians for the conflagration which he started for his fiendish diversion. Some of the leading nobles of his court were also favorable to the Jews. No less a personage than Sabina Poppaea, who succeeded to his affections after he did away with Octavia, loved to surround herself with Jews. When Josephus visited Rome to plead the cause of some priests who were arrested by the Procurator, she granted him an audience, presented him with costly gifts, and had the priests set at liberty. Very likely it was she who brought about the downfall of Seneca, the arch-enemy of the Jews. She also contributed to the success of the mission of the four rabbis who came to Rome in the interest of the Temple. But, like Octavia, she, too, fell victim to Nero's beastliness and perished from a kick of his foot while she was in an advanced state of pregnancy. More than fourteen thousand Jews gathered at her funeral to mourn her untimely death, while Nero, perhaps to soothe his conscience, had her embalmed in spices in accordance with an ancient custom of Israel.[35]

By the irony of fate, the house of Vespasian, the destroyer of Jewish autonomy, became honey-combed with the "Jewish superstition," and the *yittush* (insect) which the Rabbis say bored at the brains of Titus infected, in a figurative sense, also other members of his family. Titus Flavius Sabinus, Vespasian's elder brother, is said to have led, during his last years, a life that may be called "Jewish or Christian." His cousin, Titus Flavius Clemens (master of Clemens Romanus?), and the latter's wife, Flavia Domitilla, who was also a grand-daughter of Vespasian, had to defend themselves against the charge of "atheism"; and the fact that their two sons, Vespasian and Domitian, were in the line of succession to the throne did not avail them. Flavia was banished to the Isle of Pandatoria or Pantia. Clemens and his sons were put to death together with, according to some, Josephus and his friend Epaphroditus, "the lover of truth." The Catacomba Domitillae, laid out by Jews, bears a strikingly Jewish architectural touch.[36]

Even Hadrian, who completed the catastrophe begun by Titus, did not escape the "Jewish revenge" or poetic justice which made converts of Pharaoh, Sennacherib, Haman, and Nero. According to Isaac b. Joseph Heilo, a Spaniard who visited Palestine in 1333, there is at Beth-el, the ancient Luz and modern Bittin, an old monument which is said to be the tomb of Ahiyah the Shilonite. A legend has it that as Hadrian passed it at the head of his legions, he heard a voice issuing from the tomb: "O wretched one, what wishest

thou to do, and whither art thou going? Knowest thou not
that the victims whom thou art seeking are the children of
Abraham, the friend of God, peace be upon him?" Thereupon the terror-stricken Hadrian resolved to become a convert, and at the advice of a venerable man, whose voice was
like unto the voice which issued from the tomb, he went to
Babylon, where he who made circumcision a capital crime,
himself submitted to the rite, and died a Jew.

The hero of many a talmudic tale is a certain "Antoninus"
who has been variously identified as Marcus Aurelius, Sep-
timus Severus, Caracalla, and Helagabalus. Graetz believes that
he is Alexander Severus (222-235). Alexander was by birth
a Phoenician and was so friendly to Jews that his subjects
mockingly spoke of him as *Syrium archisynagogum et archi-
erum* (the Syrian head of the Synagogue and High Priest).
In his palace there were to be seen the statues of Abraham
and Jesus placed by the side of Orpheus, and the Golden
Rule of Hillel, "What is hateful unto thee do not to thy
fellow-man," he caused to be engraven in the court houses
and to be repeated by heralds before his legions. He allowed
the Jews to visit Jerusalem and presented a golden cande-
labrum to the synagogue in Tiberias, which he intended to
make a free city. He had high regard for R. Judah Hannasi
(the Patriarch) whom he confirmed in his rights and presented
with an estate, of which the income was to go towards the
support of the Tiberian academy, and with whom he held
frequent and intimate conversation during his stay in Syria
(231-233). At the request of Antoninus, R. Judah sent his
favorite disciple, R. Romanos, to Rome to supervise the erection of an altar which was to be a replica of the one in
Jerusalem, and to teach the priests how to prepare frankincense in accordance with the secret recipe used in the Temple.
He also removed many of the restrictions which made intercourse between Jews and Romans difficult. R. Judah was so
confident of the good intentions of his royal friend, even to
the extent of restoring Jewish independence, that he advocated the abolition of the fast of the Ninth of Ab. In him,
says Jerome, the Jews saw the fulfillment of the prediction

of Daniel (11:34): "Now when they shall stumble, they shall be helped with a little help." The Sages selected his reign as the era from which to date legal documents, and a new sanctuary in Rome was given the name the Synagogue of Severus.

One of the early visits of the Emperor to the Patriarch was on the Sabbath. As it would be expected, the meal was served cold, but the Emperor relished the cold Sabbath dinner even more than the warm one of a week-day and asked R. Judah for the reason for its better flavor. The patriarch jokingly explained that it was because for that sacred day, the Jews prepare their food with a certain condiment called "Sabbath," which is lacking in an ordinary week-day dish.

On one occasion, when the Emperor visited the *yeshibah* (rabbinical academy), he found the students, a motley crowd, sitting at the feet of the Patriarch. R. Judah introduced them to him, saying, "These are not common people. The least among them can make the dead come to life." The next time, when one of the Emperor's servants became dangerously ill, he asked the Patriarch to send him one of the students. R. Judah sent him one (some say R. Simeon b. Halafta), and he was accompanied by the curious Antoninus. Finding the servant in bed, the disciple exclaimed: "Darest thou lie while thy sovereign is standing before thee?" The psychological effect was miraculous. The servant made a superhuman effort, rose to his feet, and walked away cured. [37]

Antoninus was greatly interested in the Jewish doctrines concerning the soul and especially as regards its punishment in the world to come. Cannot the body, he wanted to know, exculpate itself by blaming the soul, without which it "lieth in the grave like a silent stone" and the soul, by blaming its house of clay without which "it flieth in the air like an innocent bird"? To this R. Judah replied:

> To what is the thing like? To a king of flesh and blood who had a beautiful orchard full of fine ripe grapes, in which he put two watchmen, one of whom was lame and the other blind. Said the lame to the

blind: 'I see fine ripe grapes in the orchard, come let
me mount on your back and we will bring them down.'
So the lame mounted upon the back of the blind and
they pulled the grapes down and ate them. After a time
the owner of the orchard came and asked what hath
become of the fine ripe grapes. The lame said: 'Have
I legs to go after them?' The blind said: 'Have I eyes
to see where they are?' What did (the king) do? He
made the lame mount on the back of the blind and
judged the two of them as if they were one. Thus also
the Holy One, praised be He, brings the soul and in-
jects it into the body and judges the two as if they
were one.

The Rabbis were so enamored of this Roman royal proselyte that they were loath to part with him, even after they
assured him a place in Paradise. The verse (2 Chr. 6:41): "Let
Thy priests, O Lord God, be clothed with salvation," they interpreted to have reference to Antoninus, "one of the righteous of the nations of the world who officiated before the
Holy One, praised be He, in this earth," and they also maintained that at the Resurrection, Antoninus will be at the head
of the legion of *gerim* who will be admitted into the presence
of the Most Holy. [38]

The most noted Roman proselyte, however, was not Antoninus, but the historical Aquila, whose spiritual monument, the
re-translation of the Bible into the Greek, endures to this day
in Origen's *Hexapla*. A native of Sinope, in the district of
Pontus, he is said to have been a nephew of Hadrian, by whom
he was greatly loved. In his youth he studied the different
systems of philosophy, delved into the mystery of magic, officiated as a priest in a pagan temple, and adopted for some
time the faith of the Christians. Still unable to satisfy his spiritual craving, he prevailed on his royal uncle to send him to
Palestine, probably to familiarize himself at first hand with
the teachings of Judaism. Hadrian complied with his request
and appointed him supervisor of the Aelia Capitolina which

was to rise on the ruins of Jerusalem. Soon after his arrival in the Holy Land, Aquila sought out R. Akiba, Rabban Gamaliel, R. Eliezer b. Hyrcanus, and R. Joshua b. Hananiah, and had them instruct him in the Bible and Talmud.

Having become an adept in the Torah, he went to R. Eliezer and, pointing to the verse (Dt. 10:18): "And (God) loveth the *ger* and giving him food and raiment," he asked if that was all he could expect if he became a convert. R. Eliezer's brusque reply was: "Is it little to have food and raiment? Is it all that the old Patriarch (Jacob) prayed for (Gen. 28:20)?" Greatly disappointed, Aquila went to R. Joshua and addressed him in like manner. R. Joshua, unlike R. Eliezer, explained to him: "By bread is meant the Torah, the bread of life.... raiment refers to the *tallit* (shawl))of good deeds...." and that, since the daughters of *gerim* may marry into the priesthood, their children will be privileged to offer sacrifices upon God's altar, set up the shew-bread, and array themselves in the robe of the High Priest. The gentleness of R. Joshua had the same effect on Aquila as that of Hillel before him had had on some of his countrymen, and he, too, embraced Judaism and underwent circumcision.

When Aquila returned to Rome, his poor appearance greatly affected Hadrian who inquired whether he had lost his fortune or suffered harm at the hands of a fellow-man. Aquila confessed that he was circumcised and converted to Judaism and made the Emperor himself responsible for the deed. "Thou didst counsel me at my parting to buy merchandise when it was as cheap as possible, and hold on to it till it would rise as high as possible. In all my travels in different countries I have nowhere seen a people held in so low esteem as the Jews, so I invested in their spiritual merchandise, and am resolved to hold on to it till it will rise to the highest heights, even as is predicted by Isaiah" (49:7):

> Thus saith the Lord, the Redeemer of Israel,
>   his Holy One,
> To him who is despised of men, to him who is
>   abhorred of nations,

> Kings shall see and arise, princes, and they shall
> prostrate themselves.

Hadrian then asked him why he could not have studied the Torah without circumcising himself. "Wouldst thou," answered Aquila, "present a valuable horse to a soldier who did not show himself willing to obey thy commands? To be worthy of God's gift of the Torah one must prove by his conduct that he is prepared to make sacrifices for the sake of His commandments."

Aquila became so thoroughly Jewish in his mode of living and thinking that he threw into the sea the share of his patrimony as tainted money, since it was realized from the sale of idols. Yet on the death of his master, Rabban Gamaliel, he burned, Roman fashion, seventy minas worth of garments and furniture. When reproached by his friends for bestowing on a Jew such a royal honor, this son of Hadrian's sister answered: "One Gamaliel is worth an hundred emperors from whom the world derives no benefits whatever."

His greatest admiration was for R. Akiba. He modeled his conduct of life after him, and he followed R. Akiba's method of interpretation of the Torah, in his new Greek version of the Bible. It was now about three hundred years since the *Septuagint* first appeared among the Greek-speaking Jews of Egypt. During these years it served as a means to keep Jews in touch with their spiritual heritage, and drew many a heathen to the religion of Israel. But the *Septuagint* also had the defect of its qualities. Its lack of strict literalness enabled the nascent Christian sect to make it a source-book of Christian theology. It was good enough to draw the heathen away from gross paganism, but it failed to impress them sufficiently with the pure Hebraic monotheism. Aquila, therefore, set himself the task of re-translating the Bible literally and in strict accord with Jewish traditional interpretation, under the vigilant guidance of R. Akiba, R. Eliezer, and R. Joshua. In his painstaking fidelity to the Hebrew text, he went so far as to give preference to the Old Phoenician script, as found on the Moabite Stone, over the more modernized Hebrew, and sometimes sinned against the syntax of the Greek in order to render more faithfully the meaning of the Hebrew.

As might be expected Aquila lost caste with the Church Fathers, and his translation was denounced by them as a work of spitefulness. His literalness also rendered his style rather cumbersome, and he was criticized for considering "not words but syllables." This gave rise to two other efforts at Bible translations one by Symmachus who, according to Epiphanius, was a Samaritan proselyte, and the other by Theodotion of Ephesus, probably a Greek proselyte, or a "Judaising heretic," as Jerome calls him. These three versions were used by Origen in his revision of the *Septuagint,* which became the standard version of the Church. Among the Jews, however, Aquila's version was accepted as authoritative, even in legal decisions. It is claimed to have been the prototype of the Aramaic *Targum* attributed to Onkelos, which to this day is revered as next in holiness to the original Hebrew (by the side of which it is usually printed). To Aquila's version R. Eliezer and R. Joshua applied the verse (Ps. 45:3):

> Thou are fairer than the children of men;
> Grace is poured upon thy lips;
> Therefore God hath blessed thee for ever. [39]

CHAPTER XIII

AT THE PARTING OF THE WAYS

THE JEWS, as we have seen, had every reason to be friendly and none to be hostile to nascent Gentile Christianity. Believing, as they did, that "whosoever denieth idolatry is *ipso facto* a Jew" and that "the righteous among the nations of the world" are as sure of a portion in the world-to-come as the faithful adherents of Judaism, they could not but be happy over every pagan who became a convert to Christianity. Such a one was at least an observer of the Seven Noahian Laws, was a "proselyte of the gate," and likely on the road to becoming, as it happened not infrequently, a "proselyte of righteousness." It was also a rabbinic principle that pagans cannot be accused of heresy. In the early controversies recorded in the Talmud between Jews and Gentiles, the Rabbis never took the offensive nor did they ever stoop to defamation. They certainly never advocated persecution of Gentiles because of their religion, but showed themselves rather lenient even when the person involved was formerly a Jew. Thus they construed the biblical statutes about an *ir hanniddahat* (a perverted city) so as to exempt a place where the majority consisted of converts. They did so also as regards an individual. They made the law in Leviticus (24:10-23) which prescribed death for the crime of blasphemy almost inoperative. They required that the alleged blasphemer should be accused by at least two witnesses who had heard him denounce the "Ineffable Name." They held that one guilty of an act of sacrilege was made liable only to excommunication in this world and were content to leave his due punishment for the world-to-come. [1]

The forbearance and readiness with which the Rabbis re-

sponded to the requests of Christians for information about
the Bible is indirectly admitted by Justin Martyr (100-65), the
first Christian apologist, and is illustrated by the assistance
rendered Origen (185-254), while engaged on his *Hexapla,*
by R. Hoshaya, head of the academy of Caesarea, and by R.
Judah II, grandson of R. Judah Hannasi. Even after the rift
between the two religions already had become irreparable,
we find Jerome (c. 337-420), the greatest student of the Bible
among the Church Fathers, in constant contact with learned
Jews. It was from them that he acquired the knowledge of
Hebrew, Aramaic, and midrashic literature, which enabled
him to produce the *Vulgate,* later to become the authorized
version of the Roman Catholic Church. Jerome had implicit
confidence in the fairness as well as the erudition of his Hebrew
teachers. He admits that "To understand this book (Job) I
procured, at no small cost, a doctor of Lydda, who was esteemed
to hold first place among the Hebrews." In another place he declares: "I got a doctor of Tiberias, in high esteem among Hebrews and with him collected everything, as the proverb goes,
from the crown of the head to the tip of his nails." He
even makes bold to recommend his method to others: "If you
observe my version to vary from the Greek and Latin, ask
the most trustworthy Jew you can find and see if he does not
agree with me." In order, however, not to defy Christian public opinion, one of his teachers "Baranina" of Tiberias would
come to him at night only, or send his information through a
certain Nicodemus. It was not until Jerome was taken to task
for his intercourse with Jews that he pleaded that his object
was to be able to confute the Jews in their religious disputations, and that loyalty to the Church cannot possibly be im-
paired "merely because the reader is informed of the different
ways in which a verse is interpreted by the Jews." [2]

The discrimination or persecution to which early Christians
were subjected were not by Jews but by Christians: the
Paulines by the Petrines and the Petrines by the Paulines.
The Jews themselves had their hands too full with the impending catastrophe to harass a group of men who, neither by their

number nor by their prominence, attracted the attention of
those outside their immediate circle. They certainly would not
send from Jerusalem, as Justin alleges, "chosen men through
all the land" to discredit Christianity. They would simply have
ignored it, as did Philo and Josephus. Paul, with his persecution psychosis, admits his disappointment when, on his arrival
in Rome, he was informed by the local Jews: "We neither received letters out of Judea concerning thee, neither any of the
brethren that came showed or spoke any harm of thee." [3]

As for the Judeo-Christians, their belief in the Messiahship
of Jesus could not possibly have been sufficient reason even
for reading them out of the synagogue, not to say for persecuting them. In Judaism, at least of that time, the *odium
theologicum* which later split Christianity into hundreds of
mutually hostile sects was totally unknown. At the beginning
of the Christian era, Jewish even more than Christian dogma-
tism was still in a state of flux. Even the belief in the coming
of the Messiah, which Jews through the ages accepted as an
essential part of Judaism, was still merely optional, as is pointed
out by R. Joseph Albo, who quotes the statement of R. Hillel
of the fourth century, that "Israel need expect no Messiah, for
they have already consumed him in the time of Hezekiah,
king of Judah." Nor was R. Akiba accused of heresy because he
regarded Bar Kokba as the promised Messiah and applied to
him the prophetic verse:

> There shall step forth a star out of Jacob
> And a sceptre shall rise out of Israel. [4]

Other instances could be readily adduced. We do not hear
that the antinomian Elisha b. Abuya was persecuted, nor his
ardent friend and admirer, R. Meir, save that their real names
were not mentioned in citing their opinions. Even after Jacob
of Kfar Sekanya became a Christian and quoted Jesus in
explaining a ritualistic question, R. Eliezer b. Hyrcanus expressed himself as pleased with his explanation, and many
Jews sought his services, among them R. Eleazar Ben Dama,

the nephew of R. Ishmael. Furthermore, R. Judah Hannasi,
who edited the *Mishnah* and devoted a whole treatise of his
code to the laws pertaining to idolatry, never referred derogatorily to Christianity. [5]

The Judeo-Christians also on their side at first regarded themselves as part and parcel of the House of Israel and were all
zealous for the Torah. James, "the brother of the Lord," was
a constant worshiper at the Temple, and "he alone was permitted to enter the Sanctuary, for he wore no wool (*shaatnez?*)
but a linen garment." We are told that while there, "he knelt
continually, beseeching God for the forgiveness of the people,
until the skin of his knees grew thick like that of a camel."
He led the life of a Nazarite and, opposed to the liberties with
Jewish ceremonials taken by Paul, the Pharisees called him
"the Just" (*zaddik*), or saint; and when Anan, the High Priest,
had him stoned, the leading citizens of Jerusalem raised such
a protest that king Agrippa deposed him from his office. [6]

The fact is that the Judeo-Christians, even after they organized a congregation of their own, did not sever their relation
with Catholic Israel. Except for their belief that Jesus was the
promised Messiah, they clung to the fundamental doctrines
and ceremonies of Judaism. They observed the Abrahamic
rite, rested on the Sabbath, celebrated the festivals, and like
strict Pharisees fasted on Mondays and Thursdays. They prayed
for the peace of Jerusalem and many of them fought against
the Romans for the preservation of Jewish independence. They
found the Bible, or what later came to be called the Old Testament, profitable for doctrine, for reproof, for correction, for
instruction in righteousness. They never faltered in their loyalty
to the "Law, the Prophets, and the Lord." To them Jesus was
the Son of God in the sense of a man of God, a righteous one,
who came "to turn men from idols to serve the living and
true God."

Such a Judeo-Christian congregation was that formed by
the Ebionites (lit., the Poor or Meek Ones) who, like many
Pharisees, stressed the virtues of humility and especially of
poverty. They were mostly humble Galileans with a small

contingent of the more erudite Judeans and more liberal Alexandrians. Their model was the sect of Essenes, who led a communistic life and believed in the necessity of frequent ablutions. Before the imminent downfall of Jerusalem they fled to Pella beyond the Jordan and to the Island of Cyprus, "grateful if their flight did not have to take place in the winter or on the Sabbath." There, too, they remembered God from afar, and Jerusalem was continually in their hearts and on their lips. They looked to James and Peter as their guides and refused to recognize Paul as an Apostle. At first they read the Bible in the original, but when the younger generation ceased to understand the language of their fathers, they adopted the translation of Aquila. Symmachus, the other translator of the Bible, is said by some to have been one of them. Jerome, who met some of their descendants in Aleppo, blamed them for trying to reconcile the "curse of the Law" with the "grace of the Gospel," and applied to them the words of Jesus about "putting a piece of new cloth unto an old garment."

From the Ebionites, or the Nazarenes, as they sometimes called themselves, later sprang the Elkesaites, who under Trajan claimed they received a new revelation in a book delivered by an angel, or the Son of God, to a just man named Elchasai. They were great advocates of baptism for the remission of sins as well as for the ailments of the flesh. They practiced circumcision, observed the Sabbath, prayed with their faces toward Jerusalem, and abstained from meat. They condemned sacrifices and taught that Jesus was the only true priest since the death of Aaron, and that Peter and James were the only Apostles. Some, however, held that Jesus was the reincarnation of Adam or some other *Zaddik,* elected by God to receive the Holy Spirit. These ideas they derived from the original Hebrew Gospel of Matthew, which it is claimed was in their possession. It is also said that they permitted the worship of idols provided the act was necessary to save life—a doctrine also held by some of the rabbis. [7]

Another group which fought for the preservation of Jewish ideals and ceremonies, though dissenting from the Jewish fold, was the *Alogi,* or "the deniers of the Word," so called because they opposed the belief expressed in the Gospel of St. John (1:1) that "In the beginning was the Word, and the Word became flesh." Its founder is said to have been Cerinthus (c. 100 C.E.), a contemporary of the Apostle and a convert to Ebionitism. By some he is credited with the authorship of the Apocalypse. He taught that Jesus was not born of Joseph and Mary, that he was not raised on the third day, but will rise with the rest of the Saints on Ressurection Day, and that the Holy Spirit which descended on him at baptism departed from him before the crucifixion. The Church Fathers report that St. John, while at Ephesus, made a hasty exit from a bath when he learned that Cerinthus was within the house. These doctrines with some modifications were propagated by Theodotus, a tanner, who came to Rome at the close of the second century, and established the very influential sect of Monarchians.

This struggle to retain as near as possible the Jewish belief of the Unity was not limited to the Ebionites and the Alogi. Among the earliest Christians there were many who held that Jesus was only a phantom, or had an astral or ethereal body, and that his crucifixion, like all the acts of his life, was only apparent. This earliest Christian heresy, which came to be known as *Docetism* (Illusionism), had already been condemned by St. Paul and St. John and later by Polycarp and Ignatius as a Judaic aberration.[8]

Closely connected with the Petrine School of Christology are the writings known as Clementine Literature, commonly attributed to Clemens Romanus, supposed to have been a disciple of Peter and third or fourth bishop of Rome. He is surmised to have been a freedman of T. Flavius Clemens (c.96). Whether the Second Epistle, the earliest extant Christian homily, the *Homilies* and *Recognitions* and the *Circuit of Peter* are the product of his pen or originated in Syria, they testify to the spirit of Hebrew monotheism which continued to prevail among the Ante-Nicene Fathers. Their doctrines are based on the Preachings of Peter (*Kerygmata*) and are not unlike those of the Ebionites. They are all anti-Pauline. Indeed, they contain many allusions to St. Paul under the guise of Simon Magus. They stress the belief in the Unity of God, and salvation by works, and that Jesus as well as Satan is an instrument of God: the one Jesus, "the true prophet," is to lead man to salvation; the other Satan, is to test him in this world ere he obtains his salvation. They inveigh against those "who have rejected Peter's teaching," which is based on the Law, "and have attached themselves to the frivolous teaching of the enemy (Paul or Simon Magus) which is contrary to the Law . . . the Law of God which Moses proclaimed, and whose eternal duration our Savior attested when he said: 'Heaven and earth shall pass away, but not one jot or tittle shall pass away.'" They insist that "Only the God of the Bible should be called God. Nor is it lawful to think that there is any other, or to call any other by that name. And if anyone should dare do so, eternal punishment of soul is his."

Much as the *Clementines* have been tampered with by various copyists and toned down to suit the theology of later times, they still are tinged with philo-Hebraic sentiments. Their detestation of Paul is only equalled by their admiration of Peter. Peter, we are told, ordained everyone to hear as the God-fearing Jews have heard. "I fled," says Clement, "for refuge to the Holy God and the Law of the Jews, with faith in the certain conclusion that, by the righteous judgment of God, both the Law is prescribed and the soul beyond doubt everywhere receives the reward of its deeds." Probably for fear of the perversion of Peter's teaching by the Gentiles, he admonishes "to take precaution for the security of the truth, that we should not communicate the books of his teachings, sent to us, indiscriminately to all, but to him who is good and discreet, and chosen to teach, and who is circumcised and faithful." The initiate should be of mature age, and be converted by degrees, so that he might be stopped whenever found unworthy. When admitted into the fellowship, he would be presented a *Kerygmata,* with the stipulation that he does not pass it on to another or make a copy of it, or allow others to copy it; and on setting out on a journey, he should deposit it with the bishop pro-

fessing the same faith as himself. A curious feature about these
sectaries was the oath which they exacted from the neophyte:

> If I break my engagement, may the universe be hostile
> to me, as well as the ether that penetrates everything,
> the God Who is over all, the best, the greatest of
> beings. And if I come to know any other god, I swear
> also by that god that I will keep the engagement that I
> have taken, whether that god exists or does not exist.[9]

While the Ebionites sought to preserve the unity of the
old and of the new Revelation by denying Jesus divinity, and
the Docetae, by depriving him of his humanity, the *Gnostics,*
or "those who know," opposed the Jewish God idea altogether.
They sought to syncretise the teachings of the Bible with the
various philosophies of the pagans, and allegorized in the
manner of Philo the stories of the Scriptures concerning the
Creation and the Godhead. They taught that salvation depended on knowing how the world came into being, and that
according to a special revelation from Jesus and his Apostles,
the Good God, who was from all eternity, caused to emanate
from Himself a number of spirits or *Aeons,* one of which
was known as Wisdom or *Achamot.* This Demiurge, the god
of the Old Testament, is a malevolent being. He made man
but refused to endow him with anything more than matter.
But without his knowledge, the Good God came down to
save mankind by revealing to them the secrets of creation. To
accomplish this end, he united himself with Jesus, the son of
Mary, at his baptism, and departed from him at his crucifixion.[10]

The most dangerous ally the Church had during the
first two centuries of its existence was the sect founded by
Marcion in Rome in 144. Like the Gnostics, the Marcionites
rejected the writings of the Old Testament. To them, Jesus,
the God of the Christians, was not the son of the God of the
Jews, who was the God of justice. He was the God of love,
who out of pity for mankind compromised with the God of
the Old Testament and chose for himself all the sinners,

among them Cain, Esau, Korah, Dathan, Abiram, and the Gentiles. They held that Apostles falsified and mutilated the original teachings of Jesus and ignored his faithful disciples. Marcion came to restore the true Gospel which, according to him, was the Gospel of Luke.

Already in the first century, one could have foreseen that the palm of victory would ultimately belong to the adherents of Pauline theology. The Jesus of the Ebionites and the Docetae was too human to satisfy the pagan cravings for a demi-god. The Jesus of the Gnostics and the Marcionites was too tenuous to satisfy the pagan desire for a Person. Pauline theology supplied the need of the majority of pagans by teaching that Jesus was neither a superior mortal nor a mere phantom but God incarnate. It fortified its position by proving that Judaism was a preparation rather than a negation of the religion Jesus came to establish. This was done in the series of booklets, chosen and edited out of many others, which at first went under the simple title *Memoirs of the Apostles* but were later given canonical rank, and became the distinctive Bible of the Christians. This was not an easy task. The *Memoirs* were originally transmitted orally and were sometimes mutually contradictory. Many of them were attributed to Apostles who had nothing to do with them. Papias, Bishop of Hieropolis and Apostolic Father, tells us how one had to be on his guard before accepting these documents.[11]

Even after the Gospels were compiled, the name sacred Scriptures was reserved only for the "Old Testament." It alone was assumed to be inspired, and out of it alone selections were read during divine services. There was no agreement as to which document was authoritative. Each group had its favorite, and sometimes went to the extent of persecuting those who preferred another. Thus some of "Paul's men" cursed those who would read any other Gospel than the one which met their approval, while John's followers would not receive into their houses or bid God-speed to one who did not accept theirs for fear of being "partakers in his evil deeds." At length, in imitation of the Synagogue, where the *Haftarah* from the Prophets supplemented the weekly

Parashah from the Pentateuch, it became customary to read selections from the Gospels also. And thus in the course of time they assumed the same sanctity as the Old Testament. By the end of the second century, the Christian world had a Bible of its own and gave it the name of the New Testament, or covenant based on the words attributed to Jesus when, at his last supper, he passed the cup to his disciples and said: "This cup is the New Testament in my blood which is shed for you."[12]

Like the Law and the Prophets of the Old Testament, this definitive Christian canon was arranged in two main parts, the Gospels and the Epistles, and its main object was to teach that all the incidents in the life of Jesus were adumbrated and predicted in the former long before his advent. Moses fled from Pharaoh in anticipation of the flight of Jesus from Herod. Moses spent forty days and forty nights on the mount as an indication of what would be done by Jesus. The same miracles that were ascribed to the Prophets were said to have been performed by Jesus, only on a larger and grander scale. Moses and Joshua dried the waters of the Red Sea or Jordan, Jesus walked upon them. Elijah and Elisha had to their credit the curing of a leper or two, the reviving of a dead body or two, and the feeding of a small crowd of followers. Jesus did all this and much more for whole multitudes. Of none of these ancients is it told that they exorcised demons; to Jesus, exorcism was a common occurrence. It was, according to their outlook, the last scene in the life of Jesus that the Psalmist had in mind when he cried out:

My God, my God, why hast Thou forsaken me? . . .
They part my garments among them
And for my vesture do they cast lots!

To the majority of the pagan converts to Christianity and to their descendants, the New Testament thereafter became the only source of religious information; but also to many of the post-Apostolic Fathers, the Old Testament, even in its

Septuagint translation, became a *terra incognita*. Of Arnobius, the great Apologist who flourished under the reign of Diocletian, it is recorded that the Old Testament seems to have been altogether unknown to him. Melito, second century Bishop of Sardis, and author of the first Christian list of the books of the "Old Covenant," had to travel East to ascertain the number and contents of the biblical books. Some accepted as scriptural works books which among the Jews had long before been declared non-canonical. They regarded the Book of Enoch, the Assumption of Moses, the Fourth Book of Esdras, Tobias, Judith, Tobit, Bel and the Dragon, etc., as part of the Law and the Prophets.

Indeed, the Apocrypha proved to nascent Christianity of no less, if not greater, value than the Bible itself. Over the Old Testament the *Septuagint,* Aquila, and Theodotion, as it were, stood guard and led many a truth-seeking pagan to become suspicious of the assertions of the Fathers. It was different with the less read books of the Apocrypha. In them, interpolations could be introduced; and to them, other pamphlets could be added with impunity. Hence these Jewish post-biblical romances and apocalypses early began to teem with words and verses and paragraphs bearing Christian coloring and anti-Jewish bias. Thus Isaiah, in his ascension to the sixth heaven, hears voices of angels invoking the Father, the Beloved, and the Holy Ghost, and is informed in the seventh heaven that the Son of God would die on a tree, descend into Hades, return to earth, ascend to heaven, and sit at the right hand of God. Jeremiah exhorts the people "to praise Jesus the Christ and Son of God, the Light of all ages, the unquenchable Light, the Life of the Faith." Ezra is consoled by the divine assurance that "My son Jesus, the Anointed One, will appear with his retinue, and will diffuse joy among those that are spared."[13]

An unbiased study of the New Testament Gospels and the Epistles will show the trend among the Gentile converts of the new religion to drift further and further away from the Old Testament and the gradual intensification of hostility toward those from whom they received it. According to the most reliable critics of the Gospels, the earliest traditions current among Christians are contained in the Gospel according to Mark. In it we find nothing about the virgin birth of Jesus or his childhood. Jesus insists that "there is none good but one, that is, God." He complains of the weakness of the flesh, and shows not a few of the infirmities of human nature. He is intolerant of the Gentiles to the extent of refusing to cast the devil out of the daughter of a Syrian woman, though he readily drove out a legion of devils from a fellow Jew and drove them into two thousand swine. He admits that he does not know the time of judgment, that he cannot tell who will sit at his right hand or at his left, and he dies while repeating in Aramaic the words of the Psalmist (22:2): *Eloi, eloi lama sabaktani.*

This naive biography of a beloved Jewish teacher was enlarged and modified in telling and retelling until it became interpolated with statements about his resurrection, his command to the Eleven to go into all the world to preach the Gospel, and his threat that whoever does not believe in him and is baptized (which seemingly would include his parents) shall be damned. His personality was sublimated, his parables were elaborated, his miracles were magnified, his denunciation of the wicked Jews was expanded to comprise all the Jews. No attention was paid to inconsistencies and contradictions.[14]

The anti-Jewish prejudice in Luke goes still further. This Apostle seems to have begrudged the Jews the honor of having produced Jesus, and therefore traces his genealogy from Adam "which was the son of God." To him, the Jewish cities of Chorazin and Bethsaida were worse than Tyre and Sidon, and Capernaum was ripe to be thrust down to hell. But the Samaritans, those traditional enemies of the Jews, whom according to Matthew (10:5), Jesus instructed his followers to shun as well as the Gentiles, are models of kindness among whom Jesus feels more at home than in his own Galilee, even though reportedly one of the Samaritan villages refused to admit him.[15]

The Gospel attributed to John and written probably about

150 C. E. is still more virulent against Jews and ignorant of
Judaism. In it, Jesus breaks with the Pharisees at the very
start. When he addresses the Jews, he speaks to them like the
"wicked son" of the Passover *Haggadah* of "your Law." God,
he believes, purposely hardened the heart of the Jews so that
they might be damned.[16]

The same tendency is noticeable in the Epistles as in the
Gospels. In the one attributed to James we hear the still,
small, but nonetheless persuasive voice of the "brother of the
Lord," surnamed the Just (*Zaddik*). Except for two references to Jesus in the introductory verses to chapters one
and two, which seem to be interpolations, it might have been
written by any of his contemporary *Tannaim* (authors of the
Mishnah.) There is in it an evident sympathy with the Jewish
viewpoint and nothing about salvation by Jesus. The author
pleads for deed, not creed. His idea of pure and undefiled
religion is reminiscent of Micah (6:6). It is: "To visit the
fatherless and the widows in their affliction, and to keep
himself unspotted from the world." To him, merely to believe that Jesus is the Messiah does not make one beloved
of God: "the devils also believe, and tremble." "Abraham
our father was justified by works." Patience under trial, upright dealing, justice to the laborer, truthfulness, and the
pursuit of peace are what count. All else is secondary and
should be left to the judgment of God. He does not generalize.
He does not indict all the scribes and Pharisees, even if they
rejected Jesus as a Messiah.[17]

More christological, yet still savoring of Jewish views, are
the Epistles ascribed to Peter, which appeal to the Saints
to lay aside all malice and all guile, and hypocrisies and envies,
and all evil speaking, and to abstain from all fleshly lusts,
and to be as holy as God is holy. Still more so is the Epistle
of Jude, who describes himself as Brother of James, presumably the "Brother of the Lord" and the bishop of Jerusalem.
They were probably indicted by Ebionites or Nazarenes when
they began to drift away from their original moorings. Not
so is the Epistle to the Hebrews, which has been variously
attributed to Paul, Barnabas, Luke, and others. In the style

of the Rabbis, and abounding in references to the Bible, the
author proceeds to prove that Jesus was both the High Priest
and the sacrificial lamb, and that all the worthies of the
Bible "died in the faith, not having received the promises,
but having seen them from afar off, and were persuaded
of them and embraced them." Thus the furniture in the
Tabernacle, and the High Priest who officiated therein, are
shadowings of things hoped for and evidence of things not
seen until they were revealed by and in Jesus, who was greater
than Moses and holier than Aaron, and who was prefigured
by Melchizedek who, "without father, without mother, without descent, having neither beginning of days, nor end
of life; but made like unto the Son of God, abideth a priest
continually." With his advent, the faith of the ancients was
fulfilled in fruition. A new covenant came into being. A new
era dawned to bless mankind. Those who did not believe in
him are like the ones who hardened their hearts in the days
of Moses, concerning whom God swore they should not
enter into His rest. The greatest sin one can commit is to
refuse to believe that Jesus is the Son of God.

> He that despised Moses' law died without mercy
> under two or three witnesses, of how much sorer pun-
> ishment, suppose ye, shall he be thought worthy, who
> hath trodden under foot the Son of God, and hath
> counted the blood of the covenant, wherewith he was
> sanctified, an unholy thing, and hath done despite
> unto the Spirit of grace? For we know Him that hath
> said, Vengeance belongeth unto me, I will recompense,
> saith the Lord. And again, The Lord shall judge his
> people. It is fearful to fall into the hands of the living
> God.[18]

The growing animosity against the Jews by the hitherto
Judeo-Christians sometimes expressed itself not only in diatribes but also in insulting argument and even in acts of violence.
The Rabbis, as a rule were loath to engage in religious disputations with those who had left the fold. Commenting on

the saying of R. Eliezer b. Arak: "Know what answer to give
to the unbeliever," R. Johanan remarks: "This refers only
to an unbelieving Gentile. It does not refer to the unbelieving
Jew, since argument will only make him the more persistent
in his folly." The Sages also warned that only those who are
as able to debate as, for instance, R. Idit, should indulge in a
controversy. They never, however, refused to accept a challenge and were sure that "on whatever the unbelievers went
astray an answer is supplied in the Scriptures alongside of it."
As a result, all the mooted questions concerning the selection
of Israel, the sonship of Jesus, the vicarious atonement, and
almost all that has been said on these and similar subjects to
this day can be culled from the controversial scraps scattered
in the tomes of the Talmud. What is of interest to us is that
the Rabbis, like Hillel, seldom if ever lost their equanimity
and were always careful not to hurt the sensibilities of their
adversaries. It is reported that once R. Judah Hannasi was
presented with a gold dinar by one of these apostates. He accepted it, "in order not to cause ill feeling," but threw it away
when his antagonist had departed. [19]

It was otherwise with the Judeo-Christians, or *Minim*, as
they came to be called by the Rabbis. Though they differed
among themselves, having as many as twenty-four varieties,
they were as one in harrying their former coreligionists. They
lived among the Jews, attended their services, and plied their
trades in the Jewish section, but always grasped the opportunity
to insult them or to do them harm. They made the lives of
many of the Sages miserable, some of whom, like R. Haninah,
the nephew of R. Joshua, R. Meir, Abba Hilkiya, R. Abahu,
and Rab Safra, barely escaped being tortured, strangulated, or
poisoned. Measures were, therefore, taken to bar the *Minim*
from association with the unsuspecting Jews. Scrolls of the
Torah, phylacteries, or *mezuzas* written by them were declared to be unfit for use and were burned for fear lest they
contain un-Jewish doctrines. Their wine, bread, or meat were
tabooed. Their testimony was not acceptable in a court of
justice. As a further safeguard against them, changes were
made in the ritual of the synagogue, and a prayer was intro-

duced into the *Amidah* (silent devotion) in which they were included among the enemies of Israel whom God was implored to "cut off." [20]

But the Gentile Christians of Rome and elsewhere, among whom the spirit of Paul dominated from the start, were no more favorably disposed to the *Minim* than to the Jews. By the Gentile Christians they were suspected as being Jews still, and their Roman pride and patriotism prompted them to regard them as barbarians and enemies of the Empire. The Apostle John complains that Diotrephes, a Gentile Christian, refused to receive the brethren, spread evil reports about them, and ejected from the assembly those who were in favor of befriending them. [21]

This being the attitude of the Gentile Christians toward their fellow-believers in the Messiahship of Jesus who were of the Jewish fold, or still observed some ceremonies of Judaism, it can be readily surmised what their attitude was toward those who persisted in proclaiming their origin and adhering to their original religion. Their bitterness became especially intense after the rebellion of Bar Kokba and its effect upon the Roman pagans, who could not distinguish between converts to Judaism and Christianity. The latter, therefore, sought to sever all ties with the mother religion, and the Fathers of the Church appealed to the Emperor to consider Christianity as wholly distinct from and in no way connected with Judaism.

It is interesting to note that even after the schism there were still some Gentile Christians who could find something to say in favor of the Jews. Aristides, a convert philosopher of Athens, who presented an "Apology" to Antoninus Pius, claiming that only Christians have the true conception of God, admits that Jews, too, worship God and imitate Him by showing compassion for the poor, by ransoming the captives, and in burying the dead, and other "such things as are acceptable before God and well pleasing also to man." This, however, became more and more an exception. Justin Martyr, in his appeals to Antoninus Pius and Marcus Aurelius, is not content with pleading the cause of the Christians. He blames the Jews for all the evil that has befallen his new coreligionists.

They, the Jews, were the authors of the wicked prejudice against the Righteous One and "us who are his." They not only killed Jesus but would kill all Christians if they were not afraid of the Government. So they inflamed the heathen to do it for them. They scourged women in the synagogue if they wished to convert to Christianity. In a word, they "treat us like enemies, as if they were at war with us; killing and torturing us when they can as you do yourselves." And addressing the Jews whom he calls Esau, he exclaims: "Jacob was hated for all time by his brother, and we now, and our Lord himself, are hated by you and all men, though we are brothers by nature."

One of the means by which the early Church Fathers endeavored to fight Judaism was by writing more or less imaginary disputations in which Jews are depicted as ignorant of their own Scriptures or as maliciously falsifying them so as to belie the claims of the Christians. Here, too, Justin Martyr was the first and greatest of his kind. In his Dialogue with Trypho, "the most celebrated scholar of the Jews," which is typical of the Christian-Jewish polemics, he tells that one day he was accosted by the famous rabbi, whose identity scholars have not yet determined, and was politely engaged by him in a discussion as to the relative merits of Judaism and Christianity. Trypho readily concedes that the rumors about the midnight meetings of Christians, when they indulge in lewdness, are mere calumnies, but cannot understand why they have abandoned the observance of the Sabbath, circumcision, and other commandments. Justin, who knew the Bible only through the *Septuagint,* then proceeds, in an abusive and superior manner, to prove that the Jews misunderstand and even falsify the Bible in order to vindicate their absurd teachings, that no one can expect to be saved by the Mosaic law, but by the new law of Christ, and that those who accept Judaism, whatever be their reason, will be damned unless they repent and acknowledge their sin before their death. "These laws of Moses," he exclaims, "have been imposed on you by Moses because of your iniquity, and the hardness of your heart. They have been given you that you may be separated from other nations and ourselves, and that you should suffer alone that which you now justly suffer; that your country may be rendered a desert, your towns delivered to the flames, and that strangers may eat your fruits before your eye; and that no one among you may be able to go up to Jerusalem."[22]

Justin does not tell us what effect this controversy had on Trypho, except that despite his harsh words the rabbi thanks him and bids him God-speed on his prospective journey. But in the *Dialogue between Jason and Papiscus,* which became quite popular, Aristo of Pella (135-170) went a step further. In it, both disputants are Jews, both ultimately recognize the evil of Judaism and are converted to Christianity.

Despite their acceptance of the New Testament, the Fathers did not regard the Old Testament as obsolete. On the contrary, they looked upon it as the foundation stone of their theological edifice. It was to them "the oracle of God," the preparation for the New Revelation which was entrusted to them. Their interpretation was christological; and to prove their understanding of the Scriptures, texts were wrested from their contexts, verses were mutilated, words were misinterpreted and forced to fit into the Procrustean bed of their exegesis. This was facilitated by resorting to the allegorical method of the Philonites. "I will endeavor to prove to you from the Scriptures," says R. Justin to Trypho, "that He Who is said to have appeared to Abraham, to Jacob, and to Moses, and is called God, is another God, different from the God Who created all things; another, I say, numerically, not in will, for I affirm that He never did anything at any time, but through Jesus. In fact, while the Supreme Being is the Creator of all things, it is His Son, Jesus, who is the manager of all things. It was he who conversed with Adam, tested Abraham, announced the destruction of Sodom and Gomorrah, appeared to Jacob in his dream on the top of the celestial ladder and to Moses in the burning bush," etc. These views seemed so self-evident that Tertullian asks:

> How can it be that God, the Omnipotent, the Invisible, Whom no man hath seen or can see, Who

dwells in light inaccessible, walked in the evening in
paradise, seeking Adam, and shut the door of the ark
after Noah had entered, and cooled Himself under an
oak with Abraham, and called to Moses from the burning bush? ... These things would not be credible concerning the Son of God, if they were not written;
perhaps they would not be credible concerning the
Father, if they were. [23]

Like the author of the Epistle to the Hebrews, the Fathers
found in the Text that the Bible anticipated every occurrence
in the life of Jesus. But if they were at a loss for a verse, they
sometimes did not hesitate to invent or interpolate one. Barnabas, for instance, refers to Isaiah as saying: "Thus saith the
Lord to His anointed, to Christ" (instead of Cyrus). Justin
quotes from the Psalms: "Say ye among the heathen, the
Lord hath reigned from the cross." They also resorted to
symbols, *gematrias* and *notarikon,* the favorite method of the
aggadists and the Philonites, to show that Jesus was hinted
at in every story, and veiled behind every letter of the Bible.
Adam, who had no parents, and Melchizedek, of whom we
are not informed that he had any, indicated that God will
assume human form without the mediation of human parents.
Enoch, who "walked with God, and was not," typified Jesus'
ascension and transfiguration. All the ceremonials of the priesthood, and all the furniture of the Tabernacle and the Temple,
were foreshadowings of his Messiahship. The sacrifices were
intended to teach that there is no remission of sin without
the shedding of blood (of Jesus). So was the entire history
of the Jewish people. Leah, the weak-eyed, symbolized the
Synagogue; Rachel, the beautiful, the Church. Jacob, says
Justin, served Laban for speckled and many-spotted sheep,
and "Christ served, even to the slavery of the cross, for the
motley and many-formed races of mankind, acquiring them
by the blood and mystery of the cross. ... Jacob was called Israel,
and Israel has been demonstrated to be the Christ, who is, and
is called, Jesus." When Jacob cursed Simeon and Levi because
"in their self-will they houghed an ox," he thought of the

Scribes and Pharisees who were instrumental in the crucifixion of Jesus, "the Ox!" The two goats which were employed in the ceremonial of the Day of Atonement were symbolic of the suffering of the Son of God. As for the cross, Moses actually used it as an object of worship when he lifted up the brazen serpent on a staff, and Ezekiel in Babylon when "he set a mark" upon the foreheads of the men that sigh and cry for all the abominations that are done in Israel. Moses also made the sign of the cross when, in his war with the Amalekites, he extended his arms and had them held up by Joshua and Hur. [24]

No aggadists have shown greater hermeneutical skill and inventiveness in their eagerness to impress the moral teachings of the Torah than the Church Fathers in their endeavor to demonstrate the "spirit and power" of Jesus, and the importance of the dogmas which became connected with his worship. To the Rabbis, too, the Bible was the immediate revelation of God; but, with few exceptions, they discouraged the extremes of literalism and allegorism. "This Torah," they said, "is like unto two paths, one of fire, the other of ice. Should one walk in the former, he is likely to burn; in the latter, he will probably be frozen. What then should one do? Let him walk in the middle." They laid down the principle that the Torah speaks in the language of men, and had no use for those who distorted the Scriptures. In Christendom, allegory became predominant in explaining the Old Testament, as long as it corroborated the truth they held and propagated. [25]

Besides the Bible and the Apocrypha, the early Fathers adapted for their own use under the name of "The Teachings of the Twelve Apostles" the old Jewish manual (*Didache*), for instructing proselytes.

Though overlaid and interpolated with Christian doctrine, its groundwork is characteristically Jewish and plainly shows a marked resemblance to the regulations prescribed by the Rabbis for the reception of *gerim*. It also shows the steps which gradually led to the hatred of everything Jewish which was implanted in the hearts of converts to Christianity from the very start. It still refers to the seventh day Sabbath as the

Kyriac (the day of the Lord, presumably God) on which
Christians are to assemble and break bread and give thanks,
and recommends them to fast, like the Jews, on the day of
the destruction of the Temple, "that we may be glad to take
our pleasure in the world to come, as it is written in Isaiah:
'Rejoice all ye that mourn over Zion.'" It insists that "the
commandments of the Lord should all be kept; none to be
added, and none taken away." Later editors, however, while
they retained much which was Jewish, warned the cate-
chumens to observe "the *kyriac* of the Lord" on Sunday and
that they should neither fast nor pray "as the hypocrites." The
same is true of the *Didascalia,* better known as "The Apostolic
Constitution." [26]

Nor did the ardent Christian missionaries overlook the Sibylline oracles which the Jews of Alexandria circulated among
the pagans in the hope of winning them to the religion of
Israel. These, too, they interspersed with prediction of Christ's
doings and sufferings and his second appearance upon earth.
"Trust that most ancient and exceedingly old Sibyl," we read
in *Cohortatio ad Graecos,* "whose books are preserved in the
whole world ... when she preannounces clearly and mani-
festly concerning the coming of our Savior Jesus Christ, which
is hereafter to occur, and concerning all things which are hereafter to take place through him." The *Cohortatio* does not indeed quote these preannouncements, but before long they
made their appearance, and in the midst of one which seems
indisputably of Jewish origin we find the stanza:

> There shall come in a cloud to the Imperishable—
> himself also imperishable,
> Christ in glory with his blameless angels,
> And shall sit on a great right-hand throne, and judge
> The lives of true, and ways of false, monotheists.

This transformation and utilization of Jewish writings for
Christian propaganda was accompanied by the transfiguration
of Jewish worthies into Christian saints. The Fathers and their
followers maintained that all the heroes of the Bible were

latent if not actual Christians, and that the Chosen People of whom it speaks were the Christian people. As the Ethiopians after their conversion made of "the strong and holy Abba Moses" a black saint, so did they fashion in the image of Christianity Abraham and Sarah, Isaac and Rebecca, Jacob and Rachel, etc. Nor did they stop at the Old Testament. If Hillel was not included in the catalogue of Christian saints, it was probably because he is not mentioned either in the Apocrypha or in the Gospels. Rabban Gamaliel, however, who is referred to in Acts as the defender of Peter, the Fathers adopted as their own and named a Gospel in his honor, the Gospel of Gamaliel. It was claimed that he accepted Jesus but continued to pass off as a Pharisee so as to retain his place on the bench of the Sanhedrin in order that he might secretly help his fellow Christians—a tradition not unlike one current among Jews that Peter pretended to be a Christian for the sake of saving his fellow Jews. Photius states that R. Gamaliel was baptized by St. Peter and St. John, together with his son "the blessed Abibas," and Nicodemus. His body, miraculously discovered in the fifth century and enshrined in Pisa, Italy, was reputed to have effected many cures. Josephus, too, it was believed by some, admitted the Messiahship of Jesus. [27]

Thus Christianity, which was the offspring of Judaism, and imbibed its monotheism, its morality, its eschatology, its terminology, its liturgy, most of its ceremonialism, and even its technique for expansion, turned against its mother. The fasts and the feasts, the Sabbath, Passover, and Pentecost were divested of their Judaic association. The first Roman synod convoked by Pope Victor I (189-99) threatened the bishops of Asia with exclusion from the fellowship of the Saints should they continue to observe Easter on the fourteenth day of Nisan. At last the seventh day of creation was abandoned in favor of Sunday, in commemoration of the rising of Jesus from the tomb. The very names Jacob and Israel were made synonymous with Christian. Tertullian advocated that Christians use biblical names so that they might prove themselves "the true and genuine Israel of God, not merely by their deeds but by the names they bear." Barnabas claimed that the Jews were divested of

the Covenant when Moses had just received it, "and their
Covenant was broken in order that the Covenant of Jesus, the
Beloved, should be sealed in our hearts in hope of His faith."
Finally, the Old Testament was declared never to have been
intended for Jews but for Christians. That Jews preserved it
was due to their stupidity, "for had they understood it aright
they would either have burned it or become Christians. They
have seized it illegally, and have dealt with it sacrilegiously."
God permitted them to possess it, explains the author of
Cohortatio ad Graecos, "lest by bringing it from our (Christian)
assembly, we should afford to those who wish to calumniate
us a pretense for charging fraud."

What the Church Fathers left the Jews as a picture of their
role in the past, present, and future were Herod, the slayer
of the innocents, Judas the betrayer of Jesus, and the Antichrist.
Thus did the Fathers dispossess the Jews of their spiritual home
even as the Romans did of their temporal fatherland. "Verily,"
as remarks Harnack, "such an injustice as that done by the
Gentile Church to Judaism is almost unprecedented in the
annals of history. The Gentile church stripped it of everything;
she took away its sacred Book; herself a transformed Judaism,
she cut off all connection with the parent religion. The daughter
first robbed her mother, then repudiated her." [28]

VOLUME II

GENTILE REACTIONS AFTER
THE RISE OF CHRISTIANITY

CHAPTER XIV

THE LEGACY OF CONSTANTINE

THE untimely death of Julian, the Apostate, filled the Roman Christian party with renewed courage and conviction. His end was pointed to as proof not only of the inviolability of Christianity but also of the truthfulness of the Nicene Creed. Constantine emerged upon the horizon as a saint, almost an Apostle. His tomb and statues were said to have been endowed with miraculous power and were worshiped as divine. The soldiers replaced upon their banners the sign of the cross which they had effaced at the command of their late Emperor. Roman and barbarian converts began to flock to the Church *en masse*.

With the re-enthronement of Constantine's Christianity as the religion of the Empire, tolerance was proscribed as treason. Athanasius, Cyril, Cyprian, and Ambrose insisted that Rome adopt the same policy toward non-Christians as Moses pursued against Canaanites. They reminded the powers that be that Jesus declared: "Think not I am come to send peace on earth; I came not to send peace, but a sword"; and "whoever will not hear the Church, let him be to thee as the heathen and the publican." They interpreted "Bear ye one another's burden, and so fulfill the law of Christ" (Gal:6:2) to indicate that every Christian was bound to watch, his brother's religious behavior. They taught that, according to Paul, the Church must see to it that unbelievers "be delivered to Satan for the destruction of the flesh, that the spirit may be saved in the day of our Lord Jesus Christ." "Compel them to enter in," according to St. Augustine (354-430), the most eminent theologian of his day, was as imperative as "Thou shalt love

355

thy neighbor as thyself," and he proved it by referring to the
Old Testament:

> If the New Testament contains no example of the
> Apostles employing force, it is simply because in their
> time no priest had embraced Christianity. But had not
> Elijah slaughtered with his own hands the prophets of
> Baal? Did not Hezekiah and Josiah, the king of
> Nineveh, and Nebuchadnezzar, after their conversion
> destroy by force idolatry within their dominions, and
> were they not expressly commended for their piety? [1]

In the days of Theodosius the Great (c. 346-95), there were
as many as eighty or ninety heretical Christian sects. He resolved to impose the Nicene Creed on all the Christians of his
domain. Thenceforth, to deviate in the least from the doctrines
and practices of the Catholic Church became as dangerous as
to be an avowed pagan. Whether one sided with the Catholic
Church or with one of the several sectarian groups—Priscil-
lianism, Donatism, Pelagianism, Arianism, Nestorianism, or
Iconoclasm—in any case recourse had to be had to the Old
Testament, and, in many instances, with what the Jews, in
their oral tradition, had said in elucidation of their own Scriptures. The Catholics and the sectarians could not escape the
Jewish literary factor. [2]

In these sectarian controversies which stirred Christendom to
its profoundest depths during its first millennium, the Jews
themselves most likely took very little, if any, part. They had
enough to do merely to maintain themselves midst the hostilities all around them; and besides, they could hardly distinguish between the subleties of Arianism, Nestorianism, Iconoclasm, etc., and Roman Catholicism. Nor would they be so
foolhardy as to meddle in a matter which did not directly concern them and which would only add to the inbred suspicion
that they were in the service of one or the other of the parties.
How dangerous it was for a Jew to give utterance to his views
is illustrated by the talmudic anecdote about Tanhuma bar
Abba, a contemporary of Theodosius. He was a liberal re-

ligionist; he taught, "When a Gentile greets thee, answer him with an 'Amen,'" and, as a controversialist, he was careful to give no offense to his opponent. Called upon to explain why Jew and Christian should not be united by the bond of a common faith, the witty rabbi replied that he, too, was in favor of such a union, but since Jews cannot "uncircumcise" themselves while Christians can become "unbaptized" he would suggest that Christians become circumcised and unite with the Jews. The Emperor admitted the reasonableness of the suggestion, but ordered that in accordance with an ancient law which prescribes the death penalty for one who disagrees with His Majesty, Tanhuma should be thrown to the lions. It is said that the beasts did the rabbi no harm and that one of the onlookers, who attributed it to the beasts being well fed, was shown that such was not the case by being himself thrown into the arena, where he was immediately torn to pieces. [3]

Nevertheless, each sect saw the hand of the subtle Jew, or the *opiniones Judaicae,* in what it regarded as the heterodoxies of the other, and they blamed him for the brutalities which they meted out to one another. Leo the Isaurian was condemned not only as another Julian the Apostate, but as a veritable Jew. Nestorius was a "perfidious Jew" to Gregory. The Chalcedonians branded their antagonists, the Monophysites, as Jews, and later returned the compliment by stating that their adversaries themselves drew their inspiration from infidel Jews. They even adduced as evidence a petition allegedly presented by the Jews to Emperor Marcian, which read:

> For a long time we were regarded as descendants of those who crucified a god and not a man. But since the Synod of Chalcedon has decided that we have crucified a man and not a god, we beg to be forgiven for this offense, and have our synagogues restored to us. [4]

How to protect the faithful Christians against the insidious influence of the Jews was suggested by the example set by Constantine when he adopted Christianity as the religion of the Roman Empire. Until his day, whatever the disabilities to which the Jews were subjected by his pagan predecessors were in consequence of their being a conquered and rebellious nation. When they behaved as good Romans should and showed the proper respect for the Emperor's statue, they were, as a rule, left unmolested. Even Theodosius the Great still admitted, "It is quite clear that no laws forbid the existence of a Jewish sect."

But the intense hatred of Constantine toward the Jews, which prompted him to speak of the synagogue as a *conciliabulum* (brothel), stamped the Jews as totally unworthy of human rights as long as they clung to the "superstition" of their fathers, and thereafter to harrow and humiliate them became a mark of Christian kings' piety. In this attitude they were, of course, encouraged, if not inspired, by the Churchmen who were usually the legislators of Christianity and who were ready to condemn when political or economic necessity sometimes prompted temporal rulers to relax the severity of their edicts. "Only against his murder would the Church, the guardian of the oppressed, lift up her voice," says a modern historian of the Jews in the medieval community. However, even in such instances there were numerous exceptions, while it is an undeniable fact that

> If an order went out for his expulsion, the Church approved, for Christian society was better without his presence; if his property were confiscated, the Church rejoiced, for his wealth had been collected by forbidden means; if his children were baptized by force, the Church (sometimes) regretted it, but doctrine forbade any attempt to restore the child to the home and religion of his fathers.

Naturally, the most drastic edicts were issued against conversion to Judaism. Constantius ordered the expulsion and confiscation of the property of all who aided and abetted Christians to embrace the Jewish religion, and Gratian deprived them of their testamentary rights. Theodosius I prohibited the marriage of a Jew with a Gentile, while Theodosius II decreed that baptized children should be endowed by their Jewish parents according to the satisfaction of the bishop. He also forbade the circumcision of (pagan) slaves. In his enmity for Jews, he abolished the venerable office of the Patriarchate on the pretext that Gamaliel VI, a descendant of Hillel Hannasi, had built new synagogues and adjudged disputes between Jews and Christians; he diverted the tax which was intended for the support of Jewish institutions into the imperial treasury (426). He did, indeed, issue a decree that "both now and for the future no one is to seize or burn their synagogues," but attached no penalty for its infraction. On the other hand, he admitted that in his role as legislator he was motivated rather by vengeance than by a sense of justice. The Jews and the Samaritans, he declared in the preamble to his Code, "have wits so ensnared and souls so damned by the monstrosities of their beastliness" that they fail to seek the Author of the great mysterious works of nature. If, therefore, "we take the law as doctor to recall them to sanity, they themselves are answerable for our harshness, for their obstinacy leaves no room for forgiveness." Hence

> Whoever has built a synagogue shall know that he has labored for the Catholic Church; whoever has wormed himself into office shall be degraded even if he has received decorations; whoever repairs a synagogue shall be fined fifty pounds; whoever corrupts the faith of a Christian shall be put to death. [5]

Theodoric, the conqueror of Italy, who was an Arian, was far more humane than Theodosius, but no better disposed to the Jews. He did, indeed, make a sincere effort to put a stop to the destruction and confiscation of synagogues and permitted them to repair the synagogue of Geneva. But each time he took occasion to berate them for clinging to their faith. "The benefit of Justice," he wrote to the Jews of Milan, "will not be denied you. But why, O Judah, dost thou seek temporal peace when, because of thine obduracy, thou art

not able to find eternal peace?" Similarly to the Jews of
Geneva: "Why do you desire that which you should avoid?
We accord you the permission you request, but we blame the
wish which is tainted with error." Such were the views of one
who is said to have stated: "We cannot command religion, nor
compel anyone to believe contrary to his conscience." [6]

But the cup of Jewish misery was to be filled to overflowing
by Justinian, the restorer of the Empire and "Lawgiver of
Civilization." A Jewish tradition has it that for a whole year
during his reign the sun never shone. If this refers to the time
when he busied himself with his famous Code, then the legend
is based more on truth than on fiction. The Jewish Dark Ages
may be dated from his day. Even Theodosius the Great refrained from prohibiting the observance of Judaism by Jews
and still had regard for the fact that there was no Roman
law which forbade the existence of a Jewish sect. Justinian
in his *Corpus Juris Civilis* collected and re-enacted all the discriminatory laws against the Jews from Hadrian onward, and
"revised" and added many of his own. Jews and Samaritans
were prohibited from leaving legacies or making any presents
except to orthodox Christians. They could not act as witness
even against each other, nor buy a piece of ground on which a
church stood, nor build a new *spelunca* (synagogue, literally,
a cave, or hole in a rock). If the Jewish Passover fell on the
same day as the Christian Easter, they were forbidden to celebrate it. Jews were not allowed to recite the *Shma,* because it
asserts that "the Lord is One"; and the Adoration, because they
did not admit that "Holy, holy, holy is the Lord of Hosts"
refers to the Trinity. Justinian also proscribed the reading from
the Book of Isaiah because his prophecies afforded some comfort to Jews in their misery; he ordered that they should use
only the *Septuagint* as their translation, and desist from their
traditional interpretation. Jews who doubted the existence of
angels or the resurrection of the body, he decreed, should be
excommunicated by their coreligionists, and their property
confiscated. [7]

Justinian also did his full Christian duty as a conversionist.
He compelled the whole community of Borion to be baptized

and turned its ancient synagogue into a church. When the
Samaritans protested the building of a church on Mt. Gerizim,
their most sacred spot, because the worshipers would mock
and attack them, he ordered their homes demolished, their
"king" Julian decapitated, and forced others to accept Christianity. The only time Justinian showed consideration for
the opinion of Jews was when one of them told him that the
vessels of the Temple, which Balisarius brought over from
Carthage to Constantinople, caused misfortune to those who
possessed them. Afraid to take a chance, he sent them in haste
to Jerusalem where he had them deposited in a church. [8]

The clergy on their part did their utmost to make Jews objects
of hate and fear, so that they would be shunned and abomin-
ated by all who beheld them. Never since Cato delivered his
famous refrain, *Delenda est Carthago,* was a people made the
subject of such ceaseless vilification as were the Jews by the
followers of the Prince of Peace. Every holiday, every Christian
rite, was utilized to implant contempt for and horror of the
Jews. All good Christians were cautioned to have no dealings
with them, as they were literally the first-born of Satan or
fiends in human shape. The Jews delineated by the Churchmen for the edification of the faithful were rather theological
caricatures than physiological figures. They know, said the
Christians, that Christianity was true, for their own Jewish
Bible told them so, but they denied it. Like Milton's Mephisto,
their consuming passion was said to be:

> To wage by force or guile eternal war,
> Irreconcilable to our grand Foe (God),
> Who now is triumphant.

St. Chrysostom, "the golden mouthed" Bishop of Constantinople, asserted that Jewish synagogues were actually the abodes
of demons, worse even than the heathen circuses, and that the
Jews keep the Holy Scriptures not to honor but to dishonor
them. "I hate the Jews," he cried in one of his fiery harangues,
"because they have the Law and despise it; and he who has
no limit in his love of Christ must have no limit in his hate

of Jews." St. Ambrose, Bishop of Milan, declared that the Jews were worse than infidels, since they denied Christ in violation of their own Law, and that mere conversation with them exposed one to "extreme pollution." St. Jerome, despite the courteous treatment he received from the Jews whom he consulted while laboring on his version of the Bible, lumped them all as Judases, was sure that their sanctuaries were synagogues of Satan, and doubted whether even their converts would be saved. To St. Hilary, of Poitiers, the Jews were originally possessed unclean demons. These were exorcised when they accepted the Law, but returned immediately after they rejected Christ. Hence it was sinful for the faithful to seek their peace, or even to answer their friendly salutation.

That God Himself deliberately deceived the Jews and gave them the Law in order to lead them to destruction, St. Jerome found in pointing to Ezekiel's statement (20:25): "I gave them also statutes that were no good, and ordinances whereby they should not live." That God denied them the ability to distinguish between good and evil, St. Gregory, "the father of medieval Catholicism" (540-604), found positively affirmed in the prefatory chapter of Job, which he uses as the text of one of his characteristic sermons:

> Who are the three hordes which stole the camels of Job? The Jews whom these hordes led away. Like camels they chew the cud; but, like the camels, they have no cloven hoofs, they do not discriminate between truth and falsehood.

But more ingeniously, St. Origen proves that the Jews were made to be inveterate enemies of Christianity from the verse, "I will move them to jealousy with those who are not a people" (Dt. 32:21). This indicated, he explained, that the Jews were always to be jealous of and seek to extirpate the Christians, who are not a people in a political sense. They never ceased, he asserted, to lure the unwary Christians into their fold, or to wreak vengeance upon those who impeded their demoniac designs. Whatever misfortunes had befallen Christendom could be traced to them: they killed Barnabas and stoned his brother Aristobulus for preaching to the Gentiles; they bribed Pilate to put to death a certain Longinus; they stirred up the pagans against Paul and Peter. According to Eusebius, Jews scourged Christian men and women when they visited their synagogues. It was believed that at their Purim celebration Jews crucified a Christian in memory of Haman and in mockery of Jesus. In the wars of the Romans against the Persians it was said that Jews purchased ninety thousand Christian prisoners just for the pleasure of putting them to death! [9]

Pari passu with these strenuous efforts to safeguard Christendom against the Jewish peril, the Church exerted itself to save the Jews from themselves by converting them to Christianity. To achieve this goal, all means from bribes to banquets to torture and banishment, and the kidnapping of infants, were regarded as permissible and even praiseworthy. To the credit of the papacy be it said that many of the pontiffs were more tolerant than the inferior clergy, and did not favor forced conversions. Of Pope Honorius it was said that he allowed baptised Jews to return to their former faith. The first pope of whose attitude to Jews we have considerable information, Gregory the Great, though an ardent conversionist, advocated the use of gentleness and protested to the Bishops of Marseilles and other dioceses against their resort to force, since such converts were not likely to be sincere. He was sure Jews were more likely to be won over to Christianity by kindness. He himself set an unusual example of tolerance when he ordered the restoration to the Jews of a synagogue which had been "consecrated" by a Jewish apostate immediately after his baptism by placing in it his baptismal robe, a cross, and a statue of the Virgin. He also ordered the payment for the synagogue buildings, which the Bishop of Palermo had "consecrated," at a price fixed by reputable persons, declaring that "if a Jew may not exceed the law, he ought to be allowed peaceably to enjoy what the law permits."

Yet even Gregory the Great could not resist the temptation to drive Jews into the Church by means which were not strictly fair or just. He congratulated Reccared on his severe legislation *contra Judeorum perfidiam* and ruled that while a pagan slave who declared his intentions to accept Christianity remained a slave, he secured his freedom if his master was a Jew. He also connived at the conduct of some converts and made special inducements to various Jews in the hope of their ultimate conversion.

One of the means whereby Jews were expected to be attracted to Christianity was by disputations, or, as they came to be more correctly called, "altercations" or "denunciations." These discussions became popular after the appearance of Justin's *Trypho the Jew*. Written copies of them were attributed to almost every leading churchman, even to some who very likely had never met a Jew. They are usually filled with insults to Jews and diatribes against Judaism, and the victory is always given to the Christian. About the sixth century these also began to be supplemented with stories or novels in which Jews were made the heroes of miraculous incidents which led to their conversion. Like the altercations, these originated in the East, one of the earliest being *Herbanus the Jew, and Gregentius*. The latter, an Archbishop of Ethiopia, summons all the Jews of the kingdom to listen to him prove from the Old Testament the truth of the doctrines of the Trinity, the Incarnation, the Cross, and the rejection of Israel. But Herbanus, their representative, parries off every attack and suggests on the third day that they be allowed to part in peace. "I see," says he, "that you have one mind and we have another. Would it not be better, therefore, for each to obey his own understanding and to be silent?"

But as the Jews gather around to congratulate the champion of their religion, Jesus appears standing on a purple cloud, surrounded by rays of glory, sword in hand and a diadem on his head, and is heard exclaiming: "Behold I appear Who was crucified by your fathers." This is followed by a blinding lightning and a crash of thunder. The heavens open, and Herbanus and the Jews are stricken with blindness. On being assured that baptism will restore their sight, Herbanus is the first to be baptized. The king acts as his godfather and confers upon him ecclesiastical and secular honors. The other Jews follow his example, and the whole kingdom is filled with joy. [10]

In the *Teaching of Jacob, the New Convert,* of the seventh century, Jacob, "faithful to Jewish traditions," tortures a deacon until he promises to accept Judaism. The deacon commits suicide, and Jacob, on examining the tenets of the deacon's faith, finds them so admirable that he resolves to propagate them among his erstwhile coreligionists. All the Jews readily respond, except one, an Eastern Jew, who insists that the Messiah had not yet come, that Jacob is a notorious scoundrel, and besides, was "not baptized in the right season" (usually at Easter). Jacob, however, pursues his missionary activities and proves to the satisfaction of all that Isaac, Joseph, Jeremiah, and Daniel were prototypes of Christ. The Eastern Jew then admits that many Jews secretly believe in Christ, among them three of the most famous rabbis, and asks Jacob for baptism.

In the *Trophies of Damascus,* the Jews of Syria challenge a monk to defend Paul's declaration that the Law was made "a curse for us" (Gal. 3:13). He does so, and then quotes numerous texts from the Old Testament to prove the Incarnation. When he refers to the misery of the Jews as evidence of the falsehood of Judaism, the leader of the Jews retorts that Christians, too, were expelled from their holy places in Palestine and that the peace which they said their Messiah came to bring had not yet been realized. But the monk scores victory by reminding him of the brazen serpent of Moses and the Suffering Servant of Isaiah. As the Jews are about to accept Christianity, the monk feigns reluctance. They would have to be better prepared before they take that important step. Toward that end they must hear him expound the Book of Daniel. As he goes on with his elucidation the Jews are deeply stirred:

> They blushed with shame, were silent still, were
> troubled, were agitated, grew somber and embarrassed,
> strayed away, ran off without stopping, fled as if fire
> pursued them, fell about like drunkards: all their wis-

dom was consumed, and they all departed, some in silence, some grumbling, some exclaiming, '*Adonai,* the monk has won!' some shaking their heads and saying to each other, 'By the Law, I believe we are wrong,' and some of the elder ones made ridiculous remarks such as 'Dear, dear, how much bacon have we been robbed of?' and the former enemies became friends of the Christians, and waited for the opportunity to be baptised, and came to the church in all sincerity and truth and received the 'seal of baptism.'

In some tales the Jews feel themselves "too sinful to be baptised," or are afraid of losing caste not only among their fellow-Jews but even among Christians, or are repelled by the conduct of those who were reputedly good Christians.

Sometimes they are trapped when they, or their children, attend a Christian service out of curiosity. It is told that a Jewish boy in Constantinople tells his father that he partook of Communion without it being known that he was a Jew. His father, a glass blower, throws him into the furnace. But his mother finds him, like Daniel, unscorched, and both are baptized. An adult Jew is converted when he secretly comes to Communion and sees a child in the wafer and blood in the chalice; another, when he smears his eyes with the blood of some monks murdered in the Monophysite controversy and receives his sight; and still another, stricken dumb when he starts to dispute with St. Severianus, finds his dumbness removed by baptism. The tale is also told of a Jew who was in the habit of listening to a daily sermon by St. Theodore of Mopsuestia. One day he could not attend and, in consequence, fell dead. When the saint heard of it, he went to the cemetery, had his decaying body dug up, brought him to life, and baptized him. The Jew, however, preferred to remain dead; and, lest he should unbaptize himself, the saint promptly pushed him back into his coffin and had him reburied as a Christian. That many Jews sinned against the Holy Ghost through ignorance and needed only to be gently or, if necessary, forcibly enlightened is the burden of a seventh century tale. In Tomey,

Egypt, two monks leave their monastery, to supply themselves with provisions, on a day sacred to the Jews as a religious holiday. On their way they visit the synagogue where they hear "Amram the Levite" expound the Law. They start a discussion and find little trouble in convincing the worshipers of the truth of the Trinity, and soon the bishop has the pleasure of leading to the baptismal font the entire Jewish population of three hundred souls. This story was committed to writing with the instruction that it be read three times a year in all churches.

The Iconoclast heresy gave rise to a new genre of story. In it, a Jew invariably steals into a church for the sole purpose of mutilating an image of Christ, of the Virgin, or of some saint, to steal a crucifix or to stab a host. But some miracle happens at the psychological moment to frustrate his nefarious designs and lead him to the cross. He is suddenly smitten with a foul disease, the image or the host bleeds, the very elements rise in protest against the sacrilegious deed, and the terror-stricken culprit flees for safety into the bosom of the Church. All of which is intended to prove the efficacy of the sacraments and statues, for, "When Jews bear witness to Christian miracles, who can remain skeptical?"

One story, composed in the eighth century, has a plot somewhat similar to that of the *Merchant of Venice*. It tells of Theodore, a Christian merchant, who lost his fortune by shipwreck. He first appeals to his Christian friends, but they refuse to come to his assistance. In his distress he turns to Abraham the Jew who, like Shylock, first upbraids him for his insulting attitude and then complies with his request. Theodore is thereafter shunned and scorned for having dealings with a Jew, and none will even say "Good morning" to him. Broken hearted, he enters a church which was formerly a synagogue, and pours out his soul before one of the sacred images. The image informs him that all will be well and that he can assure the Jew that he will lose nothing in the transaction. On hearing this, the Jew is amazed at the miraculous occurrence, accepts baptism, is made an abbot, and latter succeeds the bishop who baptized him. [11]

An interesting story is related by John of Nikions, of the

seventh century. An Alexandrian Jew is the owner of a coffer which he cannot open, but from which issue heavenly voices praising Christ and around which there is a play of lightning. At last he takes it to the bishop, who opens it without difficulty and finds in it the towels which Jesus used after washing His disciples' feet. Of course the Jew is converted.

How the Jews are frustrated in their machinations against Christianity is a favorite theme of many a tale. In one of them a Jew visits a church, bent on stealing the Host. He attends Mass and takes communion at which he touches the consecrated wafer with his tongue prior to putting it in his pocket. To his horror, the wafer remains suspended between his teeth, and he finds it impossible to close his mouth till the priest removes it. Of course, the Jew, and many coreligionists with him, are converted.

There is a similar story about a Jew who steals an image of Jesus in order to wreak vengeance "on the deceiver who has humiliated our people." The image begins to bleed profusely as soon as it is removed from its shrine, and by the time the thief reaches his home he is drenched with blood. According to one version, the Jew is traced by his bloody footsteps and is summarily stoned to death. Another version has a more inspiring ending. The Jew, who not only steals but stabs the image, is so overwhelmed by the sight of the quantity of blood which gushes from the wounds and floods the whole church, that he becomes convinced of the Sonship of Jesus and, with his entire family, embraces Christianity.

These popular stories naturally produced a special effect upon the credulous, or "soldiers of Christ." Fed on patristic literature, and the lurid tales in which they believed and with which they whiled away their idle hours, they often took the law into their own hands, recognized not even the authority of their superiors, and endured and inflicted the most excruciating pain with equal indifference. They were frequently condemned by the authorities for their ferocity and were driven from cities because, as Arcadius remarked, "their violence is such that they behave as if it were a battle in question." With a fanaticism such as has never been surpassed, these desperate men would force their way into synagogues, and, with crucifix in hand and the mob at their heels, they would denounce everything the Jews held sacred. Sometimes they would set fire to synagogues, to them the abodes of unclean spirits, or, if sufficiently attractive, take possession of them, thoroughly cleanse them, and consecrate them to Christ. Such destructions and confiscations obtained in almost every part of the Roman Empire, especially in Asia and Africa, where many Jewish communities ultimately found themselves without a house of worship. The practice was encouraged by some of the leading churchmen of the age. When Theodosius, following the Roman law, once ordered the rebuilding of a synagogue that had been demolished in Mesopotamia at the instigation of a monk, St. Ambrose condemned him for impiety, reminded him of the example of Josiah, and warned him of the fate of Maxinius. "It is monstrous," he thundered, "that Jews who despise the Roman law should be protected by that law. As for the higher law? Who will protect them: God whom they insulted, or Christ whom they crucified?" He would have been glad to have a mob do the same to the synagogue in Milan, had not God anticipated him and burned it Himself. Likewise, when the monks seized the synagogue of Antioch and the Emperor ordered its restoration, Simon Stylitis threatened him with God's vengeance and demanded the withdrawal of the decree. In both instances that most pious ruler complied.

Sometimes the monks would invade Jewish homes "to save the Holy Scriptures (which they contained) from Jewish defilement," and their Jewish inmates from eternal damnation by reducing to ashes those who resisted conversion. St. Zeno regretted that in some instances the bones of only dead Jews were burned, while there were still many Jews who could have been burned to better advantage. St. Cyril, patriarch of Alexandria, whose mob of monks tore Hypatia to pieces and plundered the churches of the Novatians, did not overlook the Jews. He gave them the alternative of conversion or exile, and the prefect who protested against the outrage was stoned to death. [12]

All the Jews, except one, of the venerable Alexandrian community, preferred banishment to baptism. But in other places the monks met with better success. In Minorca, it was claimed that, with the assistance of the relics of St. Stephen, they converted five hundred and forty Jews in eight days. Gibbon, however adds that with due respect to the relics, this feat was accomplished also with the help "of some wholesome severities, such as burning the synagogue, driving the obstinate infidels to starve among the rocks, etc." Entawos the Amorean is credited with having converted ten thousand, seven hundred and ninety-eight Jews and pagans. John of Ephesus prided himself on having turned at least seven synagogues into Christian places of worship. But most ardent, in the literal sense of the word, was Sergius of Amida. He chose to live in a village populated by Jews, where he would "gnash his teeth at them daily," exclaiming: "You crucifiers of the Son of God should not be allowed to live." When the Jews paid no attention to him, he collected a mob and burned down their synagogue; and every time the Jews rebuilt it, he burned it again. Thus, remarks a chronicler, "he continued his habitual practice of love towards God and towards strangers for forty years."

In Palestine, too, there was widespread burning of synagogues and houses; and Barsauma, at the head of a battalion of forty monks, distinguished himself by massacring the Jews who, with the permission of the Empress, went to lament at the Wailing Wall. This only relic of Israel's ancient glory became such a "detestable thing that causes appallment" to the worshipers of Christ, that when Omar, in the seventh century, went to see the site where once the Temple of Solomon stood, he found that Christians had turned it into a dump. [13]

The desecration and destruction of synagogues became an act of faith among the churchmen, and the conversion into churches of those of them which, because of their architectural appeal, were deemed worthy of preservation was celebrated with all the imposing formalities which marked the conversion of a

Jew. Before long, a ritual was composed, which the priests were instructed to use at their dedication:

> O God Who, being without temporal change, orderest all things, and bringest to a better state those things that Thou dost mark for change, look upon this church, dedicated to Thy Name, in honor of the Blessed.... Cast out of it the Jewish heresy of old, and fill it with the Holy Spirit and the truth of Thy Church: In the name of the Lord.
>
> Almighty and Eternal God, Who has deigned to cleanse this place of the violence of the Jewish superstition, and to adorn it with the loveliness of Thy Church, in honor of the Blessed ... vouchsafe, we beseech Thee, that in this church may shine forth that faith which, lifted up by the sign of the cross, has trampled death under foot, and brought to us salvation and triumph: In the name of the Lord.
>
> (Aside) O God, Life of believers, and Fountain of Grace, fill, we beseech Thee, this sanctuary with the glory of Thy Majesty in honor of the Blessed.... Let what was once a den of iniquity become the abode of Thy Word, and where a throng of unbelievers were wont to gather against Thee may Thy people by its offerings ever merit Thy favor: In the name of the Lord.
>
> (Partaking of the Sacrament) We thank Thee, O Lord, that we have been quickened by Thy bounty. We beseech Thy mercy. Make us Worthy to partake of it.
>
> (To the congregation) We beseech Thee, O Lord, to drive all the wicked spirits from·Thy people, and to turn away the enmity of the Daemons of the air from them; In the Name of the Lord. [14]

While the destruction or "reconsecration" of Jewish places of worship was easily accomplished by monks and priests

backed, as they were, by infuriated mobs and the tacit or overt
sanction of the Church, it was otherwise with the conversion
of the Jews themselves. Against them the most eloquent appeals, the most erudite arguments, the most startling stories,
the most drastic measures, the most flattering inducements could
not prevail. The vast majority stubbornly refused to surrender,
and most of those who did, did so "for a little moment until
the indignation be past," and grasped the first opportunity
that offered itself to "unbaptize themselves." The banquets of
Ferreol of Uzes did not net a single convert, and the sermons
of Avitus of Clermont secured but one. "The Samaritans who
under Justinian sought safety in conversion," complains a
chronicler, "even today vacillate in their faith," and Arsenius
whom Justinian raised to the rank of senator for defending
his former coreligionists was crucified in Egypt. The converts
under Basil I (867-86) relapsed into their old faith soon after
his death. Nor did the Iconoclasts have any better success.
Though their churches were devoid of statues and images,
those Jews whom Leo the Isaurian and his successors "compelled to enter" maintained their Jewish religious observances
in the privacy of their homes or fled to the Caucasian Mountains and the Crimean Peninsula, where they contributed to
the conversion of the Khazars to the faith of Israel. [15]

These "false brethren," even more than those who rejected
conversion outright, constituted the hardest problem with
which various synods and councils grappled during the first
Christian Millennium. At the Council of Agde, in southern
France (506), a canon was passed requiring an eight months'
cathechumenate to test the sincerity of the neophyte. At the
Council "in Trullo," at Constantinople (692), New Christians
were prohibited from accepting Jewish hospitality in any form,
and even from visiting their sick relatives or consulting a Jewish
physician. The second Council of Nicea (787) resolved that
converts whose sincerity was suspected should be deprived of
the benefits of the Church, and their children denied the sacrament of baptism,—penalties which to those tainted with Jewish
heresies would probably have been welcome were it not
for their possible effect on their Christian neighbors. Finally,

resort was had to oaths of abjuration, which, in short form, read thus:

> On behalf of both ourselves, and our wives and children, through this Declaration, we undertake for the future not to become involved in any Jewish rites or customs, nor to associate with the accursed Jews who remain unbaptized. We will not follow our habit of contracting incestuous unions or practicing fornication with our own relatives to the sixth degree. We will not on any pretext, either ourselves, our children, or our descendants, choose wives of our own race. . . . We will not practice carnal circumcision, or celebrate the Passover, the Sabbath, or the other feast days connected with the Jewish religion. We will not keep our old habit of discriminating in the matter of food. . . . With regard to the swine's flesh, we promise to observe this rule that if, through long custom, we are hardly able to eat, we shall not, through fastidiousness, or error, refuse the things that are cooked with it. And if, in all matters touched on above, we are found in any way to transgress, either presuming to work against the Christian faith, or promising in words to perform actions unsuitable to the Catholic religion, and in our deeds deferring their performance, we swear by the same Father, Son and Holy Ghost, Who is One God in Three, that whosoever of us is found to transgress shall either perish by the hand of our fellows by burning or stoning, or if your splendid pity shall have spared our lives, we shall at once lose our liberty, and you shall give us along with all our property, to whomsoever you please in perpetual slavery, or dispose of us in any other manner that seems good to you. [16]

It is hardly likely that those who regarded the belief in the Trinity as a relic of paganism would become more confirmed in that creed by being compelled to swear in the name of the Father, Son and Holy Ghost. Nor did the Church succeed in keeping even its adherents from associating with those whom she sought to place in the category of pariahs and untouchables. There were never lacking Christians who were on terms of amity and close friendship with Jews, who spoke with admiration of their deeds of kindness toward some Christians; of their sheltering in the synagogues those who fled from martyrdom; of their shrouding and burying those who had been executed; of their veneration for the saintly lives of some bishops. The Council of Paris of 829 points to the strict observance of the Sabbath by the Jews "in spite of the absence of any earthly power to compel them" as worthy of imitation by the faithful. The constant exhortations of the clergy to shun the society of the Jews are in themselves proof that not all Christians followed the example of the frenzied monks and the fanatic mobs. Indeed, it took the Church almost as many centuries to inculcate hatred toward the Jews as love for Christianity. Friendly intercourse between Jews and Christians could not be stopped. A Jew could always truthfully say, "Some of my best friends are ... Christians," and Christians, that some of their best friends were Jews. This fraternization not infrequently led to private and intimate conversation on matters of religion, or on the correct interpretation of some difficult passages of the Scriptures, and sometimes, as we shall see later, even to conversions to Judaism.

CHAPTER XV

"LA ILLAHA IL'ALLAH"

At the same time that in Europe Catholicism, as the adopted religion of the Roman Empire, was going from strength to strength, in Asia the religion of Constantine had to fight for its very existence and was eventually overpowered and eclipsed by a religion which was born in the Hejas, that part of Arabia which came in most frequent contact with Palestine.

According to biblical records, corroborated by recent excavations, there were Israelites in Arabia in the age of Joshua and Saul. In the days of Solomon, they carried on an extensive trade over land and sea from Ezion-Geber to Ophir, for the purpose of exchanging their agricultural products for "gold, silver, ivory, apes, peacocks, sandalwood, precious stones," and horses. It is claimed that the visit of the Queen of Sheba to the wisest of kings was not so much to hear his wisdom as to arrange for trading-posts and colonies for the benefit of both kingdoms. A later record also informs us that there were Arabs in Jerusalem during the celebration of Pentecost. In the course of time the Judeans who settled in Arabia, and whose numbers increased by arrivals from Babylonia, grew into independent tribes, built themselves fortified cities, such as Yathrib in the north, Sabea, Sanaa, and Mariba in the southwest, which carried on an extensive commerce with India, Persia, and Byzantium. The Wadi al-Kura was almost exclusively in their hands.

These Jews were neither Talmudists, like those of Babylonia, nor rationalists like those of Alexandria. They were simple and brave men who gloried in their past and were proud of the "rock whence they were hewn." The Banu al-Nadir and Banu Kuraiza claimed descent from Aaron and called themselves al-Kahinani. The Chaibarites traced their lineage to the Rechabites. They became deeply attached to their new home; and, except for their religion, they became in all respects like their non-Jewish countrymen. They spoke Arabic, cultivated the muses, and boasted of their feats of arms. They tilled the soil and introduced new methods of agriculture.

Their relations with the Arabs were very amicable. They taught them the art of reading and writing in the Assyrian square characters and the science of calendarization. They recounted to them the Jewish traditions, according to which the Arabs are the offspring of Shem through Yaktan, and of "the seed of Abraham" through Ishmael. These they further embellished with legends about Ishmael's founding the Kaaba, and Abraham's visit to his son when he settled in Arabia, as is indicated by his footprints still preserved on the sacred black stone. [1]

The story-loving Arabs listened attentively to these tales and gradually came to believe that they were of the stock of their accomplished kin, "the people of the Book," who "knew what was hidden from them." Many of the merchants of Hejaz and Najd carried back to their respective tribes not only the merchandise which they received in exchange for their products, but tales about Adam and Eve, Abraham, Yaktan and Ishmael, Joseph and Moses. They also imparted to them the Jewish teachings about the Unity of God, the immortality of the soul, and the speedy advent of the Messiah. Gradually it became customary for Arab women of Mecca and Medina to make vows, when their children were sick, that on their recovery they would bring them up in the faith of the Jews. The Arabs around Petra came to believe that their forbears had accepted the Torah at the same time as the Jews, while the al-Beduls pointed to their name, which signifies "those who have changed their religion," as proof that their ancestors had been followers of Judaism. [2]

The outstanding example of the pre-Islamic Hebrew-Arabic relations is furnished by Samau'el ibn 'Adiya (c 500-60), the

renowned poet and warrior of the Arabic "time of ignorance."
His mother, according to good authorities, was Arab, while
his father belonged to the Judaized tribes of Kuraiza and
Nadir. His castle near Taima which, in keeping with the
custom of his people was open day and night so as to afford
shelter to all who were in distress, attracted many travelers
to and from Syria, among them some of the leading Arab
chiefs. When prince Imru al-Kais sought to reclaim the heritage of his murdered father by winning over Justinian to his
cause, he repaired to the castle of his friend Samau'el, and
stayed there as "long as God willed." On his departure he
entrusted his daughter, his cousin, and valuable coats of mail
to the care of his friend. These Samau'el refused to surrender
when Imru's mortal enemy, Harith ibn Abu Shamir laid
siege to his castle, even though he threatened to kill his captured young son unless his demands were satisfied. "Do what
you will," was Samau'el's message to Harith. "Time always
avenges treachery, and my son has brothers." The child was
slain in the sight of his father, but the faith of Imru in his
Jewish friend was justified. Samau'el's name was immortalized
in the Arab proverb, "more faithful than Samau'el," and
Maimun Asha's address to one of his sons:

> Be like Samau'el, who, when the fierce warrior
> Pressed heavily around him with his array,
> Chose between the loss of a child and faithlessness!
> O evil choice which thou hast made!—
> But quickly and calmly did he reply:
> 'Kill thy captive; I fulfill my pledge.'

Samau'el's poems were great favorites among the Arabs,
were recited all over Arabia, and became the model for many
a poet, while Arab Christians, interpolating his songs with
references to Christianity, proudly claimed him for their own. [3]
Due probably to Jewish influence, some of the poets of
the pre-Islamic period also showed a tendency toward ethical

monotheism. Thus one of them, who seems to have caught the ring of the Psalmist, sings:

> It boots not to hide from God aught evil within our
>   breasts: It will not be hid—what men would hold
>   back from God; He knows.
> It may be its meed comes late: in the Book is the wrong
>   set down
> For the reckoning day; may be that vengeance is
>   swift and stern.

In verses attributed to Umayya b. abi's-Salt, who was an enemy of Mohammed, we read:

> Oh my soul! Thou hast no protector save Allah,
> Nor is there any other that surviveth the events of time ...
> Oh Lord, suffer me never to be an unbeliever.
> Let faith be forever the secret thought of my heart;
> Let it pervade my frame, my skin,
> My flesh and blood, so long as I live a man.

Indeed long before Mohammed appeared on the scene, Arabia became a battle-ground on which Jewish missionaries were fighting those of Christianity and Zoroastrianism for the promulgation of their religion. There was, however, something in Arab psychology which was equally allergic to Zoroastrian dualism as to Christian Trinitarianism, and which hankered after Jewish monotheism.[4]

The spread of Judaism was favored also for its teaching that the Messiah was yet to come and that the time was propitious for his arrival. This doctrine became especially appealing in the fifth century, with the breaking up of the Roman Empire and the invasions of the barbarians, which to the Jews was an indication of the beginning of the doom of Edom. The belief infected many of the Arabs, who also suffered from Roman arrogant militarism and were anxious for a deliverer. Thus Abu Ishaq tells of a Jew of Medina who promised the Arabs to pray for rain to the God of Israel if they would

donate a measure of dates and two measures of barley to
the poor. He also narrates:

> We had a Jewish neighbor, one of the Babu abd-
> Alasher. One day, while I was still a youth ... he came
> out of his house, and started to talk about the resur-
> rection of the dead, the Day of Judgment, the happi-
> ness in Paradise, and the Torments of Hell. The heath-
> en who did not believe cried out: 'Woe betide thee!
> Dost thou indeed claim that the dead arise from their
> graves, and live either in pleasant habitations or in con-
> suming fire, according to their deeds in this world?'
> 'Yes,' answered the Jew, 'I swear by the Name of Him
> by Whose Name it is to be sworn that everyone is to
> be tried by the fire of the furnace which is never
> quenched ...' Said they to him: 'Woe betide thee!
> Canst thou give us a sign that thy words are true?'
> Pointing his finger to Mecca and Yemen, he replied:
> 'A Prophet will arise in one of these places.'

Efforts like this missionary's must have met with a measure
of success. In Mecca and Medina, many began to doubt. Others
threw away their idols and adopted the Jewish custom
of praying three times daily with their faces toward Jerusalem.
Here and there men known as *Hunafa* (or *Hanifa*), who
were not unlike the "Fearers of the Lord," ceased to sacrifice
to the idols and adopted the moral code of Judaism. Here
again Abu Ishaq gives us a description of one of them, Zaid
ibn Amru ibn Nfail:

> Zaid ibn Amru was advised by a rabbi to become a
> Hanif. 'But what does *Hanif* mean?' asked Zaid.
> The rabbi answered, 'One of the religion of Abraham,
> who was neither Jew nor Christian, and worshiped
> Allah alone.' Zaid next asked a Christian and received
> the same reply. Thereupon he exclaimed: 'O God, I
> take thee to witness that I follow the religion of Abra-
> ham.' He then abandoned the cult of his fathers,
> refused to sacrifice to idols, or eat the flesh of slain

beasts, or bring up his daughters as an offering to the gods ... and constantly rebuked the evil deeds of his people.... When Zaid ibn Amru ibn Nfail grew old, he was wont to lean on the Kaaba and exclaim: 'Allah, if I but knew how to serve Thee so as to please Thee, how happy I would be to do so; but I cannot understand how.' [5]

There must have been others who, like Zaid, became dissatisfied with the worship of the jinns, of which there were three hundred and sixty images in the temple of Mecca, who abandoned the sacrifice of human beings, mainly infant girls, and welcomed the "wise men" of the People of the Book from whom they eagerly learned how to lead the good life.

Among the most notable of these was Abu Karib Assud, a contemporary of Constantine the Great. Having made secure his sovereignty over Yemen, he left Yathrib in charge of his son and journeyed eastward. He did not proceed very far when the news reached him of the assassination of his son, and he hastened back to avenge his death. In the midst of the siege, two Jewish *Khaberim*, or wise men, Kaad and Assud, came to negotiate with him concerning the city. Abu Karib was so favorably impressed with these Jewish ambassadors that he not only granted their petition but, after a discussion about their religion, accepted Judaism. In accordance with the prevailing phylarchic custom, his army followed his example.

On his return to Yemen, Abu Karib proceeded to convert the rest of the kingdom to his new religion by ordering that both the idols and the Holy Scrolls be subjected to the ordeal of the sacred fire. It is related that to the amazement of all, the idols and those who brought them were reduced to ashes, while the Torahs and and *Khaberim* escaped unsinged. What is more, the sacred fire refused to be returned to its receptacle by those who remained unconvinced; but as soon as the *Khaberim* started to chant verses from the Scriptures, it began to recede until it disappeared. Thereupon the astonished people burst out with one accord for the religion of the king and the *Khaberim*. [6]

Thereafter for nearly two centuries Yemen remained under the rule of Jewish kings. The best known of them was Yussuf, or Dhu Nuwas (515-525) who spread the Jewish faith also over Raidan, Hadramut, Sheba, and among various independent tribes. He constituted himself the defender of the Jews wherever they were oppressed. Upon hearing that two Jewish youths were murdered in Najran, he invested the city and offered the inhabitants the choice between Judaism and death. His treatment of the Christians aroused Justinian I to ally himself with Elsabaan the king of Ethiopia, whom he assured that the God of the Christians would fight on his side against the King of Yemen. Elsabaan invaded Yemen with an army of seventy thousand soldiers and a large flotilla. Dhu Nuwas, rather than fall into the hands of the enemy, turned his horse toward the sea and plunged into a watery grave. Elsabaan turned Christian and massacred the Jews and Arabs who refused to do likewise. [7]

While Christianity was thus taking root in southern Arabia, Judaism continued to gain ground in the north. In Al-Hijr, Al-Ula, Taima, Khaibar, Taif, Medina, and Yathrib, whole tribes went over to the religion of Israel. Those who did not take the final step were also indirectly and unconsciously influenced, so that it may be said that even as Judaism prepared the way for Christianity in Rome so did it prepare the way for Mohammedanism in Arabia.

Mohammed (570-632), the founder of this religion, belonged to the tribe of Koraish, which successfully defended Mecca against "the People of the Elephant," who were said to have been led by one Abramos, and came to be known as "the People of Allah." An orphan boy in his early youth, he loved to accompany the caravans which traded with Syria, Saudi Arabia, and other countries. In later life he married Hadija, a wealthy widow whose cousin was a convert to Judaism, and assumed supervision of her extensive business. While attending the various bazaars, he would seek the company of Jews and Christians and listen to their stories from the

Bible, the Apocrypha, the Gospels, and the Talmud. Whether it was due to the squabbles among the Christians concerning the creed, in which each sect branded the other as idolatrous, or to the belief that Arabs and Jews were both of the "seed of Abraham," Mohammed gave preference to the Jews. He was especially impressed by them as the people who mastered the art of writing whereby "the beneficent Allah hath taught mankind that which it knew not." Mohammed's favorite name for God was Allah, which bears a strong resemblance to the Hebrew *Eloha*. Besides, the rite of circumcision had been in practice among the Arabs from time immemorial.

Like Jesus, Mohammed never pretended to be an innovator nor to have a mission to any other people than his own. He came to recall them to the religion of Abraham, "the friend of God," and the father of Ishmael their ancestor. For some time he, together with his wife and his cousins Ali and Abu Bekr—the "Paul" and "Peter" of Mohammedanism—, worked secretly among the aliens and the poor, who were especially impressed with the doctrine that God is a *Rahman*, a Merciful and gracious One, who cares for all alike. When his followers grew sufficiently numerous, he came out in the open. The priests and the rulers became alarmed and theological debates grew hotter and hotter. At last Mohammed made the claim that he had received a special revelation. But the erstwhile camel-driver fared no better than Jesus the son of the carpenter, and those who knew him best believed in him least. The Meccans could not conceive that Allah would not choose a more imposing representative and mocked and pelted him with stones.

Finally the priests and rulers of Mecca decided to resort to force. It being against the law to shed human blood in their sacred city, they resolved to starve the Prophet and his followers into submission. This had some effect. After several months Mohammed announced that in a special revelation Allah had declared to him that it was no sin to worship the jinns. But as soon as he found himself safe again, Mohammed proclaimed that the vision was due to the machination of the devil. He did, however, refrain from preaching to the Meccans and limited his propaganda to those who came to the city as pilgrims or in pursuit of their business.

Among these strangers there happened to be a delegation of the Banu Khazraj who came to enlist the aid of the Meccans against the Banu Aus, their foes. While in Mecca they entered into secret agreement with Mohammed to visit them. After a narrow escape, Mohammed arrived at Yathrib on September 20, 622, which coincided with the Jewish Day of Atonement, the day which became distinguished among Moslems as the first day of the *Hegira,* or flight.

In Yathrib, afterwards known as Medina (*the city, par excellence*), the Jews were actively engaged in missionary work and converted many of the Banu Khazraj and Banu Aus with whom they intermarried. Mohammed mingled much with them and added further to the little store of knowledge of the Bible and the Midrash which he already possessed. He visited the synagogues and learned some Hebrew words, such as *Gehenna, Shekinah, Mishnah,* and *Zedakah,* as well as the several scriptural and midrashic sayings which he later introduced into the Koran. He also accepted and recommended to his followers many of the customs which he observed among the Jews, such as not to eat the flesh of the swine, the camel, or of any animal that dies of itself, or to taste blood. The Law of Moses he pronounced to be "a perfect rule unto him who should do right, and a determination concerning all things needful, and a direction, and mercy."

Though Mohammed regarded Jesus as "the apostle of God", he looked upon the belief in the Trinity of the Godhead and the divinity of Mary as sheer paganism. "O Jesus, son of Mary", read some of his suras, written at an early date, "hast thou said unto mankind, 'Take me and my mother as two gods beside God?'... Believe, therefore, in God and His apostles, and say not there are three gods; forbear this, it will be better for you. God is but One God. Far be it from Him that He should have a son!" Again:

They are surely infidels who say, 'Verily God is Christ the son of Mary,' since Christ said, 'O children

of Israel, serve God, my Lord and your Lord'; whoever shall give a companion unto God, God shall exclude him from paradise, and his habitations shall be
hellfire; and the ungodly shall have none to help them.
They are certainly infidels who say, 'God is the third of
three, for there is no God beside One God. . . . Christ
the son of Mary is no more than an apostle; other
apostles have preceded him; and his mother was a
woman of veracity.' [8]

It was gratifying to the Jews of Arabia to hear Mohammed
thus defend the dogma of their faith, and they were glad to
think of him as a potential Proselyte of Righteousness. Hoping that through him many more would accept the faith of
Israel, some of them volunteered to help him carry on his
mission among the Arabs. One of them even became his
amanuensis and set down his occasional "revelations." Among
his *ansar* (assistants) was Abdullah ibn Saad who is said to
have been the first to welcome him to Yathrib. To Mohammed,
however, this encouragement indicated that the "People of
the Book" were themselves ready to acknowledge him as their
Prophet or Apostle. He, therefore, counselled tolerance and
came out as a defender of the Jews against hostile Arabs.
"For the Jews their faith, for the Moslems theirs," he would
say. "Surely those who believe, and those who Judaize, and
Christians and Sabeans, whoever believeth in God, and the
Last Day, and doeth that which is right, they shall have
their reward with their Lord; no fear shall come on them,
neither shall they be grieved." He even counselled the faithful
to fraternize with Jews, intermarry with them, and assure
them that "we believe in that which hath been revealed to
you and to us." [9]

But although the Jews encouraged Mohammed in his activities among the pagans, they balked when he began to
insinuate that he was the Prophet sent to fulfill what is contained in "the ancient scrolls of Moses and Abraham." They
also refused to admit that Abraham was the founder of the

Kaaba. One of them translated the Torah into Arabic to show that Mohammed's pretensions were unfounded. Others asked him to prove his prophethood by performing some miracles. Thus Mohammed's hope for the voluntary conversion of the Jews proved a dismal disappointment.

His success at the battle of Badr (624) emboldened Mohammed to purge those whom he suspected of disloyalty, among them Asma, a Jewess, who composed satirical verses against him. She was assassinated while she lay in bed with an infant child. Abu Afak, for the same offense, met with a similar fate. Shortly after, Mohammed assembled the Banu Kainukaa, the smallest but most affluent of the Jewish tribes, and harangued them: "O tribe of Israel, fear the Lord or He will avenge Himself on you as He did on the Banu Koraish. Enter into the covenant of Islam. Know ye not that I am the apostle of God, and that I am referred to in your scrolls?" Those who refused to submit were banished from the country, and their wealth was distributed among the faithful.

It was one of these forced converts, Abdallah ibn Salan, who introduced the *Hadith* (the addenda to the Koran) as binding upon Moslems. It was he also who produced the first catechism of the new faith. He was held in such high esteem that he came to be regarded by the Moslems as the ideal proselyte.

As had happened in Christendom, the persecutions which drove many Jews to the camp of Mohammed caused also some of them to retrace their steps to the synagogue. Among these was the distinguished poet Kaab ibn al-Ashraf, one of whose parents was of the tribe of Tavy. He became a follower of Mohammed, and the Prophet thought him important enough to boast of his conquest. After the expulsion of the Banu Kainukaa, however, Kaab experienced a change of heart, declared himself a Jew, and stirred up the Banu Koraish to avenge the defeat of Badr. Mohammed was greatly indignant and, punning upon his name (*kalb*, dog), he likened him in the Koran to "a dog which, if thou drivest away hangeth out his tongue, and if thou leavest him hangeth out his tongue likewise." Unable to silence him, Mohammed delegated one of the faithful to assassinate him. The poet's head was cut off in his castle and

brought to the Prophet as he was offering his morning devotions. It was the first head of "an enemy of Allah" who died
for "the sanctification of the Name" of the God of Israel.

Shortly after this, Mohammed met with defeat at Uhud,
and the Jews proclaimed it as a mark of God's anger. This
embittered him still more and, claiming that he was executing
an order of the angel Gabriel who appeared to him in a "revelation," he decreed that the Banu al-Nadir be converted. The
Jewish tribesmen destroyed all their trees and fought desperately
until Mohammed consented to grant them permission to leave
their land, but he stipulated that they should not take their
weapons with them, nor any of their possessions. So they
tore off the doorposts of their homes on which were nailed
the sacred *mezuzot* and, except for two who yielded at the
last moment, arrayed themselves and their wives and children
in their holiday finery, and started out for Syria, Khaibar,
and Babylonia, to the accompaniment of drums and cymbals.
With them went Salama, reputed to have been one of the most
beautiful women of Arabia.

While some Arab poets celebrated this expulsion with satirical verses, others were touched by the fate of the unfortunate
exiles and expressed their admiration for the Jews. Abas ibn
Madras composed a eulogy in which he praised "their kindliness to all who were in need and distress. . . . They befriended
me during the time of ignorance. They honored me whenever
I visited them. . . . Alas for these children of Aaron who were
once exalted, but have been humiliated by those who have
enjoyed their favor and hospitality." Mohammed, however,
gloated over his victory and, in his "revelation" from Medina,
proclaimed:

> Whatever is in heaven and earth celebrateth the
> praise of God; and He is the Mighty, the Wise. It
> was He Who caused those who believed not, of the
> people who received the Scriptures, to depart from
> their habitations at the first emigration. Ye did not
> think that they would go forth; and they thought that
> their fortresses would protect them against God. But

the chastisement of God came upon them, from whence they did not expect; and he cast terror into their hearts. They pulled down their houses with their own hands, and the hands of the true believers.... This because they opposed God and His true apostle; and whoso opposes God, verily God will be severe in punishing him. [10]

Another "revelation" from the angel Gabriel sealed the doom of the Banu Kuraiza (627). Having reduced them to starvation, Mohammed made a last appeal to them to acknowledge him as the Prophet. But only one Jewish boy responded. The rest cried out: "We will not forsake the teachings of our Torah, nor exchange them for others for ever." They were given one more night to reconsider, but they spent it in reading the Scriptures. The next day, between six and seven hundred of them were marched to a trench which surrounded the city, and were slaughtered to a man. One, Alzubir, who once saved the life of a Mohammedan, was offered his pardon and the enjoyment of his possessions. He refused both and begged to be dispatched with the others, saying, "The rope should follow the bucket." Their women and children were sold to Bedouins in exchange for horses and arms. The only one who was spared was Rihana, whom Mohammed wanted for his harem. She was finally prevailed upon to accept Mohammed as a Prophet but refused to the last to become his wife. [11]

With the subjugation of Mecca and Medina, Mohammed turned his attention to the numerous flourishing Jewish communities of Khaibar. The Jews put up a brave fight, but they were betrayed by an apostate, and their castles fell into the hands of the enemy. Many of their women were distributed among the Mohammedans. The beautiful Safya, whose father was slain in battle, and whose husband and brother-in-law were murdered before her eyes, the Prophet reserved for himself. He married her on the battle-field and proved a very devoted husband. When his other wives taunted her with being a "Jewish hussy," he reminded them that her father was Aaron the High Priest and her uncle, the Apostle Moses. She became attached to him, too, and as he was dying exclaimed, "O Prophet of Allah, may my lot be with thee!" She survived him by about twenty years and died as one of "the mothers of believers," a title conferred upon the wives of Mohammed. [12]

Having crushed the Jews politically and economically, Mohammed betook himself to purge Islamism from every vestige of Judaism. He transferred the Kibla from Jerusalem to Mecca, which he claimed was from the beginning appointed to be "the place of resort for mankind, and the abode of peace." He abolished the Jewish Sabbath and substituted in its place Friday, the day when he entered Kuba. The fast of the Day of Atonement, he changed from the tenth of Ashuri (Tishri) to the month of Ramadan. He also removed the ban from eating camel-flesh, claiming that Allah prohibited it only to the Jews as a punishment for their hard-heartedness. To safeguard the Arabs against Judaic influence, he forbade the faithful to visit the synagogues, to read or hear the Jewish Scriptures, to allow Jews to attend services in the mosques or to fraternize with them in the bazaars. [13]

Yet, the religion of Mohammed remained basically the religion of the Bible and the Rabbis. It was, indeed, "that which hath been sent down unto Abraham, and Ishmael, and Isaac, and Jacob, and the tribes, and that which was delivered to Moses, and Jesus, and that which was transmitted unto the Prophets from their Lord." It insisted that God is One and that He is *Al-Rahman,* the Merciful One. To this was added the belief in angels, predestination, the resurrection of the dead, reward and punishment, the giving of alms, the control of one's passions, and the efficacy of repentance and prayers, to obtain forgiveness for all sins, even idolatry, adultery, and murder. Mohammed also stressed the virtue of peace and brotherly love and taught that one should be "like trees that yield their fruit to those that throw stones at them," that "one must not do to his neighbor as he himself would not like to be done unto," and that "deeds are judged by intentions, and reward will be made to every man according to the measure of his intention." [14]

In Islam we find the kernel of Judaism transplanted to Arabian soil. Furthermore, in the words of Renan:

> If Islamism substituted the Kibla of Mecca for that of Jerusalem, on the other hand it renders the greatest honor to the site of the Temple: the Mosque of Omar rises from the ground which was defiled by the Christians... and pure monotheism rebuilt its fortress on Mount Moriah. It is often said, Mahomet was an Arian; that is not exact. Mahomet was a Nazarene, a Judeo-Christian. Under him Semitic monotheism regained its rights, and avenged itself for those mythological and polytheistic complications which Greek genius had introduced into the theology of the first disciples of Jesus. Mahomet was a Jew at a certain period of his life, and, in fact it may be asserted that, up to a certain point, he always remained a Jew. [15]

The fact that the Jews, with whom Mohammed claimed kinship through Abraham, failed to accept him as their Prophet, rankled in his bones to the last. He seems never to have been able to get them out of his mind, and the Koran is almost as full of mention of them as are the Gospels. Sometimes he appeals to them, sometimes he argues with them; finally he denounces and curses them. Then they are no longer the People of the Book in whom the Arabs gloried. They are asses which carry books but are ignorant of their contents. Nay, they maliciously changed, deleted, or misinterpreted, at the behest of the Devil, those "revelations" which came to them and which were incorporated in the Koran. Except for the slight difference in style, the following sounds almost like an excerpt from Paul or some of the Christian Fathers:

> The Jews say, Our hearts are uncircumcised; but God hath cursed them with their infidelity, therefore, few shall believe. And when a book came unto them

from God, confirming the Scriptures which were with them, although they had before prayed for assistance against those who believed not, yet when they came unto them which they knew to be from God, they would not believe therein; therefore, the curses of God shall be upon the infidels. For a vile price have they sold their souls that they should not believe in that which God hath sent down out of envy.... When one saith unto them, "Believe in that which God hath sent down," they answer, "We believe in that which hath been sent down to us. Say, why then have ye slain the Prophets of God in times past, if ye be true believers?... Say, Apostles have already come to you before me, with plain proofs and with the miracles which ye mention; why then, have ye slain them if ye speak the truth?... Hast thou not observed those unto whom part of the Scripture was delivered? They sell error, and desire that ye may wander from the right way; but God knoweth your enemies.... O ye, to whom the Scriptures have been given, believe in the revelation which we have sent down, confirming that which is with you, before we deface your countenances and render them as the back part thereof; or curse them as we cursed those who transgressed on the Sabbath day, and the command of God was fulfilled. [16]

Unlike Christianity, Islam at first did not hunt for heresies. To a certain extent Mohammed set an example of tolerance. Among his sayings were: "My people will never agree in error," and "the disagreement of my people is a mercy from God." For the People of the Book, that is the Jews and Christians, and to a lesser degree the Magians and the Zoroastrians, he always evinced a measure of respect. They could secure exemption from conversion by paying the *jizra*, or special poll tax, and the *Kharaj*, or land tax.

Notwithstanding the restriction against polygamy and the prohibition of drinking wine and the eating of certain flesh,

Mohammed, in the ten years of his missionary activity, achieved greater results than all the Christian missionaries in as many centuries. In quick succession, one Arab tribe after another became Islamized. Yemen, too, despite its strong Christian contingent, soon fell into line. Feuds which had lasted for generations ceased. Monotheism became general. Infanticide was stopped. For the first time in history, a whole people was suddenly transformed by an ideal—loyalty to One God and His Prophet. This phenomenal success inspired Mohammed with the hope that Islam would ultimately become the religion, not only of Arabia, but of all mankind, and prompted him to send embassies with letters to the Governor of Egypt, the king of Ethiopia, and the Roman Emperor Heraclius, urging them to acknowledge Allah as the only God and himself as the greatest of Prophets (628).

Mohammed did not live to see the spread of his religion beyond the confines of Arabia. While he was laying plans for the conquest of Syria, he died as a result, it is said, of poisoned lamb fed him by a Jewess of one of the subjugated tribes. But his plans were taken up by Abu Bekr, his uncle, the first editor of the Koran, and Omar, his brother-in-law and successor (634-43).

The first country to be invaded was Syria, which Heraclius had lately won back from Persia. There Abu Bekr met the legions of Heraclius. These had been reinforced by auxiliaries of Christian Arabs, whose battalions were presented by the Emperor with a crucifix, and incited by chanting monks and praying priests displaying holy images and sacred relics. But the sign of the cross no longer brought victory to the Christian hosts despite their discipline and equipment. The Arab hordes swept over Bozra, Damascus, and Antioch, and many of their inhabitants accepted the faith of Mohammed. Soon the battle of Yarmuk decided the fate of Palestine (636), thus partly proving the truth of the prediction of an astrologer that Byzantium would fall into the hands of the circumcised. The formal conquest of Jerusalem was reserved for Omar the Vicar of the Prophet. Omar saw to it that the inhabitants were not molested, but declared the city holy unto the Moslems and decreed that thereafter Christians should build in it no new churches, nor ring their bells, nor display their crosses. He also ordered the clearing of the place where once stood the Temple of Solomon and built thereon the magnificent mosque which still bears his name.

Simultaneously with the invasion of Syria, the Arabs struck on other fronts. Before long, the crescent replaced the cross in Alexandria, the Christian metropolis of Africa, and ended the dominance of the Greeks on the Nile. The campaigns of the Arabs in ancient Babylonia planted the standard of the Prophet on the Tigris and Euphrates, and the Persians fled from their fortresses without even an attempt at resistance. Mohammed's prophecy was thus fulfilled: in the same year that Jerusalem fell, Allah rent the Persian empire into pieces.

Their success convinced the people that Islam was true. Besides, they enjoyed a well-founded reputation that a treaty with the Arabs would not be regarded as a mere scrap of paper. The Christian schismatics who abounded in Asia therefore welcomed them as benefactors and saw in the defeat of the Greeks and the Romans the just vengeance of God on their fellow-Christians of the Catholic Church. It is said that even Heraclius was a secret convert to Islam. "The hearts of the Christians rejoiced," states a Nestorian chronicler with perhaps some ulterior motive, "over the domination of the Arabs (may God strengthen it and prosper it)." "The Moslems are just, and do us no wrong or violence of any kind," wrote the Melkite (Catholic) Patriarch of Jerusalem to the Patriarch of Constantinople in 869, and Eliyya, the Metropolitan of Nizibis in the eleventh century, declared:

> Their obedience and love impress us more than the obedience of people of all other religions and kingdoms that are opposed to us, whether we are in their land or not. . . . It is clear also that the Moslems, when they have oppressed us and done us wrong, and then have turned to their law, find that it does not approve of harming and oppressing us; but people of other religions, when they honor us and do us good, and turn

to their law, find that it does not praise them for this. So the wrong doing of the Moslems toward us, and their enmity against us, and their confession that in treating us thus they are acting contrary to their law, is better for us than the good treatment of others who confess that it is contrary to their law to treat us well.

As late as the twelfth century, Michael the Syrian, Jacobite Patriarch of Antioch, sees in the success of the Arabs God's vengeance upon the Roman Catholics for their cruelty toward the other Christian sects, and claims that He

> ... raised from the religion of the south the children of Ishmael to deliver us by them from the hands of the Romans, and if, in truth, we suffered some loss ... yet it was no light advantage for us to be delivered' from the cruelty of the Romans, from their wickedness, from their anger, from their cruel zeal towards us, and to find ourselves at rest. [17]

The penetration of the Arabs into Persia sealed the fate of another of the then very widely spread religions, Zoroastrianism, or Mithraism. It, too, could not cope with the appeal made by Islam, and, reduced in numbers and worldly goods, the ancient Parsees, after a succession of hardships, finally (716) left their native land for India, where they still exist as a small but a not unhonored group. [18]

The turn of the Melkites, or those of the religion of the hated Catholic Emperors, came next and was followed by that of the Nestorians and Jacobites. These latter were of superior intelligence and brought with them to Persia the culture and wisdom which made Syria and Babylonia famous. Driven from Athens, Antioch, Edessa, and Nizibis by the fanatical intolerance of Heraclius, who ordered their noses and ears cut off and their houses pillaged, they found a home in Persia and were granted many privileges under the Abbasids. They served as physicians, astrologers, and financiers in the courts of the Caliphs. Many Melkites and Zoroastrians also joined them, and before long their Church came to rival the Church of Rome. At the time of the Moslem invasion, it could boast a hierarchy of two hundred thirty bishops scattered through Arabia, Armenia, Babylonia, Ceylon, Egypt, Khorasan, Turkestan, and other countries.

But the favors the Nestorians enjoyed under the Moslems proved more fatal to their cause than the persecution they endured under the Catholics. Lulled by a false security, or influenced by the more rational dogmas of Islam, their missionary ardor cooled off. Many turned Moslem either out of choice or to gain or retain positions of honor or emolument. We have already heard them speak in favor of the rule of the Mohammedans. Here is a statement of the Nestorian Patriarch Timothy (780-819) in praise of Mohammed:

> Mohammed deserved the praise of all the Arabs, and that because his manner of life among them was in the way of the Prophets and the lovers of God.... Then, as all the Prophets turned men away from wickedness and sins, and led them to integrity and virtue, so Mohammed turned them to integrity and virtue, so he also walked among them in the way of the Prophets...and who will not praise and honor and venerate him who fought for the sake of God not with word only, but also with the sword, most evident in his zeal for the Most High Creator? [19]

In Europe, where Christianity was dominant, such an estimate of the Prophet by a Christian would have exposed him to torture and death. There Mohammed was everywhere considered a wicked impostor and his Koran full of deceptions and immorality. Luther later summed up the opinion of Christendom when he described him as a "devil and first-born son of Satan." But this display of tolerance on the part of the Nestorians and Jacobites did not extend to the Melkites or rival non-Catholic sects. Each sect was jealous of the other. In some instances they went so far as to mutually denounce one another as spies in the service of the Greeks. [20]

However, Islam, too, before it was a century old, began, like Christianity, to split up into numerous sects, each seeking to impose its favorite doctrines upon the other. The Sunnites insisted that the unwritten traditions (*Hadith*) are equally as binding as the Koran; the Shiites, not only refused to subscribe to the oral law but denounced the Caliphs who preceded Ali as usurpers. These were further broken up into smaller sects on the question of the interpretation of the Koran, whether God can or cannot do wrong if He chose, whether He waits with His judgments until the Last Day, whether the Koran was created or uncreated, whether one may compromise with other religions in order to escape martyrdom, whether the Caliphate is a divine institution, and so forth.

Those who sought to preserve or refine the pristine monotheistic doctrine of Islam were the Mutazilites, or separatists. With the sensitiveness of Pharisees to whatever might savor of anthropomorphism, they insisted on the creation of the Koran and the freedom of the will. They also advocated the popular election of the Iman or head of the faith. For this, their books were destroyed and their property confiscated. Haroun al-Rashid, "the follower of the right cause," decreed the death penalty for believing that the Koran was created. Under Haroun's enlightened son, al-Mamun, the Mutazilites came into power and those who held that the Koran was uncreated were condemned as heretics, thrown into prison and flogged. Al-Mutawakil (847-61), however, restored the orthodox faith, reaffirmed the dogma of the uncreated Koran, the Mutazilites were excluded from all public offices, their children were forbidden to attend Moslem schools, and all were compelled to wear a distinctive dress and to nail the figure of a devil on their doors.

The same treatment was meted out to the Persian Christians of all sects. Al-Mutawakil ordered them to wear dyed garments with a patch upon their shirts, that none of them should be seen in the market on Friday, that the graves of their dead be desecrated, that their children should not learn Arabic, and that wooden images of devils be erected on their gates.

Al-Jahiz (d. 869) denounced all Christians as hypocrites who push themselves where they are not wanted. [21]

Not infrequently Christians among the Moslems were summoned to defend the principles of their faith and to explain why only "a small and despicable quantity" of Nestorians are to be found in the country of the Turks and a sprinkling of Jacobites and Melkites among the Arabs. They were ridiculed for calling themselves Hasan and Husain, Abbas, Fadl, and Ali; for believing that three times one is one, and for calling for protection on one who himself suffered crucifixion. Al-Ghazali in the *Precious Pearl* tells a story which probably was current among Moslem wits, about departed souls who went to Moses to plead for intercession. Moses, it is said, advised them:

> Go to Jesus, for he is of all the Prophets the one who offers most guarantees for certainty, the one who knows God best, the most ascetic and the wisest of them. . . . Then they went to Jesus and said to him, 'Thou art the spirit of God and the Word of God. To thee God has given the highest title in the world below, and in the world to come. Intercede, therefore, for us with God to pronounce the judgment.' Jesus replied to them, 'Men have taken me and my mother as gods in the place of God Most High. How dare I intercede for you with Him by the side of Whom they adore me, and of whom they say that I am His son and He is my Father?' [22]

Christians were hard put to it to hold their own because, unlike the disputation between them and the Jews, they could not appeal to a work which had the same authority for Moslems as for themselves. They also had to be constantly on their guard not to offend the Moslems. To avoid the possibility of being entrapped, John of Damascus (d. c. 767) prepared a guide for those who might be called upon to defend their faith. [23]

Perhaps the strongest argument against Mohammedanism was that the Bible nowhere refers to Mohammed. "If I had

found," writes a convert from Judaism to Christianity, "a
single prophecy in the Gospel concerning the coming of Mohammed, I would have left the Gospel and have followed
the Koran and I would have gone over from the one to the
other just as I have gone over from the Torah and the Prophets
to the Gospel." But the Moslems were warned that the Christians deliberately corrupted the contents of the Bible and
therefore should not be consulted. Thus al-Bukhari pleaded
with his coreligionists:

> O congregation of Moslems! How can you ask
> questions of the People of the Book, when your book,
> which God revealed to His Prophet, brings the best
> news from God. Ye read it unfalsified, and God has
> told you that the People of the Book have altered
> what God wrote, and have falsified the Book with their
> hands, and said, 'This is from God,' that they may get
> some wretched reward for it. Has He not forbidden
> you to ask those people about what you have received
> in the way of knowledge? By God, we have never
> seen any one of them asking you about what has been
> revealed to you. [24]

However, with the increasing number of proselytes from
the People of the Book, attempts were soon made to find
allusions to Mohammed in the Bible, even as in the case of
Jesus by Christian Fathers. Ali Tobari, a convert from Christianity to Islam (c. 855), thus quotes from the Book of Psalms,
which he paraphrased:

> The prophet David said in the forty-fifth Psalm,
> Therefore, God has blessed thee forever, gird on thy
> sword, O giant, because thy majesty and thy *hand*
> are the conquering majesty and *hand*. Ride thou on
> the word of truth and on the course of piety, because
> thy law and thy prescriptions are associated with the
> majesty of thy right hand; and thy arrows are sharp,
> and the people fall under thee. We do not know of any
> one to whom the features of girding on a sword, sharp-

ness of arrows, majesty of the right hand, and falling
down of people under him, are due, except the Prophet
who rode on the word of truth, humbled himself
before God in devotion, and fought the idolaters until
the faith prevailed, and David said in the forty-eighth
Psalm, 'Great is our Lord, and he is greatly *Mahmud;*
and in the city of our God and in His mountain there
is a Holy One and a *Muhammad,* and the joy hath
come to the whole earth.'

A still bolder attempt to find Mohammed in the Bible was
made several centuries later by the Jewish convert to Islam,
Saidu Hasan (thirteenth-fourteenth century). He may have
used the Hebrew text, but modified and interpolated it to suit
his purpose. Thus he quotes from Exodus (32:13) instead of
"Remember Abraham, Isaac, and Israel, Thy servants," "Remember Abraham and Ishmael, Thy servants," and comments,
"Remember the covenant with Abraham in which Thou didst
promise to him that of the offspring of Ishmael Thou wouldst
render victorious the armies of the believers. So God answered
his prayer and made the Children of Ishmael victorious over the
Amalekites through the blessing of Mohammed." Another
reference to Mohammed in the Torah he finds in the words
"m'od m'od" (Gen. 17-20), and in the name Yoshiyahu (Josiah).

The wise men of the children of Israel who comment
on the Torah explain this. Some say 'very, very'; others
say, *'Ahmad, Ahmad';* still others say 'great, great,'
...But there has not appeared of the offspring of
Ishmael one mightier than Mohammed. His name in
the books of the Prophets is Yoshiyahu. This name is
one of the names of God Almighty, and it is not
applied to anyone but Mohammed. [25]

Not to be outdone by the claims of Christianity, the Moslems asserted that the Koran, the revelation *par excellence,*
had existed from all eternity, and that the first thing to be
created was the *Nur Muhammed* (the Light of Mohammed),

which outshone the Light of the Gospels. Furthermore, they invented miracles no less numerous and marvelous than what Christians claimed for Jesus. Al-Bukhari, evidently in imitation of the Gospels, credited Mohammed with feeding a large multitude with a few loaves, with providing many people with water in the desert, healing the sick, causing rain to fall, trees to be uprooted, and animals to speak; and Abu Nuaim, who wrote a work on the *Dalail an-Nubuwwa,* or proofs of the prophethood of Mohammed, asserted:

> If anyone should say that Jesus was distinguished above other Prophets by the fact that the Holy Spirit announced him to his mother, and that he spoke of his prophethood in the cradle, we reply that similar signs took place also in the case of our Prophet. [26]

The Jews outside of Palestine at first fared somewhat better than the Christians. Omar I, the great organizer of the Mohammedan Empire, showed his high regard for the office of the Babylonian Exilarch by bestowing princely privileges upon Bustanai. He also gave him for a wife Dara, or Azdadwar, the daughter of Chosroes II. [27] This favorable situation continued till the beginning of the eighth century. With the caliphate of Omar II (717-720), the persecution of the Jews in Arabia and Palestine spread as far as Persia. Omar was determined to eradicate all infidelity from his dominions and sought by threats and bribes to convert all his Jewish and Christian subjects to Mohammedanism. He did, indeed, instruct his governors not to tear down churches or synagogues, but permitted no new ones to be built. But, as in Christendom, the executives were more zealous than the legislators. Jews were excluded from public offices and, together with the Christians and the remnant of the formerly powerful magi, were compelled to wear badges. They were deprived of their autonomy; the Exilarchate was shorn of its glory; and their places of worship were confiscated and turned into mosques.

These persecutions drove many Jews into the bosom of Islam and some of them left their mark upon its gradual development. Kaab ibn Mati, the favorite of Caliph Omar, was noted as a Mohammedan theologian and was distinguished as *al-Ahbar* (the Scholar). His teachings paved the way for the apotheosis of Mohammed as did Paul's for the deification of Jesus. To Abdallah ibn Saba may be attributed the origin of the sect which claims that Ali never died and that he will return some day to fill the world with peace and justice.

Most Jews, however, saw in the vicissitudes brought about by the Moslems indications of the immediate advent of the Messiah, and some even ventured to proclaim that they were themselves his forerunners or incarnations. Among the latter was Serene, who announced his Messiahship in the year in which Omar II died. Like Paul, he declared the Law as no longer binding and permitted marriage within the prohibited degrees of consanguinity. His fame spread beyond the confines of Persia, and Jews from distant Spain and France left for Palestine in the hope that he would soon expel the Arabs from the Holy Land. Captured by Caliph Yazid II, Serene pretended that he was merely making sport of the credulous Jews. So he was turned over to Rab Natrunai, the Gaon of Pumbeditha (719-30). The Gaon readmitted him and those of his followers who did not violate the laws of consanguinity into the fold after they submitted to the prescribed flagellation and declared their whole hearted allegiance to the teachings of the Torah. [28]

Obaya Abu-Isa of Ispahan (c. 750) did not pretend to be *the* Messiah, but the fifth and last of his forerunners, which included Jesus and Mohammed. He declared that the Messiah would come as soon as the Jews accept the Gospels and the Koran as of equal sanctity with the Torah. Unlike Serene, he was very rigorous. He abolished divorce, even in the case of adultery; ordered that prayers should be offered seven times daily in accordance with the declaration of the Psalmist (119:164), and prohibited the use of meat or wine. The miracles which he was said to have performed attracted to him so many converts that he ventured to wage war against the Persians. After nearly ten years, during which he fought at the head of an army of ten thousand, he fell in battle in 755. Most of his followers returned to the fold, but others constituted themselves a distinct sect, the Isawites. They believed that Obaya was never defeated and that he would return to finish the reformation which he had begun. The fact that despite his illiteracy he wrote, as they claimed, many books, was to them the best evidence that, like Mohammed, he was divinely inspired. A small group of the faithful still existed in Damascus during the middle of the tenth century. [29]

Another pretender to Messiahship was the disciple of Abu-Isa, Yudghan, or Judah, of Hamadan. He proclaimed himself as the Al-Rai, or (good) shepherd, and asserted that prayers and fasting would bring about the advent of the Messiah. He did not deny the Prophethood of Jesus and Mohammed but maintained that their mission was limited, while his was to establish enduring peace among all mankind. Though the Yudghanites were pacifists, one of them, Mushka, incited his followers, the Mushkaniyos, to impose the tenets of their faith by force, and all were killed in battle in the neighborhood of Koom. [30]

But, even those who were not carried away by their fervent hope for the speedy advent of the Messiah, doubted that Mohammed marked the final phase of the struggle of Judaism against paganism and the ultimate redemption of Israel from his persecutors. Rabbi Eleazer Hakkalir, the prolific hymnodist (*paetan*) of the seventh century, predicted in a hymn which later found its way into the liturgy that

> In those days and at that season, in the first month,
>   the month of Nissan,
> Yes, on the fourteenth day thereof, will suddenly
>   appear Nenahem ben Amiel (Messiah),
> Then will he say to her who is bereaved (Zion), Thy
>   children are come,
> I will set thy stones in fair colors.

Many also found an indication in the Bible (Deut. 33:2) that there would be three revelations—one from Sinai to the Jews, one from Seir to the Christians, and one from Paran to the Arabs—and that the third would inaugurate the conversion of all to the faith of the first. In an Apocalypse purporting to

be the work of R. Simeon b. Yohai, who is said to have expected the Messiah about 750, the author, foreseeing the misery
of his people under the Moslems, exclaims: "Is it not enough
what the wicked kingdom of Edom has done to us, must
we also endure the atrocities of the kingdom of the Ishmael-
ites?" Whereupon Metatron, the Prince of the Presence, replied:

> Fear not, son of man. The Holy One, praised be He,
> brings the kingdom of Ishmael only to relieve you
> from the wicked kingdom of Edom. He will appoint
> them a Prophet in accordance with His will who will
> conquer the Land for them. And they will come and
> possess it with glory. And there will be a great hatred
> between them and sons of Edom.... Is it not what
> Isaiah the Prophet foretells (21:6-7), 'And when he
> seeth a troop of camels, etc.' The rider upon the ass is
> the Messiah. He will come soon after the rider upon the
> camel (Mohammed).[31]

To the Jews of Babylonia especially, the conflict between
the Christians and Moslems was a sure sign that the Redemption
was at hand, and that "out of *Golah* (exile) will begin the
Geulah (deliverance)." According to the last of the Gaonim,
Rab Hai of Pumbeditha (939-1038), the Messiah b. David will,
with the help of the Jews of Persia, establish himself in the
Holy Land after the defeat of the Saracens and the death of
the Messiah b. Joseph, and

> ...all the nations of the earth will think what gift
> can we offer to this king, since he has little regard for
> silver and garments and vessels. Let us present him
> with his own people.... Then will Zerubbabel blow
> with the great trumpet.... And after the dead and the
> living will assemble there will appear unto them the
> plan of the House.... Thereafter will all Israel be
> Prophets...and the remnants of the nations will
> accept Judaism, as it is said: 'Then will I turn unto
> the people a clear language, etc., and they will say,
> "Come, let us go up to the Mount of the Lord," and

"out of Zion shall go forth the Law, and the Word
of the Lord from Jerusalem." ' [32]

This firm belief in the speedy approach of the "End"
prompted many of those who under pressure joined the
dominant religion to revert to their own. The Gaonic *Responsa*
have much to say about the treatment of converts to Mohammedanism who repented and retraced their steps to the fold
of Judaism. Rab Paltoi b. Abaye, the Gaon of Pumbeditha
(842-58), was one of the few who held that they be rejected
as traitors to their people. The majority of the Gaonim, like
Rab Natrunai, advocated leniency and imposed only a mild
form of penance. But besides reverts there were also quite
a few converts, that is, proselytes. Of these the greatest number came from the slave market. They were mostly Christians,
as no Mohammedan slaves were allowed to be held by Jews.
They preferred to accept Judaism so as to insure their not
being resold to either Christians or Moslems. This was particularly true of the women, since the Jews were solicitous for
the honor of their slaves, and whoever violated the chastity
of his bond woman was flogged, excommunicated for thirty
days, and unless he married her was compelled to liberate
her and recognize her son as his legitimate heir.

In the *Responsa* of the above mentioned Rab Hai-Gaon,
we read:

> In certain places there are only Egyptian (Chris-
> tian?) female slaves in the market, and the non-Jews
> permit the Jews to buy only these and no others.
> Some of them become Jewesses at once, some after an
> interval, some refuse altogether to be converted. The
> Jews have great need of their services for otherwise
> their own daughters would be compelled to carry
> the water on their shoulders from the spring, and go
> to the ovens with the non-Jewish maid servants, who
> are of low character, and thus the daughters of Israel
> might fall into disrepute and danger. In such cases
> Jews mays retain in their services female slaves without

converting them, but they must not allow them to
do any manner of work on the Sabbath. In places
where Jews are afraid lest their slaves should reveal
secrets and turn informers to the prejudice of their
masters, who for this reason, abstain from converting
them—such slaves must not be retained.[33]

Some proselytes, however, were free Christians and even
clergymen. In the Syrian Apostolic Canons of the fourth century, it is intimated that some bishops, presbyters, deacons,
and other ecclesiastics "denied the name of Christ through
fear of the Jews." Ephrem the Syrian, Aphraates "the Persian
Sage," and Jacob of Serug, "the Flute of the Holy Spirit," maintained that many of their coreligionists were led astray not
only by the machinations of the devil but by the arguments
of the Jews. Especially was this the case after Shar-Barz reduced
Galilee and Syria, captured Jerusalem, destroyed the churches
of the Christians, and carried off the "True Cross."

At about that time a monk who was doing penance on
Mt. Zion is said to have had a vision in which he saw Jesus,
the Apostles, and martyrs standing on one side in thick darkness, and Moses, the Prophets, and the Congregation of Israel
standing on the other in a sea of light. Interpreting this as
symbolic of Christianity and Judaism, the monk betook himself
to Tiberias, the center of Jewish learning at that time, and
devoted himself to the mastery of the tenets of Judaism. He
then had himself circumcised, adopted the name of Abraham,
married a Jewess, and spent the remaining years of his life in
the propagation of his new faith among the Christians. He
came to be known as Abraham the Monk. [34]

Of special interest is an epistle attributed to a certain "Father
Nestor," dating probably from the ninth century. In the introduction, the author is described as one

... who loved the Lord with all his heart, and all
his soul, and despised the religion of the uncircumcised
and their errors. He sought shelter under the wings of
the Shekinah, and chose the religion of Israel which he

was sure would secure for him life in the world to come. He was a wise man, versed in Holy Writ, and the Lord hath enlightened his darkness. Before he accepted the faith of Israel, and submitted to circumcision, he held converse with the sages of the uncircumcised, sent inquiries to them, and received their replies. These, however, convinced him the more of the darkness which enfolded them. He then penned a final epistle, and forwarded it to one of the Fathers who had been chosen to argue with him, and this is what he wrote....

Then follows "Father Nestor's" apologia in which he seeks to explain why he abandoned Christianity. He could not, first of all, conscientiously subscribe to the belief that God entered the womb of a woman, ate and drank, slept and was afraid, like an ordinary mortal, or that it was necessary for Jesus, in order to save mankind, to be crucified and lie in the grave for three days. This, he contends, would make Jesus only add to the sins of mankind instead of removing them; for to inveigle men to crucify the Son of God is far more heinous a crime than the original sin, that of Adam's disobedience, which Jesus is alleged to have come to expiate. Moreover, it does not appear as if Satan's power has in any way decreased since the advent of Christ: he still leads men astray as he did before.

Father Nestor asks:

Is Jesus to be worshiped because of the miracles he is said to have performed? Moses, Joshua, Elijah, and others did the same. As for the crucifixion, he argues: it must have been either with his consent or against it. If he consented to it, then those who played their part in the tragedy should be honored for doing his will; if not, he could not have been all powerful, and hence was no God. That he was not, the Gospels themselves bear ample evidence. They tell us that he would frequently become fatigued and sleepy, that his disciples had to arouse him to save him and themselves when their boat was about to be wrecked by a storm; that at the wedding feast his mother had to wake him when the supply of wine which he produced from water threatened to give out. Besides, Christians repudiate the Torah, which by his own admission Jesus came to fulfill: they adore images, and believe in the efficacy of relics and pieces of the cross claimed to have been discovered by the "Mother of Constantine the Little." And the author concludes these and his other arguments with the declaration of faith:

> I, Father Nestor, believe only in the God of heaven and earth, and in none who either was or will be born; and my only hope is that my soul may be united with Israel, that I may be found worthy to witness their consolation, rejoice with them in their restoration, and my lot be cast among them here and hereafter. [35]

While there are no records of converts from Mohammedanism to Judaism, it would seem that some born or bred in the religion of the Prophet also accepted the faith of Israel. The fact that the detractor of Saadia, the eminent Gaon of Sura (882-924), ventured to spread a report that he was descended from *gerim* indicates that such occurrences were not unlikely. A rumor to the same effect was circulated about his disciple, David Hababli, better known as Abu Suliman ibn Merwan Al-Mukamas, who is regarded by some as the father of Jewish philosophy, and whose polemics against Christianity are cited with approval by the great Jewish moralists of the Middle Ages. Arabian writers called him Al-Akuli, thus unknowingly suggesting that in him Judaism acquired another devotee not unlike the immortal Aquila at the beginning of the first Christian millennium.[36]

Legends also, which frequently conceal a germ of fact, refer to Moslem proselytes to Judaism. These must have been freemen, since no Jews were allowed to have Moslem slaves. Pethahiah of Ratisbon, who traveled through Persia and Babylonia between 1175 and 1190, is authority for the story that on the border of the latter there existed a nation of freebooters who worshiped "the God of Ezekiel." He also records the conversion of a Moslem prince to "the God of Baruch," the disciple of Ezekiel. This prince, he writes, once ordered his servants to dig up the grave of Ezekiel, the location of which was shown him by a certain Rabbi Solomon. As everyone who took part in the digging fell dead, an old Arab suggested that the Moslems be replaced by Jews. The Jews fasted and prayed for three days and without any mishap unearthed the sarcophagus of Baruch b. Neriah, between two marble columns, a piece of his robe still sticking out from under the lid, and a halo glowing over it. The prince, thinking that it was not mete that "two kings should lie so close to each other," ordered that Baruch's coffin be brought to his city. But none could carry it further than one mile, nor could all the horses and all the mules move it one step further. They therefore buried him there and erected a beautiful mausoleum on his grave. Some time later, while on a pilgrimage to Mecca, the prince was attracted by the fragrance which emanated from Baruch's tomb, and together with his entourage became converted to Judaism. [37]

CHAPTER XVI

THE JEWISH VIA DOLOROSA

NEXT to the ineradicable hope in the coming of the Messiah, and inseparably connected with it, was the firm faith which had prevailed among the Jews long before the *Hurban* (destruction): that the Ten Tribes which Shalmaneser transported to Assyria were never lost; that somewhere in Asia or Africa they continue to lead an independent, happy national life; and that at the advent of the Messiah they would return to Palestine and be reunited with the Judeans, never to part again. When R. Akiba ventured the opinion that they would not return, he was severely criticized by his companions. The Lord, they protested, will not cast off His people, even as He will not forsake His inheritance. [1]

The Bible gives the locality whither the Ten Tribes were deported as "Halah, and Habor, on the river of Gozan, and in the cities of Medes." But the Fourth Book of Ezra declares that thence the exiles trekked for a year and a half to *Arzarath,* where no heathen ever dwelt; and, protected by the Sambatyon, the river which dried up at their approach and resumed its wayward course after they had crossed, they established themselves again as a nation of strict observers of "the statutes which they had not kept in their own land." [2]

In the course of time there developed a tradition that this new land of Israel lay beyond the "Dark Mountains" and that the river which surrounded it would rest on the Sabbath day but would eject boulders on weekdays, and thus make it impossible for non-Jews to cross it. This legend was known to Josephus; and Pliny, who probably had heard of it from Roman Jews, incorporated it in his Natural History. Rabbi Akiba re-

408

ferred to it as proof that nature itself has regard for the sanctity of the Sabbath; and the Moslems maintained that Mohammed, with the assistance of the angel Gabriel, visited the place one night and was especially impressed with the Banu Musa, "the most righteous among the people of Moses," who lived happily in a communistic society, were never envious or sick, or molested by beasts of prey. [3]

The traveler Eldad b. Mahli, of the ninth century, who claimed to be of the tribe of Dan and to have visited the other tribes, including the B'ne Moshe, described in detail their social, religious, and political institutions. Some of them, he said, were nomads and mighty warriors, others tillers of the soil and so peaceful that their only weapons were the knives for slaughtering animals, and their only interest was in the study of the Torah. Some of their customs, however, were different from those of their Judean brethren who adopted the innovations introduced by the Rabbis. But the Church, loath to admit the existence of an independent Jewish nation, claimed, on the authority of a priest who appeared in Rome in 1122, that a certain Christian who combined the character of a priest with that of a prince, had control over the Ten Tribes, including the Sons of Moses. This was the origin of the widely-spread story about "Prester John" of whom Jewish and Christian chroniclers had much to say during the Middle Ages, and to whom Pope Alexander III (1177) addressed the epistle which begins: *Carissimo in Christo filio Johanni.*

Scholars have found it extremely difficult to determine how much truth Eldad's narrative contains. Very likely, the seed of Judaism, like that of Christianity, was sown in remote recesses by Jewish merchants who traveled over the Persian and Indian trade routes and came to be known as Radanites, probably from the Persian *rah dan* (knowers of the way), or because their headquarters were at Rhega, near Teheran. They journeyed over the seven seas and the then habitable world and supplied Christendom with the luxuries and refinements, the armor and weapons, and also the diversions and amusements to which it was, up to the time of the Renaissance, quite a stranger. An idea of the extent of their operations is given us in the *Book of Ways,* written in 847 by the Postmaster of Bagdad, Ibn Khordadhbeh. He writes:

> These merchants speak Persian, Roman (Greek), Arabic, the language of the Franks, Andalusians (Spanish), and the Slavs. They journey from West to East, from East to West, partly on land, partly on sea. They transport from the West eunuchs, female and male slaves, silk, castor, marten, and other furs, and swords. They take ship in the land of the Franks, on the Western Sea, and steer from Farama, (Pelusium). There they load their goods on the backs of camels, and go by land to Kolzum (Suez), a five days' journey, over a distance of twenty-five farsakhs (parasangs). They embark on the East sea (Red Sea), and sail from Kolzum to El-Jar (Medina), and Jedda (Mecca); then they go to Sind, India, and China. On their return they carry back musk, aloes, camphor, cinnamon, and other products of the Eastern countries to Kolzum, and bring them to Farama, whence they again embark on the Western Sea. Some take sail for Constantinople to sell their goods to the Romans; others go to the palace of the king of the Franks to place their goods.
>
> Sometimes these Jew merchants prefer to carry their goods from the land of the Franks in the Western Sea, making for Antioch (at the mouth of the Orontes); thence they go by land to al-Jabia and al-Hanaya (on the bank of the Euphrates), where they arrive after a three days' march. There they embark on the Euphrates for Bagdad, and then sail down the Tigris to al-Obola. From al-Obola they sail for Oman, Sind, Hind and China. . . Sometimes they likewise take the route behind Rome, and passing through the country of the Slavs, arrive at Khamlij, the capital of the Khazars. There they embark on the Jorjan Sea, arrive at Balkh, betake themselves from there across the Oxus, and continue their journey toward the Yourts of Toghozghor, and from there to China.[4]

So important did these merchants become in the commercial world of the early Middle Ages that the usual formula in Christian business documents was "Jews and other merchants," and in some places the market day had been changed for their sake from Saturday to another day of the week. They practically monopolized the spice market and controlled the slave trade. Their activity continued till the end of the first millennium, when the overland route was cut off by the rise of the Tartars in Asia and when the doges prohibited Venetian vessels from carrying Jewish goods and Jewish passengers.

It is probably to these Jews, more than to the Ten Tribes, that are due the "waymarks" which are discernible even to this day all the way from Persia east through India and China to the Pacific and from Ethiopia west across the Sahara as far as the Atlantic. These consist of folkways, legends, "cast of countenance," and claims to Hebraic descent which the repeated waves of Christianity and Mohammedanism could not entirely obliterate, and which led people of varied races and creeds to claim to be of the "seed of Abraham."

Strong in their insistence on Jewish ancestry are the Duranti Afghans, perhaps the leading clan in the conglomeration of races which constitute Afghanistan. According to them, they are lineal descendants of the Ten Tribes who were carried off to Arzareth which they identify as Hazara. Some prefer to be called Bani Israel, others Bani Joseph or Yusofzai. Still others trace their lineage to Kish the father of Saul, call themselves the Sons of Kais, and say that their country took its name from his son Afghan. Their unwritten law, Pukhtunwali, contains various Israelitish customs and traditions, and they still cherish the ancient animosity of the Ten Tribes toward the Judeans. Travelers assert that the men, and more especially the women, have handsome features of Jewish cast. It is, however, definitely established that the majority of the Afghan Bani Israel are of the Aryan, Mongol, or Hindu stock who accepted some Hebraic folkways and possibly religious doctrines from the Jews who had established trading centers in that region in remote antiquity, and dominated the caravan road to Kabul and Hindustan. After their conversion to Mohammedanism, they became most zealous and fanatic propagators of the faith of the Prophet. [5]

Racial reminiscences indicating the impact of Judaism are found among the Turkestani. Khiva is said to have been founded by a Jewish Persian prince whose people proselytized among the Tartars and the Mongols. Some of them still claim to be "Followers of Moses" (Moussai) and many of them fought under Temujin, that is, the Genghis Khan ("the very mighty ruler," 1154-1227) who overran Turkestan and Persia and ravaged a great part of Europe. In fact, Genghis Khan is himself believed by some to have been of the Mosaic persuasion, and Matthew of Paris states that the Tartars who followed him belonged to the Ten Tribes. [6]

The ancient history of Armenia is likewise interwoven with incidents from Jewish history probably introduced by some Armenian Jewish proselytes. It is asserted that there the ubiquitous Ten Tribes became so numerous that Shapur II destroyed ten thousand of their families in Van alone and deported about a hundred thousand more to Persia. The Armenian population must have been favorably disposed toward them, since the Midrash has it that God ordained that the Ten Tribes should pass through Armenia because there they would obtain food and drink. Moses of Chorene in the fifth century records a tradition that, at the request of King Hratchai, Nebuchadnezzar sent him a wise Jew by the name of Sambat, or Shambat, of Davidic descent, upon whom he conferred many honors. One of his offspring, Shamba Bagarat, "the mighty and wise man from among the Jews," was elevated by Vaharsaces I to the office of coronator. He took part in his sovereign's campaign against the Macedonians but stubbornly refused to accept paganism, and under Arsaces I two of his sons preferred to die for their faith. The others, however, consented not to circumcise their children and to participate in wars on the Sabbath day. Their descendants came to be regarded as the fathers of the Armenians when, in 571, they expelled the Arab marauders and established the Bagratid dynasty.

As in other places, Jews also contributed to the spread

of early Christianity in Armenia. Thaddai (Addai), the disciple of St. Thomas, was entertained while at Edessa, at the home of Tobias of the Bagarat family, who had fled thither to preserve his Jewish religion. On the other hand, Nino the nun who escaped from the persecution of the king of Armenia to Mtzket, won over Abiathar, "the chief priest of the Jews," to her faith; and Abiathar in turn became an apostle to the Jews and their proselytes, the Karthli, and through his efforts many of them as well as the pagans embraced Christianity. Some members of the Bagratid family, however, continued to cling to the faith of their fathers, and it may be assumed that a Jewish proselyting movement was going on while its dynasty lasted. This will account for the diverse ethnic clans in that region which claim to be of Jewish origin and the many customs and beliefs among them which bear the stamp of Jewishness. From there Judaism, paganized, Christianized, or Mohammedanized, penetrated into Caucasia and possibly had much to do with the conversion of the Khazars of whom we shall treat later. In the middle of the tenth century, the Arabian traveler Ibn Haukal notes in his Geography that in Atel, near the Caspian Sea, though the greatest number of the inhabitants are either Christian or Mohammedan, the king and his chief officers are Jews. [7]

An illustration of the adoption of Jewish genealogy as a result of contact with Jewish traditions is given by the Amatuni on the slopes of Mount Ararat. Moses of Chorene asserts that they were originally Persians who were brought by Arsaces to Armenia and settled in villages. In due time they became powerful clans and supplied military and ecclesiastic leaders to Armenia till the beginning of the twelfth century. The name is said to mean "new settlers" and converts, almost the same as the word *ger* in Hebrew. The conversion of the highlanders of Eastern Caucasia, Montenegro, and Circasia continued for centuries after. Pethachiah of Regensburg tells us that while in Bagdad he met ambassadors "from the seven kings of Meshech" (the Moschi of Georgia?) who came to the Exilarch with a request to send to their country some Jewish teachers, as their chiefs were resolved to accept the religion of Israel;

and that many scholars from Babylonia and Egypt repaired to this remote country to instruct its Tartar tribes in the lore of the Bible and the Talmud. An ancient legend among them, however, tells that their ancestors were fugitives from the Persian captivity who wandered northward in quest of Mt. Ararat and the remains of Noah's Ark. [8]

Some Jews left their "waymarks" among the Chinese and East Indians. The "Black Jews" in East India boast of pure Israelitish antecedents. According to their various traditions, they were sent to India to hunt for elephants or to work the gold mines during the reign of King Solomon. Gradually their complexion changed so that they could no longer be recognizable from the rest of the population. From a church legend it would appear that Jews must have been there in considerable numbers and proselyted among the native stock before the *Hurban.* It tells that St. Thomas on his missionary trip (c. 52) fell in with a Parthian Jewish merchant who was highly esteemed by the king of Gudnaphar, and went with him to Malabar where the king was celebrating the nuptials of his daughter, and a chorus of Jewish women sang songs from the Bible. Many of them became converts to Christianity, but the converts of St. Thomas denied the virginity of Mary, did not tolerate the worship of images, and among other ceremonials observed the rite of circumcision. [9]

As these Indian pioneers were almost on the point of becoming assimilated with the rest of the population, they were reclaimed in the fourth century by seven men and seven women of a band of Jews who were shipwrecked near Bombay, and they were rediscovered in the tenth century by David Rahabi of Cochin as Maharati-speaking Beni Israel or "Saturday oil pressers." They celebrated *Navyacha San* (New Year's Day) on the first day of Tishri; *Khiricha San* (pudding holiday) on the fourth of Tishri, when they ate *khir* placed near a censer with burning frankincense after saying the *Shma;* and *Darfalnicha San* (the Day of Atonement) on the tenth of Tishri, when, dressed in white, they fasted from sunset to sunset and avoided any contact with people of other denominations. On the thirteenth of Adar they had a fast, *Holicha San,* and on the fourteenth thereof, a feast on which they sent home-made sweet-meats to one another. On Passover or the *Anasi Dakacha San* (Anas-closing holiday) they buried a pot containing some favorite sour liquid. The ninth of Ab followed a meatless week during which they ate only rice served in plantain leaves. Through Rahabi they became familiar with other observances. From the Moslems they also borrowed the custom of fasting throughout the month of Elul, which they too named "Ramzan." They had neither Cohens nor Levites and knew nothing of Pentecost and Hanukkah.

Despite Rahabi's rediscovery, they remained unknown to the rest of the Jewish world down to 1760, when Samuel Ezekiel Divakar, a Jewish captain from Cochin who served in the English army, was taken captive together with several others under his command, by Tippu Sahib. Learning from the Sahib's mother that there were Beni Israel in the land, Divakar made a vow that if he should ever become free he would devote himself to the revival of Judaism among them. When he managed to escape in 1795, he immediately set about fulfilling his vow. Due to his efforts, a synagogue was erected in Bombay (1796), but he died while on his way to Cochin to obtain a Sefer Torah. His work was then taken up by the Cochin Hakham Shelomo Salem Shurabi, who was saved from shipwreck by a Beni Israel soldier. Under the English rule and with the settlement of the Sassoons among them, their spiritual condition greatly improved. They established schools and had books written for them or translated into their vernacular Mahrati. Their men have a reputation for bravery, and their women as excellent nurses. It is reported that their social, intellectual, as well as moral standards are higher than those of their neighbors, and that they have an intense love for everything Jewish. There are supposed to be about twenty thousand of them in Bombay and its environs.

In 1934 much indignation was aroused among the Beni Israel when the officers of Congregation Mussmiah Yeshua of Bombay denied them the right to be called up for the reading from the Torah on the Sabbath and holidays. The trustees of the synagogues took the stand that since they do not observe certain Jewish laws they are disqualified from the honors appertaining to Jews who adhere to all the rabbinic requirements. After protracted litigation, the High Court of Rangoon, supported by Jewish spiritual leaders of London, decided (1935) that the Beni Israel are in all respects Jews and are entitled to be treated as such by their white-complexioned co-religionists.[10]

The brown Beni-Israel are, however, themselves not free from prejudice against their coreligionists who are of a still darker hue than themselves. These Black Jews claim that their forebears came to Cochin and Malabar under Cyrus and possess a charter presented by the king of Malabar to Joseph Rabban about 750, wherein he is referred to as the Prince of Ansuvannam, is granted feudal rights over "five castes" in Ansuvannam, near Cranganore, and has permission to spread their faith among the natives.

The "five castes," composed of carpenters, braziers, smiths, gold and silver craftsmen, and distillers of cocoanut sap, made converts of many of their fellow workmen; and they, in turn, introduced into their new religion the caste system of Hinduism. Thereafter, they became divided into the *kala,* or black, to whom belonged the converted half-breeds, and the *goro,* or white. These again were split up into the noble ones, who were of the upper strata, and those who were not of noble birth. Contrary to Jewish tradition, the status of the slave among Indian Jews remained unchanged even after his conversion. He could not intermarry with his white coreligionists, nor even be called up to the reading of the Torah, nor was he allowed to wear *zizith* (fringes) and *tefilin* (phylacteries). These restrictions could be removed, however, on receipt of a certificate of emancipation followed by kissing the hands of all the white Jews of the community. But, in the synagogue he still had to sit outside on the ground in the veranda and had to wear a *kaffa* instead of a turban. Only the eighth generation of converts is eligible to marry a *goro.* To this caste also belong the Arabian Jews who settled in South India and married their women slaves, after converting them. Thus did Judaism in caste-ridden India pay the price for proselytism by establishing a caste of Untouchables among its Malayalam-speaking converts. The Jewish Untouchables, however, are very enterprising and eager to improve themselves. While the Cochin Christians register sixty-six per cent of their required attendance at school, the Black Jews furnish one hundred twenty-seven percent of their quota of school attendance.[11]

Some medieval commentators maintain that when Isaiah predicted (49:12) the restoration of the Jews from "the land of Sinim," he had in mind those who trekked a distance of ten thousand miles from the Jordan, through the Caucasus, Turkestan, and Tibet to the Yellow River in China. There are indeed indications that centuries before the Christian era Jews had trade relations with the "silkmen" who called them *Tiao Kiu Kiaou* (those who extract the sinews, Gen. 32:33). It is most likely that Judaism was there diffused by Jewish Radanites who came by sea or by the caravan route from Samarkand to Khotan to exchange the products of Africa and Europe for the paper, glass, rich cloth, and silk then made only in China. They continually increased in numbers, and at some time during their history produced men of learning and culture. Several records pertaining to them were discovered by a Catholic missionary in the seventeenth century, inscribed on marble tablets dating from the years 1489, 1512, and 1663. According to the first, seventy Jewish families arrived in China in the fifth century from "Western lands" with tribute of cotton cloth for the Emperor.They were received favorably and permitted to settle at Kai-Fung-Foo, the ancient capital of Honan. Their old synagogue was renovated in 1163 and in 1279 was rebuilt and enlarged to accommodate the increased Jewish population. It was again repaired in 1421 by the Emperor's favorite physician, and the Emperor himself presented the incense for use therein. When this synagogue was destroyed by a flood (1461) it was restored by a prominent Jew. The inscription ends as follows:

> Composed by a promoted literary graduate of the prefecture of Kai-Fung-Foo, named Kiu-chung; inscribed by a literary graduate of purchased rank, be-

longing to the district of Tseang-Fu, named Tsaoutso;
and engraved by a literary graduate of purchased
rank, belonging to the prefecture of Kai-Fung-Foo,
named Foo-joo. Erected on a fortunate day, in the middle of summer, in the second year of Hungche (1488),
in the forty-sixth year of the seventieth cycle, by a
disciple of the Religion of Truth and Purity.

The tablet of 1512 was evidently written by a Jewish missionary or a Chinese Judaizer. It reads:

Those who practice this religion are found in other
places than Peen (Kai-Fung-Foo); but wherever they
are met with, they all without exception, honor the
Sacred Writing and venerate Eternal Reason in the
same manner as the Chinese, shunning superstitious
practices and image-worship. These sacred books concern not Jews only, but all men, kings and subjects,
parents and children, old and young. Differing little
from our laws, they are summed up in the worship
of Heaven, the honor of parents, and the veneration
of ancestors.... They (the Jews?) excel in agriculture, in merchandise, in magistracies, and in warfare,
and are highly esteemed for integrity, fidelity, and a
strict observance of their religion.

The 1663 inscription, by a Chinese mandarin, afterwards
minister of state, begins with Adam, Noah, Abraham, and
Moses, tells of the settlement of Jews in China under the
Chow dynasty, and brings their history down to the fall of
the Ming Dynasty in 1642. During the sack of Kai-Fung-Foo,
the ancient synagogue was destroyed, the sacred scrolls were
torn and thrown into the river, and the Jews fled to the north
side of Noang-Ho. When, ten years later the mandarin Chao-
Yng Cheng was detailed to restore the city, the Jewish fugitives returned to their former quarters, rebuilt the ancient
temple, and pieced together the fragments of the scrolls which

had been saved from the river, made twelve copies of it, and placed all of them in a holy ark in the temple. Other sacred volumes were also gathered and repaired by the members of the community.

The lack of a Bible translation in the vernacular contributed to the deterioration of the Chinese Jewish community, and in the course of time their Judaism became diluted with Hinduism and Confucianism. They have no word for rabbi or synagogue. For God they, like the Sibyl, use the words Heaven, True Heaven, High Heaven, August Heaven, also the Invisible, the Supreme Ruler, the Ever-Living Lord, the Lord of Long Life, the Extremely Pure. They pluck the sinews of the animals they kill, observe the Sabbath and the holidays, including the festival of Purim and the Fast of the Ninth of Ab. Four days every month they devote to purification, fasting, and deeds of charity. Seven days before Yom Kippur they subject themselves to doing penance, and twice a year, in spring and autumn, they sacrifice oxen and sheep and the fruits of the season in veneration of their ancestors. The Reader of the Torah is required to cover his face in commemoration of the mask worn by Moses. They have no dogma concerning the Messiah.

When the Chinese Jewish community was first discovered by the Catholic missionary, there were still numerous evidences of their former religious activities. At one time there were probably three synagogues in Kai-Fung-Foo, and at least one each in Chin-Kiang, Hang-Chow, Ning-Po, Loyang, Ning Hsai, She-Hung, Khotan, Nanking, and Peking. The synagogue at Kai-Fung-Foo ruins, which was still in existence in the eighteenth century, was a combination of the Solomonic Temple and of a pagoda. It consisted of four courts, each of which faced the West, or Jerusalem. In the first were lavatories for ablution in preparation for services; the second contained dwellings for the attendants; and the third, rooms for guests, and the fourth was divided into two by a row of trees, in the center whereof stood a large brazen vase with incense and a marble lion upon a pedestal. The sinews of animals killed for food were extracted in a recess in the northern wall. The second division of the fourth court led to the "Hall of Ancestors," where formerly homage was paid them by sacrifices of animals and later by burning frankincense to the great men of Israel, especially Abraham, Moses, Aaron, Joshua, and Ezra. The holiest part of the synagogue was at the extreme end. There, in the Ark, were placed thirteen scrolls, the middle and most venerated of which represented Moses, and the others the twelve tribes. There was also, on an elevation, the "Chair of Moses," over which was suspended a canopy upon which was embroidered in golden Hebrew characters the *Shma*. At the door were six candelabra, a vase for incense, and a laver for washing the hands.

With the discovery of these long lost or long ago acquired brothers by their European coreligionists, several attempts were made to revive a knowledge of Judaism among them. But these efforts met with scant success, and not a few of them became, in the nineteenth century, Christians, Mohammedans, and even Buddhist priests. To a letter addressed in 1844 by the Hebrew-Christian missionary James Finn "To the Honorable Plucking Sinew Sect," the following reply was received in April 1870:

To the Chief Teacher of the Jewish Religion...

In reply to the inquiries which you therein made, we have to state, during the past forty or fifty years our religion has been but imperfectly transmitted; and, although its canonical writings are still extant, there are none who understand so much as one word of them. It happens only that there yet survives an aged female of more than seventy years who retains in her recollection the principal tenets of the faith.

Morning and night with tears in our eyes, and with offerings of incense, do we implore that our religion may again flourish. We have everywhere sought about but could find no one who could understand the letters of the Great Country, and this has occasioned us deep sorrow....

Daily with tears have we called on the Holy Name. If we could again procure ministers and could put in order our Temple, our religion would have a firm support for the future, and our sacred documents would have a secure repository.[12]

Of the once flourishing Jewry of China, embracing hundreds of thousands, only a remnant now remains whose yellow skin and almond eyes tell a story of Mongol converts to the "superior religion" of those who came from the West. From fifteen to twenty thousand of them now dwell in Canton, and a sprinkling is to be found in other places. Their present synagogue is made up of three little boats floating on the water in which the worshipers bathe before offering their devotion. They are to Europeans undistinguishable from the native Chinese, and outsiders are hardly aware of their existence as a religious entity.

But Judaism still attracts some of the Chinese, and we still hear of a conversion now and then. Outstanding among them is Salem Shalom David. Born at Feba in Hankow in 1853, he was adopted as a child by the Sassoons after the murder of his parents, and was admitted at Bombay into the faith of Israel. Later he became a devoted communal worker among the Beni Israel, and also one of the active members of the Shanghai Society for rescuing the Chinese Jews.[13]

A more recent Chinese convert to Judaism is Rosalind Phang, a licentiate of the London Royal Academy of Music, who married a Jewish journalist. She reported that hers was not the only case of a Sino-Jewish alliance. Another such case, however, came into public notice at the death of Silas Aaron Hardoon of Shanghai. His wife was a Chinese who accepted the religion of her husband, and their adopted children were brought up in the Jewish faith. Hardoon established a special fund for the translation of the Bible, as well as of the Koran, into Chinese.[14]

Some explorers find traces of the impact of Judaism and probable conversions also in the Empire of Japan. They point to two villages which bear the names Goshen and Menashe.

There is a legend that during the third century a band of strange-looking silk raisers appeared in the Flowery Kingdom and that by 471 they numbered 18,670. A temple, in front of which figures of a lion and unicorn (called "Buddha's Dogs") keep watch, is claimed to have been a synagogue, then known as "The Tent of David." It was erected by them on the spot where they first settled. The originator of the sect is said to have been found as a child in a little chest floating upon the water. They were highly respected and were known as *Chada,* or the beloved. On a site belonging to one of the *Chada* families there is a well some fifteen hundred years old, upon the curbing of which are engraved the letters "Israel." Professor Anasaki, of the University of Tokio, the chief proponent of the Japan-Israel theory, believes in the Jewish extraction of the Nipponese and that Judaism exerted some influence on Buddhism. A news item of recent date tells about a Japanese woman who married a German Jew at Nagasaki who not only became a Jewess but built and endowed several synagogues and is devoting herself to spreading her new faith in her native land. [15]

Like Asia, so is Africa honeycombed with "waymarks" and replete with traditions of the rise and fall of Jewish settlements. The pigmentation of many Jews and the practices of many non-Jews in the Dark Continent indicate that much intermarriage and interchange of religion has taken place during the centuries and that a good deal of missionary work, tacit or active, had been carried on for a long time. There can be little doubt that in their missionary zeal the Jews did not overlook Cyrenaica, Numidia, Sudan, and other places which the Rabbis identify with Egypt. The story of Ananias, who was instrumental in converting the royal house of Adiabene, is evidence that Egyptian Jews visited other lands than Palestine and proselytized wherever they went.

Reference has already been made to the Judaized Abyssinians, known as Falashas. It was probably by way of Abyssinia that Judaism expanded as far as the East Indian Archipelago. Jewish survivals have been discovered among the Hovas of Madagascar and on the isle of St. Marie to the east, where the *Zafin Ibrahim* claim to be of the "seed of Abraham." Had

Israel Zangwill succeeded in his scheme to colonize Jews in Uganda, they would have found among the natives certain legends which would have made them feel somewhat at home. One of these is that the earliest settlers who came across the Nile subdued all the tribes with which they came in contact and established a government under a king who traced his descent from David. Similar racial reminiscences are found in the country around Lake Albert Edward Nyanza and in the Tanganyika Territory. There is also a tradition that long before the Christian era some Hebrews journeyed from the great trading cities of Yemen, Aden, and Hadremut, penetrated into Somaliland, established an emporium at Zanzibar, and possibly occupied the island of Mozambique, on the eastern coast of Africa. [16]

All over the hinterland of Egypt and throughout North Africa, there are discernible traces of Jewish influence or participation in the cultural and religious life of the various people. The traveler Nahum Slouschz found in the Hara (Ghetto) of Msellata types peculiar to the pure Bedouin groups, suggesting an admixture of Arab blood. The Tunisian Jews, according to him, "are of African origin, as is evident from their type, their customs, and their ethnic names, showing that they came from the South or the Sahara." The same is true of the natives of Algeria and Morocco. The city of Ceuta is said to have been founded by Shem, the son of Noah. Heracles, father of Juba, king of Morocco, is said to have married a granddaughter of Abraham. North African folklore is especially rich in tales woven around biblical heroes such as Joshua bin Nun, David, Joab, and Solomon. Some tribes claim to be descendants of the Canaanites who fled from Palestine before the victorious Israelites. A Greek author of the sixth century quotes an Arabic historian of the fifth, to the effect that the Canaanites still maintained their identity in his time:

> They still live in the country and use the Phoeni-
> cian language. They built themselves a fort in the
> city of Numidia, in the place where Tigisis stands
> today. There, near a great fountain, are two steps of

> white stone, on which are Phoenician inscriptions,
> saying: 'We are those that fled before Joshua the
> son of Nave, the Brigand.' [17]

There is a widespread tradition in North Africa that the
Philistines with their king Jalut (Goliath?) fled before David,
passed through Egypt, and settled at Ghadames, an oasis in
the Sahara. These still hate the people of Joshua and David,
but some who claim to be descended from the Ammonites and
Moabites are friendly to the Israelites and hold the *qubba*
(tomb) of Nebi Ucha (the Prophet Joshua) in the highest
regard. In east Sudan there is a black-skinned population which
observes the Jewish Sabbath. Among some Berbers they still
leave at harvest time the sheaves which fall to the ground
for the poor and the stranger. Some even commemorate the
destruction of the Temple, and in their chants and prayers
imitate the Jewish ritual. Reheibat is still known as Reheibat-
es-Sabt (Reheibat of the Sabbath) because, up to comparatively
recent times, the inhabitants of this place continued to observe
the Jewish Sabbath. [18]
It is now commonly accepted that many Palestinian Jews
followed in the wake of the Phoenicians who traded with North
Africa either as merchants or as mercenaries or as slaves. The
Rabbis interpreted the phrase *barburim abusim* (the fattened
fowls which were imported for Solomon's table) as referring
to the big birds from the lands of the Berbers. Some talmudic
stories are also in accord with the Berber folktales. There is
one that when Joshua invaded Canaan he gave the inhabitants
the alternative either of suing for peace or of leaving the
country. The Girgashites accepted the latter; and, because
unlike the other nations they avoided bloodshed, God rewarded
them with a land as beautiful as the one they had left. The
Septuagint and the Targum identify Tarshish with Carthage.
The Ten Tribes, too, are supposed to have been deported to
Africa. There is a persistent tradition about the Aaronid priests
who refused to return to Palestine with Ezra and journeyed
as far as Africa. At a later date the Greeks and the Romans
established there many Jewish military colonies to control

the conquered people, so that it became a saying that "wherever there are memorials of Roman occupancy there also will be found remains of Jewish settlements." It is recorded that one of Titus' generals transported thirty thousand Jews into the mountainous regions of Africa where they became tillers of the soil. By the second century the African Jewish community produced several rabbis and was regarded sufficiently important by the Palestinian Jews to send thither R. Akiba to arouse public sentiment in behalf of the Bar Kokba revolution. [19]

There were, however, other factors besides their natural increase which contributed to the growth of the Jewish population in Africa. From the beginning of their history the Jews there waged more or less successful wars against paganism and directly and indirectly made propaganda for Judaism among the natives and the invaders. There are inscriptions which show that side by side with the temples of Baal and Tanit, there were temples dedicated to *Baal Shamaim* (the God of Heaven). By intermarriage and social contacts Jewish customs gradually were engrafted on pagan rites, and such theophoric names as Joab, Joal, Joas became frequent among the people. It was probably because of the many intermarriages that the Aaronids, who laid special stress on racial purity, kept aloof from the rest of their coreligionists. It is no mere accident that Alexander Severus, of Phoenicio-African descent, had statues made of Abraham, Moses, and Jesus and had the Golden Rule inscribed in public places in the form enunciated by Hillel. The *Caelicoli*, or the Fearers of the Lord, also made many converts; and it is not unlikely that, as Professor Slouschz remarks, had Hannibal triumphed over Rome, not only would the Hebrew dialect of the Phoenicians have become the language of the Mediterranean countries but Judaism the world's dominant religion. [20]

These *ultima terra* countries, as the Romans called them, formed a point of departure for Jewish expatriates to Africa's Negro Land. The fall of Jerusalem and the disastrous Bar Kokba uprising forced many Judean bands to flee as far away from Roman vengeance as they could. According to Jerome,

they established an unbroken chain of colonies "from Mauretania to India." The ruins of Tindirma still bear witness to
the enterprising spirit of these refugees. Due to their efforts,
Ghana, in French Sudan, became an important commercial
center. Some of them, known as "the masons of the desert,"
built cities, constructed canals and irrigation systems which
still exist. Others went further west, mingled with the "sons
of the soil," and impressed their rites indelibly upon the autoc-
thonous population which, however, remained as pagan as
ever. It is probably to them that the Talmud refers as "the men
of Barbary and Mauretania who walk naked in public and
say in their hearts, There is no God."

Relics of Hebrewisms are scattered among the Tuaregs, and
Hebraic ancestry is claimed by numerous Negro tribes in the
Nigeria basin, especially in the region of Lake Chad, Bornu,
and Skoto. At Ghanata a Jewish kingdom is said to have
existed from about 300 to 790, when it was overthrown by the
Moslems. At Lamlau, two hundred miles west of Timbuktu,
there was still a Jewish trade colony in 1076, and a Jewish state
at Kamnuri was known in the Middle Ages. A Hebraic flavor
is still to be noticed in the observances of the Fulani and other
tribes in the region of Cape Verd and Senegal, along the
southwestern African coast, and around the Congo and Guinea.
In the interior of Dahomey there is a Judaized community.
They have a temple in which they offer sacrifices, possess a
Pentateuch written on parchment, and observe the Sabbath
and other Jewish ceremonials. Another community, consisting
of about four hundred families and speaking Maghrabi Arabic
mixed with the local Negro dialect, claims Semitic ancestry.
They marry only among themselves or with those who profess
monotheism. Some of them call themselves *Emo Yo Quayim*
(*Am Yah Khayyim,* people of the Living God); others *Bnai
Ephraim*. An interesting description of the latter was recently
given in "An African Savage's Own Story" by one of their
own, Bata Kindai Amgoza (or Paul Emanuel) Lo Bagola, who
was carried off to Scotland when a lad of seven.

As in other places, so in North Africa, Judaism paved the
way for Christianity and Mohammedanism and continued to

compete with them during the Middle Ages. There is a cycle of legends in North Africa woven around seven rabbis who came to Demnat in the Great Atlas to convert the natives. Tertullian mentions a controversy between a convert to Judaism and a Christian which drew a large crowd, and complains that there were those among both heathen and Christians who devoted the "Day of Saturn (Sabbath) to ease and eating." Abba Arika (Rab) of Babylonia declared, "From Tyre to Carthage they recognize Israel and their Father in heaven," while Commodianus, his younger contemporary, inveighs against those who were in the habit of attending Jewish services, and asks:

> Why in the synagogue do you run to the Pharisees
> That God may be merciful to you, whom outside
>   you deny?
> You go outside, you again seek temples.
> You wish, between each, to live, but will thereby
>   perish....
> What! do you wish to be half Jew, half heathen?...
> But you go to those from whom you can learn nothing;
> You leave their doors and go thence to idols.
> Ask (of them) what is the first precept of the Law....
> Of God's precepts they will tell you only the
>   marvelous. [21]

As late as the fourteenth century the Arabic historian Ibn Khaldun (1332-1406) mentions the following tribes as more or less Judaized:

> In Ifrikia (Tunis) there were the Nefussa, an older branch of the Luata (Libyans) who professed Judaism. In Aures (Algeria) there were the Jerua. In Oran, and particularly in the region of Tlemcen, there were the Mediuna. In Morocco, the Behlula, the Riata, the Fazaz, and the Fedelua.... (The Jerua) was a people composed of many tribes which continued to live in Ifrikia and Maghreb in a state of absolute independence. Long before the first appearance of Islam in

Africa, the Jerua were distinguished for their power
and for the numbers of their warriors. ... From the
Jerua came the royal dynasties of all the Berber tribes
of the branch of the Branes.

To these may be added the above mentioned Sabbatherian
Reheibats and dark-skinned Felicis, or Krits, the Bahuzim
and other nomadic tribes who roamed over the Sahara Desert
and claimed Jewish origin. It was they and the Yhud Khaibar
who helped save Tripoli from the Byzantines, fortified the
desert with almost impregnable forts, and laid the foundation
for the superior civilization of the Moors. It was probably they
who gave rise to the belief that Africa was the locale of the
lost Ten Tribes, and the Bnai Moshe, or the "red" Jews, and
who on the eve of the Arab invasion rendered Africa ready to
become overwhelmingly Jewish. [22]

It may have been the successful missionary activity of the
Jews that added fuel to the enmity of the African Fathers
against them, and it may have been due to the Fathers that
the natives came to believe that they were descended from
the Canaanites who fled before the Israelites. St. Augustine
who, like his contemporary St. Jerome, did not despise assistance from African Jews, seldom mentions them except to
deride and denounce. In his *Tractatus Adversus Judaeos* he
tries to prove that the Jews are an ignorant lot and incapable
of comprehending their own Scriptures. All the biblical promises were, according to him, intended for the true Israel, that
is, the Christians, and all the curses for the "House of Jacob"
or the Jews, whose "lies" caused many Christians to drift
away from the *civitas Dei* (Catholicism) into the *civitas diaboli*
of the heretical sects which multiplied in Africa. They should,
therefore, be persecuted till they see the light and become
the true Israel. [23]

The result of these teachings was that the same fate which
overtook the Jews of Alexandria overtook their coreligionists
in North Africa. Their synagogues were either desecrated or
confiscated. The community of Borian which traced its origin
to the days of Solomon was forcibly converted. Communities

which resisted were ruthlessly exterminated. A Council of Carthage decreed that Christians who cling to any Jewish practices should be excommunicated, and specially drastic laws were enacted against the *Caelicoli.* [24]

But in Africa, as in Asia, the Cross steadily retreated before the rising Crescent; and when, in the eighteenth century, European missionaries were sent out to convert the natives, they had to start almost from the beginning. At the beginning of the twentieth century there was in the continent which gave birth to Tertullian, Cyprian, Arnobius, Lactantius, Optatus, Cyril, and Augustine, only one Christian nation, Ethiopia (Abyssinia), of whose total population of four million only thirty thousand were Catholics, against fifty thousand Falashas, two hundred thousand Moslems, and about three and a half million Jacobites or Monophysites.

In the latest and perhaps greatest victory of Mohammedanism over Catholicism in Africa, a most important role was played by a Jewish general and Daia, or Damia, el-Cahena of the Judaized tribe of Jerua. Beloved for her beauty, her sagacity, and her courage, this African Joan of Arc was acclaimed a national heroine, a prophetess, and a queen. Under her leadership the Moors, or Berbers, held out against Hasson and Mohammedanism for five years. But the final success of the Saracens spelled her downfall, and her warriors were either massacred or submitted to the faith of the conqueror. Among the latter were Cahena's two sons, who on their conversion were made officers in the armies against which they had formerly fought, and with twelve thousand Jews and Moors invaded Spain. At the battle of Xeres (711) the Visigoth King Roderic was defeated by one of Cahena's generals, Tarif es-Zaid, "a Jew of the tribe of Simeon," after whom they named the Island of Torifa. He was the first "Moor" to set foot on the soil of Spain.

Entrenched in their Asiatic and African possessions, the Moslems started upon a career of enlightenment which put their Christian contemporaries to shame. Already, at the cradle of Mohammedanism, Ali, the son-in-law of Mohammed, is recorded to have made statements reminiscent of the talmudic sayings of the Fathers, such as: "He dieth not who gives his life to learning"; "Eminence in science is the highest of honors"; "The greatest ornament of a man is erudition"; "The world is sustained by four things: the learning of the wise, the justice of the great, the prayers of the good, and the valor of the brave." It was not unusual among the Moslems to hear a Jew or Nestorian, while enjoying the favor of the caliph or emir, lecture on science and philosophy at their institutions of learning. Al-Mamun, the son of Haroun al-Rashid, had the works of Aristotle translated into Arabic, and Christians with a thirst for knowledge went to the schools of the Saracens to acquire the wisdom of the Greeks tabooed in their own countries, or read their works in translations made mostly by infidel Jews. Roger Bacon recommended the study of Arabic because thus only could one become familiar with science and philosophy.

However, the religious enthusiasm and cultural fervor of the Arabs soon began to decline, and jealous caliphs and ambitious emirs put a check to the promise of the early centuries of Mohammedanism. Incessant warfare had decimated the population and impoverished the land, and greedy rulers squeezed out of the masses what little they retained. In those troublous times the Great Expectation (of the Messiah) which was aroused in Judea on the eve of the *Hurban*, and which had helped to establish Jesus, and later Mohammed, was reawakened. Like Jews and Christians, save that they consulted the Koran, Suffites ransacked their sacred volume in search for the gift of miracles, and tried to discover, by the combination of certain letters, or the interpretation of various verses, the time of the appearance of the redeemer, and sought by the asceticism and mysticism to "force the end" of his absence. This supreme event, it was generally held, was to transpire some time in the fourth century of the Hegira, or about the beginning of the second Christian millennium.

So, toward the end of the first Christian millennium, dervishes were roaming throughout the Mohammedan empire and stirred up the people to prepare themselves for the new era which was soon to dawn upon mankind. After several

Mahdis appeared and as mysteriously disappeared, Obaidallah, the first of the Fatimite dynasty of North Africa, assumed the title of al-Mahdi, and at the suggestion of his vizier Yakub ibn Killis, an apostate from Judaism, made Cairo (al-Kahira) a center of Arab culture. Yakub, who is said to have descended from Samau'el ibn Adiya the poet, was particularly fond of poetry, but he was also held in high esteem as a theologian. At his death, the caliph himself attended his funeral, kept the offices of the government closed for eighteen days, and in his honor had poets recite his virtues and chant *suras* from the Koran for a month. He also made a special endowment to have Yakub's manual treating of the doctrines of the Shiites studied at his newly established al-Azhar mosque, "for all eternity."[25]

In time Mohammedanism met strong opposition, especially in Persia. There, toward the end of the ninth century, Abdallah ibn Maimun proclaimed that from the earliest times God had appointed an *Imam,* or pattern for men to follow, but that sometimes he was hidden, and his teachings had to be promulgated by deputies. The last of these was Ismail ibn Jafar, who never died. The reason why his father passed over his claim was because he was addicted to drink. His claims were taken up by Hamdan Qarmat, whose followers came to be known as Carmathians. He represented himself as the Holy Ghost, the herald of the Messiah, the messenger of Mohammed the son of Ali, or of St. John the Baptist, and taught that Islam was intended only for the uninitiated, but that the precepts and practices of the Muslims might be dispensed with by those who were enlightened in the mysteries of the Koran. Qarmat's followers penetrated into Basra and seriously threatened Bagdad. At Mecca they put an end to thirty thousand natives and pilgrims, tore the veil of the Kaaba into shreds, and carried off the sacred Black Stone to Lasha. They were greatly reduced by Saladin, but rose to power again under their leader Hassan ibn Sabah at the end of the eleventh century. Under his guidance they were organized into a secret order, resembling in many respects the monkish orders of Christendom, and pledged themselves to absolute obedience. They came to be known as the Assassins, and under their chief, commonly called "the Old Man of the Mountains," they struck terror among their neighbors, until they were destroyed by the Mongols in Persia and by the Mammelukes of Egypt in the thirteenth century.

Still Persia continued to be in the vanguard of Mohammedan reform. There Firdousi (d. 1020) used his great talents in his *Yusuf* and *Zuleikha* which he borrowed from the Bible through the medium of the Koran to glorify the ancient fire-worshipers. There flourished men like Avicenna, and singers of love and wine like Hafiz. Omar Khayyam did not hesitate to make the tavern the theme of his immortal *Rubaiyat,* which is a devastating sarcasm on the austerity and bigotry of his own sect. He is said to have contributed to the decay of the Assassins whose founder, Hassan, was his school-fellow. His opposition to the prevalent mysticism both among Mohammedans and Christians he expressed in his quatrain:

> If I myself upon a looser creed,
> Have loosely strung the Jewel of Good Deed,
> Let this one thing for my atonement plead:
> That one for two I never did misread.

Real trouble in Persia began when the Christian queen, not content with the rights enjoyed by her coreligionists, sought to convert the Mohammedans by force, and the Catholicus ordered that Christian converts to Mohammedanism be drowned in the Tigris. Soon, therefore, after Argun's death (1291) pogroms broke out against Jews and Christians all over Persia. Churches and synagogues were demolished, and Saad Abduala, accused of a plot to seize Mecca and proclaim there a new religion under the grand Khan, was executed, and his relatives were sold as slaves or imprisoned. Under Ghazan, a convert from Christianity, Jews and Christians had to wear a distinguishing sign on their heads, to pay *kharaj* tax, and were forbidden to hold public worship. Christians who baptised their children were made eunuchs and deprived of an eye. Fanatical and rapacious viziers vied with one another to convert or to enslave the people of Mordecai and Esther.

Abbas I (d. 1628) paid four hundred hecans to every male Jew who accepted Islam, and Abbas II (d. 1666) imposed the penalty of death or exile upon anyone who refused to be converted. Yet, though many submitted, most of them clung secretly to their religion. To this day the group known as *Yedidim* (friends) outwardly conform to the dominant faith but remain loyal to Judaism in the privacy of their homes. [26]

Mohammedanism also, like Christianity, did not remain reform-proof. In the eighteenth century a puritanical sect was founded by Abd-al-Wahabi which had as its goal the purification of the faith from the superstitions which had crept into it, and the peaceful conversion of the backward races in Asia and Africa. Through them, many millions in India, Burma, and China were won over from Buddhism and Confucianism. They met with special success among the Negroes in Africa where, it is said, their converts became imbued with a dignity and self-reliance "which is all too rarely found in their pagan and Christian countrymen."

Mirza Ali Mohammed, the later and greater reformer, hailed from Shiraz in Persia, where he came in contact with Jews and acquired a knowledge of the Gospels. Seeing the corruption of the *mullas* (priests) and the rapacity of the authorities, he denounced them as heretics and was thrown into jail. On release after three years' confinement, he announced himself as the *Bab*, or gate, through whom the twelfth and last Imam communicated with his faithful followers. Later he pretended to be the Imam himself. For this he was dragged through the bazaars of Tabriz and then suspended from staples set in a wall, together with a devoted follower to whom, like Jesus, it is claimed he declared: "Verily, thou art with me in paradise." His body was then thrown outside the city wall to be devoured by wolves and jackals, but was recovered by another "Joseph Arimathea" who also was martyred in 1852.

The most distinguished pontiff of the cult was Mirza Husayn Ali, who assumed the title *Baha'u'lla*, "the Splendor of God," and claimed to be he to whom the Bab referred as the one "whom God shall manifest." While he held with the other Babis that Mohammed was a true prophet and the Koran a work of divine inspiration, he taught that revelation is progressive, that women may marry again if they had no news from their husbands for nine months, that cleanliness is next to godliness, and that evil must not be met with evil. He was banished by the Turkish government to Acre (Akka), where he issued his *Kitab-i-Akdas,* and which after his death (1892) became "the most holy region" of the Babis.

Carlyle and Emerson have done much to make Mohammed a hero to many English speaking Christians, but the religion of Baha attracted a considerable number of them to Mohammedanism. Towards the end of the nineteenth century there was organized in Liverpool, England, the Society of English Mohammedans consisting of many cultured Christians. In America the Bahais started their propaganda at the World's Fair of Chicago (1893). Their missionaries now claim a following of over five thousand and a steadily growing number of converts.

While the Bahais look upon all founders of religions as prophets and all Scriptures as being inspired, they point especially to the Bible for proof of the divinity of their Babis. Baha'u'lla, in his writings, frequently refers to himself as the Tree or the Root of which Isaiah speaks in his eleventh chapter. His son and successor Abd'ul-Baha is sure that the Prophet had him in mind when he predicted that "a Branch shall grow forth out of his roots." He even adduces the Zionist movement as evidence that he is the "Branch":

> Israel, scattered all over the world, was not reassembled in the Holy Land in the Christian cycle; but in the beginning of the cycle of Baha'u'lla this divine promise, as is clearly stated in all the books of the prophets, has begun to be manifest. You can see that from all parts of the world tribes of Jews are coming to the Holy land; they live in villages and lands which they make their own, and day by day they are increasing to such an extent that all Palestine will become their home.

As yet, however, there are no indications that Jews are ready to accept Bahaism any more than Mohammedanism. On the other hand, there are records of numerous Mohammedans, Arabs, and Persians who became proselytes to Judaism. Some of them are to be found on the list of the hospitals where they had been circumcised, others among those who received stipends from the *Halukah* (fund for the support of pious and scholarly poor). In the office of the rabbinate of Tel-Aviv there is a long list of Mussulmen who applied for conversion to Judaism, and many of them have their names inscribed on tomb stones on the Mount of Olives and other Jewish cemeteries in the cities and colonies of Palestine. [27]

We now turn back again to the West. The Visigoths, whom the Moors found in possession of the Iberian Peninsula, were Germanic tribes who had been Christianized by Ulfilas (c. 311-383). Consecrated by Eusebius as bishop of the Goths, he produced from the *Septuagint* a Germanic translation of the Bible, from which he excluded the Book of Kings because "the Gothic tribes were especially fond of war, and were in more need of restraints to check their military passions than of spurs to urge them on to deeds of war." It was the first book written in a Teutonic tongue, and Ulfilas thus became the father of Gothic literature. [28]

These bellicose tribes, however, at first left the Jews unmolested in the observance of their religion. They even regarded them with reverence, and not infrequently called on them to bless the produce of their soil. They had no objection to intermarrying with them and allowed the children of such intermarriages to be raised in the Jewish faith. They also permitted Jews to hold public office, to buy heathen and Christian slaves, and even to admit these into the Covenant of Abraham.

But the Catholic Church, even while itself still struggling for a foothold in Spain, sought to isolate the Jews from the rest of the population. At the Council held in Elvira near Granada (c. 303), which was attended by Bishop Hosius of Cordova and nineteen other church dignitaries, Catholics were forbidden, under pain of excommunication, to live with Jews, to eat with them, to intermarry with them, or to invite them to bless their fields. Alaric II (485-507), who was still somewhat free from bigotry and had ordered that no action be brought against Jews on their religious holidays, decreed that Jews might not build new synagogues or buy or receive as a gift Christian slaves, and imposed the penalty of death upon the Jew who circumcised any slave in his possession.

With the conversion of Recared, Spain entered upon her career which rendered her "more Catholic than Rome," and Jews began to feel the full effect of the intolerance for which Spain became noted. The Third Council of Toledo (589) not only re-enacted all the restrictive laws which had ever been passed against the Jews but added that Jews were to be excluded from public office and forbidden to sing Psalms at their funeral services, and that the issues of intermarriages were to be brought up as Christians. Sisebut (612-20) expressed the wish that a king, who abolished the restrictions of the Jews, "shall incur the deepest disgrace in this world, and eternal torments in the flames of hell." Under him, more than ninety thousand Jews saved their property and their homes by embracing Christianity. Swintila, however, permitted those who fled to return to their native land, and the forced converts to resume the religion of their fathers.

The matter of forced baptism was taken up at the Fourth Council of Toledo (633), presided over by St. Isidore of Seville (560-636). He admitted in principle that Jews may not be compelled to enter into the Christian fold, but contended that for the honor of the Church their converts must not be allowed to revert to Judaism. He was convinced, however, that it was the duty of Christians to enlighten them and wrote *De Fide Catholica ex Veteri et Novo Testamento Contra Judaeos,* in which he endeavors to prove that the doctrine of the Trinity is based on the teachings of the Old Testament. Isidore's work evoked refutations by Jews in Latin. These the Church promptly destroyed, but excerpts have been preserved in the counter attack written at the behest of King Erwig by Julian of Toledo, of Jewish descent, who was raised to the Archbishopric and to sainthood, even though his theology was not sound enough to meet with the approval of the clergy of his day. [29]

It is said that when the messenger through whom Julian sent one of his books to the Bishop of Barcelona turned out to be a Jew, Julian was scolded by his Eminence for "making an animal the bearer of light."

Despite the decision of the Toledo Council, Chintilla (634-40) compelled the Jews to abjure their faith and to hand over the Talmud and other writings to the authorities at the peril of being flogged, stoned, or burned to death. Erwig, soon after his accession, issued a decree commanding the Jews to be baptized within the space of a year, otherwise their property would be confiscated, they would receive one hundred lashes, their skin torn off their forehead, and they would be driven out of the country. Those who remained as converts were under the steady vigilance of the clergy. When they traveled they had to obtain from the priest of the town which they left a certificate attesting to their unimpeachable orthodoxy. They also had to report to the priest immediately on their arrival at their destination. They were further required to present themselves before the ecclesiastical authorities on Jewish festivals to prove that they did not observe them, and on Christian holidays to assure them that they did. These edicts were ratified at the Twelfth Council of Toledo (681), over which Julian presided. [30]

Though France was Catholicized before Spain, the Church there found it much harder to sow the seed of intolerance than in the Iberian peninsula. The Jews, who are said to have arrived in Gaul soon after the destruction of the Temple, were received by the Franks rather hospitably, and they even won some converts. According to Renan:

> There were without doubt in Gaul Jewish exiles (of the Semitic race), but there were also groups of people who attached themselves to Judaism by conversion, and who did not have a single ancestor in Palestine. And when one remembers that the Jewries

of Germany and England have come from France,
one regrets that we do not possess more data concerning the origins of Judaism in our country. One
would probably see that the Jew of Gaul at the time
of Gontran and Chilperic was more often only a Gaul
professing the Israelitish religion. [31]

But, as in Spain, once the Church obtained a foothold in
France it began to exert every effort to put a stop to the
amicable relations existing between the Jews and Franks.
Following the edict of the Council of Elvira (305), the Council
of Vannes prohibited Christians, and especially the clergy, from
taking meals at Jewish homes. Hilary of Poitiers, we have
seen, refused to acknowledge the salutation of one whom he
suspected of being a Jew. The first official Roman document
concerning the Jews of Gaul (425) is a decree by Valentinian
III addressed to the Praetor of Gaul and the Bishop of Arles
forbidding Jews and heathens to become soldiers, to hold
public office, or to possess Christian slaves.

Clovis "the most Christian King" (481-511), like Constantine "the first son of the Church," became convinced that the
God of Clotilda was the true God because He granted him
victory, and like Constantine he remained a pagan to the end
of his life. He was, nevertheless, sufficiently Christian to exclaim, on hearing the story of the Crucifixion: "Had I been
present with my valiant knights I would have avenged his
(Jesus') injuries," and then gave free reign to the clergy to suppress all who were not of his faith. It was under him that
Arianism was exterminated in France, and that St. Avitus,
Bishop of Vienne and distinguished as the author of five books
in rhyme on Original Sin and on the Deluge and the Crossing
of the Red Sea as symbols of baptism, incited the mob to
destroy the synagogues on Ascension Day and put before the
Jews the choice of expulsion or conversion.

Thereafter, council after council discussed the treatment to
be accorded by Christians to Jews. In 506 the Council of Agde

prohibited the clergy from participating in Jewish feasts. In 533 the Second Council of Orleans forbade intermarriage between Christians and Jews, while the Third Council, which convened in the same city (538), ordered that no Jew appear on the streets for four days after Good Friday. At the Fourth Council of that place (541) it was decreed that any Jew who reconverted another Jew or made a proselyte of a Gentile, or possessed himself of a Christian slave, was to lose his property, and that if the slave preferred to remain steadfast in his Judaism he was to be condemned to perpetual slavery to a Christian master, "for it is unjust that one living as a Jew should enjoy the freedom attached to Christian birth." The Fifth Council of Paris (614) refused to allow Jews any office unless they and their families accepted "the grace of baptism" from the local Bishop.

Gradually the efforts of the clergy began to bear fruit. The Gauls began to learn that to love Jesus one must hate Jews, and to do harm to Jews became a part of the celebrations of the Church. In Chalons, Jews were stoned by the clergy and people "because they stoned Jesus." In Toulouse, on the pretext that the Jews once *intended* to betray the city to the Moors, it was customary to whip the Jews three times a year; and since it could not be ascertained whether all Jews were whipped, it was decided that they all should be whipped vicariously in the person of their rabbi, who had to stand before St. Stephen's church to receive the blow, which sometimes caused death. At Beziers, part of the Easter celebration was, after an inflammatory sermon by the bishop, to throw stones at the Jews in the street and to break the windows of their homes. These customs in certain places continued, despite the condemnation of some Councils, until the twelfth century when the bishops consented to their discontinuance on payment of an annual sum of money. In time, these outrages ceased to be confined to Good Friday or holy convocations, and often became part of the practices of loyal Christians.

Meanwhile the princes, too, came under the control of the clergy. Childebert ratified the decisions of the Third Council

of Orleans. He banished the Bishop of Uzies for being friendly
to the Jews (555), and to prove his orthodoxy the good bishop
ordered the Jews to accept baptism or be expelled from his
diocese. Chilperic graciously offered to be godfather to as
many Jews as would embrace his faith. When his Jewish
treasurer, Priscus, declined the honor, he was cast into prison,
and the noisome dungeon accomplished what the glamor
of the court and the erudition of the bishop failed to do. Priscus
asked the favor only that his baptism be postponed until after
the marriage of his son to a Jewess of Marseille. Another Jew,
however, by the name of Phatir, one of the King's godsons, fell
upon Priscus on the Sabbath day and slew him, together with
his friends (582). The murderer was pardoned but was afterwards killed by a kinsman of Priscus. [32]

The other Merovingian kings were no less zealous than Chilperic. When the Jews of Orleans welcomed Gontran to their
city by singing his Psalms in their own tongue, the king exclaimed: "Woe unto this wicked and perfidious Jewish race
that thrives only by knavery. Today they were lavish with
their blatant flattery; all people, said they, should reverence me
as their lord, and this only to induce me to rebuild at their
state's expense the synagogue which the Christians destroyed
long ago. That I shall never do, for God forbids it." At last
Dagobert I, famous as the Solomon of the Franks and who,
like Solomon, had a harem full of wives and concubines,
decreed (c. 629) that all Jews who remained unconverted by
a certain date should either leave the country or be put to
death. "Many changed their faith at that time," records Rabbi
Joseph Hakkohen, "but a large number were slain by the
sword." [33]

Yet, in spite of the fulminations of the Councils and the
clergy, many Jews and Christians continued to live together
in amity. At the funeral of Hilary, Bishop of Arles (499), Jews
sang Psalms in Hebrew, and their "Hebrew wailings" were
heard "side by side with those of other citizens." Sidonius
Apollinaris, Bishop of Clermont, was fond of Jews and employed them in his service. In a letter which he sent by a
Jew to one of his correspondents, he took occasion to state:

"He would be dear to my heart were it not for his abominable religion." In another letter he recommended a Jew to the good offices of Bishop Eleutherius, for, he said, "though still blind, as long as he lives he has a chance of conversion." It is rather remarkable that until the ninth century we hear of only two synagogues destroyed by a French mob. Nor was there lack of intermarriages between Jews and Christians. Moreover, some Christians persisted even in the observances of the Lord's Day in Jewish fashion, in the celebration of the Jewish Sabbath and attendance at the synagogue, and openly expressed their admiration for Jewish preaching. They also consulted Jewish scholars on the meaning of various verses of the Bible, and Jews not only continued to have slaves but to convert them to Judaism.

This was true especially in the "Septimania," the southern province of France, which for many years was not included in Clovis' dominion. When Wamba (672-80) decreed that all Jews should embrace Christianity, many counts and abbots took them under their protection; and Bishop Roland adopted as his wards those of their children who, to escape conversion, fled from Lyons, Chalon, Macon, and Vienne to Arles. This liberality was condemned by the ecclesiastic authorities of Spain and called forth from St. Julian of Toledo the statement that France is "a country of lack of faith, of obscene works, of fraudulent business, of venal judges, and worst of all, a brothel of Jews blaspheming our Savior and Lord." [34]

The position of the Frankish Jews was greatly improved under the Carlovingian dynasty. Charlemagne, who was bent on the temporal prosperity of his country, realizing the advantages which would accrue to it from the business abilities of his Jewish subjects, granted them some special privileges and permission to buy whatever they pleased from bishops and abbots. Charlemagne's physician was the Jew Sedechias, and his ambassador to the court of Haroun al-Rashid (797) was a Jew by the name of Isaac. One tradition recounts that he invited Jewish sages to settle in his dominions. One of these sages, R. Makhir, Charlemagne received with special honor and conferred upon him and his descendants the title of "king of the Jews." [35]

Louis the Pious (814-40) went even further than his father. He informed all bishops, abbots, counts, prefects, governors, etc., that Jews were under the Emperor's protection and should not be interfered with in the observance of their religion nor in their commercial dealings. He permitted them to settle wherever they chose, to employ Christians to do their work except on Sundays and holidays, to buy and sell pagan slaves, and the right to refuse to have their slaves baptized. They were also exempt from the ordeals of fire and water. Because Jews abstained from doing business on Saturday, the market day was changed from that day to Sunday. Louis also appointed a special magistrate to defend the Jews against the intolerance of the clergy. This he justified on the ground that:

> Although apostolic teaching ordained that we should do good to our brethren in the faith, it does not forbid us to benefit the unfaithful with our kindly service. It exhorts us rather to seek humbly our inspiration in the Divine mercy, and to make no distinction between the faithful and the unfaithful. [36]

The reactions of the Church to Louis' removal of certain Jewish disabilities was expressed by Agobard, the Archbishop of Lyons (779-840), who with St. Bernard, Archbishop of Vienne, deposed the Emperor and was in turn deposed by him. In four epistles addressed to the king, the bishops, and the clergy, he complains that these people who "are clothed with the curse as with a garment" boast of being dear to the king and the nobility, that Christian women observe the Sabbath with Jews, work with them on Sundays, and partake of their meals during Lent, and that Jews not only convert the pagan slaves but, as tax-collectors, bribe the peasants to accept Judaism by reducing or dropping taxes. Thus, he complains, "the souls that could augment the flock of the faithful, and for whose salvation public prayers are offered to God by the Universal Church on Passion Day, remain, through the obstinacy of the unbelievers, through the wickedness of the enemies of Heaven, as well as the pretended edict of the king, in the snares of Satan." His greatest grief was to see:

> The sons of light associate with the children of darkness, and the Church of Christ which ought, without blemish and without wrinkle, to present herself for the kisses of her celestial Spouse, besmirched by contact with the defiled and repudiated Synagogue. ... One should not only not make use of those who do not want to accept the Apostolic teaching, but should shake off the dust of their dwellings. In the Day of Judgment Sodom and Gomorrah will be pardoned sooner than they. [37]

Agobard's disciple and successor Amolon or Amulo repeated the same charges and, at the Councils of Meaux and Paris (845-846), also recommended that the old restrictions against the Jews be revived, that children of baptized parents be placed in Christian homes to save them from possible Jewish influence, and that Jewish slave dealers be compelled to dispose of their heathen slaves within Christian territory so that they might be converted to Christianity. He, too, vehemently inveighed against the Christians of his bishopric who fraternized with Jews, and the priests who bought wine from them for religious purposes. "We dare not," he protested, "either by our suavity, flattery, or defense, encourage the complacency of the Jews, who are accursed and yet blind to their own damnation."[38]

Other ecclesiastics went further and resorted to compulsory conversion of Jews in their diocese. The successor of Amulo in the See of Lyons, St. Remy or Remigius, reported to the Emperor that "because every Sabbath the word of God is preached in the synagogue by our brothers and priests," a number of men and women, old and young, and many of their servants accepted Christianity and invited other Jews to do likewise. Moreover, when they learned that the unconverted Jews began to send their children to Arles they reported it to the bishop. Whereupon the bishop ordered the children who remained to be brought before him, when six of them asked for baptism and forty-seven more followed their example.

It is hardly likely that there were so many willing converts in Lyons, when everywhere else they preferred to be slain or to commit suicide rather than apostatize, and the survivors returned openly to Judaism as soon as the danger was over. Nor would the reverts have been received back into the fold had they not been converted under duress. This is shown in the fact that Rabbenu Gershom, "the Light of the Exile," (960-1040) in neighboring Mayence observed full mourning for his converted son as if he had died in the faith of Israel, and from his penitential hymn in which he pleads:

> Mighty Redeemer, for Thine own sake,
> Save us who for Thee do bleed;
> See how our saints from us they take
> And there is none to intercede.

In spite of this, France of the Carlovingian dynasty under Charlemagne and Louis the Pious was like an oasis in the desert of the diaspora. Whatever prejudice and hatred there existed was fomented by the ecclesiastics, and even among them there were some whose liberal views were unique in the Middle Ages. There were Church Councils which bore witness to Jewish merits, and artists who had no compunction to represent the Synagogue as a figure of equal dignity with the Church. As late as the beginning of the tenth century Remigius of Auxerre warned his hearers in a sermon on the Crucifixion not to condemn the Jews alone but all sinners for the tragedy of Calvary, especially since God had given them until the Second Coming to repent their deed. Nor was the amity between Jews and Christians totally interrupted by the efforts of the Church to disturb it. Many Christians, we are told, attended services in the synagogue because they preferred to hear the preaching of the Jews and expressed themselves as wishing they, too, had had a lawgiver like Moses. On the other hand, Jews did not seem to fear to lend to their Christian neighbors or to read the notorious *Sepher Toldoth Jeshu,* (the medieval Jewish account of Jesus) which they usually kept hidden and are said to have counseled converts that there was no harm in admiring Jesus provided they did not believe him to be God.

Louis' liberality was especially reflected in his palace and particularly during the reign of his second consort, the Empress Judith. She made it fashionable for her courtiers to read the works of Philo and Josephus and to discuss the relative merits of Judaism and Christianity. While we do not hear of the spread of Judaism among the nobility as we do among the commonalty, we have a record of one of them, Bodo, who became a full-fledged Proselyte of Righteousness.

Bodo was a court chaplain of an old Allemanic family and noted for his learning and intelligence. In accordance with the custom of the clergy he left for Rome to receive the blessing of the Pope and to visit the graves of the martyrs. For some inexplicable reason he never returned to his native land but went to Saragossa, entered the covenant of Abraham, and assumed the name Eliezer. He also converted his nephew, married a Jewess, and became an ardent propagandist for his new faith. His apostasy caused a stir among the clergy, but it was explained to be the result of the successful machination of the devil.

There is a tradition that the founders of the Jewish communities in and around Worms and Mayence were descended from the Vangioni (who served in the Roman legions which destroyed the Temple), and their captive Jewish females whom they brought with them to their native shores on the Rhine and the Main. Another Jewish tradition claims for them a still greater antiquity. It asserts that Israelites first arrived in Germany during the affair of the "concubine of Gobeah" (Jud. 19-20) and became so attached to their adopted land that they refused to go back with the return of the Captivity under Zerubbabel. However, the more moderate claim of the Jews of Lorraine that they settled in Metz in 221 may be accepted as correct. We know that in 321 Constantine the Great issued a decree abolishing the German Jewish privilege of exemption from the burdensome municipal offices. We hear of a converted Jew who became bishop of Metz in 350, and that while Julian was at that place he condemned the bishop to prison for coercing the Jews to see the light of Christianity. In the tenth century the Archbishop of Mainz appealed to Pope Leo VII for advice on how to convert the Jews. His reply was that the Holy Trinity and the Mystery of the Incarnation be preached to them "with the utmost wisdom and prudence" but if they refused to accept it they should be expelled, "since we ought not to dwell with the enemies of God." [39]

But in Germany during the first Christian millennium, as in France, it was not all prejudice and persecution. Officially the Jews enjoyed freedom of movement, were allowed to testify against a non-Jew, and could be condemned only on evidence corroborated by one of their own. They also formed intimate friendships with some Christians, and it is recorded that Jews were among the chief mourners for Bishop Adalbert and Archbishop Mattard. The canons of some councils indicate also that there was no lack of peace and goodwill among many Christians and their Jewish countrymen.

And, as in France a century before, there occurred in Germany at the turn of the first millennium the conversion to Judaism of a distinguished ecclesiastic, a relative of the emperor, Wecelin, chaplain to Duke Conrad (ca. 1005). He, too, became an ardent missionary for his new faith and composed a diatribe against Christianity which Henry II commissioned a monk of Mainz to refute. What effect it had on his former Christian coreligionists is unknown, but in 1012 the emperor ordered that all the Jews of Mainz and neighboring communities who refused to be baptized be banished. [40]

CHAPTER XVII

DEUS LO VULT!

("God Wills It")

THE second Christian millennium dawned upon a world which was neither morally or economically an improvement on the state in which it found itself in the days of the Apostle to the Gentiles. The further invasions of Europe by the Moslems were temporarily stopped by Charles Martel at the battle of Rouen, and the consolidation of the broken fragments of the Roman Empire made the continent safer for the expansion of Christianity. But the vast majority of the barbarian converts remained as pagan after their baptism as before. The Christian moral precepts left them untouched. As a rule, those who were baptized did so at the behest of the king, who found Christ to be the mightier God, or in order to escape the divine vengeance on the Day of Wrath. Ignorance and poverty were almost universal. The miserable peasants huddled like cattle around the castle of the illiterate and fierce lord, or near the cathedral of the not much more spiritual bishop, until they were decimated by pestilence, war, or famine. Everywhere, in the words of Paul, there was "without fightings, within fears."

Even the monasteries, where those who were inclined to lead lives of piety sought refuge from the contaminating influences of the world, did not long retain their pristine purity. St. Benedict (480-543) indeed did much to raise the moral standard of Western monarchism. But his *Regula Monachorum* were too often honored in the breach and the "abodes of the spirit," whither peasants and sometimes princes retired out of fear of hell or for love of Christ, at times became nests of corruption, where ignorance, laziness, and profligacy met and mingled with saintliness and scholarliness. The wealth which flowed into them from repentant or superstitious sinners, in the belief that the supplications offered by monks would prove more efficacious than their own, only sapped their spirituality and frequently made of them mere whited sepulchres. [1]

Among the secular clergy, the standard of morality was not much higher. They were, as a rule, but little superior to their flock, if we judge by the thirteenth century *Register* of the Archbishop of Rouen. The princes of the Church also furnished an example of worldliness which was hardly surpassed by the kings and feudal lords. They engaged and led in wars, sometimes against their own colleagues, and indulged themselves in every variety of carnal pleasure. What many an honest man thought of these physicians of the soul is revealed in one of many similar anecdotes current in the Middle Ages. A certain prior of Clairvaux persistently refused the solicitation of the pope and St. Bernard to become Bishop of Tournai. After his death he appeared to a fellow monk and confided to him that, according to the assurance of the blessed Trinity, had he been made a bishop he would have been "in the number of the reprobate and damned." [2]

It was no better with the papacy itself. The Roman hierarchy degenerated into a monarchy and sought to dominate the world politically as well as spiritually. As soon as the efforts of Pope Leo I for the primacy of the Bishop of Rome over the whole Church began to be crowned with success, Rome became a battleground for temporal power between pontiffs and the princes. Each faction fought for its favorite pontifical candidate. Simony, or the buying of ecclesiastic benefices, became the order of the day. In the century after the elevation of John XII (956-64)—the first to change his name on his ascension to the throne of St. Peter—it became as risky to be a pope as to be an emperor. Many of them were maimed. Documents, such as the "Donation" of Constantine, the "False Decretals" associated with the name of St. Isidore of Seville, and the "Capitularies" ascribed to Charlemagne and Louis the Pious, (probably the work of one "Benedictus Levita," deacon of

the church of Mainz), were forged, showing that the great
Christian monarchs had surrendered their powers to the Bishop
of Rome. At last Hildebrand or St. Gregory VII (c. 1020-85)
proclaimed that:

> There is but one name in the world, and that is the
> pope's. All princes ought to kiss his feet. He alone
> can nominate and displace bishops, or dissolve coun-
> cils. Nobody can judge him. He has never erred, and
> never shall err in time to come. He can depose princes,
> and release subjects from their oath of fidelity. [3]

This was no idle boast. He deposed Henry IV of Germany for
insisting on his right to appoint bishops in his own realm, and
threatened his subjects with eternal damnation if they dared
to remain loyal to this recalcitrant son of the Church. The
emperor soon found life so unbearable that he crossed the
Alps in the dead of winter and, throwing himself at the feet
of the pontiff, implored his forgiveness. Gregory was finally
placated, but not before he had thoroughly humiliated him
by keeping him waiting barefoot, bareheaded, and clothed in
a woolen shirt, at the gates of his castle so that all might
"see and fear." The Church, however, carried her vengeance
beyond the grave. The Bishop of Liege who gave Henry an
honorable burial was excommunicated, and the emperor was
disinterred and buried in unconsecrated ground. Frederick I
of Germany and Henry II of England had similar experiences a
hundred years later in their contest for power with Pope
Alexander III.

In these stormy and brutal times, reminiscent of the days
immediately before and after the *Hurban,* there was awakened
in the hearts of many earnest Christians the ancient belief
that Jesus would appear again to establish the Kingdom of God
on earth; and since the author of the Apocalypse predicted
that this great event would transpire after the lapse of a thousand years, all hearts were filled with hope that at last the
Second Coming of Christ was near at hand when "the old

dragon ... will be cast in the bottomless pit ... that he should deceive the nations no more."

By the irony of history, the one place over which Christians had no control was the cradle of Christianity, even Jerusalem, where Greeks and Latins, Nestorians and Jacobites, Copts, Armenians, and other sects maintained their distinctive chapels and clergy. Though at dagger's point with one another, they literally "took pleasure in her stones and loved her dust," which they transported in large quantities to Europe. (The Campo Santo of Pisa was said to contain five fathoms of holy earth brought from Jerusalem in 1218.) But with the conversion of the Turks to Mohammedanism the Christians began to suffer the fate they meted out to non-Christians in their own lands. Their pilgrims were robbed and murdered, their clergy were insulted. In 1009 the Church of the Resurrection was destroyed by al-Hakim, "who made some martyrs and many proselytes." As often as it was rebuilt it was desecrated. It was felt that now if ever was the auspicious time to strike at the dragon, remove the stigma under which Christianity was smarting ever since the rise of Mohammedanism, and at the same time deal a death blow to the Greek church which refused to acknowledge the sovereignty of the Roman pontiff. [4]

Pope Sylvester II, who conferred upon the newly converted King of the Hungarians the title of Apostolic Majesty, had issued a call to all Christendom to redeem the Sepulchre "which the Prophet Isaiah (?) had said should be a glorious one, and which the sons of the destroyer Satan were making inglorious." Gregory VII also advocated the invasion of the Holy City. But both were too busy with fighting for their temporal rights to devote much attention to the Holy Land. It remained for Urban II to execute what the others planned. For this purpose he summoned a council at Placentia (1095). It was attended by thousands of clergy and vast multitudes of knights and peasants. The pope himself made the chief address. He pictured the misery of the Church in Asia and promised that whoever would abandon his house or his father, or his mother or his wife, or his children or his inheritance, for the sake of His name, would be recompensed a hundredfold and possess life eternal. For, he cried:

> With the end of the world already near, even though the Gentiles fail to be converted to the Lord (since according to the Apostle there must be a withdrawal from the faith), it is first necessary, according to the prophecy, that the Christian sway be renewed in those regions, either through you or others whom it shall please God to send before the coming of Antichrist, so that the head of all evil, who is to occupy there the throne of the kingdom, shall find some support of the faith to fight against him. [5]

A frenzy of religious fervor seized hold of the people. The cry *Deus lo vult,* or *Dieux el volt,* resounded throughout Western Europe. Peter the Hermit, a repentant sinner, set out on an ass and, in imitation of Christ, carrying a huge cross, bareheaded and barefooted, traveled all over France and Germany and, with fiery eloquence, melted the hearts of his hearers with his description of the indignities heaped upon the faithful by the infidel Saracens. Men and women enlisted by the hundreds of thousands and sewed crosses on the front and back of their garments, or even cut the holy sign deep in their quivering flesh. There were rumors of apparitions in heaven and on earth and of stars shooting down with remarkable brilliancy. Christ seemed to be ready to lead his flock in battle with Antichrist. [6]

The first experience of the crusaders was most discouraging. They were massacred mercilessly when they landed in Hungary—the newly converted nation, as yet uneducated to a holy war. They were decimated in Bulgaria, which was in sympathy with the Greek Church; and in Constantinople the Turks made a pyramid of their bones. Fire and sword, famine and disease clogged the steps of those who remained, and in their misery many cursed Christ and turned Moslem. But St. Bernard is said to have performed numerous miracles to prove that it was the will of God that holy war should continue, and Innocent III stirred up the masses by reciting the taunts of the Saracens:

> Where is your God who cannot deliver you out of our hands? Behold! we have defiled your sanctuaries ... we hold in despite of you those desirable places where your superstition had its beginning. Where is your God? Let Him arise and protect you and Himself. ... If thou be the son of God, save thyself if thou canst; redeem the land of thy birth from our hands. Restore the cross that we have taken to the worshipers of the Cross.

At last about one hundred and fifty thousand crusaders managed to capture Jerusalem, and, once in the Holy City, they removed their shoes and uncovered their heads, and in a delirium of joy exclaimed: "Jerusalem, lift up thine eyes and behold thy liberators come to break thy chains!" Then they threw themselves into the business of massacring all who were not Christians. "In Solomon's Porch and in his Temple," writes a crusader, "men rode in the blood of the Saracens up to their horses' knees." When they tired of slaughtering the Moslems they ferreted out all the Jews, herded them into their synagogues, and burned them to a man. Then they marched in procession to the Holy Sepulchre and, sobbing for excessive joy, sang a *Te Deum*.

The new government which the crusaders established was called the Latin Kingdom of Jerusalem. But it was far from being the Kingdom of God of which the zealous soldiers of Christ dreamed in 1096. It was another feudal State with all its vices and few of its virtues. It became honeycombed with mutual rivalries and fell a prey to the animosities between the Latins and the Greeks. While many crusaders were undoubtedly actuated by religious motives, many of those who remained and who arrived were adventurers who were drawn to the Holy Land for base purposes. Some native Christians began to adopt the dress and habits of the Moslem natives, and the leaders themselves succumbed to Oriental luxuries and vo-

luptuousness or degenerated into brigands who plundered caravans and held Saracens for ransom. As a result, the Kingdom
of Jerusalem began to disintegrate; and to prevent its total
collapse, a second Crusade was inaugurated in which Louis VII,
to expiate for his cruelty against his subjects, participated.

A third, fourth, and fifth crusade followed. Paradoxically
enough, Jerusalem was regained for a while by one who was
an excommunicated unbeliever and was finally lost through
a Crusade launched by the pope against him. Frederick II was
of the type of Julian the Apostate. He is said to have delighted
to speak of himself as the Antichrist, and he was suspected as
the author of the statement that the world was deceived by
three *baratores* (impostors)—Moses, Jesus, and Mohammed,
but that Jesus was inferior to the other two. He also declared
the Virgin Birth and other Catholic dogmas as "repugnant to
reason and nature." To get the support of Innocent III he took
the vow to head a Crusade in 1215, but again and again found
an excuse to evade it. Finally Pope Honorius arranged a marriage between him and the heiress of the Kingdom of Jerusalem,
and as king he embarked for Palestine, but feigned illness
and returned. [7]

At the same time that the Church was baffled in its attempts
to wrest the Holy Land from the infidels, it began to lose its
hold on many Christians in its own midst. The deplorable
spectacle which Christianity often presented, the ignorance
and immorality prevailing not only among the masses but
even among the ecclesiastics, caused some faithful followers
of Jesus in the more enlightened parts of Europe to re-evaluate
their theology and to regard the Church as no better than the
pagan dragon from which they were anxious to escape. Among
these were the Paulicians. Like the Greek-speaking Jews, they
called their sanctuaries *proseuchi*, prayer houses. They opposed
the adoration of the Virgin and the saints and denied the
validity of the sacraments and the ceremonies of the Church.
They looked upon the cross as a relic of fetishism and were
bitter in their denunciation of the monks and Roman Hierarchy. They denied the dogmas of the Trinity, the Incarnation,
and Transubstantiation and rejected the reality of the death

and resurrection of Jesus. Christ, they declared, was merely a manifestation of God, and everyone who leads a godly life is a "living Christ." They may be said to have been "Protestants before Protestantism," and the forerunners of Unitarianism.

The Paulicians came to Europe by way of Armenia, and the Greek Church had their first Apostle, Sylvanus, stoned to death. The Empress Theodora is said to have instigated the slaughter of a hundred thousand of them, and Alexius Commenus boasted that by arguing with them while at Philippolis he converted all of them to the Church. Under cruel persecution, many of them lived outwardly as Catholics, while others joined the Saracens.

Similar to their views were those of the Cathari, or "puritans." To them Rome was the Babylon; and the pope, the Antichrist of the Apocalypse. They believed only in the spiritual baptism of Christ, led a simple life, abstained from flesh diets, except fish, and ate only bread on Mondays, Wednesdays, and Fridays. Contrary to the Paulicians they were not given to allegorizing, but took both the Old and New Testaments in their literal sense and regarded Peter in such esteem that they addressed their "Perfects" by his name. But by the thirteenth century their suppression was almost complete. Their voluminous literature was obliterated, and all we know about them is from their adversaries. The names of Paulicians and Cathari were corrupted into *Publicani* and *Ketzer* (infidels), and they were accused of gross immoralities in their conventicles. Many, however, ranked them among the zealous saints who were fighting for the restoration of their faith to its Apostolic purity. [8]

The revolt against the Hierarchy was especially strong among the Albigenses. They first appeared in Aquitaine in 1010, and in 1017 we hear of them as a secret society at Orleans of which ten canons of one church and a confessor to the Queen were members. A little later we find them in Liege and Arras, in Soissons and Flanders, in many provinces of Spain, in England, Germany, and in Italy, not excepting Rome, where they were joined by not a few of the nobility, and the people affectionately called them *Bonshommes*. After vainly trying to reclaim them by fines and exile, the Church decided to resort to the more drastic measure of employing fire and sword, and in 1022, at a Council held at Orleans, in the presence of King Robert the Pious, condemned thirteen of them to be burned at the stake. Similar executions took place for more than a century and a half all over France, but the heretics persisted in their folly, continued to preach their doctrines, and succeeded in winning over some bishops and noblemen, among them the powerful Raymond VI, Count of Toulouse. Finally Innocent III pronounced them to be more wicked than the Saracens and launched a Holy War against them which was prosecuted with all the atrocities that characterized the Crusades in Palestine (1209-13). Languedoc was laid in ruins. "We spared neither dignity, nor sex, nor age," is the testimony of one of the participants. Nor was pity shown for those whose guilt was not fully established. "Kill them all; God will recognize His own!" was the order given to the soldiers, and, declares one of them, "They made a wonderful blaze, and went to burn everlastingly in hell." At Beziers about sixty thousand on both sides perished by the sword, and after the massacre the town was plundered and burned, "and the revenge of God seemed to rage upon it in a wonderful manner." [9]

Another unorthodox group formed within the Church traced its origin to Waldo, a rich merchant of Lyons. He was a diligent student of the Bible and commissioned two priests to translate it into French. Desirous to put into effect the advice of Jesus to the rich young man, he distributed his wealth to the poor and to those from whom he acquired it, and took the vow of poverty (1176). His example was followed by many of his townsmen, and the "Poor Men of Lyons," as the Waldenses came to be known, soon found many imitators not only in Northern France but in Spain and Italy.

To these devout disciples of the Ebionites the Roman Church was the "Scarlet Woman" of the Apocalypse, and as idolatrous as the cults which it displaced. They insisted that all have a right to preach, regardless of sex or ordination; that oaths are sinful and the infliction of capital punishment, even by the secular authority, is criminal; and that everyone is in duty bound to read the Bible for himself. As their doctrines began to spread in southern France, northern Spain, and throughout Italy, the Church became alarmed. Innocent III lumped them together with his hated Albigensians and consigned them to the same fate. The Bishop of Toul ordered all suspected of the heresy to be put in chains. Alphonso II of Aragon banished them from his dominions, and forbade anyone to furnish them shelter and food, while the Council of Gerona decreed the penalty of death by burning against them. But no sooner were they rooted out from Provence and Languedoc than they found refuge in the recesses of Piedmont, whence they carried on intensive missionary work all over Europe. They were, however, almost crushed in a Crusade called by Innocent VIII (1482-92) and headed by the Archbishop of Cremona. Their martyrdom, which continued till 1655, prompted Cromwell to call upon the Protestant powers to intercede in their behalf with the King of France. It also inspired Milton's famous sonnet, "On the Late Massacre in Piedmont," which is reminiscent of the Lamentations of Jeremiah:

> Avenge, O Lord, Thy slaughtered saints, whose bones
>   Lie scatter'd on the Alpine mountains cold;
>   Ev'n them that kept Thy truth so pure of old,
> When all our fathers worship'd stocks and stones,
> Forget not: in Thy book record their groans
>   Who were Thy sheep, and in their ancient fold
>   Slain by the bloody Piedmontese that roll'd
> Mother with infant down the rocks. Their moans
> The vales redoubled to the hills, and they
>   To heaven. Their martyr'd blood and ashes sow
> O'er all the Italian fields, where still doth
>   The triple Tyrant; that from these may grow
> A hundred fold, who, having learned Thy way,
>   Early may fly the Babylonian woe. [10]

This spirit of criticism and skepticism began to insinuate itself from the eleventh century onward into the very citadels of religion, the monasteries and the universities. The doctors who attracted the most students were those whose theology was the least sound from the Catholic point of view. Abelard (1079-1142), the most popular professor of his day, taught that "heretics must be coerced with reason rather than by force" and that no act is a sin unless the actor is conscious of its sinfulness, hence the Jews should not be blamed for crucifying Christ. He exposed the inconsistencies of the Fathers in his famous *Sic et Non,* without attempting to reconcile them, and declared that while the Scriptures are to be interpreted *Cum credendi necessitate,* in the writing of the Fathers, whose works are contained in books without number, if passages are deemed to depart from the truth, the reader is at liberty to approve or disapprove. He furthermore ventured to explain the Trinity in a quasi-allegorical sense and affirmed that the Crucifixion was not intended to save men from damnation but to set an example of sacrifice for an ideal. In his *Dialogue* between a Philosopher, a Jew, and a Christian, he seems to speak through the philosopher and deprecates those who claim to have a monopoly of the truth, "so that whomsoever they see differing from themselves in belief, they deem alien from the mercy of God."

Abelard's books were burned in public, and he saved himself from a similar fate by seeking sanctuary in the monastery of St. Denis. But his views were cherished by very many of his numerous disciples. The way he suggested in his *Sic et Non* served admirably to promulgate ideas which would otherwise be dangerous. Christian scholars took advantage of his subtle dialectics and, like R. Meir who could make the forbidden permissible by one hundred and fifty reasons, would remain unsuspected of heterodoxy. Thus, after having demonstrated by the most skillful arguments the truth of the Trinity, Simon of Tourney went on to say that, if he had been evil minded, he could refute the doctrine by yet stronger arguments. This became a favorite method with the students who were preparing themselves for the ministry and who, as Abelard tells us in his *Historia Calamitatum,*

> ... were calling for human and philosophical arguments, and insisting upon something intelligible, rather than mere words, saying that there had been more than enough of talk which the mind could not follow, that it was impossible to believe what was not understood in the first place; and that it was ridiculous for anyone to set forth to others what neither he nor they could rationally understand. [11]

Another very popular professor of the University of Paris whose heretical views found a considerable following was Amalric de Bene (d. c. 1204). He distinguished three periods in the Divine plan: The reign of the Father, beginning with Abraham; the reign of the Son, beginning with Jesus; and the reign of the Holy Ghost, which began with the twelfth century and is to endure till the end of time. In it, God's spirit will dwell in every human soul, and there will be no need for sacraments in order to be saved. The Amalricians included many clerics and priests, and the number of their converts was steadily growing until the bishops and doctors of the University took measures for their suppression. Some were condemned to imprisonment for life. Ten others, priests and clerics, were publicly degraded, then turned over to the secular authorities, and burned alive (1210) before the gates of Paris, together with the exhumed bones of Amalric who died shortly after his excommunication.

Amalric's views were adopted and expanded by Joachim di Floris, a nobleman who participated in the Crusades. He wrote commentaries on Isaiah, Jeremiah, and Ezekiel, and was himself regarded by many as "equal to the most illustrious prophets of ancient times." Dante assigned him a place of honor in Paradise. But fifty years after his death, there appeared in Paris a work which was attributed to him, entitled *Liber introductorius ad Evangelium aeternum* (the Eternal Gospel), with an introduction by the General of the Franciscans. It taught that not only the Old but the New Testament were abrogated, since they failed to build up the true Church of God. The pope's judgment in matters spiritual is fallible, and spiritual men need to take no account of it, it affirmed, and the Eternal Father watches over the Jews as He does over the Gentiles and "will save them from the hatred of men without it being necessary for them to abandon Judaism."

This new epoch, the Epoch of the Holy Spirit, according to the "Eternal Gospel," will be inaugurated by the Joachimite monks to whom, because they carried ropes around their loins, the Psalmist (16:6) alludes in the verse: "Excellent ropes have fallen to me as my share," and who will join "the ancient people—the Jews."

Pope Alexander IV condemned the Joachimites as heretics, and their writings were burned wherever found. But copies of the "Eternal Gospel" were secretly read by many monks and passed on from monastery to monastery. In it they found encouragement for their millenial hope for the advent of the Kingdom of God and the fulfillment of the prophecy of Jeremiah (31:31):

> I will put my law in their inward parts, and in their heart will I write it ... and they shall teach no more every man his neighbor, and every man his brother, saying: 'Know the Lord; for they shall all know me, from the least of them, saith the Lord.' [12]

It is narrated that Joachim opposed the Crusades because, according to him, the infidels were nearer the spirit of the Gospel than the Latins, and that in reply to Richard Coeur de Lion as regards the Antichrist, he stated that he is to be found in Rome where he raises himself, as the Prophet predicted, higher even than God. Such views were held by the Petrobrusians, founded by Peter de Bruis, who regarded the churches, as seats of idol worship, condemned the veneration of the cross, the dogma of transubstantiation, infant baptism, and all the Catholic ceremonies not excepting the mass. Peter was at last cast into the flames at St. Gilles, but his doctrine continued to be propagated by many monks of Cluny.

More or less the same ideas were preached by the Beguines,
a woman's organization said to have been founded by Lambert
le Bégue, a priest of Liége, for the widows or orphans of
the crusaders and the parallel communities of men known as
Beghards. They undertook to lead a communistic life, to
work at some trade, and, in the case of the women, to nurse
the sick. But as a further protest against the luxury of the
higher ecclesiastics they later turned from labor to mendi-
cancy. They held conventicles and interpreted the Bible according to their own understanding. When John XXII put
into execution the decrees which the various synods passed
against them, he found that in many places the laity took
the part of the Beguines. Their numbers, however, kept on
declining until by the fifteenth century they became almost
extinct. [13]

This mounting clamor against the dissoluteness and luxury
of the ecclesiastics finally produced the Mendicant Orders
within the Church itself, which spread with great rapidity
all over Christendom. It was pointed out that Jesus taught,
"If any man will come after me, let him deny himself";
that he counseled the young man: "Go and sell what thou
hast and give to the poor, and thou shalt have treasures in
heaven"; and advised his disciples to take nothing for their
journey, "neither bread, neither money." It may be doubted,
however, whether Jesus regarded the renunciation of riches
a virtue, or only a means of making oneself independent of
the world the better to be able to devote oneself to good
deeds. Probably he only voiced the opinion long current
among Jews. "Give me neither riches nor poverty," was the
prayer of Solomon. "The more property, the more anxiety,"
was one of the maxims of Hillel, a century before Jesus; and
a century later, R. Meir used to say, "Lessen thy toil for
worldly goods, and busy thyself in the study (or observance)
of the Torah." It was generally held: "If thou eatest thy bread
with salt, drinkest thy water by measure, sleepest upon the
(bare) ground and livest a life of trouble, yet toilest in the
Torah, if thou doest thus, 'happy shalt thou be and it shall

be well with thee,'—happy shalt thou be in this world, and it shall be well with thee in the world to come." [14]

The two chief mendicant orders came into being almost simultaneously in the closing years of the pontificate of Innocent III, who crusaded with equal zeal against the infidel Moslems and the heretic Christians. Both their founders were famed for their miraculous powers; St. Dominic was said to have been immaculately conceived and free from the taint of original sin, and St. Francis before his death displayed the *stigmata,* or wounds, which marked the hands and feet of Jesus at his crucifixion. These orders helped to win over the lower classes of society to whom they preached more by example than by word. But their success soon aroused the envy and animosity of the secular clergy. At the University of Paris, where the Dominicans and Franciscans established chairs of theology, the opposition was so great that the popes found it necessary to intervene. William de St. Amour, of the Sorbonne, in his *De periculis novissimorum temporum,* (The Dangers of Contemporary Times) attacked the mendicants as vagrants who considered manual labor a crime. He applied to them the list of vices enumerated by Paul in his Epistle to Timothy and dubbed them "men of corrupt minds, reprobate concerning the truth."

St. Amour, no doubt, greatly exaggerated the faults of his hated mendicants. But the begging friars were not an unmixed blessing to the Church. Many of them used their habit as a blind for heretical opinions which they disseminated among the poor. Many Friars Minor were suspected of Joachimism. These were either banished or burned at the stake, or condemned to the dreaded dungeon of the Inquisition.

The frequent lapses by the religious from the doctrines of the Church are best illustrated by the order of the Knights Templar. Unlike the Mendicants, these soldiers of Christ amassed enormous wealth, became the greatest bankers and usurers of Europe, and played a leading part in the politics of the Kingdom of Jerusalem. For this they incurred the ill will of the Hospitallers, a rival knightly order of monks, even as the Franciscans did of their fellow Mendicants. Philip the Fair, who coveted their possessions, soon found a pretext to precipitate their fall. It began to be bruited that these defenders of the Holy Land, whom St. Bernard delegated to smite the Moslems "without incurring sin," were infidels in disguise. Spies reported that during the secret convocations of their chapters they spat upon the cross and trampled upon it on Holy Friday; that they avowed their disbelief in Christ and left out *Hoc est corpus* in their celebration of the Mass; that they worshiped an idol named Baphomet, and the Devil in the shape of a black cat. Stories also were current that they roasted their illegitimate progeny and smeared their idols with their burning fat; that fathers would slay any of their children who obtained a glimpse of their nightly orgies, and that their Grand Preceptor declared that one hair of a Saracen's beard was worth more than all the teachings of the Church.

The Templars were examined and, under torture, many of them pleaded guilty to all the charges. Their Grand Master, Jacques de Molay, admitted to spitting on the cross but denied the other accusations. Meanwhile, Clement V, to forestall the king, issued a bull calling on all the sovereigns everywhere to arrest them, and summoned a council at Vienne to inquire into the matter. At the public trial held in Paris, many Templars retracted their confessions, but their retraction availed them nothing and they died by fire. The turn of the Grand Master came in 1314. After repeated affirmations and retractions, he recovered his courage and from the midst of the flame he summoned the pope and the king to appear within the year before the tribunal on high. Some of the Knights escaped to Africa and took service with the Moors. [15]

But voices in condemnation of the wealth of the Church and the worldliness of the ecclesiastics could not be hushed, and denials of the doctrines of the Trinity, transubstantiation, infant baptism, coupled with denunciations of the sale of indulgences, began to be heard more and more frequently. To romancers and satirists in the vernacular of the vulgar or the Latin of the learned, the Church supplied much of their material for burlesque and merriment. In the spiciest stories of Rabelais and Marguerita of Navarre, of Chaucer and Skelton, as well as Boccaccio, the monks and nuns figure as clowns and heroes of licentiousness. As for the serious writers, "it is remarkable," says Renan, "that all the authors of the times who have really transmitted the echo of public opinion, wholly sympathized with the Beguines and the Cathari" and the other heretics. This was true of some of the most loyal defenders of the papacy. Peter Damiani, in his *Liber Gomorrhianus,* pronounces all the clergy as rotten as the loin-cloth which Jeremiah hid by the Euphrates. The chronicler Salimvene jokingly defends the pope's nepotism as the fulfillment of the Scripture: "He built up Zion *in sanguinibus*" (Micah 3:10). Walter Mapes, wit and chaplain to King Henry II, depicts the rapacity, venality, and hypocrisy of the ecclesiastics, secular and monastic, in his "Bishop Golias"; and Guiot de Provence spares none who is connected with the Church in his mordant "Bible." In Italy the Goliards, or minstrels, burlesqued in their verses the mass, the creed, the confession; and the French *Trouvers* took special delight in satirizing the practice of excommunication and the use made by the Church of Hell and Purgatory as sources of revenue. In Germany the stories of "Reynard the Fox" and "Roman de la Rose" were interpolated with flings at the Holy See, and the *Minnesinger* made use of their poetic license to strike at the root of the Church. "God alone can forgive sins," sings Freidank, "and could the pope absolve me from my oaths and duties, I'd let other sureties go and fasten to him alone." Walter von der Vogelwaide (c. 1170-c. 1230), the most celebrated bard of his age, asserted not only that "Him (God), Christians, Jews and heathen serve,"—a most dangerous heresy in the Christendom of the Crusades,—but went on to sing:

> King Constantine, he gave so much—as I will tell you—to the Chair of Rome: spear, sword and crown. At once the angel cried: 'Alas! Alas! Alas! Christendom before stood crowned with righteousness. Now

is poison fallen on her, and her honey turned to gall
—sad for the world henceforth!' When will all tongues
call Heaven to arms, and ask God how long He will
sleep? They bring to naught His work, they distort
His word. His steward steals His treasure; His judge
robs here and murders there; His shepherd has become a wolf among His sheep ...

The general discontent continued to grow until in the thirteenth century it infected all classes of society. No less a
loyal member of the Church than St. Bernard of Clairvaux
denounced the hypocrisy, gluttony, and cupidity of the deacons, archdeacons, bishops, and archbishops of his time. Nor
did he spare the pope himself. "In the glitter that environs
thee," said he, "rather wouldst thou be taken for the successor
of Constantine than for the successor of Peter." No wonder
that the inarticulate masses also expressed their opposition in
their way—by their indifference and even contempt. It became a popular saying: "Viler than a priest." According to
St. Bernard, the France of his day presented a spectacle of

Churches without people, people without priests,
priests without the reverence due them, and Christians
without Christ.... The voice of a single heretic si-
lences all those Apostolic and Prophetic voices which
have united in calling all the nations into the Church
of Christ.

The opposition to the Hierarchy which had been brewing
for many years reached its peak just as the popes attained
the pinnacle of their temporal power. Arnold of Brescia, who
advocated the abolition of the papacy and the expropriation
of the wealth of the Church, obtained a large following who
looked upon him as an inspired prophet. He was seized
by the officers of Frederick Barbarossa and turned over to
Adrian IV, who had him hanged and burned and the ashes
thrown into the Tiber "for fear lest the people might collect
them and honor them as the ashes of a martyr."

Thus the Crusades, which contributed much to the increase of the papal power, also diminished the respect in which the Church was held by the populace. The debacle in which they resulted made people realize that the popes were neither infallible nor omnipotent, and their constant demands for money was coined into a proverb: "The Roman Curia cares not for a sheep without wool." Frederick II, grandson of Barbarossa, denounced the pope as a "merchant, weighing out dispensations for gold." But it remained for the grandson of Saint Louis IX, Philip the Fair, to deal the blow from which the papacy was never to recover.

This came about in the pontificate of Boniface VIII, who canonized Louis IX and whom Dante describes as "the prince of the new Pharisees." He instituted the first Jubilee indulgence in honor of the thirteen hundredth anniversary of St. Peter and St. Paul, and by his insistence on his right to tax the French clergy aroused the anger of Philip the Fair. The king accused him of heresy, simony, and immorality. The pope retaliated by excommunicating him and anathematizing his descendants to the fourth generation. Boniface was finally made a prisoner in his own palace, and but for the intervention of de Nogaret, the king's lawyer, whose father fell a victim to the Inquisition, would have been slain by an assassin. With his successor Clement V begins the so-called "Babylonian Exile" of the popes (1305-77), consisting of the seventy years during which they resided in Avignon and were wards of the kings of France. [16]

It was while the papacy was making its supreme effort for temporal power that St. Bernard of Clairvaux expressed his indignation that "to the shame of Christ, a man of Jewish origin was come to occupy the chair of St. Peter." The pope he referred to was the grandson of the Jewish fiscal agent of Benedict IX, who on his conversion assumed the name of Benedict and married into one of the noblest families of Rome. His son he named Leo, and Leo in turn called his son Peter, hence the appellation Pierleoni. After finishing his education at the University of Paris, Peter became a monk at the monastery of Cluny and rapidly rose to prominence.

Paschal II created him Cardinal Archdeacon, he was appointed by successive popes as legate to France and England, and accompanied Gelasius on his flight to France. When the throne of St. Peter became vacant by the death of Gelasius, Pierleoni received a large majority of the votes of the cardinals and nobility, and almost the whole populace of Rome rallied around him. He was consecrated in St. Peter's with the name of Anacletus II, Anacletus I having been according to some, the successor to St. Peter; while his rival Innocent II sought safety in flight to France, where his cause was taken up by St. Bernard. To be sure, the opponents of Anacletus II accused him of bribery and immorality and expatiated on the forbidding Jewish appearance of his Holiness which, it seems, was modified neither by the baptism of his grandfather nor by the intermarriages which followed. Anacletus, however, remained in full possession of the pontificate till his death; and during his reign (1130-8) he defied Lothair of Germany to unseat him, and made his brother-in-law, the Duke of Apulia, king of the two Sicilies. The Hapsburgs of Austria are said to be descendants of the family of this pontiff of Jewish blood. His marble tomb in the cloisters of St. Paul contains the inscription: "May Peter and Paul to whom you were so faithful protect you, Peter son of Leo, and welcome your soul into the glory of heaven." [17]

CHAPTER XVIII

THE BIRTH THROES
OF THE MESSIAH

As in Christendom so among the Jews of the Diaspora the belief in the advent of the Messiah was greatly intensified with the dawn of the Second Millennium. The hope magnificent which lay at the heart of Judaism, particularly since the *Hurban,* did not perish during the period of a thousand years of much suffering. On the contrary, like the jewel in the ark of Noah, according to the Rabbis, it glowed brightest when the outside was darkest. It was when the prospects were gloomiest that the Jews found refuge in the certainty that at any moment the Son of Man would appear to redeem them from their suffering and cause their enemies to embrace the very religion which they sought to extirpate. This belief proved to be the mainstay of Judaism, an inner rampart when all outer defenses were broken down. It lent strength to the weary, and courage to the faint of heart. Whenever, like the eminent poet-philosopher Solomon ibn Gabirol, they wondered: "How long will the exile last? When will the appointed season arrive?", they would, like him, seem to hear the consoling assurance: "Hope on, hapless ones, just a little longer, and the announcer will come to proclaim to Zion 'The Lord reigneth.'" This belief in the momentary advent of the Messiah was finally made obligatory by Maimonides on every Jew in the twelfth article of his creed, which reads: "I believe with a firm faith in the coming of the Messiah, and though he tarry, I will wait daily for his coming."

Certain seasons and years, however, were assumed to be more likely than others to witness the fulfillment of this age-

old hope, and some of the saintliest sages of Israel ransacked
the Bible for hints of the signs. Astrologers consulted the
hosts of heaven, and mystics held communion with the occult
powers in order to "reveal the End" of Israel's tribulation and
the coming of the world's salvation. Men like Saadya Gaon,
Rashi, Judah Halevi, Maimonides, and Nahmanides, who
discouraged "the reckoners of the End," themselves indulged
in this, to them, all important search for the hidden plan of
God. And even when their predictions were not fulfilled,
their ardor did not abate. They followed each frustration with
a new revelation and saw in every unusual occurrence the
"birth pangs," or "footsteps," of the Messiah.

The first glimpse we get of the Jews of Germany, which
is about in the middle of the tenth century, is connected with
their fervent faith in the speedy advent of the Messiah. In
Benjamin of Tudela's *Itinerary* there is a passage, evidently
an interpolation, in which we are told that when a wayfarer
comes to them they make a feast and ply him with questions
concerning "the help of the Lord which may come in the
twinkling of an eye," and whether "the time of song has
arrived." In the beginning of the eleventh century their hope
became stronger than ever. Among the Jews in Moslem
lands, the belief obtained that the Messiah would come four
hundred years after the Hegira, or in 1022. As the year passed,
the date was advanced to five hundred years. But in Christendom some calculated that since God's day is a thousand years,
the Messiah was to be expected shortly about the end of a
thousand years after the *Hurban*. In the emended Book of
Zerubbabel, which was regarded as a high authority, the year
was set as 1068, and in France a Messianic pretender actually
presented himself in 1087. But the most acceptable year was
1096, because its Hebrew numerals, *RNU,* meaning sing, are
in accord with the word used by Jeremiah when he exclaimed:

Sing (*RNU*) with gladness for Jacob,
And shout at the head of the nations....
Behold I will bring them from the north country,
And gather them from the uttermost parts of
the earth.

With the approach of that year, therefore, Messianic expectation reached its height. Then "Mourners of Zion," who always dressed in black and abstained from meat in memory of the *Hurban,* redoubled their penance and lengthened their vigils. Many Jews from all parts of the Diaspora undertook the long, hazardous journey to Palestine in order to be among the first to welcome the Messiah. It was bruited about that the Bnai Moshe were on their march to participate in the World War between Gog and Magog, and that seventeen communities of the Khazarites from distant Slavonia were about to join them. It was also reported that the miracles which were to indicate the coming of the Messiah had already appeared. [1]

By the irony of fate, 1096 turned out to be the year of the First Crusade with its untold misery for the Jews. Goaded on by rabble-rousing monks and by the prospect of pillage, many nobles and those who had hitherto been robbers now became soldiers of Christ, and, as a preliminary, began attacking "the infidels within the gates." It was claimed that Jesus said: "The day will come when my disciples will avenge my blood," and a rumor was spread that, on good authority, whoever killed a Jew would have all his sins forgiven. A German Count declared that before he started on the war against the infidels in Palestine he was determined to kill at least one Jew. Godfrey de Buillon of France vowed to avenge the blood of God upon the blood of Israel, and that he would not leave a single Jew alive in his path. Even after the leaders accepted large bribes, a chronicler tells us, they "either utterly destroyed the execrable race of Jews wherever they found them (being even in this matter zealously devoted to the Christian religion), or forced them into the bosom of the Church." [2]

Among the first victims of the infuriated mob were the Jews of Spires (May 3, 1096), on the Sabbath, when the synagogue was besieged and ten Jews were slain. In Rouen and Treves the bishops proffered their protection if the Jews would consent to apostatize, but they refused to purchase their lives at such a price. In Worms they countered *Deus*

lo vult with *Zidduk haddin* (justification of God's judgment),
and killed one another rather than submit to the faith of
the Christians. Parents slaughtered their children and then
committed suicide. None pled for mercy nor attempted to
avenge himself, except one who asked to be brought to the
bishop before accepting baptism. He then stabbed the bishop
and slew two others. Maidens and brides while calling, "See,
O Lord, our God, what we are doing to keep holy Thy great
Name," perished by their own hands or by those who loved
them. Two young girls, Bella and Madrona, sharpened the
knives for their own execution and, before they cut their
throats, repeated the benediction: "Praised be the Eternal Who
hath commanded us to give ourselves utterly to him."

Similar tragedies were enacted in Mainz, where Jews hitherto had been on intimate terms with Christians and did not
believe that their turn would come next. In Cologne, many
Jews were afforded shelter in Christian homes, but their
hiding places were soon discovered and they were slain. One
old man who was found still alive was tortured until he became unconscious and then was baptized. When he recovered
consciousness and learned what had been done to him, he
dragged himself to the Rhine and plunged in. The mob
then vented their spleen on the synagogues, and defiled the
Sefer Torah on the very day when, according to Jewish tradition, the Torah had been given to Moses on Mt. Sinai
(Pentecost, May 30, 1096). At Xanten, the attack was made
on the eve of the Sabbath (June 27). When the Jews heard
the raging fury of the mob, they finished the prayers and
killed one another, including a convert to Judaism. At Regensburg, however, the entire Jewish community was driven into
the Danube "and baptized at one wave of the hand."

An unusual incident happened in Trier. There the Archbishop admitted the Jews who had not killed themselves into
his castle, and even preached a sermon in his cathedral in
their behalf. Realizing that the catastrophe could not be averted,
and on the advice of the rabbi, he finally urged them to be
baptized. All the Jews except the rabbi decided to accept, but

reverted to Judaism the following year with the permission of the Emperor.

The bloodshed, arson, rapine, and compulsory conversions which followed in the wake of the crusaders revolted even some of the enemies of the Jews. The author of the *Universal Chronicle* denounced their leaders, Peter as a hypocrite, and Gottchaulk as a traitor. Besides, he declared, "most of the beastly remnants of Jewry" as soon as they could "after their baptism, returned like dogs to their vomit." But the Frankenstein could no longer be controlled. The masses, ignorant and superstitious, came to regard the persecution of the Jews and their conversion as a sure means to salvation. This infected even the youth. As late as 1320, after the flame of the Crusades had long burned itself out, a horde, consisting mainly of children and swine-herds led by an unfrocked Benedictine monk, swept over northern France pillaging the Jews and murdering those of them who refused to be baptized, thus writing another blood-curdling chapter in Jewish history under the title *Gezerath Haroim* (the persecution of the shepherds). [3]

The outrages of the Crusades had a depressing effect upon the Jews. Some began to doubt how a good God could deal thus with His people. R. Eliezer b. Nathan of Mayence of the twelfth century cried out in despair:

> Time after time our soul did wait,
> But the End is delayed, and no healing's in sight;
> We thought 'sing unto Jacob' to be salvation's date
> Alas, instead of healing it brought us fright.

Yet the hapless Jews continued to hope on. Their misery only helped to intensify the light of their faith in the momentary advent of a redeemer. This craving, as in the days of Jesus, soon produced numerous pseudo-Messiahs. During the First Crusade there appeared in Khazaria a certain Solomon b. Doudji who pretended to be the forerunner of the Messiah. A Karaite Jew in Palestine proclaimed (1121) that he would deliver Israel within two months and a half. In Fez, Morocco, a herald announced that the Messiah "is to be expected in 1127," and in Mesopotamia one by the name of Chad announced himself to be the Messiah. In Yemen, in 1172, a man obtained a great following among both Jews and Arabs by the miracles he performed as evidence that he was the harbinger of the Messiah. Hailed before the caliph he offered as proof of his divine mission that after having his head cut off he would come to life again. He was decapitated, and the Jews were heavily fined. But for many years some people were convinced that he would yet arise from his grave and lead them to welcome the Messiah. [4]

The most daring Messianic pretender of the Orient was Menahem b. Sulaiman, of Kurdistan, who assumed the name David Alroy. Handsome in appearance and versatile in Hebrew and Arabic lore, he was held in high esteem by Jews and Moslems alike. The rumors of the Second Crusade and that Gog and Magog were about to fight the last battle before the coming of the Messiah emboldened Alroy to summon his coreligionists in Mosul, Bagdad, and other places to storm the citadel of his native city, Amadia, preparatory to the conquest of Palestine. Summoned before the Sultan and asked if he really claimed to be the King of the Jews, Alroy answered in the affirmative. Cast into prison, he escaped three days later and returned to Amadia, it is said, in a miraculous manner, having accomplished a journey of ten days in one day. He was finally killed (c. 1163) by his own father-in-law, and, as was to have been expected, the Jews paid dearly for "forcing the end."

Alroy's death, however, did not stop the Messianic extravaganza. In Bagdad two of his devotees spread a rumor that Alroy was alive, and that he would meet his followers in Jerusalem whither they would be carried on angels' wings. After entrusting these two with all the jewelry and money they possessed, all assembled on the roofs to await the arrival of the angels, the women holding on to their children lest in their flight they should be parted. Dawn came, but the angels failed to appear. The hoax was made much of by the Mohammedans, and the Jewish apostate Samuel ibn Yahyah utilized the episode in a taunting polemic against Judaism. Still, numerous Jews continued to adore the memory of Alroy, called themselves "Menahemites," and looked forward to his ultimate reappearance.[5]

Such pretenders and impostors were not limited to the Orient. In 1087 a Messianic movement was started in Leon, then an important Jewish community, by one who proclaimed himself the Messiah. On moonlit nights he jumped from tree-top to tree-top, so that it might seem as if he "came with the clouds of heaven." He and many of his dupes were slain by the French, but not a few of the survivors believed that he was merely translated to heaven to appear soon again.

In Cordova, Spain, Ibn Arye, a miracle worker who claimed to be the Messiah, appeared ten years after the First Crusade (1117) and "because of him," writes Maimonides, "Israel came very near destruction." But the leaders of the community took the situation in hand before it grew too serious. They led him to the synagogue where he was flogged and excommunicated, "and thus (the Jews) saved themselves from the Gentiles, though not without very great difficulty." Ten years later a certain Moses of Morocco, on his return from Spain, proclaimed that the Messiah had already arrived and would reveal himself on the night of Passover. He, therefore, advised his coreligionists to see their property and to borrow whatever they needed from their neighbors, as did the Children of Israel on their exodus from the land of Egypt. Many followed his advice and were reduced to starvation. Moses fled and died in Palestine. [6]

Besides Messianism, what helped not a little to comfort and strengthen the Jews during the distressing times of the Crusades was the study of the Kabbalah, which stemmed from the same root and was watered and nurtured by their tears. Indeed, the Kabbalah was to Judaism what the philosopher's stone was to science. It did not achieve the expected result, but it contributed toward making the lot of the harassed Jews more bearable. It opened to the Jews a world peopled with angels ready to do their bidding and about to establish the Kingdom of God on earth.

These millenarian speculations and mystic interpretations of the Bible were embodied in a book which appeared in the thirteenth century under the title of *Zohar* (splendor). It claimed to be the product of the saintly Rabbi Simeon b. Yohai who was a victim of the Hadrianic persecutions, but its real author is supposed to have been Moses de Leon of Spain. According to de Leon, it was the injunction of R. Simeon that his work be made public in the last generation before the advent of the Messiah. This generation he found by computing the numerical value of the Tetragramaton (the special name of God, J H V H) to be the one in which he lived, or the year 1300. Somewhere about that time, he declared, all nations would unite to destroy the Jews, but when all hope will seem to be lost, the Messiah will bestir himself in his abode, known to Kabbalists as the "Bird's Nest," which is in the Lower Paradise:

> He will cry and weep so loud that the firmament above will tremble, until the Holy One, blessed be He, will send word that He will destroy the wicked nations and avenge the wrongs of His people. He will then appear in Galilee, the place first destroyed by the Romans, and vanquish all the nations that will assemble in Jerusalem. He will disappear for a while, and reappear to rout those who will come together in Rome, to war against him. After many signs and wonders the Messiah will emerge victorious, and 'the Lord will rejoice in His works.' Those who will survive the cosmic catastrophe will be endowed with new souls. They will become new creatures, and join the Jews in the worship of the God of Israel. Then will be inaugurated the great Sabbath, the Seventh Millennium, concerning which it is written (Isa. 4:3): 'He that is left in Zion, and he that remaineth in Jerusalem, shall be called holy, even everyone that is written unto life in Jerusalem.' [7]

It is interesting to note that even in the most trying days of the Crusades the Jews did not despair not only of their own liberation, but of the ultimate regeneration of the human race. According to the *Zohar* there is in every soul an emanation (*nizuz*) of God, which is ever craving to be reabsorbed into its original source. Whenever a Gentile feels inclined to embrace Judaism, God selects a soul from those which abide in Bithiah, Obadiah, Aquila, and other proselytes, kisses it, and sends it down to enter the body of that person, and thus helps the holy "spark" to break through the "shells" (*Klippot*) which imprison it. Even as it is written (Isa. 43:7):

> Everyone that is called by name,
> And whom I have created for My glory,
> I have formed him, yes, I have made him. [8]

But while at present Jews must be on their guard against proselytes who seek to join them out of superstitious fear or some ulterior motive, as did the "Mixed Multitude" who were responsible for the worship of the Golden Calf, it will not be so in the days of the Messiah. Then, not only Christians and Mohammedans who have already approached the tip of the wing of the Shekinah, though they are still under the influence of Mars, but all will see the Seventh Window in the highest heaven opened, and the Star of Jacob will shine forth over all the world. Then will all the nations of the earth clamor for the God of Israel and the words of Isaiah (11:10) will be fulfilled: "The root of Jesse, that standeth for an ensign of the peoples, unto him shall the nations seek; and his resting place shall be glorious."[9]

The mysticism and Messianism of the thirteenth century found their leading exponent in Abraham Abulafia of Saragossa, Aragon. A brilliant student of the Talmud and an admirer of the works of Maimonides, he dreamed of "hastening the End." At the age of twenty he set out to locate the River Sambatyon and to discover the Ten Tribes. However, he proceeded no further than Acco. He returned to Spain and immersed himself in the study of the Kabbalah, and before long he evolved a mystic philosophy of his own. His asceticism and his evident sincerity attracted numerous disciples, who with him devoted themselves to unraveling the hidden secrets of the stories, laws, words, letters, even the jots and tittles, of the Torah. At last Abulafia began to believe that he was commissioned by God to become the redeemer of his people and decided to appear as the predicted Messiah by the year 1290.

As a preparation for the great event and in obedience, he claimed, to an inner Voice, Abulafia set out for Rome on the eve of Rosh Hashanah, 5041 (1208), for the purpose of converting Pope Nicholas III. Apprised of his intentions, the Pope issued an order that Abulafia be seized and burned at the stake. Nothing daunted, he continued on his journey only to learn that the pope had succumbed to an apoplectic stroke the night before Abulafia reached Suriano. He, therefore, proceeded to Rome to convert Nicholas' successor. There he was thrown into prison by the Minorite monks, but for some unknown reason was allowed to leave a month later. Now more than ever convinced that he was endowed with supernatural influence, he went to Palermo where he secured a large following among Christians through his claim that the mystery of the Trinity was merely another phase of the Jewish Unity. [10] This made the Kabbalah and particularly the Zohar, a favorite study of Christian scholars.

Despite Abulafia's failure to convert the pope and his condemnation by R. Simeon b. Adret, two other adventurers appeared in Spain. One of them, Nissim b. Abraham, of Avila, proclaimed 1295 as the year of redemption, and the people made ready to welcome the Messiah. After fasting and distributing large sums in charity, they dressed in white and repaired to their synagogues to hear the sound of "the great trumpet "Shofar Gadol" announce "the year of redemption." Instead, they found little crosses fastened on the doors and pews. This may have been either a practical joke played by skeptics on their credulous brethren, or a Christian hint of what Messiah Jews should look for. In consequence of their disappointment, some did go over to Christianity. [11]

Though as a result of the Messianic hysteria and the mental aberration caused by the terrorizing crusaders, some Jews were driven into the bosom of the Church, by far the vast majority of them continued to cling as tenaciously as ever to the faith of their fathers. The problem of their conversion remained as unsolved when Catholicism became the greatest power on earth as when it was still hiding in the underground Catacombs of Rome. The Jew, like Mordecai of old, refused to bow to Haman even when he was raised to royal estate.

Of course, the Church could have decreed a Crusade against the Jews and cut the Gordian knot with one stroke of the sword of which she was now in full possession and of which she made good use without the least compunction. She could have exterminated them even more easily than she did the Nestorians, the Arians, the Catharists, and the Waldenses. But strange to say, the very fact that they had never accepted Christ was in their favor. It deterred her from punishing them for not accepting him in the way she dictated. They were, therefore, tolerated first because Paul predicted that they would ultimately see the light and hence should be allowed to exist so that his prediction would be fufilled. But even more than this, they were to serve as proof to the veracity of the tragedy of Calvary. According to St. Bernard of Clairvaux, "They are living symbols for us, representing the Lord's Passion. For this they are dispersed in every land, so that, while they pay the just penalty of their great crime, they may be witnesses for our redemption." Innocent III also affirmed: "It is pleasing to God that they be oppressed by the servitude they earned when they raised sacrilegious hands against Him who had come to confer true liberty upon them." [12]

Apparently the clergy were too glad to have such an object lesson with which to impress their congregations. Thus, in Beziers the bishop preached a sermon during the Easter season in which he reminded the people that "they could observe around them the grandchildren of those who condemned Jesus and denied the existence of Mary the Mother of God," and proceeded that "Whenever their hearts were agonized by the thoughts of the insults offered to their Savior, they had his blessing, and the Governor's license, to avenge themselves on the Jews—but only with stones."

The preservation of the Jews was, therefore, regarded as much the duty of the Church as was their conversion. Hence, she now and then raised her voice against the wanton slaying of Jews, and at the Council of Mayence the faithful were reminded that the slaying of a Jew was murder, "since war is not made even on enemies abroad unless they have broken the peace." Pope Alexander II expressed his indignation at the Archbishop of Narbonne who approved the massacre of the Jews in France and Spain, and rebuked the crusaders who foolishly wished to kill those whom the Divine Mercy had predestined to salvation. St. Bernard also denounced the behavior of the frantic mob led by fanatic priests, and Gregory IX described their treatment of the Jews as "horrible and outrageous, an offense against God and a dishonor to the Holy Chair through whose privileges the Jews are protected." The Council of Bourges (1236) even went so far as to assert that "Faith must be kept with Jews and no one may use violence against them; for the Church protects the Jews, since, as it is written, 'she desires not the death of the sinner.'" But the pope who exercised the greatest influence on Church legislation with regard to Jews was Calixtus II. In his bull *Sicut Judaeis non,* he deplores that the Jews prefer "to remain hardened in their obstinacy rather than acknowledge the prophetic words—and the eternal secrets—of their own Scriptures... Nevertheless, in view of the fact that they begged for our protection and our aid, and in accordance with the clemency that Christian piety imposes, we grant their petition and offer them the shield of our protection." He then proceeds:

> We decree that no Christian shall use violence to force them to be baptized as long as they are unwilling or refuse.... For surely none can be believed to possess the true faith of a Christian who is known to have come to Christian baptism not willingly, and even against his wishes.... (That) no Christian shall pre-

sume to wound their persons or kill or rob them of
their money.... Furthermore, while they celebrate
their festivals, no one shall disturb them in any way
by means of sticks or stones, nor exact from any of
them forced service, except that which they have been
accustomed to perform from ancient times...that
no one shall presume to desecrate or reduce the
cemetery of the Jews, or with the object of extorting
money to exhume bodies there buried. [13]

Hence, after the tenth century, there began to be witnessed in Christendom a strange conflict between the temporal
and spiritual lords concerning the right of protecting the Jews.
Henry IV permitted those who had been violently baptized
during the First Crusade to return to their faith. He also tried
to save the property looted from the Jews by the crusaders,
among them the Archbishop of Mainz and his relatives, and
included the Jews in the General Peace of 1103. Frederick
Barbarossa, a devout Catholic, insisted that "It is the duty of
our imperial office, demanded alike by justice and reason to
...assiduously protect the Jews of our empire who enjoy a
special claim in our regard in that they belong to our imperial
treasury (*servi camerae nostrae*)." Louis VII, Henry VI, and
Frederick II took action against the blood accusation long
before the popes denounced it as a libel. On various occasions
the sovereigns prohibited the monks to force their way into
the synagogue to preach their conversionist sermons, and defended the right of the Jews to revert to Judaism after their
forced baptism.

An interesting instance of royal protection is furnished by
Denys Quinon, Procurator of the Jews under Charles V. In
the charter granted the Jews on their return to France, it was
stated that they were not to be compelled to attend church
in order to listen to conversional sermons. But as the clergy,
some of whom were themselves apostate Jews, persisted in
their preaching, Denys petitioned the king to confirm his
order. His argument was that the Jews had not the habit of
going to church, and obtained no religious satisfaction from

their attendance, besides being in considerable danger of bodily harm, or at least of abuse and derision from the rest of the congregation when they saw the Jews there. His petition was granted. [14]

To be sure, the temporal powers did not insist on their right to protect the Jews for humanitarian reasons. They protected them not as human beings but as their private property. If they sometimes opposed their forced conversion it was mainly because, as their tax collectors, they would thereby lose not only their own possession, which reverted to the Church, but money loaned to others. For as long as Jews remained unconverted, any time a prince found himself in need of funds or wished to curry the good will of his subjects, he did not hesitate to confiscate their property or to absolve their creditors. In 1349 Emperor Charles IV assigned to the Archbishop of Trieste the property of the Jews of Alsace "who have already been killed or may still be killed," and offered to the Margrave of Brandenburg the three best Jewish houses in Nuremberg "when there is next a massacre of Jews there." The Jews always paid, and paid dearly, for the privilege to live and to earn a livelihood whenever that privilege was granted them. Frequently, too, this protective policy was prompted merely by the sovereign's relation to the pope. Thus, Philip the Fair, who at first instructed his officials to turn over to the Inquisition any Jew "who handled the Host, blasphemed the sacraments, circumcised a Christian or led him to heresy, built new synagogues, sang too loudly in them, or possessed the Talmud," changed his policy during his quarrel with Boniface VIII (1293-7) and forbade the Inquisition to meddle in any matters which concerned the king. These matters included "usury and fortune-telling."[15]

Regardless, however, of the claims of the secular authorities, the Church, by virtue of her mission to guide all men to eternal happiness, insisted on her superior right and persisted in her assumption of jurisdiction over the Jews in order to protect them not only against enemies from without but against themselves. But here she found herself faced by the dilemma of how to prevent the witness, whose mere presence served as a reminder of the truth of the crucifixion, from bearing evidence which might prove more damaging than favorable. For as infidels Jews were not only exempt from conforming to Christian rites, they could express with impunity opinions which would put a Catholic in jeopardy of his life or liberty. Besides, the Jews were like "the demon that holds the key to the sanctuary." They could readily quote the Bible, which most Christians could not. And, indeed, many heretics, taking advantage of the license given to infidels, spread their subversive doctrines disguised as Jews.

With the waning enthusiasm for crusades and the steady increase of heretical sects, the Church determined to concentrate her efforts more and more on converting the Jews. Hitherto Christians who wished to acquire a knowledge of Hebrew would consult some Jewish scholar. This was done from the times of Jerome down to Rabanus Maurus, though they either hid this activity or were careful to state that they did not accept this information they received. But in the course of time, such relation became strictly prohibited; and in 1198 a Cistercian monk in Catalonia was chastised because he took lessons in Hebrew from a Jewish teacher. To enable students to pursue the study of the language in which the Bible was written, the better to fit themselves for the conversion of the Jews, Hebrew courses were introduced into the universities. To this Raymond de Penaforte, the General of the Dominicans (d. 1275), perhaps the most rabid conversionist of his time, later added Arabic, so as to reach not only Jews but also Saracens. He also introduced what came to be known as the *Index,* with the object of expunging from Jewish literature whatever was deemed unfavorable to the teaching of Christianity.

To further allay the ghost of Judaism and win over the Jews themselves, The Church reinstituted compulsory religious disputations. Except for the controversies ordered by Constantine the Great and Basil I, few such, if any, were formerly held with the sanction of the State or on the initiative of the Church. Sometimes they were even called for by Jews themselves, and St. Peter Damiani wrote tracts "to close the mouths of those Jews who frequently debate on Christian doctrines." Occasionally Christians too would, perhaps out of curiosity, ask Jews for their opinions about the Trinity, the Virgin, the Saints, auricular confession, and the efficacy of relics. Now such private conversations were declared to be dangerous even for the purpose of making the Jews see the light. Berthhold of Regensburg warned the faithful against "the treacherous babble of the stinking Jews." "You are ignorant," said he, "ignorant with respect to the Bible as the Jews are learned, and they can always throw up to you that your own faith is weaker than theirs." Gregory IX also forbade Christians to engage in controversies with Jews, while Alexander IV decreed that no lay person should enter into an argument, either in private or public, with Jews concerning the Catholic faith, and that whosoever shall act to the contrary "let him be bound in the fetters of excommunication."

The public disputations conducted at the command and under the surveillance of the Church were rather condemnations than disputations. As their object was both to convince the Jews of their errors and confirm the Christians in their truth, the Jews who were compelled to participate in them were doomed to lose from the start and put not only themselves but their community in danger of violence if they uttered anything remotely suggesting that Christianity was not the true religion. Theirs was the task which, according to the Rabbis, God assigned to Satan to "break the barrel and yet retain the wine." Once under St. Louis, when the Jews were ordered to hold a disputation with the clergy at the monastery of Cluny, a knight who was accorded the privilege to start the controversy asked their spokesman whether he believed that Mary, "who bore God in her body and arms," was a virgin and the mother of God? The Jew, of course, answered in the negative. Whereupon he was at once struck down since, as the knight explained, some good Christians hearing his reasons might be influenced by them. Furthermore, Louis IX decreed that "no one, unless he be exceptionally well instructed, shall be allowed to dispute with a Jew; but if a layman hear the Christian law reviled, he shall defend it with his sword, of which he shall force as much into his body as he can make enter." [16]

The earliest of compulsory controversies in the second Christian millennium took place in France, the cradle of the Crusades and the Inquisition. It was ordered by Alduin, Bishop of Limoges (1019), and lasted for a month but netted only three converts, and those who remained unconvinced and unbaptized sought safety in flight. With the establishment of the preaching orders, these controversies became more frequent, more violent, and reaped a greater harvest of souls. One of the most famous of them was convoked at the solicitation of the apostate Nicholas Donin of La Rochelle. Having been excommunicated by R. Yehiel of Paris, he converted, joined the Dominicans, and denounced the Talmud as a work full of blasphemy against God, vilification of Jesus and Mary, and hatred of Christians. Happy to have a Talmudist's own testimony, Pope Gregory IX ordered the ecclesiastical authorities to seize all the copies of the Talmud on the Sabbath during Lent (1240) and deposit them with the Dominicans and Franciscans. The decree was generally disregarded in Christendom. But Louis IX, who started on his way to saintship, summoned four rabbis to appear at the royal palace in Paris to disprove the charges in the presence of the Queen Mother, the Bishop of Paris, and a host of Dominicans. Nicholas served in the capacity of referee. In vain did R. Yehiel adduce proofs that the term *"goi"* in the Talmud does not refer to Christians and that the word *"minim"* in the Eighteen Benedictions alludes to apostates to paganism. His arguments were of no avail, and despite the intervention of the Queen Mother and the Archbishop of Sens, R. Yehiel was exiled and twenty-four cart-loads of Talmud manuscripts were consigned to the flames (June 17, 1242). This established a "legal precedent" until 1757 when, also at the instigation of apostates, the last seizures and burnings of the Talmud took place in Kameniec, Podolia. The martyr R. Meir of Rothenburg, in a dirge commemorating the event, called upon Aaron and Moses to declare whether God connived at this talmudic auto-da-fe because He really had given "a new Torah." [17]

Twenty years later a public disputation took place in Barcelona. The villain in this tragedy was Pablo Christiani, also an apostate and a Dominican who journeyed about in southern France and argued with the Jews. Meeting with little or no success, he induced Raymond de Penaforte to arrange for a public debate, and Jayme I of Aragon ordered no less a notable than R. Moses b. Nahman (Nahmanides) to participate in the controversy.

The disputation, which lasted four days (July 20-4, 1236), was graced by the presence of the king, his courtiers, and many eminent ecclesiastics. Pablo, confident of his victory, singled out Nahmanides as his main controversialist, since his defeat would mean the greatest blow to Judaism. The king indeed graciously granted the Rabbi freedom of speech. The venerable sage, however, refused to take advantage of this permission, but without the least offense to Christianity explained why his people cannot accept Jesus as the promised Messiah, and why the haggadic utterances of the Rabbis of the Talmud should not be taken as proof of their convictions. His arguments, according to the Hebrew account, so impressed the king that he bestowed upon him various royal gifts.

To make sure that his statements would not be distorted, Nahmanides had them copied in a pamphlet entitled *Vikkuah* (controversy). Pablo, however, construed some of them as blasphemous, and Clement IV commanded the Jews to submit all their books for investigation. Jayme again showed himself favorable to the Jews. He permitted them to have these volumes expurgated by themselves. But the pope prevailed against the king, and the ecclesiastical Council solemnly declared:

> It is true that the arguments of the Jew had been found unanswerable by the Christian. But the fact that the Christian had not been clever enough to find answers, by no means proved that answers did not exist.... Besides, it is certain that the Jew's arguments were put into his head by his master, the Devil. The Christian, not being in league with the Devil, has no one to whisper answers to him.

Nahmanides, like R. Yehiel before him, fled to the Holy Land, while Pablo continued with renewed zeal his missionary efforts among the Jews who were compelled to listen to his harangues in the synagogues, and to pay the expenses of his travels.

Another apostate who was instrumental in bringing about a public disputation with all its bitter consequences for the Jews was Abner of Burgos, who on his baptism assumed the name of Alfonso de Valladolid. He is described by his contemporaries as a man of little faith, but ambitious and out for whatever would promote his worldly welfare. To continue in the good graces of his former coreligionist, he wrote a pamphlet *Iggereth Haggezerah* (Epistle on Fate) in which he justified the step he took by claiming that the stars at his birth ordained that he should embrace Christianity. This was answered in a biting satire by Issac ibn Pulgar, whereupon the renegade became vindictive and raked up anew all the accusations which the Church Fathers and their successors levelled against the Jews. In particular he denounced the "Velamalshinim," the ancient prayer for the discomfiture of Jewish sectaries and *dilatores* and, after a public disputation, he succeeded in securing a royal decree ordering that the offending prayer be deleted (1336). [18]

More imposing for its pomp and splendor and length of time was the public disputation convoked by Benedict XIII with the sanction of King Ferdinand at which he undertook to convince the Jewish representatives from Aragon and Catalonia that the Talmud itself maintains that the Messiah had already come in the person of Jesus. For that purpose he appointed his physician, the renegade Geronimo de Santa Fe, who while a Jew was known as Joshua al-Lorqui, to dispute with R. Joseph Albo. The discussion began with a sermon by Geronimo based on the text from Isaiah (1:19-20):

> If ye be willing and obedient,
> Ye shall eat the good of the land;
> But if ye refuse and rebel,
> Ye shall be devoured with the sword.

It dragged on for twenty-one months (February 1413-November 1414). But as the stiff-necked Jews continued to refuse and rebel, the exasperated French pope issued a Bull (May 11, 1415) compelling the Jews to hear Christian sermons at least three times a year—during the Advent, at Easter, and in the summer. Benedict, however, instead of converting the Jews *en masse* was himself deposed and with his fall Geronimo de Santa Fe disappeared from the scene. [19]

In addition to public disputations, the Church abetted and encouraged polemics in writing. In these, too, Jewish apostates were conspicuous for their industry. They wrote in Hebrew, Latin, and the vernacular, and supplied material for the churchmen who, ignorant of Judaism, aspired to follow in the footsteps of Jerome, Origen, and other Church Fathers. These polemical dialogues were often the result of actual controversies, though sometimes embellished. Some of them are also distinguished by the fantastic claim that the much abused Talmud, as well as the Old Testament, taught that Jesus was the Messiah. The honor of this discovery belongs to Moses Sefardi, who, on his conversion (1106), assumed the name Petrus Alfonso, the names of the saint on whose day he was baptized and of his royal godfather Alfonso VI, whose physician he was. Moses—Peter's series of dialogues between Moses and Peter and similar tracts were highly praised and much used by his successors. His fame, however, rests on his *Disciplina Clericalis* (A Training School for the Clergy), which was translated into many languages, including Hebrew, and which was utilized by the clergy in their sermons. Most of its thirty-three tales were adopted into the *Gesta Romanorum,* the most widely read of medieval story books and which Joseph Jacobs remarks "might almost be called *Gesta Judaeorum.*" [20]

Petrus Alfonso's attempt was bettered by Raymond Martin, a Dominican (d. 1284), the author of *Pugio Fidei* (Dagger of the Faith) and other works, wherein he tried to show that the Rabbis of the Talmud, the Midrash, Rashi, Ibn Ezra, Maimonides, and Kimhi also believed in Jesus as the Messiah and the only begotten Son of God, and the Talmudists corrupted the text of the Bible. But the most popular polemic during the Middle Ages was first written in Arabic in the twelfth century by the son of a rabbi of Fez, Abu Nasr ibn Abbas. The author was a student of philosophy, mathematics, and a traveler. In the city of Maragha he claimed to have seen two visions in which Mohammed appeared to him, and he embraced Mohammedanism. In Toledo, however, he was baptized and wrote a treatise "Concerning the Advent of the Messiah, Whom the Jews Vainly Await." This was translated by Alphonsus Bonihominis, supposed to be the pseudonym of the Dominican convert Paul de Valladolid. He also translated or compiled ibn Abbas' better known *Ifham al-Yahud* (Confutation of the Jews), under the name of *Epistola Samuelis Maroccani,* which went through many editions in Latin, German, Italian, and appeared in English (1649) under the title: "The Blessed Jew of Morocco; or the Black Moor Made White." Ibn Abbas claims that Mohammed is indicated in the words *bim'od m'od* (lit., exceedingly) in God's blessing of Abraham (Gen. 17:2). [21]

It was but natural that Jewish apostates should play an important role in the polemic against their former coreligionists. Their knowledge of the original sources of Judaism crowned them, in the opinion of Christians, with the halo of experts, while they themselves felt that they could thus best take revenge on those who naturally regarded them as renegades and that they could, at the same time, prove their loyalty to their new religion. No wonder that the epitaph of Victor von Karben, who instigated the expulsion of the Jews from the lower districts of the Rhine, boasts:

> Victor, formerly a Jew, wrote in the year 1509
> four works against the errors of the Jews.

Hand in hand with her unconcealed efforts to convert the Jews, the Church resorted to the indirect method of driving them into her arms by reducing those who resisted to the status of pariahs. "To wish to please Christ's enemies means to treat Christ himself with contumely," was the admonition of Gregory VII to Alphonso X. But besides, the Church was in constant dread *ne Judaismo cohianture,* lest the flock of Christ be captured or contaminated by Judaism. Hence, as Peter of Cluny advised, the Church proceeded to punish them according to their baseness. In this, many popes themselves set examples of hate and contempt for the Jews even on occasions when the latter did them homage. When Innocent II was welcomed by them to Paris (1139) with the scrolls of the Law, his Holiness' response to their address was: "May the Lord God Almighty tear away the veil that conceals your hearts." Gregory VIII (1187), like his namesake a century before, threatened the Count of Nevers who protected them with excommunication, declaring that "the Jews, like the fratricide Cain, are doomed to wander through the earth as fugitives and vagabonds, and their faces must be covered with shame. They are under no circumstances to be protected by Christian princes; but are on the contrary to be condemned to serfdom." The most hostile legislation against the Jews since the days of Constantine was framed at the fourth Lateran Council (1215), inspired and convened by Innocent III. In it the old laws were re-enacted that no Jew should employ Christian nurses or servants, and that any Christian who even lodged in a Jewish home should be put under the ban. It forbade converts from Judaism to practice Jewish customs, and Jews to show themselves during the processions at Easter. It decreed that Jews should pay, besides an annual tax for each family, tithes to the Church on property they acquired from Christians. It was at the Lateran Council that Christendom adopted the old Moslem decree that Jews be compelled to wear a badge in front and back of their coat or hat "so that those who were thus marked might be recognized from all sides." The badge was to be of a round piece of red or yellow cloth, "four fingers in circumference ...in keeping with Moses' command that Jews wear a peculiar dress." This law was first enforced by St. Louis prior to his departure for the Second Crusade. [22]

Thereafter, the Jews became a prey to all, and were denied the most elementary rights of human beings. In order to avoid insults and injury to their life, they were ordered to live like lepers outside the camp, cooped up in what later became known as ghettoes. But even there they were not left in peace. Though it was forbidden to rob or kill them, yet in the event of a robbery or murder, Jews could not testify against the Christian malefactor; and when their evidence was found necessary, they were required in many places to take an oath *more Judaico,* by standing barefoot on the hide of a swine. Whoever spoke a good word concerning them, or did them a deed of kindness, or meted out justice to them, was suspected as at least a potential if not actual heretic or Judaizer. The great Franciscan Roger Bacon (1214-94) was thrown into prison because he disapproved of conversion by force and declared that "there were at the time of the crucifixion many holy and good men among the Jews." For having pleaded the cause of the Jews against the Parisian mob which massacred the parents and carried their infants to the Church for baptism (1380) Hughes Aubriot, Provost of Paris, was stigmatized as a Judaizer, accused of immorality, and condemned to life imprisonment in the Bastille. [23]

To make matters still worse, the Church began to heap new calumnies in addition to the old ones. Until the eleventh century Jews were blamed for stabbing the Host, for being in league with the Saracens or heretics, for dabbling in black magic, and causing droughts and earthquakes. Their moral integrity was unassailed even when each Christian sect accused every other sect of the grossest immoralities and the most fiendish perversions. In the twelfth century the heinous ritual murder accusation which the Romans first invented against the Christians was launched by a Jewish apostate against the Jews. Innocent III firmly believed that Jews were bent on "murdering the followers of Christ." This belief became so widespread that the Archbishop of Mayence exacted an oath from the Jewish community that they would not kill Christians to use their blood in preparation for Passover!

Jews were also charged with poisoning the wells during the spread of the Black Plague. During the crusaders' invasion of Worms a corpse, which had been buried for a month, was dug up and dragged through the streets, was said to have been killed by Jews who then boiled him and threw the concoction into the wells so as to poison the people who drank from them. In 1321, according to a Hebrew letter said to have been discovered in the house of a Jew of Parthenay and translated by a Jewish apostate, lepers and Saracens were planning to destroy the entire Christian population of Europe by poisoning the wells. The fact that the Jews, probably because of their dietary laws and their hygienic habits, mostly escaped the ravages of the epidemic in which more than a fourth of the Christian population perished, only served as evidence of their guilt, and over three hundred fifty congregations in France, Switzerland, Germany, and Poland were exterminated. The Bishop of Erfurt indeed protested that the Jews had been put out of the way for mercenary reasons, and the Strasbourg Chronicler, who witnessed the burning of two thousand Jews on the Sabbath (St. Valentine's Day, 1349), put himself on record that "If they (the Jews) had been poor, and if the nobility had not been in their debt, they would not have been burnt." But it sufficed for the blood-thirsty mob as a pretext to destroy the hated race. Sings Henricus of Erfurt:

> The pestilence like fury broke,
> And took its thousands of our folk;
> The earth against us fiercely turned,—
> And many Jews were therefore burned. [24]

The most effective instrument for the extirpation of heresy and the conversion of Jews was the Holy Inquisition. That any deviation from the dogmas of the Church was a capital offense already had been declared by Paul, who after he transferred his zeal from Pharisaism to Christianity asserted that unbelievers should be "delivered to Satan for the destruction of the flesh, that the spirit may be saved in the day of our Lord Jesus Christ," and who himself set an example by delivering Hymeneus and Alexander to Satan that they may learn not to blaspheme (1 Cor. 5:5; 1 Tim. 1:20). It is not unlikely that Paul meant only excommunication, since Christians then lacked the power to actually penalize one for his unbelief. But Moses' injunction to inflict the punishment of death upon any who deserted the true faith was later accepted as the law, and St. Optatus of the fourth century insisted that the treatment meted out to the worshipers of the Golden Calf was binding upon Christians. During the first Christian millennium, however, the Hierarchy as a rule refrained from condemning heretics to death. It held that *Ecclesia abhorret a sanguine* (the Church abhors bloodshed), and imposed only such penalties as stripes, fines, disqualification from office, or exile.

It was Innocent III who contended that "high treason against God" deserved no less a penalty than high treason against the temporal ruler and, strange to say, it was Frederick II, himself a heretic, who prescribed capital punishment for the crime of heresy. Gregory IX (1227-41) further perfected the method of Inquisitorial procedure. Innocent IV, in his bull *Ad Extirpanda*, permitted the Inquisitors to extort confession by torture, and the fiery zeal of St. Dominic and his preaching friars, nicknamed *Domini canes* (the hounds of the Lord), developed heresy-hunting into an art.

The Inquisitors went around from place to place calling upon the inhabitants to confess if they knew any heretics. The faithful were warned to obey the command: "Bear ye one another's burden, and so fulfill the law of Christ." This was interpreted to mean to report all suspects at the peril of being participants in the crime. The accused was never notified of his guilt, nor was he allowed an advocate to defend him. Anybody could be a witness against him, even his wife and his children and slaves of the tenderest age. It is reported that Gregory IX was highly pleased when mothers testified against their children. On the other hand, no one could refuse to testify on pain of being himself suspected of heresy, nor could he retract anything he had said against the defendant.

The accused was condemned from the start, but the trial was frequently prolonged by efforts to determine the degree of his guilt, and especially to discover who were the other *participes crimine.* To accomplish this, resort was frequently had to torture, but the testimony thus extracted was regarded as freely given. There never was an acquittal. Those who confessed and became "reconciled" were condemned to do penance, to be scourged, or to wear the *Sanbenito* (the garb of the penitent), or to be banished or imprisoned for life. The obstinate heretic was sentenced to be turned to the "secular arm," which meant to be burned alive. All this was said to be in agreement with the judgment which God, the "First Inquisitor," passed upon the Adam and Eve for their first disobedience—that they make themselves girdles (!), suffer toil and pain, be expelled from the Garden of Eden, and be doomed to death. The death penalty by fire which Nero and Caligula invoked against the early Christians, and Constantine against Jews who dared molest a convert to Christianity, was preferred to other modes of execution because it involved no shedding of blood, and at the same time would be in fulfillment of the saying of Jesus (John 15:6): "If a man abide not in me, he is cast forth as a branch, and is withered; and men gather them, and cast them into the fire, and they are burned." The Inquisitors, however, absolved one another, in order to remove the semblance of sin.

Since the Inquisition was instituted to deal with Christian delinquents, it could not legally proceed against Jews. But once established, it began to wind its tentacles around the members of the unfortunate race until, in spite of the protests of the temporal powers, it obtained exclusive control over them. Beginning as a guardian of the faith of converts, Clement IV extended its authority to include "Jews who seduced Christians from their faith," and Gregory X added Christians who harbored or helped "Jewish converts who returned to their vomit." A more direct blow to Jews was given by Alexander IV, who included usury in the category of heresies under the surveillance of the Inquisition. Long before the Church forbade money-lending on interest, Jews were prohibited by their own law to charge interest on loans; and though the Old Testament (Ex. 22:24; Lev. 25-36; Dt. 23-20; Ps. 15:5, etc.) excepts a "stranger" from the ban, the Rabbis

of the Talmud and their followers drew no line of demarcation between a Jewish borrower and a Gentile. "Whoever
lends money to a foreigner on interest will be destroyed," declares Rashi, the illustrious French rabbi of the eleventh century. In the twelfth century, however, force of circumstances
compelled the Jews to disregard the injunction. "In the present time," says R. Eliezer b. Nathan of Mayence, "where Jews
own no fields or vineyards whereby they could live, lending
money to non-Jews for their livelihood is necessary and
therefore permissible." The same reason is given by R. Isaac
of Vienna of the thirteenth century. "It is permitted to take
interest from them (the Gentiles)," he declares, "because it is
necessary for our livelihood, and we cannot tell what taxes
the king will exact from us.... Threatened as we are by ex-
orbitant demands and needing as we do huge sums for bribery,
money-lending is the price of our existence." To the Inquisitors,
however, this furnished another pretext for mulcting the Jews,
and while they usually connived at the "pope's usurers" among
the faithful and even among the clergy, they showed no pity
when Jews were concerned. [25]

The Jew thus became to the Church not only a soul to be
saved but a sponge to be squeezed. She inherited his possessions
when he became converted, and she confiscated them when he
stubbornly refused to be converted. And when any other
"legal" pretext to despoil him failed, she was never at a loss
to invent one. Thus, in order to extort additional money, the
Inquisition changed the style of the Jewish badge and compelled the Jews to replace the old with the new.

It is not surprising that despite the untold martyrs who
during the Middle Ages sacrificed themselves for "the sanctification of the Name," there was a considerable number who
yielded under pressure and permitted themselves to be baptized in order to save their lives. These, however, with rare exceptions, were reduced to utter poverty and were turned out
upon the world to eke out a pitiful existence from "Christian
charity." Their plight was taken up in a Council at Tours
(1233), where fear was expressed lest "poverty should compel
converted Jews to return to their vomit." But this consideration

had no effect upon the temporal and even spiritual rulers. The utmost they did was to allow some converts a small pension —four pence a day under Philip the Fair—or to permit them to stay at the *Casa dei Catecumeni*. The usual way was to give them permission to beg. There are letters still extant bespeaking for converted Jews the generosity of their new co-religionists, even ordering the burgomaster to appoint two citizens to introduce them and to allow them free passage throughout the Empire. [26]

Strange to say, despite the supreme efforts of the spiritual and temporal powers to force them into the bosom of the Church, most of those who accepted baptism did so as a last resort and as a rule turned back to Judaism the moment they could induce those in authority, usually by a large bribe, to permit them to do so. This they did even during the crusades, with the permission of Henry IV and Frederick II. But many more of them must have done so even without the sanction of the law.

Contrary to what we might expect, the Middle Ages were not altogether free from intermarriages, if we may judge by the exactments of the Church and the Synagogue. The issue of such marriages were as a rule raised as Jews, and the Rabbis frequently decry any discrimination against them. Says R. Judah Hehasid (d. 1217) in his book of the Pious (*Sefer Hasidim*):

> It is preferable to marry the offspring of a prose-lyte of righteousness who is modest, honest, and charitable than one both of whose parents are full-blooded Jews but destitute of these virtues; for children of such proselytes are themselves likely to be righteous and merciful. [27]

Still more remarkable are the conversions which took place when to be discovered as a Judaizer meant certain torture and death, and, even if not discovered, was to be condemned to wear the badge, to live in the ghetto, and to be denied even the elementary rights of human beings. That their records are not more extensive need not surprise us. For obvious reasons, neither the Church nor the Synagogue would deem it advisable to give publicity to such occurrences, even if they came to their notice; the former, because it might influence others to do likewise; the latter, because of the danger to which a report of that kind would expose, not only the individual concerned, but the entire community. Yet there are facts which indicate that France and other lands in the Middle Ages harbored many Jewish *gerim* even as they did Christian heretics. Innocent III, Gregory IX, Clement IV, Nicholas III, and other pontiffs constantly complained not only of Christians who treated the Eucharist as if it were nothing more than a piece of plain bread, but of "Christians who go over to the rite of the Jews and Jews who lure these Christians to it." Nicholas IV deplores the habit of Christians who contribute candles to and join in the services of the synagogue, and the Council of Beziers (1276) protested vigorously against the Jews "whose perfidy has fraudulently deceived many simple-hearted Christians, and maliciously drawn them into their own error." Martin IV, who was himself approached by Abraham Abulafia on the matter of conversion, reprimanded the French clergy for not being more active in suppressing Jewish missionary activities, and Honorius IV (1285-7) asserted that Jews seduced the faithful and bribed the apostates to revert to Judaism, and then hid them or sent them to where they could live as Jews without being detected. [28]

These and similar statements were no doubt exaggerations of actual facts, some of which are corroborated by Jewish writers. Thus R. David Kimhi of Narbonne (1160-1235) states in one of his polemical works: "And verily I have seen French *gerim,* saints and sages in their practices, who became proselytes because of the contradictory passages in the Gospels." R. Simon ibn Latif of Toledo refers to many Gentiles who turned to Judaism. R. Isaac Males was burned at the stake (1278) for receiving into the Jewish fold one by the name of Perrot, whom the community of Toulouse buried in its cemetery. And R. Simon Duran of Majorca tells of a French prince who came to him for instruction with the object of embracing Judaism. [29]

Most of these proselytes were no doubt obscure people, who possibly were in the service of Jews and lived and died in the ghetto. Some of them, however, mastered not only the Hebrew Bible but also the intricacies of the Talmud. The Tosafists quote the opinion of an "Abraham the *Ger*" of the twelfth century regarding the duties of a convert. An "Isaac the *Ger*" was the author of a work of exegesis; another, of uncertain name, wrote a polemic against Christianity, and one Jehosiphia composed several hymns in Hebrew.

To one of these medieval proselytes to Judaism we are indebted for one of the finest responsa of Maimonides. Apparently a Mohammedan by birth, he assumed on his conversion the name of Obadiah and devoted himself to the study of the Talmud. Once he differed from his teacher, and the latter made an uncomplimentary remark about his pagan ancestry. The Moslem *ger* reported it to Maimonides, and the sage replied in a very affectionate epistle. He calls him "Master and teacher, Obadiah the enlightened and intelligent." He tells him that Abraham was the father not only of those who are his children according to the flesh, but also of all who are of his faith, even as is written in Isaiah (6:3): "Neither let the alien, that hath joined himself to the Lord, speak, saying, 'The Lord will surely separate me from his people,' " and he assures him that "there is absolutely no difference between us and thee; for the Creator hath also chosen thee from among the nations. Let not," he continues, "thy pedigree be light in thine eyes, for if we pride ourselves upon our connection with Abraham, Isaac, and Jacob, thou mayest pride thyself on being connected with Him Who spake and the world came into being," and he proceeds:

> When thy teacher called thee a fool for denying that
> Moslems are idolaters, he sinned grievously, and it is
> fitting that he ask thy pardon, though he be thy master. Then let him fast and weep and pray; perhaps he
> will obtain forgiveness from God. Was he intoxicated

that he forgot the thirty-three passages in which the
Torah commandeth concerning the *ger*? Even if he
had been in the right and thou in error, it was his
duty to be gentle; how much more when thou hadst
the truth and he the error! And when he was saying
that a Moslem was an idolater, he should have been
conscious that he was talking to a proselyte of righteousness and was putting him to shame, for our sages
have said: 'He who gives way to his anger shall be
esteemed in thine eyes as an idolater.' And how great
is the duty which the Torah imposes on us with regard to *gerim!* Our parents we are commanded to
honor and fear; to the Prophets we are ordered to
harken. But one may honor and fear and obey without loving; while in the case of *gerim* we are bidden to
love them with all the force of our heart's affection.
And he called thee 'fool'! Astounding! A man who
left father and mother, forsook his birthplace, his
country, and its power, and attached himself to this
lowly, despised, and enslaved race, and recognized the
truth and righteousness of this people's Torah, and
cast the things of this world from his heart—shall such
a one be called 'fool'? God forbid! Not witless but
wise hath God called thy name, thou disciple of our
father Abraham, who also left his father and his
kindred and went Godwards. And He Who blessed
Abraham will bless thee, and will grant thee to behold
all the consolations destined for Israel; and in all the
good that God shall do unto us He will include thee,
for the Lord hath promised good unto Israel. [30]

Another *ger* by the same name was a Christian. Of him
we know both the land of his birth and the date of his
conversion, from an annotation on the margin of a memoir
written in Hebrew and found among *Genizah* fragments. It
reads:

> Obadiah, the Normandy *ger,* who entered the Cove-
> nant of the God of Israel in the month of Elul, in the

year 414 according to Shtarot, which is 4862 since the
Creation (c. 1102). It is in the handwriting of Obadiah the *ger* himself.

From Obadiah's record of his life we learn that he visited
the important Jewish community of Aleppo and journeyed
by way of Syria and the Holy Land to Egypt, carrying cre-
dentials from the Rabbi of Aleppo. The welcome he received
is evidenced by the fact that while in Damascus he was appointed trustee of the community chest and entrusted with
the office of collecting the weekly contributions for the relief
of the needy. About 1121, he met in Palestine a pseudo-
Messiah by the name of Solomon, a Karaite, who subsisted
exclusively on fruit and milk, and predicted that the Redemption would begin in two and a half months after he announced
it. But Obadiah refused to join his followers because Solomon
was a Levite! "It is nineteen years now," he writes, "since I
accepted the Covenant of the God of Israel and I have never
heard that Jews expect to be redeemed by a descendant of the
Tribe of Levi but through Elijah the Prophet and the anointed
king of the seed of David, king of Israel."[31]

For all we know, this Obadiah may have been a crusader
before he became a recruit of the Lord of Israel. There is no
doubt, however, about another convert to Judaism. Among
his captives at Ramah, near Jerusalem, was a beautiful Jewess
with whom he fell in love. When he threatened to take her
life if she continued to spurn his offer of matrimony, the
maiden bared her neck and begged him to dispatch her with
his sword. Thereupon the knight threw away his weapon,
promised to do her no harm, restored her safely to her parents,
and, out of his great love for her, accepted her faith. He then
took her to be his wife and became a leader in the Jewish
community. [32]

There were proselytes among those who were martyred
during the massacres by the crusaders in France and other
places. One of them was the son of a Christian mother, Master
Jacob b. Sulam, of Mayence. He was raised in the Jewish
faith but, because of the stigma of his non-Jewish birth, he

was sometimes looked down upon by the elite. During the havoc wrought by the mob and the destruction of the holy scrolls, he grasped a knife and, calling to all around: "Until now ye have belittled me, behold what I will do," cut his own throat for the sake of "our Mighty One, Whose Name is the Lord of Hosts." In the *Memorbuch* of Mayence are inscribed ten proselytes—seven men and three women. Among the names of those who died for "the sanctification of God's Name at the time of the Lord's anger," there is "Rabbi Isaac, son of Abraham our father," who hailed from Wurzburg; and "Isaac, son of our father Abraham," who left a fund for rearing the young in the faith for which he sacrificed his life. Of a Rabbi Abraham of Augsburg we are told that he "rejected the gods of the peoples, and broke off the heads of the images, was confident of life eternal, and was burned for the Unity of the Name" (November 12, 1265). "Abraham b. Abraham," it is recorded, was a Prior of the "barefooted" (*Yehefim*) Minorites. It is not certain whether it was his martyrdom or that of another *ger* of the same name which inspired the elegy of his fellow-martyr Mordecai bar Hillel which begins:

How great is the good which Thou hast appointed
    for those who walk in Thy paths,
Who sacrifice their lives as the choicest of
    Thine offerings;
Thou hast chosen Abraham for Thy sweetest savor,
Frankincense for Thy nostrils, and whole-offering
    for Thine altar.[33]

Some of the proselytes in the Middle Ages were probably foundlings like *Asufi* of Egypt, Babylon, Greece, and Rome, whom for one reason or another Christians abandoned among Jews. A convert of this kind is the heroine of Jacques Halevy's grand opera *La Juive,* and of Emma Lazarus' tragedy *The Dance to Death.* In the latter, the whole Jewish population of Germany in the fourteenth century is condemned to death by fire unless baptized within five hours. They refuse to save their lives at the price of apostasy and go to their death attired in their best, singing and dancing and carrying with them the scrolls of the Torah. With them goes also Liebhaid von Orb, the long lost daughter of the governor, who believes she is a Jewess. The governor is apprised of her Christian birth by her foster father, who seeks to save her. But he refuses to accept the testimony of a Jew, and when at last he discovers the truth it is too late. She has already danced with the rest into the flames.[34]

To the Jews of the Middle Ages, this infiltration, small though it was, of "aliens who have joined themselves to the Lord" was like a shaft of light in the thick darkness of their existence. It gratified their pride and vindicated their unshakable faith in the ultimate conversion of the rest of mankind. Hence their scholars continued to include "the laws concerning *gerim*" in their codes, and their common folks to spin stories about princely proselytes. Even the Zohar could not withhold references to Gentiles who embraced Judaism; while R. Avigdor Kara, whose elegy on the martyrs of Prague (1389) was included in the services for the Day of Atonement, implored God to save His people if not for their own sake then for the sake of:

> Obadiah, Naaman, the Kenite,
> Rahab and Ruth, the Ammonite,
> And all who embraced His law of light.

CHAPTER XIX

THE CHURCH TRIUMPHANT

THE yellow badge and the Ghetto, the fantastic accusations and the constant humiliations, and the brutal harryings of the fanatical monks and mobs which caused considerable numbers of Jews to seek refuge in the bosom of the Church seemed, in the thirteenth century, to sound the death-knell of Judaism. Yet, despite the efforts of the Church, the seed of hate and prejudice against the Jews did not always fall on fertile soil. There were princes and rulers like Rainard II of Sens, "the king of the Jews," or William II (Rufus) of England, or Frederick II of the Holy Roman Empire, who refused, either for humanitarian reasons or out of opposition to the assumptions of the Hierarchy, or, in most instances, because they were concerned more for the state of their exchequer than for the fate of Jewish souls, to submit to the behest of the Holy See, and did not interfere with the religious predilection of the Jews, even if they did not approve of it. They appointed the Jews to high offices and intervened, usually at a price, in their behalf, sometimes even to the extent of permitting them to revert to their former religion after they had been baptized. Thus when some Jews of Aragon tried to rescue a Jewish boy from a couple of monks who intended to convert him, the King, in consideration of a gift of twenty-five hundred solidi, absolved them "whether they were guilty of the crime or not." Nor were the pontiffs themselves more law-abiding than the princes. They, too, had more confidence in the financial ability and medical skill of the Jews than of their own coreligionists and often entrusted to them their worldly treasures and sacred persons.[1]

There were, moreover, many Christians in various walks

501

of life who ignored the ban against associating with Jews.
Chief among these were the students of the Bible. Already
in the sixth century it was found that either through the
ignorance or the carelessness of the copyists, the text of the
Vulgate became greatly corrupted; and for the next five
centuries attempts were made by many scholars to remedy
the evil. But the various emendations only made confusion
worse confounded. Much progress was made in France under
the supervision of Stephen Harding, but more especially by
the Preaching Friars of the thirteenth century. The Dominicans had their *Correctoria,* the most important of which was
the one of Hugo of Saint-Cher (1236). But Roger Bacon, the
Franciscan, pronounced them "the worst corruption, the destruction of the text of God," and either he or his pupil William de Mara produced the *Correctorium Vaticanum* (ca.
1282). There were other *Correctoria* more or less authoritative
among certain groups of churchmen.[2]

The reason for the difficulty to restore the correct text of
the Vulgate lay in the fact that the scholars did not possess
the original manuscript of St. Jerome. In order to reconstruct
his translation they, therefore, had to consult Jews who were
familiar with the Hebrew or the interpretations of Hebrew
commentators. This was true of Harding, of whom we are
told that he "even had recourse to the Rabbins in order to
settle the reading of the Old Testament." William de Mara
refers not only to the Talmud but to the glossary of Menahem
b. Saruk and the "perus" (*perush, commentary*) of Rashi.
Rashi was indeed the inspiration of many a Christian Hebraist,
from Andrew of St. Victor (d. 1175) to Nicholas de Lyra
(1270-1349), whose influence on Luther is suggested in the
familiar couplet:

> *Si Lyra non lyrasset*
> *Lutherus non saltasset.*
> (If Lyra had not played the lyre,
> Luther would not have danced.)

Another study which helped to bridge the gulf between
Jews and Gentiles was the Kabbalah. This mystic *Hebraica*

veritas was, like the Old Testament on which it is founded, long believed to affirm the truth of Christianity, and this belief was confirmed by statements in the *Zohar*. It speaks of the *Adam Kadmon* (the aboriginal man) who, like Christ, was both finite and infinite. It refers to the triune nature of God, as is indicated in the threefold mention of His Name in the *Shma* (Dt. vi, 4). It depicts the Messiah as taking upon himself all the sins of Israel and vicariously atoning for them by his suffering. It was, therefore, both in the interest of Christianity and in the hope of supplying themselves with additional ammunition in their warfare against Judaism that Christian theologians cultivated a knowledge of the Kabbalah by consulting Jewish scholars or the works they produced on the subject. Judging by an anonymous letter of a Christian Hebraist, surmised to have been Roger Bacon, where they could not come in direct contact with Jews in their own country, Christian scholars would write to those of Spain and Germany for the books in which they were interested. [3]

These Judeo-Christian contacts were not, however, limited to the realm of the Bible and Kabbalah. The growing interest in secular knowledge which began in the twelfth century and culminated in the Renaissance prompted many seekers for truth to sit at the feet of Jewish teachers and read the works of Jewish authors on medicine, astronomy, and alchemy. The Jews, who hitherto were the transmitters of the luxuries of the East to the nations of the West, became also the intellectual intermediaries between Moslems and Christians. They were employed as translators from the Arabic by the great patrons of learning, among them Frederick II, Charles and Robert of Anjou, Raymond of Toledo. The work of their scholars rendered into Latin usually by converts, or under Christian names, were studied in the universities and monasteries. Roger Bacon, criticizing the translators of philosophic works states: "In the same way Michael Scot claimed the merit of numerous translations. But it is certain that Andrew, a Jew, labored at them more than he did." [4]

The chief contributors to Christian thought of the Middle Ages were Solomon ibn Gabirol (1021-58) and Moses Maimonides (1135-1204). The latter's *More Nbukim,* translated into Latin under the title *Dux Neutrorum,* became a great favorite among the leading scholastics of the thirteenth century. Such authorities as Alexander of Hales, Albertus Magnus, and Thomas Aquinas, in their *Summas,* refer to him by name and sometimes adopt his conclusion. Ibn Gabirol, whose *Mekor Hayyim* ("Fountain of Life") was translated with the help of an apostate, under the title *Fons Vitae* (c. 1160), was not known as a Jew. William of Auvergne, Bishop of Paris, the fourth greatest scholastic of his century, even claims that Avicebron, or Avicebrol, as ibn Gabirol came to be called, must have been a Christian Arab. It was only through the discovery of a Hebrew abridgement of the original Arabic that the fact was established that Avicebron was no other than ibn Gabirol and the author of the *Fons Vitae.*[5]

Removed from the vigilance of the Church, and the reserve which of necessity they had to maintain in the forced public disputations, these Jewish physicians, scientists, or financiers would meet their Christian interlocutors on an equal footing and in their friendly conversations did not hesitate to give expression to their views on the miracles of Jesus, the mystery of the Trinity, the Transubstantiation, the character of the Mosaic institutions, and on some of the statements of the Talmud. Snatches of stories and remarks which enlivened these intimate conversations between Jews and Gentiles are still extant. We are told that when Pedro of Aragon once stated to his Jewish physician that Jews must regard Christians as unclean because they would not drink the wine touched by them, the latter took a swallow of the water in which were washed the king's feet, thereby showing that the reason was not physical impurity but a religious prohibition. On another occasion, when they discussed which is the true religion, Judaism or Christianity, his Jewish interlocutor told him the parable of the two similar jewels which a father left to his two sons—which is probably the original story of the three rings used by Boccaccio and later by Lessing. It is said that once Alfonso XI of Castile condemned the business methods of the Jews. Whereupon his Jewish visitor repeated to him the popular adage: "If one mouse eats the cheese, people say the mice have done it," so if one Jew does what is wrong all Jews are blamed for it. "And," he added, "it is not Jewish ethics but Christian legislation which drives some poor Jews to illegal acts in their desperate struggle for a livelihood." [6]

Sometimes these conversations were enlivened with that wit and wisdom which dull the edge of prejudice and carry more conviction than the strongest arguments. Thus when Benedict XIII taunted R. Astruc Levi of Daroca about the haggadic statement that the Messiah was born on the day of the destruction of the Temple, the latter replied: "Lord and Pope, you believe so many improbabilities about your Messiah, should we not be entitled to one?" There is preserved a colloquy between the distinguished physician of Salamanca, R. Hayim ibn Musa, and one of his ecclesiastic friends who wanted to know why, if Judaism is the true faith, God did not permit the Jews to remain in the Holy Land. To this, Ibn Musa retorted: "If Christianity is the true faith, why do Christians no longer possess the Holy Sepulchre? Jews at least might say that it is God's punishment for the sin of rejecting Christ; but Christians who accept him, and can by means of confession and absolution and his expiatory power render themselves free from sin, how can they account for God's thus depriving them of the sole of relics of His son and their Messiah and bestowing them upon infidel Saracens?" [7]

Especially noted for their repartee were members of the family of Nathan l' Official. Among those with whom they discussed religious matters were the Bishops of Sens, Mans, Meaux, Anjou, Poitiers, the confessors of St. Louis and his Queen, Gregory X, and numerous friars and Jewish apostates. Asked why the exile which followed the crucifixion lasts so long, while that of Babylon, which was in punishment for idolatry, endured only seventy years—a point which Christian controversialists adduced in favor of Christianity—Nathan replied: "During the first Temple, Jews worshipped images which had little duration, wherefore their punishment was short; but the worship of Jesus who lived just before the begin-

ning of the Diaspora endures to this day. Hence the continu-
ation of their punishment." To the question why the verse,
"And God saw that it was good," is lacking in the account
of the second day of Creation, Nathan answered: "It was because on that day occurred the division of the waters, which
God foresaw would be used by Christians for baptismal purposes." Even more bold, though less poignant, was the reply
of R. Solomon b. Reuben to an apostate who sought to prove
the dogma of the Trinity from the Hebrew Bible: "Had
you a Quaternity to prove, you would demonstrate it quite as
strikingly and convincingly from the Old Testament."[8]

While as Hebraists, mystics, scientists, and physicians, Jews
not infrequently gained access to the highest spheres of society,
as merchants they came in contact with the middle and lower
strata of the people among whom they lived. Despite the prohibition of the Church against dealing with Jews at the peril
of excommunication, Christians continued to trade with Jews
since their own coreligionists exacted much greater profits
and higher rates of interest than the latter. In Italy where, at
the instigation of the Franciscans, the *Monti di Pieta* put
Jewish money-lenders out of business, the latter were soon
given special inducements to resume their occupation. In
this way some Jews and Christians learned to know, and became friendly with, one another. Even during the Crusades
the outrages against the Jews were committed mostly by
outlaws or serfs whose knowledge of them was derived from
fanatical friars or priests or the lawless element which infested the city. The merchants and the middle class burghers
remained, as a rule, friendly, and frequently afforded shelter
to their Jewish neighbors in times of trouble. These amicable
relations would naturally lead to religious conversations, and
even an inadvertent or unintentional remark by a Jew might
have started a spiritual upheaval. As James Darmesteter has it:

> Many a man entering some squalid house in the
> Ghetto to pawn his goods or to seek his horoscope,
> but tarrying there to talk of the mysteries of the uni-
> verse, emerges with a disturbed soul, ripe for the stake.
> The Jew knows how to unveil the vulnerable points

of the Church, and in order to do so he has at his service, besides the knowledge of the Holy Writ, the formidable sagacity characteristic of the oppressed. . . . It is he who forges all that deadly arsenal of reason and irony which was destined to become the legacy of the skeptics of the Renaissance, of the libertines of the great century. The sarcasm of Voltaire is but the last faint echo of a word murmured six centuries before, in the shadow of the Ghetto, and earlier still in the times of Celsus and Origines, at the very cradle of the religion of Christ.[9]

The discomfitures of the Church were not, however, due merely to the unwillingness of some Christians of high or low estate to obey her behests. Sometimes it was brought about by the very weapons and men on whom she relied for the realization of her aspiration. Thus, the main reason which prompted Clement V to introduce the study of Hebrew into the universities was not so much in order to verify the correct text of the Vulgate but the better to solve the problem of the conversion of the Jews. But it was soon realized that the teachers of that language, some of whom were apostates, were seeking to Judaize, and John XXII deemed it advisable to order that the teachers of Hebrew should be kept under strict surveillance. And indeed it was the study of Hebrew that led some Christians to reject the authority of the Church and was, to some extent, the forerunner of the Reformation. It was even more so with the cultivation of the Zohar and Jewish mysticism. Joachim di Flor, the putative author of *The Everlasting Gospel;* Raymond Lully, the Spanish "Doctor Illuminatus" of Spain (1235-1315), whose ardent zeal for converting the Saracens as well as the Jews earned him a martyr's death in Tunis, and Johannes Eckhart (c. 1260-1327), the two latter mystics and Kabbalists, were the forerunners of some of the heretical sects of the thirteenth century and of the Reformers of the fifteenth. Luther acknowledged his indebtedness to Eckhart's teachings in his *German Theology.*[10]

Perhaps the worst defeat suffered by the Church in her warfare against the Synagogue was due to the public disputations. Not only were no Jews convinced by them, not even those who deemed it advisable afterwards to be converted, but the Christians who were present during the controversy were thereby given a chance to hear heretical views which otherwise they never would have heard. The aftermath of these disputations was in many instances worse for Christianity than for Judaism. Many an humble cleric or friar within the walls of a convent was started on the road to heresy by the faltering reply of a Jewish disputant; and many a layman began to scrutinize his theology who otherwise would rest content with the orthodox creed as taught by the priest. That knight was not altogether wrong who asserted that "some good Christians, through a misunderstanding of the arguments of the Jews, would become infidels."

This was still more the case with the polemics carried on in tracts and tomes by Christian zealots and Jewish apostates. The Jews retorted in kind, and produced replies whose influence was even more lasting and far-reaching than the spoken word. They, too, wrote manuals for the purpose of providing Jewish disputants with texts, methods, and arguments against the assaults of Christian conversionists. True, most of these were written in Hebrew, but many were composed also in Latin and the vernacular, or translated into them. Even in the original they were not inaccessible to the steadily increasing number of Christian Hebraists, and were to be found in the monk's cell as well as in the nobleman's castle.

The primary object of these polemics, however, was not so much to convert Christians to Judaism as to confirm the Jews in their faith and fortify them against the attacks of the clergy and their own apostates whose one great passion was to save them. Their authors themselves, such as Anatolio of Italy and Gerson b. Jacob of Germany, pleaded with their coreligionists never to be the first to start an argument with non-Jews, nor to seek for proselytes among them. Some rabbis, in fear of the consequences, even dissuaded prospective proselytes from accepting Judaism and made *Takkanot* (regulations) requiring that Jewish propagandists or Christian converts be reported to the authorities. R. Isaiah of Troki would prohibit Jews even to expound the Old Testament to Christians for fear that it might start the latter on the road to Judaism. But despite the caution of the rabbis, and the ruthless persecution of propagandists and proselytes by the Government, their morale was not broken, and there were, all through the Middle Ages, Jews who not only defended but preached their faith in the hearing of Gentiles.

Outstanding among the polemic and apologetic pamphlets which were produced in consequence of Judeo-Christian controversies are those of R. Joseph Kimhi (1105-70). Noted as poet, exegete, grammarian and translator, he fled from Spain during the persecutions by the Almohades and settled in France. There, at the request of his pupils he composed a little dialogue between a Jew and an apostate, the *Sefer Haberit* (Book of the Covenant). In it he points out that if a religion is to be known by its fruit or effect, Judaism must be superior to Christianity. Jews live up to the Ten Commandments, they do not perjure themselves, they do not rob, nor steal, nor murder; their lives are chaste and their homes cheerful; they educate their children and are hospitable to strangers—virtues which were then very far from common among Christians. Jews never take usury from their own coreligionists and take it from Gentiles solely because it is the only way they are permitted to earn a living; while among Christians, even clergymen do so and from their own flock. He also attacks the unreasonableness and total lack of biblical authority of the doctrines of the Virgin Birth, the Atonement, the Trinity, and the Sonship of Jesus.

But as a controversialist R. Joseph was surpassed by his son R. David (1160-1235), whose commentaries on the Bible were held in very high esteem by Christians no less than by Jews. His comments on the Psalms, to which Christians resorted as text-proofs of their doctrines, contain numerous criticisms of Christianity. The censor ordered them to be expunged, but they were collected and published under the title *Teshubot Lanotzrim* .(Replies to Christians). The *Vikkuah* (dispute), also attributed to him, was likewise condemned by the clergy, but like his commentaries, was frequently quoted by the Reformers in confirmation of their unorthodox opinions.[11]

The famous controversies of Paris and Barcelona also brought forth tracts that helped to weaken the cause which they were intended to strengthen. The *Vikkuah* by R. Yehiel of Paris, the *Mahazik Haemunah* (strengthener of the Faith) by R. Mordecai b. Joseph of Avignon, and Rashi's commentaries to which Christian exegetes frequently resorted, argued the baselessness of the Christian assertions concerning the teachings of the Bible. Raymond Martini's attack on Judaism and defense of Christianity were refuted by R. Moses Nahmanides and R. Solomon b. Adret and R. Jacob b. Reuben's *Sefer Milhamot Adonai* (Book of the Battles of the Lord) became so popular that Alfonso of Valladolid found it necessary to refute it in his *Battalos de Dios* (1336).[12]

For a masterpiece of Jewish polemics we are indebted to Joshua Allorqui, the pupil of a rabbi, who became a bishop, Paul de Santa Maria. Like Paul the Apostle, Joshua started out as a devout Jew and wrote a stinging satire on Christianity and a pungent rebuke to Jewish apostates, but like Paul, he later renounced Judaism and penned bitter diatribes against his former coreligionists. Of special interest is the polemic of Profiat Duran (R. Isaac b. Moses Efodi). He was one of the forced converts, and together with another victim laid plans to flee to Palestine and return to his ancestral faith. The latter, however, lost his nerve and urged his friend also to remain a Christian. Duran's answer was the epistle *Al Tehi Kaavoteka* (Be not like thy fathers, 1396), in which he shows up the weakness of Christianity.[13]

Once the "battle of the books" was started, the Jews entered the lists with characteristic zeal despite the danger to which they thus exposed themselves under the vigilant eyes of the minions of the Inquisition. R. Meir b. Simeon of

Narbonne wrote his *Milhemet Mizvah* (the Obligatory War) in the shadow of the dread Tribunal. R. Isaac Nathan composed his biblical concordance *Meir Netib* (the Illuminator of the Road) to facilitate the use of the Bible in the warfare with Christianity, and excoriated Jewish apostates and Christian missionaries in his *Tokahat Mateh* (the Rebuke to a Misleader) and *Mibzar Yizhak* (the Citadel of Isaac). This polemic activity became especially strong in Spain during the fourteenth and fifteenth centuries, when Jews were not always content with merely defending their faith but ventured to take the offensive. Thus R. Joseph ibn Shem Tob, who was martyred in 1460, drew from the New Testament material for his "Doubts Concerning the Religion of Jesus," while others went to the patristic literature for ammunition against Christianity. Hasdai Crescas and his disciple Joseph Albo composed treatises in Spanish to prove to Christians the unreasonableness of the doctrines of the Church; and R. Shem-Tob b. Isaac ibn Shaprut translated and commented on portions of the Gospels to expose their untenability to the Jews (*Eben Bohan,* the Tried Stone, c. 1385); R. Hayyim ibn Musa, who waged war against Nicholas de Lyra, in his *Magen Veromah* (Shield and Spear) laid down the rules whereby his coreligionists could give to their arguments not only a biblical but a logical and scientific foundation.

This religio-literary campaign spread as far as Africa, where it embraced Mohammedanism as well as Christianity. R. Simon b. Zemah Duran, who fled from his native Majorca after the persecutions of 1391, wrote his *Keshet Umagen* (Bow and Shield) to prove that Jesus was a strict observer of Judaism. His equally famous son and successor in the Algerian rabbinate, R. Solomon b. Simon Duran even dared acclaim the religious superiority of Judaism to Christianity by comparing the moral conduct of average Jews with that of even the Christian clergy.[14]

Probably the most influential and certainly the best known of the Jewish polemics of the Middle Ages is *Hannizahon* (the Victory) by R. Yom-Tob Lipmann of Muehlhausen.

An apostate by the name of Peter charged that the verse, "For they bow down and pray to naught and vanity, unto a god that cannot save," (Isaiah 45:20) originally incorporated by Rab of the third century in the Adoration (Alenu) with which Jews always conclude their services, was intended as an aspersion on Christianity. As a result many Jews were imprisoned, among them R. Yom-Tob Lipmann, and eighty of them were martyred (1400). R. Lipmann succeeded in disproving the apostate's assertion and was set free.

Thereafter the rabbi devoted himself to teaching his people how "to answer a defamer." Versed in the Latin language, he read the Gospels and the Fathers; and, equipped with a biting satire, he collected whatever had been written by the polemists who preceded him, and all the simple but clever sayings current among the masses of his time. These he arranged according to the days of the year, each of which he prefaced with a verse from the Bible, and concluded with a concise resume of the teachings of Judaism.

Among R. Lipmann's attacks on Christianity are:

> If Jesus was born of a virgin, why does the Gospel give the genealogy of Joseph, the husband of Mary? Why did God delay the birth of Jesus for thousands of generations, and thus condemned innumerable pious men and women to suffer damnation for a fault which they had not committed? Why did God wait for Mary when there were before her Sarah, Miriam, Abigail, Huldah and many more equally deserving of the privilege? If through Jesus' crucifixion the curse of original sin is forgiven, why is the earth still bringing forth thorns and thistles, and women bringing forth children in sorrow, as in the days of Adam and Eve? (Gen. 3:16, 18).

Though it was carefully guarded by the Jews, *Hannizahon* somehow became known to the clergy, and numerous professors of Hebrew or theology, Catholic or Protestant, deemed it their duty to refer to or write on the tract of "R. Libman."

It was translated and published in Latin (1644) by Father Theodor Hackspan (1607-1659), who grabbed it from a Jew when the latter, while arguing with him, was searching it for a fit answer to his remarks. [15]

Disappointed in her every effort, the Church at last began to realize that the "witness" could neither be muzzled, bribed, nor intimidated, that degradation, isolation, and disputation could never make him see the light, while his presence might endanger the salvation of her own flock. The only way to protect herself against him was, therefore, to expel him. Such a policy had already been recommended by Leo VII at the beginning of the tenth century. In his reply to the query of the Archbishop of Mayence as to the best way to deal with the Jews, he advised that he should have "the religion of the Holy Trinity and the mystery of the Incarnation preached to them with all wisdom and prudence.... If they voluntarily submit to baptism, thanks be to God; but if they refuse, they should be expelled from the domain, since no commerce should be held with the enemies of God." But as long as they were found to be useful as middle men they were permitted to stay. In the thirteenth century, however, the Cahorsins and Lombards (the "Pope's usurers") began to take over the business of money-lending, and Jews ceased to be a necessary evil. By banishing them the Church would therefore achieve a double purpose: Christian merchants would be rid of shrewd rivals and their coreligionists would be protected from the contagion of heresy. [16]

Minor expulsions had indeed not been infrequent before. Jews were banished from the royal domains of France (1182), from Vienna (1196), Mecklenburg (1125), Breslau (1226), Frankfurt (1241), Brandenburg (1243), and Munich (1285). But the first country to make a clean sweep of all its Jews was England where, according to Pseudo-Josephus, they were found already at the time of the treaty made by Hyrcanus and Augustus. They certainly were settled there soon after the Norman Conquest (1066) and seem to have gotten on with their Christian countrymen quite amicably. Contrary to Jewish custom, they would drink with them and join them in such un-Jewish diversions as deer hunting. They lived in stone mansions and kept Christian domestics. Of William, the sacristan of St. Edmund's Abbey, we are told that he was to the Jews "a father and a patron," received their wives and children in the refectory in times of war, and permitted them to wander "through the altars and round the shrine while the Solemnities of the Mass were being celebrated." They also did not hesitate to express their opinion on the dogmas of Christianity and the miracles of the saints. There is the story of a witty Jew who was journeying with an archdeacon by the name of Peche and his deacon who was called Dayville, whose deanery extended from Bad-place to Bad-pass. "It will be a wonder," said the Jew, "if chance bring me safe from this country whose archdeacon is Sin (*Peche*), whose dean is the Devil, which you enter by a Bad-place and go out in a Bad-pass." When the monks of Canterbury fell out with their archbishop, the Jews of the community sent food and drink to the convent and prayed for them in their synagogues. It is recorded that at the funeral of Hugh, Bishop of Lincoln,

> The Jews, too, weeping and wailing and declaring that he had been a mighty servant of the Lord, paid him honor by running alongside and weeping so that they compelled us to notice that with this man the words of God were fulfilled 'The Lord gave him the blessing of all the nations (Ecclus. 44:25).'

William Rufus is said to have permitted on several occasions Jewish converts to return to Judaism and threatened "by the face of Luke" that unless Christians could refute the Jews he would join the latter sect. Henry I seemed to have greater confidence in the loyalty of the Jews than in that of the Christians, protected them as "the King's bondsmen," and once, at the trial of an ecclesiastic to which a rabbi was invited he exclaimed: "Welcome, Bishop of the Jews! Receive him among ye, for there is scarcely any of the bishops of England that has not betrayed his lord, the Archbishop of Canterbury, except this one. In this Israelite bishop there is no guile." Henry II also sanctioned the special privileges granted the Jews by his father, and these were later reconfirmed by Richard I. The regents of Henry III insisted that "the bishops have nothing at all to do with our Jews," and ordered that Jews should not be made to plead in Christian courts, and that Christians who, in obedience to the order of the Church, would refuse to sell them food, should be imprisoned. [17]

It would seem that down to the time of Richard I intermarriages between Jews and Christians did not arouse the popular indignation we would expect. There is the case of Jurnet of Norwich (1186) who married a Christian heiress Myrild, daughter of Humphrey de Havile, who probably embraced the faith of her husband. He and his wife were indeed deprived of all their possessions but continued as before to live among, and to do business with, their Christian neighbors.

Even the religious disputations prior to 1096 are conspicuous by the friendly tone which runs through them. We need but refer to the specimen adduced by Joseph Jacobs in *The Jews of Angevin England*. In it Brother Gilbert, Abbot of Westminster, reports to Anselm, the Archbishop of Canterbury, his dispute with a Jew who used to come to him as a friend. He describes him as a man "well versed even in our law and literature and practiced in the Scriptures and in disputes against us." He gives the Jew's arguments as well as his own without the usual epithets which mark Christian polemics. Nor does he claim, as was customary, that his disputant was at last convinced, though he states that one of the listeners was converted to the faith and became a monk.

But here, too, the Church never abandoned her hope to make the Jews see the light of Christianity. It is truly touching to read Anselm's letter to the Prior and Archdeacon of Canterbury in behalf of a Jewish convert:

> With the most affection of my heart, I order you and beg your religion to take care of this Robert, with joyful piety and pious joyfulness with which all Christians ought to help and assist one fleeing from Judaism

to Christianity.... Let him rejoice that he has passed
from perfidy to the true faith, and prove by our piety
that our faith is nearer to God than the Jewish. For
I would prefer, if necessary, that there should be spent
in this all that belongs to me from the rents of the
archdeaconry, and even much more, rather than that
he who has fled out of the hands of the devil to the
servants of God should live in a misery among us. [18]

As, however, the Jews continued to be obdurate and sometimes even dared "attack" their adversaries by defending their
own views, voices began to be heard favoring the discontinuance of disputations with Jews while waiting for an opportune time to get rid of the whole mass of them. Thus
Peter of Blois in the preface of his *Contra perfidiam Judaeorum,* addressed to the Bishop of Worcester, writes (c. 1198):

You have made long and anxious complaint in
your letters that surrounded by Jews and heretics
you are attacked by them and have not read the
authorities in the sacred Scripture by which you can
refute their calumnies and answer their cunning
sleights. It is right, says the Apostle, that there should
be heresies and schisms so that those who have been
proved may be manifest. Wherefore life is allowed to
the Jews of today, because they are our treasures
while they confirm the prophecies on our faith and
the law of Moses. We read the Passion of Christ, not
alone in their books but in their faces.... As for what
you say that you desire to dispute with Jews so as to
convert them and turn them to the faith, I commend
you the less for that for you beat the air, exhausting
yourself with foolish and vain zeal. God indeed has
placed a limit to them which they may not exceed.
Their hour is not yet come, but He has blinded them
till the time when the heathen are converted to the
faith. Hence it is what is said by Isaiah. 'Go and blind
the heart of this people, etc.' It seems to me wiser for
our faith to conceal the injury done to it for the time

rather than enter into discussion with a people stiff-necked and of a stubbornness truly bestial.

By the middle of the twelfth century the Church in England began to realize that her efforts to attract Jews into the fold by sweet reasonableness and material assistance were of little avail, and she decided to resort to harsher measures. Jewish children would sometimes be snatched by monks, carried off to a church or monastery to be baptized and raised as Christians. Priests became busy in disputations with rabbis at which, in the words of William of Malmesbury, the latter "received nothing but confusion, though they often boasted that they had been conquered not by speech but by deeds." We can judge of the gentleness, if not the reasonableness, with which these disputations were conducted by the record of an attempt to convince a Jew of the truth of the immaculate conception from nature. Jews like Christians then believed in the existence of barnacle geese, which are born on trees without the mediation of parents. The missionary, therefore, triumphantly calls on his Jewish hearer: "Be wise at length, wretched Jew, be wise even though late. The first generation of man from dust without male or female.... thou darest not deny in veneration of thy Law.... But the fourth, in which alone is salvation, from female without male, that with obstinate malice thou detestest to thy own destruction. Blush, wretch, blush, and at least turn to nature." [19]

Yet, while the Church began to doubt whether the conversion of the Jews could be achieved by disputations, she did not give up hope of accomplishing her purpose by depriving them of their elementary human rights. She permitted them only one pursuit, money-lending, and then punished them for being usurers. She did her utmost to enforce the provision of the Lateran Council (1179) which prohibited Jews to employ Christian servants "even for the purpose of tending their children, or for services or for any cause," and ordered that a Christian's testimony against Jews should be preferred to that of a Jew. Walter Mapes, Archdeacon of Oxford, when he took the oath to dispense justice to all, added, "to all, except to Jews and white monks (Cistercians)."

Gradually the credulous and fanatically religious masses became disposed to accept any rumor, no matter how absurd, concerning the villainy of "the enemies of Christ," such as that Jews would cast evil spells upon Christians, and celebrate their festival of Passover by drinking the blood of Christian children or putting some of it in their unleavened bread. Ironically enough, this slander invented by the Greek pagan Apion was resurrected in England (1144) more than a thousand years later by a converted Jew, Theobald of Cambridge. The disappearance of a Christian lad, William of Norwich, gave the renegade an opportunity to assert that Jews use the blood of Christian children at their "annual sacrifice" during the Feast of Unleavened Bread. The libel seemed at first so absurd that the Jews were not even tried. But as the monks soon proclaimed that the boy martyr was performing miracles, the story, with local variations, spread all over England and abroad. In songs and ballads it was told, both in English and in French, how a Jew-boy, murdered by his father, because he became a convert to Christianity, sang hymns to the Virgin after his death. The relics of such martyrs began to be sought after as an unfailing source of revenue by different churches and monasteries. The monks of Gloucester boasted for their institution a young St. Harold "whom Jews made a glorious martyr unto Christ" (1186), and the clergy of Bury St. Edmunds announced that they possessed a little St. Robert "martyred by the Jews on the 10th of June" (1181). Not to be outdone, the Winchester community adopted as a boy-martyr one who was employed and befriended by a Jew and found slain. This craving for martyrs at the hand of Jews became so deep-rooted that during the massacres at Stamford (1190) a youth who plundered the Jewish victims and was robbed and killed by a fellow plunderer was immediately canonized, and his body was said to perform miracles till the great Hugh, Bishop of Lincoln, put a stop to the reverence paid it and the revenue which it produced. [20]

By a strange coincidence the best known of these so-called
boy-martyrs who caused so much innocent Jewish blood to
be shed also went by the name of Hugh of Lincoln. His
body was found in a well belonging to Jopin, the Jew (1255),
who, on the priest's promise that his life would be spared,
"confessed" that the boy had been crucified by a number of
prominent Jews. Jopin was later dragged around the city
tied to the tail of a horse and hanged. Ninety-two other Jews
were carried to a London jail, and eighteen of them were executed and their property confiscated. The others saved themselves by paying a heavy ransom. "Little Sir Hugh" was buried
with great pomp in a shrine in the Cathedral of Lincoln, and
many miracles were attributed to him. His martyrdom became the theme of stirring ballads in French, Scottish, and
English, calling upon the populace to avenge, in the words of
Chaucer's Prioress:

> Yonge Hugh of Lincoln, slayn also
> With cursed Jewes, as is notable. [21]

We can easily imagine the effect of these ballads at that
time if we recall the confession made six hundred years later
by Charles Lamb in his essay on Imperfect Sympathies: "I
cannot shake off the story of Hugh of Lincoln. . . . A Hebrew
is nowhere congenial to me. . . . I do not like to see the Church
and the Synagogues kissing and congeeing in awkward pos-
tures of affected civility."

Before the end of the twelfth century the comparative
safety and prosperity of English Jewry was reduced to the
same level as that of their coreligionists in France and
Germany. They were hated by almost everybody, and safe
nowhere, so that St. Bernard, in a letter in which he con-
gratulates the English on the zeal of God which burns in
them, pleads:

> You should not persecute the Jews, you should not
> slay them. You should not even put them to flight.
> Consult the divine pages. I know that it is written

prophetically of the Jews (Ps. 59:12): 'The Lord will show unto me about mine enemies. Do not kill then, never will my people be forgotten....' If the Jews are altogether ground down, how in the end shall their promised salvation and conversion prosper?

But the plea of the Saint was of no effect. The hate ceaselessly inculcated by the Church became in England, too, a Frankenstein which she herself was frequently unable to subdue. During the coronation of Richard Coeur de Lion (September 3, 1189), when Jewish representatives came to bring a tribute to their new king, the crowd, fearing lest the Jews cast a spell upon him, drove them off with sticks and stones and beat some of them to death. As the riot grew, "a pleasing rumor," writes an Augustinian canon, "spread with incredible rapidity through all London that the King had ordered all Jews to be exterminated." The Jews barricaded themselves in their homes, but these were pillaged and then set on fire, and it was "only satiety or weariness that calmed the fury of the rioters." Similar scenes were enacted in York, Norwich, Stamford, St. Edmonds, and other places. Everywhere synagogues were destroyed, homes were burned, manuscripts were torn, and many Jews were massacred even when they pleaded for "Christian grace." [22]

When the report of the riots reached the king he was furious not because of the massacre of the Jews but because of "the insult to his royal majesty and for the great loss to the treasury," for the gentry and the abbots saw to it that the records of their indebtedness to the Jews be destroyed during the disturbances. He ordered the Royal Chancellor, Bishop of St. Ely, to make a thorough investigation and punish the malefactors. But while three were hanged for destroying Christian houses, those who perpetrated the most horrible atrocities escaped with little, if any, punishment.

Even those who condemned the outrages against the Jews and, like St. Bernard, quoted the Psalm as proof that it is wrong to slay Jews, saw in them "a pious augury" for the reign of Richard. William of Newbury, who does not seem to have been in sympathy with the "bold and greedy men who carried out their own cupidity with savage joy," declares that "the fate of the blaspheming people (the Jews) ennobled the day and place of the king's consecration ... since the Omnipotent often fulfills His own goodwill by the will and bad acts of even the wickedest of men." He does indeed plead that the crucifiers of our Lord Christ should be allowed to live among Christians "as a continual and most helpful remembrance by all of the faithful of our Lord's Passion ... and thus the Jews ought to live among Christians for our own use, but serve as for their own iniquity. But," he continues, "the Jews in England under Henry II were by an absurd arrangement happy and renowned far more than the Christians, and swelling very impudently against Christ, owing to their good fortune did much injury to Christians, wherefore in the days of the new king the lives which they possessed by Christ's clemency were put in danger by his just judgment, though by the beautiful arrangement of his justice those have no excuse who brought slaughter upon them by a secret rising." [23]

The temper of the populace, however, was probably better indicated by Richard of Devizes who sarcastically remarks on Winchester which "alone spared her vermin": "It never did anything in a hurry.... It did not want to vomit forth the load on its stomach ... till at an opportune time she might once and forever evacuate the whole mass of disease." Robert of Gloucester sings of the London massacre with unfeigned delight:

> The wretched wicked Jews they weened well to do
> And a rich present they prepared with great pride
> And sent it to the noble King, but small thanks them
>   betide.
> For the King was somewhat vexed, and took it for
>   great shame,
> That from such unclean things as them any meat to
>   him came.

And bade them put out of court, and to the wretches
    shame do
There was many a wild serving-man that was ready
    thereto,
And they went into Jewry and wounded and tore
    men too
And robbed and burnt houses, and many of them slew.

Despite the pall of hate which thereafter hung over English
Jews they continued to cling with grim determination to the
heritage of their fathers. Out of a list of some seven hundred
and fifty, states Jacobs, only seven converts occur, and only
one, that of a Jewess. Most of those who saved their lives by
conversion during the massacres reverted to Judaism as soon
as things somewhat quieted down, and some who hitherto
were missionaries experienced a change of heart by the very
ordeals through which their former fellow-Jews had to pass.
Thus, R. Joseph Bkhor Shor tells of an apostate who tried
to persuade him to be baptized on the strength of the Isaiahnic
prophecies concerning the Servant of God (Chaps. lii-liii).
"O fool," replied the rabbi, "Let thine ears hear that which
thy mouth uttereth: If he (Jesus) is God would he be termed
servant?" Thereupon the apostate rent his clothes and rolled
himself in ashes, and repented.

Richard I did not insist that those who had been converted
during his coronation should remain Christians. Hoveden the
Chronicler tells that Benedict of York, who barely escaped
death by submitting to baptism by the Prior of St. Mary, was
once asked by the King who he was. He answered, "I am
Benedict, the Jew, from York," and, to the chagrin of the
Archbishop of Canterbury, the King did not demand "Christian justice." Benedict-William died shortly after, probably
as a result of his injuries, and was refused burial on both the
Jewish and the Christian cemeteries, the former, Hoveden informs us, because he had turned Christian, the latter because,
"like a dog to his vomit, he had turned to his Jewish de-
pravity."

Nor did the massacres put a stop to the conversion of

Christians to Judaism. During the more tranquil years which preceded Richard's coronation, such cases were more numerous. R. Ephraim of Bonn tells in his Valley of Tears (*Emek Habbakah*) that in a certain city of England there were many proselytes, and that a whole congregation of them, consisting of twenty-two men, "hallowed the Name of the Unity (1190)." Girard of Cambridge also relates:

> A certain monk of the same (Cistercian) order, or rather a certain demoniac in our own times, being as it were tired of the Catholic faith... at last caused himself to be circumcised with the Jewish rite, and as a most vile apostate joined himself to his damnation to the enemies of the cross of Christ. Also on the northern border of England... a certain brother, likewise in our own days, by a similar error, or rather madness... fled with ruinous and ruinbearing ways to Judaism, the home of damnation and the asylum of this depraved reprobation.... But I myself am persuaded that those two wretches did not leave the truth ... out of mere devotion or desire of increasing their religion.... But because they could no longer bear the harshness and rigour of that order, and instigated by the spirit of fornication they committed this crime. [24]

We may take it that these friars escaped the consequence of their deeds, for Girard would certainly have gloated over it. What he does tell us is that Walter Mapes, who denounced the Cistercian Order as covered with "the stains of deliberate vice and cupidity," facetiously said: "It is remarkable that those two wretches, since they wished to leave their former faith, as being so perverse and infested with so many poisonous vices, did not become Christians, adopting a safer.and more salubrious plan!"

Shortly after (1202), Bonefand, a Jew of Bedford, was charged with having "maliciously and against the peace of our lord the King, caused to be ementulated (circumcised?) Richard the nephew of Robert of Sutton." The case was tried by a jury of the hundred—a rather unusual proceeding, which found Bonefand not guilty, and Richard was turned over "to the King's mercy." Twenty years later, however, a deacon who devoted himself to the acquisition of Hebrew, was burned at the stake (April 17, 1222) for accepting the faith of Israel and marrying a Jewess.

The most outstanding English proselyte of the thirteenth century was Robert de Reddingge (or Reading), a Dominican of unusual attainments. Preparing himself to become a missionary to the Jews, he took up the study of Hebrew, the better to be able to convince them of their misinterpretation of the Scriptures. But his studies only led him to doubt the truths of Christianity, and finally to go over to Judaism. After submitting to the rite of circumcision, he assumed the name of Haggai, and married a Jewess (1275). When summoned before the ecclesiastical authorities, he defended himself with great eloquence and erudition. There is a story that the Archbishop of Canterbury, after degrading him from his office, turned him over to the Sheriff of Oxfordshire, and that the latter, swearing by the throat of God that he would be revenged on such a blasphemer, ordered him to be burned immediately, remarking, "I am only sorry that this fellow goes to hell alone." [25]

By the thirteenth century the influence of the Church, long resisted by the State, began to be marked both in the enactments of the secular authorities and the methods of their enforcement. Jews who would not or could not pay immediately the confiscatory taxes imposed on them had their wives and children seized, their eyes gouged, or their teeth extracted. The law requiring them to wear a distinctive badge was enforced with utmost rigor. They were forbidden to build new synagogues, or to worship in their old ones in voices audible to the Christians, to eat meat during Lent, or to employ Christian nurses or servants. Christians who had any dealings with them were promptly excommunicated. At the same time Henry III built a Domus Conversorum for the maintenance of converts to Christianity (1232).

Jewish misery became so great that in 1254 they pleaded

for permission for the Jewish community to leave the country. But Henry III still regarded them too valuable to his treasury to allow them to depart, and even ordered his officials to keep a careful watch over those who tried to escape. However, after the Jews had been drained of their wealth by the riots of 1262-6, the only justification for permitting them to stay was the possibility of their conversion. To accomplish this objective Duns Scotus, the *Doctor Subtilis,* suggested that the Jewish children be baptized by force, and the parents who refused to be converted be transported to some island where they should be permitted to follow their own religion until the fulfillment of the Isaiahnic prophecy about the "remnant that will return" (4:22). Other means, however, seemed more practical. Blasphemy was made punishable by death, and in 1274 a Jew was burned at Norwich for his "insolence." Jews were also ordered to listen to the harangues of the Dominicans against their religion (1280). In 1282 the Archbishop of Canterbury confiscated all the synagogues in his diocese, and at the call of Honorius IV the bishops of York and Canterbury prepared still more drastic measures against "the unchecked fanaticism of the Jews." At last the inevitable doom came. At the insistence of the Queen Mother Eleanor, Edward I issued an edict (July 18, 1290) without the Parliament's approval, that the Jews of England should be banished, the debts owed them by Christians cancelled, and the property they left behind confiscated. On the eve of All Saints Day the once proud and prosperous English Jewish community went into exile. But their ill fate followed them. Many were robbed and thrown into the sea. One captain, it is said, ran his ship against a sand-bank, made those whom he conveyed disembark, and, with the rising tide, sailed away, shouting to the unfortunates: "Cry unto Moses, who led your ancestors safely through the Red Sea, to bring you back to dry land!" England became, or was believed to have become, rid of all Jews.

Of the sixteen thousand who were banished from England some went to Flanders, but the majority sought refuge in France, the land of their fathers, whose language they spoke and whose customs they retained, there to meet a similar fate a century later. It was like the proverbial jumping from the frying pan into the fire. The bigoted St. Louis had long before decided on either their conversion or expulsion, and tolerated them only because of the financial exigencies of the Crusades. His grandson, the rapacious Philip the Fair, who prohibited the repairing of synagogues and the acquisition of copies of the Talmud, held on to the Jews until, by the beginning of the fourteenth century, the Jewish sponge had been squeezed dry, and then decided on their banishment. Fearing that they might hide the treasures he believed they possessed, he issued secret instructions that they be suddenly arrested on the ninth of Ab (July 22, 1306). While in jail they were notified that they were to leave the country and that they could take with them only the sum of twelve sous each. "The clergy," says Milman, "in their zeal for the faith, and the hope that their burdens might be lightened, approved this pious robbery and rejoiced that France was delivered from the presence of this usurious and miscreant race." [26]

Ten years later, after economic necessity prompted Louis X to reinvite the Jews to France, the Jews became exposed again to the same treatment as they had received under Philip the Fair. Synagogues were broken into, and sacred scrolls carried off and desecrated. Jewish homes were frequently entered in the name of the King and robbed of their contents. The ritual murder libel also reared its ugly head in France, and when some lepers who were accused of poisoning the wells put the blame on their fellow-outcasts, the Jews, it was readily accepted as true. It was also alleged that Jews were in league with the Moslems of Tunis and Granada to destroy Christendom. As a result, massacres became of frequent occurrence; and soon after the death of Philip (1322), the Jews were expelled once more.

After the disaster of Poitiers the Jews were recalled again by Charles V (1361) and offered many privileges. They were exempted from listening to Christian sermons and were not to be prosecuted even for the gravest crimes committed before their previous exile. But they were not permitted to enjoy these privileges for any length of time. A wealthy Jewish convert to Christianity, Denis Machault, was alleged to have been persuaded by his former coreligionists to return to Judaism. At the instigation of the clergy the leading members of the Paris Jewish community were tortured, and a confession was extracted to the effect that they were implicated in the escape of Denis. The defendants were condemned to the stake, but Parliament commuted the sentence to flogging in three public places on three successive Saturdays, after which all the Jews were to be banished and their property confiscated. "Moved by piety and fearing the evil influence of Jews on Christians," the king approved the decree on the Day of Atonement (September 17, 1394). He was, however, humane enough, despite the protests of the clergy and the populace, to allow them three months of grace to dispose of their belongings and to collect their debts. At the end of the year they were all marched to the frontier and ordered to leave, and France, too, like England, became a land without Jews. [27]

CHAPTER XX

CONVERTS AND REVERTS

WITH the conquest of Spain the Moors entered upon a career which for several centuries outshone even that of their co-religionists in the East. Their Emirs were zealous patrons of literature and science. Cordova, Seville, Granada, Toledo, Barcelona, and many other cities were models of architectural beauty and refinement of manners, and contrasted sharply with the filthy and miserable hovels of the populace and the barbarian behavior of the knights and ladies in the tinselled courts of Christian kings. Unhindered by a generally benighted clergy, their universities allowed full scope for the study of the various sciences and philosophy. Students with a thirst for knowledge flocked to them from all parts of Christendom. It is said that Sylvester II (Egber) was himself at one time a scholar at the University of Cordova.

Free from the terror of persecution which hung like a pall over the Jews in Christendom, their coreligionists in Spain collaborated with their Moorish neighbors, and shared in their contributions to knowledge. They rivaled them in their love of poetry and were the authors of some of the finest verses. It is recorded that there was not a youth, nor woman, nor child, in the city of Cordova who could not repeat the songs of Abu-abhan Ibrahim ibn Sahal. Jews were among the professors at the universities, among the officers and soldiers of the army, among the counselors and viziers of the caliphs. Indeed, Islam at that time stood nearer Judaism than Christianity, not only theologically but ethically, and both Jews and Moslems spoke with derision of "the woman (St. Mary) worshipers and polytheistic (Trinity) savages beyond the Pyrenees."

528

The first invasion of the Berber Almoravides ("Marabouts"), however, marked the beginning of the end of Moslem toleration. According to their tradition Mohammed had permitted the Jews to continue in their faith till the coming of their expected Messiah, or about five hundred years after the Hegira. As the time for the end of that period arrived and their Messiah had not yet come, Yusuf ibn Teshufin ordered all the Jews of Lucena, the leading Jewish community in Spain, to accept the religion of the Prophet (1107). However, he permitted them to remain Jews temporarily only on payment of a large sum of money. But worse times were in store for the Jews with the arrival of Abdallah ibn Tumart (1112), who claimed to be the Mahdi, or the incarnation of Mohammed. He insisted upon the simple life, upon the avoidance of any form of pleasure, including poetry, music, and painting, forbade the study of philosophy, and preached a war of extermination against all who were not strict Almohades or Unitarians. His successor Abdulmumen extirpated the Almoravides, suppressed the Christians, and addressed the Jews as follows:

> You do not believe in the mission of Mohammed, the Prophet, and you think that the Messiah who has been announced to you will confirm your Law and strengthen your religion. Your forefathers, however, asserted that the Messiah would appear at the latest about half a century after the coming of Mohammed. Behold, that half century has long passed, and no Prophet has arisen in your midst! The patience with which you have been treated has come to an end. We can no longer permit you to continue in your unbelief. We no longer desire any tribute from you. You have only the choice between Islam and death.

Abdulmumen was at last prevailed upon to permit many Jews to emigrate to other lands, but he destroyed all their synagogues. Those who neither left nor became converts to Islam were to be sold into slavery. Many Jews, as well as Christians, therefore, assumed the mask of Mohammedanism. Among them was our poet Ibrahim ibn Sahal. Of these early "Marranos" some ultimately became as fanatical as the Almohades, others retained their disguise but hoped and prayed for the time when they would be able to revert to Judaism.[1]

The *Reconquista,* or reconquest, of Spain by the Christians brought much misery to the Jews. But when peace was finally established, Jews were treated rather favorably. The forced converts to Mohammedanism were permitted to return to Judaism, and among the first to take advantage was ibn Sahal. During the Crusade against the Saracens of Spain (1063) when many Jews were massacred, the Viscount of Narbonne and the clergy did their utmost to protect them, and Pope Alexander II strongly condemned the Archbishop for his seeming approval of the deeds of those who "foolishly wished to kill those whom the Divine Mercy had predestined to salvation." Alfonso VI is said to have waited to launch the battle of Zacala (1068) till the close of the Sabbath. Alfonso I of Aragon, who at first tried to appease the Moors by oppressing the Jews (1114), also granted them equality with his other subjects. In the thirteenth century James I assured the Jews of Lerida that they would not be disturbed by Inquisitors, and excused them from attending conversional sermons outside their quarters. In Castile, Jews were treated like Christians in all legal matters. The Jews, on their part, also became attached to their Christian rulers who for a time pursued the liberal policy of some of the caliphs. The deaths of Ferdinand III, the conqueror of Castile (1252)—whose tombstone bears a Hebrew epitaph—and of James I, the conqueror of Aragon (1276), were profoundly mourned by their Jewish subjects.

With the completion of the *Reconquista* and the firm establishment of Roman Catholicism in the Iberian Peninsula, the Church, now at the zenith of her power, began to enforce her anti-Jewish policy with renewed zeal. Already Gregory VII reprimanded Alfonso VI for his favorable treatment of the Jews of Castile. "We admonish your Highness," wrote he, "that you must cease to suffer the Jews to rule over Christians. ... To wish to please Christ's enemies means to treat Christ himself with contumely." In 1250 Innocent IV issued a bull forbidding Jews to build new synagogues, to associate with Christians, or to attend them as physicians, or to employ Christian nurses, and they were required to pay tithes toward the support of the clergy. They had to wear a distinctive badge, on pain of suffering the infliction of ten stripes, and were liable to the penalty of death and confiscation of property for the attempt to make proselytes. The clergy, too, did their utmost to implant and nurture in the hearts of their flocks an implacable hatred toward the Jews. They spread or countenanced the wildest rumors about them. To treat a Jew with common decency became a sign of Judaizing. Don Pedro, of Castile, nicknamed "The Cruel" because he protected the Jews in their rights, was said to have been the substituted child of a Jewess, and his court was dubbed the "Jewish court." On his defeat (1369) his bastard brother, Henry of Trastamare, ordered his execution while taunting him as "the Jew, the son of a harlot, who calls himself King of Castile," and Urban V expressed his delight in the characteristic message: "The Church must rejoice at the death of such a tyrant, a rebel against the Church, and a favorer of the Jews and Saracens. The righteous exult in retribution." [2]

The miserable end of Don Pedro marked the beginning of the crowning tragedy of the Jews in Spain. Thereafter the hitherto "paradise of the Jews" was turned into a veritable hell for them. In some places they had to pay a special tax of thirty dineros in memory of the "thirty pieces of silver" paid for the betrayal of Jesus, and those who failed to do so were either tortured or sold as slaves. Dominican and other monks, accompanied by mobs of hoodlums, would break into synagogues and by insults and assaults compel the congregations to listen to their conversionist sermons. In Valencia the knights of St. John broke a door through the wall of the Jewish quarter "in order to introduce crucifixes into the streets of the Jews with a view to raising riots." Besides these religious propagandists the Cortes and the grandees who were envious of the prosperity of the Jews constantly demanded that they be deprived of their every right—even that of shaving or cutting

their hair—and that they be expelled from the country as traitors. At last, goaded into frenzy by Archdeacon Ferrand
Martinez, the Queen's confessor, the rabble of Seville massacred most of the thirty thousand Jews of the city or sold
them to the Moors as slaves (Ash Wednesday, 1391). The rest
saved themselves by accepting baptism. Of the three synagogues
of the community, two were converted into churches. [3]

Similar scenes were subsequently witnessed in Castile, in
Aragon, in Valencia, in Catalonia, and were re-enacted on
the Balearic Islands. Everywhere there were burnings, torture,
enslavement, forced conversions. The number of these victims is said to have exceeded fifty thousand; while those who
"clamored for admission" into the church are estimated to have
been about two hundred thousand. It is claimed that, despite
the multitude of the neophytes, the holy chrism remained un-
exhausted till all were baptized!

But the end was not yet. In anticipation of the Day of Judgment which he believed was at hand, the Dominican Fray
Vincent Ferrer set out on a mission to finally purify Spain once
and for all, both of its social degeneracy and Jewish heresy.
Everywhere he was followed by a mob of Flagellants before
whom he painted with fiery eloquence the horrors of the
second coming of Christ to judge the world, and challenged
them to do their Christian duty to extirpate heresy, Judaism,
and Mohammedanism. He would appear in the synagogues
with a *Sefer Torah* (sacred scroll) in one arm and a crucifix
in the other, calling upon the congregation to come to Jesus,
and not infrequently he reinforced his harangues by the more
convincing arguments of the mob. He is credited with the
conversion of more than twenty thousand men, women, and
children.

Once, however, the stain of Judaism was washed away by
the waters of baptism, these erstwhile outcasts found all gates
thrown wide open for them and their children. They were
welcomed into the highest ranks of the Hierarchy as well
as the most exclusive circles of the nobility, and mixed their
blood with royalty itself. According to the *Libro Verde de
Aragon* and the *El Tizon de la Nobleza Espanola,* not a few

of them intermarried with the grandees of Aragon and Castile. The "New Christian" Luis de Santangel was made treasurer for the kings of Aragon. Pedro de la Caballeria was partly responsible for the marriage of Ferdinand of Aragon (of Jewish descent) and Isabella of Castile. The former Rabbi Solomon Halevi, who had been driven into the Church by the massacres of 1391, became Paul de Santa Maria, Archbishop of Burgos and Chancellor of the Kingdom. As confessor to Ferdinand and Isabella he favored the expulsion of the Jews from Spain, but as one who induced Isabella to finance the expedition of Columbus he was instrumental in preparing for them a refuge in which they were to flourish as they had not even in the golden period of Spain. [4]

The Church indeed had no illusions about the sincerity of converts who submitted to baptism by brute force. Many a *bon mot* was passed around in the monasteries at the expense of seemingly "voluntary" neophytes. In the Rhineland in particular, where hate more than zeal for conversion was the predominant factor, Conrad of Megenburg used to say that the "faith of a converted Jew is like the droppings of a sparrow: hot when it falls, but cold by the time it hits the ground." There they used to repeat a favorite story of a certain Everhard, a thirteenth century convert, who became a canon in Cologne. On his death-bed, when he was offered the Sacrament, he asked that a cat, a mouse, a dog, and a hare be brought into his room. Pointing at them he said: "Look at these animals. They have never seen one another before. Yet the cat chases the mouse, and the dog the hare. They follow their instincts, and you may as well expect that a Jew will not follow his instinct and turn Christian." The Church, however, was building for the future, sure that if not the parents then their children would ultimately outgrow their ingrained antipathy. In Majorca Jews were offered as much as two thousand libras (c. $1,500) for accepting Christianity which reward, however, they were denied after they were once converted and could no longer "unbaptize" themselves. [5]

But with the growing number of those who were returning to their Judaism the Church began to fear for the safety of

her home born as well as adopted children, and Jewish apostates or their descendants were most conspicuous for their
zealotry. Specially noted was the Franciscan Friar, Alonso
de Spina, Rector of the University of Salamanca. His fanatical
hate of Jews, whether public or secret (*Judios publicos, Judios
ocultos*) knew no bounds. His *Fortalicium Fidei* (1460) is a
rehash of the most malicious libels ever circulated about them.
He predicted that unless the Jews were destroyed they and
their myriads who had been locked up in the Caspian region
since the time of Alexander would join Antichrist and destroy
Christendom. He lamented that ravaging wolves were permitted to mingle with the flock of the Lord. He was sure that
if the *Conversos* were investigated, "countless numbers of them
would be condemned to the stake; for countless numbers com-
bine the adherence to Jewish customs with the observance
of the Christian religion." He was indeed opposed by another
friar of Jewish extraction, Alonso de Orepesa, General of the
Geronimite Order, whose learning and saintliness carried great
weight in the Councils of the Church. But the ceaseless agitation of Tomas de Torquemada (also of Jewish descent),
a Prior of the Dominican monastery, and the appearance of
tracts which made light of the Catholic creed, finally stifled
all opposition, and under Ferdinand "the Catholic" (a descendant of a Jewess), the Inquisition, which Alfonso X of
Castile and Ferdinand II of Aragon allowed to fall into desuetude, became a *fait accompli* (1478). [6]

The Marranos did not at first realize the seriousness of
the situation. They had so many Christian friends, even relatives, and were themselves so opulent and powerful, that they
feared no more danger from the new than from the old Inquisition. Yet, for greater safety, they held a meeting in their
favorite church in Seville, and organized themselves into a
Self-Defense society. Unfortunately, the daughter of a prominent Marrano, Diego de Susan, who, because of her exceeding beauty, was known as *La hermosa hembre,* confided to her
Christian lover that the Conversos were conspiring against
the Christians. This was followed by the arrest of many and
the burning alive of six men and women (Feb. 6, 1481). But

poor *La hermosa hembre* paid dearly for her indiscretion. Her
father, himself, became a victim of the Inquisition and she
adopted a life of shame. It is rumored that at her request her
skull was nailed over the door of the house in which she
plied her trade, where it remained until the nineteenth century,
seemingly uttering cries of grief from its grinning jaws.

The Marranos of Toledo endeavored to imitate the example of those of Seville, but their plot, too, was discovered.
Those caught were marked with a cross on the forehead
and the words "Receive the Sign of the Cross which ye have
denied and lost." They were also fined a fifth of their property
for the war with the Moors, deprived of their capacity to hold
office, and sentenced to flagellate themselves with hempen
cords six Fridays in succession. Others including many ecclesiastical dignitaries were burned alive. By the irony of fate,
among the first victims of the Inquisition at Aragon (1485)
was Francisco de Santa Fe, son of the notorious apostate
Geronimo de Santa Fe. Another of the same family met a
similar fate a little later in Barcelona. The Bishops of Segovia
and Calahora, both of Jewish descent, were, at the instigation
of Torquemada, sent to Rome for trial, and either died of a
broken heart or of torture in prison. The bones of the grandmother of Alfonso de Cabaleria were exhumed and burned.
Her great grandson, however, married the granddaughter
of King Ferdinand, and thus infused Jewish blood into the
house royal of Aragon. It is calculated that during the fifteen
years of his office as Chief Inquisitor, Torquemada condemned
more than eight thousand Marranos, and Jews who were implicated with them, to be burned alive, and more than six
thousand in effigy. Before the end of the fifteenth century
nearly thirty thousand persons are said to have been put
to death by fire by the Inquisition, while several hundred thousand were either penanced or otherwise punished. [7]

As the Inquisition showed no pity for the living neither
did it have regard for the dead. Not even pregnancy was
sufficient cause to spare a woman from the ordeal of a
trial. Its mottos were, "Arise, God, judge Thy cause," and
"Catch ye foxes for us!" (Ps. 74:22; Cant. 2:15). In keeping

with the bull of Innocent VIII, those who escaped from its clutches were extradited from any part of the Catholic world. If they died before they were condemned, their bones were exhumed and burned after a mock trial. If they could not be found they were burned in effigy. It was made incumbent on every Converso to denounce a fellow Converso who was suspected as a Judaizer. Offers were also made of a part of the property of the condemned Conversos (sometimes amounting to fifty per cent) to those who would help expose his guilt, and rabbis were ordered to excommunicate those of their community who failed to do so. When R. Judah ibn Virgo of Seville preferred to flee rather than turn informer, the Inquisition pursued him to Lisbon and tortured him to death. To facilitate the labor of the Inquisition, manuals modeled after the one by Bernard Gui (or Guidonis, d. 1331) were issued which described the characteristic habits of the Jews:

> Putting on clean or festive clothes, clean and washed shirts and hairdress; arranging and cleaning their house on Friday afternoon, and in the evening lighting new candles, with new tapers and torches, earlier than on other days of the week; cooking on the said Fridays such food as is required for the Saturday, and on the latter eating the meat thus cooked on the Friday, as is the manner of the Jews; keeping the Jewish fasts, not touching food the whole day until nightfall, and especially the Fast of Queen Esther, and the chief fast of Cinquepur (Yom Kippur), and other Jewish fasts, laid down by their Law ... and on the said fast days asking pardon of one another in the Jewish manner, the younger ones to the elder, the latter placing their hands on the heads of the former, but without signing them with the sign of the cross ... Saying Jewish prayers ... with the face turned to the wall, moving the head backwards and forwards as the Jews do; cutting the nails and keeping, burning or burying the parings; cleaning or causing meat to be cleaned, cutting away from it all fat and grease, and

cutting away the nerve of the sinew of the leg ...
killing oxen as the Jews do, covering the blood with
cinders or with earth; giving the Jewish blessing before
eating, called the *baraha*; reciting certain words over
the cup or vase of wine, after which each person sips
a little, according to the custom of the Jews; not eating pork, hare, rabbit, strangled birds, conger-eel,
cuttle fish, nor eels or other scaleless fish, as laid down
in Jewish law ... pouring water from jars and pitchers
when someone has died ... making divinations for
children born to them, on the seventh day; not bap-
tizing them, and when they have been baptized scrap-
ing off the Chrism put on them in the sacrament of
baptism.... If they give Old Testament names to the
children, or bless them by the laying of hands; if
women do not attend church within forty days after
confinement; if the dying turn towards the wall; if
they wash a corpse with warm water; if they recite
the Psalms without adding the *Gloria Patri* at the
close; who say that the dead Law of Moses is good,
and can bring about their salvation, and perform
other rites and ceremonies of the same.

The zeal of the minions of the Inquisition was such that
the most innocent act which remotely resembled a Jewish
custom or the mere prattle of children was sufficient to subject even a genuine Christian to the horrors of the rack, the
strappado, the *aselli,* the *cordeles,* or garrotes, so that many
who "confessed" and perished were later found to have been
innocent. The victim was doomed from the moment some
inadvertent word or act of his impressed an informer or enemy
that there was ground for suspicion. R. Menasseh b. Israel
tells of a Portuguese nobleman, who, to prove the worthlessness of the Inquisitorial procedure, made an Inquisitor under
torture confess to a crime for which he condemned his physician.

Gradually the mere fact that one was a new Christian, or
a descendant of Conversos, was enough to make him an ob-

ject of suspicion and loathing, and to torture or burn him became a national sport. Mobs delighted "to shave the *Nuevos Christianos*" by setting fire to the beards of old men. It was regarded an honor to light the first faggot which was to burn the bodies but save the souls of these hopeless heretics. They also came to be spoken of as *Marranos,* a word of uncertain derivation but supposed to stand for swine, or to be a corruption of *anathema maranatha.* In some parts they were also nicknamed *Alboraycos,* probably from Al-Burak, Mohammed's charger which is claimed to have been neither horse nor steed, suggesting that they were neither Jews nor Christians. [8]

Nor was there a more amicable feeling towards the Nuevos-Christianos among those of the upper classes. As the market became, so to speak, glutted with amibitious Conversos seeking to be assimilated with the Old Christians, protests began to be heard from the haughty Hidalgos against the fusion of tainted blood (*mala sangre*) of the Jews with the pure blood (Limpieza) of the original Spaniards. Animosity to Jews became racial rather than religious. The Cortes and the clergy clamored for their exclusion from the army, from the university, and from holy orders. The Bishop of Cordova formed a Christian Brotherhood which admitted no Conversos. A research bureau was instituted by the Inquisition to investigate the pedigrees of the Conversos and ascertain who of them were "half New Christians," "quarter New Christians," or "part New Christians." The Moriscos fared no better than the Marranos, but being less "dangerous" their expulsion was delayed till the opening year of the seventeenth century. They would not even convert them. When St. Francis Xavier was about to baptize a Mohammedan child in Goa, India, (1452), the Spanish Colonists insisted that "Mussulmans were unworthy of so great a blessing."

At length the impoverished Jews, debarred from the professions, the trades, and commerce, ceased to be a financial asset, and heresy-hunting was no longer profitable. "In our days," complains an Inquisitor, "there are no more rich heretics." Then a convenient child-martyr at La Guardia effected the same result for Spain as Little Sir Hugh for England and Simon of Trent for France. After burning some fugitive Marranos, who returned to Toledo on Torquemada's promise that they would be pardoned (February 1492), Ferdinand and Isabella, realizing that "the infected limb had to be amputated to save the rest of the body," signed the decree (March 30) expelling all the Jews from their dominions within four months.

It is said that on the eve of the issuance of the evil decree, Don Isaac Abrabanel obtained an audience with their majesties and offered them a magnificent bribe. But the ever vigilant Torquemada appeared in the nick of time and, flinging a golden crucifix before them, exclaimed: "Judas sold his Master for thirty pieces of silver, now you would sell Him again for three hundred thousand ducats of silver. Here He is; take Him and sell Him."

The terrible blow of the edict staggered but did not stun the unfortunate Jews. The great majority were seized with religious frenzy and resolved to hold on to their ancient heritage at all costs. "Let us be steadfast and strong for our faith and the Torah of our God," they cried to one another. "If our enemies let us live, we shall live; if they kill us, we shall die; but we will not profane our Covenant, nor let our hearts turn back. We will go in the Name of the Lord, our God." And forth they went, carrying away with them naught but some of the stones of the cemeteries, where rested the bones of their fathers. They went, two hundred thousand or, according to some, as many as eight hundred thousand of them, to the sound of pipes and drums, on the ninth of Ab (August 2, 1492) (the day of Jewish mourning for the destruction of the first Temple by the Babylonians and the second by the Romans), from the land where they lived and had thrived for more than fifteen hundred years, and to whose prosperity they contributed in no small degree. But their misery did not end with their banishment. On one ship which some took passage for Africa the plague broke out, and the captain put them all off on a desert island to die of starvation. Many sank with the vessels, which were overloaded with the human freight, or perished in the flames which broke out on the decks. Many were robbed and beaten or ripped open to investigate whether they had swallowed their jewels. One girl was attacked before the eyes of her parents, and then the ravager cut her throat "lest she should give birth to a Jew"—a picture of the Inquisition which forced Jews to embrace Christianity and then routed them out with fire and sword for fear lest they revert to Judaism. The synagogues which they left behind were either demolished or turned into churches. Among the latter were the two magnificent sanctuaries of Toledo that were renamed El Transito and Santa Maria la Blanca. Like England and France, Spain at last was left without Jews. [9]

In Sicily, which became a dependency of the crown of Aragon in 1412, the Jews were mostly artisans and for centuries had enjoyed comparative freedom. Frederick II protected them against the crusaders and ordered that no discrimination be made between them and the other nationalities. But clouds foreboding evil began to overcast their sky in the thirteenth century. In Marsala they had to take part in the services on Christmas and St. Stephen's Day, after which they would be followed by the mob and stoned on their way home. In 1366 they were forbidden to decorate their synagogues, and ordered to tear down those which had been decorated before the law was issued. In 1369 Frederick III imposed upon them the wearing of a badge of a piece of red cloth, and in 1392 they were confined in ghettos. Under Alfonso V, they were compelled to listen on conversionist sermons, and prohibited to emigrate to the Holy Land. Then, in 1491, a rumor was spread that during a religious procession before Christmas in Castiglione a certain rabbi threw a stone through his window and broke the arm of the crucifix. The rabbi was at once killed, and Ferdinand praised the murderers for their meritorious act. On January 12, 1493, despite the appeal of the Royal Council not to deprive the Island of its skillful craftsmen, they were expelled. They were permitted to carry off only one garment, one mattress, one blanket, a pair of used sheets, and three taros for traveling expenses. At their departure, however, many Christians went up to the roof-tops at Palermo and waved them a last, fond farewell.

In Sardinia, also, the Jews enjoyed equal rights during the domination of the Romans, the Goths, and the Vandals, and when a Jewish apostate placed the images of saints in the synagogues of Cagliari, Gregory the Great himself ordered their removal. But after 1430 Jews began to be subjected to the same treatment as their brethren had received in Spain. In 1481 it was decreed that if a Jew was accused of an offense against Christianity he should have his hands cut off; and if he employed a Christian servant he, as well as the servant should receive two hundred stripes and pay a fine of two hundred ducats. Before the end of the fifteenth century, however, these barbarous laws became superfluous. For Sardinia, too, was rid of its Jews.

Not content with banishing the Jews from her own possessions, Isabella compelled the principalities of Italy to do likewise and endeavored to make Henry VIII promise not to let the Spanish refugees remain in England. She met with greatest success in neighboring Portugal, where Jews had resided for more than a thousand years and, under the Moors, had been free to practice their religion undisturbed. Even when Alfonso Henriques became the first Christian king of Portugal (1139-85), Jews still enjoyed royal protection, were entrusted with honorable and lucrative positions, and privileged to wear coats-of-arms. It is said that when St. Vincent Ferrer was about to invade Portugal to preach his gospel of hate against the Jews, King Don Joao I sent word to St. Vincent that he might enter the kingdom but on condition that he do so with a crown of glowing iron upon his head. When the King's attention was called by Rabbi Moses Navarro to the bulls of Clement VI and Boniface IX which prohibited forced conversions, he issued an order condemning the practice and had the bulls proclaimed all over Portugal.

But the Church would not long tolerate such "un-Christian" conduct, and Alfonso II died under a ban. Alfonso III was deposed because he permitted Jews to hold Moorish slaves and, worse still, he had ordered Christians to pay the debts they owed to Jews. Still, most of the kings continued their favorable attitude and employed Jews as councillors and physicians. They granted them a substantial amount of autonomy and exempted them from taking an oath *more Judaico* and from appearing at court on their Sabbaths or holidays. Alfonso V (1438-81) loved to associate with Jewish scientists; and on his death, according to Don Isaac Abravanel, "all Israel was filled with grief and mourning; the people fasted and wept." His son and successor, Joao II (1481-95), also was a patron of Jewish scientists and welcomed R. Abraham Zacuto, the refugee Professor of Astronomy at the University of Salamanca, as well as the other exiles from Spain.

But the poison of religious prejudice was spreading all the time. In 1449 the populace stormed the Judaria of Lisbon and put several of its denizens to death. Alfonso ordered that the ring-leaders be severely punished. This, however, only intensified the anti-Jewish agitation of the Cortes and the clergy. Jewish apostates, like Bonafus de la Caballaria, author of *Zelus Christi contra Judaeos et Saracenos,* also played their traditional part in fomenting hate against their former coreligionists. Joao, at last, changed his humanitarian attitude and allowed only those refugees to remain in his dominion who either by their wealth or by their craftsmanship could contribute to the success of his African campaign. The one hundred thousand who did not belong to this category were exiled and exposed to the most gruelling experiences. Women and girls were attacked in the presence of their husbands and parents by the captains and crews of the vessels in which they sailed and then thrown into the sea. Those who could not get away were sold, or given away, as slaves.

Joao's successor, Manoel the Fortunate (1495-1521), was like him at first favorably disposed towards the Jews. He not only restored liberty to the enslaved but refused to accept a gift offered him by the Jewish communities in appreciation of his favors. But the rulers of Spain objected to the Infanta's marriage unless he purged his country of Jews and heretics. He, therefore, issued an order that all Jews be banished except the young ones who were to be retained and raised as Christians at his expense.

This decree was executed on the first day of Passover, March 19, 1497, amidst most heartbreaking scenes. Many Christians took pity on their unfortunate countrymen and helped the parents conceal their children. Some Jews in their last parting embrace squeezed their little ones to death or threw them into the river and then killed themselves, so that they might die together as Jews. The remaining twenty thousand were driven like cattle to Lisbon, where they were once more offered the right to remain and to enjoy many privileges besides, if they would allow themselves to be baptized. The appeal was reinforced by two converted brothers who attained high rank as physician and churchman respectively. When all inducements failed, the Jews were dragged by their hair and beards and baptized. Only seven managed to save themselves. Chief Rabbi Simon Maimi, who resisted to the last, was buried alive up to his neck and died a lingering death seven days later.

The one avenue of escape offered the Jews who would not abandon their faith was to emigrate to the recently discovered island of Sao Thome on the western coast of Africa. To further spur on their settlement in that notoriously insalubrious spot, Joao II shipped thither seven hundred Jewish children (c. 1484) in the hope that the parents would follow, and so they did. They were joined also by many of their Spanish coreligionists who, with the permission of the Government, sent over two hundred thousand Negro slaves before them. Those who were spared from the beasts and the plagues not only reverted to Judaism but converted also their slaves and many native women whom they married. They also made proselytes at the trading stations in the interior and sent them to Fez for instruction in their new faith. When St. Francis Xavier arrived on his mission to convert the natives he was shocked to find many former Conversos and their slaves and neighbors living openly as Jews, and immediately appealed to the home Government for the establishment of the Inquisition in that part of Portugal. After some time, a branch of the Inquisition was opened at Goa (1560) and was kept busy with the prosecution of Judaizing pagans and heretical Christians till the invasion of the Dutch several centuries later. By that time, however, the Judaizers had already been suppressed. But many Negroes still retained traces of the customs and beliefs of the *Judeos*. Those belonging to this group are described by explorers as "grave and reserved, as compared with other Negroes; and wealthy, having most of the trade in their hands." [10]

The story of the Canary Islands is similar to that of Sao Thome. When the Spaniards first penetrated into the "Fortunate Islands," they found the aboriginal Guanches, a white, fair-haired and blue-eyed race, maintaining a certain form of Monotheism. With the establishment of the Spanish rule (1402), many Marranos sought refuge in that distant land, reverted to Judaism, and erected a synagogue. With them went also a number of wives and husbands of Old Christian families, who revolted against the oppression of the Church or outrightly accepted the Jewish faith. But the long arm of the Inquisition soon reached them, too. In 1504 a Holy Office was set up in Las Palmas, and auto da fes began to be held at frequent intervals, until the crypto-Jews either fled or became assimilated with the Christian population. [11]

The mass conversions in the Iberian Peninsula were the greatest victory over Judaism Christianity had known since Constantine the Great first undertook to win them over to the religion of love by violence. But the victory was only apparent. Most of the stiff-necked people remained Jews in all but name, and Christians in nothing but form. The water of baptism did not extinguish the love for Judaism which burned within them and only drove them to practice it in secret. Outwardly they submitted to the discipline of the Catholic Church, but secretly they continued to be loyal to their ancestral faith. They would baptize their children, attend mass, and go to confession, receive the Sacraments, and die in the "odor of the Church." But, as a rule, in the privacy of their homes they observed, as much as they could, all the minutiae of the Jewish ceremonials and were ever planning to flee to where

they could practice the teachings of their religion in the
open. Usually they would circumcise their male children; and
in cases where the parents failed to do so, their offspring
would submit to the rite even at an advanced age. Some of
them would abstain from meat altogether so as not to have
to eat forbidden food. Others refrained from it at least on
Sabbaths and holidays. Some ate no leavened bread throughout the year in order to have an excuse for not eating it on
the holiday of Passover. In the privacy of their homes they
would cover their heads during prayer, wash their hands
before meals, and prepare food on Friday for the Sabbath,
on which day they would rather freeze than kindle a fire. On
Sabbath eve they would light "the candle of the Lord" in
the cellar, so that it might not be seen, and on Rosh Hashanah
they would sound the Shofar in the woods or mountains
where they would not be heard by the outside world. After
baptism they would "unbaptize" themselves or their children
by washing off the holy water. They would admit no outsider
into the deathroom at the last moment, so as to give the dying
man an opportunity to disavow his Christianity, and whenever feasible they would bury the dead among their own
people, or at least in virgin soil.[12]

Children were usually warily informed of the tenets of their
faith and their racial origin when they reached the age of
thirteen, and were impressed with their duty to observe the
peculiar customs of their group and to marry only in their
own circle. This developed a sort of *Limpieza* among the New
Christians and drove some of the Conversos completely into
the Church. Raphael Cortes de Alfonso, or Cabeza-Loca (Crazy-
head) as he was nicknamed, was ostracized from his own community because he married an Old Christian. He avenged
himself by reporting to a priest that one of the Conversos was
trying to win him back to the Law of Moses (1685), and after
a trial which dragged on for three years, many were condemned to the stake or sent to the galleys.[13]

The Marranos had to be constantly on their guard against
spies and informers (*malshinim*). It should be remembered
that it was mainly owing to the betrayal by Henrique Nunes,

a New Christian, that the Inquisition was introduced into Portugal. Nunes was assassinated as a *Malshin* by two Marranos disguised as monks. But the Church pronounced him a martyr and conferred upon him the title *Firme Fe* (*Firm Faith*). [14]

In the course of time many Jewish beliefs and customs were forgotten among the Marranos, or fashioned after the manner of the Church; and the Judaism of these crypto-Jews became a sort of Free Masonry whose words, signs, and tokens were noticed, or had meaning only to the initiated. Like Masonry, too, secrecy came to be regarded as an essential element of their Judaism, so that even when, centuries later, the danger was removed, it was found hard to convince them that a Jew might practice his religion in public without being guilty of profaning it. But whatever of Judaism they retained, they clung to with all their heart and soul, and in their zeal for it they frequently dared incur the vengeance of the Church not only for professing but for propagating the religion they were believed to have abjured. The archives of the Inquisition contain many records of youths and maidens of tender age, born and baptized as Christians, who, when put to the test, preferred death for "the sanctification of the Name" of the God of Israel. Martyrdom had as little terror for these Jewish Christians in Christendom as it did for the Roman Christians among the pagans. Some even coveted it and added a new benediction for the privilege: "Blessed be Thou, O Lord our God, king of the universe, Who has sanctified us with Thy commandments, and hast bidden us to sanctify Thy Name among the many." There were some who, after fleeing to safety, would return, at the risk of being apprehended, for the sole purpose of instructing those who stayed at home in the creed and customs of Israel. Other rabbis or "theologians" went from house to house to attend to the rites which the members of the community either could not or would not perform themselves. One of them is said to have circumcised three thousand *Anusim,* young and old, during his clandestine visits to his native land. In Toledo a friar on his pastoral rounds found as many as thirty men in one house recovering from their circumcision. Especially zealous were the Marranos of Portugal, where the Inquisition outdid in brutality its older sister in Spain. When in Lisbon it was rumored that after a mass celebrated for the cessation of the pestilence, a crucifix at the altar shone brighter than usual, a Marrano explained the phenomenon as resulting from the reflection of the lights (1506). In 1539 a placard was found affixed to the Cathedral and other churches of Lisbon stating "The Messiah has not come. Jesus is not the Messiah. Christianity is a lie." Though a reward of ten thousand escudos was offered for the apprehension of the culprit, the criminal was never caught. Instead, another notice was found posted on the door of the Cathedral declaring "I am neither Spaniard nor Portuguese, but an Englishman. You will not discover my name even if you offer twenty thousand instead of ten thousand escudos." To save face, the authorities finally fixed upon a Marrano as the one who perpetrated the outrage and, having obtained his confession by torture, burned him alive.[15]

The multitudes of Marranos who managed to escape from the clutches of the Inquisition, and the many more thousands who were compelled to stay behind, constituted no less a problem to the Synagogue than they were to the Church. There were the ultra orthodox who felt, as the Novatians did toward the *Lapsi,* that despite their conversion under pressure they forfeited their status as Jews and should be regarded as apostates, since according to the Talmud one should prefer martyrdom to conversion. Most of the leading authorities, however, were of the opinion that the rabbis of the Talmud had in mind converts to paganism and refused to put in the same category converts to either Christianity, with its code of Mosaic ethics, and Mohammedanism, with its creed of the Unity. To them they preferred to apply the other dicta of the Talmud: "The Merciful One forgives him who is coerced"; and "though he has sinned, he is still to be considered a Jew." They drew a distinction between *m'shumadim,* or apostates, who to ingratiate themselves with the Church abetted and even invented most malicious libels against their former coreligionists, and the *Anusim* who were Christians by compulsion. They were careful not to reproach them for their weakness and treated them as if they had never relinquished the true faith. The precedent for this was set by R. Gershom of Mayence, "the light of the Exile," whose son died in the "odor of the Church"; and R. Abraham ibn Ezra, whose son became a Moslem. R. Solomon Izhaki (Rashi) in particular championed the cause of the forced converts of his day and pleaded that they be not alienated, since "they became Christians only through the fear of death." In answer to various inquiries he wrote:

> It is necessary to decide in favor of those who follow the Jewish law in secret and are not suspected of transgressing the religious precepts which the Christians oblige them to observe outwardly. At bottom they fear God. They weep and groan over the constraint put upon them, and implore pardon of God. But if there is a suspicion that they committed transgressions without having been forced to do so, even if they have repented with all their heart, and all their soul, and all their might, they cannot bring evidence *ex post facto* concerning facts which they witnessed before they repented . . . . Let us be careful not to take measures for isolating and thereby wounding them. Their defection was made under the menace of the sword, and they hastened to return from their wandering . . . . Even if a Jew becomes a convert voluntarily, the marriage he contracts is valid. All the more is this true in the case of those who are converted by force.[16]

A similar attitude was taken by Maimon and his still more famous son R. Moses (Maimonides). The latter, according to some, temporarily assumed the mask of Mohammedanism. In his Letter of Consolation, in which R. Maimon exhorts his coreligionists in Morocco not to let go of the Torah which is like "a rope stretched from earth to heaven" and is sure to save them from being submerged in the "sea of suffering," he appeals to them also not to be intolerant of those of their brethren who, under pressure, do not hold on to that spiritual rope with both their hands. "He who clutches it with his whole hand has doubtless more hope of ultimately saving himself than he who clings to it with but part of it; still he who holds on with the tips of his fingers has more than he who lets go of it altogether."

Equally sympathetic is Maimonides in his "Epistle Concerning Apostasy" (*Iggeret Hashmad,* or *Maamar Kiddush Hashem*). It is written in Arabic in response to a statement made by a zealot that any Jew who recites the Mohammedan creed, even if he does it by compulsion, is guilty of blasphemy and cannot be counted as a Jew,—an opinion shared by some of the Maghreb. Maimonides, though only about twenty-five years of age, felt called upon to upbraid this excessive zeal. The rabbis of the Talmud, he maintains, never excluded anyone from the synagogue who "confessed and forsook" his transgressions; nor did the Prophets deny the idolatrous Israelites the privilege of being counted members of the house of Israel. He refers to such eminent saints and sages as R. Meir and R. Eleazar who are said to have feigned paganism in times of persecution, and proceeds:

> The Talmud indeed ordains that a Jew should rather suffer martyrdom than commit the three capital sins: idolatry, unchastity, and murder. This obligation applies also to the lesser sins, if the intention of the persecutor is to make him give up his religion . . . . Every Jew is in duty bound to sanctify the name of God . . . . But he who does not possess the stuff of which martyrs are made, even in regard to committing one of the three capital sins, in order to save his life, cannot be considered an idolater,—he merely did not perform the precept concerning the Sanctification of the Name. Nay, even one who actually worshiped an idol, as long as he did it under compulsion, cannot be held liable; for how could the involuntary transgressor be put on a level with the wilful violator of his faith. . . . Besides, we must make a distinction between a transgression by mere word, and one by deed.

The present persecutions differ from those to which the Rabbis said one should rather submit to martyrdom than yield.... We are not now required to perform an idolatrous act, but only to recite a formula in which the Moslems themselves are aware we do not believe, but do it in order to please the Government.... Now, he who sacrifices himself rather than acknowledge that man (Mohammed) as God's messenger certainly performs a most meritorious deed. But if one should ask us whether he should be martyred or converted, we would advise him to convert rather than be martyred, and leave the land. This advice I give to myself, to those I love, and to all who consult me: remove from these places and go to where one may live according to his religion, and observe his Torah unhindered. Those, therefore, who are compelled to remain should not regard themselves as if they are profaning the Name of God, nor should one despise those who out of necessity must violate the Sabbath. ... If, however, they believe that they need make no preparation for a departure because of the speedy advent of the Messiah, they are sinners, for no one knows the time of his coming, nor are religious duties dependent on his coming. [17]

Other defenders of the *Anusim* in the fourteenth century were R. Simon b. Zemah Duran (*Rashbaz*) and R. Isaac b. Sheshet Barfat (*Ribash*). Both fled for safety to Algeria where the fugitives, who themselves sacrificed so much for their religion, were inclined to make no distinction between *Anusim* and *meshumadim*. Some of them even turned over the refugee Conversos from Majorca to the officers for deportation. *Ribash* pleaded against condemning all *Anusim* indiscriminately and urged that those who did not accept Christianity voluntarily be treated in all respects as Jews. *Rashbaz* would not even require "proofs" of their sincerity. His motto was the saying of the Fathers: "Judge not thy neighbor until thou art in his place." [18]

These views were accepted by the majority of the Jews in Spain and Portugal, long before the expulsion. They not only did not estrange the Marranos but welcomed them to their homes and their synagogues, and made every effort to hold them in the fold by cords of love. Of a certain pious man it is told that he would make clandestine visits to the Conversos and offer them his share in the bliss of the world to come if they would but repeat the *Shema* every day. To remove any doubt about their fitness to participate in Jewish services, they recited on the eve of the Day of Atonement, the *Kol Nidre* formula by which they were absolved of vows made under duress, and assured the less liberal of their brethren that "In the tribunal of heaven and the tribunal of earth, by the permission of God, praised be He, and the sanction of this holy congregation, we hold it permissible to unite in prayer with the *abaryanim*" (transgressors). In Italy, a special supplication was offered on the Sabbath for "Our brethren, the forced ones of Israel (*Anusim*), who are in trouble and captivity, may God have mercy upon them and pity them for the sake of His great Name, and lead them forth from oppression into freedom, and from darkness into light, and say ye Amen." [19]

Regardless, however, of the attitude of some of their more conservative co-religionists, the *Anusim* looked upon themselves as *bona fide* members of the house of Israel. Indeed, there were many who considered themselves even more loyal to the faith since they were constantly running the risk of being discovered and exposed to the vengeance of the Inquisition. Besides, they firmly believed that they were following the advice of Isaiah (26:20): "Hide thyself for a little moment, until the indignation be overpast," for they were convinced that the Messiah was already knocking at the door; in fact, that he had already been born in Constantinople and that very soon not only would they become Jews in the open, but all mankind would embrace Judaism. For this belief they found confirmation in the fall of Constantinople (1453), which indicated the speedy victory of the Unity over the Trinity, and in the discovery of America where, it was said, the Ten Tribes were already massing for the war of Gog and Magog, or Armageddon.

A strong impetus to this belief was given by the most illustrious Jew of his time, the scholar, statesman, and financier, Don Isaac Abravanel. Having failed in his supreme effort to avert the catastrophe from the Jews of Spain, the aged sage and saint set himself the task "to strengthen the feeble hands, and to uplift the stumbling feet," with the comforting assurance that "their night of darkness" was at last to end. With this aim he wrote *Mayane Hayeshua* (The Wells of Salvation), *Yeshuoth Meshiho* (the Salvation of His Anointed), and *Mashmia Yeshuah* (the Proclaimer of Salvation) (1496-8). In these, among other things he announced that the Messiah was born on the eve of the expulsion of the Jews from Spain, and that, according to the most reliable authorities, he would appear in the year 1503, restore the Jews to Palestine, rebuild the Temple, reintroduce the spirit of Prophecy, and convert the Gentiles. These booklets were widely read and helped much to maintain the morale of the despairing *Anusim*. [20]

As in former years, these Messianic expectations only added to the toll of Jewish martyrdom. In 1500 a girl of fifteen stirred up the *Anusim* by asserting that she had been taken up to heaven and shown the martyred Conversos seated on thrones of gold, proclaiming that the Messiah was already on his way. The result was that thirty-eight of those who impatiently cast off their Christian mask were sent by the Inquisition to join their martyred colleagues. A tailor, or cobbler, by the name of Luis Dias of Setubal who announced himself as the Messiah attracted a following of Old and New Christians from all over the land. He was seized but released on promise that he would retract. However, he was soon discovered with a "Master Gabriel" preaching the "Law of Moses" and making proselytes, and he and eighty-three of his disciples, Jews and Christians, were burned at the stake (Lisbon, 1542).

This Messianic craze found reverberation in distant Germany, where a certain Asher Demmlein called upon his countrymen to prepare for the Messiah who would appear in

1502, preceded by a column of fire and a column of smoke, to lead them unhindered to the Holy Land. In response, many Jews in Italy and Germany, and some Christians, too, acclaimed him a prophet, abandoned their occupations, spent their time in ceaseless prayer, and in mortification of their bodies, and gave away their possessions to the poor. The grandfather of the Chronicler David Gans smashed the oven in which he used to bake his unleavened bread for the Passover in the conviction that next year he would bake his matzos in Palestine. But when the "year of penitence," as it came to be known, passed, and the Messiah failed to materialize, some Jews accepted the Christian Messiah, while others attributed this disappointment to the insufficiency of their atonement.

The most interesting of the Marranos who laid claim to Messianism was undoubtedly Diogo Pires (1501-32), of Lisbon. In addition to an excellent secular education, he secretly received instruction also in the Bible, the Talmud, and the Kabbalah. Due to his unusual attainments he was appointed at an early age to a high position in the court of justice, and was a great favorite at Court. But his thoughts were always with the *Anusim,* and his constant yearning was for the Messiah to come and deliver them. When a certain David Reubeni arrived in Portugal and presented himself as the ambassador of the Ten Tribes to arrange for united action against the Turks, Diogo readily joined him. He had himself circumcised, assumed the name of Solomon Molko, and went about proclaiming the happy tidings that the Messiah was about to appear. His enthusiasm proved contagious, and the joy with which he was everywhere received exceeded all bounds. Molko soon began to believe that he himself was the Messiah, and in conformity with an old Jewish tradition that the Messiah would come from among the poor and sick of Rome, he journeyed to the Eternal City, dressed himself in rags, soiled his face, and for thirty days lived among the beggars by the banks of the Tiber. The fulfillment of his prophecies concerning the inundation of Rome and the earthquake of Lisbon added to his self-assurance, and his sermons in Italy drew large

crowds of Jews and Gentiles, some of whom were high dignitaries of the Church. Even Clement VII and some of his
cardinals became attracted to him. But some prominent Jews,
fearing the consequences, denounced him to the Inquisition,
and, despite the pope, he was condemned to the stake. In a
mysterious way, however—supposed by the pope's substitut-
ing another in his place—the pseudo-Messiah managed to
escape and with Reubeni, who was then in Italy, set out on
a visit to Charles V and Francis I, hoping to convert them to
Judaism. Instead, they were both carried in chains to Mantua,
where Molko's sentence to death was executed (1532). At the
stake the German Emperor offered to grant him his life if
he would recant, but Molko replied that he longed to become
"a burnt offering of sweet savor unto the Lord"; and that if
he had anything to repent of it was that he had been a Christian in his youth. Many Jews in Europe and Asia persisted in
the belief that Molko somehow escaped again, and some even
claimed to have seen him in the body eight days after his
execution. Reubeni, not being under the jurisdiction of the
Inquisition, remained in jail for three years and finally perished by poison. [21]

It must be stated that not all the Spanish and Portuguese
clergy and nobility approved the action of the Inquisition.
There were not a few who were bitterly opposed to it and
tried to protect the Jews and Marranos to the extent of their
ability. The first Inquisitor-General of Aragon was slain in
the Cathedral of Saragossa (1485). Fernando Cutinho, councilor of the supreme court and later Bishop of Silvas, insisted
that "no compulsion and persecution can make a sincere
Christian out of a single Jew." He was of the opinion that
anyone converted under duress was legally still a Jew and
should not be treated as a heretic. In the case of a Marrano who
was hailed before him on the charge that he had insulted the
Virgin, the Bishop angrily exclaimed: "The provost who
brought the action and all the witnesses ought to be tortured; for no witnesses are ever called that have not been
bribed with money or otherwise. I will have nothing to do
with the matter. I need not act the part of Pontius Pilate.

Let other, young men, pass judgment." When in 1531 Portugal was shaken by an earthquake, and the monks seized the opportunity to put the blame on those who harbored Jews and Marranos, Gil Vincente, regarded as the Portuguese Shakespeare, reminded them that they could best serve the king and the Church by preaching love and not by inciting the mob against innocent men and women.

There were also some prominent Christians who not only opposed the Inquisition but were in sympathy with its victims. These, when found trustworthy, would be invited to the *divinum mysterium,* and thus sometimes started on the road which led to heresy and even to Judaism. Pedro Fernandez of Alcaydete, treasurer of the Cathedral of Cordova, was sentenced by the Inquisition (1481) to die at the stake for frequenting the society of Marranos and other suspected heretics, for preaching to them the Law of Moses, for observing Jewish holidays and disregarding those of the Church, and for seeking comfort while in sickness or danger in the reading of the Old Testament. The Marranos' ardent faith in the speedy advent of the Messiah also lured many to join these dreamers of the better order of society. Among the zealous followers of the "Prophet of Setubal" were the popular poet Goncalo Eannes Bandara and the high Government official Gil Vaz Bugalho, neither of whom had Jewish blood in his veins, and both of whom died for "the sanctification of the Name." But the Marranos exerted a no less subtle influence on many who remained in the Church. Either because it afforded them an opportunity for study, or in order to disarm suspicion, many of the *Anusim* educated their sons for the priesthood. The result was that these men in holy orders undermined from within the foundations of the faith they were expected to protect and promulgate. Even when they did not convert others to Judaism they sowed in the heart of many the seed of Protestantism. [22]

One of the most interesting characters of this type was Diogo da Assumpção, of an ancient Christian family (1579-1603). As a young Franciscan monk he developed a fondness for the Old Testament and began to doubt the truths of the dogmas of Christianity At last he became convinced of the superiority of Judaism and planned to flee to France or England, far from the clutches of the Inquisition. He was, however, apprehended and thrown into jail. In spite of the tortures to which he was subjected for two years, he refused to listen to the exhortation of the pious priests or reveal those who shared his views. He also observed the Jewish Sabbaths and fasted, as was the habit of the *Anusim,* on Fridays. His last wish was to die in the Law of Moses "in which he lived ...and to which he looked for salvation." He was burned alive in Lisbon in the twenty-fourth year of his life. His fellow-*Anusim* formed a religious society in his honor, called "The Brotherhood of S. Diogo," and kept a light perpetually burning before the Holy Ark in his memory. His conduct was contagious, and his example was imitated by many who were before indifferent. [23]

Another martyr whom the Marranos "canonized" was Diego Lopes of Coimbra, which became a stronghold of crypto-Jews. Fixed to the stake for proclaiming himself a Jew (1580), the chains with which he was tied were said to have suddenly dropped into the flames while his body was nowhere to be seen. The clergy and the populace attributed this strange phenomenon to the machination of the devil who, they affirmed, carried him off body and soul before they were parted. To the *Anusim,* however, he became another Elijah who ascended into heaven in a chariot of fire.

At Coimbra, too, a secret society of Judaizing priests, physicians, and mathematicians was formed by Antonio Homem, whose great-grandfather was forcibly baptized in 1497 but whose mother belonged to an Old Christian family. He was a graduate in Canon Law of the University of Lisbon and was appointed a member of the faculty of the University of Coimbra, whither many *Anusim* were wont to send their sons. His reputation for learning and eloquence was nationwide, and he was one of those who were called to discuss the proposed canonization of Queen Isabella of Portugal. At the same time he was carrying on Jewish propaganda among the professors and students of the university. When the secret leaked out he was sent by the Inquisition to Lisbon, where he was condemned "as a contumacious and negative" heretic and was garroted and burned (May 5, 1624). The house in which he conducted the services was razed to the ground and on its site was erected a pillar bearing the inscription *Praeceptor Infelix*. But the *Anusim* honored him by organizing a fraternity in his memory by the name of Confraria de S. Antoni. [24]

Other distinguished martyrs were Captain Manual Fernandes Villareal and Antonio Cabicho. The former distinguished himself as one of the leading litterateurs of Portugal and was rewarded for his championship of the House of Braganza by being sent as Consul General to Paris, where he was befriended by Cardinal Richelieu. On his return to his native land it was reported that, when in France, he went with his wife to celebrate Passover at Rouen. Under torture he recanted and implicated several New Christians and his own wife. But the Inquisition would take no chances with him, and he was garroted (1652). [25]

Cast in a more heroic mold, Antonio Cabicho loudly proclaimed his adherence to the Law of Moses even while he was on his way to the pyre. As a high wind deflected the flames from his body, the populace amused themselves by pelting him during his agony with stones and sticks. With him perished his faithful clerk Manoel de Sandoval, who, proclaiming his belief in the only God, the Father, declared that he was happy to die "in the religion of my master!" [26]

Don Lope de Vera was a Spanish nobleman by birth and had no Jewish contacts. While a youth at the University of Salamanca, he took up the study of Hebrew and became sufficiently proficient as to read the Bible in the original. When he tried repeatedly to win over his brother to his changed views on religion, the latter reported him to the Inquisition. He then boldly announced his intention to become a Jew. While in jail he circumcised himself with a bone and insisted on being called Judah the Believer. He also refused to use any animal product for food or even a quill pen for writing, and his only reply to all the exhortations and threats of the Inquisitors would be *Viva la ley de Moisen* (Long live the Law of Moses). After five years of brutal floggings and all sorts of efforts to make him see the light, he was finally condemned to be burned alive. On his way to the pyre he joyously recited prayers in Hebrew, and even in the midst of the flames he was heard to chant the Psalm, "Unto Thee, O Lord, I lift up my soul." He expired (July 25, 1644) at the age of twenty-six like another R. Akiba, proclaiming his whole-souled love for the One God of Israel. [27]

These gruesome scenes were sometimes lit up with a garish light of grim humor. When Diego de Susan, father of La Hermosa Hembre, was led to the stake for his part in the plot against the Inquisition, he turned to a bystander and pointing to the halter which was fastened around his neck, one end of which was trailing in the mud, remarked: "Be so good as to lift up the end of this Tunisian scarf of mine." Various pleasantries are also recorded of Balthasar Lopez, (who had himself entered the Covenant of Abraham at Bayonne and was making propaganda for Judaism among his kinsmen. When he, together with fifty-seven other Judaizers, was being led to his execution at the Gate of Jesus (1654), the priest urged him to confess so that gates of Paradise might be opened to him freely. "Freely?" retorted Lopez, "I must have struck a bad bargain, since the confiscation of my property cost me two hundred thousand ducats." [28]

One of the many younger martyrs was Alonzo Lopez. At the age of sixteen he was apprehended at the Port of Palma by the vigilantes of the Inquisition, who were in search of Conversos suspected of escaping and reverting to Judaism. Under torture he admitted that he had been born and baptized in Madrid and then taken by his father to Oran in Africa, where both of them were circumcised. Despite the assurance of the Inquisitors that many notable rabbis now acknowledged the sonship of Jesus, Alonzo insisted that "he was a Jew, a son of Israel, and that he waited for the Jewish Messiah." After several years of fruitless endeavor, the patience of the Inquisitors was exhausted, and he was burned at the

Gate of Jesus (January 13, 1675), in the presence of more than thirty thousand spectators.

It was probably among the *Anusim* that the legend developed of a Jewish forced convert who accepted the gift of the papacy in order to do whatever possible to alleviate their persecution. Such legends were indeed not unknown before. The Talmud tells of a Jew who in times of trouble pretended to be a pagan, won the confidence of the authorities and managed to frustrate their hostile designs. A similar story was current about Simon Caiaphas, or Peter, the first Bishop of Rome. We have seen that he always championed Judaism against the antinomianism and anti-Semitism of St. Paul. It was probably to counteract this impression of the Jewishness of the Prince of Apostles that there was later produced the so-called Gospel of Peter, which is filled with fierce hatred of the Jews. But the Jews held on to the old tradition and claimed that Peter remained loyal to his faith and sought to protect his people. It is said that after the Crucifixion, Christians everywhere would attack, kill, and maim as many Jews as they could or sell them as slaves for "thirty pieces of silver." St. Peter went to Rome, assumed the papacy, and at least once a year, during the Great Assembly, he would preach on good will to Jews. While there, he had a tower built secretly on the summit of a huge rock whither he would retire as often as pontifical duties permitted, to worship the God of Israel. In this retreat he would also compose hymns which he would send by a faithful servant to his brethren in Jerusalem. Some of these hymns were incorporated in the rituals for the Sabbath and the Day of Atonement, among them the inspiring *Nishmat kol hai* (the soul of all living) and *Eten t'hilah* (I will give praise).

It was natural that the Jews of France and of the Iberian Peninsula should attribute to some of their forced converts the same motives and conduct that were attributed to St. Peter. This was believed in the case of Don Abraham, the last Rabbi of Castile. But the one who captured the popular fancy was a certain Andreas or Elhanan, supposedly the son of the famous R. Solomon b. Adret of Barcelona. As a child, it was said, he was abducted by a priest, educated in a monastery, and was later elevated to the papacy. One day, while heading a delegation to Rome, his father noticed a birthmark on his Holiness' face and burst into tears. At the Pope's insistence, R. Solomon disclosed the secret; and the monk who reared him was sent for and admitted that Andreas was not, as was believed, the child of a nobleman but of the rabbi. Thereupon the Pope renounced Christianity and, to expiate the sin of his living as a Christian, ascended a tower in the market-place, delivered a harangue against Christianity, and leaped into the flames. The Christians attributed his conduct to a mental derangement and dubbed him "the insane and heretical Pope." [29]

In the French version Andreas is said to have been the son of R. Simeon b. Isaac, "The Great," of Mayence. Though kidnapped as a young child he doubted the story of his Christian descent, and at last he forced his attendants to reveal to him the secret of his birth. When he learned the truth he convoked his cardinals, and from the top of a tower publicly denied the doctrines of Christianity, and then leaped to his death.

The most dramatic, and perhaps the most popular of the versions, is the one current among the Jews of Germany. In it, Elhanan is kidnapped by a priest while his father, R. Simeon, is attending services at the synagogue. The boy is brought up in a monastery, where he distinguishes himself as an unusual scholar and becomes a cardinal. His handsome appearance and reputation for wisdom and sanctity make him the unanimous choice for St. Peter's throne. But in the midst of his glory he cannot suppress his yearning for his father; and in order to get to see him, he advises the Bishop of Mayence to enact such drastic laws against the Jews that would cause them to send a delegation to Rome to plead their cause. As he expected, a Jewish delegation soon arrived consisting of R. Simeon and two other rabbis. The pope immediately recognizes his father, enters with him into a talmudic discussion, and invites him to a game of chess of which he was exceedingly fond. From the way the pope plays the game, R. Simeon suspects that he must have learned it from Jews, and cleverly leads him on to talk of his early life. The pontiff at last reveals that he was born a Jew and regrets that thus far he had been too weak to abandon the life of honor and luxury which he had enjoyed as a Christian. But he is determined to be a hypocrite no longer. His only fear is whether God will pardon him the sin of his past. R. Simeon assures him that God in His mercy always forgives those who return to Him in truth. Whereupon Elhanan revokes his former edicts against the Jews, and, after writing a book against Christianity which he orders every candidate for the papacy to read, clandestinely returns to Mayence and disappears among his former coreligionists.

The story of the Spanish and Portuguese Conversos, and the proselytes who from time to time joined them, constitutes indeed one of the most stirring episodes in all history. Hundreds of thousands of them had long ago become completely assimilated with their Christian neighbors, without a trace of their former Jewishness remaining; others were forced to remain an ethnic group, a sort of caste of untouchables, by the intense hatred which did not abate even after they became devout, sometimes fanatical Catholics. Yet at least fifty thousand of them grimly clung for half a millennium to the frail craft of their crypto-Judaism in the midst of the raging billows of Catholicism which overwhelmed them. Scattered in small groups in the rural districts of the Peninsula, and cut off from all contact with their coreligionists, they came to regard themselves (like the Falashas of Abyssinia, or the Tiao Kiu Kiaou of China) as the sole remnant of the seed of Abraham, and the only guardians of a sacred treasure which must be kept concealed from the eyes of the outside world, even after the Inquisition had been discontinued. Neither did the outside world, Jewish or Christian, know of them. They did not even, like the "lost" Ten Tribes, live in the myths and legends of the Jewish masses, until, in a most fortuitous manner, they happened to be "discovered," and reclaimed by the larger remnant of Israel during World War I.

In 1917 Samuel Schwarz, a Russo-Jewish engineer, while on a business trip to Belmont, in the hill country of Portugal, was warned by his contractor to avoid the company of a certain *Judeu* (Jew). On inquiry he found that the person referred to was married to an Old Christian and did not associate any longer with the Marranos. This aroused Schwarz's curiosity, and he searched out several crypto-Jews. When they heard him recite Israel's ancient watchword: "Hear, O Israel, the Lord our God, the Lord is One," the word *Adonai* (Lord) attracted their attention, and an old woman who was the leader of the group quickly covered her eyes with her hands in the traditional manner, and acknowledged him a Jew. Thus by the name wherewith God introduced Himself to Moses, this one Hebraic survival of the sacred tongue among the Marranos served to make one Jew known to his long lost fellow-Jews.

But the "enlargement and deliverance" of the *Anusim* came from one of their own, Arturo Carlos de Barros Basto, born near Oporto, in 1887. A scion of an old New Christian family, he chose the profession of a soldier, attained to the rank of captain, and was among the first to hoist the Republican flag on the town hall of Oporto (1910). He also introduced the Boy Scout movement into Portugal and became known as an author of note.

Yet all his activities could not silence within him his nostalgia for the faith of his fathers. He devoted himself to the study of Hebrew, and when the war was over he went to Tangiers and formally entered the Jewish fold. He returned to Oporto and began to urge his coreligionists to throw off their secrecy and to establish a synagogue. His efforts at last met with success, and in 1924 the Chief Rabbinate of Palestine received a letter from Lisbon in which the Marranos, after describing their condition, state: "We wish to participate openly and honestly in the lot of our people throughout the world, for we belong to it by blood, race, and spiritual life."

In response to their appeal, several Jewish organizations of England and France undertook to collect funds for the support of the institutions necessary to provide religious instruction and inspiration for old and young. Synagogues were built in Oporto and Braganca, and Jewish public worship was introduced in places where such services had meant certain torture and death for more than four hundred years. Soon a rabbi from Salonica was imported, an Instituto Teologico Israelita was founded to train their own rabbis, and Captain Barros-Basto, the "Apostle to the Marranos," started the magazine *Ha-Lapid* (The Torch) in order to reach those who live in remote places, with the result that a considerable number of Marranos,—farmers, workingmen, professionals, merchants, and soldiers—have declared themselves openly as members of the Household of Israel. It was due to a Marrano professor of the University of Madrid that Spain voted at the Council of the League of Nations (1922) in favor of the English mandate for Palestine. Reborn Spanish Jewry was also represented by a delegate to the Zionist Congress at Zurich, Switzerland (1929). Recently they even made several Christian proselytes, among them the noted Spanish singer Conchita Supervia, who was married to a prominent Anglo-Jewish merchant. The erstwhile harassed and tortured crypto-Jews who shrank from the least public notice of their Jewishness are now openly professing their Jewish religion. [30]

CHAPTER XXI

IN THE WAKE OF THE EXILES

WHILE the exiles of the Iberian Peninsula were bemoaning their banishment as the greatest calamity that had befallen them since the *Hurban,* the *Anusim,* who were compelled to stay behind, envied them the opportunity thus afforded them to go to where they could observe their religion free from the daily dread of the emissaries of the Inquisition and even in the broad light of day. They were happiest when, by bribery, they could escape and join those who were compelled to leave. But when they could not evade the law by bribery they resorted to trickery. Sometimes on the plea of a holy pilgrimage to Rome, or under the pretext of going on a permissible business trip to a place not on the restricted list, they would start out on a journey and at an auspicious moment change their itinerary and return no more. When this was impracticable, they would first ship their wives to the nearest non-Christian lands and later send on their children so that at least their household, if not themselves, might be saved to Judaism. These lands were naturally those of the Moslems. R. Obadiah di Bartinoro reports that on his visit to Cairo in 1484 he found:

> About fifty householders belonging to the *Anusim* that were in Spain. All are truly penitent. The majority of them are paupers, having left their houses and their substance and their sires and their grandsires, who observed the laws of the Gentiles, to come to take refuge under the wings of the Shekinah. [1]

By far the most fortunate were those who cast their lot among the Turks. Bajazid II welcomed them with open arms, and is said to have exclaimed: "You call Ferdinand a wise King, he who has made his country poor and enriched ours!" They were employed as court physicians, as interpreters and ambassadors, and their rabbis were granted the same privileges as the representatives of Christianity. Turkey became to the victims of medieval totalitarianism what the United States is to modern refugees, without the latter's quotas and restrictions. The *Anusim* saw in it another Promised Land, and invited their coreligionists in Christendom to come and join them. Thus Isaac Zarfati writes at the conclusion of the fifteenth century:

> Turkey is a land in which nothing is lacking. If you wish, all can go well with you. Through Turkey you can safely reach the Holy Land. Is it not better to live under Moslems than under Christians? Here you may wear the finest stuffs. Here everyone may sit under his own vine and fig-tree, while in Christendom you may not venture to dress your children in red or blue without exposing them to the danger of being beaten or flayed red. [2]

Similarly, in what has since become a classic of Portuguese literature, *Consolacam as Tribulacoēs de Israel* (1533), Samuel Usque, a fugitive from the Inquisition, describes his new home as:

> A wide and spreading sea, which our Lord opened with the wand of his mercy (as at the Exodus from Egypt), that the tide of thy present disaster, Jacob, as happened with the multitude of the Egyptians, should therein lose and exhaust itself. Here the gates of freedom and equality are ever open and shall never be closed against thee. Here thou mayest renew thy inner life, change thy condition, strip off and cast away false and erroneous doctrines, recover the ancient truths, and abandon the practices which by the violence of the nations among whom thou wast a foreigner, thou wast compelled to imitate. In this

realm thou art highly favored by the Lord, since therein He granted thee boundless liberty to begin the
complete repentance of thy sins.[3]

In response to these glowing accounts, many *Anusim*
began to flock to the lands of the Turks. Safed, Salonica, and
especially Constantinople, where Constantine the Great would
tolerate no Jews, became important Jewish centers. On their
arrival the Conversos would immediately throw off the mask
of Christianity and assume Jewish names. Many had themselves circumcised and went through the marriage ceremony
again, if they could not have had these ceremonies performed
before. Stephen Gerlach, the German chaplain at the embassy,
states that by 1574 as many as ten thousand returned to the
fold in the Turkish capital and that, according to rumor,
Selim II himself accepted the Jewish faith.

Among those who sought refuge in the Turkish empire
were some of the wealthiest and most prominent *Anusim* of
Spain and Portugal. One of them was Joao Miguez (d. 1519)
who, with his aunt Beatrice de Luna, settled in Constantinople.
Here they proclaimed themselves Jews and assumed, respectively, the names of Joseph Nasi and Gracia Mendesia. Before
long Joseph was created Duke of Naxos and Prince of the
Cyclades, and virtually ruled the empire. Through his influence and that of his aunt and mother--in-law, Suleiman the
Magnificent (1520-66) sent a strong protest to Pope Paul IV
against his treatment of Jews who were Turkish subjects, and
the Pope found it advisable to make amends. Suleiman also
quickly put a stop to the blood-accusation which was being
agitated among the Greek Christians in Amasia, Asia Minor,
by ordering that the ring-leaders should be put to death if
the victims were found innocent, and that all such cases be
tried before the Sultan himself. In addition, he presented
Joseph with a tract of land on the Sea of Tiberias, for the
establishment of a Jewish colony.

Alvaro Mendes was another Marrano who became very
prominent in Turkish politics. Created Knight of Santiago
by Joao III, he became in Constantinople one of the greatest

statesmen of his time. He was also prime mover in the alliance between England and Turkey against Spain and was made Duke of Mitylane for his services. [4]

These Marranos and their coreligionists made cultural contributions to their adopted country as teachers, translators, and publishers of books in Latin, Greek, Italian, Syriac, and Hebrew. But though many of them prospered in their new home, their love for their fatherland remained as intense after their exile as before. Spanish and Portuguese was to them almost as sacrosanct as Aramaic became to the Jews after the Babylonian captivity. They not only cultivated it as a literary language and added to it some of its choicest masterpieces, but they introduced it into the prayerbook and never exchanged it for another tongue. To this day they persist in using it as their vernacular (Ladino) and write it in Hebrew characters. Nor did they bear a grudge against those from whose wanton cruelty they suffered so long. When Sebastian of Portugal met with a crushing defeat in Africa (1578), the remnant of his forces were happy to be sold as slaves to the descendants of the Marranos, knowing that they would receive nothing but kindness at their hands. Donna Gracia, we are told "did not withhold her favor even from her enemies." [5]

It may seem strange that next to Mohammedan countries, the *Anusim* should have chosen Italy as their haven of refuge. The fact is that the land which was first to make Christianity the religion of the state was until the rise of Protestantism the most liberal country in Christendom. There the influence of Frederick II, who pronounced the dogmas of the Church as "repugnant to reason and nature," persisted long after he had been declared the Antichrist. There the pantheistic philosophy of Averroes (d. 1198), whom Petrarch described as "a mad dog barking against the Church," found ready acceptance. There also the followers of the Eternal Gospel, the Fraticilli, the Apostolici, the Beguins, and the other reform sects which took up the cudgels against the Church, thrived longer than anywhere else, and Catharism was openly professed. Matthew Paris called Milan "a home of all heretics, Paterines, Luciferians, Publicans, Albigenses, and usurers." To these may be

added the Ghibellines and not a few of the Guelphs whom
Dante placed, together with Frederick II and a cardinal, in
the Inferno far below

> Him who made
> That commentary vast, Averroes.

A remarkable light on the tolerance which prevailed in Italy
during the fourteenth century is thrown by Boccaccio (1313-
75) in his *Decameron*. His "Abraham the Jew" is a princely
merchant of Paris, a past master of the Law, and withal a very
loyal and upright man. He has an intimate friend, Jehannot
de Chevigne, who is greatly distressed at the prospect that the
soul "of so worthy and discreet and good a man should go
to perdition for default of faith," and does his utmost to persuade him to be converted. Finally, Abraham promises to be
baptized after a pilgrimage to Rome to see God's Vicar on
earth and those who are nearest to him. He then continues,
"If these appear to me such that I may, by them, as well as
by your words, apprehend that your faith is better than mine,
even as thou hast studied to show me, I will do as I have
said; and if it be not so, I will remain a Jew as I am."

Jehannot, who knows the state of Christianity in Rome, tries
to dissuade him, or to induce him to be baptized first, but
all in vain. Abraham hastens to Rome and diligently observes
the conduct of the pope, the cardinals, and other prelates.
Unfortunately, Boccaccio tells us, he finds that "all, from the
highest to the lowest, are most shamefully given to the sin
of lust ... that the interest of courtesans and catamites is of
no small avail there in obtaining any considerable thing, ...
that human, nay, Christian blood no less than things sacred,
whatsoever they might be, whether pertaining to the sacrifices or to the benefices of the Church, are sold and bought
indifferently for a price.... All this, together with much else,
which must be left unsaid, was supremely displeasing to the
Jew, who was a sober and modest man, and him seeming
he had seen enough, he decides to return to Paris."

Jehannot despairs of Abraham's conversion. To his amazement the Jew informs him that after witnessing the utter cor-

ruption, lust, covetousness, and gluttony which are in evidence everywhere in ecclesiastic Rome, he is resolved to be baptized. For, says he, God must be especially partial to Christians if he permits them to prosper in spite of all the diabolical things of which they are guilty:

> Meseemeth your chief pastor and consequently all the others endeavor with all diligence and all their wit and every art to bring to nought and banish from the world the Christian religion, whereas they should be its foundation and support. And for what I see that this whereafter they strive cometh not to pass, but that your religion continually increaseth and waxeth still brighter and more glorious, meseemeth I manifestly discern, that the Holy Spirit is verily the foundation and support thereof, as of that which is true and holy over any other. Wherefore, whereas aforetime I abode obdurate and insensible to thine exhortations and would not be persuaded to embrace thy faith, I now tell thee frankly that for nothing in the world would I forbear to become a Christian. Let us, then, to church and there have me baptized, according to the rite and ordinance of thy holy faith.

No Jewish polemist passed such scathing criticism of Christian ethics as did this eminent son of the Church. Boccaccio condemned the Christianity of his day in the very forefront of his masterpiece. Nor did he stop with his aspersion of Christian morality. In another story, Saladin seeks to entrap the Jew Melchizedek as a pretext for depriving him of his wealth. He poses to him the question: which is the true religion, Judaism, Christianity, or Mohammedanism,—expecting, of course, to hear him say Judaism. The Jew, however, does not commit himself but tells him the story of the three rings, which has been current among Jews and later adopted by Lessing in *Nathan the Wise,* implying that the best religion is the one which does most for mankind.

The tolerant spirit which pervaded Italy is also shown in the fact that there the Inquisition never took root, and its chief activities were directed solely towards political rather than religious dissenters. There were indeed tortures and burnings and banishments, but one who enjoyed the protection of an influential doge or nobleman could air his views without incurring serious danger. There the Holy Office was burned in Rome soon after the death of Paul IV, and his statue was cast into the Tiber. The universities of Padua and Mantua were seed-plots of free thought, even atheism. It became proverbial, "The better the grammarian the worse the theologian," and Lord Burley advised parents: "Suffer not young men to cross the Alps" lest they be infected by unbelief. It was in Italy that Lorenzo Valla exposed the forgeries of the letter of Abgar to Jesus, and the *Donation of Constantine* upon which were based the pretensions of the Hierarchy to temporal power, and where he challenged the correctness of the supposedly inspired Vulgate. Yet he was appointed secretary of the Curia and Canon of St. John Lateran. Pomponatius, too, in whom, it was said, "The soul of Averroes found its incarnation," was in great favor with Leo X, who excommunicated Luther. People there were not concerned with the creed as long as one said nothing against it. Their motto was: "Think with the few, speak with many." There were some, however, who did not hesitate to speak with the few, and one of them was Pico della Mirandola (1463-94).

Mirandola was one of the many Christians who believed that the *Zohar* (the great repository of Kabbalah) would ultimately lead Jews to accept the dogma of the Trinity. At the same time he sought to expunge from Christianity whatever savored of paganism and formulated nine hundred theses as a defense against all disputants. Among these were the theses that neither the cross nor any images are to be adored, that Jesus did not physically descend into hell. His *conclusiones philosophicae, cabalisticae et theologicae,* made a stir among scholars, and were promptly suppressed by Innocent III. Scenting danger, he gave up his pursuit of knowledge, destroyed his poetical works, and betook himself to write against Jews, Moslems, heretics, idolaters, and unbelievers. This, together with the influence of his friend Lorenzo the Magnificent, restored him to the favor of the Church, and he was absolved.

Others went further than Mirandola, boldly denied the divinity of Christ, and made Italy not only the cradle of the Renaissance but of the Reformation and even of Unitarianism. Of the latter was Bernardino Ochino (1487-1564), the most aggressive Unitarian of his day, who started as a monk of the order of the Observantines, became vicar-general of the Capuchins, and later joined the Protestants. He was successively expelled from Geneva, from Augsburg, from Canterbury, and from Zurich because of his denial of the dogma of the Trinity, and as the putative author of *De tribus impostoribus* (Moses, Jesus, Mohammed) which had been variously attributed to Averroes, Frederick II, Machiavelli, Boccaccio, Pomponatius, Erasmus, Servetus, and Spinoza. He finally found a refuge in Poland, only to be banished in 1564, and died in solitude and obscurity in Moravia. [6]

Laelius Socinus and his nephew Faustus Socinus, who came under the influence of Ochino, did not indeed go as far as their master. But both were champions of toleration and progress. Laelius, a student of Hebrew and Arabic, denounced "the idolatry of Rome" wherever he went. Faustus rejected the sonship and worship of Christ and emphasized the doing of the work of Christ. He also advocated the outlawry of war and the abolition of capital punishment. [7]

Italy, too, had set a precedent of kindness to Jews when they were persecuted in other Christian lands, and they felt that the nearer they were to the throne of St. Peter the safer they were from Christian attacks. When they were expelled from England, Nicholas IV pleaded for them in his *Orat mater ecclesia* (1291) and invited them to Rome. When they fled from France, Boniface IX reduced the taxes of those who lived in Rome, ordered that they be treated fairly, and protected them in the observance of their Sabbath. While in other Catholic lands Hebrew books were consigned to the flames, in Italy Hebrew printing presses were permitted to be set up soon after they were invented. Martin V (1417-31) not only forbade the forcible conversion of Jews or their minor

children and the disturbance of their services, but, like Calixtus II and Gregory IX issued a bull which read:

> Whereas the Jews are made in the image and like-
> ness of God and a portion of them one day will be
> saved; and whereas they have besought our protection
> following in the footsteps of our predecessors, we com-
> mand that they be not molested in their synagogues;
> that their laws, rights, and customs be not assailed;
> that they be not baptized by force, constrained to
> observe Christian festivals, nor to wear badges, and
> they be not hindered in their business relations with
> Christians. [8]

The same liberality was shown by several other popes and
high Churchmen. Sixtus IV (1471-84) studied Hebrew under
R. Elijah Levita, and other prominent Gentiles sat at the feet
of R. Elijah (Cretensis) Delmedigo and R. Obadiah Seforno
to acquire a knowledge of the Kabbalah. Religious discussions
were frequent and amiable. Moses b. Solomon of Salerno read
the *Moreh Nebukhim* of Maimonides to Nicolo Paglia, and
his own views of Christianity as given in his *Taanot* (Complaints) to prominent clergymen. Ercol I was so pleased with
the arguments in favor of Judaism advanced by Abraham Faris-
sol in his *Magen Abraham* (Shield of Abraham) that he urged
him to make a resume of it in Italian. In Pavia, a Jewess who
had a quarrel with her husband decided to spite him by joining the Church. After she had been fully prepared by the
priests, she was seized with remorse and refused to proceed
with the baptism. The Bishop of Pavia not only did not punish
her but pleaded with her husband to take her back, assuring
him that her behavior during her absence was so exemplary
as not to disqualify her from *even* being the wife of a *Cohen*
(a priest). [9]

The lack of prejudice against the Jews was conspicuous particularly among the learned. Jews were admitted as students to
the universities and graduated as *doctores*. Once, when a quarrel broke out among the scholars of the University of Padua,
R. Elias Delmedigo, who lectured on philosophy, was appealed

to, and his decision met with the approval of all. Jews were welcome guests in the palaces of the nobility. The Duchess of Tuscany was a great friend of Donna Benvenida, the wife of Samuel Abravanel, and was in the habit of calling her "mother." Christians also frequently went to listen to the sermons of rabbis or the chanting of the cantors. Salamoni Rossi stood in high favor at the court of Mantua where his sister was a singer, and he was the *maestri di capella* and collaborated with the cantor of the Cathedral of St. Marks in several of his religious compositions.

Strange to say, the ones who were opposed to the settlement of refugees from Spain and Portugal were themselves refugees, for fear lest the newcomers might cause the prejudice from which they had escaped to take root in their new home. Not so with the native Christians. Alexander VI welcomed them, and Paul III (1534-49) guaranteed them protection for a period of five years, which guarantee was confirmed by his successor Julius III (1552). Fra Paolo Sarpi, a leading Italian theologian, even asserted that Marranos should not be considered backsliding Christians since their conversion was effected by force. Ercole I granted the Marranos who landed at Genoa (1493) special privileges. Ercole II even allowed them to revert to their ancestral faith (1534), and the Grand Duke of Tuscany issued an order stating:

> We desire, moreover, that during the said time no Inquisition, Visitation, Denunciation or Accusal, shall be made against them or their families, even though during the time they may have lived outside our dominions in the guise of Christians, or with the name of being such.[10]

But as so often happened in the history of the Church, this liberal movement which put Italy in the vanguard of the Renaissance and the Reformation was finally crushed by the steadily growing forces of reaction which followed the rise of Protestantism. The Neapolitan Cardinal Caraffa reported to Paul III that Italy was on the verge of becoming Protestant, and that in the sack of Rome (1529) was to be seen the finger of God and His wrath on a sinful nation. Italy, he insisted, must be purged of her heretics *à la* Spain. The Spanish Inquisition was introduced in Rome (1543), and the Society of Jesus, or the Order of the Jesuits, was approved by Paul III. This new Order undertook complete charge of the education of the youth. Its members who were to act as teachers "were not . . . to teach or suffer to be taught anything contrary to the prevalent opinions of acknowledged doctors current in the schools." The Vulgate was to be the only authorized version, and the Septuagint used only in so far as it did not conflict with the Vulgate. As a further protection against any possible infiltration of unbelief, the *Index Librorum Prohibitorum* was promulgated, and the faithful were enjoined to destroy all books which did not have the imprimatur of the proper ecclesiastic authorities.

With the enthronement of Caraffa as Paul IV (1559), the Church declared herself in a state of war with the entire non-Catholic world. The Jesuits and Inquisitorial spies became busy everywhere. Unorthodox monks, priests, and laymen were thrown into jail. The liberal Cardinal Contarini died of poison. Ochino barely escaped with his life, as did Giacomo Aconzio, whose *Stratagems of Satan* was among the earliest works to be placed upon the *Index*. Giordano Bruno was burned at the stake (1600), and Galileo perished "without the shedding of blood" in one of the filthy dungeons of the Inquisition. Those who were *reputati Luterani* had to flee. Many of those who belonged to the old Waldensian communions in Calabria and Montalto were hanged, drowned, or sent to the galleys, and their women and children sold into slavery. Sixty-one printers of supposedly latitudinarian works were put under the ban, and all their publications suppressed. Forty-eight editions of the Bible were also placed upon the *Index,* among them being not only the Waldensian version of the thirteenth century, but the more correct translation of Brucioli (Venice 1530-2) based on the Hebrew and Greek. Even the editions of the Fathers, annotated by Erasmus, were destroyed, and the study of Greek and Hebrew proscribed—Greek because it was connected with paganism, and Hebrew, because it might lead to Judaism.[11]

With the declining years of Paul III, the heretofore somewhat favorable lot of the Jews began to change for the worse.
The Pope, who at the beginning of his pontificate welcomed
the Marranos into Italy, now determined to drive the Jews
into the bosom of the Church. He increased their burden of
taxation, and offered many privileges to converts. He also
granted the new Christians the property of their unconverted families, and prohibited their marrying among themselves or being buried among their former coreligionists. The
result was a steadily increasing number of apostates who displayed their zeal for their new faith by maligning the old.
Among these were two grandsons of R. Elijah Levita, one of
whom became a canon and the other a Jesuit. Not content,
however, with abandoning their faith, they denounced the
Talmud as the source of all heresies and the cause of the
Jewish refusal to accept Christianity, and precipitated the destruction of all the copies of the Talmud by order of Julius III.
(Rosh Hashanah, 1553)

The cup of Jewish misery became full to overflowing during the papacy of Paul IV. In his bull *Cum nimis absurdum*, he
re-enforced all the ancient restrictions, confined the Jews in a
ghetto, and is said to have secretly given orders to burn down
their quarters. He compelled them to work on the restoration of the walls of Rome without remuneration, and to contribute towards the maintenance of their apostates, and forbade
them to have more than one synagogue in any city. They
were also forbidden to trade with Christians except in old
clothes, to own real estate or be addressed as Signor, and, to
add to their humiliation, they had to wear a yellow hat. In
his pontificate the ancient custom was renewed of imprisoning
Jews for a certain period each year, forcibly fattening them, and
then compelling them to run naked on the first day of the
Carnival for the amusement of the stone-throwing and mud-
slinging mob. A stop to this sport was put by Clement IX (1668)
in return for an annual contribution of two hundred ducats,
which the Jews continued to pay till 1847. Under Paul IV
Sixtus Senensis, who after his conversion entered the Order
of Franciscans, was charged with heresy and sentenced to

die at the stake, but was saved by the Dominicans and sent with another apostate, Joseph Morc, to preach to the Jews of the Papal States. At his instigation twelve thousand Hebrew volumes were consigned to the flames in Cremona. The exception was made in favor of the Zohar which, it was believed, propagated the mysteries of the Trinity. Several years later, however, it, too, was put on the *Index*. [12]

Paul IV was a worthy forerunner of Pius V and Gregory XIII. The former ordered all the Jews expelled from the Papal States, except Rome and Ancona, in punishment for their propensity to "magic." The reason he gave for the exceptions was that in Rome Jews were needed to put Christians in mind of the Passion of Jesus, and that they might also become less wicked by being in the vicinity of the Holy See. In Ancona, they were permitted to stay for the less altruistic purpose of carrying on trade with the infidels. Gregory XIII, among other enactments, decreed in his *Sancta mater ecclesia* that at least one hundred Jews and fifty Jewesses above the age of twelve should attend weekly conversionist sermons, preached mostly by apostate friars or priests, either in a church or a synagogue. As the listeners did not always pay the proper attention, Innocent XI introduced the appointment of inspectors whose duty it was to maintain the interest of the congregation by striking the inattentive ones upon their fingers with a long pole. [13]

How Christians and Jews looked upon the forced attendance on Holy-Cross Day is admirably depicted by Robert Browning, whose insight into the Jewish soul was hardly surpassed by George Eliot. He first gives us an excerpt from a diary kept by the Bishop's secretary in 1600:

> Now was come about Holy-Cross Day, and now must my lord preach his first sermon to the Jews: as it was of old cared for in the merciful bowels of the Church, that, so to speak, a crumb at least from her conspicuous table here in Rome should be, though but once yearly, cast to the famishing dogs, under-trampled and bespitten-upon beneath the feet of the guests. And a

moving sight in truth, this, of so many of the besotted blind restive and ready-to-perish Hebrews! How maternally brought—nay, for He saith "Compel them to come in," haled as it were, by the head and hair, and against their obstinate hearts, to partake of the heavenly grace. What awakening, what striving with tears, what working of a yeasty conscience! Nor was my lord wanting to himself on so apt an occasion; witness the abundance of conversions which did incontinently reward him: though not to my lord be altogether the glory.

As against this, Browning depicts what was going on in the mind of the Jews thus driven to church:

Bow, wow, wow—a bone for the dog!
I liken his Grace to an acorned hog . . .
Aaron's asleep—shove hip to haunch,
Or somebody deal him a dig in the paunch! . . .
See to our converts—you doomed black dozen—
No stealing away—nor cog nor cozen!
You five that were thieves deserve it fairly;
You seven that beggars will live less sparely . . .
Give your first groan—compunction's at work;
And soft! from a Jew you mount to a Turk.
Lo, Micah,—the selfsame beard on chin
He was four times already converted in! . . .
Groan all together now, whee-hee-hee!
It's a-work, it's a-work, ah, woe is me!
It began, when a herd of us, picked and placed,
Were spurred through the Corso, stripped to the waist;
Jew brutes, with sweat and blood well spent
To usher in worthily Christian Lent,
It grew when the hangman entered our bounds,
Yelled, pricked us out to his church like hounds;
It got to a pitch, when the hand indeed
Which gutted my purse would throttle my creed:
And it overflows, when, to even the odd,
Men I helped to their sins help me to their God.

But while the Bishop is gratified with his success to "soften their obstinate hearts, to partake of the heavenly grace," the Jews employ the tedious hours by repeating under their breath "Ben Ezra's Song of Death" with its comforting assurance:

> The Lord will have mercy on Jacob yet,
> And again in his border see Israel set.
> When Judah beholds Jerusalem,
> The stranger-seed shall be joined to them;
> To Jacob's house shall the Gentiles cleave.
> So the Prophet saith and his sons believe.

The worst sufferers from the Reaction were the Marranos who on their arrival in Italy hastily threw off the Christian mask, and stayed to rest or to recoup their fortunes before continuing their journey to places under the domination of the Turks. Paul IV and his successors treated the letters of protection granted them by Paul III as scraps of paper. Lists of those who reverted to Judaism were collected at the Holy Office for proceedings to be taken against them. Those who repented and professed the Catholic faith were sentenced to be deprived of their estates and deported to Malta. Those who remained steadfast to the end were extradited to the country of their origin or burned on the Campo dei Fiori, made famous by the execution of Giordano Bruno.[14]

Among the victims of the reactionary policy pursued by Gregory VIII were the Neofiti. They had been known as crypto-Jews, yet lived unmolested in Apulia ever since the forced conversion of their ancestors toward the end of the thirteenth century. But in 1572 those who did not cease Judaizing were burned in Rome or saved themselves by fleeing to the Balkans.[15]

The martyrdom which caused the profoundest grief among the Jews of Italy was that of Gabriel Henriques, alias Joseph Saralbo. A native of Serpa and a goldsmith by trade, he settled in Ferrara about 1548 and devoted himself to reclaiming his fellow-Marranos to Judaism. With this object in view, he mastered the art of circumcision, and the number of those whom he initiated in the Covenant of Abraham is variously estimated between eight hundred and three thousand. At last he was caught with seventeen others, and after more than a year of confinement, during which the Holy Office at the Santa Maria Sopra Minerva repeatedly offered him not only his life but certain favors if he would recant, he was conducted to the Campo dei Fiori to be burned alive for being "obstinate and pertinacious in his shameful opinion of Judaism." He remained steadfast to the end and urged his brethren in the faith not to mourn for him, since he was going gladly to meet immortality. With him also perished Diego Lopez, another "wretch" who, being a Christian, had himself circumcised and followed Judaism. He, however, was mercifully hanged first and then burned.

For many years Saralbo's memory was cherished by his coreligionists as that of a saint, and Hebrew poets vied with one another in composing elegies in his honor. These elegies contain no reference to Christianity or the Church, but from between their lines is an audible, piercing, sorrowful refrain:

> Though quenched be the fire, from weeping I will not
> tire,
> That thus to the knife is put the dove's life![16]

The vigilance of the Church extended not only to those who had been baptized by a priest with at least a show of consent but to all upon whom the sacrament was thrust. Any superstitious nurse or drunken rascal who sprinkled a few drops of water on the head of a child or unwary adult at home, on the street, or in the synagogue, was declared to have complied with the requirement of the inviolable sacrament. Even the mere wish of a relative, no matter how remote, was sufficient to make one liable to be held as a convert, and it was not unusual for children to be torn from the bosom of their parents and carried away to the Casa to be brought up as Christians. This continued till the latter part of the nineteenth century, and the Church is said to have thus netted more than two thousand Jewish souls in Rome alone. Once, in a friendly conversation with a Dominican, a Jew jokingly remarked that he would not mind his children being baptized if the pope were to act as their godfather. To his astonishment he was soon called up to make good his declaration. The Jews courageously protected their children but their "revolt" was easily crushed, and His Holiness Urban VIII led the Jew's boy of seven and another child in a magnificent procession to the baptismal font.

A similar episode, with the same result, took place as late as the middle of the nineteenth century and created a sensation in Europe and America. A servant-girl, in the employ of the Mortara family in Bologna, informed a priest that four years previously, when little Edgar was very ill, she had secretly baptized him so as to save his soul if he should die. The priest reported the matter to Rome, and the Inquisition issued orders that the child be taken from his parents and raised as a Christian. On June 23, 1858, at ten o'clock at night, Mortara's house was invaded by papal soldiers who demanded the six-year-old boy. The parents tried to prove that the child had never been seriously ill and that the nurse acted out of spite. The Governments of Austria, France and Germany interceded in their behalf, but to no avail. Edgar was brought up a Catholic, became an Augustine monk, and adopted the name Pius in honor of Pius IX. It is believed that the Mortara incident contributed in a measure to the downfall of the Papal States and that Pius IX had this in mind when he told the young priest in 1867: "I have bought thee, my son, for the Church at a very high price."[17]

The Jews, with the courage of despair, sometimes fought bravely in defense of their homes and altars, but, as we might expect, they always were made to pay dearly for their temerity. In 1558 the apostate Joseph (Philip) Moro who, with Sixtus, instigated the burning of the Talmud, forced his way into the synagogue of Recanati on the Day of Atonement and set up a crucifix on the Ark of the Law. The crucifix was immediately removed, and the apostate had to leave. But the whole city was stirred up, and a massacre was averted only by the intervention of the mayor who had two of the principal members of the community flogged in order to placate the ire of the people. Another similar "revolt" was crushed in like manner in Rome in 1639.

In spite of this, Marranos continued to relapse into Judaism on their arrival in Italy. Spanish and Portuguese visitors continued to find many whom they knew as monks and priests in their native lands now wearing the Jewish badge in the ghettos of Rome and Venice. In 1574 the Inquisitional Tribunal of Lisbon secured, through a New Christian, the names of thirty householders who were living openly as Jews in Ferrara. A century after the Spanish expulsion, Livorno, or Leghorn, became a veritable "little Jerusalem."[18]

These *Anusim* were not content with merely practicing Judaism; they were inflamed with a passion to reclaim to the faith of their fathers those who were too timid to appear as Jews in public and to defend Judaism against Christianity. One of the most outstanding of them was Filotheo Elijah Montalto (d. 1616), a native of Portugal who first settled in Leghorn and later moved to Venice. Distinguished as a physician, he was offered the post of Professor at the University of Padua. He preferred, however, to accept the invitation of Maria de Medici, who exempted him from any service on Saturday, and was appointed Councilor. Besides being an author of various works on medicine and science, which earned him a reputation among the greatest of his time, he composed a treatise on the Fifty-third chapter of Isaiah, the main Christian biblical support for the Messiahship of Jesus, published several polemics against Christianity, and carried on an extensive correspondence with Marranos on the matter of their return to Judaism.[19]

To Montalto may be given credit for the conversion of the young poet Paul de Pina, of Lisbon. Bent on becoming a monk, he left for Italy (1599) with, as he believed, a letter of introduction to Montalto from a relative, Diego Lopez Lobato, the physician of the Court of France. The letter read: "Our cousin Paul de Pina is going to Rome to become a monk. Your grace will do me the favor to put him on the right road." At the solicitation of Montalto, de Pina consented to postpone his trip to Rome and to go, instead, to Brazil. Thence he returned to Portugal, still as a conforming Christian. But the martyrdom of Diogo da Assumpçao,. which occurred about that time, decided for him, as it decided for several others, to embrace the cause for which the former gave his life. De Pina hastened to Amsterdam (1604), embraced Judaism under the name of Reul Jessurun, and became a prominent member of the Jewish community. With him was converted also Diego Gomez, who adopted the name of Abraham Cohen. De Pina's family later intermarried with English nobility, and among its members was Erskine Childers, the Irish patriot who was executed for the share he took in the Irish Rebellion of 1922.[20]

Among other zealous missionaries of, and to, the *Anusim* of Italy, suffice it here to mention Immanual Aboab, of Portuguese birth, who settled in Venice, one of the prominent Jewish polemists of his time, whose *Nomologia* (1625) was held in high regard; Abraham Curiel of Venice, a captain of three vessels, who settled in Safed, and spent the last years of his life in poverty and in the study of the Torah; Jacob Curiel, of Pisa, the charge d'affaires of the king of Portugal, who devoted himself to settling the difficulties between the Sefardic and Ashkenazic congregations in the city of his adoption. Rodrigo Mendes da Silva, Privy Council to the king of Spain and acclaimed as "the Spanish Livy" for his numerous historical works, left for Venice where, at the age of seventy he was circumcised and assumed the name of Jacob. Unlike other Marranos, he continued to raise his hat at the mention of the names of Jesus and Mary and would kiss the robe of any priest with whom he happened to speak, even after he proclaimed himself a Jew.

Besides the reversion of the *Anusim* to their ancestral faith, there were not lacking among Italian Christians those who leaned to the religion of Israel. In 1546 it was discovered that a group of over forty learned. men were wont to meet clandestinely at Vicenze and to propagate their Unitarian principles. About 1550 a secret conference of delegates from forty communities declared its belief that "Jesus was not God, but man;

born of Joseph and Mary, but endowed with divine powers."
Since burning was for the time being prohibited, each of these
heretics who was caught was weighted down with a stone and
cast into the Tiber. Those who managed to escape joined or
established Unitarian congregations in Geneva, Poland, and
Transylvania.[21]

As in other lands, so in Italy persecutions only helped to fan
the flame of heresy. Perugino, who started out as a sincerely
religious painter, became a sceptic after the martyrdom of Sa-
vonarola. Among the seventy-eight victims who, in the century
following, expiated their heresies at the stake, there were
people of all shades of opinion and of all classes of society,—
friars and professors, peasants, and noblemen. But thousands
more who were equally guilty avoided the vengeance of the
Church by keeping their convictions to themselves or con-
fiding them only to most intimate friends. David Nasi, the
brother of Don Joseph Nasi, tells in the introduction to his
Hodaat Baal Din (the Admission of the Prosecutor) that the
Duke Francisco Bentivoglio, whose hospitality he enjoyed, frequently confessed to him his doubts of the truths of Christianity
and delighted in having him read from the works of the Jewish
polemists with whom the Duke seemed to be in entire agreement.[22]

There were, however, some who made no secret of their
convictions regardless of the consequences. At the height of
the Catholic Reaction, Cornelia da Montalcino, a Franciscan
Friar of Rome noted for his learning, adopted the religion of
Israel and bravely met his fate at the Campo dei Fiori (September 4, 1557). In the early Records of the Society for Dow-
ering Brides of the Spanish and Portuguese Community at
Venice, reference is made to the daughter of a Marrano burned
in Rome "for the sanctification of the Name," and to a certain
Esther, "daughter of Abraham our father." Similar instances
are reported in the centuries that followed. Among those of
the nineteenth century is that of a young Italian physician who
served as counsel for the Venetian Republic, at Jerusalem,
and was a member of many scientific institutions. On the

eighth of Nissan 5651 (1891) he applied for circumcision at the
General Bikkur Holim Hospital in Jerusalem. Assuming the
name of Abraham Pinto, he settled in Jaffa and devoted himself to attending to his many patients, without pay. His sister
also became a Jewess and married a Sefardic Jew in Egypt.[23]

CHAPTER XXII

THE AFTERMATH OF THE RENAISSANCE

THERE was really nothing essentially new in the religious upheaval which came to be known as the Protestant Reformation. All its teachings had been preached and fought for before. But till the sixteenth century they were limited to small groups which were easily suppressed by the powerful machinery of the Church. The Renaissance made conditions more favorable for their acceptance among the wide masses and their rulers. It developed a rugged individualism and a national consciousness unknown before. The printing press made possible the free circulation of books among many who would otherwise have depended upon the *ipse dixit* of the priests. More effective still was the discovery by the Humanists that some of the doctrines which the Church had maintained, based on the Bible and the Fathers, were the result of a misinterpretation of the sacred sources.[1]

At first, however, the Reformation limited itself to the removal of what it considered the most glaring abuses of the Church. It abolished celibacy and confession, pilgrimages, penances, the worship of relics and saints, and some fasts and feasts. It did not touch the dogma of the Trinity nor the doctrine that salvation can be had only through the acceptance of Christ. Nor did Protestantism prove any more tolerant or enlightened than the Catholicism whose persecutions it condemned. If the rivers of blood which the older religion shed are longer and wider than those of the latter, it is because the latter's history is shorter and humanizing influences in Protestant lands were stronger. It was felt that

> The Spanish Inquisition
> Will not do in our days,
> You will have to be content
> To torture non-believers in other ways.

But Protestants, too, in whatever country they won ascendancy hounded not only Catholics and Jews but those who differed in some minor details from themselves. Whatever else they rejected, they retained the very principle which made the name of Church from which they broke away odious, viz., that is the right and duty of the Hierarchy to coerce the dissenter into its fold even at the price of his liberty, property, and life. According to Lecky, wherever the Protestants attained to power

> ... they immediately established a religious tyranny as absolute as that which they had subverted ... it may, I believe, be truly said that there were more instances of partial toleration being advocated by Roman Catholics than by orthodox Protestants.... It may, I believe, be safely affirmed that there was no example of the consistent advocacy or practice of toleration in the sixteenth century that was not virulently generally denounced by all sections of the clergy, and scarcely any till the middle of the seventeenth century.[2]

For the first, large-scale effect of the Reformation we have to go to Switzerland. This country, which was the first democratic state in Europe, became, already in the fourteenth century, a center of the mystic or pietistic movement which looked upon the Church practices as of little importance. It was there that the Society of *Gottesfreunde* (Friends of God) found its most active propagandist in Nicolas of Basel. It was there that Erasmus secured a printer for his Greek New Testament, and Coverdale for his English Bible. It was there also that the labors of the Humanists were turned into the channel of religion, and the first mass renunciation of allegiance to the Holy See of Rome took place.

One of the main factors in the revolt against the Church was a political one. Toward the end of the fifteenth century the hardy mountaineers of the Swiss Confederation acquired a reputation as the best soldiers in Europe, and agents of the popes and the kings at war were vying with one another to secure their services. Serving in war proved highly remunerative to the soldiers and those who hired them out, and most of the Swiss fighting-men became mercenaries. As soldiers in the papal armies, they lost much of their respect for the papacy, while the pope, finding their services necessary, did nothing to suppress any symptoms of an incipient revolt.

These inarticulate masses found their champion in Ulrich Zwingli of Zurich (1484-1531), an admirer of Pico della Mirandola and Desiderius Erasmus, and a student of Hebrew. His admiration for the language grew with the progress he made. Again and again in his commentary on the Bible he speaks of the beauty of that tongue and the necessity for mastering it in order to understand not only the Old but also the New Testament. Unlike Luther, who found Hebrew distasteful and corrupt, Zwingli declares:

> After I had begun not merely to understand Hebrew but to cherish it, I found the Holy Tongue beyond all belief cultivated, graceful, and dignified. . . . Indeed I may dare say that if one conceives its dignity and grace, no other language expresses so much with so few words and such powerful expressions; no language is so rich in many-sided and meaningful forms of expressions and modes of imagery. For no language so delights and quickens the human heart as this, which abounds in beautiful adornment of figures and symbols.

He blames much of the error in the Creed of the Catholics and Protestants on a misunderstanding of the Hebrew Bible and the "Hebraism" in the Gospels, for "the writers of the

New Testament were Hebrews, and they transferred the peculiarities of their mother-tongue into the Greek." Furthermore:

> The ignorance of Hebrew forms of expression has led to an erroneous interpretation of many passages of Scripture. . . . Hence . . . dissension, impudent declamations upon things which one does not at all understand, and violent invectives against the opponent. For the words being understood according to the rudiments of grammar but the thoughts not being at all comprehended, the interpreter . . . gives way to assumptions, and the fabrication of foolish allegories, while he ought to have turned his attention to the investigation of antiquity, and made himself thoroughly conversant with the customs and modes of thinking of each particular age in which the authors may have lived and written.

His study of Greek and Hebrew, in order "to learn the teachings of Christ from the original sources," convinced him that the Vulgate, which the Church held as inspired, contains many errors, and that St. Jerome "twists the Gospel in regard to invocation or intercession of the saints, as he does often in other places." On the other hand, the Septuagint, the version which Luther pronounced as "extremely poor even though liberal," Zwingli held in high esteem and refers to it quite often in his commentaries on the Old Testament. He also consulted the interpretations of the Rabbis. The result of his labors he embodied in his translation of the Bible into Swiss-German which appeared in 1530, four years before Luther's version, and was used by Coverdale in his first rendition of the Bible into English.[3]

Equipped with a thorough knowledge of the original source Zwingli, as soon as he settled in Zurich, began to attack as unbiblical the prevalent customs and practices of the Church, the adoration of saints and relics, and the celibacy of the clergy. He showed that the Jewish feasts and dietary laws were trifling when compared with the forty days' fasts of

Lent and abstention from meat on Fridays "and the enforced leisure of feast days" of the Catholics. His anger was especially aroused by the appearance of an indulgence seller who came to town to push his trade, and he succeeded in persuading the Council to order him to leave. As a former chaplain in the mercenary armies, he denounced the practice of hiring out young men as soldiers and cried, "No wonder that the cardinals at Rome wear red hats. Wring them and out will pour the blood of our citizens."

Zwingli called upon the Council to act as umpire in a discussion of sixty-seven theses, among them that unbaptized infants are not in danger of damnation and that the bread and wine of the Eucharist are to be regarded merely as symbols of Christ's body and blood. The people refused even to discuss them, and the canton of Zurich betook itself to carry out the work of Reformation. The churches were denuded of their pictures and images. Their walls were whitewashed, the relics removed and buried. The bishop was deposed, and the wealth of the monasteries was turned over to schools. The services were simplified, and the Lord's Supper was solemnized four times a year, merely in memory of Christ. In 1524 Zwingli publicly celebrated his marriage in the Cathedral and thus completed his rupture with the Church. In 1525 the last Catholic mass was observed in Zurich.

With the exception of Socinus, Zwingli was the only one of his contemporaries who condemned the execution of Servetus. He showed his reverence for the Prophets by calling his theological seminary the "Prophecy," and he defended the Old Testament against those who regarded it as inferior to the New. "Christ," he would say, "submitted himself and his teaching to it, and the Apostles used no other Scripture, indeed they could not, since until after the beginning of their preaching there was no Scripture as yet other than that drawn from the Old Testament." Nor was he prejudiced against even the pagans. Writing on Pindar he remarks, "May God grant that we learn from the heathen poet to understand the truth promulgated by the Hebrews, and to set her gracefully before the minds of men." Shortly before his death he expressed his belief that in the future assembly of all the virtuous, Abel, Enoch, Abraham, Isaac and Jacob will mingle with Socrates, Aristides, and Antigonus, with Numa, Camillus, the Scipios, and the Catos, and every good and holy man who has ever lived— a thought which the Rabbis uttered more than a thousand years before when they said, "The righteous of the nations of the world have a share in the future life."[4]

The example of Zurich was followed by Berne, where, after a heated debate, the town council resolved to accept Zwinglianism, and soon also by Basel where the way was prepared by John Oecolampadius, a distinguished Greek and Hebrew scholar, and a former follower of Luther. Other cantons fell into line, and Zwingli was sanguine enough to hope that "within three years Italy, Spain, and Germany will take our view." These successes alarmed the five "Forest Cantons" which remained loyal to the old faith, and when a Zuricher was caught preaching the Word of God within one of them, they promptly burned him at the stake. This was a signal for war (1529), and in the civil strife which ensued Zwingli, who served as a chaplain, fell on the battlefield. The victorious Catholics avenged themselves on the Reformer by having his body quartered and burned with dung, on the place where now stands a big boulder with the inscription:

'They may kill the body but not the soul':
So spoke on this spot Ulrich Zwingli, who
for truth and the freedom of the Christian
church died a hero's death, October 11, 1531.[5]

For Zwingli the Old Testament served not only as the authority in matters pertaining to religion but also in those of government; and like the Puritans, he founded a theocracy like that set up by Moses in the Pentateuch. There were, however, many in his party who did not think he went far enough. They questioned the authority of the town council to decide on debated subjects and insisted on the literal interpretation of the Bible. The most radical among them were the Anabaptists, who in imitation of Jonah went through the streets with portentous uproar, crying: "Woe! Woe! Woe! to

Zurich!" and warned that there "can be no full satisfaction through Christ." They were mostly poor and untutored people but had among their leaders ex-priests and ex-monks and excellent Hebrew scholars, such as Felix Manz, Hans Denk, and Ludwig Haetzer, and George Blaurock, called on account of his eloquence, "the second Paul."

Zwingli did not try to suppress them, but as was his wont, he called for a public debate before the town council. The main discussion centered about infant baptism, which the Anabaptists singled out as their main objection. The town council decided that children must be baptized as heretofore and that parents who did not perform this rite should be punished. But the radicals refused to obey and organized themselves into a separate sect. Finding that neither fines nor imprisonment had any effect, the council imposed upon the culprits the penalty of death by drowning. Accordingly, Manz was thrown into the Limmat, and Blaurock, who was not a citizen of the Canton, was scourged and banished, then was caught by the Catholic authorities, and burned at the stake in the Tyrol. Another who was banished and met with the same fate was Ludwig Haetzer. A student of the Bible, which he read in the original Hebrew, he wrote various tracts to propagate his views in Latin and German, with the motto, "O God, set free the prisoners." He also wrote a pamphlet on the conversion of the Jews and, in collaboration with Hans Denk, translated the Prophets into German five years before Luther (1528). Soon after his banishment from Basel he was seized at Constance and beheaded. He is acclaimed by the Unitarians as their proto-martyr.

Liberal though Zwingli was when compared with the other Reformers, he was no less prejudiced against the Jews than they were. He was careful to disclaim any Jewish influence. To him, too, the only salvation for the Jews lay in their conversion to Christianity. Hence Zwinglian Switzerland, like the Calvinist cantons, continued the Catholic tradition concerning the Jews late into the nineteenth century. Intermarriages were forbidden, their families were restricted, and the poor were not allowed to marry at all. They were driven out repeatedly from Berne, Zurich, and Basel, and in 1622 were expelled "forever" from the Confederation, only to be recalled when they were found indispensable to the economy of the country. But in the eighteenth century, protests began to be heard, here and there, against the disabilities of the Jews; and when Johann Heinrich Pestalozzi was urged to grasp the opportunity of converting the destitute Jewish children who were among those on whom he tried out his educational theories, the famous educator replied:

> I must disagree with you, my dear Heinrich, when you are so inconsiderate as to ask that I convert to Christianity these poor Jewish orphans. In this you are lacking insight. In matters of one's belief, neither compulsion nor force should be used. For centuries Christianity has been taught. Still, what contradictions there are when it comes to apply principles of Christianity to Jews! For, Christianity sinks low and loses its purity and greatness whenever it is face to face with Jew-hatred. The only good I desire to inculcate is true love of man, and if you want to help me you must rid yourself of that basest of all feelings—hatred of the Jew.

Such voices began to be heard more and more frequently with the progress of the nineteenth century. But it required the refusal of France, Holland, and the United States to conclude commercial treaties with Switzerland to cause the *Bundesrath* to abolish all restrictions against Jews, and to finally declare in the Constitution: "No one . . . shall be punished in any way whatever for his religious views. . . . The exercise of civil or political rights shall not be abridged by any conditions or provisions of a confessional or religious nature."

With the death of Zwingli, the progress of Zwinglianism came to a halt and has remained stationary ever since. But a more popular, though a less liberal, leader of the Reformed Church was soon to arise in the French-speaking cantons, one who hailed from France, John Calvin.

France, "the first daughter of the Church" and the first
to organize the Crusades, was in fact less submissive than the
other Catholic countries, and it was because she proved such
an *enfante terrible* that Mother Rome found it necessary to
subject her to the discipline of the Inquisition long before
she introduced it into Spain, Portugal, and Italy. But her spirit
of revolt remained indomitable. It manifested itself in the
"Babylonian Captivity" and the Schism which gave her a
pope of her own, and was expressed in the Pragmatic Sanction of Bourges, the Magna Carta of the liberties of the
Gallican Church. It it said that Pope Julius was so enraged
at Louis XII for insisting on the ancient rights of the
Church of France, that shortly before his death he was about
to fulminate a bull depriving him of his title of "Very Christian King" and transferring it to Henry VIII of England.

True, the Crusades, the Inquisition, and the wars which
followed sapped her mental and moral vitality, and by the
fifteenth century France found herself no better than most
other states in Christendom.   Excessive cruelty was meted
out for the most trivial offenses, especially for the crimes of
heresy and blasphemy. Superstitions of the basest sort obtained
credence both among the populace and the higher classes.
The belief in magic and witchcraft was rampant; relics of all
kinds were worshiped. The knife wherewith, it was claimed,
a Jew stabbed a consecrated wafer, was adored, according to
a doctor of the Sorbonne, more than the precious body of
Jesus Christ himself. The study of the Bible in this period
was neglected, and even among the learned the writings of
the Fathers usurped the place of the Prophets and the Apostles.
Robert Etienne tells of doctors of the Sorbonne who were
totally ignorant of the Holy Scriptures. He quotes one of
them as saying: "I am amazed that these young people keep
bringing up the New Testament to us. I was more than
fifty years old before I knew anything about the New Testament."

However, unlike in Italy, once the Renaissance seized hold
of the French it did not stop with the rebirth of the arts and
letters. After a few centuries of subterranean influences, the

ghosts of the Cathari and Albigenses began to stir with new life. Independent thinking began to reassert itself. People began to scrutinize the Church and to pass judgment on the clergy. An entry in the Diary of Louise de Savoy shows the trend of the time even in circles which are usually conservative:

> In the year 1522, in December, my son and I, by the grace of the Holy Ghost, began to understand the hypocrites, white, black, gray, smoky and of all colors; from whom may God, by His clemency and infinite goodness, be pleased to preserve and defend us. For, if Jesus Christ be not a liar, there is no more dangerous generation in all human kind.[6]

Of Louise's children, Francis I, a munificent patron of the New Learning, surrounded himself with artists and scientists and scholars irrespective of their religious opinions. He founded the College de France and invited R. Elias Levita to occupy the chair in Hebrew. He permitted a Hebrew printing press to be established in Paris and ordered a Latin translation of Maimonides' *Guide of the Perplexed,* the original of which had been burned by the Dominicans three centuries earlier. Like her royal brother, Marguerite of Navarre was unintimidated by priests and monks, and bravely protected those whom they suspected of heresy.[7]

The first fruit of the French Reformation was the Pagninus Bible (Lyons, 1528), the result of twenty-five years of labor by a Dominican friar; and the version of Jacques Lefevre d'Etaples (1530). Lefevre also asserted that the doctrine of Transubstantiation was un-biblical, and that, contrary to the teachings of the Church, the "Three Marys" were not identical. For this he was condemned by the doctors of the Sorbonne. But he had friends in high places, among them Bishop Briconnet, who is said to have exhorted his friends: "Even should I, your Bishop, change my speech and teachings, beware that you change not with me." With his encouragement and assured of the protection of royalty, Lefevre applied himself assiduously to the translation of the Bible into French, which became the basis for all subsequent versions in that language.

The success of this effort surpassed the expectations of the bishop and his protege. Everywhere copies of it were eagerly bought and read. Some priests read from it to their flocks on Sundays and feast-days. In obscure hamlets and many out-of-the-way places, those who were not illiterate pored over the installments of the Scriptures as they appeared fresh from the printing press and waited impatiently for the other parts to follow. As a result, people who until then accepted their religion almost exclusively on the dicta of the priests began to discuss the correctness of the teachings of their faith.

The Gallican Church at first made no attempt to stop the movement. The abbots, curates, and monks of sixteenth century France were little concerned about the beliefs of their flocks so long as they repeated the creed and observed the ceremonies. Jean Desperiers, author of *Cymbalum Mundi,* a satire on Christianity, and Pierre Gringoire, who ridiculed the pope and the clergy, were allowed to die a natural death despite the raillery of their heresy. Francois Rabelais, a Franciscan and later a Benedictine monk, and still later a fully ordained priest was not degraded because of his defamatory *Pantagruel* and his veiled advocacy of Unitarianism. Men like Jean Bodin (1530-96) and Michel Montaigne (1532-92), who, by the way, were partly of Jewish descent, ventured to advocate freedom of conscience and speak in praise of Judaism, yet enjoyed royal and ecclesiastic favors. Bodin revered the Old Testament so highly that many questioned whether he believed in the New. In his symposium *Heptaplomeres,* which greatly influenced Milton, Grotius, Leibnitz, and other savants of the centuries following,—men of different faiths assemble in the home of a devout Catholic merchant in Venice to discuss various religious and political problems; but most of the burden of the controversy falls upon Diego Toralba, the philosopher, and Solomon bar Cassus, the Jew. The latter, through whom Bodin was seemingly giving utterance to his own ideas, is a man of unimpeachable purity of character, capable of great sacrifices for the weal of his fellow-men, and endowed with a sublime tolerance for the religions of all mankind. Montaigne, a still more powerful intellect than Bodin, does not hesitate to complain: "Our religion (Catholicism) is made to extirpate vices; it protects, nourishes, and incites them"; and "There is no enmity so extreme as the Christian." He also points to the futility of religious persecution, as illustrated by the treatment of the Jews in Portugal. Some of the weaker sort, he says, did indeed embrace Christianity to save their lives; but "even to this day, which is a hundred years since, few Portuguese can yet rely or believe them to be real converts; though custom, and length of time, are much more powerful counsellors in such changes than all other constraints whatever."[8]

With such promising prospects the Reformation might have spread all over France had not its friends put a check to it by the methods which they employed to expedite it. The agitation for "new doctrines" became too tumultuous. The movement began to grow too rapidly. The Church became terrified, and, as in Italy, a Counter-Reformation was the result. The Sorbonne doctors and the Parliament of Paris, at the instigation of the Franciscan monks, condemned and ordered the surrender of all suspected literature. Bishop Briconnet lost courage and denounced the Reformists as plotters against the social order. Lefevre, with his zealous disciple and co-worker, Guillaume Farel, took refuge in Strassburg and spent his last years in the palace of Marguerite of Navarre, bemoaning that "When I ought to desire death, I have basely avoided the martyr's crown, and have betrayed the cause of my God."

There were others, however, who welcomed the martyr's crown rejected by Lefevre. A woolcarder by the name of Jean Leclerc, inspired by Lefevre's French Scriptures, tore down the papal bull which offered indulgences in return for prayer and fasting, and substituted for it a placard in which the pope figured as Antichrist (1524). He was whipped, branded and banished. But he continued with even greater vehemence to denounce the papacy and to condemn the adoration of sacred images. Finally he was seized and sentenced to have his head encircled with red-hot bands of iron before his body was consigned to the flames. It is reported that not one cry of anguish escaped his lips during his agony; but before he expired the bystanders heard him calmly repeat (Ps. 115:4): "Their idols are silver and gold, the work of men's hands."

Leclerc's work was taken up by Jacques Pauvan, whom Briconnet, during the period of his liberalism, had invited to help him enlighten the masses. He preached that baptism is only a symbol, that holy water is no better than ordinary water, that the Mass is no prophylactic against sin, and that the truth is to be found only in the plain words of the Holy Bible. Hailed before the doctors of the Sorbonne, he at first retracted but soon reasserted his opinions and was sentenced to be burned at the Place de Grave. His last words made such an impression that one of the doctors declared: "It had been better to have cost the Church a million of gold, than that Pauvan should have been suffered to speak to the people." A similar fate was meted out to a shoemaker of Tournay, Jean Chastellain, and a certain hermit of Livry. As the latter withstood the flames with remarkable fortitude, the priests assured the spectators that he was one of the damned who was entering the fires of hell while still on earth.[9]

For some time the Italianized Francis I halted between the orthodoxy of the Church and the liberalism of the College de France. He rejected the petition of the doctors of the Sorbonne to prohibit the publication of books with heretical content and did his utmost to save the life of Louis de Berquin, the propagandist of reforms. But his jealousy of Charles V and his need of money led him to throw the scale in favor of the Catholic princes of Germany, and what the entreaties and inducements of the pope could not effect was accomplished by the impatience and violence of the Reformers themselves.

For, instead of listening to the counsels for moderation of Erasmus and Melanchthon, the impatient French Reformists set out to convert their countrymen by force of arms. In imitation of the Hebrew Prophets fighting the battles of the Lord against the worshipers of Baal, they smashed sacred statues, desecrated places of worship, and posted pasquinades and distributed broadsides in which the pope and the clergy were condemned as "false prophets, damnable deceivers, apostates, wolves, false shepherds, seducers, liars, traitors, thieves, more detestable than devils." The height of their audacity was reached when a placard was found affixed to the door of the bedchamber of Francis lampooning the holy Mass (1534). [10]

This outrage finally decided the king on his future policy. His first step was to issue an edict "absolutely prohibiting any exercise of the art of printing in France, on pain of the halter." A strict censorship was at once instituted, and Protestant Bibles and books together with their churches were consigned to the flames. Those whose religious views were not quite sound were apprehended and condemned without the formality of a trial. On the testimony of spies, many were convicted of plotting the assassination of the king or of poisoning the wells, and were tortured until they implicated others or became "reconciled" to the "King's religion." The Christian "New Catholics," very much like the Jewish "New Christians" in Spain and Portugal, conformed to the State religion outwardly but clung to their principles in secret. Those of them who were discovered were sent to the galleys or stake, and on their death were thrown into the common sewers, while their children were carried off by the dread dragonnades and raised as Catholics.

As many of the French Reformers as were able sought safety in the French-speaking sections of the Swiss Confederation, and among them was John Calvin (Jean Cauvin, 1509-64), who was later hailed as "the most Christian of his time" by millions of his countrymen. Coming under the influence of Pierre Olivetanus, Nicholas Cop, Jacques Lefevre, and Giovani Alciati, who ultimately became a Unitarian, Calvin grew dissatisfied with the creed of the Church and at Basel, "the Athens of Switzerland," consecrated himself to the task of cleansing the people from "the filth of the papacy" and of vindicating those "whose death was precious in the sight of the Lord."

The distinctive teaching of Calvin was that Adam, who was made in the image of God, *i.e.*, spiritually perfect, blotted out this image and incurred the curse of God by his disobedience. This "original sin" and its consequent curse inheres in his descendants, and they must all suffer eternal damnation; but God in His mercy predestined some to be saved. The only means to join the host of the Elect is to kill the Old Adam through mortification of the flesh. But thus partaking, as it were, in the passion of Christ one will share also in his resurrection. Jesus' righteousness will then be imputed to him, too, and he will be saved.

Calvin retained two of the Sacraments: baptism as a sign of initiation, and communion as a symbolic reminder that he transfused his spirit into his followers as if he became part of their flesh and blood. He denied the dogma of Transubstantiation and denounced the adoration of statues, the invocation of the saints, and other Catholic observances as the device of the devil. Calvin also revised the first French translation of the Bible made by Pierre Olivetan and had it published with funds generously supplied him by Waldenses. Due to Calvin's boundless energy, Geneva became to nascent Protestantism what Rome was to Catholicism. From her great university, which he helped found, went forth the most zealous apostles of the new doctrine. His *Institutes of the Christian Religion* (1535) were accepted all over western Europe as "holy doctrines which no man might speak against," and were adopted, with slight modifications, in Holland, Scotland, England, and America.

But the greatest trials and triumphs of his sect were to be experienced in France, where its followers came to be known as Huguenots. First meeting in secret in Paris (c. 1550), they grew within a decade to more than two thousand congregations, and in defiance of the Government they sang Psalms in the vernacular and distributed caricatures of the pope and bishops. The massacre of St. Bartholomew's Day (1572) did not terrify them. The revocation of the Edict of Nantes (1685) did not subdue them. Just when it seemed that France was Catholic to a man, they appeared as a great multitude bold enough and strong enough to dictate terms to the king. This continued until the fall of the Empire when, with the end of religious discrimination, they assumed an important place in the progress of their nation.

While in Basel, Calvin received an urgent request to settle in Geneva as preacher and leader. There, in spite of opposition, he started on the realization of his dream to make Switzerland a theocracy patterned after that of Judea. He regimented the citizens in the minutest details of their lives and passed drastic laws condemning anyone who did not accept his interpretation of "the word of God" to banishment and death. The reformer who protested against the king's intolerance was himself not more liberal when it concerned his own doctrines. Within five years he meted out fifty-eight sentences of death, seventy-six of exile, and innumerable imprisonments. Among his victims were some of the most advanced Reformers of Italy and his close friend, Sebastian Castellio—the latter because he did not admit the inspiration of the Song of Songs. Significant is the role he played in the execution of Miguel Serveto, better known as Michal Servetus (1511-53).

Servetus was born in Aragon and was sent by his father to study law at Toulouse. There, at the age of seventeen, he first became acquainted with the Scriptures. Ten years later, while at Louvain, he also took up the study of Hebrew, until he was able to read the Jewish commentators on the Bible and the Jewish polemics. The latter developed in him an aversion to the papacy, "the beast of beasts and most abandoned of harlots." He was particularly repelled by the doctrine of the Trinity, which to him was sheer paganism. "I am unable to restrain from tears," says he, "when I read the replies which are made concerning this (the Trinity) by Rabbi Kimhi, against the Christians. For I see the absurd reasons with which they combat him and I cannot choose but weep." "In the place of one God," he writes elsewhere, "you have a three-headed Cerberus; in place of faith, you have a fatal dream; and good works, you call worthless pictures." Rome, he claimed, in order not to appear to Judaize, preferred to heathenize. The "false prophet Mohammed" has a more truly scriptural attitude toward Christ than have Christian Trinitarians. "All those who believe a Trinity in the essence of God, are Tritheists, true Atheists."

Besides his opposition to Trinitarianism on biblical grounds, Servetus also blamed this dogma for the refusal of the Jews to accept Christianity. "The Hebrews," he claims, "being supported by so many authorities, deservedly wonder at the Tripartite Deity that is introduced to us," and urges that in disputing with Jews no reference should be made to the belief that Jesus is the actual Son of God. Strangely enough, his views did not go so far as to allow those who were forcibly converted to revert to their former faith. For, he says, "if a man can become a complete man, after the heart of God, only in Christianity, then, according to Hebrews 6:4-6, he who, after he has become a Christian, reverts to heathenism or Judaism, sins against the Holy Spirit." It was in keeping with his own practice strictly to conform to the usages of the Catholic Church, even when they were no longer conceived as divinely ordained.

The opinions Servetus expressed in his books and confidential correspondence excited the indignation both of Protestants and Catholics, and one of his letters to Calvin sealed his fate. Calvin had already regarded the statement of Servetus in his edition of Ptolemy's Geography, that Judea is not "a land flowing with milk and honey" as blasphemous, and that it necessarily inculpated Moses and grievously outraged the Holy Spirit. He was outraged still more by his statements in his *De Trinitatis Erroribus.* At last an opportunity presented itself to do away with this dangerous heretic once for all. Servetus' *Christianismi Restitutis,* which had been rejected by the publishers, finally appeared in a mysterious manner. Unable to do him any harm in Geneva, Calvin sent a sheet of it to France, denouncing its author as a Judaizer, "a veritable rabbi," who had encompassed "the ruin of many poor souls." Servetus was hailed before the Inquisitor-General of Lyons. He defended himself by saying that the views he expressed were intended only for the purpose of discussion. Nevertheless he was imprisoned, but effected an escape to Geneva through the connivance, it is said, of the

Catholic authorities. However, he was recognized by some friars at the church where he attended vesper services, and was condemned to be burned at a place which, as if to add insult to cruelty, was near the cemetery of the Jews. When his end approached, Servetus asked Calvin's pardon. But Farel, the friend of Calvin, pointed out that Servetus in his agony cried out, "Jesus Christ, Thou Son of Eternal God, have mercy on me," and not "Thou Eternal Son of God," and Calvin refused to forgive "that obscene dog who, with the utmost impudence, asserted in one word that there was no harm in what he said." [11]

Among the more prominent men who, like Servetus, suffered for the cause of Unitarianism, was Sebastian Castellio. At first a friend of Calvin, he denounced the murder of Servetus and declared that to discuss the difference between the Law and the Gospel, gratuitous remission of sin or imputed righteousness, is of no more importance than to discuss whether "a prince was to come on horseback or in a chariot, or dressed in white or in red." Castellio was expelled from Geneva and from Basel, and died in neglect and poverty, remembered only by Socinus and Montaigne. Even more tragic was the fate of Valentino Gentile, the Unitarian who was beheaded in Bern. It is said that before he died he expressed himself as honored in being martyred for the glory of the Father, whereas the Apostles and other martyrs died only for the glory of the Son. [12]

Calvin had many friends among Jews, or ex-Jews, who helped spread his doctrine. One of them was Isaac la Pereyra, an eminent jurist and theologian. Marco Perez, who escaped the clutches of the Inquisition for Judaizing, became the head of the Calvinist consistory in Antwerp and had at his own expense a translation made into Spanish of the Bible and the *Institutes* for distribution among his former countrymen. Another former Jew, John Immanuel Tremmelius, who was a Catholic before he became a Protestant and was professor of Hebrew at the University of Strassburg, translated Calvin's catechism into the sacred tongue in the hope, no doubt, of converting the Jews to his new religion. [13]

As far as is known, there were no Jews in France after the

fourteenth century. There were indeed some *Juifs deguises* (secret Jews), officially designated as "Portuguese merchants," to whom Henry II granted letters patent; but when, in the beginning of the seventeenth century, some undisguised Jews began to penetrate into the forbidden territory, Louis XIII issued an edict (1615) forbidding Christians to shelter or converse with them under penalty of death and confiscation. Louis XIV expelled them from the newly-acquired colony of Martinique but found it advisable to permit them to stay in the annexed province of Alsace-Lorraine. However, their condition there remained most intolerable until the eighteenth century. [14]

Meanwhile the spirit which exacted the Edict of Nantes from Henry IV (1598), in which for the first time since Constantine the Great a Catholic nation granted freedom of conscience to a heretical group, kept marching on. The ideals of tolerance and equality advanced by Montaigne and Bodin gained an even larger following even among the clergy. Richard Simon, a priest who was aroused by the condemnation of a Jew to the pyre on the accusation of ritual murder, became interested in Judaism and translated into French R. Leon da Modena's *Historia dei Riti Ebraici.* Simon's contemporary, Charles Louis Montesquieu, in his *Esprit de Lois,* which some rank as the greatest book of the eighteenth century, hurled his accusation against the Church's intolerance. "I cannot help remarking, by the way," he says, "how this (Jewish) nation has been sported with from one age to another: at one time their effects were confiscated when they were willing to become Christians; and at another, if they refused to turn Christians they were ordered to be burned." His righteous indignation reached its height when he wrote on the effect of compulsory conversion. His "Humble Remonstrance to the Inquisitions of Spain and Portugal" which he put in the mouth of a Judaizing maiden of eighteen, is one of the noblest protests against religious persecution in all literature.

Some of Simon's works were consigned to the flames, and Montesquieu's *Esprit de Lois* was condemned by the Sorbonne and put on the *Index* by the Church. But the Church was no longer the power she was in the Middle Ages. Not only the Philosophers but loyal Catholics like Abbe Gregoire insisted on tolerance, and the Revolution brought about, if not the *fraternité, at least the liberté* and *égalité* of all Frenchmen, regardless of their creeds. At last, in 1831, King Louis Philippe ratified the resolution of the Chamber that Judaism, like Catholicism and Protestantism, be supported by the State treasury and be granted a subsidy for the training of rabbis at the Seminary of Metz!

Conversions to Judaism, however, took place long before all religious discriminations were removed. Already about 1730 many of the *Juifs déguisés* began to profess the religion of Israel openly. But even before, there were some, Christians by descent, who abandoned Catholicism for Judaism. To be sure, they could not have been very numerous, but there must have been many others who did not have the courage to face the inevitable consequences. Only recently there was discovered a Spanish document which tells the story of a wealthy French nobleman, Roueries, who accepted Judaism at the time when the Counter-Reformation was at its peak. He was the possessor of three chateaux in the neighborhood of Lyons and was probably influenced by the *Anusim* who settled in that neighborhood. To them he left his fortune, of thirty thousand ducats, and, with his two sons made his way to Venice where he became a Proselyte of Righteousness (1575). Thence he went to Constantinople and joined the pensioners of Don Joseph Nasi. When his Christian countrymen taunted him that his money would never be returned by those whose religion he assumed, he replied: "I did not come to seek the Hebrews, but the God of the Hebrews and their Law. Of them you can assuredly say no ill." There is also a record of a certain Jean Fontanier, a royal secretary and a strenuous advocate of the recalling of the Jews to France, who was first a monk, then a Calvinist, and was later burned at the Place de la Greve for Judaizing.[15]

In the annals of Jewish martyrdom there are few episodes more stirring than the story of Nicholas Antoine. Born about 1602 at Briey, Lorraine, he received his education in schools under the supervision of the Jesuits. By the time he attained the age of twenty, he experienced a decided leaning towards Protestantism. Under the influence of Paul Perry, the eloquent Reformist of Metz, he matriculated at the Calvinist seminary at Sedan, and afterwards at Geneva, and prepared himself for the Protestant ministry. But the study of the Bible in the original, to which he devoted himself most ardently, led him to doubt the doctrines of the new faith, and he consulted the rabbis of Metz about receiving him into the Jewish fold. Refused on account of the consequences to which such an act might lead, he decided to go to Italy where, they told him, one could become a Jew without imperilling himself or the Jewish community. The rabbis of Venice, however, were no more encouraging than those of Metz. It was, they informed him, no less dangerous in Italy for Jews to admit a Christian into their fellowship than in France. The rabbis of Padua even added that conversion was unnecessary for salvation, since anyone who lived a good life and believed in the Only One could regard himself a Jew, even if the world took him for a Christian.

Disappointed, Nicholas returned to Geneva, became an instructor in philosophy at the Academy, and observed as much as he could, or knew, of the precepts of Judaism without the formality of conversion. In lieu of a *mezuzah,* he wrote over his door passages from the Pentateuch, and recited his prayers in Hebrew. As pastor at Gex, on the Franco-Swiss border, he never referred to Jesus and never drew from the New Testament any texts for his sermons.

One Sunday, while speaking on the verse in the Second Psalm which the Christian version renders "Kiss the Son," he took pains to impress upon the worshipers that God is a Spirit and could not have a son. The Lord of the Manor, who happened to be in the audience, reported it to Geneva. The community became aroused. Its most prominent theologians tried to convince him of his errors, but Nicholas refused even to argue with them. He merely kept on chanting the Seventy-fourth Psalm, and when they stopped he announced himself a Jew. The amazed theologians pronounced him insane, and he was put into an asylum. While there he drew up a profession of his faith, accompanied by eleven philosophical objections to the doctrines of the Trinity. He also made an attempt to perform the rite of circumcision upon himself. On April 11, 1532, he was summoned before ·a tribunal of fifteen pastors for another examination. But Nicholas refused to retract or excuse himself and proudly declared that he was a Jew and that he asked for nothing better than to die for Judaism. Thereupon ensued a heated discussion among the theologians. Some suggested that he should be only unfrocked and banished; others agreed that such mildness would encourage heresy. The latter decision at last prevailed, and on April 20 sentence was pronounced that he be put to death by strangulation and burning. The sentence was executed the same day.

Nicholas proved a hero to the end. As he was led through the streets to the Place de Plianpalais, loaded with chains, he refused to listen to the pleadings of the pastors to say the word that would save his life and continued to repeat to himself: "Come, Come! Let us die for the glory of the great God of Israel, Who is One and without compare"; and when one of the pastors mentioned the Trinity, he kicked violently the faggots which were heaped up about him. It was noticed that even after he was garroted there was still feeble motion in the limbs when the flames reached the body. The onlookers concluded that his "body suffered the pains of both sentences, while his soul went to suffer another more terrible still in the next world." [16]

Very likely the Jews of Metz, Venice, and Padua never learned that the Christian whom they were afraid to admit into the household of Israel joined the host of martyrs headed by R. Akiba, who was reputed to have been of proselyte ancestry, for the story came to light only recently. So did the story of another French proselyte of righteousness, Aaron d'Antan, in Provence, through his correspondence with the Royal Librarian at Berlin (1661-1739). Probably there were other proselytes who lived and died unknown and unnoticed by the people with whom they cast their lot. [17]

In the nineteenth century the story is told of the widow and the daughter of one of Napoleon's marshals who accepted Judaism while at Athens. These noble proselytes became

ardent Zionists long before the movement was heard of; and
as a result of their efforts, the titular Duchess of Piacenza (d.
1855) bequeathed a considerable fortune for the promotion of
the Zionist work and a plot of ground in the Valley of Olym-
pia for the erection of a synagogue. In 1868 we hear of another
proselyte who was the secretary of the Suez Canal Corporation.   Attracted to Judaism, he had himself and his eight-
year-old boy circumcised in Alexandria, Egypt, assumed the
name of Abraham Israel, and became a strictly observant Jew.
When some time later the child died, his father buried him
temporarily in the Christian cemetery (there being then no
Jewish one), but as soon as he was able, reinterred the body on
Mount Olive, overlooking Jerusalem. To this should be added
the name of Sarah, who is buried in the cemetery of the colony
Zichron Yaakob, in Palestine, and whose epitaph reads:

> And Ruth said: 'Entreat me not to leave thee, and to
> return from following after thee; for whither thou
> goest, I will go; and where thou lodgest, I will lodge;
> thy people shall be my people, and thy God my God.'
> The proselyte Sarah Mathilde Klein, born in Paris in
> 1864, and died in Zichron Yaakob in the 2003rd year
> of our Exile, Nisan 22d, '682 (1892).[18]

To present day France belonged the distinction of having
an ordained rabbi who at first prepared himself for the priesthood. Aimé Palliere was born in 1875, and until the age of
seventeen he knew of Jews only from the household Bible
and its illustrations by Doré. One day, while on a vacation, he
happened to pass a synagogue. Curiosity prompted him to
enter. It was at the *Neila,* or concluding service, of the Day of
Atonement. The solemnity of the services profoundly affected
him, but he soon forgot about it and continued to prepare
himself for the priesthood at the Catholic University of Lyons,
where Abbé Augustin Lemann, a converted Jew, was his professor of Hebrew.

By chance, there fell into his hands R. Leon da Modena's
book on Jewish observances in the translation of the Abbé
Richard Simon. The book produced in him conflicting emo-

tions. Torn between his love for the religion of his fathers
and the appeal of the religion of the people of the Bible, he
attached himself to various Christian sects and joined the Salvation Army in the hope that its humanitarian work would
give him the peace for which he was yearning. Finding that
neither the preachments of the Evangelists nor the tambour-
ines of the Salvationists could put a stop to the struggle within
him, he decided to submit again to the Church. But as he
was taking Communion, a voice within him cried: "Do you
believe in the Real Presence?.. Do you believe in the Incarnation, in the divinity of Christ?" He turned to the Hebrew
Bible, and, to use his own words:

> Through the Hebrew syllables, with their sonorous
> cadence, something of the soul of Israel reached me. A
> biblical passage, or a shred of prayer out of the ritual
> which I succeeded in translating, spoke to me of Ju-
> daism in a more penetrating manner, and menaced
> my faith more than could have all the learned dis-
> courses of a convinced and informed Israelite with
> the best intentions in the world.

Finally Palliere left for Leghorn, sought out R. Elijah
Benamozegh, and confided to him his craving for the religion
of Israel. To his disappointment, the Italian saint and sage
dissuaded him. It was no longer for fear of the dire consequences which would have inevitably followed during the Middle Ages; but, the rabbi explained, the acceptance of Judaism is
not necessary for the salvation of a Gentile. Anyone who observes the seven Noahian laws is sure to have a portion in the
world to come. Besides, he thought, Palliere could do more
for the cause of true religion by remaining within the camp,
and avoid inflicting pain on his aged mother.

But Palliere thought otherwise. He wanted to join actively
and openly in Israel's mission to be a light to the nations and to
share in the conquests which are to be made "Not by might,
nor by power, but by the spirit of the Lord." So he became a
Jew and joyously accepted the "yoke of the Torah" in its
entirety. Later he even became a rabbi and was invited to

occupy the pulpit of the Rue Copernic synagogue in Paris. Due to him more Hebrew was introduced into the ritual and many ancient customs have been revived. His great hope was to make loyal Jews out of those who, unlike himself, were Jews by birth but lukewarm to their heritage. He edited the work of his master, R. Benamozegh, *Israel and Humanity* (1914) and published *Foi et Reveil* and a number of articles on the universality and reasonableness of Judaism, under the pseudonym Loetmol. He was especially active in the French Jewish youth movement of which he was president, and was also interested in Zionism. Unlike Paul, the sometime Jew, who preached to Gentiles the abolition of the Law, Palliere preached to the Jew the preservation of the Law and pleaded with non-Jews to retrace their steps from Rome to Jerusalem.

In spite of this, Palliere was beloved not only by his fellow-Jews, but by his former Christian co-religionists, and his sermons and articles not infrequently appeared in Catholic publications. His autobiography, *Le Sanctuaire Inconnu* (Paris, 1926), which tells of his spiritual Odyssey, has been translated into German (*Unbekannte Heiligthum,* Berlin, 1928), into English (*The Unknown Sanctuary,* New York, 1928), and also into the Greek, and is recognized as a valuable addition to Jewish inspirational literature.[19]

The land that contributed most to reversion to Judaism was Holland, the birthplace of Charles V, the bitter enemy of all who did not belong to the Catholic Church. There the Reformation was inaugurated by Desiderius Erasmus, who himself was opposed to it but who contributed to its success by *The Praise of Folly* and especially his *Colloquia,* in which he belabored his fellow-monks with such devastating sarcasm that he is described as "the glory of the priesthood and its shame." But what shook the theological edifice of the Church was his critical edition of the New Testament (1516), from which it became evident that the Vulgate, which the Church pronounced to be inspired, contained numerous errors, and that the verse, "For there are three that bear record in heaven, the Father, the Word, and the Holy Ghost: and these three are One" (John 5:7), upon which ultimately rests the dogma of the Trinity, is an interpolation. The sage who feared lest the study of Hebrew would promote Judaism contributed to the same result by the cultivation of Greek.[20]

Erasmus was optimistic enough to hope that the "philosophy of Christ" would gradually sweep away the ancient political and theological abuses of the Church, and refused to be drawn into the conflict which broke out in Germany. But there were others who would wait no longer. Dirk Coornhart, the famous Dutch writer, turned against the Church because of her brutal treatment of those whom she suspected of heresy. There were those who sided with Lutheranism, Anabaptism, and especially with Calvinism, and in 1512 Herman van Ryswick, formerly an Inquisitor, was burned at the stake for preaching Unitarianism. "To exterminate the root and ground of the past," Charles V introduced the Spanish Inquisition into Holland. But unlike its effect in Spain, this dread institution only made matters worse. Nobles and burghers, nicknamed "the Beggars," rose in protest against it, and their protest was followed by wild anti-Catholic riots. Philip II found it necessary to send a Spanish army under Alva, and the "Spanish fury" broke out in all its fiendishness. Men were burned, women were buried alive. But the resistance of the Protestants remained unbroken. Everywhere infuriated mobs wrecked altars, smashed images, and damaged churches and cathedrals, and the magistrates refused to interfere, till William of Orange, known as William the Silent, united the Dutch provinces (1576) and proclaimed freedom of worship throughout the land.

Thereafter, with rare exception, Holland became a haven of refuge for all who in their own land were harassed because of their religious views. Thither fled the Puritans from England, the Huguenots from France, the Mennonites from Bohemia, the Socinians from Poland. Under Frederick I, the University of Halle, which he founded, opened its doors even to Jews and Moslems, "provided they refrained from spreading their convictions among their fellow-students," and in 1795 the National Convention proclaimed that "no Jew shall be excluded from rights or advantages which are associated with citizenship in the Batavian Republic, and which he may desire to enjoy." [21]

Jewish refugees from Spain and Portugal trickled into Holland while it was still under Spanish domination, and lived as Catholics in constant dread of the Inquisition. With the elimination of the Spaniards, whole shiploads of them began to arrive at the port of Amsterdam, eager to revert to Judaism. One group of ten men and four children, too impatient to wait till they reached Amsterdam, put in at the port of Emden, sought out Rabbi Moses Uri Levi, and begged him to admit them into the Jewish religion. As he would not venture to do it in Germany, he followed them to Holland where, it is said, he received as many as two hundred forty-eight men into the faith of Israel. [22]

The suffering which the Dutch endured during the regime of the Catholics infused in them a spirit of tolerance such as was not witnessed before in Christendom. They not only sympathized with the Jews, as they did with the Protestant refugees from France or England, they fraternized with them, attended their services. Personages like the stadtholders, William III, and William V, did not deem it beneath their dignity to be the house guests of some of them. Rembrandt (1609-69), an intimate friend of R. Menasseh b. Israel preferred to live near or in the Jewish quarter, and loved to make etchings and paintings of Jews in various moods. He also painted some of his own folks and passed them off as Jews. Thus, his "Jewish Bride" is said to be a portrait of his sister, and his "Philo, the Jew," a representation of his father. His delineation of Jews, and especially of their rabbis, forms an agreeable contrast to the caricatures of them drawn by Christians through the ages. [23]

Sympathy with the Jews developed in Holland into admiration of their history and their literature. This was especially true of the French Huguenots, who fled thither after the revocation of the Edict of Nantes. One of them, Pierre Juriu of Rotterdam, in *The Fulfillment of Prophecy* (1685), branded all the persecutors of the Jews as Antichrists, and predicted that the Jews were destined to lead the world to the true religion. Jacob Christian Basnage (1653-1725), noted as a skilled diplomat, compiled *L'histoire et la Religion des Juifs* (Rotterdam, 1706), in which he treats impartially of the vicissitudes of the Jews down to his own time, and declares in the Prospectus thereto:

> In the decay and dregs of centuries men have adopted a spirit of cruelty and barbarism towards the Jews. They were accused of being the cause of all the disasters which happened, and charged with a multitude of crimes of which they never even dreamed. Numberless miracles were invented to convict them, or rather the better to satisfy hatred under the councils and princes, by means of which people may judge of the malice of the former and the oppression of the latter. Men did not, however, confine themselves to the edicts, but everywhere military executions, popular riots and massacres, took place. Yet, by a miracle of Providence, which must excite the astonishment of all Christians, this hated nation, persecuted in all places for a great number of centuries, still exists everywhere. ... Peoples and kings, heathens, Christians, and Mohammedans, opposed to one another in so many points, have agreed in the purpose of destroying this nation, and have not succeeded. The bush of Moses, surrounded by flames, has ever burned without being consumed. The Jews have been driven out of all the cities of the world, and this has only served to spread them abroad in all cities. They still live in spite of the contempt and hatred which follow them everywhere, while the greatest monarchies have fallen, and are known to us only by name.

Basnage's *History*, written in fashionable French like his Catholic contemporary Richard Simon's *Ritual*, was the first Christian work whose writer did not regard the history and literature of the Diaspora as unworthy of attention except to malign and ridicule. Yet it enjoyed a large circulation, passed through various editions, and was translated into several languages. Though it is not without faults, it stands out as a monument to the candor, sincerity, and humanity of its author. Among the other works written, not in order to convert or humiliate the Jews, but to describe them as they are was a translation of the Mishnah, with the commentaries of Maimonides and Bertinoro, into Latin by William Surenhusius (1698-1703). While everywhere else Christians and apostate Jews condemned the Oral Law as a cesspool of blasphemy and moral corruption, this young scholar of Amsterdam expressed his conviction that it is superior to the classical literature and is on a spiritual level with the Bible. According to him

> He who desires to be a good and worthy disciple of Christ must first become a Jew, or he must first learn thoroughly the language and culture of the Jews, and become Moses' disciple before he joins the Apostles, in order that he may be able through Moses and the Prophets to convince men that Jesus is the Messiah.

Surenhusius not only sought to familiarize his countrymen with the teachings of the Jews; he was also a valiant champion of their rights. Christians, he complained, learned all they knew of God and religion from the Jewish Scriptures, and they repaid their debt with revilement and persecution. They acted "like highway men, who having robbed an honest man of all his clothes, beat him to death, or send him away with scorn." He was proud and happy that his own country, unlike the rest of Christendom, offered asylum to the harassed Jews, and he assured the senate of Amsterdam that they will never regret their kindness:

> In the measure in which this people once surpassed all other peoples, you give it preference, worthy men! The old renown and dignity which this people and the citizens of Jerusalem once possessed are yours and the Jews are sincerely devoted to you because they are not overcome by force of arms but won over by humanity and wisdom; they come to you, and are happy to obey your republican government.

The Dutch Jews prized highly the goodwill of their countrymen and the freedom they enjoyed in their new home. Yet they excommunicated Benedict Spinoza (1632-77), who offended more against traditional Judaism than Maimonides or Gersonides. The act was prompted by fear lest his views would jeopardize their standing among the conservative Christians. Their fear, however, was unfounded. Spinoza's doctrines were indeed vehemently attacked by some Christians, but his sins were not visited even upon himself, not to say upon other Jews. Many Christians continued to the last to be devoted friends of this son of Israel whom the Synagogue rejected and the Church did not win over. John de Witt, the Grand Pensionary of the Netherlands, bestowed upon him a pension. The Amsterdam physician Louis Meyer was with him at his death and became the editor of his posthumous works. His earliest biographies were written by men who were diametrically opposed to each other. Jean Maximilien Lucas, a French refugee, author of *La Vie et L'Esprit de M. Benoit de Spinoza* (1719), was supposed to be a freethinker or a Rosicrucian. Johann Koeler Colerus was a German who came over to preach Lutheranism to the Hollanders. He was by no means in agreement with the subject of his biography, as he showed in the treatise *The Resurrection of Jesus Christ from the Dead,* wherein he attacked Spinoza and his followers (1705). But he wrote of him with a respect bordering on admiration, and his book, translated into French and English, became very popular. Whether they approved of his views or not, the Dutch were proud of their Jewish philosopher and agreed with the sentiment expresssed by an unknown poet:

> Renowned Spinoza's features
> No faithful brush portrays,
> But, Wisdom being immortal,
> His works will live always.[24]

Spinoza's writings exerted but little influence on his own people; his *Tractatus Theologico-Politicus* and *Ethics* and his correspondence with the leading intellects of his day greatly furthered the cause of Deism and Unitarianism all over Europe. His treatise *De Deo et Homine* became the Gospel of a sect, which preached the amalgamation of Judaism with Christianity.

No less, if not more, popular among non-Jews than Spinoza was his teacher R. Menasseh b. Israel. Among the intelligentsia this rabbi's writings were familiar from Spain to Brazil. His *Conciliador*, written in Spanish and translated into Latin by his pupil Denis Vos, was eagerly read by Christians as well as Jews. His *De La Resurreccion de los Muertos* was complimented by the Roman Church by placing it upon the *Index Expurgatorius*. But R. Menasseh's main interest was in the "lost sheep of Israel." He made it a point to inquire if immigrants, newly arrived from Spain or Portugal, were of New Christian descent and would spare no pains to persuade them to come back to the faith of their fathers, as he and his family had done. To those whom he could not reach personally he would send chests of books and urge them to familiarize themselves with their contents and impart their knowledge of Judaism to others. [25]

Before long Amsterdam became a veritable Dutch Jerusalem, to which clandestine Jews and Judaizing Christians flocked from all nations. "It is a daily occurrence in our city," writes a contemporary chronicler, "to see men from all nations and tongues come from the most remote corners of the earth to behold the glory of the Lord and the glory of our holy and pure Torah." Some of them we have met already. Others we shall come across later. Here we shall refer to a few who have made important contributions to their community and State. Abraham Zacuto, known as Zacutus Lusitanus (1575-1642), was born in Lisbon as Manoel Alvares and studied at various universities in Portugal and Spain. After practising medicine for about thirty years in his native city, he suddenly left for Amsterdam with his wife and five children, embraced Judaism, and became an intimate friend of R. Menasseh. Distinguished as one of the most skilled practitioners and theorists of his time, he was consulted by leading scientists from Holland, England, Italy and France, and his works on the praxis and history of medicine ran through one edition after another.

Jacob Rosales, like Abraham Zacuto, was a native of Lisbon and friend of R. Menasseh. He achieved a great reputation as a physician and numbered among his patients the Archbishop of Braga, the Duke of Braganza, and the Commander of the Order of Santiago. He was also a mathematician and astronomer and was on intimate terms with Galileo. His conversion to Judaism in Amsterdam (1625) seems not to have affected the esteem in which he was held as a man and physician, for we find him attending on the Prince of Denmark and the Empresses Leonora and Maria, and raised to the dignity of Count Palatine by Emperor Ferdinand III. He was denounced to the Inquisition by one of its informers, who added, however, that according to Rosales' belief one could be saved by the law of Jesus as well as by the Law of Moses.

Joseph and his son Ephraim Bueno were both eminent physicians, patrons of R. Menasseh, to whose *De la Resurreccion de los Muertos* they contributed laudatory sonnets. Ephraim also subsidized R. Menasseh in his venture as a publisher and issued, in conjunction with Jonas Abrabanel, a Spanish translation of the Book of Psalms. He also translated parts of the Jewish liturgy, was one of the editors of the *Shulhan Aruk,* and co-founder of the society of *Torah Or.* Rembrandt entertained great admiration for him and perpetuated his likeness in his famous portrait *The Jewish Doctor* (c. 1647).

Abraham Farrar, born in Oporto (c. 1600), was another physician who became a Jew in Amsterdam. As a diligent student of the Torah under the Haham Mortara, he drew up a compendium in Portuguese of the six hundred and thirteen precepts of the Mosaic Law in order that "all of us who come from Portugal and Spain, and for our sins do not understand Hebrew, shall rightly know what they are." He also indulged in friendly discussions about the Christian religion with the Hamburg theologian Johannes Mueller. So did Dionysius Musaphia (c. 1606-75) physician-in-ordinary to Christian IV of Denmark, who, after his conversion in Amsterdam, assumed the name of Benjamin and wrote the *Zeḳer Rab* on Hebrew synonyms (1635), which enjoyed great popularity down to the nineteenth century.

Another distinguished Spaniard was Diego Barrassa, or de Barros. In addition to being a physician and scientist, he was a linguist and astronomer. After his conversion he devoted himself to writing a commentary on the Bible and served as the member of the Board of the Talmud Torah.[26]

Not all of the Amsterdam proselytes were Spanish or Portuguese Marranos. Some were former *bona fide* Christians, and even monks. Among the charges brought against Uriel Acosta, who after risking his life to accept Judaism in Amsterdam, turned against it, was that he had dissuaded two Christians —a Spaniard and an Italian—from embracing the faith of Israel. Vincente de Rocamora (c. 1600-84) had been a Dominican friar, noted for his piety and eloquence, and confessor to the Infanta Maria, afterwards Empress of Austria. In 1643 he fled to London, circumcised himself with his own hand, took the name of Isaac, and gave much of his time to the charitable and cultural activities of the Jewish community. Another ex-friar was the Franciscan Henriques Solis, who in Amsterdam became Eleazar de Solis, and whose effigy was burned in Lisbon in 1640. Thomas de Pinedo, after being trained in Madrid became a Jesuit, assumed the name of Isaac and distinguished himself as a philologist and classical scholar. Antoni Enriques Gomez was a powerful rival of Calderon. He wrote more than twenty comedies, some of which had been acclaimed by enraptured audiences. For his gallantry and service he was made a captain in the army and Knight of the Order of San Miguel. However, he and his son, also famous as a Spanish litterateur, made their way to Holland and became proselytes to Judaism. He was tried *in absentia* by the Inquisition of Seville and condemned to burn in effigy (April 13, 1660). Gomez was also a poet of no mean rank. While he still lived in France as a Christian he composed a touching elegy on the death of a martyr Lope de Vera y Alarcon. His epic, based on the story of Samson, is reminiscent of Milton's *Samson Agonistes* and probably expresses what he was prepared to do under circumstances which demanded sacrifices for his new faith:

> I die for Thy holy word without regret,
>   for Thy teachings, true and sublime;
> I die for Thy holy people, Thou lovest yet,
>   And wilt love till the end of time. . .
> I die for Israel consecrated from birth
>   To make Thy Name known in all the earth. [27]

One or two others we cannot omit mentioning in this connection. R. Jacob Judah de Leao was either a Marrano himself or of Marrano descent. Though born in Hamburg (1603) he was educated in Amsterdam and was a schoolmate of R. Menasseh. After spending some years in his native city he returned to Holland, where he officiated as rabbi and teacher in the Amsterdam Talmud Torah (religious school). He engaged in numerous controversies with Christian clergymen on Judaism and Christianity. His irrepressible hobby was the Temple of Solomon, so that he came to be known as "Templo." He searched the Bible and the Talmud for data pertaining to the ancient sanctuary and executed a model of it and its sacred vessels on a reduced scale. It was exhibited before Charles II of England, and his description of it in Spanish and Hebrew was in a few years translated into Dutch, French, German, Latin, and English. He also designed numerous engravings to illustrate the *Mishnah,* coat of arms for the English Freemasons, and translated the Psalms into Spanish. [28]

Among the converts or reverts who were zealous defenders of Judaism were Captain Joseph Semah Arias, the translator of Josephus' *Contra Apionem* into Spanish; and Juan Carrasco, an Augustinian friar of Burgos. Carrasco's *Apology of Judaism* (Hague, 1733) was included by Daniello of Leghorn in his collection of controversies between Jews and Christians, and by Wiffen, who took him for a Protestant, in his *Collection de Reformadores Espanoles*. But the past of many, if not most, who gave up high and secure positions for the sake of Judaism frequently remained a secret. It is doubtful, for instance, whether the philologist, poet, and adventurer Solomon Bernich, a French monk, who appeared in Holland about 1760, was or was not of Jewish descent. Similarly as regards Abraham Cohen de Errera (d. 1639). He is said to have been a descendant of Gran Gonzalo de Cordova and while representing the Sultan of Morocco at Cadiz was captured by the English in a raid on that port. When set free at the intercession of the Sultan with Queen Elizabeth, he went to Amsterdam, accepted Judaism, and immersed himself in the study of mysticism, on which he wrote two works, *Puerta del Cielo* and *Casa de Dios*. In his will he requested that these works be translated into Hebrew by R. Isaac Aboab, and left a considerable amount for their publication. They were partly rendered into Latin by Baron von Rosenroth and were highly regarded by the historians of the Kabbalah.[29]

There were a number, however, whose non-Jewish extraction is less doubtful. In the earliest registers of the cemetery of the Spanish and Portuguese community of Amsterdam, the inscription "children of Abraham our father" occurs quite frequently. The illustrations to one of the *Haggadahs* published there are known to have been engraved by a proselyte. In the liturgy of 1687 there is a special section devoted to the regulations for "the circumcision of proselytes."

In the Scandinavian peninsula, where Lutheranism early gained a firm foothold, Catholics and Calvinists suffered under severe disabilities. Though Queen Christian of Sweden corresponded with R. Menasseh b. Israel and had as her minister Manuel Isaac Texeira, no Jews were permitted to settle permanently unless they were converted. Charles XI was in constant fear of "the danger of the eventual influence of the Jewish religion on the pure Evangelical faith." The first two Jewish families, consisting of twenty-eight persons, who sought admittance into Sweden (1681) were all baptized in the presence of the king, the dowager queen, and several high officials. In Denmark, Holger Paulli, supposedly of Jewish extraction, in anticipation of the second advent of Jesus in 1720 urged the

European rulers to compel the Jews to become Christians and deport them to Palestine to start the re-establishment of the Jewish State.

Yet the Scandinavians, also, contributed to the roll of proselytes to Judaism. An interesting case occurred in Denmark. After the death of Jens Gedelöche it was discovered that he was a proselyte to Judaism. Whereupon the authorities ordered that his remains be removed from the Christian to the Jewish cemetery. Since, however, he was never formally converted, the Jewish community later disinterred him and buried him outside of their own "House of the Living." [30]

In Sweden, besides R. Isaac Papon (d. 1600), who is described on his tombstone in Eybeschuetz as *ben avinu Abraham* (Son of our Father Abraham), an entire noble family, the Graanbooms, or Granboms, abandoned their evangelical faith for Judaism. The first of them emigrated to Holland at the age of sixty-nine with his wife, a son of twelve, and a daughter of fourteen. The son, who was renamed Aaron Moses Isaac, devoted himself enthusiastically to the study of the Talmud and attained such proficiency that the Amsterdam community appointed him to the headship of its Etz Hayyim Academy. He was also made one of the *dayyanim* (ecclesiastical judges) after the death of R. Saul. In 1797 he became rabbi of the new congregation Adat Yeshurun, and on his death, in 1807, was succeeded by his son, R. Israel Graanboom. [31]

R. "Isaac, b. Abraham Ger," as he signs himself, was the author of *Zera Yizhak* (the Seed of Isaac) on the study and observance of the Torah, and his son, R. Israel wrote *Melitz Yosher* (*The Advocate of Right*) in defense of some innovation introduced by his father into the Amsterdam community.

CHAPTER XXIII

IN CENTRAL EUROPE

OF all the non-Latin countries, Austria proper was the only one where the Renaissance stopped short of the Reformation. To be sure, there was a certain amount of religious friction, but the Hapsburgs and later the Jesuits made any concerted opposition to the Church impossible. Every movement towards a revision of the faith was nipped in the bud, and even the French Revolution had little effect. Austria, as someone said, "in a time of universal effervescence... produced only musicians and showed zeal only for pleasure."

A legend has it that eight hundred and fifty-nine years after the Deluge one Abraham and his wife Sussana, with their sons Salim and Ataim, founded there a kingdom (*Judeisapta*) in what came to be known as Austria, which existed until 210 B.C.E. In all likelihood, Jews arrived there, as in other countries, in the wake of the Roman legions as merchants and interpreters, and settled in Vienna, which was then on the main highway of European trade. By the end of the eleventh century Jewish settlements were scattered all over the land; and in the twelfth century, one Shelom, or Solomon, was appointed by Leopold V Master of the Mint and manager of his financial affairs. On the pretext that he had put in jail one of his Christian slaves who stole and then took up the cross, Shelom and fifteen other Jews were killed by the crusaders. Leopold proved himself well deserving of the title, "the virtuous," which his countrymen bestowed upon him. Though himself a crusader, he executed two of the ringleaders of the mob, and thus probably averted a general massacre. Shelom's successor was also a Jew, and, like another Joseph, played an important part during the famine of 1235, and the war with Emperor Frederick II. [1]

Frederick II took the Jews under his special protection and granted them a charter, or Privilege (1238) which provided among others, that they be exempt from the duty to furnish horses for the royal retinue; that in their internal affairs they should be governed by their own laws; that their persons and property be protected the same as those of Christians, and the desecration of their cemeteries and stoning of their synagogues be severely punished; that they should not be forced to submit to trial by ordeal, but could clear themselves from an accusation by an oath; and that they should not be condemned on the testimony of Christians alone. It also imposed heavy fines on the baptism of Jewish children without the consent of their parents, or of slaves without the permission of their masters; and required that three days be given mature converts during which their sincerity to embrace Christianity would be tested. Still more liberal was the charter of Duke Frederick II, the Magna Carta of Austrian Jewry, issued after he regained possession of his country. In this charter it was explicitly stated that every Jew was to enjoy freedom of movement throughout his domain, and that "he should pay at every toll station only as much as any other resident of the particular place wherein the Jew resides." The Duke's liberality is attested to in the lines of Tannhauser:

> Jews, Christians, Greeks, Welsh and pagans many,
> Were ever found in his place;
> Hungarians, Poles, Russians and Bohemians
> And all who loved to live a life of grace. [2]

This favorable situation made Vienna the largest Jewish community in Austria-Germany. But their good fortune came to an abrupt end under the reign of the Hapsburgs (1272). Cries began to be heard that the Jews enjoy more privileges than Christians; that they fill the land with the "stench of unbelief, and that they ought to be burned, or sold at the rate of thirty for a penny." Charges of ritual murder and of Host desecration became of frequent occurrence, and Jews were not only burdened with unbearable taxes, but often forfeited the principle and interest of the debts due them by Letters of Annulment (*Totbrief*) which were granted the Christian borrowers.[3]

One faint ray of light pierced the darkness of Austrian Jewry under the reign of Albrecht II. Desirous to protect them against mob violence, he appealed to Benedict XII to investigate the truth about the miracles allegedly performed by a desecrated Host. The fact that the result of the investigation was never made known is sufficient evidence that the Jews were found not guilty. Albrecht also was instrumental in saving thousands of Jews from the massacres which everywhere followed in the wake of the Black Death (1349). For this he was nicknamed "Benefactor of the Jews" (*Fatuor Judaeorum*).

Albrecht's rule, however, was only a brief lull in the storm which broke out anew after his death. Since the possessions of a Jew on his conversion passed to the Duke, rapacity as well as religious zeal prompted them to "persuade" Jews to accept Christianity, if necessary by force. In 1370, all Jews in the ducal lands were thrown into jail, and their property confiscated. Only one young maiden and a forty-two year old man submitted to baptism, but the latter soon reverted to Judaism and was burned at the stake. The worst was yet to come. Under Albrecht V the Jews were accused of conspiring with the Hussites and supplying them with arms against the Church. Resort was also had to the unfailing device of Host desecration. In 1420 a rumor spread that a Christian woman, the wife of a sexton, had been enticed by a Jew several years before to steal a Host in order to make sport of it. Thereupon the Jews were imprisoned and stripped of everything they had, and interrogated as to where they hid other valuables. Those who did not "confess" were hanged by chains over a fire. Their children were whipped before their eyes until their blood flowed, their young men were rolled about in barrels until they died or were loaded into boats without oars and pushed away from the banks to drown in the Danube. Those who were imprisoned in the synagogues asked each other's forgiveness, recited the *Vidduy* (the Confession), and then killed each other. The last survivor, who had been chosen by lot, poured the oil of the Perpetual Lamp upon the altar, and, after setting fire to it, committed suicide (Sabbath of Sukkot, 1420). The others who were rounded up went to their deaths as if to a wedding, crying out, "Soon we shall see the light of Paradise," and calling from the midst of the fire, "Hear, O Israel, the Lord our God, the Lord is One!" (March 12, 1421). A Latin inscription on the spot where this occurred commemorates "the expiation of the terrible crimes committed by the Jewish dogs who paid the penalty upon the stake." [4]

The *Wiener Gezerah* (evil decree of Vienna) lingered long in the memory of the Jews, and Austria came to be known as *Erez Haddamim* (the Bloody Land). They did, however, begin to settle there again at the invitation of Frederick III who, finding himself in dire financial straits, granted them a "Privilege" with the express permission of Pope Nicholas V (1451), and in 1623 they were even promised, for a consideration, of course, protection "forever." But expulsions followed inevitably on the heels of each invitation. The Church continued to foment the prejudice of ·the populace. Frederick was dubbed the "King of the Jews," officers who protected them were refused communion and absolution, and students indulged in their pastime of harassing Jews with greater frequency and cruelty than ever before. Through the influence of the Jesuits, it was decreed (1630) that two hundred Viennese Jews, including at least one-third women and one-fifth children of both sexes, should be compelled to attend conversionist sermons delivered by monks every Saturday afternoon, and those who stayed away had to pay a fine which was set aside for the support of apostates. As late as 1760 Maria Theresa issued an order that all unbearded Jews should wear a yellow badge on their left arm.

Joseph II, though affected by the new spirit of tolerance which became fashionable at the time, never emancipated himself from the old prejudice against non-Catholics, and especially Jews, which he inherited from his bigoted mother. Acclaimed by some as "the humanitarian upon the throne," he was averse to putting Protestantism and Judaism on an equality with

Catholicism. His primary aim in granting his *Toleranz patent* (Patent of Toleration, 1782) was not to ameliorate the condition of his Jewish subjects but to make Christians of the Jews. In 1824 he rejected the appeal of the Viennese community for permission to build an up-to-date synagogue because it might attract a better attendance. On the other hand, he refused permission to print Mendelssohn's commentary on the Bible instead of Rashi's because he did not want his Jews to become "naturalists" (atheists). [5]

The battle against the Jews and Judaism continued in Austria during the nineteenth century, and every attempt at emancipation was followed by reaction. The revolution of 1848 was followed by laws renewing the former prohibitions against keeping Christian domestics, assuming Christian names, and many other civic and cultural restrictions. The liberal laws promulgated in 1867 aroused a storm of protest among the people, instigated by the clergy. In 1871 August Rohling issued his notorious *Der Talmudjude* ("the Talmud Jew"), in which he falsified many tenets of the Talmud, and in 1883 he even reasserted that the Talmud enjoins the use of Christian blood in the celebration of certain rites. Blood libels were actually staged in Tisza-Eslar, Hungary (1882) and Polna, Bohemia (1899), in the latter of which Professor Masaryk proved the innocence of the defendant.

To escape constant persecution and ostracism, many Jews of Austria, like those of Germany, submitted to baptism or proclaimed themselves *Konfessionslos* (religionless). Some, who from a feeling of loyalty or self-respect hesitated to take the final step, had their children baptized in their infancy. Mixed marriages, too, became the *Wiener Mode,* with the result that quite a number of Jews were "ennobled," and mixed their blood with that of the oldest nobility or even of the reigning family.

Yet, during all the vicissitudes of their history, the Jews of Austria had also their share of reverts and even converts. After the *Wiener Gezerah,* many who saved their lives by baptism returned to Judaism as soon as an opportunity offered itself. There were also some Spanish and Portuguese *Anusim* who for varied reasons chose Austria as the place in which to revert to their ancestral faith. A very unusual case was that of Diego Lopez Pereira, who, of all people, became a favorite of the bigoted Maria Theresa, and was created first Baron d'Aguilar and a privy councilor to the Empress.

Pereira was noted as a financier and a farmer of the tobacco revenue. As the head of the tobacco monopoly of Austria, he was called by Charles VI to Vienna. He agreed to come only on condition that he and his family be permitted to live there as Jews. On his arrival (1730) he declared himself and his household of the religion of Israel, and assumed the name of Moses. Thereafter he devoted himself to the amelioration of the lot of his coreligionists in Austria, Hungary, Bohemia, and Moravia, even at the risk of losing favor with the Empress, and protected Jewish refugees from other lands. When the rumor of his reversion to Judaism reached Spain, the Government at once demanded his extradition. But Pereira and his ten children managed to escape to London, where h: died in 1759. [6]

The story of Christianity in Bohemia and Moravia, the non-Germanic provinces which became the possessions of the Hapsburgs, is altogether different from that of Austria. Though converted to Christianity later than their German neighbors, they possessed a translation of the Bible by the middle of the ninth century. They were also receptive to new ideas and welcomed the Wycliffites, who fled from England, and the Waldenses, who escaped from France. It was among them that the Protestant revolt was started, which later assumed world-wide proportion and deprived the Church of half her empire.

The leader of this revolt was John Huss. His life span fell at a time when the Hierarchy passed through the most serious crisis of her existence. Gregory XII and Benedict XIII were engaged in a life and death struggle for the control of the Holy See. Each attributed to the other the basest motives and behavior, and each was supported by a college of cardinals and fanatic partisans. After more than thirty years of bitter strife, a Council was convoked at Pisa (1409), without the authorization of either pope, to put an end to the ecclesiastic war and to save the Hierarchy. The Council found both pontiffs guilty of immorality, heresy, and sorcery, and the populace acclaimed its findings by burning the popes in effigy with parchment mitres on their foreheads. A new pope, Alexander V, was elected in their stead, but the deposed pontiffs refused to surrender their authority; and in their stead, there were now three. However, even the legitimate pope proved no improvement on those whom he replaced; and his successor, John XXIII, was forced to abdicate at the Council of Constance (1415).[7]

During most of these turbulent years, Huss played the part of a faithful son of the Church and was regarded as such. After his graduation from the University of Prague, he was appointed to a lectureship at his *alma mater,* promoted to the deanship of the faculty of philosophy, and then to the office of Rector. Because of his fervid eloquence, he was also made curate of the chapel of Bethlehem. Before long, however, rumors reached the archbishop about Huss' deviation from the straight and narrow path.

It is said that in his connection with the university he used the writings of Wycliffe as his textbooks, and that he declared the miracles allegedly performed in a shrine near Wittenberg to be forgeries of greedy ecclesiastics. He also bitterly opposed the religious war decreed by Alexander V against the King of Naples, and especially the indulgences which he promised to all who should participate in the Crusade. Furthermore, Huss was an ardent Bohemian patriot and fought against the special privileges enjoyed by the Germans, who looked upon Czechs as their inferiors and were in control of the university as well as of the benefices of the Church.

Huss thus aroused against himself the enmity of the State, and the Church, and he was soon made to feel the strong hand of their powers. He was deprived of the right to exercise his clerical functions, ordered to abjure his Wycliffe heresies and to surrender all his writings, to be burnt in the palace of the Archbishop, at the peril of being denounced as a contumacious son of the Church and suffer excommunication.

Huss, however, was not intimidated. "In the things which pertain to salvation," he maintained, "God is to be obeyed rather than man," and with even greater vehemence he continued to inveigh against the immorality and cupidity of the priests, the sale of indulgences, the doctrine of Transubstantiation, and the institution of auricular confession. He reinforced his preaching with his *De Ecclesia* and *De Sex Erroribus,* the latter of which he posted on the walls of the chapel of Bethlehem.

At last the disaffection in Bohemia began to assume threatening proportions, and the newly convoked Council of Constance found it advisable to invite Huss to vindicate his views. In a letter of safe conduct the king assured him that no matter what judgment were passed, Huss would be permitted to return safely to Bohemia. But once enticed to Constance he was put in chains, and when his case came up for hearing he was denied the right to employ counsel to defend himself, or to speak in his own behalf. He was ordered to recant in public and to retract whatever statements against the teachings of the Church he had made in writing or on the platform. Upon his refusal, the King himself proposed that he be sentenced to the stake (July 6, 1415). He was accordingly degraded from the priesthood as "an accursed Judas who has consulted with the Jews," his soul was officially consigned to the devils in hell, and he was handed over to the secular authorities, while the Council unconcernedly proceeded to the other business of the day. As he was being tied to the stake he was urged for the last time to recant. But Huss, calling upon God to witness that the one great object of his preaching and writing was to reclaim men from sin, merely chanted prayers and expressed his faith that "He who hath delivered Jonah from the whale's belly, Daniel from the Lion's maw, and the three youths from the fiery furnace," will also deliver him if it be to His glory. He stopped only when his mouth was choked by the smoke.[8]

At the news of the martyrdom of Huss the nobles of Bohemia and Moravia issued a *Protestatio Bohemorum,* in which they affirmed that those who convicted him and their followers were "liars, vile traitors, and calumniators of Bohemia and Moravia, the worst of all heretics, full of all evil, sons of the devil." The uprising became a revolution. German professors were expelled from the university, and German priests were banished from their parishes. Furious fighting broke out in Prague and other places, and Martin V issued a bull in which he proclaimed a Crusade "for the destruction of Wycliffites, Hussites, and all other heretics of Bohemia." But though one army after another of mercenaries was hurled against them, the Hussites were almost always victorious and their enemies fled before them. At last the Holy See accepted a compromise, and the Hussite creed was legitimatized in Bohemia and Moravia (1434).

Unfortunately, the Hussites, who had been united when threatened by a common enemy, split among themselves when the danger seemed to be over. The most advanced Reformers called their citadel Tabor, and the pond near it Jordan, and, like the English Puritans, looked upon themselves as the Chosen People who were commissioned by God to fight the battles of the Lord not only against the German Edomites, Noabites, and Amalekites, but against the Czechish Utraquists who were more moderate in their reforms. They were defeated at the battle of Lippan (1434), and in their turn the Utraquists were suppressed when Austria gained control of Bohemia. Most of the dissidents were executed or exiled, their literature was almost entirely destroyed by the Jesuits, and the country when almost depopulated was saved to the Church. But a remnant remained, and Huss' influence did not altogether cease. Like all Reformists he left behind him an enduring monument in the translation of the Bible into the Czech tongue, in which he was guided by the commentaries of the rabbis. This Bible became the version adopted by that small but faithful band, the *Unitas Fratrum,* whose traditions, with some modifications, were carried on to this day by the Bohemian or Moravian Brethren, until it was superseded by the famed Bible of Kralice, Moravia (1593). It was their guide in all matters of creed and life, and their bulwark against the Catholics and Protestants, both of whom were bent on their extermination. Their zeal for the Word of God is described by a sixteenth century German historian to whom Huss is "worse than a Tartar, a Turk, a Sodomite, or a Jew," as follows:

> Furriers, shoemakers, tailors and that class of mechanics by their frequent attendance at sermons and their zealous reading of the Scriptures that had been translated into the vernacular tongue, were led to open discussion with the priests before the people; and not men only, but women also, reached such a measure of audacity and impudence as to venture to dispute in regard to the doctrines of the Scriptures, and maintain these against the priests. [9]

Hardly were the Hussites suppressed in Bohemia than a new schism threatened to develop in Moravia, a fief of the Bohemian crown. The barons who were in need of peasants and artisans welcomed all refugees from religious persecution, and among them the Anabaptists, who were ostracized by Catholics and Protestants alike, and were soon joined by Balthazar Huebmaier. He was distinguished as a Hebraist, and at a very early age was appointed professor of theology and preacher at the cathedral of Regensburg (where he demolished a synagogue to build a Christian chapel). But he gave up his posts when he espoused the views of Zwingli, which views he changed again for those of the Anabaptists, which views he preached to ever increasing masses. In Zurich he was arrested shortly after his arrival, was convicted of heresy, tortured, and expelled. He went to Nikolsburg, and his influence grew steadily. It seemed as if he was to make Moravia a center of Anabaptism.

But like many Christian sects, the Anabaptists soon split among themselves. A certain illiterate Hans Hut of Franconia came with a message that Christ would shortly come again to establish His kingdom, that the elect would receive a two-edged sword to exterminate the wicked and the day would be presaged by the irruption of the Turks into Christendom. He found an associate in another prophet, Jacob Wiedeman, and wherever they went people deserted their homes, placed their goods in common, and awaited the day of the coming of the Lord. Hut was imprisoned by the barons, but escaped to Augsburg. He was, however, captured by the Catholic authorities and tortured to death. Huebmaier was taken to Vienna and burned at the stake; and his wife, with a great stone tied to her neck, was thrown into the Danube. [10]

The Anabaptists finally settled in Austerlitz, where they were permitted to live in their own way. There they established communist colonies after the model of the Essenes. They married exclusively among themselves. Everyone worked according to his ability, and everyone received according to his needs. They proved themselves excellent farmers and artisans, and prospered exceedingly. Their fanaticism, however, turned their settlements into places of ceaseless strife and contention, each one spying on his neighbor to see whether he conformed to the teaching of their religion. The government, too, as soon as the danger of a Turkish invasion passed, began to take steps against them. They went from place to place, only to be banished. They were burned, beheaded, and drowned, but remained steadfast to their Anabaptist faith. But after Bohemia and Moravia were subdued by the Catholic forces, the Jesuits took them in hand and against these forces they could not long prevail. It is said that the depopulation of the country, due mainly to the extermination of the Anabaptists, was so frightful that the Moravian diet passed a statute permitting every man to take two wives, so that the country might be repeopled. [11]

The Jews of Bohemia and Moravia had reason to look forward to better treatment at the hands of the Hussites and Anabaptists, who, like the English Puritans, were saturated with the spirit of the Old Testament, whose founder they called "Magister in Israel," and whose successor, they claimed, "ruled like a judge in Israel." Indeed, even while Catholicism was in complete control of the country there were periods when, despite the bulls of the popes, Jews of the Kingdom enjoyed not only protection but some privileges. As early as 1124 a certain Jacob, who was forcibly converted, was not molested when he continued to live publicly as a Jew, and though he removed the Christian symbols from the synagogue, he escaped with the paying of a fine. The regulations of Ottakar II (1254) reaffirmed and even surpassed in their liberality those of Duke Frederick II. They provided that a Jew could be tried only in the synagogue, and no Christian could testify against him except in company of a Jewish witness, that he could not be compelled to transact business on his Sabbaths and holidays; that the desecration of Jewish cemeteries was punishable with death and confiscation of property; that a Christian who accused a Jew of ritual murder and was unable to support his charge with the testimony of three Christians and three Jews should suffer the same punishment as the Jew would have suffered. Charles IV protected Jewish reverts from the vengeance of the Church, and in 1356 reaffirmed the regulations of Ottakar II. [12]

But the favor of the Kings did not reflect the sentiment of the general populace. The people, goaded on by the clergy and spurred on by rumors that the Jews desecrated the Host or killed a Christian child for ritual purposes, or poisoned the wells, frequently robbed or murdered the Jews, demolished their synagogues, desecrated cemeteries, and exterminated whole communities (1298, 1305, 1389, 1391).

Nor were the Hussites, who were fighting for their own freedom of conscience, inclined to think of granting the same right to their Jewish countrymen. They did, indeed, accept their help in time of distress. They were heartened by the fasts and prayers which, at the order of R. Jacob Moelin, the Jews observed during the march of the crusaders. They welcomed them during the siege of Prague, in the construction of a moat at the Vyschrad, and joined them in singing the hymns composed for the occasion by R. Avigdor b. Isaac Karo. But when the Taborites captured the city (1421) they put before the Jews the choice between martyrdom and apostasy. Many Jews who preferred the former threw themselves and their wives and children into the flames. [13]

Needless to say, the Church poured out her wrath upon the Jews the moment she regained control of the country, and punished them not only for their infidelity but for abetting the Hussites and for supplying them with money and ammunition. When, in 1522, a procession of the Jews went out to meet Louis II, the last Polish King of Bohemia (with the scrolls of the Torah carried by the rabbis under a silken canopy), he touched it only with his whip. In 1557 King Ferdinand swore that he would never tolerate any Jews in Prague; but finding them necessary to the welfare of his Kingdom, he was released of his oath by Pius IV. To salve his conscience he decreed that the Jews and their children should attend once a week a sermon by a Jesuit father at the Salvator-Kirche. [14]

The history of the Jews of Bohemia and Moravia, after they became united with Austria under the Hapsburgs (1526), is, like that of Austria, a congeries of expulsions and readmissions when the state of the exchequer made their presence necessary, of "voluntary" and forced conversions and not infrequent reversions. An interesting case of the latter is that of Hayyim Engelsberg. Having broken into one of the synagogues of Prague he escaped punishment through baptism. He was also accorded a friendly reception by the Emperor and nobility at Vienna when he undertook to convert his former coreligionists, but not meeting with much success, he lost favor with the ecclesiastics and being caught, with two other apostates, in the act of breaking into the vault of the archdukes, was condemned to be hanged. On the scaffold he confessed that when he had received the holy sacrament he had wrapped the Host in his handkerchief and had thrown it upon the ash heap. Thereupon the mob fell upon the Jews, killed some of them, and plundered the homes of many. Engelsberg himself was mutilated while he recited the *Vidduy* and was burned on the same spot where Jewish martyrs met a gruesome death two hundred years before. [15]

While as a rule only the lower strata of the Jewish community could be induced to join the Church, some of the saintliest Christian men and women of Bohemia were seeking admission into the house of Israel. These Judaizers, one of whom, Ian Pita, was burned at the stake, continued under cover for many years. A rumor had it that two of the great luminaries of Austrian

Jewry, Ignatz Kuranda (1812-84), the champion of equality, and Adolf Jellinek (1821-93), reputed the most eloquent rabbi of the nineteenth century, were both descendants of Hussite converts to Judaism.[16] In the reign of Joseph II, encouraged probably by his reputed liberalism, disguised figures began to appear at the services on Jewish holidays and disappear soon after they were over. A government investigation revealed the fact that they were mainly country folks who first adopted the Jewish Sabbath as their day of rest and then were anxious to associate with Jews in order to learn the other doctrines of Judaism. To put a check to the movement the Emperor issued a decree in his own hand ordering that if they considered themselves Christians they should return to the Christian Sabbath; if Jews, they should submit to circumcision. To the amazement of the authorities they accepted the latter alternative. In fact, it was discovered that many of them had already undergone the rite, and regarded the decree as a privilege to be grateful for rather than a punishment. Thereupon the Emperor ruled that as Jews they should be ejected from their homes and farms, since none but Christians could own real estate, and the peasants in a body departed from the villages wherein their ancestors had dwelt long before the Hapsburgs came to Bohemia. The government then appealed to the rabbis to dissuade them from abandoning their Christian religion, and one rabbi induced some of them to stay in the Christian fold by assuring them that once they assumed the obligations of a Jew they would be expected to observe all the six hundred and thirteen commandments or be accounted as sinners. Most of them, however, clung to their new faith and continued to propagate it among their fellow peasants. According to a press report from Prague as late as 1935, "hundreds of Christian peasants in the villages of Carpatho-Russia are besieging the rabbinate to circumcise them and to convert them to Judaism so that they may go to Palestine."[17]

For the oldest organized group of Sabbatarians and Unitarians, as well as for the greatest number of proselytes in modern times, outside of Russia, we must go to Hungary, the most centrally located country in Europe, which has given

Bohemia more than one of her kings, and which Church historians affectionately called *Regnum Marianum* (Realm of Mary).

Jews had settled among the Hungarians already at the time when the Romans served as soldiers under Arpad, who subdued them. They managed to live amicably with the Huns, who invaded the land in the fifth century, and the Magyars, who wrested it from them in the ninth century. The letter which Hasdai ibn Shaprut addressed to King Joseph of the Chazars (c. 960) was first to be delivered to the Jews living in Hungary with the request that they pass it on to their royal coreligionists in Khazaria. As late as the twelfth century there was still be found in Hungary the "Chalisier" who claimed descent from the Tartar proselytes of Southern Russia. As in other lands, they engaged in commerce, especially with Bohemia, held non-Jewish slaves, sometimes intermarried with their non-Jewish neighbors, and raised their children in the Jewish faith. [18]

Probably in few other lands did Catholicism find it so hard to establish itself as in Hungary. Even after the country became converted under Duke Geza (970-97) at the instance of his Catholic wife, most of the people for centuries persisted in their heathen customs and offered sacrifices to the pagan gods. The new religion had to be spread by the sword, and defended by foreign ecclesiastics and German mercenaries. Later Catharists, Albigenses, and Waldenses won over many of the populace, and some of the princes, to their heresies. The views of Wycliffe and Huss were propagated there by Jerome of Prague a century before the Lutheran Reformation. Through the influence of Biandrata, the physician-in-ordinary to Sigismund, the king, his mother, and many nobles, declared themselves against the doctrine of the Trinity. With the invasion and subjugation of Hungary by the Turks (1526-1686), the cry was frequently heard: "Where are the old Magyar saints? Why do they not defend the realm against the infidels?" It seemed at one time as if Hungary were on the point of turning Unitarian or Mohammedan. [19]

The Church, of course, kept a vigilant eye on Hungary as

elsewhere, and never ceased to prod the princes to crush heresy wherever it appeared. Already the Synod of Szabolos (1092), summoned to remedy the abuses of the clergy, took measures to protect the faithful against un-Christian influences, and decreed that no Jews or Moslems should be permitted to marry Christians or keep Christian slaves. These prohibitions had to be repeatedly re-enacted, and in the Diets of 1523 and 1525 the penalties of confiscation of property and death at the stake were decreed for all who deviated from the path prescribed by the Church.

But the heretics refused to capitulate, and when in power, meted out to the Catholics the same measure the latter had meted out to them. Calvinism, Lutheranism, and Anabaptism won many adherents. Nor were there lacking decided tendencies towards the denial of the Trinity, the acceptance of the seventh day Sabbath, and even the doctrines and practices of Judaism. In 1529 the anti-Romanists became sufficiently powerful to order the expulsion of the Catholic clergy and the diversion of the property of the Catholic Church to secular purposes. Finally, the restrictions were removed at the Diet of Torda in Transylvania by the decree of John Sigismund (1557), and Hungary became the first European country where freedom of conscience, speech, and worship were accorded to all people under the first, and thus far the only, known "Unitarian" king to rule a Christian nation. True, this term had at first no theological connotation. It merely signified that the representatives of the various religious bodies at the Diet were united in a league of tolerance for one another's creed. But when the more orthodox withdrew, the name was retained by the anti-Trinitarians to designate their belief in "One only God and none else besides." As such, it was officially adopted at the convention of 1638.

For about half a century Unitarianism flourished in Hungary and bade fair to become the dominant religion of the realm. Its chief apostle was Francis David (1510-79), a Catholic priest who turned Lutheran, then Calvinist, and later joined Biandrata and devoted the rest of his life to war against Catholics, Lutherans, and Calvinists. In a debate at the palace in the presence of King Sigismund, the court, and the clergy (March 8-16, 1568), he was acclaimed the victor, and the whole population of Kolozsvar (Klausenberg) accepted "the Religion of Francis David." Thousands of others in Transylvania and Hungary did likewise, and appointed David their Bishop.

Under David, Unitarianism made rapid strides. The press poured out anti-Trinitarian literature. The Dominican monastery at Kolozsvar became a Unitarian university. The number of congregations grew apace, and before the end of the century there were about four hundred and twenty-five Unitarian churches in Hungary. But trouble arose soon among them over the question as to the place to be assigned to Jesus in their ritual. All agreed that he should not be worshiped as God, but some still felt that he should be given an exalted position similar to that of Mary, as among the Catholics. Biandrata was among the latter, and since David would not be persuaded, he sent for Socinus to labor with him. Socinus warned David and his followers that their views "might lead men back to Moses and Judaism." But they remained unmoved. After the death of Sigismund Augustus (1572) the controversy became even more bitter. His successor, Stephen Bathory, came under the influence of the Jesuits and deprived the Diet of its jurisdiction in matters religious. Protestant and Unitarian ministers were ousted from their churches. David was thrown into jail, after he preached a sermon in which he declared, "Whatever the world may say, it must some day become clear that God is but One," and five months later he expired in the dungeon of Deva. Unitarianism courageously struggled on for another generation, but Rome finally triumphed, and with the assistance of the Hapsburgs drove the Unitarians either back to the Church or to the duplicity of the Spanish and Portuguese Marranos.[20]

Socinus' warning that David's brand of Unitarianism might lead to Judaism seemed to be realized among the Szeklers, originally the most savage of the "three nations" of Transylvania. Under the leadership of Chancellor Eossi and Bethlen (1588) they abolished baptism, adopted the dietary laws of the Pentateuch, and instituted the observance of the seventh day Sabbath and other Jewish festivals. Bethlen's successor inaugurated a

reign of terror against Szeklers. Their property was seized and
confiscated, many of them were "legally" executed. One of
them was stoned to death by the mob, and his wife pilloried
in the market place and banished from the country. Under
Marie Theresa the schools and colleges of the Sabbatarians were
closed, their presses and books were destroyed, and their child-
dren torn away from their parents and dispersed in Catholic
homes and institutions. Many of them fled to other lands. Yet
about thirty-two thousand still remained to continue their heroic
struggle for freedom of worship.

To what extent Bethlen and Eossi themselves Judaized is
unknown, but Simon Pechi, Eossi's adopted son, who at one
time rose to the governorship of Transylvania, went the whole
length of becoming a full-fledged Jew. To his enthusiastic
propaganda is credited the conversion of twenty thousand
peasants to his faith. At last he was imprisoned but managed
to escape to Turkey and found work as a compositor in the
printing house established by Donna Gracia near Constantinople. In the course of time he became proficient in Hebrew
and translated the Jewish Prayer Book and other literature into
Hungarian.[21]

Pechi was not the only Hungarian *ger* who was instrumental
in spreading a knowledge of Judaism and its literature among
his new coreligionists. Some scholars are of the opinion that
"Hgr" which follows the name of Abraham, the exegete, in
unvocalized Hebrew stands for *Hagger* (the proselyte) rather
than Hagar, the Hungarian, another proselyte, and they have
the authority of Hebrew etymology.[22] Moses b. Abraham
Avinu (our father) was remarkable in that he became proficient
also in Yiddish. A scion of a Nickolsberg family by the name of
Hasse, he went to Amsterdam where he was circumcised, accepted the Jewish faith, married the daughter of a certain R.
Israel, and worked as a printer (1686-7). By 1690 he had a
printing establishment of his own in which he published a
series of devotional books in Hebrew and Yiddish. In 1709
we find him in Halle, Germany, where in 1712 appeared his
Tolaath Moshe, or *Weltbeschreibung* ("The Worm of Moses,"
or "The Description of the World"), containing an account

of the Ten Tribes drawn from various sources in Yiddish. In 1714 he printed the prayer book *Tefillah L'Moshe* and the *Zera Berak* by Zedekiah Baruk. Because of his alleged anti-Christian statements his shop was closed, his books were confiscated, and he himself was imprisoned. But due to the effort of influential Jews, he was released and returned to Amsterdam, where he published various books, among them the talmudic treatise *Rosh Hashanah*. His children were brought up not only in the faith but in the trade of their father and participated in the printing of the Talmud in Frankfort on the Oder (1717-19). His daughter Ella was probably the youngest typesetter in the history of typography. A composition of hers in rhymed Yiddish appended to the *Tefillah L'Moshe* reads:

> The Yiddish letters I set with my hand,
> I, Ella bath Moshe, of Holland
> My years are only nine, please bear it in mind,—
> And condemn not a child if a mistake you'll find.

Like Ella, her sister Gella also lent a hand to her father's printing, and left an account of herself and family in another prayer book:

> Of these beautiful new prayers, from beginning to end
> I have set each letter with mine own hand....
> A virgin I, less than twelve years of age.
> Wonder not that I must labor who am so young in
>   years:—
> The daughter of Israel hath for ages been shedding
>   tears!
> My beloved masters withhold not your patronage,
> Nor begrudge a few cents for this book to spend,
> Remember on them doth our living depend.... [23]

A record of a would-be convert is found in the *Responsa* of R. Akiba Eger (1761-1835), wherein the rabbi, who insisted on compliance with the law of the State which prohibited conversion to Judaism, commends his correspondent for refusing to circumcise a Christian and expresses himself as averse to teaching Judaism to non-Jews. R. Moses Gaster, on the other hand, speaks with approval of a woman by the name of Kovochi whom he met in 1888 who "by sheer miracle, had survived the tortures inflicted upon her for the sake of her Jewish faith" and has transmitted her love for her new religion to her children.[24]

The removal of the ban on conversion to Judaism by Austria in 1868 and by Hungary in 1895 produced unexpected religious alignments among the people of the dual monarchy. Many Jews who were driven by anti-Semitism into the Christian fold retraced their steps and flew back "like doves to their cotes." Among the more prominent of them were the Baroness of Koerner, who married Baron Popper; the composer Arnold Schoenberg, who was reconverted by R. Louis Germain Levy in Paris in 1933; and Jolan Foldes, the novelist whose stirring story *The Street of the Fishing Cat* was awarded the prize in the All-Nations Prize Novel Competition. Quite a sensation was caused in Budapest in 1936 when Baron Peter von Hatvany, the sugar magnate of Hungary, announced to R. Hevesi his determination to return to Judaism and bequeathed a large portion of his fortune to the Jewish community.[25]

Perhaps it was "the call of the blood" that prompted Archbishop Franz Cohen (d. 1888) to bequeath all his possessions to the Jewish people of Kromeriz, Czechoslovakia. His palace has since been turned into a synagogue and the income from his estate applied to the support of the charitable organizations of the community.[26]

The effect of the new law was marked especially among the Gentiles. It is reported that one hundred fifty-seven non-Jews were admitted into the Jewish faith in 1869 alone, and their number since then grew into several thousand. Statistics for Hungary show that between August 1919 and 1928 there were conversions of five hundred sixty-seven men, four hundred eighty-one women, and eighty-eight children. During the ministry of R. Chayes, the Vienna Bet Din accepted an average of four hundred *gerim* per annum. Several Sabbatarian and other Christian communities also proclaimed themselves openly as Jewish. In 1928 the once numerous proselyte congregation of Boezoed Ujfalu, which had clung to Judaism for about three hundred years, consisted of but fifty families; and as they found themselves unable to support their religious institutions, the local rabbi appealed in their behalf to world Jewry and assured their continuous existence. In 1926 it was reported:

> That the number of re-converts completely cancel out the number of Jewish apostates. Still more interesting is the fact that instead of preventing intermarriage, it only decides the non-Jewish contracting party to go over to Judaism, since the Jews would not go over to Christianity. This is a very notable reaction against the ruthless wave of anti-Semitism sweeping through the country. [27]

At least one of the recent Austrian *gerim* who deserves special mention is R. Jacob Abraham, lately on the staff of Bikkur Holim Hospital of Jerusalem. While still a student in an Austrian academy, he was attracted through his study of Hebrew to the Jewish religion and became a proselyte in the "court" of *Zaddik* of Sadagura in 1908. He left the following year for Palestine, where he found employment as a proofreader in a Hebrew printing establishment. Still more dramatic was the career of Gavor Gedman. At the age of twenty-seven he participated in the outrages committed against the Jews by the awakening Magyars after the World War. While he and his brother were pillaging a Jewish home he found a book, which turned out to be a Hungarian translation of the Bible. He took it, with the other loot, to his house, and, to use his own words, "I started to read it, and as I read I began more and more to realize what a great people the Jews must be to have produced it, and how we Christians have sinned against them in our terrible persecutions. At last my conscience would give me no rest until I resolved to expiate my crime by becoming one of them." After an inner struggle he ran away from home, embraced Judaism, and became a *Bahur* (Scholar) in one of the *Yeshibot* (Talmud Schools) of Hungary. [28]

Among the Jews of Bohemia and Hungary there have always been current various tales in which the hero is a proselyte to Judaism. One of them is the story of the Jews of Prague being saved from destruction through the love of a baker's apprentice for a Jewish maiden. Because they would not bake leavened bread on Passover, it was customary for Jews to buy it from Christians on the first night after the conclusion of the festival. In the course of his work the apprentice learned that the Gentile bakers conspired to put poison in the bread and immediately informed his sweetheart, who in turn notified the rabbi. The latter ordered that contrary to custom, they should eat mazzot for a day longer, and thus saved the Jews. The young man then declared his intentions to become a proselyte, was sent to Amsterdam, and after his conversion was married to his Jewish sweetheart. [29]

A more touching contribution to Jewish folklore was made by the Jews of Hungary. The hero is Prince Emerich, who fell in love with Hannah, the beautiful daughter of the famous R. Issac of Tyrnau (d. 1427), author of the popular *Minhagim l'kol hashanah,* whom he first saw at a carnival. The prince persisted in his courtship, but Hannah would not marry one not of her faith. Suddenly the disappointed lover disappeared, to the great sorrow of his mother and friends who mourned him as dead. Actually, Emerich settled in Poland among Jews, where he passed off as one of the Spanish *Anusim* who came to learn the religion from which he had been torn away as a child. There he assumed the name of Abraham, and after acquiring a knowledge of Judaism and of the Talmud, he returned as a Polish *Bahur* (Talmud student) to Tyrnau, and was admitted into R. Isaac's Yeshibah. It was not long before he and Hannah announced their engagement.

Something told Emerich's mother to attend the wedding of the rabbi's daughter, and she was shocked to find her long lost son in the groom. When she came to, she urged him to admit that he was the prince, but Emerich insisted that he never was anything but a Jew. When her entreaties were of no avail, the princess decreed that unless he confess he should be burned at the stake. The sentence was executed, and

Emerich-Abraham went up in flames with a smile on his face and the "*Shema*" on his lips.

The Jews, of course, paid dearly for the love which prompted the prince to embrace their religion, and to become a martyr for its sake. They were all thrown into jail; but as they were about to be massacred, the prince appeared to his mother in a dream and warned her against committing such an atrocity. She, therefore, commuted their sentence to expulsion. The entire community then left Tyrnau, and followed their rabbi and his daughter into exile, grateful to have escaped with their lives. [30]

CHAPTER XXIV

THE PROTESTANT REVOLUTION

UNLIKE France, Switzerland, and Holland, the religious upheaval in Germany was greatly accelerated by the economic condition of the country. The cupidity of the Roman Curia weighed especially heavy on the Germans, already a prey to more than three hundred petty princelings who were claiming a right to sponge upon the peasantry. These successors to the robber barons of former times who, we are told, "looked upon robbery as a trade, and considered it rather an honor to be wolves," became especially oppressive during the fifteenth century as their military exploits began to be less and less lucrative and as their poor serfs, rendered sullen and resentful by crushing taxes and forced labor, were ready to put the entire blame on the Church. The old sallies of the Minnesinger began to be repeated with ever increasing bitterness. People began to murmur about the "tricks" of the papacy "to extract the money from our pockets as if we were barbarians." A young shepherd who denounced the pope as a villain drew thousands of approving listeners. Demands were openly made that priests be killed and the wealth of the Church be divided among the members of the community. [1]

To this discontent with the policy of the Church there was added the lingering effect of the mystic or pietistic movement which was inaugurated in Germany in the thirteenth century by Meister Eckhart and his Brethren of the Free Spirit. But, strange to say, in Germany more than anywhere in Christendom, the Reformation which there culminated in a revolution was expedited by a controversy over the Talmud between a Jewish renegade and a Christian humanist, and was propagated to a considerable extent by Jews who saw Christianity in the light of the flickering faggots of the Inquisition.

The counterpart of the Spanish Dominican Vincente Ferrer was the German Franciscan John Capistrano, who had been commissioned by Nicholas V to preach against the insubordinate Hussites and "the disbelieving Jews." Everywhere he and his fellow monks went, burnings and expulsions became the order of the day. Ancient Jewish communities were depopulated, and children by the hundred were carried off and raised in the Christian faith. But owing to German disunity, many Jewish communities continued a precarious existence in villages and towns and thither fled those who were banished from the larger centers. The Dominicans, not to be outdone by the Franciscans, and to gain prestige for their Order, undertook to convert these. With this in view, the Prior of the Order in Cologne engaged as his tool a certain Johannes Pfefferkorn, who had served time for burglary and, on his release, presented himself and his family for baptism in Cologne. Pfefferkorn then wrote a number of defamatory attacks on the Talmud, and at the instigation of the Dominicans, Maximilian issued an order, which was read in all synagogues on the first day of the Feast of Tabernacles (April 10, 1510), that all the Hebrew books found there and in Jewish homes be seized and destroyed.

The heart-broken Jews made bold to appeal to the Emperor, and through the help of the Archbishop of Cologne succeeded in having a commission appointed to investigate the charges. It consisted of Pfefferkorn and another apostate, Victor of Carben, the Prior of the Cologne Dominicans, and Johannes Reuchlin. Reuchlin, "the phoenix of Germany" (1455-1522), was famous for his devotion to the Kabbalah and his mastery of Hebrew, which he studied under the court physician Jacob b. Yehiel Loans and under R. Obadiah Seforno. His admiration for the sacred tongue "in which God, angels and men spoke together as friends talk face to face," he expressed in a eulogy *De Mirifico Verbo*, which he followed with one of the first Hebrew grammars in Latin. Reuchlin was at that time no special friend of the Jews. He, like many others, believed that they were a depraved and superstitious lot and that the Talmud was the source of their spiritual degradation. But having been called upon to act as judge, he made a thorough investigation; and to the surprise of the commission, Reuchlin's opinion turned out to be the reverse of what they had expected. He declared that instead of burning the Hebrew commentaries on the Bible, they should be studied in order to better understand the Scriptures; that the *Zohar* contains affirmations of the doctrines of Christianity; and that the prayer-books should not be destroyed, as long as those who use them are permitted to remain Jews. Furthermore, he argued, that if there is aught in Jewish literature derogatory to Christianity, there is much more in Christian literature insulting to Judaism. Besides, according to the rulings of the Church, Jews were not to be regarded as heretics, and hence cannot be accused of blasphemy. He even went so far as to ask protection for the Jews on the ground that, according to the old law, they were citizens of the German Reich.

In reply to Reuchlin, Pfefferkorn, with the assistance of the Dominicans, issued a scurrilous pamphlet, *Der Handspiegel* (the hand-mirror), abusing the Jews and accusing their defender of having been bribed by them. Reuchlin retorted in *Der Augenspiegel* (the eye-mirror), in which he exposed Pfefferkorn as a liar and thief, who blackmailed Jews and Jewish books in order to extort money. He also dug up an obsolete teaching of the Church, according to which "a Christian must love a Jew as his fellow-man and neighbor." This shifted the attack from the Talmud to Reuchlin. The Dominicans accused him of Judaizing and heresy, while the Humanists rallied to the defense of their master. Unable to wreak vengeance on their enemy, the monks resorted to the never-failing libels of ritual murder and Host desecration as a result of which many Jews were tortured, thirty burned at the stake, and two, who submitted to baptism, were "mercifully" beheaded (Berlin, 1510). After four years of warfare the Emperor ordered that *Der Augenspiegel* be confiscated, and

Reuchlin write an apology. Reuchlin complied, but his "apology" was more damning than his attack.

This "battle of the books," which excited all Germany, indicated that there were even some ecclesiastics who would not allow their prejudices to get the best of their judgment. Even the Bishop of Spires aligned himself on the side of Reuchlin. But the credit belongs chiefly to the Humanists. In 1515 they issued a volume *Epistolae obscurorum virorum* ("Letters of Obscure Men"), in which they exposed in the Church Latin of the Middle Ages the gullibility, superstition, cupidity, and lasciviousness of the monks and clergy of their day. When this volume was suppressed, another even more devastating appeared from the pen of Ulrich von Hutten. It is related that when Erasmus read it he laughed so heartily that he burst a boil on his neck and so cured himself without the aid of a physician. In a certain sense this is what the *Epistolae* did to the spiritual boils of Christianity—it helped to laugh many of them out of existence. [2]

One man who did not laugh was the morbid monk Martin Luther (1483-1546). The son of a Saxon peasant, he was reared in the Catholic teaching that only by "good deeds"— by which was meant praying, mortification of the flesh, pilgrimages to the shrines of the saints and observing of the sacraments, can one escape the torment of hell. He matriculated at the University of Erfurt, a center of Humanism, but also a place where Hussites sometimes whispered their anti-clerical propaganda in the ears of the students. Luther avoided both the Humanists and the Hussites, and at the request of his father prepared himself for the profession of the law. To everyone's surprise he suddenly appeared in the monastery of the Augustine Eremites and became a monk.

The motive which prompted Luther to make this decision has been variously explained. Judging from his later self-revealing writings—which, however, are largely colored by his passions of the hour—he was in constant dread of hell-fire, and his horrors of Satan's snares led him to seek sanctuary in the holy precincts of the monastery where the devil would be least likely to have dominion. There he scrupulously de-voted himself to prayer, fasting, maceration, and other mortifi-cations which he added of his own volition, and wearied the Confessional with his fear of being "gallows-ripe." There, too, he began to read the Bible which, he states, he had not studied in his earlier years. He also took up the study of Hebrew and of the Kabbalah, in which, however, he never became proficient.

Once, while Luther was lecturing on St. Paul's Epistle to the Romans at the University of Wittenberg, it suddenly occurred to him that the word *justitia* in the Vulgate rendition of the verse "the just shall live by his faith" (Romans, 1:7, from Habakkuk, 2:4), means, as most Jewish commentators understood it, faith in God's righteousness. But to him it sug-gested that only by faith can one obtain salvation, and he began to fear lest the excessive "good works" which he imposed upon himself were but a "Satanic delusion," a trick of the powers of darkness to effect his damnation. Thereafter his scrupulosity gave way to spiteful breaches of monastic disci-pline. He began to abandon Breviary and to discard the ob-ligatory recitation of the daily Office, and finally came to the conclusion that the doctrine of "good works" is a snare and deception.

His confidence in the infallibility of the Hierarchy shaken, Luther began to scrutinize the conduct of those who were at its head. Among the many abuses in which they indulged, the one which aroused him to open revolt was an Indulgence pro-claimed by Leo X to obtain funds for the building of St. Peter's Cathedral in Rome. Luther, who saw in Indulgences, as in all "good works," a machination of Satan to make men put their trust in something else than faith, drafted ninety-five theses, posted them on the church door (1517), and challenged anyone to defend them. He succeeded better than he had ex-pected. The "theses" were copied and widely circulated in German and Latin, the sale of Indulgences rapidly declined, everywhere controversies raged, and the press was busy pub-lishing pamphlets defending the rebellious friar. To stir the people further Luther wrote three pamphlets, in the first of which, entitled *To the Christian Nobility of the German Nation,* he urged the princes to do away with the pope and and the priesthood, since every Christian is a priest in his own right and needs no other intermediator between him and Christ, and to take over all church property in Germany; in the second, which he called *The Babylonian Captivity of the Church,* he asserted that according to the Scriptures there should be only three Sacraments—that of baptism, the Eucharist, and penance, and condemned transubstantiation as a "monstrous phantom"; and in the third, *The Freedom of the Christian Man,* he amplified his doctrine of justification by faith alone.

Leo X was at first inclined to treat the whole matter as merely a monkish aberration, and delayed taking a hand until after the imperial election of 1519. But the papal nuncio of Charles V issued a statement declaring that Luther "brought together all previous heresies in one stinking mess," and forbade his writings to be printed, sold, or read "since they are foul, harmful, suspected, and come from a notorious and stiff-necked heretic." Luther was summoned to appear at the Diet of Worms under a safe conduct of the Emperor. After hearing his famous address—the genuineness of which is doubtful—the latter declared his outrage that "a single monk, led astray by private judgment, has set himself against the faith held by all Christians for a thousand years or more and impudently concludes that all Christians up till now have erred," and ordered him to return to Wittenberg. Within a few days after his departure an edict proclaimed Luther an outlawed heretic, decreed that all his books be burned, and threatened all his sympathizers with extermination. But the edict was ignored, his books were read more than ever, and he himself was spirited away by his friends to the safe keeping of Frederick the Wise's castle of Wartburg.

Luther was pugnacious yet cautious, radical or conservative, mystical or rational as it suited his purpose, capable of asceticism yet craving for self-indulgence, extremely morose and excessively hilarious. He was impetuous and rude, arrogant and stubborn, and could hate to the verge of insanity. Like

Paul, whose theology he adopted, his animosity for those with whom he formerly cast his lot surpassed all bounds once he turned against them. He would be pleased with nothing less than that "all bishops should be murdered, and all religious foundations and monasteries razed to the ground." If this could not be done he would at least have the satisfaction of cursing them. Raging like a madman he writes:

> I will curse and scold the scoundrels until I go to my grave, and never shall they hear a civil word from me. I will toll them to their graves with thunder and lightning. For I am unable to pray without at the same time cursing. If I am prompted to say 'Hallowed be Thy Name' I must add, 'Cursed, damned, outraged be the name of papists.' If I am prompted to say, 'Thy Kingdom come,' I must perforce add, 'Cursed, damned, destroyed must be the papacy.' Indeed I pray thus orally every day and in my heart without intermission. [3]

While Luther raged against the Church, another professor of theology at the Wittenberg University, less eloquent but more cultured, who visited Rome, Andreas Bodenstein von Carlstadt, experienced the same revulsions to the Church as he, and rushed to the defense of his ninety-five theses. He also led in the public disputation of Leipsic in which Luther took part, and he went even further in his advocacy of reform. He declared that nuns and priests should be compelled to marry, that the mass should be abolished, and that all true Christians are directly inspired by God. Accordingly, soon other friars doffed their cowls, fled from the monastery, and incited the mob to attack those who remained, and amid derisive cheers demolished the windows and the altars, desecrating holy pictures and images.

Luther became alarmed at the ascendancy of Carlstadt and the turn which the Reformation seemed to take. Disguised as a horseman with buckled sword and long hair, Luther hastened to Wittenberg, where he at once began to preach against Carlstadt's innovations. His sermons had the usual effect. Carlstadt was deprived of his office and died in exile and poverty. [4]

Thereafter, Luther became the hero of Germany. The prospect of sharing the wealth which hitherto flowed from Germany to Rome also acted as an incentive for the nobility to embrace the new doctrines, and at the Diet of Spires (1529) they issued a vigorous protest against the assumptions of the papacy—whence they came to be known as "Protestants"— and declared themselves ready to defend their cause with the sword. Charles V quickly summoned a new diet at Augsburg at which he promised "to reform what required to be reformed, that there may be in future only one pure and simple faith, and that, as all are disciples of the same Jesus, all may form one and the same Church." A makeshift compromise was patched up, but when the danger seemed to be over, the Pope and the Emperor resolved on a holy war; and, as during the Crusades, a pardon was promised to all who would join in stamping out "the accursed sect of Luther."

For a while it appeared as if the Emperor, who was joined by the Kings of France and Hungary-Bohemia, was about to be victorious, and that Lutheranism would share the fate of the heresies in other lands. But at the critical moment the King of Saxony managed to wrest victory from defeat, and Charles V saved his life by fleeing to Spain. There the sick and disheartened Emperor, who inherited a taint of insanity, retired to a monastery, where he lived in quasi-monkish fashion, and occupied himself by busily, though ineffectively, trying to regulate the many clocks with which he filled his pretended prison so that they keep the same time. He died while expressing his regret that he had not burned Luther at the Diet of Worms in 1521. With his abdication the conflict between Protestantism and Catholicism in Germany came temporarily to an end. At the Diet of Augsburg, in 1555, the principle was laid down that the religion of the ruler was to be the religion of the state (cujus regio ejus religio), and permission was granted the Lutherans to retain whatever property they had seized from the Church prior to 1552.

But while the Lutherans won the war against the Church, they lost the peace among themselves. The doctrine of the duty of each individual to interpret the Bible according to his own light, by which Luther justified his revolt against the Church, proved a two-edged sword. In their search for scriptural truth, many found Luther no more infallible than the Holy See. The Holy Ghost stubbornly refused to guide all alike in their interpretation of the Bible. Already at the Diet of Augsburg some pronounced Luther's "Confession" as unscriptural, and assumed the name of German Reformed. These were followed by numerous other small groups, the most radical of which were the Anabaptists. They were given that name because they opposed infant baptism and insisted that there was no warrant in the Bible for the doctrine of salvation by faith. Some even rejected the doctrine of the Trinity, maintaining that Jesus was "only a holy Prophet and not at all God; that all we had by Christ was that he taught us the way to heaven; that he took no flesh of the Virgin, and that the baptism of infants was not profitable." They refused to take an oath, advocated the abolition of capital punishment, preached tolerance towards those who differed from them, believed in communism, and were opposed to war. They were also strong believers in the speedy advent of Christ. For their catechism they adopted the Teachings of the Twelve Apostles.

While Luther was concealed at Wartburg, three representatives of those who styled themselves the "Prophets of Swicken," appeared in Wittenberg. One of them was a weaver, another an apostate priest, and another, Thomas Muenzer, a Lutheran pastor who claimed to have been under the direct influence of the Holy Ghost. Muenzer and his followers maintained that "the foundation and genuine epitome of all divine truth and will is in the books of Moses." His fiery eloquence and his violent language gained him many adherents, among them Carlstadt and the faculty of the university. His doctrines spread over Saxony and Thuringia. All who were discontented with the prevailing conditions flocked around him and demanded the abolition of peonage and establishment of the Kingdom of God in accordance with their pattern.[5]

The Anabaptists and the peasants who joined them had no doubt that Luther would sympathize with the new movement. Did he not teach that it is the duty of every believer to interpret the Scriptures according to his own light, and was he not himself the son of a peasant? Were not the reforms they requested "established in the Old Testament" and will he not "help abolish serfdom and establish equality even as Christ has delivered and redeemed us all, without exception, by the shedding of his precious blood, the lowly as well as the great?" They therefore organized themselves into an Evangelical Brotherhood, and in 1525 they drafted twelve articles in which they demanded their human rights by sacking castles and monasteries and committing atrocities against the burghers of the cities. Luther called upon the peasants to remember the injunction of the Gospel that servants should obey their masters. When they refused to listen, he declared that rulers have unlimited authority over their subjects and "may force them and drive them as we force and drive pigs and wild beasts." "Treat them like mad dogs," he cried. "Stab, strangle, and slay as best you can the thievish murderous hordes of peasants. Whoever dies fighting for authority is a martyr before God." The undisciplined peasants with their rude farm implements for weapons were easily routed. About one hundred and fifty thousand of them were slain, and the residue sank back to the state of slavery in which they were before the Reformation.

But the Anabaptists were not defeated. A few years after the end of the Peasants' War we find them in the free city of Strassburg, led by Melchior Hoffman, proclaiming the Second Advent of Christ due in 1533, and that from Strassburg as the new Jerusalem he and the "saints" would march forth to conquer the world for the Kingdom of God. When the year passed and Melchior's prophecy was not realized, it began to be whispered that Strassburg was too sinful a city to become the capitol of God. Jan Mattys, a Dutch baker, who gave himself out as another Gideon, decided on Muenster in Westphalia, where Lutheranism was under a cloud, to be made "the New Zion." The city went wild with excitement.

Anabaptists fought Catholics and Lutherans until they gained control of the city (1534), and held out against the superior forces of the bishop until they were overpowered. John of Leiden, one of the apostles of Mattys, then assumed the leadership and proclaimed himself King David. He also appointed elders according to the tribes of Israel. Furthermore, he legalized polygamy and set the example by taking sixteen wives, though he recommended to others to be content with only three. After a long siege, the Anabaptists were starved into submission. However, they did not surrender before only three hundred of them remained and on promise that they be given safe conduct to leave the city. This promise was not kept, and "King David" and two of his leaders were tortured, executed, and suspended in iron cages from the tower of St. Lambert, where they remained until 1881. The Anabaptists, however, were not exterminated, and their doctrines, with modification, are still preached by the Mennonite and Moravian brotherhoods, as well as by many English and American Baptists. [6]

Luther's chief reform consisted in the abolition of relics, shrines, pilgrimages, and the invocation of the saints. In other respects he deviated less from the Roman Church than any of the other Reformers. Indeed, his was Roman Catholicism best suited to the Teutonic taste. He retained the mass, but the celebration of it was in German, and substituted consubstantiation for transubstantiation or the actual transformation of the wafer and wine into the flesh and blood of Christ. In place of the authority of the pope, he indeed set up the authority of the Bible, but according to the interpretation which he thought should be given unto it. Nor was he any more tolerant than the Church from which he seceded. He had no more charity for the Calvinists than for the Catholics; and as for the Swiss Reformers, they were to him no better than parricides and matricides. All of them he condemned as "not only liars but the very incarnation of lying, deceit, and hypocrisy," and he would "no more make peace with them than with the Devil." Like the Hierarchy, he claimed for his own Church *extra ecclesiam nulla salus.*

The political principle *cujus regio ejus religio* rendered Lutheranism vulnerable to a still greater degree. It put a secular princeling in the place of a universal pope and gave him the authority to prescribe the mode whereby to obtain eternal salvation. Hence, it was not unusual for little principalities to change their religion to suit the conviction or predilection of each new ruler, and it is recorded that some had done so within a short period five and six times.

Personally, too, Luther estranged from himself many who sympathized with him when he first started on his career as a Reformer. Philip Melanchthon, his gentle collaborator and successor, was constantly reproving him for his vehemence and vulgarity and was glad when death freed him from the *rabies theologorum*. Other humanists deserted him and returned to the old Church, among them Erasmus, who previously defended him against the Pope's bull of excommunication. To this refined and gentle scholar, Luther's manners were revolting, as well as his doctrines of justification by faith, and he feared that Lutheranism would bring about the ruination of secular studies and the corruption of morals. The Wittenberg Reformer savagely retaliated by denouncing him as a skeptic, an Epicurean, and a slanderer of Christ.

One of the accusations from which Luther recoiled with horror was that he was a Judaizer, an accusation which every Christian sect hurled against another from the time of Paul to this day. This was true in so far as well-founded observation had it that, in some instances, "Lutheranism led to Calvinism, Calvinism to Unitarianism, Unitarianism to Sabbatarianism, and Sabbatarianism to Judaism." Luther himself was vehemently opposed to anything that in his estimation savored of Judaism. In contrast to Zwingli, he preferred the Vulgate to the Septuagint. He was repelled by the Kabbalah, nor did he have the patience to master the Hebrew tongue, though he admitted that without a knowledge of it there could be no understanding of the Scriptures. He himself admitted, "I am no Hebrew grammarian, nor do I wish to be one." To him, Hebrew grammar was a concoction of the Rabbis, which was sufficient reason for avoiding it, and he stated that "after the Babylonian Captivity the language was so corrupted that it cannot be restored."

However, Luther could not altogether escape Jewish influence in his work as a Reformer. What little he knew of Hebrew he acquired from the grammar of Reuchlin, which was based on the work of R. David Kimhi. In his translation of the Bible, he followed closely the *Postilla* of Nicholas de Lyra, who depended largely on the commentaries of Rashi; and even though he was unwilling to give them credit and never omitted an opportunity to vilify them, he borrowed considerably from the Rabbis. But more especially was he influenced by Jewish apostates. Several of them taught Hebrew at the University of Wittenberg, and one of them, Antonius Margaritha, the son of a rabbi, supplied him with ammunition against Judaism in a work entitled *The Entire Jewish Faith* (1530). He also appropriated much material from the writings of Jewish renegades of former times, especially Paul of Burgos' *Perfidy of the Jews.* [7]

The mistake made by Luther, as by other Reformers, was his belief that since he was fighting the traditional enemies of the Jews with weapons forged from the Scriptures, the Jews would flock to his standard and join him *en masse.* He was also encouraged by his conviction that Jesus would reappear in 1558 when the whole world would accept him as their king. He, therefore, at first assumed the role of a champion of the rights of these "brothers-in-blood of the Savior," and called upon Christians to remember that

> Through them (the Jews) alone the Holy Ghost
> wished to give all books of the Holy Scriptures to the
> world. They are the children; we, the guests and the
> strangers. Indeed, like the Canaanite woman, we
> should be satisfied to be the dogs that eat the crumbs
> which fall from their master's table.

These sentiments Luther elaborated with his usual exuberance in a tract entitled *Das Jesu ein geborner Jude sei* (That Jesus was born a Jew, 1523), written explicitly in the hope to

"attract some of the Jews to the Christian faith," in which
he declared:

> Our fools, the popes, bishops, sophists, and monks,
> these coarse blockheads, dealt with the Jews in such a
> manner that any Christian would have preferred to
> be a Jew. Indeed, had I been a Jew, and had I seen
> such idiots and dunderheads expound Christianity, I
> should rather have become a sow than a Christian.
> For they have dealt with the Jews as if they were
> dogs and not human beings. They have done nothing
> for them but curse them and seize their wealth. I
> hope that if the Jews are treated friendly and are in-
> structed kindly through the Bible, many of them will
> become real Christians and come back to the ancestral
> faith of the Prophets and Patriarchs.
>
> My advice, therefore, is to deal kindly with the
> Jews and to instruct them in the Scriptures so that they
> come over to us. So long as we use violence and
> slander, saying that they use the blood of Christians
> to get rid of their stench and other nonsense of a
> similar nature, and treat them like dogs, what can
> we expect of them? How can we hope to win them
> over and improve them if we prohibit them to work
> among us, and trade and mingle with us, and force
> them into usury. If we wish to help them we should
> deal with them not according to the papal law but
> according to the law of Christian charity. We must
> welcome them in our midst, permit them to work and
> trade among us. They will then have an opportunity
> to witness Christian life and doctrine. Should, how-
> ever, some of them still remain stubborn, what of it?
> Not every one of us is a good Christian.

The tract became very popular. It went through nine
printings in German and one in Latin during the first year
of its publication. Also, a certain Urban Regius, in a Hebrew
epistle to the Jews of Braunschweig, called their attention to

Luther's teachings and appealed to them to accept Christianity. But Luther learned to his disappointment that the Jews on their side, far from flocking to the Protestant baptismal font, looked upon the Protestant movement as an admission that they were in the right when they formerly refused to turn Catholic. Indeed, Joseph d'Arles, a French Kabbalist, proved by means of *Gematriot* that the Reformation was to inaugurate the realization of the Jewish Messianic expectations, and on the strength of this belief three German Jews approached Luther with the proposition that he lead the way and accept Judaism! [8]

Having waited impatiently for nearly two decades for the Jews to see the light, Luther launched out in a tirade against them with all the vehemence and abuse of which he was past master. His anti-Judaism was hardly surpassed by his anti-papalism. His hatred of the "damned, rejected race" became an obsession with him. He dismissed Andrew Boeschenstein, a convert and Hebrew teacher of Melanchthon, from his professorship at the Wittenberg University for being an "arch-Jew." In his table-talk, in his letters and pamphlets *Concerning the Jews and Their Lies, Concerning the Shem Hamphoras,* and the *Race of Christ* (1544), he poured out his wrath on the people which is *Stocksteineisenteufelshart,* harder of heart than sticks and stones and iron and the devil combined! "If I had the power over them," he raged, "I would assemble their most prominent men and demand that they prove that the Christians do not worship the One God, under the penalty of having their tongue torn out through the backs of their necks!" The only way for Christians to treat the Jews, he insisted, was to

> Set their synagogues on fire, and whatever does not burn up should be covered or spread over with dirt so that no one may ever be able to see a cinder or stone of it ... in order that God may see that we are Christians. ... Their homes should likewise be broken down and destroyed. ... They should be put under one roof or in a stable, like gypsies, in order that they may realize that they are not masters in our land,

as they boast, but miserable captives, as they complain
of us incessantly before God with bitter wailing. . . .
They should be deprived of their prayer books and
Talmuds, in which such idolatry, lies, cursing, and
blasphemy are taught. . . their rabbis must be forbidden to teach under the threat of death. [9]

Luther's former appeal in behalf of the Jews, notwithstanding its popularity, was soon forgotten; but the vicious
outbursts of his later years fanned the age-old hatred of the
Jews, and ever since rendered Protestant Germany the most
anti-Semitic country in Christendom. Jews, it is true, were
no longer burned alive, and after the massacres and forced
conversions of Passau, Bavaria, in 1478, precipitated by the libel
of Host desecration, that historic pretext was no longer resorted to, for the miracle of the Eucharist was no longer
believed in. But reasons for their persecution were never
lacking. The study of Hebrew continued to be pursued not
in order to gain a better understanding of the Bible, but to
"expose" the barbarism of the hated race. R. Lipmann's *Book
of Victory* and other Jewish polemics were held up as proof
of Jewish arrogance and their contempt of Christians as of
Christianity. Scholars like Buxtorf, Muenster, and Hackspan
resurrected old manuscripts and rummaged through the Talmud for derogatory statements against Gentiles. One of the results of these labors was a virulent attack on Judaism by the
apostate, Samuel Friedrich Brenz, in *Juedischer abgestreifter
Schlangenbalg* ("The Jews Stripped Serpent-skin," 1614). It
evoked a reply from Solomon Zebi Hirsch in *Der Juedischer
Theriak* (The Jewish Antidote, 1615). But the detractors of Judaism continued their work of defamation, and the government did its full share to encourage them. When Johann Andreas Eisenmenger published his notorious *Endecktes Judentum* ("Judaism Exposed," 1700), which has become the bible
of anti-Semitism ever since, and consented at a price to destroy
it, it was reprinted by order of Frederick I of Prussia. In his
judgment, it was a defense of Christianity and would prevent
apostasy to Judaism.

An interesting exception was Johann Christian Wagenseil, a contemporary of Eisenmenger. He, too, undertook to expose the Jews and wrote his *Tela Ignea Satanae,* in which he republished the Jewish works against Christianity. He also appealed to Protestant princes to intensify their efforts to convert the Jews, although he did not approve of the use of force. At the same time he refuted the charges of ritual murder, or that the Talmud teaches hatred of Christians or any other people, and admitted that Jews are no less, if not more, honest than Christians. Like Balaam, Wagenseil came to curse and blessed instead. [10]

Centuries of oppression had so cowed the Jews of Germany that they ceased to expect any humane treatment at the hand of Christians. But the spirit of liberalism which emanated from France finally penetrated also into Germany, and Frederick the Great, "the philosopher upon the throne," and admirer of Voltaire, was more concerned with the rehabilitation of the Vaterland than the salvation of Jewish souls. He, therefore, promised to grant them certain rights as soon as they proved themselves "useful citizens." But the more enlightened Germans did not wait for the *Patent* which he issued in 1750. The leaders of the *Aufklaerung* (Enlightenment) began to welcome them on terms of equality and sat at the feet of Moses Mendelssohn (1729-86), who carried off the prize offered by the Berlin Academy of Science for an essay in which Immanuel Kant was one of the competitors. Distinguished men and women flocked to hear the lectures of Marcus Herz, and were fascinated by the charms of his wife Henrietta. The peak of German liberality was reached when in 1779 appeared Gotthold Ephraim Lessing's *Nathan the Wise,* with its plea that men should be judged not by their creeds but by their deeds, and the appeal of Christian Wilhelm Dohm for conferring upon the Jews all the rights enjoyed by the Christians (1781).

The Jews were so carried away by these unexpected signs of liberalism that, not to be outdone by their Gentile countrymen, they were willing to give up their heritage of Judaism. The genial sun of good-will accomplished what the storm of hate never could. Some of them began to look upon Christianity as simply a symbol of German patriotism and submitted to the formality of baptism, while others, like some of their Gentile friends, even boasted of their atheism.

There were also a few simple souls who, like David Friedlaender, offered to accept Christianity provided they would not be expected to subscribe to the dogma of the Trinity, or of Jesus as the incarnation of God. This conditional surrender was rightly rejected on the ground that Christianity without a supernatural Christ would be Judaism under a different name. Yet it was just what the Hegelian and Tuebingen Schools were teaching, and what David Friedrich Strauss elaborated in his *Life of Jesus*. By the irony of fate, this latter work was saved from suppression through the efforts of Johann Neander, a Jewish convert, who, being consulted as the most distinguished Church historian of his time by the government, insisted that "scholarly works are to be fought with the weapons of science, not by the power of the State." [11]

But while the government no longer stooped to convert the Jews by force, the German intelligentsia, unlike that in other countries, advocated measures some of which had been resorted to by the medieval Church, and others which have later been implemented by the Nazis. A Professor Friedrich Ruehs advocated the complete segregation of the Jews, their deprivation of citizenship, restriction on their marriages and births, and even their wearing a special badge. Another Professor Jacob Friedrich Fries (1816) predicted that if Jews be not exterminated, all Germans would be their slaves within forty years. Still another, Hartwig Hundt--Radowsky in *Der Judenspiegel* (1819) suggested that all male Jews be emasculated and all Jewish women be placed in houses of prostitution. To these and their ilk, converted Jews were even more to be feared than those who still followed the faith of their fathers; and they made them feel, that, notwithstanding their baptism, they were unwanted in a Christian community. No wonder that many apostates regretted their mis-step and that Heinrich

Heine, the most noted of them, expressed the disappointment and the nostalgia of them all when he wrote:

> I am very sorry that I had myself baptized.... Is it not foolish? Scarcely am I baptized than I am decried as a Jew..... I remember the Psalm, 'We sat by the rivers of Babylon,' which you recited so beautifully, so touchingly, that even now I am on the verge of weeping, but not only for the Psalm. Indeed, the Jews are of the stuff of which the gods are made; today they are trampled under foot, tomorrow they are worshiped; while some of them creep about in the filthiest mire of commerce, others ascend the highest peak of humanity, and Golgotha is not the only mountain on which a Jewish God has bled for the salvation of the world. The Jews are the people of the spirit, and whenever they return to their spirit they are great and splendid and put to shame and overcome their rascally oppressors... Whilst among the Jews there is every possible caricature of vulgarity, there are among them also the ideas of the purest humanity. And as they once led the world in the new paths of progress the world has perhaps still to expect further discoveries from them. [12]

Until the first World War this spirit of exclusiveness and persecution was justified on the ground that Germany was a Christian State. Julius Stahl, a baptized Jew, proposed that Jews be prohibited the use of any names connected with Christianity, such as Peter or Paul. But gradually there emerged a new reason which made it impossible for a Jew to escape his Judaic heritage even by conversion to Christianity. Already about the beginning of the nineteenth century Johann Gottlieb Fichte advanced his philosophic opinion that the Germans were the most unmixed of people, their language the purest and best, and their mission was to be a *Herrenvolk*. This idea of a Chosen People differed from the one promulgated by the ancient Hebrews and their descendants in that instead of emphasizing the ideal of service to the rest of mankind, it preached the subjugation or enslavement of all who were not Germans or "Aryans." Strangely enough, a convert to Christianity, named Wilhelm Marr, reinforced this assumption in a pamphlet entitled *Der Sieg des Judentums Ueber das Germantum* ("The Victory of Judaism over Germanism," 1873), and an English expatriate, Houston Stewart Chamberlain "established" it on a scientific basis in his *Foundations of the Nineteenth Century* (1899), which met the enthusiastic approval of Wilhelm II. [13]

At last German arrogance and the will to dominate, necessarily pent up during the tolerant nineteenth century, burst out in all its fury under the neo-paganism which followed the debacle of World War I. In their humiliation, the defeated war lords found the Jew the most convenient scapegoat upon whom to lay the blame for the frustration of their ambitious plans. Treischke's saying, "the Jews are our misfortune," became Germany's slogan. The hatred fostered by Catholicism and nurtured by Lutheranism against Judaism was now directed against the Jews. Jews were no longer blamed for crucifying Christ, but, on the contrary, for producing him and, through him, foisting Christianity on the "Aryans." To avenge these ancient "wrongs," every trace and manifestation of the Jewish genius, be it a treatise on medicine or mathematics, a musical composition or a philosophic dissertation, was to be ruthlessly destroyed. Pastors who prayed for Jews, and judges who meted out justice to Jews, were apprehended by the Gestapo and thrown into concentration camps. The mere association of a Jew and an "Aryan" exposed both parties to severe punishment for *Rassenschande* (race disgrace), and the least streak of Jewish blood was enough to brand one a pariah and an outcast. The one hundred and fifty thousand German Jewish converts to Christianity were classified according to the amount of Jewish blood which was supposed to course in their veins, regardless of the sincerity of their belief or their contributions to the culture and prestige of their country. [14]

But if a drop of Jewish blood is enough to contaminate "Aryans," Jews can boast of not a few precious Nordic drops of blood which by the same token should ennoble them. For nothwithstanding the bitter hatred of the Germans for the Jews, some of them, at the peril of their lives, continued to be attracted to Judaism since the Reformation, as they were during the era of Catholicism. The story of German converts to Judaism in the face of the fierce anti-Semitism of the Teutons is one of thrilling and absorbing interest. Thus, in 1492 twenty-four Jews and Jewesses were burned alive at Judenberg near Sternberg in Mecklenberg, on the charge that they induced a priest to embrace Judaism and desecrate a Host. In the sixteenth century Michel Jud, allegedly the illegitimate son of a count of Regenstein, was raised as a Jew and played an important part in political as well as commercial affairs of the Germany of his day. Of the proselytes of that century, one had been a student at Wittenberg who fled to Constantinople (c. 1551), studied Hebrew, knew both Greek and Arabic, "got in among the Jews and accepted their faith." Another, Conrad Victor, a professor of the classic languages at the University of Marburg, emigrated to Salonica (1607), embraced Judaism, and assumed the name of Moses Predo. After a residence of seven years, he appealed to the Duke of Hess to show himself as tolerant as the Sultan and grant him permission to return and join his wife. The permission was, as we would expect, refused, and Moses died in Salonica without seeing his wife again. [15]

Johann Peter Spaeth (d. 1701) was born in Venice and brought by his father to Augsburg. There he was raised in the Catholic faith. After writing an important work in defense of Romanism, he was converted to Lutheranism and was commended for his devotion and erudition by the head of the board of theological studies of the University of Augsburg. At the same time, Spaeth was deeply perturbed by the inhumanity of the Christians to the Jews. His sense of justice sickened at the trumped up charges of the blood ritual and other slanders. Having investigated and found them false, he began to doubt the other beliefs of Christianity as well. He did not, however, take the final step all at once. Trying in vain to remain in the Christian fold, he joined the Mennonites; but an unusual episode precipitated his decision to give up Christianity altogether. A crucifix which dropped from his pocket was picked up and returned to him by a Jew with the remark "It is Israel, the man of sorrow!" At this, there flashed on the mind of Spaeth the description of the Suffering Servant in the fifty-third chapter of Isaiah, and its application to the Jews. "The Jews," thought he, "bore the sins of the heathen, while they were daily persecuted by them. From time immemorial they had been treated in a shameful manner and the same sort of thing happens nowadays." He thereupon left for Holland, became a Jew under the name of Moses Germanus, and wrote considerably in favor of Judaism. Spaeth was one of the zealots who took up the cudgels against Benedict Spinoza for his unorthodox views.

Abraham *Ger Sedek*, another German proselyte, hailed from the vicinity of Hamburg. In Jewish sources he is described as "a prince and great one" in his native land, who "recognized his Creator" at the age of forty-eight, and in order to serve Him unhindered emigrated with his daughter to Amsterdam. There he was joined by his son Simeon, a general in the royal army, and he and his family set out for Palestine. Fearing to pass through Germany they journeyed by way of Poland, only to be seized by the Russians. Simeon, however, managed to escape and traveled through various lands to collect funds for the redemption of his father and sister. At Algeria he put all his belongings in a boat which was to transport him to Morocco, but during the night a storm wrecked his vessel and all his effects were lost. Simeon's adventures were attested to by the rabbis of Algiers in a letter concerning him to their colleagues in Fez (1712) [16]

A German who at least for a time lived as a Jewish Marrano was a certain Brent of Eighelsdorf, near Koenigsberg. The son of devout Protestants, he became deeply interested in the Hebrew Bible and found that the original texts did not substantiate the dogmas which theologians claimed to have been derived from them. A little later he took up the study of the Talmud under Rabbis Tevel and Wulff of Halle, and while still nominally a Christian he began to observe the dietary laws, kept the Sabbath and festivals, went to the synagogue, associated mainly with Jews, and was a frequent guest at their weddings and other religious ceremonies. In 1749 he went to Holland with various commendations from the Jews of Halle. There he had himself circumcised in the presence of ten men and assumed the name Yohanan Brent. During his convalescence he received the tender care of the entire Jewish community, as well as gifts in clothing and money, and was voted a stipend of two florins a week for the rest of the year.

For two years Brent stayed in Holland and occupied himself with the practice of medicine. But his unrequited love for a Jewish maiden decided him to return to Nuremberg. He married a Christian and died, apparently, in the Protestant faith (1789). He contributed, however, to the spread of Unitarianism by translating from the Hungarian Szent Abraham's Catechism (1766) and by stressing the teachings of Moses and the Prophets in his lectures at the various universities.

Halle was among the places where the Jews were most persecuted. They suffered there during the Crusades, were peremptorily expelled from there in 1493; and in 1724, twenty years before Brent's arrival, their newly built synagogue and houses were demolished by the students of the University. Yet Halle is noted in Jewish history not only for its Jewish publications but for the fact that some who participated in them were proselytes. Reference was made in another place to the activity of Moses b. Abraham and his family as Hebrew and Yiddish typesetters. The converts Israel b. Abraham and his sons Abraham and Tobias followed the same occupation. They had presses in other parts of Germany, and we find them working at their trade at Koethen, Jessnitz, Wandsbeck, and Neuwied, Offenbach as well as Salonica.[17]

One whose conversion caused a stir throughout Germany in the eighteenth century was Joseph Abraham Steblicki (1726-1807). Raised as a Catholic at Nikolai, Silesia, he attended a Jesuit college and was in turn teacher in the schools of his native city, city treasurer, and member of the city council. After retiring from active life he devoted himself to the study of the Bible, and before long he began to observe the seventh day Sabbath and the dietary laws. In 1785 he had himself circumcised, assumed the name Joseph Abraham, and appeared at the services on the Day of Atonement, dressed in the white gown (*kittel*) worn by Jews on that sacred day. In accordance with the law still in force at the time, conversion to Judaism was a capital offense, and the authorities who instituted proceedings against him urged that the law be enforced; but for some reason, Frederick II ordered the proceedings to be quashed. The question then arose whether as a Jew, Steblicki should still have the right to reside in the city and whether he should be made to pay the special taxes imposed on Jews by birth. The problem, however, was solved by the official decision that he was mentally unbalanced. Steblicki retained the affection of his family and friends as well as the high regard of the Jewish community, until his death. He figures as the hero in David Samoscz' *Ger Zedek* (Breslau, 1816) and M. A. Hertzberg's *Der Neue Jude* (The New Jew, Gleiwitz, 1845). [18]

Hamburg was one of the Germanic cities which tolerated neither Jews nor Catholics. To the horror of the Protestant clergy, they discovered there early in the seventeenth century many immigrants who passed off as Catholics but who were secretly practicing the tenets of Judaism. The matter was brought before the senate; but realizing the advantages to the city of the settlement of these enterprising merchants, the only action taken was an order that they should not observe their religion publicly, and should pay a special tax for their protection (1611). By 1650, however, when Catholic public worship was still prohibited, these Marranos publicly reverted to Judaism and established an active Jewish communal life with a Talmud Torah and an officiating rabbi.

One of these reverts was Dom Francisco de Sampio (d. 1666), alias Francisco de Mello, who came from Antwerp, where he represented the Spanish government as consul. At the suggestion of his wife, whose family intermarried with the highest nobility of Portugal, he submitted to circumcision at the age of seventy, as did their two sons (Good Friday, 1647), and took the name Abraham Senior Texeira, while his wife called herself Sarah. Despite the demand of the imperial government for their extradition, the Texeiras, under the protection of the senate, remained unmolested and moved in the exclusive circles of the society of their adopted city. When Christine of Sweden visited Hamburg in 1654 she stayed at their home and appointed Abraham her financial agent.

Texeira showed his liberality by supplying the copper roofing for the church of St. Michael. But his chief delight was in his own religion. He contributed lavishly for the construction of a new synogague, founded Jewish benevolent societies, and served as president of the congregation. His son, Isaac Hayim Senior, followed in his footsteps and was ever on the alert to help his coreligionists politically and financially. In his later years he moved to Amsterdam, where he held the office of president of the Spanish-Portuguese community to the time of his death (1705).[19]

Some German proselytes of the nineteenth century played an important part in the resettlement of the Jews in the land of their fathers. One of them, who later took the name of David b. Abraham Klassen, left his native Tugenhof with a son and daughter, and at the age of forty presented himself for circumcision at the Rothschild Hospital in Jerusalem. An experienced farmer, he became superintendent of Gan Montefiore, near Jaffa, the first pre-Zionist experiment in the reclamation of Eretz Israel for Jewish settlers. Both he and his daughter Hannah "the proselyte" married zealous Zionists, and with the scrolls of the Torah which his Jewish wife presented him as her dowry he organized a congregation of his Jewish laborers. Klassen and his wife are buried on Mt. Olive, and on their tombstones are respectively inscribed the following epitaphs:

> Here lieth the true Proselyte of Righteousness who entered under the wings of the Shekinah, a wholehearted and righteous man and one that feareth the Lord, David ben Abraham of blessed memory (Klassen). He departed with a good name on Monday the sixteenth of Tammuz, '625 (1865). May his soul be bound in the bond of life.

Here lieth the woman Mirka daughter of R. Simeon
wife of R. David Klassen the *Ger,* departed the 23rd of
Adar I, '646 (1886). May her soul be bound in the
bundle of the living ones.[20]

Perhaps the best known of the more modern German proselytes is Nahida Strumhoefel, who established a reputation as a
literary woman under the name Nahida Remy (1849-1928).
Ever since she read the Old Testament, at the age of ten, she felt
herself drawn towards the people whose early history it records. But she became especially interested in them during the
outburst of anti-Semitism in the eighties. She plunged into
Jost's and Graetz's histories of the Jews, devoured the *Juedische Familienpapiere* (Jewish Family Papers) of Wilhelm
Herzberg, delighted in the company of Professor Moritz Lazarus under whose guidance she delved deeply into the writings of Zunz, Jellinek, Geiger, and other sages of German
Israel, and wrote tracts on various Jewish topics, such as Jewish
women, prayers in the Bible and Talmud, humanitarianism
and Judaism, etc. After reading Moses Mendelssohn's Jerusalem she resolved to become a Jewess and started out for Geneva
to enter into the fold of Judaism. On her way she stopped at
Freiburg to pay a visit to Professor Lazarus, who was quite ill.
Before long, his former disciple became both his coreligionist
and his wife, and won a place in the affection of the Jews as
Nahida Ruth Lazarus. [21]

It was on the eve of the reign of terror inaugurated by the
Nazis that German Jewish apostasy reached its peak. Of the
thirteen thousand and three hundred who embraced Lutheranism between 1900 and 1935, the large number, nine hundred
and thirty-three, was recorded in 1933. This may be explained
on the ground that the terrified Jews expected to gain physical
security by joining the established Church. Finding that this
availed them little, since the Nazis were less against the Jewish
religion than against the Jewish race, the number of converts
began to decline, though some very poor Jews in their desperate
plight still accepted Jesus with the dole offered them by Protes-

tant and Catholic missionaries. On the other hand, some who had already become Protestants retraced their steps back to the synagogue. Dr. Boreslav .Kornfeld, the publicist, who was baptized by his parents when a child, returned to Judaism on his escape from a concentration camp. Emil Ludwig did likewise soon after the rise of the Third Reich. Professor Joseph Setina, of Chemnitz, even underwent the rite of circumcision. Dr. Theodor Lessing, who as a Christian convert married into German nobility, reverted to his ancestral faith, in which he was joined by his wife, and met with a martyr's death at his Marienbad villa, whither he fled from Nazi persecution.[22]

There were also some "pure Aryans" who, notwithstanding Nazi ruthlessness, sought admittance into the household of Israel, nor did the Draconian Laws against *Rassenschande* stop intermarriages. In Frankfort alone there were sixty-one such unions in 1933 and twenty-two in 1934. The Rabbinates of Czechoslovakia and Vienna were appealed to by hundreds of German girls to admit them into the religion of their Jewish sweethearts in the hope that the government would then allow them to become their wives. Hundreds of others wished to become Jewesses so as to be permitted to retain their positions in Jewish homes or places of business. Many fled to Poland or Palestine and there embraced Judaism, and there are records of some who proclaimed themselves Jews in protest against Nazi brutality, and of daughters of Nazi officials who fled to Palestine or Poland where they embraced Judaism. Thus Kurt Neuman, a German settler in the Jewish agricultural colony Quatros Irmanos, Brazil, accepted the faith of Israel to prove his condemnation of Hitlerism. But there were some who were actuated by even superior motives, among them Marguerite von Kummel, who at the start of Hitler's rabid anti-Semitic campaign (1934) went to Palestine, became a Jewess, and committed suicide—a victim of her hate of Nazism and love for Judaism.[23]

CHAPTER XXV

AMONG THE SLAVONIANS

WITH the exception of Bohemia, Poland was the only Slavonic country which was affected by the backwash of the Reformation. Her Christianization was begun by Mieczyslav I (965), a vassal of the German Emperor, whose favors he sought; and at the insistence of his wives, the first of whom was a sister of the King of Bohemia. Four hundred years later Jagellon, the Prince of Lithuania, who for the preservation of his kingdom also married a Catholic princess, embraced her faith (1384), and the two countries were united under one ruler. This union made Poland an important factor in European affairs and started her on the road to becoming, for some time, a dominant power in Christendom.

The German priests and Teutonic Knights who undertook the Christianization of Poland looked upon the country as an outpost of Germany and ruled their charges with an iron rod. They treated them as bondsmen, despoiled them of their possessions, and knocked out their teeth if they complained or failed to observe the prescribed rites. As a result, riots frequently broke out among the populace, convents and churches were destroyed, and priests and nobles were massacred. As the number of native clergymen increased, the Polish ecclesiastics insisted that their German colleagues be excluded from their benefices. Finally, Boleslav II, who received the crown from the pope, was compelled to flee for safety to Hungary, and the combined armies of the Poles and Lithuanians succeeded in crushing the power of the Teutonic Knights at the battle of Tannenberg (1410). [1]

It was Casimir the Great who first raised his country to a

671

high rank in the European system. He promoted agriculture
and commerce, constructed highways, and established courts
of justice throughout the land. He also founded schools
for the masses, established the University of Cracow for higher
education (1364), and opened his country to all who were willing to develop its various resources. When he heard that the
Bishop of Cracow put him under the ban, he had him drowned
in the Vistula. Under him, Poland became the freest country
in Christendom, and thither flocked all who were persecuted
and harassed for their religious convictions. Jerome, the colleague and co-worker of Huss, was invited to the University
of Cracow. Many of the nobility also declared themselves Hussites and demanded that the estates of the Church be expropri-
ated for public purposes. [2]

Calvinism and Lutheranism were introduced into Poland
chiefly by the efforts of young *Szlachta* (gentry) who had
studied abroad. From Prague, Padua, and especially Koenigsberg, Wittenberg, Goldberg, and Leipsic they returned filled
with enthusiasm for the subversive new doctrines and found a
ready following among the lower clergy who smarted under
the treatment of their arrogant bishops. Many of them began
to break their vows of celibacy, appointed Protestant preachers
on their estates, and ordered their peasants to attend the services. In Danzig, Catholic churches, monasteries, and convents
were seized and converted to secular purposes; and in Cracow,
a non-sectarian organization was formed for the purpose of
"evangelizing" the entire country. With the accession of Sigismund II, who married the daughter of Prince Radziwill,
Calvinism gained great momentum among the *Szlachta,* and in
1550 the first Calvinist synod in Poland was held at Princzow.
At the diets of 1555 and 1558 the *Szlachta* demanded absolute toleration for all sects (save the anti-Trinitarians) and the
exclusion of Catholic bishops from the Senate. It is estimated
that the number of Catholic families who abandoned the
faith during these years was about two thousand, while the
Catholic churches converted to Protestant uses (mostly Calvinist) were two hundred forty in Great Poland, four hundred
in Little Poland, and three hundred twenty in Lithuania. [3]

That the Calvinist *Szlachta* found it necessary to exclude the anti-Trinitarians from their demand for absolute toleration shows that, as in Hungary and Czechoslovakia, there were also in Poland many who went as far as the acceptance of Unitarianism. This doctrine was indeed publicly preached by Pastoris, a Belgian priest, in Cracow (1546). Peter of Goniond, at first a violent opponent of Protestantism, later adopted similar views while in Switzerland and Moravia, and after the Synod of 1556 gained a considerable following among the upper classes. A strong impetus to the Unitarian movement was given by fugitives from Italy, some of whom first came under the influence of Calvin but ultimately went beyond him in their liberal creed. Among them were Biandrata, Ochino, Faustus Socinus, and Gregorius Pauli, a minister at Cracow. At the Conference of Petrikove in 1562 many ministers and nobles formally renounced the doctrine of the Trinity. A year later, forty-two ministers organized a Unitarian Church at Cracow. At the same time they pledged themselves never to go to law, or take an oath, or participate in war under any circumstances. These principles were given permanency in the Rakovian Cathechism (1605), which for two hundred years remained the authority on Unitarianism.

As everywhere else, the Reformation in Poland was stimulated by the translation of the Scriptures into the vernacular. The first attempt at a Polish version of the Bible, made in 1455 for the fourth wife of Jagellon, contained only the Pentateuch, Joshua, Ruth, and Kings. In 1521 there was added "Speeches of the Wise King Solomon" (Proverbs) and in 1522 the Book of Ecclesiastes. Thereafter renditions of the Bible became of frequent occurrence. John Seklucyan, a Catholic priest at Posen, who became a rabid Protestant, translated the New Testament in 1551. A committee of lay and clerical scholars prepared and published at the expense of Nicholas Radziwill a complete version in 1553. But Simon Budny, Radziwill's pastor in his newly built Calvinist church, and familiar with the Hebrew language, issued another translation of the Bible at Nieswiez, in 1570. This led to the standard Protestant Bible which came to be known as the Danzig Bible.

Unfortunately, the very elements seemed to fight against the Reformation in Poland. The superstitious peasants were easily intimidated by the orthodox clergy, who pointed to numerous calamities that threatened or overtook the land, the Tartar invasions and the epidemics, conflagrations and famines which followed in their wake, as the vengeance of God on heretics. The fact also that the worst Polish enemies were Protestant Swedes and Germans made heresy synonymous with treason and opposition to the Church tantamount to enmity to the State.

The final blow to Protestantism in Poland was given by the Jesuit monks, who established themselves there under Cardinal Hosius in 1564. They opened schools, organized religious brotherhoods, filled positions as military chaplains and as professors at the secular academies. Like their rivals, they also published a Catholic translation of the Bible (1597) and preached in the vernacular, and endeared themselves to the populace by their patriotism and self-sacrificing service in times of trouble. With the enthronement of Stephen Bathori, their influence reached its peak. One of their order, John Casimer, was made king (1648-68) and received from the pope the title *Rex Orthodoxus*. Jesuits became confessors and chaplains to princes and *pans* (noblemen), and brought about the suppression of the Arians, Socinians, and other sects. The entire Protestant literature was destroyed. The Bible, the translation and publication of which was made possible by the munificence of Nicholas Radziwill, was burned by his own son who had embraced Catholicism, and only two copies of it are now extant. [4]

The only people who defied the zeal and machinations of the Jesuits were the Jews. They appeared on the Polish horizon long before the country was Christianized. In the ninth century, according to legend, a certain Jew by the name of Abraham Prokhovnik was proclaimed king when the noblemen could not agree on a successor to the throne. It is said that in 905 Prince Leshek, who discussed with a Jewish delegation from Germany the principles of their faith, invited them to settle in his country and granted them various privileges. At all events, some Jewish merchants from Germany visited Poland at an early date for business reasons and decided to stay. Their little "commercial colonies" were steadily enlarged by fugitives from neighboring countries, by the Khazarites from the south, and the victims of the Crusaders of the eleventh and twelfth centuries, so that after the expulsion from Spain Poland became the greatest Jewish center in the Diaspora.

For several centuries the Jews enjoyed a high degree of freedom and autonomy. They were employed as tax-gatherers and were in charge of the coinage, which they stamped with Hebrew words and even such inscriptions as "Rejoice Abraham, Isaac, and Jacob!" They owned Christian slaves. Mechislav the Old issued, in 1173, strict injunctions forbidding any violence against the Jews. Boleslav the Pious promulgated in 1264 a statute which secured "for all time" the personal and religious freedom of the Jews. He also made it obligatory on Christians to hasten to the rescue of a Jew who was attacked, "as soon as they hear his cries," prohibited the kidnapping of Jewish children for the purpose of baptism, and imposed upon a Christian who falsely accused a Jew of a murder for ritual purposes the same penalty as would have been meted out to the Jew had the accusation been found true.

Especially favorable to the Jews was Casimir the Great, "the peasant king." He confirmed the Magna Carta of the Jewish liberties issued by Boleslav and added many and even more beneficent enactments. He was solicitous about defending the Jews in all their rights and, to make sure that they would suffer no discrimination, took them out of the jurisdiction of the ecclesiastical courts. He made the murder of a Jew punishable by death, removed the restriction which kept Jews from entering the houses of Christians or visiting the municipal baths. The extent of Casimir's tolerance can be judged by the story that he fell in love with a beautiful Jewess named Estherka, by whom he had two sons and two daughters; and while the sons were brought up as Christians, he permitted the daughters to be raised in the Jewish faith. So grateful were the Polish Jews to their royal benefactor that, at the marriage of his granddaughter, one of their merchants at Cracow presented her with one hundred thousand florins in gold, a gift equal to the dowry she had received from her grandfather.

It was the same in Lithuania under the reign of Gedimin. We are told that at the funeral of the grand duke Vladimir Vasilkovich "the Jews wept.... as at the fall of Jerusalem, or when being led into the Babylonian captivity." Withhold, too, who in 1389 issued a charter similar to that granted by Casimir the Great, was for a long time after his death remembered by the Jews for his tolerance and generosity.[5]

But while the kings and dukes, who were mainly interested in the economic needs of their country, were favorably inclined toward the Jews, the Church was unalterably opposed to granting them any rights so long as they refused to embrace Christianity. Two years after the promulgation of the Charter of Boleslav a resolution was adopted at the ecumenical Council of Breslau stating:

> Whereas Poland is a new plantation on the soil of Christianity, there is reason to fear that her Christian population will fall an easy prey to the influence of the superstitions and evil habits of the Jews living among them, the more so as the Christian religion took root in the hearts of the faithful of these countries at a later date and in a more feeble manner. We, therefore, more strictly enjoin that the Jews residing in the Diocese of Gnesen shall not live side by side with the Christians, but shall live apart, in houses adjoining each other or connected with one another, in some section of the city or village.

To make the segregation complete, Jews were ordered to dispose of their homes in the Christian quarters, to wear a special hat, or a red badge, not to appear on the streets during Church processions, to have no more than one synagogue in any town, and not to keep Christian slaves or even wet-nurses. On the other hand, Christians were forbidden, on pain of excommunication, to invite Jews to their homes or to trade with them. A Jew living with a Christian woman was to be imprisoned and fined, while the woman was to be whipped in public and banished from the town.

For a long time this great Charter of the ecclesiastics for the persecution of the Jews remained inoperative. The princes and magnates continued to treat the Jews humanely. The *szlachta* and the *khlops* (peasants), being still "feeble" in their Christianity, persisted in being feeble in their hatreds. Some Jews dressed like Christians, even to the extent of wearing golden chains and carrying swords, lived among Christians, and employed Christian servants. They pursued their trade with their Christian countrymen at home and abroad, and sometimes even occupied responsible posts. There is a tradition that like Prokhovnik, a certain Saul Wahl, a favorite of Prince Radziwill, was proclaimed by the *szlachta* king of Poland and reigned one night.[6]

Slowly but surely, however, the poison of prejudice injected by the clergy took effect; and with the decline of the power of the kings, the seed sown by the Church began to bear bitter fruit. Rumors of ritual murders and the desecration of the Host began to be set afloat. *Schuelergelaufs* (attacks by seminary students), riots, and massacres became more and more frequent, and the charge of poisoning the wells, imported from Germany, caused the slaughter of ten thousand Jews (1348). Casimir the Great was nicknamed by the clergy "Ahasuerus" and denounced as a Judaizer, and his successor, Louis of Hungary, who was under control of the Church, threatened to expel all the Jews who refused to accept Christianity.

Under Vladislav Jagellon, Louis' son-in-law, and a convert from paganism to Catholicism, the Jews of Poland suffered their first persecution. Accused of having pierced three hosts in a Dominican church in Posen, the rabbi and thirteen Jewish elders were roasted on a slow fire (1399), and the Jewish community was fined to pay a yearly tax for the support of the Dominican church. In Cracow, where a priest announced from the pulpit that Jews had killed a Christian boy and made sport over his blood, the rabble plundered their goods after setting fire to their homes. Some of them were forcibly baptized,

while the children of the slain were raised as Christians (1407),
and the Synod of Piotrkow (1542) decreed that

> Whereas the Church suffers the Jews for the sole
> purpose of recalling to our minds the tortures of our
> Saviour, their numbers shall under no circumstances
> increase.[7]

With the arrival of Capistrano from Germany (1543), the
intensification of the Catholic reaction, and the machinations of
the Jesuits, the lot of the Jews in Poland grew from bad to
worse. They were blamed for the Reformation which turned
many faithful Catholics into "Judaizers" and "semi-Jews." They
were accused of being in league with the Tartars and the
Turks, the Swedes and the Russians. The people were told that
the victory of the Teutonic Knights over the Polish troops
(1554) was a visitation for the "godless" privileges which were
enjoyed by the Jews. Casimir IV and Alexander Jagellon,
who started out as liberals, found themselves compelled to
yield to the pressure of the Church. Jews were expelled from
Lithuania and their synagogues converted into chapels, or for
secular uses, while those of the Jews who accepted baptism
were granted special privileges and dubbed "Jerusalem nobles."
After the passing of the Jagellon dynasty, even the last vestiges of the former rights of the Jews were swept away. Children were carried off and converted at the whim of any *pan,*
and men were quartered, dismembered, flayed alive, or nailed
to the gallows on the flimsiest pretext, or just for fun. In 1663
the apothecary Matathias Califari was butchered and burned
in Cracow on the statement of a "friendly" Dominican that
he was guilty of blasphemy. On the testimony of a repentant
apostate that they "tampered" with his new religion, the
brothers Hayyim and Joshua of Lemberg suffered the deaths
of martyrs. Joshua, who committed suicide while in jail was
dragged through the streets tied to the tail of a horse and then
cremated. The worst fate was reserved for Rabbi Hayyim, the
wealthy, generous, and scholarly head of the rabbinical academy of Lemberg. When he refused to listen to the Jesuit who

offered to reprieve him if he accepted Christianity, his tongue
was torn out and, while still living, he was quartered and then
burnt on the eve of the feast of Shabuot, May 13, 1728.[8]

The one time when Jews and Poles fared alike was when the
savage Greek Catholic hordes of Cossacks, Ukrainians, and Tartars led by Bogdan Chmielnicki invaded Poland. To avenge
their wrongs at the hands of the Polish *pans,* they vented their
fiendish hate upon the Jews, both being the "desecrators of our
holy religion." Jews who refused to be converted were mutilated and left to die a lingering death. Many were burned,
buried, or cast into wells alive. Women and maidens were
violated in the sight of their husbands and parents, and infants
slit open in the arms of their mothers. It was not an unusual
sight to see a Pole, a Jew, and a dog strung up on the same
tree above a placard:

> *Lakh* (Pole), *Zhyd* (Jew), and hound
> All to the same fate bound.[9]

Despite all this, the number of Jewish converts who stayed
in the Church was insignificant. Many young women whom the
Cossacks forcibly converted in order to marry them committed
suicide. Rabbi Nathan Hannover, a contemporary Chronicler,
writes in his *Yeven Mezulah* (The Miry Depth) about some of
the expedients to which these unfortunates resorted in order to
escape the contamination of the Cossacks. One beautiful girl
to whom a Cossack proposed marriage assured him that she
possessed a magic power which rendered her bullet-proof, and
was shot by him. Another promised to marry him at the church
which stood on the other side of the bridge, and when they
reached the bridge she jumped into the water below. In Nemi-
row alone, about six thousand sacrificed their lives for "the
sanctification of the Name." Those who survived the massacres
were soon permitted by John Casimer, the "cardinal king" who
hated Greek Catholicism, to return to their religion, and to circumcise children who had been distributed among the Christians, and to be reclaimed by the community to the faith of
their fathers. The women whom the Cossacks violated were

reinstated by the *Vaad,* or Council of the Four Countries, and their offspring were brought up, and regarded, as Jews. [10]

Times of wholesale martyrdom were always auspicious for Messianic pretenders, and the terrible tragedy in Poland was no exception.

At that time there appeared in Smyrna Sabbatai Zevi (1626-76), a descendant of Marranos, whose absorption in Messianic calculations led him to the belief not only that 1648 would mark the "beginning of the End," but that he himself was to be the Messiah who would redeem Israel from all his trouble. His handsome appearance and saintly living attracted many followers, despite the sentence of excommunication passed upon him by the rabbis of the city. After several visits to Salonica, Alexandria, and Athens, where he gained devoted adherents as well as bitter antagonists, he betook himself to Cairo. There he heard of a Jewish orphan girl Sarah, who as a child of six had been confined in a monastery and raised as a Catholic but later escaped to Leghorn and resumed her former religion—claiming to be the destined bride of the Messiah. Sabbatai sent messengers to bring her to Cairo and married her. Returning to Smyrna he "revealed" his Messiahship on Rosh Hashanah, 1665, amidst the blowing of horns, while the congregation shouted, "Long live our king, our Messiah." Probably in imitation of Jesus, he soon began to sign himself "first-begotten son of God, Sabbatai Zevi, Messiah and redeemer of Israel," and, in keeping with his Messianic role, he proclaimed that with his coming the old law ceased to be binding, and that most of the regulations of rabbinic Judaism were no longer to be observed.

Encouraged by the adulation of his followers, Sabbatai left for Constantinople to dethrone the Sultan and partition the world among those whose souls were reincarnations of the souls of the kings of Judah and Israel. His arrest by order of the Grand Vizier contributed to his prestige, since it was expected that the Messiah would have to suffer tribulation before his mission could be accomplished, and even Moslems and Christians joined the crowd of his adorers. For an unknown reason, after two months of imprisonment he was transferred to Abydos. There he held court like a king with Sarah as his reigning queen, and thence he sent word to the Jews of Poland that he would avenge their massacres by the Cossacks.

Sabbatai, however, was doomed to be betrayed by one of that country. A certain Nehemiah Cohen, who claimed to be a prophet, accused him of treasonable designs; but through intercession of the Sultan's mother, he was conveyed to Adrianople and turned over to the Sultan's physician, a Jewish convert to Mohammedanism, who persuaded him to follow his example. On September 13, 1666 Sabbatai donned the white turban of a true believer and took the name of Mehmed Effendi. His wife Sarah also went over to Mohammedanism and assumed the name of Fauma Kadin, and received rich presents from the Sultana. Nehemiah Cohen, who while in Turkey passed off as a Mohammedan, fled back to Poland, threw off his turban, and disappeared from the scene in which he acted the part of Judas in the tragi-comedy of the seventeenth century "Jesus." [11]

Sabbatai's apostasy by no means shook the faith of his followers. Some of them were convinced that it was not he but a phantom who embraced Mohammedanism; or that he did it for some profound reason, unfathomable to the vulgar. Though a pensioner of the Sultan, he continued to keep in touch with Jews, and published a work in which he predicted that the Redemption would come "under the Zodiacal sign of the fish." At the same time he assured the Sultan that he strove to win the Jews over to Mohammedanism. However, when surprised in the act of singing Psalms and expounding the *Zohar* to some Jews, he was banished to Dulcigno, in Albania, where he died on the Day of Atonement, 1676.

If, Jesus-like, Sabbatai had his Judas, he also had his Paul and Apostles. Among them was a certain former Portuguese Marrano, Miguel Cardoso, who reverted to Judaism in Venice, assumed the name of Abraham, and settled down to practice as a physician in Leghorn. Highly cultured and a *bon vivant,* he took up the study of the *Zohar* and other works of the Kabbalah, began to dream dreams and see visions, and proclaimed himself a prophet and even the Messiah ben Joseph, the forerunner of the Messiah ben David. With the appearance of

Sabbatai he became one of his most zealous supporters. He traveled extensively, everywhere gaining adherents by his eloquence. He also sent circulars and wrote numerous tracts in behalf of the cause, justifying Sabbatai's apostasy by quoting from Isaiah liii, that the Messiah had "to be counted among sinners in order to make atonement for the sins of Israel"— a doctrine which, no doubt, still clung to him from the days when as a Christian he was taught about the vicarious atonement of Jesus.

After Sabbatai's death, his brother-in-law, Jacob Querido, assumed the name of Zevi, announced himself as the incarnation of Sabbatai as well as of the Messiah ben Joseph, and introduced many innovations which appealed particularly to the young. As the rabbis and the majority of the Jews were bitterly opposed to his teachings, Querido and his partisans severed their connection with the Jews and organized a sect of their own. They called themselves *Maaminim* (believers) or *Haberim* (associates), and denounced the other Jews as *Kofrim* (infidels). To this day, the *Donmeh* (apostates), as they came to be known by their former coreligionists, live outwardly in every respect like Mohammedans, visit the mosques, make pilgrimages to Mecca, and fast on the Ramadhan. But they still pray partly in Hebrew and partly in Ladino (the "Yiddish" of the Sefardic Jews) in a secret *kal,* or meeting place, and marry only among their own. Their creed consists in believing in the Unity of God and the Messiahship of Sabbatai Zevi. They are given to the daily reading of the Psalms and insist on chastity and charity. Among their festivals the most sacred is the Ninth of Ab, the birthday of their Messiah. They regard the Ladino as a holy language and are, as a rule, well versed in the Bible and the *Zohar,* which to them are of equal sanctity. There are about ten thousand of the *Donmeh,* mostly in Turkey, with Salonica as their center. In the course of time they split up into three sects, the largest being the Yakubis, or the Jacobites, named after Jacob Querido. They expect the momentary return from heaven of their founder, and send a woman and her children every Saturday to the seashore to watch for his arrival. It was rumored that Kemal Pasha was, or was descended from, one of their members.

In England, Italy, Germany, and Holland, the Sabbatai Zevi delusion stirred the Jews to their profoundest depths, but nowhere as much as in the Polish provinces which fell a prey to the savage hordes of Chmielnicki and Gontha. Even after the Messianic debacle had caused a rude awakening everywhere else, they held on to their forlorn hope with the tenacity of despair. They refused to concede that the Messiah had failed them and that they would not be redeemed soon, to be carried off on a cloud to Jerusalem. Some fasted for days, denied food even to their little ones, bathed in ice-holes, and prayed ceaselessly for the realization of the great event. The intensity of their belief became endemic. A contemporary Ukrainian writer reports that "faint-hearted and destitute Christians, hearing the stories of the miracles performed by the false Messiah and beholding the boundless arrogance of the Jews, began to doubt Christ." On the walls of the churches in Moghilev on the Dnieper inscriptions appeared acclaiming the Jewish Messiah "Sapsai." A certain Hayyim Malakh gave out that as the Children of Israel were kept in the wilderness forty years before they entered the Promised Land, so would Sabbatai return forty years after his death to perform his promise of their final deliverance. In anticipation of his coming, a party of one hundred and twenty Jews led by R. Judah Hasid started on a pilgrimage to Jerusalem (1700) and were joined by others from Germany, Austria, and Italy to the number of thirteen hundred. The death of Judah Hasid and the frustration of their hope drove some of them into the Mosque and others into the Church. Yet Hayyim Malakh continued his propaganda in Podolia and Galicia, and the Shebsen, as his followers were named, persisted secretly in clinging to their heresy despite the efforts of the leading rabbis to suppress them. [12]

From among these secret Sabbathians in Podolia came Jacob Leibovitz, better known as Frank, an appellation usually given to Europeans by people in the East. To protect themselves against the onslaughts of the orthodox, he and his followers informed the Bishop of Kamenetz-Podolsk that when they spoke of the Messiah they referred to God and that the Zohar teaches the doctrine of the Trinity. They failed to state that by the Messiah they meant Sabbatai Zevi, and by the Trinity merely the Kabbalistic conceptions of the Deity. The Bishop, regarding them as potential Christians, ordered a disputation to be held between the Zoharists and the Talmudists, at which he decided in favor of the Frankists, imposed a fine on their opponents, and consigned all the copies of the Talmud in Podolia to the flames (1757).

Elated by his success, Frank began to pose as the successor to Sabbatai and proclaimed that he and his adherents would accept Christianity, even as Sabbatai and his followers embraced Mohammedanism, in order to hasten the "End" by sinning! Thereupon, five hundred and fourteen Frankists had themselves baptized in a church of Lemberg. The occasion was marked with great solemnity, many of the Polish nobility acting as godfathers and bestowing their names upon the neophytes. The conversion of Frank himself took place in Warsaw (1759) in the presence of the royal family, with King Augustus III acting as godfather.

Somehow it leaked out that the Trinity professed by the Frankists was not quite identical with that taught by the Church, and that to his followers Frank was the *Santo Senior,* the Holy Lord, or second person of the Trinity. Frank was arrested and sent to a monastery in Chenstokhov, where he lingered for thirteen years. This, however, only confirmed his adherents in their belief that he was the suffering Messiah, and a reincarnation of the prisoner of Abydos. The belief was reinforced in numerous mystical epistles in which he claimed that he had descended into hell to expiate for their sins, and that he was to "rid the world of all the laws and statutes which have been in existence hitherto." Released by the Russian commander who occupied Chenstokhov in 1772, he went with his family to Moravia, whence he moved to Germany where he assumed the title of Baron von Offenbach and lived in the style of a nobleman enriched by the gifts of many pilgrims who came to consult him and his beautiful daughter Eve, "the Holy Lady." For some time after his death his followers constituted a distinct group known as the "Neophytes," but gradually they intermarried and merged with the Catholic population. Eve died in poverty and obscurity in 1816.[13]

Meanwhile, during the period when freedom of thought and expression prevailed in Poland, Jews came forth with pamphlets defending their views and assailing those of their enemies.

Such a polemic, *The Retort,* was written by R. Jacob Nahman of Belczytz, court physician to Sigismund III (1581). It was evoked by *The Christian Dialogues* (1575) and *Catechism* (1580) of Martin Chechovitz, a former Catholic priest who joined the Bohemian Brothers in Vilna and held religious disputations with "genuine and pseudo-Jews." It was written in Polish, showing that at least some Jews were masters of the language of their country as well as of the sources of Christianity. [14]

More effective than *The Retort,* and ranking among the best of Jewish polemics, was a work written in Hebrew by the Karaite Isaac b. Abraham of Troki, near Vilna. Since he was a member of the Jewish sect which rejected the Talmud, Christians assumed that only a little argument was all that was necessary to make him "see the light," and Catholics and Protestants engaged him in religious disputations. Isaac's *Hizzuk Emunah* (The Strengthening of Faith, 1593), in which he shows himself conversant not only with the Gospels but also with Patristic literature, was soon supplied by a Rabbinite with Talmudic references and translated into Spanish and German. Since there was no one bold enough to print this "dreadful treatise," it was widely circulated among Christians in manuscript form. But its popularity was further stimulated by Johann Christoph Wagenseil, Professor of Oriental Languages at the Altdorf University. Determined to devote his considerable knowledge of Hebrew to the cause of Christianity, Wagenseil collected and translated into Latin six Jewish polemics, including *Hizzuk Emunah,* under the title *Tela Ignea Satanae* (The Fiery Arrows of Satan, 1681), with comments "so that Jews be not fortified in their errors." The work, however, served a contrary purpose. It was employed by the free thinkers of the eighteenth century as a source-book in their assaults on the Christian dogmas. Of it Voltaire said, "Not even the most determined unbelievers have brought forward any arguments which could not be found in the *Strengthening of Faith* by Rabbi Isaac." [15]

It is hardly likely that Isaac b. Abraham was himself a proselyte as Professor Gotthard Deutsch surmises. However, references to Polish proselytes are not only in the Memorbuch of Mayence, among those who were martyred during the Crusades, but also in various *Pinkosim* and *Responsa*. Numerous traditions and folktales also preserve the stories of more or less prominent personages who embraced Judaism either out of love for a fair maiden, out of admiration for Jewish steadfastness, or out of conviction. These are corroborated by the constant complaints of the Church and the regulations of the State. About 1539 an apostate Jew claimed that many Christians had adopted Judaism and were being sheltered by the Jews of Lithuania. In 1548 the Bishop of Vilna reported that Catholic women frequently married Jewish men and raised their offspring in the faith of the fathers. We know that many Polish Christians who were bent on conversion went or were sent to Turkey, and that a number of them fled to the one liberal country in Christendom—Holland. [16]

One of the better known proselytes of Poland was a certain Catherine Melcher Zaleshovska, the wife of an alderman, whom the Bishop of Cracow tried his utmost to bring back into the fold. It is recorded that though she was eighty years of age when condemned to the stake for her crime, she "went to her death as if it were a wedding (1539)." [17]

Another woman proselyte was Anna Constance, a descendant of Schleswig-Holstein nobility, the wife of the wealthy Baron of Hoimb, and probably the most influential lady in the court of Augustus "the Strong." Sentenced to be jailed in Pilnitz on a charge of Judaizing, she escaped to Berlin and thence to Halle, where she was seized, pronounced insane, and imprisoned in the fortress of Stolpen (1716), where she spent the last fifty years of her life with the Old Testament as her constant companion. She also acquired a knowledge of Hebrew, the Midrash, and Talmud, and learned to converse in Yiddish with the rabbis of Bohemia on Jewish topics. She was a strict observer of the Sabbath and festivals, and had her poultry killed and prepared in accordance with the Jewish dietary laws. A large part of the income from her estates in North Germany she devoted exclusively to the old Jewish favorite benefactions (*Pidyon Shebuim*) (redemption of captives) and *Hakhnasat Kallah* (endowing brides).[18]

The most outstanding Polish *Ger Zedek* is undoubtedly Count Valentine Potocki, the son of a distinguished nobleman. Sent by his father to Paris to finish his education, he met there his countryman Zarembo, also of noble lineage, and the two became close friends. Once they entered a tavern for refreshments, and while there they heard an old man instructing a small boy in a tent in the yard. On inquiry they were informed that the book used was the Holy Scriptures written in the original Hebrew. They asked the old man to translate it to them. He did so with avidity, and the youths soon became so engrossed in it that they began to neglect their other studies. For this the old man reproached them, but young Potocki remonstrated that he had no right to scold them for searching after the truth.

While out for a walk one day, Potocki confided to Zarembo that he had become convinced that the Jewish religion was the only true one and that he had resolved to become a Jew regardless of the consequences. To his surprise Zarembo confessed that he, too, was thinking of doing the same. After some hesitation they decided to cast lots. The result was in favor of conversion, but still Potocki hesitated since it would mean the giving up of the respect and comforts to which he had been accustomed. To make sure of himself, he went to Rome and spent considerable time in communion with bishops, cardinals, and even the pope. These contacts, however, only deepened his conviction that Judaism was the only true religion. So he fled from Rome to Amsterdam, became a Jew, and assumed the name of Abraham b. Abraham.

After Zarembo waited in vain for his friend's return, he went back to Poland, married the daughter of a well-known nobleman, Tishkewitch, and sought diversion in the social whirl of his circle. But the thought that Valentine might have carried out his resolve made him ashamed of his own weakness, and his health began steadily to decline. On the advice of physicians he went to Koenigsberg, whence he left with his wife and son of five, for Amsterdam, where on the day after their arrival, he and his boy entered the Covenant of Abraham. Some time later his wife, who at first was greatly alarmed, also became a Jewess and accompanied him to the Holy Land, where they lived happily as devout and God-fearing Jews.

The fate of Count Potocki was quite different. He, too, left for Palestine, but a nostalgic feeling drew him back to Lithuania. There he settled in the town of Ilye, spent all his time in the study of the Torah, and was regarded as a saint. Once he reprimanded a boy for misbehaving in the synagogue, and when the boy grew impertinent R. Abraham slapped him and told him that he acted like a *Shegetz* (one of non-Jewish descent). Thereupon the lad's father, a tailor, informed the authorities that the reputed R. Abraham was in reality a proselyte. Potocki was immediately arrested and deported to Vilna; but neither his Jewish friends nor the clergy and the bishop could induce him to revert to Catholicism. As torture proved of no avail, he was sentenced to be burned alive in the center of the city, on the very day of the giving of the Torah (Shabuot, 1749). No Jews were present when the tragedy took place save a youth by the name of Zishko who, being beardless, was not recognized by the mob. He reported that R. Abraham b. Abraham remained steadfast to the end and that before he expired he pronounced the Hebrew benediction: "Blessed be Thou who sanctifiest Thy Name among the many." [19]

With the dismemberment of Poland, nearly a million Jews passed over to the control of the Russians where a thousand years before a whole region along the Don, the Volga, the Caspian and Black Seas, including the "mother" city of Kiev, was dominated by a dynasty which accepted the faith of Israel. This people, known as Khazars, was a conglomeration of

Turks, Finns, Huns, Scythians, and Slavs in addition to Armenians and Georgians. They helped the Greeks to hurl the conquering Persians back to their border, subjugated Armenia, defeated the Ugers (Hungarians), drove the Bulgars from the Ukraine, and won control over the sea of Azov. They levied tribute on Russia and are said to have claimed lordship over twenty-five nations.

Into Khazaria, which like many pagan lands was free from persecution, fled many Jews from their Mohammedan and Christian enemies, and by dint of their industry and intelligence soon inspired respect among their pagan neighbors. As merchants, physicians and interpreters they came in touch with all classes, especially with the nobility and the Khagan who resided at Atel on the Volga.

Somewhere in the eighth century, a Khagan named Bulan is said to have dreamed that an angel appeared to him and urged him to seek for the true religion without telling him which it was. The same happened also to the viceroy. When the news spread about, the Byzantine emperor and the Mohammedan caliph sent theologians and envoys with costly gifts to induce the Khagan to accept their religion while the Khagan himself invited a learned Jew to take part in the disputation. After the various champions presented their arguments, Bulan asked each of them to tell him what they thought of the religion of the adversaries. Whereupon the Christian stated that Judaism is superior to Mohammedanism, while the Mohammedan maintained that Judaism is preferable to Christianity. This made Bulan decide in favor of Judaism, and his example was followed by four thousand of his nobles and many more of his subjects. [20]

His successor Obadiah built numerous synagogues, established *yeshibot* (religious schools), and invited renowned Talmudists to his land. He made Khazaria the most tolerant country then known, and introduced peace and equality among the inhabitants, the only exception being that the reigning prince should always be of the Jewish faith, and that while Jews, Christians, and Mohammedans were represented at the

Supreme Court by two judges each, the pagans were represented by only one judge.

The country prospered exceedingly, and its fame spread over Europe and Asia. In the Byzantine court the Khagan's correspondence was given precedence over that of the pope and the Carlovingian emperor. Justinian II, when he fled from Kherson, took refuge in the palace of the Khagan, where he met and married his daughter Irene, famous for her beauty. Leo IV, called Khozer (775-80), had thus some Jewish relatives, and it was with the aid of Khazarian troops that he vanquished the Bulgarians.

The news of the conversion of the Khazars reached Spain at the time when Hasdai ibn Shaprut was treasurer of Abdulrahaman III, Caliph of Cordova. On hearing it, the minister immediately addressed a letter of inquiry to the Khagan. He received a reply from Joseph, the then Jewish Khagan, in which the Khagan describes how Bulan and his noblemen came to embrace Judaism.

> Know and take notice that I live at the mouth of the river (Volga), and with the help of the Almighty I guard the entrance to this river, and prevent the Russians, who arrive in vessels, from passing into the Caspian Sea for the purpose of making their way to the Ishmaelites (Moslems). In the same manner I keep the enemies on land from approaching from Bab-al-Abwab. . . . Our eyes are (turned) to God and to the wise men of Israel who preside over the academies of Jerusalem and Babylon. We are far away from Zion, but it has come to our ears that on account of our sins, the calculations (concerning the coming of the Messiah) have become muddled, so that we know nothing. May it please the Lord to act for the sake of His great Name. May the destruction of His Temple, the cutting off of the divine service, and the misfortunes that have befallen us, not appear small in His sight. May the words of the Prophet be fulfilled (Mal. 3:1: 'And the Lord Whom ye seek shall suddenly come to His Temple').

Another Khazar epistle, confirming in the main the above, but omitting the story of the dream, was recently discovered in the Cairo Genizah. The Khazars are supposed to have been the descendants of Togarmah, the seventh son of Noah, who is also claimed to have been the ancestor of the Turks. But the Jews of Persia and Arabia preferred to find in them the "lost" Ten Tribes come to life and power again, they called the Don River Al-Sabt (Sambatyon) and Kiev, which is situated on it, Sambatas.

For centuries the Khazars held dominion over Hungary, Poland, and Russia, and made these countries havens of refuge for the persecuted Jews from the lands of the Mohammedans and the Christians. Kiev became a talmudic center, and a saying obtained: "Out of Kiev shall go forth the Torah, and the word of the Lord from Starodub." [21]   •

But five years after Khagan Joseph penned his famous epistle, the prosperity and peace of the Khazars began to decline. Hordes of savage "Tartars" and daring Norsemen began their invasion of Slavonian territories. Little by little they were dislodged from their possessions on the Caspian and Black Seas, but held out for some time in the Crimean Peninsula, where they still had a King David in 1000. In 1016 the descendants of the Jewish royal family fled to their coreligionists in Spain. Many of the Jewish Khazars, however, continued to live in the Crimea and organized themselves into a *Kahal Kozer,* to be distinguished from the Kahal Gregas, the Byzantine Jews who still kept on settling there. R. Pethahiah of Ratisbon, who visited them about 1175, describes them as *minim* "who do not believe in the traditions of the sages, eat their Sabbath meal in the dark, are ignorant of the talmudic forms of the benedictions and prayers, and have not even heard of the Talmud." It is evident that he refers to the Karaites who must have become a majority. In the fifteenth century they had their own overlord, Khoza Kokos. But the majority of the early Khazar proselytes were scattered over the neighboring countries, introducing Jewish ideals among their Christian neighbors. Some estimate that from sixty to seventy per cent of the Jews of Southern Russia are not of Semitic descent.

The conversion of the Khazars to Judaism helped, according to a Church legend, to convert the Russians to Christianity. According to it,

> When Vladimir had announced his intention to abandon idolatry (c. 986), he received a visit from Khazarian Jews, who said to him: 'We have heard that the Christians have come to preach their faith, but they believe in one who was crucified by us, while we believe in the one God, the God of Abraham, Isaac and Jacob.' Vladimir asked the Jews: 'What does your law prescribe?' To this they replied: 'To be circumcised, not to eat pork or game, and to keep the Sabbath.' 'Where is your country?' inquired the prince. 'In Jerusalem,' replied the Jews. 'But do you live there?' he asked. 'We do not,' answered the Jews, 'for the Lord was wroth with our forefathers, and scattered us all over the earth for our sins, while our land was given away to the Christians.' Thereupon Vladimir exclaimed: 'If God loved you, you would not be dispersed in strange lands. Do not wish to inflict the same misfortune on me!'[22]

Whatever be the reasons for his rejection of Judaism and Mohammedanism, Vladimir's selection of Greek Catholicism was prompted less by the soundness of its creed than by the pomp and splendor of its ritual. The ten ambassadors whom he sent to Constantinople to learn about "the religion of the Greeks" reported on their return that the celebration of a festival which they witnessed while there so fascinated them that "we no longer knew whether we were in heaven or on earth." He was also informed that the young princess Anna, the daughter of one of the emperors, would be a likely prize for his acceptance of the faith of her people. So without much ado he sent an embassy to Basil and Constantine offering to become a Greek Catholic in return for their willingness to have him as their son-in-law, and the emperors, who were in need of an ally against the Romans, reluctantly consented. Vladimir was baptized in Kherson, and his marriage to

Anna was solemnized immediately after. Thereupon all the idols were collected and burned in huge bonfires, and the statue of the supreme god Peroune was dragged through the street, scourged with whips and pelted with mud, and thrown from the top of a precipice into the Dnieper. At the same time, all the inhabitants of Kiev and vicinity were ordered to repair to the banks of the river, where Vladimir took his seat on an elevated throne, surrounded by a large number of ecclesiastics from Constantinople; and, at a given signal, the whole multitude waded into the stream and was baptized by the clergy on the shore in the name of the Father, the Son, and the Holy Ghost. [23]

It is interesting to note that the first Bishop of Novgorod, appointed by Yaroslaw (1035), was a certain Lucas Zhidyata (Lucas the Little Jew) of whom it is said that he seldom referred to the creed, constantly stressed the importance of the Ten Commandments, and drew his texts mostly from the Old Testament. Lucas may have seen the light at the same time as the Russian pagans. But we know that simultaneously with the adoption of the "Orthodox," or Greek Catholic, faith, Russia also adopted the Byzantine policy regarding the Jews. Those of them who were already in the land were forced to be converted, all others were kept out. Feodosi (1057-74), the abbot of the Pechera monastery, preached to his flock to live in peace with all, friend and foe alike, "but not with these foes of God" (the Jews) who "hold a crooked religion." His one great ambition was either to convert them or be made a martyr by them. To accomplish this end, he would secretly and unexpectedly visit the Jews at night to argue about Christ, or otherwise to irritate them. But to his chagrin, Jews stubbornly refused either to be converted or to kill him and thus make of him a holy martyr. The metropolitans and clergy were no more successful than he. But their harangues had their effect on the Christians, and in 1113 we hear of a bloodthirsty mob plundering the Jews of Kiev. As late as 1526 the Muscovite ambassador to Rome declared that Russians "dread no one more than the Jews, and do not admit them into their borders." [24]

This was no doubt somewhat of an exaggeration. There were always some Jews in Kiev, among them fugitives from the fire and sword of the Crusaders. In the fifteenth century, Ivan III employed several Crimean Jews in his diplomatic negotiations with the Khan. One of them, Khoza Kokos, preferred to write his letters in Hebrew, until the Grand Duke of Muscovy requested him to correspond with him in the Russian or "Basurman" language. Another was Zechariah Guizolfi, a Genoese Jew, who married Bikhakhanim, the reigning princess of the Taman Peninsula, and was known as "the Prince of Taman" (1484-1500). Ivan III also invited Master Leon to cure his sick son. Unfortunately, the child died, and the physician paid for his failure with his life. [25]

As in the rest of Christendom, Jews were feared and hated in Russia because they were suspected as adepts of the black arts, enemies of all Christians and ardent missionaries. To Sigismund Augustus' request that Lithuanian Jews be allowed to do business in Russia by virtue of the commercial treaties between the two countries, Ivan the Terrible replied:

> It is not convenient to allow Jews to come with their goods to Russia, since many evils result from them. For they import poisonous herbs into our realm, and lead astray the Russians from Christianity. There-upon the King should no more write about these Jews.

He also ordered (1563) that all the Jews of the recently occupied city of Polotzk be converted to the Greek Orthodox faith and those who resisted baptism be drowned in the Dniva. The Polish Prince Vladislav was invited to become the Czar of Russia (1610) on condition that no Roman Catholics be allowed to convert the Russians nor build churches of their own, and that no Jews be permitted to enter the Muscovite Empire under any circumstances. Even the "enlightened" Peter the Great, who called several Jewish finance agents into his new capital, St. Petersburg, and showed particular favor to Lipman Levy, a banker from Courland, could not rid himself of his Russian Judeophobia. "I'd rather see in our midst," he declared, "nations professing Mohammedanism and paganism than Jews. They are rogues and cheats. It is my endeavor to eradicate evil and not to multiply it. They shall not be allowed to live or to trade in Russia, whatever efforts they make, and however much they may bribe those near me."

Catherine I issued an ukase expelling them from Little Russia (1727) despite the protests of the Cossacks who found them useful as traders. Elizabeth Petrovna, bent on the conversion of all the Mohammedans and Roman Catholics to Greek Catholicism, declared (1741) that:

> From our whole empire, both from the Great Russian and Little Russian cities, villages, and hamlets, all Jews of the male and female sex, of whatever calling and dignity they may be, shall, at the publication of this our ukase, be immediately deported with all their property abroad, and shall henceforth, under no pretext, be admitted into our Empire for any purpose; unless they be willing to accept the Christian religion of the Greek persuasion. Such, having been baptized, shall be allowed to live in our Empire, but they shall not be permitted to go outside the country.

When the merchants of Little Russia and Livonia remonstrated that the expulsion of the Jews meant the ruination of their trade, the Empress swept away all their arguments with the laconic statement: "From the enemies of Christ I desire no benefits." She expelled her body physician, Antonio Sanchez, who was a member of the Academy of Science, when she discovered that he was guilty of the "crime" of being a Jew. The same policy was pursued by Catherine II, who was as notorious for her immorality as Elizabeth was for her piety.[26]

Yet, by the irony of fate, Russia was destined to become the home of the largest Jewish community in the Diaspora. Her conquest of Poland brought her face to face with Jews of Little and White Russia, of Lithuania and Ukraine, and they soon had a taste of the pogroms which continued spasmodically down to the twentieth century. But the nineteenth century dawned with a promise of respite for the unfortunate

Russo-Polish Jews. Alexander I, who came under the influence of French enlightenment, showed his good will toward them on several occasions, and, encouraged by his example, voices began to be heard pleading that instead of seeking to save their souls the government should exert itself to treat them like human beings. Among these voices was also, for the first time, that of a Jew, Judah Leib Nyevakhovich, who in a Russian pamphlet entitled *The Cry of the Daughter of Judah* (1803) protested against "the deep-seated hatred of the Jews in Russia," and assured the Russians that "the Jew who preserves his religion undefiled can be neither a bad man nor a bad citizen."

But the fact that Napoleon, the dreaded enemy of Russia, was granting equality to the Jews who came under his control, was utilized by the Greek Church to drive the somewhat liberal Czar into submission. While Alexander was making his well-intentioned plans to improve the lot of his Jewish subjects, the Holy Synod, which proclaimed Napoleon as the Antichrist, gave as proof that his main object was "to put the Church of Christ to shame," the fact that

> He established the Great Synhedrion of the Jews, that same ungodly assembly which had once dared to pass the sentence of crucifixion upon our Lord and Savior, and he now planned to unite the Jews,—whom the wrath of the Almighty hath scattered over the face of the whole earth, so as to incite them to overthrow the Christian Church and proclaim the pseudo-Messiah in the person of Napoleon.

At last the Czar was prevailed upon to change his policy and to regard himself as an instrument of Divine Providence to convert the Jews,—whom the partition of Poland providentially put in his charge. By a ukase of 1817, "Israelitish Christians" were granted crown lands in the southern and northern provinces, full civil equality, and exemption from all burdensome taxes. In 1820, a large tract of land in the Government of Yekaterinoslav was set aside specifically for Jewish converts, with a "Curator" and a staff of officials to assist in its administration. At the same time, Alexander decreed the expulsion of the few remaining Jews from St. Petersburg (1818), forbade the employment by Jews of Christian servants, and the leasing to them of Christian farms (1820). He also banished over twenty thousand Jews from the villages of the Governments of Vitebsk and Mohilev, and from the border-zone, into the already overcrowded and impoverished towns and hamlets of the Pale.

Drastic as were these measures, Nicholas 1 (1825-55), the "terrible incarnation of autocracy," found them too mild and thought of what to him seemed a new means of driving the Jews into the bosom of the Greek Catholic Church. Hitherto Jews all over Christendom were singled out from the rest of the population by a garb or a badge. Poland was the exception. There they were permitted during the Middle Ages to dress in Polish fashion, and to this fashion they clung even after the Poles themselves abandoned it. Nicholas was of the opinion that by compelling them to discontinue their distinctive Judeo-Polish dress, they would ultimately cease to cling to their distinctive religion. Again, while everywhere in Christendom Jews were refused admittance into the army (though they had to pay a tax for being "exempt"), he decreed that Jewish communities supply conscripts to serve for twenty-five years, commencing from the time they reached the age of eighteen. An exception was made in the case of the Karaites who, according to Nicholas, left Palestine before the Christian era, and therefore had no share in the Crucifixion.

Thereafter, there were re-enacted on Russian soil scenes which were hardly surpassed in the Spain and Portugal of the Middle Ages. The Russian tragedy was the greater in that Jews themselves were compelled to act as the spiritual executioners of their brethren and children. Since no Jew would willingly deliver his child to the "Moloch" of the army of the Czar, Russian Jewry became infested with *Moserim* (informers), who preyed upon their coreligionists for a price, and would seize anyone who was unfortunate enough to lack a protector, or could not pay blackmail. The *Poimaniki*, or captured recruits, were frequently children of seven or eight. They would be assembled in the synagogue where, arrayed in *tallit* (prayer-shawl) and *kittel* (shroud), they would be placed before the Holy Ark and, amidst burning candles and the sound of *shofar,* they would be administered the oath of allegiance. This done, they would be quartered in the homes of Christians and watched over by a special officer till they commenced their arduous journey to the remotest parts of Russia, including Siberia.

The following description of the experiences of the *Poimaniki* or *Cantonists*, as they were usually called, is given by the historian Simon Dubnow:

> Having arrived at their destination, the juvenile conscripts were put into the cantonist battalions. The 'preparation for military service' began with their religious re-education at the hands of sergeants and corporals. No means was neglected so long as it bade fair to bring the children to the baptismal font.... The children were first sent for spiritual admonition to the local Greek-Orthodox priests, whose efforts, however, proved fruitless in nearly every case. They were then taken in hand by the sergeants and corporals, who adopted military methods of persuasion.
>
> These brutal soldiers invented all kinds of tortures. A favorite procedure was to make the cantonists get down on their knees in the evening after all had gone to bed and to keep the sleepy children in that position for hours. Those who agreed to be baptized were sent to bed, those who refused were kept up all night till they dropped from exhaustion. Then children who continued to hold their own were flogged, under the guise of gymnastic exercises, subjected to all kinds of tortures....
>
> The majority of these children, unable to endure the torments inflicted upon them, saved themselves by baptism. But many cantonists, particularly those of maturer age (between fifteen and eighteen), bore their martyrdom with heroic patience. Beaten almost

into senselessness, their bodies striped by lashes, tormented to the point of exhaustion by hunger, thirst, and sleeplessness, the lads declared again and again that they would not betray the faith of their fathers. Most of these obstinate youths were carried from the barracks into the military hospitals to be released by death. Only a few remained. [27]

Many blood-curdling stories were brought back by the survivors of these slaughtered innocents. One is to the effect that during a military parade in the city of Kazan the battalion chief drew up all the cantonists on the banks of the river, where the Greek-Orthodox priests stood in their vestments, ready for the baptismal ceremony. At the command to jump into the water, the boys answered in military fashion, "Aye, aye!" dove under and remained till they were drowned. In most cases, however, they died less dramatically in the barracks, brigs, and hospitals for refusing to recite the creed, or to eat pork, or the cabbage cooked with lard. It is estimated that of all the recruits, scarcely half remained alive. Of those who survived, about a tenth retraced their steps to the Jewish fold. These *Nikolayevski Soldati* (Soldiers of Nicholas), with their uncouth demeanor, and ignorant but sincere adherence to Judaism furnished much material for folk-songs and tales, and (such is the Jewish sense of humor) for numerous jokes, among their more polished and learned coreligionists in the Pale. One of them, however, Wolf Nachlass, who became a *Cantonist* at the age of ten and resisted for a number of years the tortures and temptations of the conversionist corporals, finally had his resistance broken (1845), and not only did he become a convert but won over five hundred fellow-Cantonists to the religion of the Czar, who graciously thanked him in person. [28]

Another direct action was taken by Nicholas through a "Jewish Committee," all the members of which were Christians. This committee established a school of Rabbinics and Yiddish in Warsaw in order to prepare missionaries to the Jews. It also undertook, under Abbe Chiarini, a translation, or rather a defamation, of the Talmud (Paris, 1830). This was supplemented with an ukase ordering all Hebrew books to be transported to St. Petersburg, under a police escort, for investigation as to whether or not they contained anything at variance with imperial enactments. Finding this procedure too burdensome, he commanded that the condemned works be "delivered to the flames on the spot (1886)." Cartloads of Hebrew books were thus destroyed by fire or thrown into store-houses, there to rot until the censor, frequently illiterate and prejudiced, should decide whether they be spared or not.

A ray of light pierced through "darkest Russia" with the coronation of Alexander II (1856-81). The *Tzar Osvoboditýel* (Liberator Czar), who evinced his humanitarianism in the emancipation of nearly twenty-two millions of his enslaved *muzhiks* (peasants), the abolition of capital punishment, and the reformation of the barbarous system of Russian justice, took to heart also the lot of his Jewish subjects. He rescinded the decree concerning juvenile conscription, permitted the captive children (except those who had embraced Christianity) to return to their parents, and discontinued the usual phrase *kromye Yevreyev* (excepting the Jews) from enactments in favor of the population. Interested in the Jews as subjects and not merely as potential converts to Christianity, he withdrew the grant of monetary assistance from those of them who embraced the Greek Catholic or any other Christian persuasion, and repealed the law which prescribed immunity or a mitigation of the sentence for criminals who embraced Christianity.

And again, as during the early days of Alexander I, there appeared among the Russian intelligentsia champions of the Jews who sought to counteract the influence of the Church and to dilute, if not destroy, the poison injected in Russian literature by Pushkin, Gogol, Lermontoff, and Turgenief. They discarded the opprobrious term *Zhyd* for "Jew" and adopted the more respectable epithet *Yevrey*. They advocated the erasing "of the bloody boundary-line separating the Jews from humanity." "Where are religion, morality, enlightenment and the modern spirit," asked Nicholas Pirogov, the superintendent of education, "when these Jews who, with courage and self-sacrifice, engage in the struggle against prejudice centuries old, meet no one here to sympathize with them and extend a helping hand to them?"

Unfortunately, the benign efforts of Alexander II, like those of Alexander I, were of short duration. The reactionaries who managed to convert his liberal predecessor into a tyrant were soon in the saddle again. The peasants were turned into peons, and the measures intended to put Russia abreast of the times were thwarted and perverted by mercenary officials. Alexander's counsellors attributed all the national troubles to his incipient reforms, and the intimidated czar resumed the road which Russia trod under Ivan the Terrible and Nicholas I, and which ultimately led to the extirpation of the Romanoffs.

As had often happened before, Jewish apostates contributed not a little to the intensification of prejudice against their former coreligionists. Aenikin in his *Derek Selulah* ("The Paved Road," St. Petersburg, 1835) and Buchner in his *Der Talmud in Seiner Nichtigkeit* ("The Worthlessness of the Talmud," Warsaw, 1848) appealed to the Jews to become assimilated with the Christians for material reasons. But Jaesu Brafman went much further. Embittered against the officials who were about to draft him into the czar's army, he indicted his *Kniga Kahala* (Book of the *Kahal,* Vilna, 1869), in which *à la* Pfefferkorn, he declared that Judaism taught its adherents to violate all the laws of God and men; that it fostered fanaticism and prejudice against the Christian religion, and that the *Kahal* (community) is a clandestine organization whose object is to subvert the government and destroy Christianity. This diatribe, published at government expense and freely distributed among the officials, became the basis for the notorious *Protocols of the Elders of Zion* (1919). Brafman's success prompted Hippolyte Lutostanski, a Roman Catholic priest of unsavory reputation who turned Greek Orthodox, to compose treatises on "The Use of Christian Blood by the Jews" and "The Talmud and the Jews," both masterpieces of malice which served as textbooks for official anti-Semitism.

With the new attitude of the government, the powers of

darkness which were held in check during the brighter days of Alexander's reign began to bestir themselves anew. On the pretext that Jews had stolen a cross from a church fence and stoned the church building, the first of a series of *pogroms,* or massacres of Jews, broke out in Odessa on Palm Sunday, 1871, and the spectre of the blood-libel was resurrected in distant Mutais, Caucasus (1873). With the accession of Alexander III (1881) and the appointment of his ministers Constantine Pobyedonostsev and Nicholas Ignatzev, Russian history became "a long list of martyrs and a register of convicts." Pogroms were adopted as part of the policy of the government, in the hope that "one-third of the Jews emigrate, another third embrace Christianity, and the remainder die of starvation."

With this end in view, Jews were deprived of every available means of making a livelihood. Those, however, who abjured their faith were freed from taxation for a period of five years, and received a bonus of from thirteen to thirty rubles; their marriage to their Jewish wives annulled, and their wives were prohibited to marry again. The water of baptism absolved them also from any crime of which they may have been guilty, even murder and rape. The only Jewesses who were permitted to live in the capital of Holy Russia were those who plied the "profession" of a prostitute, or could show the yellow tickets as evidence of the same. This policy was continued by Nicholas II and was abandoned only when the Romancff dynasty, and its mainstay, the Greek Orthodox hierarchy, were crushed by the new, and no less ruthless, tyranny of the Bolsheviki.

Needless to say that to escape their unbearable lot, many Jews sought refuge in the Greek Orthodox Church. These Russian *Anusim,* of whom there were thirty thousand in Moscow and St. Petersburg by the middle of the nineteenth century, are described by Dr. Max Lilienthal as follows:

> I made the acquaintance of many of them, and learned of their inexpressible pain and tortures of conscience. While on the one hand they try to appease their uneasiness by the fair prospects that are opened

to their children, by the satisfaction that they are exempt from the continual reactions and exceptional laws to which their former coreligionists are exposed; on the other hand, when in the company of Jews, they show themselves so awkward and uneasy that we cannot help but pity them. They despise the heathen idolatry of the Russian Church, but do not dare, for fear of Siberia, to betray themselves by a single word. Their heart still clings with all the Jewish fervor to the holy *Shema Yisrael*, but nevertheless they feel attracted by the wealth and luxury that surrounds them. They try to conceal their Jewish jargon and do not wish to be reminded of their Jewish origin, but nevertheless on the Jewish New Year's Day and Day of Atonement remorse pursues them like an evil spectre, and thus their life is one of uneasiness, repentance, luxury, and apprehension.[29]

For these converts accepted Christianity not because they would be saved from hell in the world to come but to escape the Russian hell in this world. What they were after was not salvation but a certificate of baptism, and this they sought to procure in any way possible. Some obtained it by proxy without ever having seen the priest or studied the catechism or entered the portals of a Christian sanctuary. Many became professional converts and did a thriving business by assuming the names of, and receiving the sacraments for, those who themselves never deviated in the least from the narrow path of Judaism. Others kept up their work in behalf of their faith and people as before. Daniel Chwolson (1819-1911), the eminent Orientalist who became professor at both the University of St. Petersburg and the Seminary for the training of priests, remained one of the staunchest defenders of Jews and Judaism. His treatise on the blood accusations is one of the best vindications of Israel ever written. Gregory Bogrov did more than anyone else to expose the horrors of Nicholas' "reforms." One of the finest Hebrew poets during the *Haskalah,* or Russo-Jewish Renaissance period was Constantine

Schapiro, who resorted to baptism in order to be able to pursue his trade as a photographer in St. Petersburg. Gregory Peretz, one of the leaders in the struggle for the liberation of the Russian masses, was also one of the champions of the rehabilitation of the Jews, thus being the forerunner of the Zionist movement which reclaimed many Jews to Judaism. [30]

One thing seems obvious, Greek Catholicism never of itself appealed to the converts of Russian Jewry. Those who would escape their disability by conversion showed their predilection, whenever possible, by joining any other church than the *Pravoslavnian* (orthodox). Some hoped that by abandoning the distinctive Jewish rites without professing a belief in the Trinity, they would be granted the human rights for which they longed, and organized such societies as the *Bibleitsi*, or the Spiritual Biblical Brotherhood, founded in Yelisavetgrad by Jacob Gordin (1879), and *Novy Israel* (New Israel), established in Odessa and Kishinev by Jacob Priluker (1885), which rejected the Talmud, the dietary laws, the rite of circumcision, and the ancient form of worship. They also transferred the traditional Sabbath to Sunday. Another who sought an avenue of escape, Joseph Rabinovich, advocated the formation of a "Congregation of New Testament Israelites." These movements, however, never made much headway and ultimately led their proponents themselves to the Christian fold. Priluker went to England and became a Protestant missionary to the Jews, while Gordin emigrated to America and became the foremost Yiddish playwright in the United States. But some Jewish converts were instrumental in spreading the doctrines of Protestantism in the Empire of the Czars and outside of it. One of these Hebrew-Christian missionaries to the Christians was German-born Adolph Philippi, who was elected professor of theology at the University of Dorpat (1841). Of him, the Lutheran Encyclopedia states:

> If Dorpat and Rostack are even today strongholds of
> sound Lutheranism, and if the Church in the Baltic
> provinces and the province of Mecklenburg is firm in

its Lutheran faith, these conditions are in large measure due to the fulness of faith and the vigorous personality that characterized Philippi. [31]

But while the Russian giant was wrestling with the hapless
Jews, the Jews, without any effort or intention, won many
voluntary recruits from the camp of the enemy. Russia, with
her entrenched Greek Catholicism, in which the Renaissance
and the Reformation had produced scarcely a ripple, has furnished more proselytes to Judaism than any other country in
Christendom. In Russia, Judaism, or some semblance of it,
made its appeal not only to a few individuals, but to whole
groups, and today there are all over the world hundreds of
thousands of former Russian Orthodox Christians who are
strict observers of the religion of Israel.

Dissatisfaction with the doctrines of the Greek Orthodox
Church began almost simultaneously with the conversion of
St. Olga. By the beginning of the fifteenth century the prevailing religious unrest had already produced several dissenting sects. One of these, the Strigolniki, so called after its
founder Carp Strigolnik, whose center was in Novgorod, abrogated many of the rites of the Greek Church and denied the
divinity of Christ. Whether the Jew Skaria (Zechariah), who
was reputed to have studied "astrology, necromancy, and various other magic arts," was in any way connected with this
movement is uncertain, but by 1475 we hear of the *Szydovstvoichy,* or the "Judaizing Heresy." Led by the priest Denis
and the Archbishop Aleksey, who took the name Abraham
and called his wife Sarah, many Russians, including priests,
monks, and mechanics, accepted the Jewish day of rest as their
Sabbath and some of them even submitted to the rite of circumcision. Among the Judaized courtiers of Ivan III was
the Secretary of State Fedor Kuritzyn, the Archimandrite
Zosimus, the Monk Zacharias, the Czar's daughter-in-law,
Princess Helena, and his grandson Dimitri who in 1498 became heir apparent. It seemed as if Russia was on the eve of
becoming another Khazaria, when the Church Council, with

the assistance of the Czar, started a war of extermination against the *Szydovstvoichy* sect. Kuritzyn was burned at the stake, Zosimus was pronounced "a son of the devil" who should not be granted the privilege to sit "on the holy seat of the martyrs," while Princess Helena was degraded. The knout, the jail, and the stake produced their salubrious effect on the rest, and the heresy seemed to have been suppressed.

But, in fact, the *Szydovstvoichy* sect never died out in Russia. Sometimes people were Judaized through intermarriage. A Jewess who, during the Cossack invasion, was forced to marry a Greek Catholic came ten years later to the Catholic city of Slutzk, and her husband, his brother, and their children accepted the faith of Israel. Some conversions were also due to the direct missionary activity of the Jews who were forcibly baptized. According to the Patriarch Nikon (1671), Jews who had been admitted as monks into the Voskreusky Monastery not only "fostered there their old religion" but influenced the young "popes" to follow their example. An additional impetus to proselytism was given in the seventeenth century by the "reform" introduced by the Patriarch in making the sign of the cross with three fingers instead of the customary two. This opened up a religious controversy which resulted in driving many into the ranks of the *Raskolniki* (heretics). Out of these came the *Dukhobortsi* (Carriers of the Spirit) who spurned the priesthood, denied the right of the state to interfere in matters of religion, and taught, like the Anabaptists, that every man by his own efforts to live up to the best within him may effect the salvation of his soul. Under Peter the Great, they were everywhere flogged, tortured, and burned. But many of them preferred to have their right arm cut off rather than make the sign of the cross. Many also committed mass suicide by shutting themselves in their buildings and setting them on fire. As soon as the persecution slackened, the survivors came out into the open. But their little communities were wiped out by Catherine the Great, who had the men conscripted to military service, running as long as twenty-five years. [32]

Russia, too, had her *Ger Zedek par excellence* in the person of Alexander Voznitzin, who was married to a member of the Romanoff family and lived in Moscow as a retired captain of the navy. He was fond of reading the Bible, and frequently consulted priests and monks concerning the meaning of certain verses. Not satisfied with their explanations, he decided to take up the study of Hebrew. By chance he came across Baruk Leibov, a tax-farmer from Smolensk, who visited the capital in the interest of his business. Baruk had already been under a shadow. In fact he had been expelled from Moscow by order of Catherine I for having built a synagogue for the Jews who resided in the village of Zverovich, much to the annoyance of the Orthodox priest. Voznitzin nevertheless invited him into his home, and his secret visits became more and more frequent. Soon the Moscow Synod received the information from Voznitzin's wife that her husband had become alienated from the Pravoslavny creed, scoffed at the ikons, and was on the road to embracing Judaism. The captain's house was raided, and the incriminating evidence was found of "a small garment with fringes on the four corners," and a Slavonic Psalter from which the pictures of Jesus and the Saints had been torn out.

Voznitzin was thrown into jail, and on being searched they found no crucifix on his person. Baruk was at once put in chains, and a heavy watch was set around him to guard against the "trickery of the Jews" who might obtain his release. Meanwhile, twenty witnesses were summoned to court including the captain's wife and servants. A Jewish apostate testified that a piece of torn paper, which Voznitzin was seen throwing out of his pocket, contained a Hebrew blessing in Latin characters. It was further learned that in 1736 Voznitzin and Baruk left together and stopped on Friday evening in a farm house which they did not leave till Saturday night; that during the day Voznitzin sat with covered head and read from a book; and that during their entire stay they ate nothing but bread and honey; that thence they went to Smolensk, where Voznitzin underwent an operation, and frequently attended divine services at the synagogue. It was also reported that Voznitzin would speak irreverently of Jesus and the Virgin; that he would have his servants confess only to God and not to the "pope," and that one day he collected the holy ikons on one of his estates and threw them into the river.

The news that so distinguished an officer in the Royal Navy had turned Jew spread like wildfire in the upper circles of Russia, and intensified the horror of "Jewish seduction." Czarina Anna Johanovna, as protectress of the true faith, took personal charge of the case and ordered that the captain and his "seducer" be brought to judgment before the Chancellery for Secret Inquisitorial Affairs in St. Petersburg, and the trial began on March 22, 1738. Voznitzin, who while in Moscow pleaded not guilty, confessed, under torture, that he was guilty of blaspheming Jesus and his Holy Mother, of having been circumcised, and of belonging to the Jewish faith. Baruk, too, admitted that he pointed out to him the difference between the original text of the Bible and the inadequacy of the Slavonic translation, and that at Voznitzin's request he obtained the Mohel who operated on him. These confessions so shocked the czarina that though the law required the application of the "dibe" (garrot) three times in order to obtain all the details available, she ordered to dispatch the criminals at once so as to rid Russia from such base wretches as quickly as possible, and declared:

Seeing that Voznitzin and Baruk Leibov have confessed, the first to profaning the name of Christ, falling away from the true Christian faith, and accepting the Jewish religion, and the other that by his misleading words he enticed him to Judaism, there is no further need for a hearing. In order that the disgraceful blasphemous matter should not be prolonged any further, and that those who, like the blasphemer Voznitzin and the misleader Baruk, shall never again dare entice any others, both should be punished for their crime against God, with death by burning so that seeing them suffer, other ignorant people and God-

blasphemers shall not turn away from the Christian
law, and seducers, like Baruk, shall not dare lead them
astray from their Christian faith and convert them to
their own.

The Russian *auto-da-fe* took place on Saturday (July 15,
1738), in the public square of St. Petersburg, at eight o'clock
in the morning, in the presence of a large crowd of spectators. It is said that when Voznitzin noticed that Baruk showed
no signs of nervousness he told him, "Baruk, *nye toropis* (don't
be in such a hurry)." His wife, "for her righteous information
against her husband," was granted, in addition to her legal
share, an estate with one hundred peasants. As for the other
witnesses, the Holy Synod decreed that since they did not
testify against Voznitzin till after his wife's information, they
forfeited the privilege of being given their freedom. But the
matter did not end with the execution of the "criminals." It
was followed by the expulsion of Jews from Little Russia, and
Elizabeth Petrovna's decree prohibiting Jews to reside in any
other part of Russia unless they accepted Greek Catholicism
and promised never to leave the country. [33]

It was in the reign of Catherine II that a Judaizing movement, eclipsing that under Grand Duke Vladimir and surpassing that of the Khazars, started among the Russian peasants
and working classes. Beginning in many instances merely as
Subbotniki, or Seventh Day Sabbath observers, many of the
sectaries gradually added on other Judaic beliefs and ceremonials, until they came to reject the doctrine of the Trinity,
discarded the New Testament, adopted the dietary regulations
and the rite of circumcision. Strangely enough, they became
especially numerous in the districts of Tula, Voronezh, Bobrov,
Orlov, and Saratov, where no Jews were allowed to reside.
Trusting in the liberality of Alexander I, fifteen hundred
peasants openly avowed their Jewish faith at the beginning
of the nineteenth century, made bold to ask for permission to
have a synagogue and a cemetery, and to protest against "the
oppression which they had to undergo at the hands of the
local authorities, both ecclesiastic and civil, on account of their

confessing the Law of Moses (1817)." But their appeal only served to call the attention of the government to the seriousness of the situation. A commission, appointed to investigate, reported an amazing number of Judaizers in the villages and cities of Great Russia.

Various reasons were given by these sectaries for abandoning their Christian faith. Most of them believed that they were merely reverting to the religion of their fathers, the Judeans or the Khazarites. Some arrived at their decision by reading the Scriptures. One peasant informed the czar's commission that he and his fellow Judaizers were induced to change their faith by "a holy old lady." "Bring her here," ordered the officer. "She is very old and cannot walk," replied the peasant. "Then let her be carried in." In a few minutes he brought an old Bible wrapped up in a napkin and presented it with the words: "This is the holy old lady who pleaded with us to become Judeans."

And perhaps the simple peasant was right. It was neither the Jews nor reminiscences of the Khazarites but the Bible itself that converted the thousands of Greek Catholics into Judaizing Russians. Alexander I, who was inclined at first to "Westernize" his Empire, seeing that the more advanced nations had their Bibles translated into the vernacular, decided to do the same and in 1813 founded the Bible Society whose chief object it was to render the Scriptures into modern Russian as well as into the languages and dialects spoken among his subjects. Later, when the czar experienced a change of heart, the Society was liquidated and the holy volumes were confiscated and fed to the flames, and it was not before 1856 that the Holy Synod deemed it advisable to remedy the loss. Meanwhile many got the habit of reading the Bible and disputing the correctness of traditional interpretations and the dogmas which were based on them. This led to various sects, all of whom, however, were at one in their opposition to the doctrines and practices of Greek Catholicism, and in their readiness to be martyrs for the faith as they found it in the pristine Church before it became "a tool of Satan."

To prevent the further spread of the heresy, the Archbishop

of Voronyezh and the Minister of Religion proposed, with special reference to the Subbotniki or Sabbatarians that,

> The chiefs and teachers of the Judaizing sects are to be impressed into military service, and those unfit to serve deported to Siberia. All Jews are to be expelled from the district in which the sect of Sabbatarians or 'Judeans' has made its appearance. Intercourse between the Orthodox inhabitants and the sectaries is to be thwarted in every possible manner. Every outward display of the sect, such as the holding of prayer meetings and the observance of ceremonies which bear no resemblance to those of Christians, is to be forbidden. Finally, to make them an object of contempt, instructions are to be given to designate the Sabbatarians as a *Zhydovskaya* (Jewish) sect, and to publish far and wide that they are in reality *Zhyds* (Jews), inasmuch as their present designation as Sabbatarians, or adherents of the Mosaic Law, does not give the people a proper idea concerning the sect, and does not excite in them that feeling of disgust which must be produced by the realization that what is actually aimed at is to turn them into *Zhyds*.

The proposals of the Archbishop and the Minister of Religion were sanctioned by Alexander I in 1825, and thereafter nothing was too brutal for the clergy and the police to "uproot the Judean sect." Their settlements were laid waste. Thousands of them were banished to Siberia and the Caucasus or flogged to death. But the New Israelites, as they preferred to call themselves, seemed to thrive on the blood of their martyrs. Even those who, unable to endure their lot, returned to the Orthodox faith did so in most instances only outwardly. It is estimated that while in 1818 they numbered only three thousand seven hundred seventy-one, by 1825 they had increased to twenty thousand. Today they may be counted by the hundred thousands. Some students of the movement believe that these more or less Judaized Russians have grown to such proportions as to "more than compensate for all the losses which Judaism has had." [34]

The above mentioned *Dukhobortsi,* like the Subbotniki, became specially active in the early reign of Alexander I. Their leader, the Cossack Yevlamp Katelnikoff was not only a great preacher but a good organizer, and through him the study of the Bible, especially of the Old Testament, became more widespread than ever. To put a stop to the movement Katelnikoff and his daughter were immured in a monastery, his leading followers were thrown into jail, and the rest were banished to a remote spot in Caucasia. There, however, the sect won many adherents under their leader Peter Vasilovich Verigin. The sect finally decided to leave Russia and look for a haven of safety abroad, and with the assistance of Count Leo Tolstoi, who donated the income from his "Resurrection," and of American Quakers, who contributed fifty thousand dollars, the first shipload of *Dukhobortsi* arrived (1899) in Canada, where they now number about sixteen thousand. [35]

Still another sect which the *Raskolniki* brought into being was the society of Brotherly Love. Its "Apostle" was Nicholas Sozonovich Ilain, Captain of Artillery. As a young officer stationed in a small town in the Pale, he enjoyed discussing religion with the rabbis, the Lutheran pastors, and the Catholic priests. On being transferred to the Aral district, he devoted himself to the study of theology and published his *Tidings of Zion* and *The Ray before Sunrise,* in which he advocated the adoption of the biblical dietary laws, the observance of the Seventh Day Sabbath, and the abolition of graven images. For this he was immured in a monastery. There he came in contact with Zechariah Sharri, one of the cantonists who had accepted Christianity at the stroke of the knout, and rejected it when his conscience began to trouble him. The two found solace in the company of each other until they were released in the somewhat brighter times of Alexander II. Sharri then went to Riga and Ilain to Mitau, where they carried on a vigorous propaganda and made thousands of proselytes. After Sharri's death, however, his followers dispersed, some going back to the original fold, the rest becoming assimilated with other Judaizing heretics. [36]

The most numerous as well as remarkable of the several heretical sects today is the *Subbotniki,* or Sabbath observers. Early in its history it split up into the *Subbotniki Talakrini,* or respecters of tradition, the *Subbotniki Starejudai,* who recognize only the authority of the Bible, and the *Bezshapochniki* (hatless). They are all Unitarians and strict observers of the Seventh Day Sabbath and the Jewish festivals, abstain from forbidden food, and are especially fond of the Psalms. They are hard working people, lead the simple life, and for their scrupulous probity are known as the Honest Ones. But because they do not wear hats when they pray or eat, some of them organized into a group of *Subbotniki Shapochniki* (wearers of hats, like the "true" Jews) and finally accepted Judaism *in toto.* [37]

The Subbotniki Shapochniki, because of their close resemblance to Jews, were regarded by the government as specially "dangerous" and were made the target for most discriminatory legislation under Nicholas I. Their children, like those of the Jews, were frequently taken away from them and they themselves deported to the wild regions of Siberia, Caucasia, and the frontiers where Russia was waging a perennial war against Turkey or Persia. But the change of habitation had no effect on their religious convictions. It only helped to infect the Christians of their new habitat with the bacilli of the heresy which they carried with them from the old home. Seeing that the whole city of Alexandrovsk went over to their faith, the government later decided to transport them nearer home, where its surveillance might be more effective. But the Caucasian administration interceded, and these industrious people were permitted to remain to help develop the newly acquired province. These, like their predecessors of long standing, came to regard themselves as lineal descendants of the Ten Lost Tribes, and the cantonists who reverted to Judaism and converted their Christian wives and children discarded the last vestiges of their former religion and became strictly orthodox

Jews. They abhor the missionaries who are sometimes sent to win them back to Greek Catholicism and envy the "true" Jews with whom they believe God is not as exacting as with those who are not of the seed of Abraham. [38]

Worse than the lot of the exiles to Caucasia was that of the Subbotniki who were banished to the bleak and frozen regions of Siberia. This was reserved for the peasants of the diocese of the Archbishop of Voronyezh. The adults were separated from the children and deported to the tundras of Irkutsk, where they were isolated from both Jews and Christians. Any who were caught smuggling in their children or fraternizing with Jews were exiled further to the still more rigorous and wild regions of Turchansk and Minusinsk. But the Subbotniki not only held their own, but even continued to increase. Many Russians, whom the authorities had overlooked or connived at, voluntarily joined them in their new home. Many of the children who had been forcibly detained in their native villages somehow evaded the vigilance of their priestly guardians and went in search of their parents in the steppes of Siberia. Some of them died on the way. Those who reached their goal but could not locate their parents settled among the sectaries and many of them ultimately adopted the Jewish religion.

The communities of these proselytes present a modern picture of the *Kehal Gerim* which is referred to in the Talmud. In the larger towns they usually form a ghetto of their own. But not infrequently they huddle together in little villages like those of Zima and Taiturka in the government of Irkutsk, where they have their institutions under the guidance of their rabbis and *shohetim* (ritual slaughterers) and lead the life of their Jewish coreligionists in the towns and hamlets of the Pale.

The best known of these villages is Judena, in the district of Yeniseisk. It was founded by a group of ten families who were already Proselytes of Righteousness, and several who were still in the stage of *Molokani* (observers of the dietary laws) whom Alexander I "invited" to settle on forty acres of arable land and some acres of forest land. Despite the priests' frequent visitations, and their distance from Jewish contacts, their zeal for their new faith did not lag. The first thing they did during the brief spell of religious freedom enjoyed in Russia in 1905 was to build themselves a synagogue. They have even produced a "Zaddik" (Jewish saint) of their own in the person of Timofey Mikhailovich Bandariov, a native of Caucasia, who as a lad was belfryboy and acolyte to the local priest. His contact with Jews was for some time limited to the two Jewish merchants of the village whose conduct and intelligence he found far superior to those of the local priests. Gradually he became convinced that their theology was also more biblical than that of the Christians, and at the age of forty he had himself circumcised, declared himself a Jew, and assumed the name David bar Abraham, which became corrupted into Bandariov. Banished to Siberia he settled in Judena, and devoted himself to the cultural and economic improvement of his fellow Molokani. He also became noted as an author. His writings, which evoke high praise from the sage of Krasnaye Syelo, include *Work, Idlers and Parasites, Cain and Abel,* and *Leo N. Tolstoi.* Tolstoi seems to have been in sympathy with the movement. These books, however, were promptly suppressed by the authorities, and any copies of them wherever found were destroyed.

The later years of his life Bandariov spent mainly in preparing his last will and testament, and, in accordance with the command of Moses (Dt. 27:3) he inscribed it on the two huge stones taken from the graves of two Tartars who are said to have been buried alive for refusing to surrender to their enemies. These stones, which now mark his tomb, came to be regarded as his Ten Commandments, and are consulted by his followers as his teachings concerning their duties to God, to country, and to fellow-man. [39]

No sooner was the hope for freedom of conscience introduced into Russia (1905) than many other secret Judaizers and Sabbatarians came out from their hiding places and proclaimed themselves Israelites. They hailed from the regions of the Volga and the Don, where the Cossacks held sway; and appeared in multitudes in the provinces of Tambov and Yekaterinoslav,

Kherson and Kiev, Podolia and Volhynia, Twersk and Kuba.
The number of these *Yudistvuyuschy,* as they called themselves, was estimated at no less than one hundred thousand,
while that of the *Molokani* and *Subbotniki,* who in most
instances were on their way to complete Judaization, was pre-
sumed to be as high as two million. The reaction which soon
set in drove many of them under cover again, but many more
left their possessions, which were sometimes considerable,
and with their families sought refuge in Canada, the United
States, South America, and Palestine. Of those who emigrated
to America, over a hundred families settled at Bayle Heights,
near Los Angeles, California. The three hundred Cossack
families from Kuba who established themselves in a co-
operative colony in Uruguay, made such a success of their
enterprise that the government recommended them as models
for emulation by the natives.[40]

The Zionist movement which infused new hope into the
hearts of the miserable dwellers in the Pale, and caused many
indifferent and even converted Jews to retrace their steps to
the synagogue, profoundly affected also the Judaizing Russian Christians. To numerous Cossacks on the Volga, Theodore
Herzl appeared as the promised Messiah, and whole villages
emigrated to "Palestinka." Hundreds of families from Caucasia and Siberia are now settled in Jerusalem, Jaffa, Tel-Aviv,
Rishon l'Zion, and other colonies. They were among the first
to rehabilitate Galilee, and became fishermen on the Sea of
Kinneret. They proved themselves both industrious and excellent agriculturists and adaptable to, and lovers of, the land
of Israel. Their children speak Hebrew and feel insulted if
they are referred to as *gerim.*[41]

Among other more or less prominent individuals who groped
their solitary way to Judaism we may single out the daughter
of a Polish Count who played an important part in the uprising
of 1830, and a youth who belonged to the noble family of
Tishkevitz, which two centuries before had produced the proselyte of righteousness, Zarembo. There was also a general of
a corps of Cossacks, Mikhail de Lusinian, a former prince of
Cyprus, who became a convert to Judaism at the age of thirty,

took the name of David, and died in St. Petersburg in 1912. The motive which prompted Doctor Krassilnikoff of Odessa to cast his lot with the Jews to the extent of adopting their religion and even their Yiddish dialect was strange indeed. He was one of the *Narodnichestvo,* or public spirited men and women of the Russian intelligentsia during the reign of Alexander II who undertook to raise the economic and cultural standard of their countrymen regardless of race and religion. In his intense idealism, Krassilnikoff held himself responsible for the misery of his fellow-Russians of the Jewish race and felt it his duty to expiate for the horrors perpetrated on them by his people. His conversion, like the wearing of the Jewish arm band by the Dutch and Belgians under Nazi domination, was intended not only as a protest but a sort of vicarious atonement for the transgressions of his State and Church: "If they flog a Muzhik," he would say, "let them flog me, too; if they martyrize the Jews, let them make a martyr of me also," which the Russian officials probably did.

By the Treaty of Versailles, Poland and Lithuania were given their autonomy. But though they both drank of the same bitter cup as did the Jews while under the iron heel of Czarist Russia, and despite the special provisions to protect the rights of minorities, the Jews in these countries fared no better than before, while Russia, by "liquidating" all religion as the "opiate of the people," dealt a staggering blow to both Judaism and Christianity. Yet even in Bolshevik Russia and Nazified Poland and Lithuania, there were not lacking some who sought after the God of Israel. In 1927 the rabbinate in Warsaw and Kaunas found it necessary to convoke a conference to deal with the many applications of would-be *gerim.* Strange to say, when the candidates for conversion whose applications were rejected appealed to the government, it rebuked the rabbinate for imposing difficult conditions on intending proselytes. The government itself, however, was hostile to converts as to Jews, and public opinion was even more so. Theodor Leschek, who became a proselyte and took the name Abraham b. Abraham, was dismissed from his professorship at the Tarnow High School on the unsupported

718   GENTILE REACTIONS TO JEWISH IDEALS

charge that he was a communist. In 1931 the Supreme Tribunal also reversed the decision of the Minister of Education in the case of Stefan Raczynski, whose petition to the Warsaw rabbinate had been denied, stating that rabbis may only reconvert Jews who had been baptized but not convert native Christians to Judaism. [42]

Notwithstanding the restrictions and the obstacles put in their way, both by those whom they wished to leave and by those whom they wanted to join, the converts continued to come. They came as individuals, they also came in multitudes. In 1933 one hundred and fifty Polish peasants from a village near Lutzk applied to the Palestine office in Warsaw for certificates to enable them to proceed to Transjordania, where, like the Sabbatarians who settled in lower Galilee, they intended to embrace Judaism. In 1935 a delegation representing fifteen hundred peasants who called themselves New Jews or Israelites reported to the Warsaw rabbinate that their group "feels like Jews" and observes all the laws and customs of Israel and, in the name of their leader, the peasant woman Olga Krilitchuck, asked for a subvention to maintain a *shohet*, a *mohel*, and a rabbi. [43]

The story of Prince Richard Zaslavski and his wife is of unusual interest. Richard was raised at the czarist court in the Greek Catholic religion. Before he left for the front in 1914 his mother confided to him that she was the daughter of a Warsaw Jew and that thirty years ago she eloped with his father, embraced his faith, and became his wife. Two years later Richard was made a prisoner of war and sent to a concentration camp in Austria. He was released when the Poles invaded Austria and made a major in the army. In the military office he met Zoshe Sove, a Jewess who had become a Roman Catholic, and they fell in love with each other. After comparing their past, both decided to return to Judaism. The Warsaw rabbinate readily readmitted Zoshe into the faith of her fathers, but hesitated in regard to Richard. A *mohel* in Ruzhani, however, consented to perform the rite of circumcision, and in April 1924 Richard was received into the household of Israel. [44]

What happened in Nazified Poland took place on a larger scale in Soviet Russia and in her former possessions. In the Ukraine two hundred and seventeen peasant "Israelites" applied to the Commissariat for Foreign Affairs for permission to emigrate to Palestine (1922), and when "real" Jews feared to instruct their children in Hebrew and the Yevseks, former Jews, sought to destroy the faith of their fathers, these Christians taught Judaism not only to their own, but also to the Jewish children. Some conversions were no doubt prompted by motives of matrimony. Rabbi Mase of Moscow reported that till 1923 he had officiated at the marriages of three hundred sixty-seven converts. The wife of the Zionist leader of Warsaw, Dr. Noah Davidson, was the daughter of the czarist General Russki. Such cases, however, were not as common as one would be likely to expect. There were at least as many who were inspired by religious convictions. Thus Father Simone of Cracow became Abraham b. Abraham only after his admission into a talmudic academy (1930). Some even undertook the dangerous task of missionizing among their former coreligionists. Alexander Ciovanu was arrested in Bessarabia for "diverting coreligionists from the true faith" by spreading among them the distinctive doctrines and observances of Judaism. [45]

Sometimes those who themselves had participated in pogroms, looted Jewish homes and places of business, slew Jews and dishonored their wives and daughters, experienced a change of heart and accepted the religion of their victims. Thus in 1925 there appeared before the Warsaw rabbinate eleven Russians who begged not only to be accepted into the Jewish faith, but to be instructed how to do penance for the horrors they had committed against the Jews when, as members of a frenzied mob, they had invaded the Jewish quarter and, with cross in one hand and a hatchet in the other, satiated their thirst for the blood and property of the defenseless Jews. The rabbis, after repeated refusal, finally granted their request, and the eleven bandits are now law-abiding and devoted Jews.

The story of the Cossack leader Costi reminds one of the

talmudic traditions concerning Pharaoh, Jethro, Nebuzaradan and Hadrian, and of the talmudic "dream proselytes." He was in command of one of the regiments of Petlura, who was guilty of the most horrible outrages against the Jews in Bessarabia. One night, after a day of carnage and loot, he dreamed that his father appeared and said to him: "My son, why do you lend your hand to the murder of innocent Jewish men, women, and children?" Costi resigned from his regiment and became a convert to Judaism under the name of Abraham b. Abraham. Alexander Wolodsky, the son of a general in the Czar's army, and himself an officer under Kolohak, the leader of the White Terror and the ruthless foe of the Jews, finally landed in the camp of Israel.[46]

In 1937 the Jewish press published the story of a Christian Pole, who after the pogrom of Brest-Litovsk, came to the local rabbi and informed him that as a result of the pogrom he had firmly resolved to become a Jew and to share the suffering of the Jews. The rabbi refused to accede to his request to be officially converted, but the Pole's determination to demonstrate his solidarity with Jews grew daily, and finally he went to Cracow where, after due preparation, he embraced the Jewish faith.[47]

Among those who became "Proselytes of the Gate" if not "Proselytes of Righteousness" because of the persecutions of Jews by Christians, a prominent place must be accorded to A. S. Bershadsky (1850-96), whose father was a priest and whose mother was a descendant of a Cossack hetman who massacred the Jews under Bogdan Chmielnicki. A less distinguished man but one imbued with perhaps even greater love for Jews was Yakim Richko. When his fellow-Christians began to suspect him of sympathy with Jews, they deprived him of his cow and few belongings. As this seemed to have no effect, they beat him and dragged him to the top of the belfry and prepared to hang him. At this, Yakim intentionally or by accident imitated the bark of a dog. His tormentors, who believed that he was bewitched by the Jews, fled in panic from the presence of their victim. Thereafter

Yakim's bark saved hundreds of Jewish lives. His one grand passion was to settle in Palestine among the Jewish colonists. But he died shortly before he started on his pilgrimage.[48]

Trakhim Werchola, a Ukrainian peasant, was another of those whom the misery of the Jews precipitated into the fold of Judaism. Almost single handed he fought against the Petlura hordes who slaughtered twelve hundred Jews in one day at Proskurov. Then he fled and disappeared among the Jews of Lemberg.

Werchola was no exception. Had Petlura not been killed by Schwarzbard in Paris to avenge the brutal murder of his relatives, he might have witnessed some of his partners in the massacres of Jews in the Ukraine, repentantly join those whom they were bent on exterminating. One of them was his own godson, Mendel Meir Einfield, of Piontek near Lodz. Stolen as an infant by a band of gypsies, he was sold to the wife of Petlura. The White Guard leader became the god-father of the child and raised him as a Christian, and implanted in him his own hate of the Jews. When World War I broke out, Einfield, unaware of his descent, joined Petlura's gang, specialized in pogroms against Jews, and boasted of the murder of scores of them. While pursuing his bloody work, so Einfield declared on the eve of his conversion, he dreamed night after night of an old Jew who revealed to him his origin, even the village where he was born, and demanded to know why he was bent on the extermination of the people from whom he was descended. When Einfield corroborated the information given him in the dream, he adopted or reverted to the religion of his ancestors, became an ardent Zionist, and passed the remainder of his life in Palestine.[49]

Perhaps even stranger is the story told to the Palestine office in Warsaw by one who applied for a certificate to enter Palestine "to atone for the sins he committed against the Jews." He was born a Jew in the neighborhood of Kalish, Poland, and was left an orphan at the age of ten. Raised as a Christian, he was made an officer, married a Christian woman, organized pogroms, and shared with his soldiers the plunder they carried off from Jewish homes. But the death of his wife and children within a short time of one another led him to believe that perhaps it was in punishment for the terrible crimes he had committed against the Jews, and he was anxious to right the wrong as much as he could by becoming a Jew and aiding in rebuilding the Land of Israel. The Palestine office afforded him the opportunity.

It is pleasant to turn from those whom Russian fanaticism drove into the Orthodox Church and made into *pogromchiks* to one who, born in the odor of Russian Orthodoxy, became a "Ruth of the Volga Steppes," and contributed to modern Hebrew some of its most precious poetic gems. Yelisavetta Ivanovna Shirokoff was born in 1889 to a teacher in a rural school in Riazan, and at an early age evinced an aptitude for languages and poetry. She first came in contact with Jewish life when, as a student in Moscow, she visited some of her Jewish classmates. The Zionist ideal which then fascinated many a Jewish youth appealed to her poetic soul, and she became anxious to participate in the rebuilding of the ancient Land of Israel and in reviving the language spoken by the Hebrew Prophets. With this in view, she devoted herself with unsurpassed zeal to the study of Hebrew, and before she reached the age of twenty-three she began to translate into her native tongue the poems of R. Yehudah Halevi and Hayyim Naham Bialik. In 1922 she made her debut as an original Hebrew poet, and since then has published several little volumes of poetry of rare beauty, filled with lyrical grandeur and the sublime pathos of the psalmists' genius. "Elishevah", her adopted *nom-de-plume,* not only became the wife of a Jew, but a Palestinian Jewess, singing the songs of Zion like a veritable daughter of Zion, and inspired and stayed by the one hope

... That the generous-hearted folk
Will not refuse a tiny meal of its great wealth.
And, when I die, thus will say: 'She was a stranger
who left her birthplace, for she loved so much the
    Jewish people.

A gift of love is good to God, may she find rest
In the shadow of the eternal walls of Zion, our strength;
May she sleep a trustful sleep, be brightly blessed,
And from heights of heaven Judea's sun shine on
    her ever.'[50]

CHAPTER XXVI

THE BATTLE FOR THE BIBLE

(FRANCE, GERMANY, ENGLAND)

ONE thing in which all the Reformers shared alike was an insistent demand on the restoration of the Bible to the people. In this there was no difference between those who followed Calvin and those who agreed with Servetus. Nor was the early church opposed to it. The abundance of biblical translations into the various vernaculars at the beginning of the second millennium indicates that they were done with the sanction of the Hierarchy. At that time there were, besides the Septuagint and the Vulgate, biblical versions in Coptic, Ethiopic, Armenian, Syriac, French, Irish, and Slavonic, dating back to the sixth and seventh centuries. King Alfred himself is supposed to have translated the Bible into Anglo-Saxon, and Charlemagne is said to have ordered three German clerics to render it into German. The eminent grammarian, Aelfric, who lived at the dawn of the eleventh century, had translated into English all of the Pentateuch, Joshua, Judges, Kings, Job, and Esther, besides the Apocryphal Judith and the Books of the Maccabees.

But with the advent of the thirteenth century the Church began to realize that the reading of the Bible by the masses was not an unmixed blessing. Long experience had shown that their "searching" the Scriptures almost always resulted in Anti-Papism, Anti-Trinitarianism, Iconoclasm, and even Judaism. What was worse, these students of the Bible refused to hide their light under a bushel, and became ever more determined to make others see it. Their missionaries penetrated into Flanders, Spain, Lombardy, Germany, and England, and everywhere attracted large crowds because of their moral zeal and knowledge contrasted often with the loose lives and ignorance of many of the clergy.

In order, therefore, to maintain the authority of the Church it was decreed that none should read or teach the Word of God unless duly commissioned so to do. The Council of Toulouse (1229) made it a criminal offense for a layman even to harbor a copy of the Bible in his home. Innocent III, being informed that in the diocese of Metz "multitudes of laymen and women, carried away by I trow not what, desire to know the Holy Scriptures, had the Gospels, the Epistles of St. Paul, the Psalter, the Moralities on Job, and several other books translated for them into French," immediately ordered the bishop to proceed against the violators of the law with all the means at his command, stating:

> The Divine Law has wisely decreed that any beast touching the Holy Mountain should be stoned to death; this typifies that common people may not presume by their intellect to attain to the sublime heights of Revelation and to preach to others.... There remains for you, therefore, but one thing to do, namely to obey. Do so voluntarily, and you will not be compelled by force.

The first to strike a telling blow in behalf of the "open Bible" were the Waldenses. They claimed it to be their sacred duty to spread a knowledge of the Scripture among the masses. They pointed to the story of Eldad and Medad:

> We read in the Old Testament, in the Book of Numbers, Chapter II, that two men, called Eldad and Medad, having received the spirit of God, prophesied in the camp of Israel. This caused a great commotion. A young man ran to tell Moses: 'Eldad and Medad do prophesy in the camp.' Hearing this, Joshua, the son of Nun, answered and said: 'My Lord Moses, forbid them.' But Moses answered: 'Enviest thou for my sake? Would God that all the Lord's people were prophets, and that the Lord would put His spirit upon them.' [1]

But the longest and strongest battle for the Bible was fought in England. There the humanities of the Renaissance made but little progress. There the Reformation started with a plea for social justice and was inspired by the biblical concern for the poor, the widow, and the orphan, and its teachings of human equality. John Bull's rallying cry was:

> When Adam dolve, and Eve span,
> Who was then a gentleman?

Langland in his version of *Piers Plowman* castigates not only the vices of the priests but their indifference to the plight of their flocks. This also is the *Leitmotif* of Chaucer's *Canterbury Tales* wherein he portrays the brawny hunting monk, the wanton, beggarly friar; the summoner with his wallet "bretfull of pardons, come from Rome all hot"; the prioress with the motto *Amor vincit omnia* engraved on her brooch, while the "poor parson" is neglected and threadbare despite that "Christ's lore and His Apostles he taught, and first he followed it himself." To this was added the opposition to the papacy as a foreign institution and the policy of the "French Pope" to place his Roman favorites in English bishoprics and abbacies. The complaint most frequently heard was that

> The brokers of the sinful city of Rome promote for money unearned and unworthy caitiffs . . . . the present aliens who neither see nor care to see their parishioners, despise God's service, convey away the treasure of the realm, and are worse than Jews and Saracens. . . . God gave his sheep to be pastured, not to be shaven and shorn. [2]

This demand for social justice found a champion in John Wycliffe. As a prebendary of Westbury he espoused the policy of John of Gaunt and was nominated one of the royal envoys to Brugas to protest against the Pope's appointments of foreign bishops and other ecclesiastics to offices in England. But he did not stop here. He urged that profligate priests should be disqualified, since "undirstonding of hooly writ withouten charite

that keepeth Goddis heestis, makit a man depper dampned."
He also assailed in numerous tracts in Latin and English the
pardons, indulgences, absolutions, pious pilgrimages, worship
of images, and the whole gamut of Church practices. Finally
he took the momentous step (1380) of attacking the doctrine
of Transubstantiation.

Wycliffe's fame as a preacher drew the masses like a magnet
despite the Church's condemnation, and by many he came to
be looked upon as "the most holy of all men of his age."
Through him Oxford became "a fautor of heretics," and at
one time the scholars rose up in arms and threatened death to
anyone who would do him harm. He was especially beloved
by the "poor" zealots, known as Lollards, who in long, russet
robes, with staff in hand, preached in churches and grave-
yards, in streets and private homes, against the pope and the
clergy, against Transubstantiation and auricular confession,
against war, capital puishment, and private ownership. How
widely accepted their teachings became can be judged from
the complaint of a contemporary that "every second man on
the street is a Lollard." [3]

At first the Church deemed it the wiser policy not to take
extreme measures against Wycliffe and demanded only that
he retire from Oxford. But the reformer refused to be silenced.
He continued to appeal to the King and Parliament to deprive
the clergy of their special privileges and demanded the right
to teach the doctrine of the Eucharist as he interpreted it. At
the same time he labored on a revision of his translation of
the Bible. Summoned to appear before the papal court he
declared:

> I am always glad to explain my faith to anyone, and
> above all to the Bishop of Rome; for I take it for
> granted that if it be orthodox he will confirm it, if it
> be erroneous he will correct it. I assume, too, that as
> chief Vicar of Christ upon earth the Bishop of Rome
> is of all mortal men most bound to the law of Christ's
> Gospel, for among the disciples of Christ a majority
> is not reckoned by simply counting heads in the fash-
> ion of the world, but according to the imitation of

Christ on either side. Now Christ during his life upon earth was of all men the poorest, casting from him all worldly authority. I deduce from these premises, as simple counsel of my own, that the pope should surrender all temporal authority to the civil power and advise his clergy to do the same.

But more than his opposition to her dogmas, what aroused the wrath of the Church against Wycliffe was his translation of the Bible into the vernacular. It was the first serious attempt to render into English, as it was then spoken, the entire contents of the Scriptures. But it was more. Wycliffe was not merely a translator but a commentator and propagandist, and his introductions abounded with condemnations of the Church. His version, therefore, aroused a storm of protests, and he was condemned as a heretic and as one who profaned what is most holy.[4]

The battle over the Scriptures went on for several centuries. There were those who arraigned themselves on the side of the Church and used the original Hebrew as a source of doctrine and authority. There were, on the other hand, many who followed in the mood of Wycliffe, and consistently appealed to the original texts for the claims they made.

It would be a mistake to think that Hebrew learning on the part of Christian scholars had narrowed itself or had suffered such a restriction as to become only an agent of reform for Christian doctrine and polity. Nor are we to look upon the counter-Reformation of the Catholics with their interest in the same Jewish materials as if all this were merely and likewise a logical consequence of Hebrew interests of the previous centuries. The contribution of Hebrew learning and materials as they were being accumulated and shaped was vast for all men—Protestant and Catholic. The political and social reverberations of the Reformation went on with increasing fervor and with great alacrity.[5]

In time even the Anglican Church became as abhorrent to some of England's subjects as was the Church of Rome. The Puritans demanded that the Reformation be carried further than it had gone and that England govern herself politically and ecclesiastically after the model of ancient Judea. The Puritans, in their veneration for everything biblical, according to Macaulay:

> ...paid to the Hebrew language a respect which they refused to the tongue in which the discourses of Jesus and the epistles of Paul had come down to us. They baptized their children by the names, not of Christian saints, but of Hebrew patriarchs and warriors.... They sought for principles of jurisprudence in the Mosaic law, and for precedents to guide their ordinary conduct in the books of Judges and Kings. ...Morals and manners were subjected to a code resembling that of the synagogue, when the synagogue was at its worst state. The dress, the deportment, the language, the studies, the amusements of this rigid sect were regulated on principles not unlike those of the Pharisees who, proud of their washed hands and broad phylacteries, taunted the Redeemer as a Sabbath-breaker and winebibber. Some precisians had scruples about teaching the Latin grammar, because the names Mars, Bacchus and Apollo occurred in it. The fine arts were all but proscribed. The solemn peals of the organs were superstitious.... The extreme Puritan was at once known from other men by his gait, his garb...and above all by his peculiar dialect. He employed, on every occasion, the imagery and style of Scripture. [6]

Evidently the great English historian was prejudiced against Puritanism and ignorant of Pharisaism. But that the Puritans were absorbed in the Old Testament and modeled their conduct after the Hebraic pattern, there can be no doubt. They were indeed "Christian Israelites" theirs being, in the words of Heine, a "Judaism which allowed to eat pork," a diet, however, from which some conscientiously abstained. They forebore to bow to the name of Christ, abolished the organ and choir, and did away with the Book of Common Prayers. They not only adopted the Hebrew nomenclature but observed Sunday with all the strictness of the biblical rabbinical Sabbath. They also regarded themselves as God's Chosen People, a Kingdom of priests and a holy nation, whom, like the Children of Israel from Egypt, He liberated from the bondage of popery, and looked upon the rest as "Amalekites and Baalites." Their one great regret was that they were not lineal descendants of Abraham, Isaac, and Jacob. Their most eminent representative, John Milton, would even reintroduce "That great covenant (circumcision) which we still transgress," while John Bunyan tells us that "finding in the Scriptures that they (the Jews) were once the peculiar people of God, thought I, if I were of their race my soul must needs be happy." It was probably this wish that later became father to the belief held by many Englishmen that they were indeed the offspring of the Ten Lost Tribes of Israel.

These presumptive Israelites were as opposed to Episcopalianism as to Catholicism, but as long as the latter seemed to be the more dangerous they united their efforts with the former. After the death of Elizabeth, however, the Anglican Church began to introduce many of the practices of the Church from which it seceded, set up a prelate with the power and legal pomp of the pope, subject only to the King who, it was maintained, ruled by right divine and could do no wrong. To the extreme Puritans this was no better than popery and idolatry, and like the ancient Israelites they determined to cut it off root and branch.

The opportunity came under Charles I who, though a zealous Episcopalian, leaned toward Rome. Guided by Archbishop Laud, he set out to make not only of England, but of Scotland and Ireland as well, a Protestant Spain, with the Star Chamber as another Inquisition. But England was not Spain; and although some nobles and ecclesiastics favored the policy of the King and his Archbishop, the vast majority were bitterly opposed to it. The national and religious conscience of the people was stirred to its profoundest depths. At last, when the Parliament which Charles had repeatedly dissolved was convoked again, it showed that the non-conformists were in a great majority. The hated Star Chamber was abolished, Laud was imprisoned, and later expiated for his cruelty by being beheaded on Tower Hill (1645), the Book of Common Prayer was interdicted, and Charles was sent to the scaffold that "all the people shall hear, and fear, and do no more presumptuously."

The chief actors in this tragedy were the Puritans at the head of whom was Oliver Cromwell. Despite their inrooted veneration for the monarchy, the Puritans were not intimidated by the concept of divine kingship. On the contrary. "It is lawful," wrote Milton, "and has been so through all ages for anyone who has the power to call to account a tyrant or a wicked King and after due conviction to depose and put him to death." It was pointed out that in the Bible neither Moses nor Joshua assumed the prerogative of kingship, that for centuries after the Israelites settled in the Holy Land they were ruled only by judges, that Gideon refused the crown, and Samuel insisted that only God was to be King, and later anointed David in place of Saul. Moreover, Elisha the Prophet commissioned Jehu to "smite the house of Ahab" and Jehoiada the priest commanded the slaying of Queen Athaliah.

Such an army as the one led by Cromwell had never been witnessed in Christendom before. Unlike the crusaders they were not lured by Indulgences nor by the opportunity to rob and rape their adversaries. While as soldiers they submitted to the most rigid discipline, when off duty all ranks were ignored and a corporal could admonish a less devout general. They never forgot the Mosaic admonition (Dt. 23:15): "The Lord thy God walketh in the midst of thy camp. Therefore shall thy camp be holy." All non-combatants were protected and, according to Macaulay it was acknowledged by the most zealous Royalists that:

> In that singular camp no oath was heard, no drunkenness or gambling was seen, and that, during the long dominion of the soldiery, the property of the

peaceable citizen and the honor of woman were held
sacred. No servant girl complained of the rough gallantry of the redcoats. Not an ounce of plate was taken
from the shops of the goldsmiths. But a Pelagian
sermon or a window on which the Virgin and Child
were painted, produced in the Puritan ranks an excitement which it required the utmost exertion of the
officers to quell.[7]

Cromwell did not aspire to kingship. His aim, as he said,
was the establishment of "union and right understanding
between the godly people, Scots, English, Jews, Gentiles,
Presbyterians, Anabaptists and all." He also protected the
Huguenots and Waldenses in France. But in England he
sought to establish the domination of Puritanism. He forbade the use of the Book of Common Prayer as savoring of
popery, and prohibited the "Scottis Kirk" to participate in
the secular affairs of the nation. He was especially severe on
the Catholic Irish. He regarded them as idolaters; and while
he did not compel them to convert, he interdicted the reading
of the mass and hunted down their priests.

The Puritans did not long enjoy their supremacy. The
execution of Charles I caused him to be regarded as a martyr
to the Established Church, raised its prestige, and two years
after Cromwell's death, Charles II was welcomed into England amid the wildest demonstrations of joy. The Anglican
Church was restored, and the authorities were ordered "to
arrest, fine, flog, exile and burn" all non-conformists. As a
result, "thousands of Puritans fled to America where as
Pilgrim Fathers, they laid the foundation of the Democracy
which, in the words of Lecky, was cemented by the 'Hebraic
Mortar.' "

Far as the Puritans went in their advocacy of reform in
the Anglican Church, there were others who went further
still. Chief among these were the Baptists, the first to question
the authority of the State to impose any form of religion upon
the citizens. "The Lord's people," says Robert Browne, "is of
the willing sort. They shall come unto Zion and inquire the

way to Jerusalem, not by force nor compulsion, but with their faces thitherward." They also rejected infant baptism, holding that the rite in itself is not productive of grace but is merely a symbol of the regeneration of the individual concerned. But the sect which next to the Puritans contributed most to the establishment of a Government in the spirit of the Hebrew Prophets was the sect which styled itself the Seekers for Truth, "in scorn by the world called Quakers."

The name "Quaker" originated as a nickname conferred upon the members of the organization "because of their trembling at the word and power of the Lord as many of His servants and Prophets have done" (cf. Isa. 66:8, Ps. 2:11). Its founder, George Fox, repelled by the formation of the established Church, evolved a system at variance with all the existing forms of Christianity. While not openly abandoning the dogma of the Trinity and the sonship of Christ he insisted that there is in every man an "Inner Light" by which he is to be guided. This Inner Light is present in all human beings, whether they heard of Christ or not. It was, says Fox, this divine principle in Nebuchadnezzar, an idolator, that caused him to say, "Blessed be the God of Shadrach, Meshach, and Abed-nego." Quakers formulated no creed, no ritual. They had no ordained ministry or a paid clergy, and no ceremonials. Their religion was based on personal righteousness. They held with the Prophets that what God requireth is only to do justly, to love mercy, and to walk humbly. Hence, they insisted on dressing simply, helping the poor, being strictly honest and scrupulously truthful even to the extent of taking no oath. They were especially opposed to all war as incompatible with the Inner Light or the "Mind of Christ."

These ideals the Quakers propagated with the zeal of the Hebrew Prophets, and very often in the manner peculiar to them. Sometimes they would walk barefoot, or put on sackcloth, or undress altogether. They would remove their hats only at prayer, and would "thee" and "thou" even royalty. They refused to pay tithes, since the money went to the support of the clergy of the established Church; called their days and months not by their heathen names but by their numbers (as First Day for Sunday, First Month for January). They were so careful not to introduce popish or Episcopal practices that they would open their shops on Christmas and Good Friday, thus subjecting themselves to the resentment of the populace. They married only among themselves and kept out of politics. Like Israel, whom they took for their model, they strove to be "a peculiar people." They were anxious "to dwell alone, and not be mixed with the nations" (Num. 23:9). [8]

The missionary activity of the early Quakers was not limited to England. Some of them ventured to go to Rome to enlighten the pope, others went to Holland and Germany to preach to the Protestants, while still others traveled to Moslem countries to convert Mohammedans. Everywhere, however, their gospel fell on deaf ears. In England they were subjected to most inhuman persecution. They were accused of plotting against the Government, of being blasphemers, wizards, and witches. They were flogged, tortured, banished, or burned. This, however, they endured with almost superhuman patience, and unlike other non-conformists persisted in holding their assemblies in the open and by sheer force of passive resistance obtained from the Government legal recognition of their rights to worship according to the dictates of their conscience. [9]

Still even the Friends (Quakers) regarded themselves as in the framework of Christianity, though their references to the historical Christ were very few and far between. There were, however, some since the reign of Henry VIII who went much further than the most extreme Reformers. To them Puritanism, Baptism, and Quakerism served as a bridge to Unitarianism. According to Hooper, there were in the conventicles some who dared not only to deny that Christ is the Messiah, but also "to call that blessed Seed a mischievous fellow and deceiver of the world." We hear of a group calling itself the Family of Love which held that "Christ does not signify any one person but a quality whereof many are partakers." One Matthew Hamout, a playwright who "denyed Christe," had his ears cut off and was burned in 1579. A few years later John

Lewes Francis Kitt, a young clergyman, and Peter Cole, a tanner, met the same fate "for denying the Godhead of Christ and other detestable heresies." Especially was Anti-Trinitarianism or Unitarianism prevalent among the *literati,* such as Sir Walter Raleigh, Robert Greene, and Christopher Marlowe. Among the papers of Thomas Kyd was found one containing "vile heretical conceiptes denying the divinity of Jhesus Christe our Saviour." Shakespeare ridiculed both Puritans and Catholics. But he prudently refrained from taking sides with either in his plays or sonnets. There is good ground to surmise that Francis Bacon, though nominally a conformist, was, if not a Deist, at least a Unitarian. His plea for toleration is an indication that he did not believe that Christianity was the sole means of salvation—the underlying cause of most Christian intolerance.

There can be little doubt that John Milton was essentially a Unitarian. To him the formalism of Episcopalianism was as revolting as the pomp and display of Catholicism and the "New Presbyter" but "the Old Priest writ large." For the Episcopal clergy he had nothing but contempt. He accuses them of being "learned in nothing but the antiquity of their pride, their covetousness and superstition," and he compares them to Satan:

> So clomb this first grand thief into God's fold,
> So since into His Church lewd hirelings climb. [10]

It remained for John Biddle (1615-62) to become the father of English Unitarianism. A master of the free school of Gloucester, he was much esteemed for his diligence in his profession and high moral life. While still a student of theology he wrote *XII Arguments drawn out of Scripture,* wherein the commonly received doctrine touching the Deity of the Holy Spirit is clearly and wholly refuted. But the book was seized and ordered by Parliament to be burned by the hangman. But his *Confession of Faith touching the Holy Trinity, The Testimonies of Irenaeus, etc., Concerning the One God and the Persons of the Trinity*, and his *Two-fold Catechism* had a wide circulation, and his adherents grew in number both among the clergy and the laity. At the instigation of a Baptist pastor he was again put to trial, but was rescued by Cromwell who sent him to one of the Scilly Islands with a stipend of one hundred crowns a year. He finally died in prison. [11]

In the eighteenth century the battle against the Athanasian Creed spread to the Universities of Oxford and Cambridge and flared up in Parliament. William Whiston, the translator of Josephus into English (for which he was deprived of his professorship!), and others pleaded for the omission of the creed to which they no longer subscribed. Many of the clergy of the Established Church publicly confessed that they could not conscientiously recite it. "Brethren," one of them is reported to have said, "this is the creed of St. Athanasius, and God forbid it should be the creed of any other man." It was retained, however, for the sake of harmony and was recited with mental reservation. Unitarianism drew into its fold the cream of English intelligentsia and impressed more or less, such minds as those of Bentley, Locke, Newton, Berkeley, Addison, Pope, Swift. Finally the Act of Blasphemy was repealed (1813), and congregations which avowed their sole belief in the Unity of God and the humanity of Jesus were established, unhindered, all over England and the colonies. [12]

Even in Calvinist Scotland, where in 1697 a youth of eighteen was hanged for declaring that "Trinity in Unity is as much a contradiction as a square circle," and that orthodox Christianity was a delusion which would not last till the year 1800, Robert Burns warned the Kirk:

> Orthodox, orthodox,
> Wha believe in John Knox,
> Let me sound an alarm to your conscience:
> There's a heretic blast,
> Has been blawn in the wast,
> That what is not sense must be nonsense.

The heyday of Puritanism marked also the heyday of Adventism. The belief became widespread in the speedy restoration of the Jews to the Holy Land where, it was averred, they would accept Christianity and crown Jesus their King. In a tract called "News from Rome," it was reported that a hitherto unheard of Hebrew tribe already started from "the mountains of Caspy" on its way to recover the Holy Land, and that a Jew serving in that army, "called Caleb Shilocke, prognosticated many strange accidents which shall happen in the following year, 1607." In a pamphlet, "*Nova Solyma*," which appeared in London in 1648, it was stated that the Restoration had already taken place fifty years before, and a description was given of the Messianic State established on Mount Zion. It was generally held by almost all the Protestant sects that Jesus would make his appearance in 1666, in keeping with the verse in Revelation (13:18): "Let him that hath understanding count the number of the Beast; for it is the number of a man; and his number is six hundred, three-score and six," which number added to the thousand years which had already elapsed since the birth of Christ gave the year 1666. [13]

Inflamed by these rumors and prognostications, a Welshman named Evins set forth the claim that he was actually Christ (1644). A Yorkshireman called James Naylor, who from Puritanism drifted into Quakerism, gradually arrived at the conviction that he was the reincarnation of Christ, and gathered around him many disciples. After serving several terms in jail, he entered Bristol in imitation of the manner in which Jesus is said to have entered Jerusalem. He rode on horseback in the nude, "with lank hair reaching below his cheeks," attended by seven followers who sang "Hosanna! holy, holy! Lord God of Sabaoth!" He was arrested, together with his followers, was convicted of blasphemy, and sentenced to be whipped through the streets, his tongue bored with a red-hot iron, his forehead branded with the letter "B" (blasphemer), and then to suffer imprisonment with hard labor for two years. Also a certain Methodist-Sabbatarian, Joanna Southscott of Devonshire, proclaimed herself the expectant mother of "Shiloh," and in anticipation of this happy event her one hundred thousand followers fitted out a cradle becoming the dignity of the Infant Messiah. Shiloh did not materialize, but Joanna's sect lingered on till the end of the nineteenth century. [14]

While these dreamers never resorted to force, there were those who were determined to establish Christ's Kingdom by violence. They claimed that the time had come to introduce the Fifth Monarchy as successor to the four pagan monarchies —the Assyrian, Persian, Grecian, and Roman, wherein the Law of Moses would become the law of the State. They went so far as to resort to a *coup* d'etat, and under the leadership of Thomas Venner, a cooper who was also a preacher, a band of fifty made an attempt to seize possession of London (1661). Most of them were killed in battle, and Venner and ten of his followers who were taken prisoners were executed for high treason. [15]

The Puritan veneration for the Old Testament and their ardent Messianic expectations aroused a new interest in the Jewish people. Since from times of old it has been assumed that the conversions of the Jews would be a condition precedent to the second advent of Christ, it was felt to be the sacred duty and privilege of Englishmen to bear a part in this great consummation. Hence, from 1584 downwards, preachers and laymen began to voice in books and pamphlets their profound love for Israel and their hope for the *World's Great Restauration, or the Calling of the Jewes* (London, 1621), which cost the author and the publisher a term in prison, expressed the belief that "The Lord give them grace, that they may returne and seeke Iehovah their God, and David their King, in these latter dayes." Henry Jessey, a Baptist minister, author of several tracts concerning the second coming of Christ, was of the opinion that Daniel's "little horn" was not other than King Charles, and that the Jews would be converted by 1658. He even collected money from charitable Englishmen for the prospective settlements of Jews in Palestine and he dedicated his "Glory of Jehudah and Israel" to the "honoured representatives of the nation awaiting its redemption as a testimony to the noble traits of the Jews." In anticipation of the great event two other Baptists who resided in Amsterdam, Joanna Cartwright and her son Ebenezer, urged Lord Fairfax and the General Council to repeal the Statute of Banishment, and to readmit the Jews "to trade and dwell in the Land as they do now in the Netherlands." A direct appeal to the Jews to be converted, in order to hasten the advent of Jesus, was also made by the Quaker George Fox in *A Visitation to the Jewes* (London, 1650); while Margaret Fell, who subsequently became his wife and was a good Quakeress in her own right, addressed herself to Menasseh ben Israel in a tract, *The Call of the Jewes out of Babylon which is the Good Tidings to the Meek, Liberty to the Captives, and for the opening of the Prison Doores* (London, 1656), and followed it up with a pamphlet four years later in Hebrew and English, entitled *A Loving Salutation to the Seed of Abraham.* [16]

It is not unlikely that in removing the restrictions on the resettlement of the Jews in England Cromwell expected that through the Jews England would gain a commercial advantage over her rival Holland. But there were Englishmen also who were prompted by humanitarian and religious reasons. One of them was Leonard Busher, a leader of the Brownist group of the Puritans, who found shelter in Leyden. His *Religious Peace; or, a Plea for Religious Liberty* (1614), published for presentation to James I, was probably the first appeal of its kind in England. Even more persistent was the voice which emanated from beyond the ocean. In Roger Williams' *The Bloudy Tenet of Persecution for cause of conscience discussed, etc.,* those of the Jewish faith are explicitly referred to. His appeal was reinforced by Hugh Peters of Salem, Massachusetts, in a pamphlet (1646): *A Word for the Army, and Two Words to the Kingdom, to clear the one and cure the other,* wherein he pleaded that "strangers, even Jews, be admitted to trade and live with us." In 1648, the year in which many Jews believed the Messiah would be revealed, the Council of Mechanics passed a resolution that freedom be granted to all, "not excepting Turkes, nor Papists, nor Jewes." In the same year appeared a little pamphlet by Edward Nicholas, entitled *An Apology for the honourable Nation of the Jews, and all the Sons of Israel,* in which England is admonished not to continue her maltreatment of God's people, and to make amends for her wrongs in the past:

> Now that we all show ourselves compassionate, and helpers of the afflicted Jews; and pray that the same authority that proceeded against them formerly... will repeal the severe laws made against them; that our receiving them again, and giving them all possible satisfaction, and restoring them to commerce in this realm, may be an example to other nations that have done them, and continue to do them, wrong; till which time (God putting their tears into His bottle) God will charge their suffering upon us, and will avenge them on their persecutors.

At the same time that the way for readmitting the Jews to England was thus being prepared by Gentiles, there appeared on the scene a rabbi from Holland, Menasseh b. Israel (1604-57), the son of a Marrano who was baptized Manoel Dias Sosiro, and while yet an infant went with his family to Amsterdam. There the father and his two sons underwent the rite of circumcision, and respectively assumed the names of Joseph, Ephraim, and Menasseh, and the patronym of Ben-Israel. Young Menasseh early distinguished himself for his eloquence and erudition, and his numerous works, written in Latin, Spanish, Portuguese, and Hebrew, exerted an influence beyond the circle of his own coreligionists or the confines of his own country. Withal, as a product of his age, he was a student of the Kabbalah, and a believer in the speedy appearance of the Messiah.

About 1642 a certain Aaron Levi, who as a Marrano went by the name of Antonio de Montezinos, returned from a business trip to South America and brought the news that he had discovered some of the Ten Lost Tribes. They were settled, he reported, around Quito, in Equador; they made allies of the local Indians and converted them to their own faith; and they would readily join others in a war against the Spaniards. Aaron Levi also asserted that he heard them pronounce the *Shema* and made an affidavit to the truth of his assertion.

Aaron Levi's declaration elicited great interest among Jews and gentiles alike. Both believed that the resurgence of the Ten Tribes would be the prelude to the advent of the Messiah, though to each the Messiah presented the fulfillment of a different hope: to the Jews, that the Messiah would lead the whole world to embrace Judaism; to the Christians, that under him all would be converted to Christianity. [17]

Based on the statement of Aaron Levi, John Dury and Thomas Thorogood, both friends of R. Menasseh b. Israel, all wrote books proving that the Millennium was at hand. Other Christian divines appealed to the famous Amsterdam rabbi to set an example for other Jews by his conversion to Christianity. But Menasseh b. Israel, who was no less interested in Aaron Levi's report than they, had views of his own. He pieced together the prediction in Daniel (12:7) and in Deuteronomy (28:64) and arrived at the conclusion that prior to the advent of the Messiah, the Diaspora would have to extend "from the end of the earth even unto the other end of the earth." As England, according to some Jewish commentators, was "the end of the earth" (*finis terrae*), the Messiah cannot be expected until she would readmit the Jews into her domain and thus make the dispersion universal. These ideas he developed in a little book in Spanish and Latin called *Spes Israelis,* and dedicated it to the English Parliament (Amsterdam, 1650).

Menasseh b. Israel did not live to reap the fruit of his devoted labors. His "Humble Address" which he presented to the Lord Protector, and his moving petition for the authorization of the Resettlement of the Jews, was not officially acted upon owing to the strenuous opposition of many influential Englishmen. William Prynne, author of the voluminous and gloomy *Histrio-Mastix,* and in his *Short Demurer* admonished that "it is now a very ill time to bring the Jews when the people were so dangerously and generally bent to Apostacy and all sorts of Novelties in Religion; and would sooner turn Jews, than Jews Christians." Others rehashed the old libels against the Jews and asserted that Jews are a menace to society, that they use the blood of Christian children for their Passover ritual,

impoverish every country by their excessive usury, and are un-
remitting in their efforts to convert Christians to Judaism.
However, the Committee of the Council of State decided that
Jews might be readmitted on seven conditions, among them
that they print nothing in disfavor of Christianity; that they
do not hinder their own from accepting Christianity, nor attempt to convert Christians to their own faith. At a subsequent
conference which Cromwell convened at Whitehall, it was
declared that there was no statute which excluded the Jews
from England. While the Jews were thus not "invited," as
Menasseh b. Israel had hoped, their presence was connived at,
and Charles II granted them a formal charter of protection
(1664). [18]

It is doubtful, however, whether England ever was without
Jews even after the Expulsion of 1290. A certain Doctour
Armand was tried by the Privy Council in 1562 as "esteemed
to be a Jewe, and judged to ryde through the streets on a
carte." Besides those who were accommodated at the *Domus
Conversorum* either before or after their pretended conversion
we find references to "visitors" or "strangers" suspected to be
"juis." One such, a native "Portugal," was Edward Brampton,
a name he assumed in honor of King Edward IV, the ex-
officio godfather of converts. He married a rich widow, became Governor of Guernsey in 1482, was knighted in 1484,
and played an important part in the politics of his adopted
land. Also, Nathanael, "a Jew borne," had the honor of
having John Foxe preach on the occasion of his conversion
(1578). The best known Jew, however, is the Marrano Rodrigo Lopez, said to have been the prototype of Shakespeare's
Shylock. He settled in England in 1559 as body physician of
the Earl of Leicester, and became court physician to Queen
Elizabeth. Having aroused the ire of the Earl of Sussex, he
was charged with "compounding to poison the Queen," and
was hanged, drawn, and quartered in 1594.

Some Jews, however, managed to retain their faith for some
time before they were detected and then escaped without
being converted. Such was Jacob Barnett, secretary to Casanbon
at Oxford. On being discovered he was urged by his employer

to accept Christianity. Barnett staved off the ordeal of baptism as long as he could and then set a date for the ceremony. But when the appointed day arrived he was nowhere to be found, and the frustrated Privy Council had to content itself with entering on their records that Jacob Barnett, a Jew, was banished (1613). That the Jews must have already become notorious for their resistance to conversion is indicated in Marvell's *Coy Mistress,* where the ardent lover protests:

> I would love you ten years before the Flood
> And you should, if you please, refuse,
> Till the conversion of the Jews. [19]

To the honor of the English people be it said that though the Jews resettled there uninvited, they were never maltreated. Their lot was certainly not worse than that of the Christian commonalty who were not of the nobility, and it continued to improve as the years passed by. There were naturally objections raised by some every time a step was taken to remove some of the civil disabilities against the Jews. But the more humane feeling toward the Jews constantly gained ground, until at the turn of the eighteenth century the demand for granting them all the rights and privileges of citizenship could no longer be ignored. From all sides came words in praise and admiration of the Jew. Richard Cumberland portrayed him as but little lower than the angels. Walter Scott depicted Rebecca as a paragon of female loveliness and virtue. Samuel Coleridge sang of the two ragged Jewish maidens whose

> Soul-subduing looks might cheat
> The Christian of his pride,

and Byron in his *Hebrew Melodies* sought to shame the Gentiles of their pride and belief that their prosperity is proof of the truth of Christianity by putting in the mouth of the Jew:

> If the bad never prosper then God is with thee!
> If the slaves only sin, thou art spotless and free!
> If the exile on earth is an outcast on high,

Live on in thy faith, but in mine I will die!
I have lost for that faith more than thou canst bestow
As the God who permits thee to prosper doth know.

These poets, playwrights, and novelists were reinforced by
the publicists and statesmen of that time. William Hazlitt asked
if the Jews from whom Christendom had received its ideas
of God and morality and the founder of its religion are still to
be punished for the crime committed by their coreligionists
nearly two thousand years ago? Basil Montague ridiculed the
wild rumor that Jews will convert the cathedrals and churches
into synagogues, and poked fun at the Philistine of his time
who still goes forth "with his helmet of brass on his head,
and his coat of mail weighing five hundred shekels of brass
and his staff like a weaver's beam" to do battle against the God
of the armies of Israel. But more than any other did Thomas
Macaulay employ his powerful eloquence "for terminating
old hostilities and ... for blotting out from the statute book
the last traces of intolerance." In essays and addresses he appealed to the English sense of justice and their deep-rooted
reverence for the Bible not to discriminate against the people
of the Bible. "Sir," cried he in his famous speech on Jewish
disabilities:

> Sir, in supporting the motion of my honorable
> friend I am, I firmly believe, supporting the honor
> and interest of the Christian religion. I should think
> that I insulted that religion if I said that it cannot stand
> unaided by intolerant laws. The whole history of
> Christianity proves that she has little indeed to fear
> from persecution as a foe, but much to fear from perse-
> cution as an ally.... Let not us, mistaking her char-
> acter and her interests, fight the battles of truth with
> the weapons of error, and endeavor to support by op-
> pression that religion which first taught the human
> race the great lesson of human charity.

After a hard struggle Macaulay was privileged to witness,
a year before his death, the last vestiges of Jewish disabilities

removed, and with the phrase, "So help me, Jehovah" in the place of "the faith of a Christian," Baron Lionel de Rothschild took his seat as the first Jewish member of the English Parliament.

But many Englishmen did not remain content with merely removing the civil disabilities from their Jewish countrymen, or even with being "spiritual Semites" (a phrase made popular in 1938 by Pope Pius XI), who were claimed by the Church as her adherents from earliest times. They maintained that they were in very deed the lineal descendants of the Israelites of the Bible, and that in them are being fulfilled the promises given the ancient Hebrews which those who are assumed to be the "seed of Abraham" have forfeited. It was them whom Isaiah had in mind when he spoke of the remnant of God's people in "the Isles of the Sea," who glorify the Lord in the regions of light,

"Even the name of the Lord, the God of Israel."
(11:11; 24:15)

In support of this contention there grew up a tradition based on an ingenious interpretation of the Bible which became to several million Englishmen "the Gospel truth." According to it, when Shalmaneser subjugated the Ten Tribes, many of the coastal tribes (Asher, Manasseh, Ephraim, Dan, and Simeon) escaped in their boats and fled to the isles of the north and west of Europe. The men of Dan settled in what is now Ireland, and came to be known as Tuatha de Daanans, while the Simeonites became the Simonii or Cimerii of ancient Wales. The more adventurous of them, however, joined the other tribes and made their difficult way overland from the East. For a knowledge of their journey we are indebted to the Danites who were wont to name places after the name of their eponym (Jud. 18:12, 29). They must have sailed over the Danube, the Dniester, the Dnieper, and the hundreds of other rivers whose names in ancient geographies contain the syllables "dan" or "don," until they reached Denmark, or Dan's last resting place—Mark in Anglo-Saxon meaning "boundary" or "descendants."

Not so those who stayed in Ireland. They regarded their new home merely as an asylum, or *Arzaret* (another Land of Israel), and called themselves Gauls (Heb. *golim,* exiles), or Saccae (Heb. *Succot-ites,* dwellers in booths), or Hibernians (after Heber the Kenite?). The Gadites, or Getae, whom Strabo describes as "a righteous nation" but fierce and savage in battle, settled in Scotland, and called themselves "Maesi," or followers of Moses. Especially did the Simonii or Cimerii of Wales retain many memories of their past. David was a favorite name among them, and when they accepted Christianity David became their patron saint. During their long journeyings, however, they forgot their Hebrew tongue, even as did those who remained in Babylon, and adopted the language of the natives, even as was predicted by Isaiah (28:11):

> For with stammering lips, and with a strange tongue
> Shall it be spoken to this people.

The Danish invasion of England was thus rather a reunion of the scattered tribes than the subjugation of a people by an enemy. It was only necessary that they appoint a king of the Davidic dynasty to fulfill the promises: "The sceptre shall not depart from Judah," and: "There shall not be cut off unto David a man to sit upon the throne of the house of Israel" (Gen. 49:10, Jer. 33:17). This came to pass after Nebuchadnezzar carried off into captivity Zedekiah, the last ruler of Judea.

According to the Anglo-Israelites, Zedekiah left behind him his daughter, Tea Tephi, over whom he appointed Jeremiah as guardian. The Prophet took her with him when he joined the refugees who fled to Egypt. He also managed to save her royal escutcheon, the harp of David, and the *Lia Phail,* Stone Wonderful, or *Eben Shetiyah,* the foundation stone of the Temple on Mt. Zion. Tea Tephi married Heremon, the prince of the Tuatha de Daanan, and thus united the Lion of Judah with the Unicorn of Joseph, which became characteristic of English heraldry. David's harp was preserved at Tara, the capital of Ireland, and became a source of inspiration to Erin's Bards ever after. The Lia Phail was transferred by Fergus I from Tara to Dunstaffnage, thence by Kenneth to Scone, thence by James I to Westminster, and upon it the English kings who are anointed like David, have ever since been crowned.

Tea Tephi became famous in Irish ballads, and her tomb at Tara was regarded as a shrine for many centuries. Equally renowned in Irish story became her guardian Jeremiah. According to a widespread tradition, he opened a school and had as one of his pupils their celebrated monarch Fin McCoyle. Several of their kings bore his name, and his bust was set up in the capitol of Dublin, while an ancient Bard records:

> There is not a hut the Isle around
> But where a Jerry may be found.

The Anglo-Israelites point to the name British or Britain as a corruption from the Hebrew *Brith-am* or *Brit-ish* ("People, or man of the Covenant"), and see in it an allusion to the prophecy in Isaiah (42:6; 49:8). They also see in the name Saxons an abbreviation from Isaacsons, as Amos (7:9, 16) preferred to call the House of Israel. "The evidence that we are this blessed Israel," writes one of them, "is most clearly given by our being named or called 'Saxons'....We are acknowledging ourselves to be the sons of Isaac, and complying with Scripture by being called under another name" (Isa. 65:16). But their greatest support they draw from the peculiarities of the English and their institutions. The English have nothing in common with the European nations. Even as Balaam spoke of the Children of Israel:

> Lo, it is a people that dwelleth alone,
> And is not reckoned among the nations (Num. 23:9),

so did Shakespeare describe the British:

> I' the world's volume
> Our Britain seems as of it but not in it.

And even as the Rabbis claimed, not without reason, that Aramaic was nearest the language of the Torah and next to it

most holy, so did they maintain that English is best adapted
for a translation of the Scriptures because it abounds in Hebrew
roots. The aboriginal Irish called their altars Betal, or Bothal,
as the Hebrews did their Beth-El. The battle cry of the ancient
Saxons was "Alleluiah" and the joyous acclaim of the Norsemen was "Huzzah," later corrupted into "Hurrah," which
no doubt was derived from *Hosannah*. Many of their laws bear
a Semitic stamp. Their customs pertaining to marriage and
inheritance, their periodic redistribution of the land, of letting
the fields lie fallow, of having cities of refuge, of Gavelkind,
of the Witenagemot, so similar to the biblical *Krue haedah*
(assembly of the representatives of the people, or parliament,
the Sanhedrin of later times), all bespeak a Hebraic beginning.
For centuries, however, they allowed themselves to fall into
innocuous desuetude until the real Britons, the Covenanters,
came into power and reclaimed their heritage. "When the
Puritans gave special opportunity to the development of our
Hebrew tendencies," states an Anglo-Israelite, "the very
nation seemed to recover itself as only Israel could have done.
It was as though by second nature we recalled the past." [20]

The claim to Israelitish ancestry deepened in the English
the sense of their duty to convert the Jews, and made them
most active in their effort to spread the Gospel among them.
In 1807 they organized the London Society for Promoting
Christianity among the Jews. The New Testament was translated into Hebrew (1817) and Yiddish (1821), and numerous
novels were written in which the hero, or heroine, marries
out of the faith, sees the light, and finds temporal and eternal
happiness by accepting the faith of the Christian mate. The
joy of these zealous "Evangelicals" over a stray lamb which
joined their fold was given expression in the following "Lines
to a Converted Jew":

> O snatch'd from error's gulf through grace,
>   From sin through Christ set free!
> Welcome thou child of Israel's race
>   The Christian welcomes you.

Through thee may Israel seek the Lord,
And Jews prove Christians true;
For Christians love the Jewish name,—
The Savior was a Jew. [21]

It may be noted that these efforts met with hardly any success, that few if any Jews have ever been converted by reading the New Testament in Hebrew or Yiddish. The D'Israelis, Ricardos, Aguilars, and others accepted Christianity out of a desire to be in no way distinguished from the majority of their countrymen. Hence they almost always became Episcopalians. The poor, mostly immigrants, were usually attracted by the material benefits which they obtained together with the salvation of their souls. Yet some converts earned a place of distinction among the leading scholars and propagandists of their new faith. Such were, to mention a few, Alfred Eldersheim, whose *Life and Times of Jesus the Messiah* ranks high in the voluminous literature on that period; Isador Lowenthal, a missionary to the Moslems, who translated the Gospel into *Pushtu,* and Christian David Ginsburg, the eminent Masoretic scholar. The first Anglican Bishop of the United Church of England and Ireland (1841), who also took a prominent part in the translation of the Anglican liturgy into Hebrew, was Michael Solomon Alexander. He was also an ardent member of the London Society for the Promotion of Christianity among the Jews. [22]

As against these Jewish converts to Christianity there were a number of English gentiles who not only proclaimed the Unity of God but actually embraced Judaism. John Evelyn tells in his Diary (1641) about a Kentish woman he met in Amsterdam whose husband, a Burgundian Jew, translated for her instruction several books of their devotion. In the records of the State Trials of Scotland there is an entry of the trial on June 15, 1681, of Francis Borthwich of Edinburgh, who "was studious to make a shameful apostasy from the most holy faith and he professed and openly declared himself to be a Jew and was circumcised and ... did rail against our Lord and Saviour

Jesus Christ, denying Him to be God, and affirming Him to be a mere man ... and he did with great and hurried execrations wish all manner of judgments to befall him, if ever he should return to the Christian religion." But such occurrences would naturally be more frequent in England where, after the middle of the seventeenth century, there was a synagogue with a *Haham* and the Jewish services were not infrequently attended by gentiles. Samuel Pepys records such a visit in his Diary under date of October 14, 1633, probably on the Feast of the Rejoicing of the Law when all decorum was relaxed, and there was "disorder, laughing, sporting, and no attention, but confusion." But we have a more agreeable description by one who visited the synagogue the previous year, in which we are also informed that while there he counted "about or above one hundred right Jews, one proselyte among them." [23]

Some of these converts belonged to the upper strata of English society. Rumor had it that Lady Hester Lucy Stanhope (1776-1839), the brilliant grand-daughter of the first Lord Chatham and niece of William Pitt, was inclined to, if she was not officially a convert to, Judaism. There is greater certainty about another English noblewoman, Elizabeth Jane Caulfield (1834-82), the only daughter of the first Lord Athlumney, and the wife of the third Earl of Charlemont. She was a regular attendant at the synagogue of Belfast, which was near her country home, or at the Bayswater and Central Synagogue while in London. and frequently sought the advice of rabbis in matters of religion. A woman of great talents, she utilized her unusual accomplishments for the benefit of Jewish and general philanthropies. [24]

Perhaps the most remarkable of English proselytes was George Gordon, (1751-93), the younger son of the third Duke of Gordon, and a relative of Lord Byron, whom Dickens is assumed to have had in mind when he wrote *Barnaby Rudge*.

George Gordon served successively in the army and the navy, and was elected to Parliament when England was agitated by the question of the removal of Irish disabilities. He was the instigator of the "No Popery" riots, the President of the Protestant League which fought against Catholics, and one of the leaders who sought to overthrow the monarchy in France. He defended Cagliostro in the celebrated Diamond Necklace Case, and championed the cause of the Dutch against the Austrians. In the midst of all his various activities he was taking stock of Christianity as a whole, and arriving at the conclusion that both Catholicism and Protestantism were idolatrous, decided to make the "unreasonable and imprudent step," and applied to Chief Rabbi Tebele Schiff, of London, to accept him into the Jewish faith. As the rabbi, unwilling to violate the condition upon which the Jews were readmitted into England, refused to grant his request, Gordon went to Birmingham where he prevailed upon a certain R. Joel to convert him to Judaism (1787). The next five years he devoted to perfect himself in the knowledge of Judaism and came to be known as "the pious R. Israel b. Abraham." On his return to London he mingled almost exclusively among his new coreligionists. In consequence of a book he wrote against Marie Antoinette, he was lodged in Newgate. While in jail he would pray every morning, afternoon, and evening in the Hebrew tongue, and every Saturday he held services in his room amidst a *minyan* (quorum) of Polish Jews. "His Saturday's bread was baked according to the manner of the Jews; his wine was Jewish (untouched by gentiles); his meat was Jewish (according to the rabbinic requirements), and he was the best Jew in the Congregation of Israel." On his prison wall were to be seen the Ten Commandments in the Hebrew language, the bag of the *tallith*, or fringed prayer garment, and the phylacteries. At the expiration of his sentence the rich Jews refused to guarantee bail as security for his future good behavior, for fear of being suspected of having contributed to his conversion. After a life filled with frustrations Gordon died of a broken heart and was buried in the family vault on Hampstead Road. [25]

Macaulay, in his address on the removal of Jewish disabilities, points to the treatment of Lord Gordon as proof of the Jewish aversion to proselytism. And, indeed, other Christians had the same experience as Lord Gordon. English Jewry, as a rule, refused to admit those who clamored for conversion to Judaism.

In 1751, when several Christians expressed their intention to be converted, the wardens of the Spanish and Portuguese Synagogue addressed a letter to the Ashkenazic congregations, warning them of the danger of admitting them into the household of Israel. In 1752, the three then existing congregations, Bevis Marks, Duke's Place, and Hambro Shool, resolved not to sanction conversions. Rabbi Hart Lyon also declared that to marry a non-Jewess "is tantamount to abandoning the faith even if she should become a Jewess." Proselytes, however, continued to trickle into the Jewish community either out of religious conviction or through the mediacy of intermarriage. This happened most frequently in the provincial cities, where Jews were few. "Several romantic cases are on record," writes Lucian Wolf, "where a Jewish pedlar would induce some one of the gentile lassies among his customers to share his humble fortunes and embrace the religion of his fathers." A notable instance is that of Moses Abrahams and Martha Haynes, daughter of a Dorsetshire farmer (1781). Martha became a zealous Jewess, and through a daughter who married Samuel Yates, was the ancestress of Sir Herbert Samuel, the first High Commissioner of Palestine. [26]

To be sure, even where the Jewish contracting party retained the faith of the fathers, the children, in many instances, were raised in the religion of the majority. Hence, as in Spain, Jewish blood mingles profusely with that of the English nobility, not excepting royalty itself. The present Marquess of Crewe and Viscount of Galway is an offspring of Kitty Villareal, who married out of the faith in 1731. A descendant of Hannah Norsa became the forbear of the issue of the Duke of Gloucester. It was well stated that "the blood of the Inquisitional martyrs, and of the despised Tudesca, and of Charles Stuart, and of Nell Gwynne, are united in some of the foremost British families." But the opposite is true also, and both processes continue to this day among the high and among the lowly. In a register of English female proselytes from 1809 to 1816, they not only raised their children in the Jewish faith but thirty-nine of them also converted their children by the former husbands after their marriage to Jews. [27]

Among the prominent English proselytes of today is the
Honourable Venitia Stanley, youngest daughter of Lord Shef-
field, and the niece of the Catholic Bishop of Emaus, who
became the wife of Edwin S. Montague, one time Secretary
of State for India (1917-22). Almost all the Rothschilds who
married out of the faith remained in the Jewish fold, and
raised their children in the religion of their fathers. Hannah
de Rothschild (d. 1890), daughter of Baron Mayer Nathan de
Rothschild, who continued as a steadfast Jewess even after
her marriage to the Earl of Rosebury, bequeathed her love
for her people to her son, Neil Primrose. A Member of Parliament, he was an ardent Zionist, and when the British War
Office organized a Jewish regiment in the Holy Land he was
among the first to serve under General Allenby. He was
killed in action in the campaign for Jerusalem, and was buried
in the Jewish cemetery at Ramleh. Another Rothschild by
marriage, a proselyte, is Barbara Hutchinson, daughter of the
Recorder of Hastings. A convert who greatly assisted her husband in his outstanding Jewish religious and educational work
was Florence Ward, Vice-Mistress of Girton College, the second
wife of the eminent scholar Claude G. Montefiore. Eva Violet,
daughter of Lord Melchett (who had married a Catholic lady
and raised his children in the faith of their mother), after
her marriage (1933) to Lord Reading's son, formally entered
the Jewish fold at the liberal synagogue in London. Her
brother, the second Lord Melchett, is one of the very enthusiastic workers in the cause of the Jewish people. He was among
the first to lodge a protest against the treatment of the Jews
in Germany, took an especial interest in Jewish sports, and
was honorary president of the World Maccabee Organization.[28]

Some Englishmen were attracted to Judaism through
Zionism. One such is Mrs. Israel Zangwill. It is said that the
original of *Daniel Deronda* was Colonel Albert Edward Gold-
smid, whose parents had concealed from him the fact that
he was a Jew and revealed it to him only when he was about to
marry a supposedly Gentile young lady. It turned out that
the girl was also of Jewish descent, and the happy couple

went to Palestine for their honeymoon, where later their daughters Rachel and Carmel were born. The Colonel became an ardent Zionist and one of the founders of the Maccabeans. He also took an active part in the organization of the Jewish Lads' Brigade in London and the provinces. [29]

George Eliot was probably a Unitarian or Deist. Laurence Oliphant (1829-88) was a mystic. As a humanitarian he took a leading part in the administration of the Mansion House Fund for the relief of the victims of the Russian pogroms in 1882, and conceived the idea of founding a Jewish settlement in the district of Gilead and of expioiting the mineral deposits of the Dead Sea. When the Sultan refused the necessary firman he with his wife settled among the Jews in Haifa and devoted the remainder of his life to the study of the Kabbalah. [30]

A unique personality was Carl Joubert, a collateral descendant of Grote, the historian of Greece (1867-1906). Having gone to Russia at the age of twenty, to attend to his father's business, he championed the cause of the Russian Christians, but he was especially impressed with the piety and almost superhuman endurance of the Russo-Polish Jews. While in Warsaw he made his home with a poor artisan and took up the study of Hebrew and the Talmud, in which he became so proficient that R. Isaac Elhenan Spector, of Kovno, pronounced him worthy to be a rabbi in Israel. Later he applied for admission into the Jewish community, and on his return to London joined the congregation of the Hammersmith Synagogue. After his death, it was learned that he was the author of the articles on "Zionism and Anti-Semitism," which appeared in the *Quarterly Review* in 1902 over the signature of "A Quarterly Reviewer," and which were later issued in book form under the title of *Aspects of the Jewish Question*. [31]

It need not be assumed, however, that all the modern English proselytes were lords, ladies, and litterateurs. As against those who attracted attention because of their social standing or their unusual achievements, there are hundreds who, if they attracted any notice it was by reason of their conversion. Thus we learn that in the single year of 1928 the London *Beth Din* (Jewish court) had to deal with one hundred sixty-seven applications for admission into the Jewish fold. In South Africa not only Boers but also Kaffirs sometimes seek to become Jews, and the congregations of Johannesburg, Sydney, and Melbourne found it advisable to protest against conversions with a view to matrimony. Whatever may be the truth about the ancient Anglo-Saxons being descended from the Ten Lost Tribes of Israel, there can be no doubt about many Israelites of today being offspring of Anglo-Saxons. [32]

CHAPTER XXVII

IN AMERICA:
THE MODERN MELTING POT

WHATEVER merit there may be to the claim that Columbus was of Jewish descent and even a Marrano, there is no doubt about the religion of some of those who made his expedition possible. The only one of the high officials belonging to an old Christian family and directly connected with the epoch-making discovery was the royal secretary, Juan de Coloma, whose wife, however, was descended from the noted Jewish family, the De la Caballerias. The first European to behold the New World was the Marrano sailor Rodrigo de Triana, and the first to set foot on the new soil was the interpreter Luis de Torres, who was baptized just before sailing.

Columbus deemed it important to begin his account with the statement that the permission granted him to undertake his quest for the discovery of the Indies was "in the same month in which their Majesties issued the edict that all Jews should be driven out of the kingdom and its territories." He might have added that he set sail within a day or two of the departure of the last Jewish exiles, to whom the New World was to become a veritable Land of Promise. Nor was it long before they were found in considerable numbers throughout Spanish and Portuguese possessions from Cuba to Argentina on the Atlantic, and from Chile to the Philippine Islands on the Pacific.

But the tentacles of the Inquisition of Old Spain reached out to the settlements of New Spain, and its Green Cross peered from its niche upon the flames and demons of the sambenitos of the penitents of America as it did upon the victims of the auto-da-fes of Europe. The Spanish Government was suspicious of the intent of those who applied for leave to go to the colonies for the purpose of trade, and it was only after a great expenditure of gold that they were ever allowed to embark. But they were closely watched by the emissaries of the Church and the State, and after the bull issued by Paul III forbidding Lutherans as well as Conversos from settling in the New World, the Marranos were in constant danger of deportation.

The methods whereby the Iberian statesmen tried to keep the Marranos within the Church differed according to the policies of their Government. While those of Spain were not permitted to go to the New World, those of Portugal were driven thither by sheer force. To the Government of Portugal Brazil was, like Siberia to Russia, a penal colony to which were deported those who were considered too dangerous to be allowed to remain at home. These latter were joined by many who went there of their own volition, and before long they became leaders of commerce and owners of plantations with numerous slaves. Their industry and ability were recognized by the Dutch and the English both of whom vied with each other for their support and cooperation in their rivalry with the Portuguese. Both granted special inducements "to the people of the Jewish nation" who would come to settle in their colonies. [1]

At first, the victims of the Inquisition were sent for trial to the mother land. In 1515 a certain Pedro de Leon and his family were brought to Seville to be prosecuted on the charge of Judaizing; and, in 1528, at the first auto-da-fe held in the New World, Harnando Alonso, one of the *conquistadores* who helped Cortes to subjugate Mexico, was burned there at the stake together with another Judaizer. By the middle of the sixteenth century the Church found enough backsliders in South America to justify the establishment of Inquisitorial tribunals in Peru and Mexico to cope with "the cursed sect of Jews and Judaizers which had for some years been corrupting the faithful flock." Other tribunals were later introduced in other parts of Spanish and Portuguese America.

Soon the age-old prejudices against, and dread of, the Jews, which dogged their steps in the Old World, were imported into the New. Judaizers were depicted by the clergy as objects of horror, fiends who delighted in mutilating crucifixes, in desecrating holy images, and in bringing on, by their wizardry, hurricanes and earthquakes. In a book published in Mexico in 1648, titled *Third Exaltation of the Divine Mercy,* "for having cleaned and purified this city and kingdom of the heresy of the cursed sect of Judaizer" it is related that an image known as "Lord of Izquimiquilpan and Christ of the Poor Lead Mines," had become blackened "due to the fact that so many Jews were performing abominations throughout the land." One day this image is said to have detached itself from the cross, and the winds blew and the earth trembled until the Jews were discovered and punished. Thereafter, only sounds of music were heard in the church, and voices that prayed. Three stars also appeared above the cupola, the bells rang of themselves, a great light shone, and the Image became miraculously renewed.

To recognize these so called infernal Judaizing minions of the devil, learned priests composed manuals based on previous works and reports extracted from penitents, or volunteered by apostates and replete with a medley of distorted facts and imaginary beliefs. "Judaizers abstain from pork, turn to the East when they pray, light candles on Friday evenings, and change bed linen on Saturdays. They eat meat when Christians subsist on fish, and fast when Christians feast. They never mention the name of Jesus Christ nor His Holy Mother, and when they say Our Lady del Carmen they really invoke the prophet Elijah of Mt. Carmel. They bleed all kinds of flesh and eat the forequarters only...and, filthily, they do not (*sic*) eat the animals of cloven hoof.... On Saturday they do not remove their hats, though they get their heads broken for such discourtesy.... They believe that adulterous Jewesses appear for judgment before God with their heads covered with a dirty cloth ... that the souls of the dead become birds, and come to drink or bathe near the corpse, and for this they place a jar of water and a clean towel ... and for fear of the Holy Tribunal they put in secret places of the corpse the gold that should be placed, according to their belief, on the eyes and mouth." [2]

For some reason the American Inquisition stood even more in fear of Judaizers than the parent institution and permitted only such priests as had at least two degrees to visit the suspects so as to be able the better to wrestle with the powerful demons of whom they were possessed. They were instructed to regard no action or expression as too trivial for their investigation. Anyone who, having observed a person perform one or more of the alleged customs of the Jews, or who, having heard him declare the beliefs attributed to them failed to report it immediately to the authorities; anyone who absented himself from mass, or stayed away from an auto-da-fe, was liable to suffer the same penalty as the condemned. Children were exhorted to denounce their parents, parents to report on their children, and husbands and wives to have no compassion on their guilty spouses. Simon Perenis, an artist, was found guilty as a Judaizer because he inadvertently remarked that he preferred rather to paint a lady of flesh and blood than a pale and unattractive Madonna. There is a tradition, that while in his cell he became very ill. When, out of pity, his request for a palette and brushes was granted he locked himself in his cell, refusing to admit even the guards who brought food, and, despite the semi-darkness of the cell, produced the image of "Our Lady of the Pardon" which hangs in the cathedral of Mexico. "In view of the miracle whose vile agent he had been," we are told, he was pardoned—to the extent of being burned.

The Judaizers were no less clever in eluding the vigilance of the spies of the Church than the latter were to entrap them and as in the days of the Hadrianic persecutions developed a language of signs and tokens comprehensible to none but their own. Those, however, who were unfortunate enough to fall into the hands of the Holy Tribunal showed, in most instances, that they were of the mettle of their coreligionists in Spain and Portugal. Many of them proudly confessed their Judaism and stubbornly refused to implicate others even under the most horrible tortures. One of them, " a vile member of the cursed sect" who, according to the document in the National Archives of Mexico, "arranged marriages between Jews and Jewesses, investigating whether or not each was really following the laws of Moses...boasted that his mother had been punished by the Inquisition of Seville and had not revealed the names of any Judaizers, adding that no one was obliged to confess more than his own faults and that this is what each should do, in order to leave some out of prison to help them."

Sometimes the very torments which they had to endure imbued the Judaizers with a spirit of bravado which made them defy the Church, and joke about their fate. Juan Mendes, reads another document, "thirty-two, with evident sign of circumcision," confessed under torture that he had his doubts about the dogmas of Christianity. This, he stated, may have been the call of the Jewish blood which ran in the veins of his mother. But, he added, blood or no blood, had he known of the laws of Moses he should surely have accepted them. It was reported that Thomas Trevino of Sobremonte (arrested in April, 1625 in the city of Mexico, on the testimony of one who "on account of the scruples he feels and for the unburdening of his conscience" watched him closely) after his dinner or supper, in answer to the prayer "Praised be the most Holy Sacrament" would say, "Much good may it do your worships." It was related that he was accustomed to read from a small book like The Hours, but never allowed anyone to lay hands on it; that he did not take off his hat when he saw the cross; that he would not confess, and seldom went to Mass.

> He further proved his perfidy...by marrying a Jewess...The day of the wedding...he invited many of those who shared his wicked laws, and celebrated it with Jewish rites and ceremonies, putting on his head at the meal a cloth, and beginning the courses with a certain dish of cakes and honey, basing himself for this upon certain Apocryphal history, which he said was Scriptures, and which commended this rite.

He beheaded the chickens to be served at the table
... with a knife. He repeated three times upon behead-
ing the chickens ... a certain ridiculous prayer, with
his face turned toward the East ... and this perfidious
Jew washed his hands after eating, three times with
cold water, so as not to remain *treso* (*trefah*) which
means tainted.

Trevino somehow managed to gain his freedom but was
arrested again in 1643 together with his wife and two children. His son, little Rafael, with "visible mark of circumcision," testified under torture, that when very young ...

His father, who was a rabbi, performed upon him
the ceremony ... and while he was recovering, his
father would light a candle and remain in his room,
praying every night until dawn ... and from June to
December ... fasted with his father every Thursday
and sometimes Mondays. ... In the year 1640 he made
a journey with his father to the city of Zacatecas,
and his father told him that he would take him and
the family to some place where each man lived as he
wished, and that he was only waiting for some poor
people to get out of the Tribunal dungeons in order
to aid them.

As a result of this testimony little Rafael was placed in
a monastery, while Trevino lingered in jail for a period of
five years. During all this time and despite the torture, he
persisted in denying his guilt. But the night before he was
to be executed he declared himself happy to die a Jew without
the benefit of "pardon," that is, of preliminary strangulation.
Informed that he would be burned the following day, he
nonchalantly remarked that this was incorrect, since according
to the Jewish way of reckoning time, from eventide to eventide, he would die on the same day.

Trevino's courage did not forsake him to the last. He refused
to carry the cross in his hands in the procession to the stake,
and he had to be gagged to stop him from reiterating his

attachment for Judaism. However, he managed to make himself heard, and it was related that his "blasphemies" were so shocking that even the mule on which he was made to ride "bucked and kicked and refused to hold him . . . because he was a dog Jew and possessed of the devil." He was therefore put on a broken down horse with an Indian mounted behind him who struck him on the mouth to stop his blasphemies. Thus he was led to the stake where, "because he had surpassed the patience of our Holy Mother the Church," he was roasted on a slow fire (April 11, 1649). As the flames crept slowly upward, he drew the faggots as close and as high as he could with his feet, and, with his last breath, shouted: "Dogs of priests, pile on the wood higher! I paid enough for this fire!" (His fortune, which was considerable, was confiscated by the Church.) [3]

Isaac de Castro Tartas, a youth of twenty-one, was another victim who attracted considerable attention. He was born in France in 1626 to a Portuguese refugee who assumed the name of Abraham, studied at the Universities of Paris and Bordeaux, and lived for a while in Amsterdam. From there he went to Brazil, and thence to Bahia, then in the hands of the Portuguese. There he was arrested as a Judaizer and sent to Lisbon for trial, during which he proudly proclaimed his Judaism, all attempts to reconvert him to Christianity notwithstanding. To relieve his parents' anxiety, he wrote to them, after his arrest, not to worry if they did not hear from him for some years as he was going to Rio de Janeiro to try to reclaim to Judaism some relatives living there. With five others he was burned at the stake (December 15, 1647). As the fire leaped up around him his voice was heard, above the crackling of the flames, proclaiming the *Shema,* or Jewish profession of faith: "Hear, O Israel, the Lord our God, the Lord is One!" This made such an impression upon the populace that the Inquisition hesitated for some time afterwards to burn persons alive. Among the Jews he was mourned as a saint. [4]

To win over as many as possible to Judaism was indeed held to be the holiest task of the Judaizers. Of the Mexican

martyr Duarts Rodreiguez, who escaped from Portugal to
Peru, it was reported that on his journeys he made it a point
to assemble all the Jewesses and preach to them on Judith
and Esther. A most ardent propagandist was Francisco
Maldonaldo da Silva, a prominent surgeon of Conception de
Chile. He was brought up as a good Catholic by his father,
a native Portuguese, who himself had a narrow escape from
the clutches of the Inquisition. When he attained the age of
eighteen there fell into his hands the *Scrutinium Scripturarum*
of the renegade Pablo de Santa Maria. It called to his attention the very views which it set out to confute. The reading
of the Bible, and his father's explanations of it, completed his
Judaization. He circumcised himself with a pair of scissors,
took the name of Eli, and began to preach his new religion to
his sisters, who were ardent Catholics. The latter denounced
him to the Holy Office, and, early in 1627, he was sent to Lima
for trial. He refused to be sworn on a crucifix, and as the
ablest theologians could not shake him from his faith, he was
turned over to the "secular arm" and for condign punishment (1633).

In prison he not only observed as many of the ceremonies
of Judaism as was possible under the circumstances, but resolved to be a Nazarite. As such he fasted at frequent intervals, and allowed his hair to grow long. Instead of listening to
the monks who came to argue with him on matters religious he
attempted to convert them to Judaism. One day, by fashioning a rope out of the maize husks which he ordered instead
of bread, he managed to get out of his cell through the window, broke into the other cells, and by his fiery eloquence converted two Old Christians who were lodged there for minor
offenses. This precipitated his doom, and on January 23rd he,
together with ten other *Judaizantes*, was marched to the Plaza
to the sound of hymns and prayers chanted by the clergy,
and in the presence of the Indians and Peruvians who flocked
from great distances to see the spectacle, was burned while
exclaiming: "This is the doing of the Lord God of Israel, so that
I may now look upon Him face to face." With him were also
consumed the two paper books which he skillfully scraped

together while in prison, in which he wrote with ink made from charcoal and pens cut out of chicken bones, a vindication of the faith for which he died a martyr.

In this struggle against insurmountable odds women played a part no less, if not more conspicuous, than men. Though they could have hidden their Judaism much more easily than the men, they very seldom flinched from proclaiming it. They were, even more than the men, interested in seeking mates of undoubted Jewish ancestry and in seeing that the children were properly indoctrinated in their religion.

One fourteen-year-old girl, noted for her beauty, was suspected of Judaizing because of her laxity in going to Mass and observing communion and confession. Her stubborn refusal to denounce her accomplices rendered her, according to the Chronicler, "the most notable case in the records of the Inquisition, both here (in Mexico) and in Spain." She was sentenced to spend two years in an Inquisitor's house to be instructed in the faith, and then exiled.

The hopes which seized hold of many Jews in the New World that the Messiah was to make his advent in 1642-3 was especially cherished by the women. Many of them fasted and prayed to be found worthy to become the mothers or grandmothers of the hoped-for redeemer. In the Auto-da-Fe of 1649, Blanca Enriquez, who together with her children and grandchildren was condemned to a martyr's death, was the most obstinate of all Judaizers. Her house became a little sanctuary where Judaizers would assemble for services to hear her husband explain the doctrines of their faith and to read from the Prophets as "his tears fell line by line." She believed that one of her progeny would bear the expected Messiah. However, she was prepared for the worst, and taught not only her family but her slaves how to act under torture should they be caught by the Inquisition.

The effect of her teachings was shown in the lives of her children. One of her daughters, the expectant mother of the Messiah, when she began to feel the pangs of parturition is said to have made "nine Stations to a painting of Saint Moses." The child venerated as the promised Messiah all through New

Spain, fell a victim to the Inquisition at the age of twenty-eight. The same hope and frustration was experienced by Donna Blanca's granddaughter, Blanca Juarez, who was processed in the 1649 Auto-da-Fe at the age of twenty-two, and sentenced to imprisonment for life after serving two years in the house of an Inquisitor. She is reported to have been

> ...so austere an observer of their laws...that they thought her a saint...and they bathed her and dressed her in white...and she ate unleavened bread and bitter roots...and she would gather with the women and they would take their pleasure in speaking of rites and ceremonies.....In prison...she became ill ...and was absolved...but having recovered...it was found that she had kept silent about many sins ...and that she had communicated with other prisoners under the name of Little Dove, and in the tongue of Angola, with the slaves that serve in the dungeons.

Another daughter of Donna Blanca, Beatriz Enriquez, was a pillar of the little congregation which met at the house of her father. Her main effort was to inure them to the danger which lurked for them in every nook, and to teach them how to cope with the Tribunal. To encourage them by her example she would lift up her arms and ask them "to look at them and to see how good she had them for the torture."

A niece of Donna Blanca, who was married twice, was reported to have remarked that she loved her second husband more than the first because his father had been burned by the Tribunal in Portugal. While in prison she communicated with other prisoners under the name of Big Dove, and joked with them about the sambenitos that they would have to wear, saying that "she did not mind if hers were not studded with diamonds, but that she would like an edging of yellow satin, since, being of very white skin, it would be most becoming ...and it was agreed among them that they would all ask for sambenitos with edging."

Donna Blanca poured out her spirit even on her servants and slaves. One of them, the mulatto Esperenza Rodriguez, who became the wife of a German sculptor, was accused of Judaizing. Following the instructions of her mistress she feigned insanity. She kept kissing a large doll which she made from pieces of her clothes, saying it was her child, and cried for it when it was taken away from her. At last she broke down under torture, confessed and begged for mercy. She was sentenced to prison for life with confiscation of goods and flogging.

Donna Isabel de Rivera, the wife of Francisco Botello, was suspected of Judaization because she was heard to remark, "It is too bad the Judas effigies of Holy Week parades should be made so ugly." After her husband's arrest she refused to take the Sacrament or go to Mass, openly expressed her gratitude to him for teaching her the ways of the Jews, and her contempt for the Holy Tribunal which she said was not at all holy, but was after her husband's money. In jail she ministered indefatigably to the prisoners, taught them to recite old Jewish prayers and admonished them not to abandon the Jewish religion. Botello, who never yielded under torture, was at last burned, while Donna Isabel, after spending four years in religious hospitals, was condemned to life service for the Inquisition, with confiscation of goods. [5]

The readiness and generosity with which the Marranos welcomed anyone who was willing to revert to, or accept, the religion of Israel was sometimes taken advantage of by charlatans of the type of Fray Jose Diaz Pimiento, a native Cuban, who became a monk. According to the records of the Inquisition, he appeared in Curacao in 1615 and confided to Jews that he was fleeing from the Inquisition and would revert to his ancestral faith if he were supplied with a certain amount of money. At Palma the Jews provided him with a Negro slave and literature from which to study the "one hundred and thirty-two" precepts of Judaism. From such as the Bible in vernacular Spanish and books called *Oronio* and *Talamontcin,* these which treated of the genealogy of Our Lady he learned that the Virgin had been the wife of Senor Joseph; that the latter had not been the father of our Lord Jesus Christ, but someone called Juan Pandera. Thereupon he tore up his Rosary, saying, "If these things are of God, let flowers grow out from them." As no flowers grew, he entered the covenant and assumed the name of Abraham. His conversion was celebrated with a great feast, and he was presented with a purse of pesetas. A trip to Bahia netted him five hundred pesetas more.

The smattering of Hebrew which Pimiento acquired enabled him to extract more money from other Jewish communities, until he was seized, put in chains, brought before the Tribunal of Carthagena as a renegade priest, and sentenced to the Auto da Fe in the convent of Santo Domingo. Since he recanted he was ordered to go to Spain. On arriving at Cadiz he made good his escape, but was apprehended at Xerez, and imprisoned in a convent. From there he sent letters, signed Abraham Diaz Pimiento, begging for loans and giving as references some prominent Jews of Jamaica and Curacao. Once more he escaped, but the Inquisition got hold of him again and put him in prison in Seville. There he denied his Judaization while under torture. But later he experienced a change of heart and confessed to the alcaide that he still believed in "only One God, the Creator of all things, and One in person only." He also refused to add the *Gloria Patri* to the fifteen Psalms of Ascent which he frequently recited, and repeated the prayers taught him by the Jews of Curacao. He declined to sign his confession on the Jewish Sabbath. At the last moment, however, his courage failed him. He re-accepted the Catholic faith, confessed his sins before the vast crowd which came to see the burning, and begged pardon for the bad example he had given them. For this he was granted the privilege of being strangled before burning (July 25, 1720). To this the chronicler adds: "It must be remembered that no bad odor resulted from the burning, as happens in other cases."

Tried with Pimiento were five Judaizantes: a woman of seventy, with her son of twenty-eight and daughter of nineteen, and two others. Four of them being reconciled were sentenced to perpetual imprisonment and the penitential garb. Of Melchor de Molina, the fifth, it was testified, that he reproached those who wished to start on a journey on the

Sabbath, saying: "Do you not know that the Sabbath, according to our Law, is so sacred that nothing can be done on that day, to such an extent that if one raises his hand to head on the Sabbath in order to scratch himself, his hand retains the position so that he cannot move it till evening?" He was condemned to two hundred lashes, seven years in the galleys, and perpetual imprisonment afterwards.

One of the latest victims of the American Inquisition was Antonio Jose da Silva of Brazil, known as *O Judeo* (the Jew). He was born in Rio de Janeiro in 1705, to a family of zealous Judaizers, and studied law at the University of Coimbra whence he graduated at the age of twenty-one. In the same year he was suspected of Judaizing, was tortured until he became crippled, and was ordered to appear as a penitent at a public Auto-da-fe. Thereafter he devoted himself to literature, produced many popular dramas, and was considered the Portuguese Plautus. But his fame availed him little when he was again suspected of backsliding. He was re-arrested, together with his pregnant young wife, on the testimony of a Negro slave-girl, that he changed his linen and abstained from work on the Sabbath, and observed fasts which were not prescribed by the Church. As he remained negative under torture he was released to the secular arm. In spite of the efforts of many personages of distinction in the political and literary world, and the intervention of the king himself, he was garroted and burned, this on the same day that one of his comedies was produced at the principal theater of Lisbon (October 1, 1739).

The number of processed Judaizers began to decline in the eighteenth century. This was not due to the changed attitude of the Church. In Portugal the Inquisition continued to function till 1821, and in Spain a Judaizing schoolmaster was garroted on July 26, 1826. Nor was it for lack of suspects, for in 1754 a Jesuit priest reported that there were in Buenos Aires alone between four and six thousand Judaizantes. Most likely the Marranos in the New World, like those of the Old, had by that time become more circumspect. Many of them also fled to the inaccessible interior, penetrated into the jungles of Yucatan, and though they sometimes married with the Indians, they clung desperately to the few relics of Judaism stored away in their memories and distorted by time and environment. Others remained within the Church, but retained their love for things Jewish, and waited for an opportunity to proclaim themselves as of the Jewish people. As late as 1919 the South American Zionist Congress held in Buenos Aires received a request from fifty-five persons living in Cura-Cautin to be admitted into the Association. They did not know there were any Jews left in the world. They were mostly small farmers or woodcutters who still celebrated most of the Jewish festivals, spoke of God as *Adonia,* called themselves *Sabbatarios* (Sabbath observers) or *Cabanistas* (dwellers in booths). They were also inspired by the hope that some day they would return to their home in Zion. Remnants of these fugitives are still to be found in various parts of South America. There are about three thousand Jewish Indians in Mexico whose life is no different from the others of the race. Some of them are organized into small congregations with a synagogue and rabbi. Others are being reclaimed and helped to a better knowledge of their Judaism, which became diluted with Catholicism, by the more recent Jewish settlers from Europe. Many kept their Jewishness a secret till after the Mexican Revolution in 1910. They have given their country some of its outstanding leaders. The renowned mural painter Diego Rivera's grandfather was a Spanish nobleman married to a Portuguese Jewess, and his mother was half Spanish and half Indian. In a recent interview he declared: "My Jewishness is a dominant element in my life. Wherever I have gone I have acknowledged myself a Jew. Whatever disabilities our people have suffered I have experienced with them. From this has come my sympathy with the downtrodden masses which motivates all my work." [6]

Early in the seventeenth century, in order to promote the sugar industry, the Dutch Government invited Jewish settlers to the West Indies and offered them, not only freedom of worship but exemption from taxes for a period of seven years, and for twelve years if they established plantations with fifty or more slaveworkers. As a result, many Marranos from Europe and South America began to flock to this new Promised Land. Curacao soon became a Jewish colony, a *Jodenwijk* (Jewish Borough) and foreign powers appointed Jews as their consuls at its port. It also became, according to the complaint of the Inquisition at Cartogana, the "nest of all heretics," and a refuge for those who were discontented with the Spanish rule. In Recife, the present Pernambuco, or *Cais des Judios* (Port of Jews) there were at one time more Jews than Christians. In 1642 they invited Isaac Aboab de Fonseca, "the first American rabbi," to be their spiritual leader. As they were at liberty to convert others to their religion, many of the Negro slave population which in some places was fifteen times as large as the white population were made proselytes to Judaism. According to the census of 1788, there were among one thousand three hundred and eleven white Jews no less than six hundred and fifty Negroes and mulattos, more or less Judaized.

It is interesting to note that despite the treatment these former Marranos received at the hands of the Portuguese, both in the Old World and the New, they retained a love for the land and language of their origin. When, in 1797, a Portuguese ship was seized by a French privateer and put in at Surinam, they welcomed the sailors in their own language, housed and fed them, and sent them back to their native shores, free of expense. This treatment so impressed the Portuguese Government that the Secretary of State addressed the following letter to "Doctor David Nassy and the heads of the Portuguese Nation, residing in Surinam":

> ...I am commanded by His Royal Highness to thank you in his name for this noble deed. His Royal Highness had noted with much pleasure that the Portuguese Jewish nation still remember their former fatherland. It would be pleasing to the Prince if all of them or some should come back to settle again in Portugal, where they would enjoy the greatest security and repose, since under the rule of the august and enlightened Prince who rules over us, none of the causes now exist which formerly necessitated their banishment. [7]

The reception given to the Jewish fugitives from the new
Spain and new Portugal when they landed (1654) on the shores
of New Amsterdam, the present New York, gave little promise
of the bright future which was in store for them in North
America. Peter Stuyvesant, the then Governor had little use
for "the hateful enemies and blasphemers of the name of
Christ." But due to the exertions of the Netherland Jews who
were influential in the affairs of the Dutch West India Company, he reluctantly consented to admit them on condition
that "the poor among them should not be a burden to the
Company or community, but be supported by their own nation." They were also prohibited from holding public services,
or to participate in the duties and privileges of the other citizens.

The Jews, however, were no exception. The mutual anti-
pathies which rendered Old World Christendom an arena in
which each sect sought to exterminate the other, were transplanted into the New. In many instances the prejudice of one
Christian against another of a different sect was, if possible, even
more intense than against the Jew. Peter Stuyvesant, who was
a member of the Dutch Reformed Church, was no less intolerant of Lutherans than of Jews. As regards Roman Catholics,
in 1700 every priest who entered the colony of New York was
in danger of being hanged. As late as 1777 John Jay, who was
of Huguenot stock, attempted to have the Constitution of New
York grant civil and political rights to all, including Jews, "except the professors of the religion of the Church of Rome." [8]

It was the same in the other Colonies. In Puritan Massachusetts, citizenship was denied to all who were not conforming
Puritans. Quakers, not being regarded as "of the people" were
branded, whipped from town to town at the cart's tail till they
reached the boundary and were banished. If apprehended again
they suffered the loss of ears, the mutilation of the tongue, and
death. A similar fate awaited the Baptists, while Catholic
priests were liable to imprisonment for life. In the colonies
where Episcopalianism was the established Church, as in Virginia, Catholics could not own land, or be witnesses in a
court of law, and the children of those who had not been
married by an Anglican priest were regarded as illegitimate.

The most liberal colonies were founded by a convert to Catholicism and a dissident from Puritanism. In Maryland, the Lords Baltimore, who were forbidden to live in Virginia because they would not take the Oath of Supremacy, guaranteed equal rights not only to Catholics but to all citizens including the Jews, and restored to liberty Dr. Jacob Lombroso who, under the Puritan regime, had been convicted for denying the divinity of Jesus (1656). This first attempt at the separation of State and Church was, however, of short duration. Under William and Mary, when the Anglican Church became the State Church of Maryland, Catholics, Quakers, Unitarians, and "pagans" were deprived of their civil rights. It was not until 1826 that the "Jew Bill," initiated by Solomon Etting and Bernard Gratz, was passed by the legislature, and all discriminatory laws against the Jews were at last removed.

Baptist Roger Williams in Puritan Massachusetts, like Catholic Lord Baltimore in Episcopalian Virginia, suffered much for his religious principles. He was anxious to establish a place where people would enjoy "full liberty of religious concernments." He therefore founded Rhode Island, where he hoped, as he stated in the preface to *The Bloody Tenant,* that the following principles would be accepted as self-evident that

> (1) God requireth not an uniformity of Religion to be enacted and enforced in any civil state. (2) It is the will and command of God, that ... a permission of the most Paganish, Jewish, Turkish, or Anti-Christian conscience of worships be granted to all men in all Nations and Countries; and they are only to be fought with that Sword which is only (in Soul matters) able to conquer, to wit, the Sword of God's spirit, the Word of God. (3) True civility and Christianity may both flourish in a state or kingdom, notwithstanding the permission of diverse and contrary consciences, either of Jew or Gentile. [9]

In Rhode Island, indeed, as in Maryland, the experiment at first proved a failure. Catholics were soon deprived of their rights and were not enfranchised until 1784, and no person, who did not profess the Christian religion was admitted into the colony after 1663. But despite these discriminations, there was something in the air of North America which softened religious acerbities and promoted friendships among Jews and Christians. Thus the Reverend Ezra Stiles eulogizes Aaron Lopez, his fellow-citizen of Newport, "whose beneficence . . . to his nation and to all the world is almost without parallel":

> He was my intimate friend and acquaintance! Oh! how often have I wished that sincere, pious and candid mind could have perceived the evidence of Christianity, perceived the truth as it is in Jesus Christ, known that Jesus was the Messiah predicted by Moses and the prophets! The most amiable and excellent characters of a Lopez, a Menasseh b. Israel, of a Socrates, and a Gengenelli (Pope Clement XIV d. 1774) would almost persuade us to hope that their excellency was infused by Heaven and that the virtuous and good and all nations and religions, notwithstanding their delusions, may be brought together in Paradise on the Christian system, finding grace with the all benevolent and adorable Emanuel who with his expiring breath and in his deepest agonies, prayed for those who knew not what they did. [10]

And not even in England did the Puritans so completely identify themselves with the Children of Israel as did those of them who settled in America. In Jewish history they found an adumbration of their own history. They, too, had a "Pharaoh" in James I, an "Egypt" in England, a "Red Sea" in the Atlantic, and a "Canaan" in America. No wonder they accepted the Mosaic Code as binding upon themselves as it was upon Israel. In the colony of New Haven it was ordered (1639) that "the judicial laws of God as they were delivered by Moses ... shall be accounted of moral equity and generally bind all offenders," while in the Plymouth colony it was enacted (1654) that

> It was the great privilege of Israel of old and so was acknowledged by them, Nehemiah the 9th and 10th,

that God gave them right judgments and true Lawes.
They are for the mayne so exemplary, being grounded
on principles of moral equity as that all Christians
especially ought alwaies to have an eye thereunto in
the framing of their politique constitutions. We can
safely say both for ourselves and for them that we have
had an eye principally unto the aforesaid platforme in
the framing of this small body of Lawes.

While the Puritans conformed to many of the Mosaic regulations outwardly, the Quakers, who first made their unwel-
come appearance in Massachusetts in 1656 (and were promptly
thrown into prison till they should be deported) came to
make America a home for the Friends as well as for all the
oppressed and persecuted. The opportunity came when William Penn, who next to Fox was the most distinguished Quaker,
obtained a grant of land with the right to make all necessary
laws. Penn proceeded at once to try his "Holy Experiment,"
and in 1683 laid out the city which he named Philadelphia or
Brotherly Love. In it, as in the rest of the colony of Penn-
sylvania, equal justice was extended to all regardless of race or
religion. A treaty of peace was made with the Indians who were
paid fairly for their land, and slaves were emancipated after
fourteen years' service so that by the end of the eighteenth
century slavery was practically extinct among the Friends. The
success of this Holy Experiment drew a steady stream of
Friends from the mother country, who gradually spread all
over the land. Penn was also instrumental in introducing religious and political freedom into New Jersey, and was associated with John Locke in drawing up a charter for Carolina,
providing that "heathens," Jews, and other dissenters from the
purity of Christian religion," be given the same rights as the
rest of the population.

The trend of liberalism and regard for social justice continued to grow with the passing years. Even among the more
orthodox sects it was felt that the Hebraic rule (Num. 15:16),
"One law and one ordinance shall be both for you and for the
stranger that sojourneth with you," should be adopted as a

basic principle. George Washington objected even to the word
toleration, suggesting as it does that it is "by the indulgence
of one class of people that another enjoyed all the exercise of
their inherent rights." The height of liberality was attained
when the State not only divorced itself from the Church, but
declared, as did the Senate of the United States, that "the Government of the United States of America is not, in any sense,
founded on the Christian religion." [11]

The leading spirits of the Revolution period were as a
rule religious liberals. Paine and Jefferson were probably Deists.
Benjamin Franklin's credo, as he tells us in his *Autobiography,*
was that there is "One God Who made and governs all things,
and Whose most acceptable service is doing good to man."
But the greatest progress was made by Unitarians of whom the
Adamses and Madison were the chief exponents. Priestley's attacks on the orthodox theology were everywhere read with
approval. In New England all reference to the Trinity was
eliminated from the ritual of the Episcopalian King's Chapel.
A Salem rector, who continued to read the Athanasian Creed
despite his known views, justified himself by saying, "I read
it as if I did not believe it." Channing pronounced the doctrines of Atonement as a "gallows erected at the center of the
universe for the public execution of a god." Emerson's *Divinity
School Address* (1826) and Parker's *Transient and Permanent
in Christian Theology* (1841) found an echo in many a conservative house of worship. The ablest and most eloquent ministers, the students who returned from Cambridge and Oxford,
most of the leaders in literature, education, and social welfare,
organized themselves into groups which published periodicals
and issued tracts in which the supernatural character of the
person and office of Jesus was unequivocally rejected and his
humanity alone stressed. Their Christianity was no longer "a
religion about Jesus but the religion of Jesus, which is summed
up in love to God and love to man." The view has been increas-
ingly gaining ground among many Christians that the sole
criterion for admission into the Christian brotherhood should
be not what a man thinks of Christ but whether he leads the
Christ-like life. [12]

With the discontinuance of the persecutions by Church and State, scores of new sects came into being, all of them reactions to some episode, or teaching, or suggestion found in the Old Testament. There are, or were, for instance, the Shakers, who taught that God is bisexual, because according to the Bible he created male and female "in his image." They worshiped with dancing and shaking of the entire body, even as David did when he brought back the Holy Ark (I Sam. 6:16). There are those of the "True Church of God" who, to demonstrate the truth of the words of St. Mark (16:17-8), expose themselves to the bites of venomous snakes, and drink poison and hold in their hands a red hot iron, just to prove the strength of their faith; and there are those of the Christian Science cult who teach that evil and sickness are delusions which can be dispelled by a true knowledge of God. It remained for a certain Joseph Smith, the son of a Vermont farmer, to connect the Bible with the aborigines of America, and to add still another volume to the sacred Scriptures, *The Book of Mormon* (first published at Palmyra, 1930).[13]

The bearer of this new revelation who felt called upon to begin the ingathering of Israel foretold by Isaiah (11:10-6) was an unlettered youth to whom a celestial messenger by the name of Moroni disclosed, in 1823, that God had a great work for him to perform. It was nothing less than the translation of a volume containing the fullness of the Gospel of Christ as he taught it, after his resurrection, to the Nephites, a branch of the House of Israel which settled in America ages before its discovery by Columbus. This record was for centuries buried in a hill called Cumorah and when Smith unearthed it, it was engraved on plates of gold covered with characters in the "reformed Egyptian tongue," and the Urim and Thumim by means of which they were to be translated into English.

According to the Book of Mormon, America was populated by two great waves of immigration; the first was by the Jaredites, who arrived after the confusion of tongues which followed the building of the Tower of Babel and who settled between the Gulf of California and the Isthmus of Panama. The Nephites came from Jerusalem just prior to the Babylonian captivity and landed on the coast of Chile. They came here because it was destined to be the Land of Zion, choice of all other lands, where a New Jerusalem would be built by the ingathered Israelites prior to the second coming of the Messiah.

The Nephites grew to be a great and prosperous people, but after the death of the Prophet Lehi, of the tribe of Ephraim, they split into two hostile camps with regard to his successor. Internecine war reduced their numbers and impoverished their culture. They became spiritually benighted, and even dark in appearance, and when they were rediscovered, their degenerate descendants were found to be a horde of savage Indians, or the "Lamanites."

Among the articles of faith, formulated by Joseph Smith, the prophet and revealer of the Latter Day Saints, were the belief that men would be punished for their own sins, and not for Adam's transgression; that the Book of Mormon is equally, with the Bible, the word of God; that there is to be a literal gathering of Israel and a restoration of the Ten Lost Tribes, that Christ would reign personally upon the earth, and "that the earth will be renewed and receive its paradisaic form." Another principle of the creed of the Mormons is that marriage is necessary for the salvation of women and the perfection of men, and that the glory of the saints is in proportion to the number of their children, since they provide abodes for spirits who long to be embodied. [14]

Joseph Smith is represented as the lineal descendant of Joseph of old, ordained to the Aaronic and Melchizedek priesthood by the Apostles Peter, James and John. His work is said to have been prophetically indicated by David when he sang (Ps. 85:11): "Truth shall spring out of the earth," by Isaiah when he exclaimed (45:8): "Let the earth open that they may bring forth salvation," and by Ezekiel when he joined together the stick of Judah and the stick of Joseph (37:15-20) in a hint of the union of the Book of Mormon with the Judean Bible.

By all the numerous sects which from time to time appeared and disappeared, flourished under persecution and wilted in the sunshine of tolerance, the Jews were affected the least.

Some conversions there naturally took place before as after the Revolution. Under British rule we hear of Isaac Miranda, an "apostate Jew or fashionable Christian proselyte," who was a judge in the Court of Vice-Admiralty; and of Judah Monis who, after his baptism, taught Hebrew at Harvard and wrote the first Hebrew grammar published in America (1735). There was also a Reverend Mr. Hideck (or Heidek), "the lately converted Jewish rabbi," who went from Charleston, South Carolina, to convert the Cherokees to Christianity, who had the belief that the American Indians were the Lost Ten Tribes of Hebrews. After the Revolution the number of those who drifted into the various denominations became more and more limited to foreign-born "Hebrew Missionaries," who labor with hardly any success or to those who seek an escape from the still prevailing prejudice against Jews into the fashionable Episcopalian or the more Hebraic Unitarian sect. Of the estimated one hundred and fifty thousand Jewish converts to Christianity during the last hundred and fifty years, few if any became Catholics save through intermarriage, while by far the largest number joined the Christian Scientists.

On the other hand, though the Jews refrained from propaganda for their faith, a number of Christians accepted Judaism and in some communities the most zealous workers in behalf of the faith of Israel are born Christians who became "Proselytes of Righteousness".

Already at the beginning of the nineteenth century the question of proselytism came up for discussion at a meeting of the K. K. Beth Elohim Congregation of Charleston, South Carolina, and a resolution was embodied in its Constitution of 1820:

> The Congregation will not encourage nor interfere with making proselytes under any pretense whatever, nor shall any such be admitted under the jurisdiction of the Congregation, until he, or she, or they, produce legal and satisfactory credentials, from some other Congregation, where a regular Chief, or Rabbi and Hebrew Consistory is established, and, provided he, or she, or they, are not people of color.

The political reaction which followed the German abortive revolution of 1848 had a telling effect on American proselytism. Many Jews and Christians were forced to seek refuge in the United States, most of them liberals in religion as in politics. Here their common suffering and struggles as immigrants in their new home, as well as their common language and culture, bridged over the gulf created by their ancestral faith. Intermarriage became frequent, the children in many instances were raised as Jews, and sometimes even adults accepted the religion of Israel. Rabbis reported from various parts of the country that they were approached by Christians with a view to their conversion to Judaism. "There is perhaps no other country in the world," wrote Rabbi Illoway in 1865, "where the Hebrew communities are so frequently increased by numbers of proselytes as in this country." [15]

The problem of proselytism to Judaism was at last taken up at the rabbinical conference held in Philadelphia in 1869. It was recognized that in the United States Judaism has a golden opportunity to gain converts if it would but remove the obstacle of circumcision which keeps back many males from seeking admittance into the House of Israel. After various conferences, at which the question was argued, the rabbinical conference held in New York City put itself on record that it

> ... considers it lawful and proper for any officiating rabbi, assisted by no less than two associates, and in the name and with the consent of his congregation, to accept into the sacred covenant of Israel, and declare fully affiliated with the congregation any honorable and intelligent person who desires such affiliation, without any initiatory rite, ceremony, or observance whatever; provided such person be sufficiently acquainted with the faith, doctrine, and religious usages of Israel; that nothing derogatory to such person's moral and mental character is suspected; that it is his or her free will and choice to embrace the cause of Judaism, and that he or she declare verbally, and in a document signed and sealed before such officiating

rabbi and his associates, his or her intention and firm resolve—

1. To worship the One Sole and Eternal God and none besides Him.

2. To be conscientiously governed in his or her doings and omissions in life by God's laws, ordained for the child and image of the Father and Maker of all, the sanctified son or daughter of the divine covenant.

3. To adhere in life and death, actively and faithfully, to the sacred cause and mission of Israel, as marked out in Holy Writ. [16]

The rabbis, especially those of the Reform wing of Judaism, were very optimistic as regards the ultimate spread of their religion. R. Isaac M. Wise, an opponent of Zionism, was convinced that "the teachings of Reform Judaism will be the religion of the twentieth century." Rabbi Barnard Felsenthal, an ardent Zionist, also was sure that "through the silent innate power of divine Judaism, through the writings of inspired leaders in Israel, yes, even through the mere fact of our existence, we shall exert an influence upon the religious development of the world." With this in view, the Union of American Hebrew Congregations has undertaken the publication of tracts, and the Anglo-Jewish press is printing articles elucidating the main teachings of the faith, and the Jewish Chautauqua Society is giving courses in Judaism at various higher institutions of learning all over the land.

The Sunday services introduced by various congregations were reported "in almost every instance," to be attended "by a considerable number of non-Jews, who in that way are given enlightenment on Jews and Judaism, and are afforded an opportunity for possessing themselves of our conception of religion."

More perhaps than any efforts of the rabbis is the contribution made by intermarriage to swell the number of proselytes to Judaism in the New World. Among the earliest proselytes in this country was Elizabeth Whitlock. She married Moses Mordecai, one of the signers of the Non-importation Resolution and, after his death, became the wife of Jacob I. Cohen of Richmond, Virginia. One of her sons, Jacob Mordecai, was a partner of Haym Salomon, the financier of the Revolution. [17]

Early in 1806 Jeanette Picken, the beautiful and talented daughter of a Philadelphia school-mistress, met Abraham Hyman Cohen, son of the "Jewish priest" of Philadelphia's Mikveh Israel synagogue at the home of a mutual Christian friend, and the young folks fell deeply in love with each other. Fearing the possible consequences, young Cohen was summoned before the Trustees of the Congregation and was made to promise under oath that he would marry only within the faith. Thereupon Miss Picken declared herself willing to become a Jewess, and after spending thirty days in the home of a Jewish family where she was "instructed in the rites and ceremonies of the Jewish household duties, with dietetical prohibitions," she was then formally admitted into the Jewish faith. Shortly thereafter, as Sarah Jeanette, she was married to Abraham Cohen "according to the law of Moses and Israel." Sarah found the Jewish rites and ceremonies very admirable, and saw in the Jewish religion "nothing but what the most devout Christian could conform to." But at the birth of her first son, she felt compunction about inducting him into the Covenant of Abraham, and when he died in 1814 she was told by her Christian friends that his death was a punishment for her abandoning Christianity. This preyed on her mind to the extent that she became ill, saw visions of a frowning Christ, and heard the angels in Paradise sing: "Though thy sins be as scarlet they shall be white as wool." When her second child Henry Luria also died, she broke with Judaism and after several years left her husband with three of her four daughters, one of whom later married a Jew, and remained in the Jewish fold. Her husband died in Richmond, where he officiated as minister of Congregation Beth Shalom.

Some years later the former Jeanette Picken, or "S. J. Cohen," as she signed herself, wrote a little book entitled *Henry Luria; or, the Little Jewish Convert,* to caution the young against "their entering into a union where great disparity exists, especially in religious matters." In it she pleads:

> Take warning by what I write; let my example, my sufferings and sorrow, be the beacon light to guard you from such dangers. Not that I write this in any bitterness of feeling, for I have experienced all kindness and affection from the Jewish people, and especially those of my husband's kindred, of whom many are still living in Baltimore, Philadelphia, South Carolina, Georgia, etc., and some holding high positions, an honor to their name, religion and country. I love them still, fondly love them, as a part of that nation to which my dear husband belonged, to which he clung with undying tenacity during his life, and with his last breath reiterated, 'Shamong! Israel! [18]

At about the same time a Christian woman of Philadelphia was thus repenting her entrance into Judaism, a Jewish woman of Charleston, South Carolina, was doing her penance for her acceptance of Christianity. As a young girl she fell in love with a Christian young man and embraced his religion. For some reason, she soon regretted the step she took. When she decided to go back to her faith and her people, she sent the following petition to the Board of Trustees of K. K. Beth Elohim, of Charleston:

Gentlemen:

> Relying on your generous sympathy with one, who though she committed a great error, appears now before you a penitent, I take the liberty to request your aid in reinstating me in the religion of my forefathers. You are aware, Gentlemen, that some twelve years ago, I abandoned the religion of my forefathers and became a Christian. I was then young and inexperienced, living entirely among a Christian community, all of which overcame my understanding and I took the step of which I have for the last six years deeply repented. I am convinced of the truth of our holy religion, and

it is my utmost desire again to worship with you at the same altar, at which your and my ancestors worshiped, and am willing to undergo any penalty you may feel inclined to inflict. As the representatives of a Congregation who are Israelites and who believe in that sacred Law of Moses, which commands kindness and charity to all mankind,—in the name of that God Who revealed Himself to His chosen people, I conjure you not to dismiss a penitent, but to receive her as one who went astray and is anxious to return to her flock.

With my best reliance on your generous sympathy,

I remain, yours

(signed) ....

Her petition was granted, and after going through the formality of having the story of her relapse told during the Sabbath services, she was re-admitted into the synagogue and lived to a good old age, a happy and respected member of the Jewish community. [19]

There are many who claim that Adah Isaacs Menken (1835-68) was born Adelaide McCord, the daughter of James McCord, a merchant of Millemburg, Louisiana. If this be true, then she was one of the most remarkable of women proselytes to Judaism. Her fascinating personality won her the admiration of men like Charles Dickens, Charles Read, and Victor Hugo, Algernon Swinburne, and Alexander Dumas. Her career as an actress, dancer, and adventuress was amazing. She appeared with such stars as Edwin Booth, James Hackett, and James Murdock; and, as Mazeppa, she thrilled Europe and America. On her marriage, in 1856, to Alexander Isaacs Menken, she also assumed the biblical name Adah. Her devotion to her new faith and people she beautifully and passionately expressed in a poem, "Hear, O Israel!" included in her book *Infelicia,* dedicated to Charles Dickens. She also studied Hebrew, and wrote many articles on Jewish topics for *The American Israelite.* It is said that she never forgot to light her Sabbath candles, and that the rabbi who attended her before she expired found a Hebrew Bible under her pillow. She was buried in Paris in the Pere LaChaise cemetery, where also lies Rachel the tragedienne, and on her simple slab was inscribed: "Thou Knowest." Together with Sarah Bernhardt, whose Jewish ancestry is also disputed, she is included by David Belasco among the "Fifty Best Actors and Actresses that Ever Lived," and Clement Wood gives her a high place in his *Poets of America.* [20]

The one who will go down in American Jewish history as the *Ger Zedek par excellence* is undoubtedly Warder Cresson (1798-1860), a well-to-do Quaker of Philadelphia. A student of the Bible, he became deeply interested in the people of the Book, and at the age of thirty wrote *Babylon the Great Is Falling,* against Catholicism. Through the influence of the missionaries who were laboring among the Jews and Mohammedans in the Holy Land, he was appointed as the first American Consul in Jerusalem (1844).

In Palestine Cresson's Jewish sympathies became more and more pronounced, and instead of spreading Christianity among the Jews he severely criticized the methods of the missionaries. Before long he became intimate with the prominent rabbis of the community, took up the study of Hebrew, acquired a familiarity with the Talmud and the *Zohar,* and at the age of fifty (1848), he formally entered the Covenant of Abraham, under the name of Michael C. Boaz Israel.

His conversion to Judaism caused a stir in Philadelphia. When he returned there to settle his affairs, many would stop to gaze at him as he took his daily walk to offer his devotions at the synagogue. His family, with the exception of one son who joined him, turned against him and regarded him as mentally unbalanced. A commission in lunacy had him placed in an asylum for the insane. Cresson appealed to the higher court. Over one hundred witnesses among them physicians and psychiatrists, and members of the missionary society were heard. The pros and cons of this unusual case were discussed by the press of the country. The Supreme Court finally declared him to be sane and sound, and reversed the decision of the lower court. Cresson then disposed of his property, leaving most of it to his family, and went back to Jerusalem.

In Jerusalem Cresson adopted the habit of a Sefardic Jew, married into a prominent Sefardic family, and "The American *Ger Zedek*" became a leader of the Jewish community. By many he was regarded as a saint. Appeals were made to him to intercede, by his prayers, for the suffering and the sick, and stories became current among the masses of his ability to perform miracles. When he died, November 6, 1860, all the places of business in Jerusalem were closed, and the entire Jewish community followed after his coffin. He was buried on the Mount of Olives, and his grave has become a shrine to which many repair to offer prayers.

Cresson was a militant Jew and wrote various tracts and articles denouncing the missionary efforts to convert Jews to Christianity. In the history of Zionism he will be remembered as one of the very first, if not the first, who advocated the founding of Jewish agricultural colonies in Palestine. He made many appeals to the Jews of the world and himself established a colony in the vicinity of Jerusalem. He felt that "All that is now wanted is a sufficient sum of money to commence with, and then, willing, industrious hearts and hands, and all will go well, and peace and plenty will soon succeed the present state of poverty and suffering."

There is a record of a certain Warder Cresson, Jr., who as a child had been converted with his father, studied the Talmud in Polish *yeshibot,* was appointed *dayyan* (assistant rabbi), and became famed as a *lamdan* (scholar). He may have been the son or son of the son of the above mentioned Warder who sided with his father when the rest of the family preferred to have him pronounced insane rather than see him a follower of the faith of Israel. [21]

The *Occident,* a periodical published in Philadelphia from 1843 to 1869, contains numerous references to Christian converts to Judaism. One of them reads:

As we stopped for a few hours at Baltimore on our journey southward, on the 27th of February (1855) we learned that a young man from Germany had been accepted and received as a proselyte on that very day. We understand that he was admitted only after a long and careful probation.... There is, by the by, a worthy proselyte residing in Baltimore, who joined our standard at Amsterdam, some years ago. He had been connected with a missionary society we think at Basel, Switzerland, and in this strange school he learned to appreciate the truth of our religion, of which he has been a humble and consistent follower ever since. He is called Abraham Rump, and his name deserves to be put in record, that he may be remembered among those who shall be for a memorial in the house of God. [22]

In the same city, one of the leading families which contributed to our country some of its most noted physicians, and to American Israel some of its most illustrious leaders, is descended, on the mother's side, "a non-Jew, a German of a family of distinction in the state of Hanover who was converted to Judaism." [23]

The wave of immigrants which swept over the United States after the Russian pogroms in the early eighties of the nineteenth century contained not only Jews but also Russian and Polish Christians, many of them Subbotniki, to whom reference has already been made. In the old country they felt closer to Jews than to Christians and frequently accepted the Jewish religion after their arrival in America. Others drifted into the so-called Ghetto whose denizens spoke or understood their language and were accustomed to the same mode of living. They found a cordial welcome among those who had every reason to bear a grudge against everything Russian or Polish. They were given work in their sweat shops and factories, they drank tea with them from their samovars in their homes; and when they brought over the other members of their families they were helped by the Hebrew Immigrant Aid Society which frequently also provided them with shelter and comfort on their arrival. Many of these Slavonians benevolently assimilated to the extent of adopting the Yiddish dialect, sometimes even the Jewish religion.

Another group which sometimes supplies *gerim* is the Italian, many of whose members follow similar occupations as Jews, especially in the needle industry. Intermarriage between Italians and Jews is not unusual. But conversions also are recorded in which the love element played no part. Thus we read of one Peteriglicini, of Corona, Long Island, who had himself and his three sons, ranging in age from three to seven, circumcised at the Beth Israel Hospital in 1915. [24]

Conversions, however, are limited neither to immigrants, nor to Slavs and Italians. The spiritual unrest which produced in the United States alone, during the brief period of its nationhood, more sects than during the entire history of Christianity, prompted many of the native as well as of the foreign born to seek refuge in Judaism. The reasons are as various as they were in the days of the Sages of the Talmud. Some of them were: "Proselytes of love," some "Proselytes of dreams," some because they found in Judaism the only religion which satisfied their thirst for the Living God, and afforded them the spiritual comfort they craved. It is hardly feasible to enumerate them all. We shall cull only the few stories which have more or less human interest, as they appeared in the American Jewish press in recent years.

In the *Yiddisher Tageblatt* of about a quarter of a century ago, there is a report of three conversions which took place almost simultaneously. One proselyte was a Turk, who accepted the Jewish faith in the presence of two hundred people. After the operation he delivered an edifying talk in the manner of an old fashioned *maggid* (preacher), based on the text (Ex. 15:26): "If thou wilt diligently harken to the voice of the Lord thy God ... I will put none of the diseases upon thee, which I have put upon the Egyptians; for I am the Lord that healeth thee." Another was a German Lutheran who became a Baptist, then a Seventh Day Adventist, and finally concluded "that there is but one God, and that is the Jewish God." The third was Rufus L. Perry, a Negro lawyer of Brooklyn, whose thesis in French on *Human Dignity According to the Concep-*

tion of the Talmudists earned him a gold medal, and a membership in the *Societé Academique d'Historie Internationale.*[25]

The latter part of 1923 has quite a record for proselytes. On September 4, there was the conversion in New York of McDonald, an Irishman, in his early twenties. On the 5th, several conversions took place in Boston. On the 6th, the wedding ceremony was celebrated of one whose mother was herself a convert, but refused to give her consent to the marriage until the prospective bride became a Jewess. On the 27th, a young American woman embraced Judaism at Sinai Temple in San Francisco, while a French girl did the same in another part of the country. Before the year was over, a woman and her two children were converted in Troy, New York. An Irishman who wished to become as good a Jew as any, insisted, when he abandoned Catholicism for Judaism, on changing not only his Christian name but also his patronym from Healy to Schwartz! Similarly, according to the New York Law Journal, a man named Edwards changed it to Ulman, stating: "I wish to cast my lot with the people of my mother's faith. . . . I want to live unequivocally and without reservation of any kind as a member of the Jewish faith." [26]

In Detroit, Kalman Wagner reverted to Judaism and converted his Christian family because of a dream. As an orphan child of seven he had been taken in by a Christian minister, raised as a Christian, became the organist of his benefactor's church, and married his daughter. Ten years later he dreamed that his father reproached him for not remaining in his faith. He told the dream to his wife, and the entire family officially accepted the Jewish religion and assumed biblical names (1916). A woman of Burlington, Vermont, who first discovered that she was of Jewish birth at the age of forty-two, writes to the editor of a Jewish daily: "All my life I have been drawn to the Jewish religion of my father with my whole heart. . . . I am willing to give up everything for the faith which I claim to be mine. I can't seem to be able to use just the right words to express the longing that is in my heart. But I hope that you can interpret my feeling."[27]

The call of family tie led to the conversion of an Italian

Christian to the religion of his son. One day a woman came
to the Yeshibah Torah Hayyim of East New York and begged
that her son of ten be admitted as a student of that institution.
The boy proved to be a bright and studious lad, and made
rapid progress in his Hebrew studies. His devotion to Judaism
infected his father, and on the same day when Michael celebrated his *Bar Mitzvah*, Vincent became a full-fledged Jew. [28]

A more pathetic story is that of Henry Hirschfield, whose
father, a convert to Christianity, married the daughter of a
Polish landowner and reared his children in the Catholic faith.
When he arrived in the United States at the age of seventeen, he lived as a Jew, married a Jewess, and raised his family
as Jews. But the thought that in Warsaw his official status
was that of a Christian preyed on his mind, and at seventy-
seven he made the six thousand mile trip to the Polish capitol
to correct the record. The rabbinate accepted his application
for his reinstatement into Judaism. But before the issuance of
the Government certificate, he died at the home of his Catholic
brother and was buried in the Catholic cemetery. [29]

As against these *Gerim Gerurim,* as the Sages of the Talmud
would have called them, we read of numerous proselytes who
adopted Judaism for its own sake. Indeed, in many a community in the United States some of the strictest observers of
Jewish ceremonies and of the most zealous laborers in the
vineyard of Judaism happen to be born Christians. Mrs. William B. Ziff, the daughter of a Protestant minister, after her
conversion, went with her children to Palestine to raise them
in a strictly Jewish atmosphere. Mrs. Jennie C. Donley, of Cold
Water, Michigan, who has been instrumental in the conversion
of other members of her family, writes a year after her conversion:

> The past year has been the best of my life. It seems
> as if I have entered another new world. It would be
> the greatest privilege to worship with the 'Chosen of
> God,' but has never been possible, and in this my soul
> is afflicted. Yet the Lord is ever near, and His Sabbaths
> bring sweetest rest. I am seeking the Lord with all my

heart. Pray for me, my dear rabbi, that He may search
my heart and give me wisdom to understand His
teachings, for I am so ignorant and so unworthy of
the least of His blessings, and He bestows so many
upon me and fills my soul with His glory. I have met
these Jewish people and they are fine, like all Israel,
and a blessing. I have renewed my membership in the
Jewish Publication Society. The pamphlet of Sermons
you sent me last year brought me great joy. I read
them again and again. Can you tell me where I can
get the sermons for this year? You know I never *hear*
a sermon, but it is a wonderful blessing to read them.
I cannot number the blessings I have received through
Israel. It is no use for me to try to enlighten the people.
I had better just worship God. He does the work. I
lend my literature to those who are willing to read
it. [30]

American Jews, like their French coreligionists, can boast of
at least one Catholic priest who openly proclaimed his preference for Judaism. In a series of articles which appeared in
translation in one of the Yiddish papers Father Duffy presents
an *apologia pro vita sua*. He expresses his unstinted admiration of the Church whose loyal son he had been for a period
of sixteen years, and the self-sacrificing labors of her consecrated men and women. But he could no longer conscientiously subscribe to the dogmas upon which she insists depends
one's salvation. The pomp and splendor of the Eucharist Congress in Chicago broke down his last reluctance to leave the
faith of his fathers, and after trying out various Christian
sects he finally found peace and comfort in the shadow of
the synagogue. [31]

In America some of the fairest appreciations of Judaism were
written by Christians. Foremost among them is the work of
Professor George Foote Moore of Harvard, whose *Judaism*
(1930) is perhaps the best exposition on that subject ever written, and of Professor William Orton of Smith College, who
finds in the ethics of Judaism, the outgrowth of "experience and

history, not out of metaphysics and theology," a challenge to the modern world. The article on Jesus in the *Universal Jewish Encyclopedia* is written by Dr. R. Travers Herford, the author of works on the Talmud and the Pharisees, and is so unorthodox from a Christian point of view that he is taken to task by a Jewish apostate for being a *Shabbos Goy* (a Gentile employed by Jews to do their chores on the Sabbath). In America, too, some leading lights in the literary, scientific, and artistic world openly joined the Congregation of Israel. Temple Ohabei Shalom of Boston numbers among its most faithful members another professor of Harvard and his wife, a near relative of a bishop, both of whom possess "an amazing fund of Jewish learning," according to the rabbi who converted them. They participate regularly in the services, and take an active part in the affairs of the Brotherhood and Sisterhood of the Congregation. Peter J. Walter, the artist, who was raised a Catholic, became a Jew and brought up his children in the Jewish faith. In 1929 he decided to make his conversion public, and, in accordance with the Orthodox Jewish requirement, remarried his Jewish wife three months later, according to "the Law of Moses and Israel." Constance Gideon, of Scotch descent, became a proselyte to Judaism after her marriage to Henry Gideon. She has been collaborating with her husband in interpreting Yiddish folk-songs, and her collection, "From the Cradle to the *Chuppe*," reveals a profound sympathy with and penetration into the soul of the Jewish people. The wife of Naphtali Herz Imber, author of the *Hatikvah*, has the distinction of having inspired one of his Hebrew doggerels:

> Thou saidst like Ruth:
>> 'Thy people, thy God, are mine';
> So I said unto thee:
>> 'Peace, so is my life thine.'[32]

A Ruth of a different type is Ella MacKenna Friend, wife of the noted portrait painter Leo Mielziner, and mother of Jo Mielziner, the scenic artist of the Theatre Guild, and Kenneth MacKenna, the actor,—whose biography of Professor Moses Mielziner of the Hebrew Union College is an important contribution to American Jewish literature. In the film world there is Norma Shearer, the widow of Irving Thalberg, of the Metro-Goldwyn-Mayer Corporation. She is a member of the B'nai B'rith Synagogue of Los Angeles, and a faithful observer of Jewish rites. So also is Agnes Wayburn, who, before she became Mrs. Schlessinger, was a member of the famous Floradora Sextet.[33]

There is a story of a certain Israel Rosenberg who made his way to the Hawaiian Islands (1887) and attracted the attention of the reigning prince, David Kalakana. His Majesty is said to have become so interested in Judaism that he began to study Hebrew, so as to be able to read from the *Sefer Torah* which "Rosey," as the natives called him, brought with him. He also granted him a tract of land for the purpose of establishing a synagogue in Honolulu. "Rabbi Rosey," however, disappeared as mysteriously as he arrived, and the only mark he left behind is the Sefer Torah which Princess Kawananakoa keeps among her most treasured possessions, and lends to the Jewish community for use during their services.[34]

It remained for the Negro race to add its ingredient to the melting pot of American Israel. That some of the slaves held by Jews of the South adopted the religion of their masters is indicated by the above-mentioned resolution of the Charleston, South Carolina, Congregation not to admit "people of color" into its membership. Until quite recently one could still meet a colored man or woman who tried to the best of his knowledge to observe the Sabbath and Jewish festivals. It was not, however, until the beginning of the twentieth century that the United States was to witness the remarkable sight of Negroes embracing Judaism *en masse.*

The first colored Jewish congregation in the United States was founded in 1899, when Rabbi Leon Richlieu, an Ethiopian, founded the Moorish Zion Temple. His services were attended by many Negroes and before long they declared themselves of the Jewish faith. Their numbers were swelled by Judaized Negroes from the West Indies, and Negro-Jewish congregations were organized in Chicago, Cleveland, Newark, Youngstown, Asbury Park, and other places. Now in "Little Africa" in Harlem alone their membership is estimated to be over two thousand, and as they are more missionary-minded than their white coreligionists, their numbers are steadily growing. The "Congregation of the Commandment Keepers," which has Chief Rabbi A. W. Matthews as its rabbi, recognizes Jesus but only as one of the Prophets. On the other hand the members of the Kahal B'nai Abraham, under the leadership of Rabbi A. Isaiah Ford, are strict observers of all the ceremonies of the Jewish religion. They accept none into the fold before his record is investigated, and only after he has received an intensive course in the teachings of Judaism.

The relation of the white Jews to their dark coreligionists is rather cordial at times. Some of the white Jews contribute towards the support of their institutions, accept their children in their Talmud Torah, and some send their own children into the Hebrew schools of their darker brethren. Except for the natural disinclination to intermarriage, they show that among Jews the bond of religion often transcends the difference of race. Colored pupils have sometimes been singled out for special distinction in white Talmud Torahs. At the commencement exercises of the Institutional Synagogue Hebrew School, Vertella S. Valentine, a Negro Jewess, was valedictorian of a large class of white Jewish graduates. Among some Negroes the belief is prevalent that by accepting Judaism they are merely returning to the religion of their forefathers who were of the Tribe of Judah, and that the white Jews are the offspring of the Ten Lost Tribes. Some also claim that their first patriarch Ham, like his brother Shem, was a Jew by conviction. All of them, however, identify themselves with the hopes and aspirations of the white Jews, participate in the activities of Zionism, and feel with the victims of Nazism. Rabbi David Kohl, of the *Chevrah Anshe Sh'horim* (Society of Black Men) of Cleveland, exhorts his flock thus:

You are Jews. Judaism is your religion and Hebrew is your language. For these past four hundred years you have been worshipping foreign gods and you have been ground down into subjugation. You have been among strangers all these years. The white Jew, too, has been among strangers. He has been in Golus. Study his history and you will see that he has had pogroms in Russia, Poland, and throughout Europe just as the Negro has had burnings and lynchings in the South. The Jew and the Negro must welcome each other, for the Jew is the best friend that the Negro has. ... The time has come to break the yoke! to join hands with Jacob and shout: *'Shema Yisrael, Adoshem Elokenu, Adoshem Echad!'* [35]

We have recounted the history of Gentile-Jewish relations and their special bearing upon proselytes from earliest times to the present. [36] We have found it necessary to pursue our paths horizontally and vertically. In the course of our researches, we reckoned, to a great degree, with the Jews, both as a people on their own soil (twice before in Jewish history) and as a scattered folk in many parts of the world and among other and diverse peoples. Whenever possible we permitted the documentary material to speak for itself.

In these times, when the Jewish people has undergone so cataclysmic an experience, it is tempting to try to conjecture the future course in this unbroken thread of Gentile-Jewish relations. Geographically, Palestine was always at the juncture of three great continents, historically it was the cradle of the three great monotheistic religions. Even before the establishment of the State of Israel, Palestine was the meeting place of many peoples. Today, with the permanent political and sovereign status of so many of the erstwhile scattered people of Israel, it may not be too much to envisage Israel as the instrument, par excellence, in the convergence, borrowing and interplay of ideas as well as of commerce between East and West. It seems in place to ask, What changes, if any, may we expect from the non-Christian peoples now resident in Israel, in their attitude toward historical Christianity? May we not anticipate a more sympathetic, historical, and even scientific appreciation of the ethical and moral nuances in Christian thought? On the other bank of the stream, it is not too much to look for a renewal of former historical approaches and a widening of Christian use of the old and the new, and even of more recent ethical and religious emphasis. As for the Arabs, whose medieval ancestors were leaders of, and partners with, the Jews in much of the transmission of the ideas of the East to the countries of the West, it certainly can be hoped that their commingling as equal citizens in the new democratic State of Israel will help to renew former intellectual relations and that the give and take between Arabs and Jews will redound to the benefit of the entire Near East and all its peoples.

THE END

NOTES

NOTES

(Editor's Comment: It is remarkable that under the strain of his illness the late Rabbi Raisin could muster the determination and drive necessary to complete this large work. The present editor was informed that our author wrote out the footnotes in the last days of his illness. All bracketed statements in these notes, made necessary in many cases because of the incompleteness of the footnotes, are those of the editor. It is to be noted, however, that a large sampling of the documentation and of the references to sources indicated that the work was done thoroughly and conscientiously.)

EDITOR'S PREFACE

1. Herman Hailperin, "Intellectual Relations Between Jews and Christians in Europe Before 1500, Described Mainly According to the Evidences of Biblical Exegesis, With Special Reference to Rashi and Nicolas de Lyra," *University of Pittsburgh Bulletin, The Graduate School, Abstracts of Theses,* (Pittsburgh, 1933), Vol. IX, pp. 128-145. See also Hailperin, Review of Beryl Smalley, *Hebrew Scholarship Among Christians in XIIIth Century England as Illustrated by Some Hebrew-Latin Psalters,* in *Historia Judaica,* Vol. II, pp. 122-125 (1940); also Hailperin, "Nicolas De Lyra and Rashi: The Minor Prophets", *Rashi Anniversary Volume* (New York, 1941), pp. 115-147; Hailperin, "Saadia's Relation to Islamic and Christian Thought", *Historia Judaica,* Vol. IV, (1942), pp. 1-15; *Ibid.,* "Jewish 'Influence' on Christian Biblical Scholars in the Middle Ages", pp. 163-174; Hailperin, "The Hebrew Heritage of Mediaeval Christian Biblical Scholarship," *Historia Judaica,* Vol. V, (1943), pp. 133-154; see also, by the same author, five lectures on Maimonides in *A Rabbi Teaches.* (New York, 1939), pp. 105-171.

2. Among older works may be cited H. Graetz, *Die jüdischen Proselyten im Römerreiche unter den Kaisern Domitian, Nerva, Trajan und Hadrian,* (Breslau. 1884); N. Samter, *Judenthum und Proselytismus,* (Breslau, 1897); I. Weil, *Le Prosélytisme chez les Juifs selon la Bible et la Talmud,* (Strassburg, 1880). Two more recent excellent special studies are Bernard J. Bamberger, *Proselytism in the Talmudic Period,* (Cincinnati, 1939) and William G. Braude, *Jewish Proselyting in the First Five Centuries of the Common Era* (Providence, R. I., 1940).

3. I am indebted here to Dr. Max Kadushin for his brilliant discovery of this characteristic quality of the biblical-rabbinic mind. See his *Organic Thinking, A Study in Rabbinic Thought,* (New York, 1938), pp. V-IX, 14, 22, 188 f., 194, 203ff., 211 f., 219f.

4. *Ibid.,* p. 215.

INTRODUCTION

1. *Baba Bathra* 16 b; M. Lazarus, *The Ethics of Judaism,* (Phila., 1900), I, 261-263.

2. *The Christian Church,* Eng. Tr., London, pp. 128f. [This is Pt. 6 of *The History of the Origins of Christianity,* London, 1890].

3. [*The History of the Decline and Fall of the Roman Empire,* (New York, 1906), II, 265 f.]

4. Isa. 43:21.

CHAPTER ONE

Pp. 1 — 22

1. [Job 38:7; *cf.* Isa. 45:18]; Gen. 14:17 f., 18:20 f., 20:5, 23:6; Mal. 1:2.

2. [Deut. 32:4, Exod. 34:7, Ps. 103:11 f., 145:8f].

3. [Gen. 18 and 23, 43:12, Exod. 18:7, Josh. 6:22 f., 9:3 ff., I Sam. 15:6, II Sam. 10:1 ff., 21:1 ff., I Kings 20:32, II Kings 6: 22, II Chron. 28:10-15].

4. [Num. 20:14 f., Judg. 11:24 ff., Deut. 32:8].

5. Exod. 17:8-16; Deut. 25:17-19; *Tan. B.* V, 45.

6. Deut. 23:4-9; *Num. Rab.* 21:5.

7. *Mekilta,* Beshallah 2, (*ed.* Lauterbach), I, 201; *Soferim* 15:7 (*ed.* Higger), pp. 281 f.; *Mekilta,* Nezikin 18 on Exod. 22:20 (*ed.* Lauterbach), III, 138. [The words, "pagan proselytes are dearer to God than Jewish saints," may be found in *Mishnat Rabbi Eliezer,* (*ed.* H. G. Enelow), p. 302].

8. Lev. 19:17 f.; Exod. 23:4 f.; Deut. 22:1-4; Prov. 24:17, 25:31; Job 31:29 f.

9. Exod. 21:5-6; 22:2; Lev. 25:39, 42, 55; Deut. 15:16 f.; Jer. 34:8; Amos 2:6.

10. Exod. 21:20-27; Lev. 22:11; Deut. 5:14; Job 31:13-15; Ecc. 17:21.

11. Gen. 15:2; 17:20; 35:8; Ruth 2:4-8; I Chr. 2:34 f.

12. Gen. 17:5, 21:8, 25:23; Exod. 20:6; Num. 14:12; Deut. 4:6-8, 26:5; Isa. 1:4; Jer. 7:28.

13. Exod. 3:2-8, 20:21; Isa. 6:3, 19:19-25, 66:1; Zeph. 2:11; II Chron. 6:32. On I Sam. 26:19, see Targum and Commentators.

14. I Sam. 15:22f.; Isa. 1:10-18; Jer. 3:16, 7:22, 22:16, 31:31ff.; Hos. 6:6; Amos. 5:21ff.; Mic. 6:6-8; Pss. 15, 24:1-5, 50:7-17, 51:18f.

15. Exod. 20:10, 23:12; Lev. 19:34; Deut. 10:18f., 14:29, 16:11f., 24:18-21, 26:12f.; Jer. 7:6, 22:3-5; Ez. 22:7; Mal. 3:5; Job 31:32. See Lazarus, *op. cit.,* I, 228-231.

16. Exod. 12:19, 43-49, 22:31; Num. 9:14, 15:16, 26; Deut. 1:16, 14:21, 24:17, 27:19; Josh. 20:9; Ez. 47:22-30. See Driver, *Deuteronomy,* (1885), pp. 165f.

17. Gen. 18:20-23, 20:17; I Kings 8:32f.; Isa. 56:7f.; II Chron. 6:32f.

18. Isa. 2:2f., 11:6f., Jer. 31:33f.; Hosea 2:20f., Micah 4:1-4. See M. Buttenwieser, *The Prophets of Israel,* (New York, 1924), pp. 318f.

19. See E. C. Baldwin, *Our Modern Debt to Israel,* (Boston, 1913), pp. 164f.; *Midrash Mishle* and *Yalk.* on Prov. 30:1.

20. Tobit 4:7-15, 12:7-10, 14:5-7. See Renan, *op. cit.,* pp. 122ff.

21. Book of Enoch, (*ed.* R. H. Charles, Vol. II, pp. 163-277), 10:16-29, 20:20,

89:39-48; G. G. Fox, *Judaism, Christianity and Modern Social Ideals*, (Ft. Worth, Texas, 1919) pp. 79f.; J. Klausner, *Haraayon Hamashihi Beyisrael*, (Jerusalem, 1921) pp. 18-32.

22. See I. Abrahams, *Hebrew Ethical Wills*, (Phila., 1926) pp. XIX-XXVI; L. Ginzberg, *The Legends of the Jews*, II, 201-222; R. H. Charles, *The Testaments of the XII Patriarchs*, in *op. cit.*, pp. 282-367.

23. Ecclus. 4:10, 7:1-3, 20-21, 34-35, 10:6f., 19, 28:1-7.

CHAPTER TWO
Pp. 23 — 61

1. Hos. 12:8; Joel 4:6.

2. [*Gen. Rab.* 3:7 and 9:2]; Wisdom of Solomon 11:24-26 [*ed.* R. H. Charles, I, 554].

3. *Berakot* 31a, *Shabbath* 30a, *Taan.* 22a, *B. Bath.* 60b, *Ab. d'R. N.* 34:9; S. Singer, *Authorized Daily Prayer Book,* p. 299.

4. *Mid. Hag. Shemot* 32; (Beshallah 17:6, Jethro 19:13); *Esther Rab.* 14; *Aboth* 3:6.

5. *Shab.* 133b; *Sotah* 14a; *Gen. R.* 18:2; *Pesik. R.* (Buber) 139a; *Lev. R.* 35:3. Though the Bible could have furnished the Rabbis with many instances of God's severity they confined their *imitatio Dei* solely to His mercy and righteousness; see, in this connection, S. Schechter, *Some Aspects of Rabbinic Theology*, (New York, 1910), pp. 203f.

6. *Gen. R.* 58:13; *Sifre Deut.* Par. 49; Schechter, *op. cit.*, pp. 26f., Herford, *The Pharisees*, (New York, 1924), pp. 157ff.; *Exod. R.* 9:16; *Mid. Hag. Shemot* 9:16; *Tanh. Vaera* 11.

7. *Sanhedrin* 39b, 98b; *Gen. R.* 27:4.

8. *Gen. R.* 36:9, 37:6, 42:8; *Lev. R.* 17:6; *Num. R.* 8:3, 17:3, 19:32; *Deut. R.* 5:14;*Yalk. Reub.* 1:42; *Tan. Hukdth.* 25; *Nid.* 61a, *Nazir* 23b, *Eliy. R.* (*ed.* Friedmann) 29:144f.; *Baba Kam.* 38b; *Sanh.* 46a; 49a; *Shab.* 32a, 88b; *Sotah* 42b; *Yoma* 23a.

9. *Berakot* 7a, 10a; *Ab. Zar.* 4b; *Taanit* 23b.

10. *Sanhedrin* 56b; *Pesik. R.* (Buber) 51a; *Gen. R.* 22; *Exod. R.* 9:8; *Ecc. R.* 75.

11. *Mekilta* on Exod. 22:30; Lazarus, *op. cit.*, pp. 205ff.; Schechter, *op. cit.*, p. 63; *Ruth R.*, Petihta, 1:1.

12. Ibn Ezra on Josh. 19:18; *Pesik. R.* 74; *Mid. Hag.*, (*ed.* Friedmann), Jethro, 20:2; *Jer. Megillah* 9, 39; *Bab. Kam.* 83a.

13. *Pesik. R.* (*ed.* Buber) 167b; *R. H.* 17a; *Tos. Sanh.* 13:1f.; *Sanhedrin* 110b; *Ruth R.* 3:2.

14. *Yalk.*, Lek Leka 76, Bo 212; *Mid. Shoher Tob* on Ps. 117; *Sanh.* 105a; *Jer. Mak.* 2,36.

15. *Suk.* 49b; *Mid. Teh.* 1:10; *Gen. R.* 16:9; *Yeb.* 79a; *Sanh.* 105a; *Maim. Hil. Melak* 8:11.

16. *Hil. Melak.* 8:11, 10:12. [See *Sanhedrin* 59a, 77a; *Sifra*, Ahare Mot XIII, *ed.* Weiss 86a].

17. *Berak.* 34b; *Kid.* 72b; *Lev. R.* 32:7; *Kohel. R.* 4:3; *Ab. Zar.* 24a; *Tan.,* Noah 19.

18. [*Shebuot* 35a; *Sanh.* 71a; *Mekilta* (*ed.* Lauterbach, III, 67); Matt. 15:6].

19. [*Sotah* 44b; *Sanh.* 2a, 20b; *Maim. Hil. Melakim* 5:1-2].

20. [*Gen. R.* 48:3, (*ed.* Theodor), I, 479f.; *Maim. Hil. Melak.* 9:8].

21. [*Berakot* 28a; *Bab. M.* 49a; *Seder Eliya. Rab.* (*ed.* Friedmann), p. 140; *Gitt.* 10b; *Bab. Kam.* 113a].

22. Schechter, *Some Aspects,* 215; G. F. Moore, *Judaism,* II, 188f.; [Ginzberg, *Legends* II, 53f. and V, 340].

23. [J. D. Eisenstein, "Gentile"], *J. E.,* V, 624f.

24. *Ibid.,* p. 625.

25. [*Gen. R.* 49:9, *ed.* Theodor, p. 510]; *Num. R.* 20:1; *Sifre Debarim* 96; *Midrash Tehillim* on Ps. 17:14, [*ed.* Buber, 134]; *Beza* 32b; *Esther R.* 3:5; *Gittin* 59b.

26. [*Jer. Demai* 4, 6 (24a); *Ket.* 15b; *Eliy. Rab* (*ed.* Friedmann), p. 36]; *Hil. Melakim* 10:12.

27. [*Mekilta,* Shirata 3, *ed.* Lauterbach, II, 25].

28. [James Drummond, *Philo Judaeus,* II, 286f.].

29. *Gen. R.* 1:7, 24:8; *Abot* 2:16, 3:15, 4:3; *Berakot* 43b; *Sanh.* 76b; *Shab.* 88b; Schechter, *Studies in Judaism,* Second Series, (Philadelphia, 1908), pp. 168, 171, 270.

30. *Berakot* 17a.

31. *Berak.* 17a; [M. Higger, *The Treatises Derek Erez,* (New York, 1935), pp. 82-85].

32. *Abot.* 1:15, 2:16, 3:16; *Berak.* 17a; *Kidd.* 33a; *Gittin* 62a.

33. *Abot* 3:2; *Sanh.* 82b; *Megil.* 15b.

34. Schechter, *Studies,* II, 292; Halevi, *Kuzari* 4:23; Maimonides, *Epistles* (Leipzig, 1859), p. 23; Bahya, *Hob. Hal.,* Shaar Haper., 9:1-3; Anatoli, *Malm. Hat.,* Toledot, (Lyck, 1866), p. 256; Abraham Bar Hiyya, *Hegyon Hannefesh,* 8a.

35. K. Kohler, *Jewish Theology,* (New York, 1918), pp. 439f.; H. G. Enelow, *Selected Works,* III, 509.

36. *Abot* 4:1; Singer, *Daily Prayer Book,* p. 291.

37. Singer, *op. cit.,* pp. 290-292; *Union Prayer Book,* [Cincinnati, 1947, Vol. I, p. 34].

38. *Taan.* 21b; *Megil.* 6a; *Tanh.,* Tisa, 17; *Gen. Rab.,* 89:8.

39. [Higger, *op. cit.,* pp. 248 ff.]

40. [*Zech.* 4:6].

41. [Morris Silverman, *High Holiday Prayer Book,* (Hartford, 1948), pp. 153, 159, 161].

CHAPTER THREE

Pp. 65 — 83

1. Gen. 17:1f., 14:22, 28:3, 43:14; Exod. 6:3.

2. Gen. 13:8, 14:24, 18:23f., 20:17.

3. A. H. Godbey, *The Lost Tribes A Myth—Suggestions Towards Rewriting Hebrew History,* (Durham, N. Carolina, 1930), p. 571; [Gen. 14:19].

4. Gen. 14:13, 40:15, 43:32.

5. Book of Jubilees 29:11, (*ed*. Charles), p. 57; *cf. Shabbath* 67a-b.

6. [Hastings, *A Dictionary of the Bible*, III, 415f.; G. A. Barton, *Archaeology and the Bible*, (Philadelphia, 1933), p. 221].

7. Gen. 12:6, 8; 13:3-8, 17:23, 21:33, 24:3.

8. Gen. 23:7, 12, 31:19; 34; 35:24; Exod. 3:13; 32; Deut. 10:22; Josh. 24:2.

9. Lev. 24:10. Num. 12:1, 31:32f.; Deut. 20:14, 21:10ff.

10. Jud. 3:5, 13:2f., 16:4f., 21:12.

11. Jud. 5:14; II Sam. 1:13, 3:3-5; I Kings 3:1, 11:1, 14:21, 31, 15:10; II Kings 8:18, 26; I Chron. 2:34, 4:18, 11:46; II Chron. 11:21.

12. I Sam. 13:19f.; Godbey, op. cit., p. 515, [quoting R. N. Salaman, *Palestine Exploration Fund*, 1925, pp. 33-47; 68-79, in article, "What Has Become of the Philistines?"].

13. Exod. 23:29; Josh. 15:63; Jud. 1:21-35, 3:1-6, 8:22f., 17:6, 12; I Kings 11:4-8.

14. Josh. 11:17, 13:17; Jud. 3:3; II Sam. 5:20; II Kings 4:42; I Chron. 5:8.

15. I Kings 22:11; I Chron. 7:10, 8:33, 9:39f., 14:7; II Chron. 18:10.

16. Josh. 9:23; II Sam. 6:10f.; I Kings 11:5-8, 15:12f., 22:44; II Kings 12:4, 14:4, 15:4, 35; I Chron. 16:38; II Chron. 20:23; Ez. 44:7.

17. [I Kings 1:8, 26, 45; 2:35; I Chron. 29:22].

18. II Kings 11:26f.; II Chron. 15:1f., *Sanhedrin* 102b.

19. I Kings 18.

20. Hosea 6:9; 9:7.

21. I Kings 15:9f., 22:43; II Chron. 15:1f., 17:7f.

22. II Kings 10-12; II Chron. 22, 24.

23. II Chron. 29; Prov. 25; *Sanh.* 94a-b.

24. II Chron. 33:1-3; II Kings 21:1-16, 22:8f.; *Sanh.* 103a-b; *Levit. Rab.* 17; Driver, *Commentary on Deuteronomy*, (New York, 1895), pp. XIII, XXV, LXI; Deut. 4:6f., 6:4f., 10:12, 13:3, 30:6, 5:15, 7:1f., 10:16, 12:2f., 13:2f.

25. II Kings 23.

26. Jer. 44:15f., *Bab. Kam.* 16b.

27. Jer. 1:18.

CHAPTER FOUR
Pp. 84—101

1. Jud. 6:31; Micah 4:5.

2. Exod. 2:11f., 8:6, 9:16, 29, 14:18, 19:6, 32:12; Lev. 19, 26, 34; Num. 10:29f.; Deut. 7:7f., 9:28, 10:18, 27:1-8, 28:10, 29:9-14, 31:10-13, 32:27, 37, 33:3; Josh. 4:24, 8:30-35.

3. Isaiah 30:15; Hosea 1:4; Zech. 4:6; I Kings 5:14, 17:9f., 19:15; Jer. 10:11; II Kings 18:26; Isa. 36:11; J. L. Katzeneleson, "Hareligia Vehapolitilka etc.", in *Hatekufah*, Vols. 24 and 25, pp. 321f., and 38f.

4. Amos 2:1-3; Isaiah 13, 15, 16, 17, 19, 20, 21, 46, 47; Jer. 1:5-10; 25; 46; 47; 48; 49.

5. Zeph. 1:14., 2:1-4, 3:9; Joel 3:1-6; Amos 8:11; Isaiah 2:2f., 11:10, 19:8f., 23:14f.

6. Jer. 1:4-9, 4:2, 12:14, 31:26f.

7. Gen. 14:18; Ps. 110:4; Deut. 26:5; Josh. 5:13-15.

8. Josh. 9:3f.; II Sam. 21:1f.

9. Ezra 2:58, 7:24, 8:20; Neh. 3:7, 26; 7:46ff., 10:29; *Yebam.* 78b-79a; *Kidd.* 70a; *Num. Rab.* 8:3; Godbey, *op. cit.,* pp. 501-507.

10. Num. 10:31f., 24:21f.; Jud. 4:11, 5:24.

11. I Sam. 15:6f., 27:10, 30:29.

12. I Chron. 2:55.

13. II Kings 10:15-17, 23; Jer. 35; 41:1f.; Neh. 3:14f.

14. *Sanh.* 106a; *Niddah* 61a.

15. II Kings 17:24f., Josephus, *Antiquities* IX. 14:3; X. 9:7.

16. Isaiah 65:1f.; Jer. 41:5f.

17. Ezra 4:3; Neh. 1-6; Deut. 11:29; 27:12; Josh. 8:33.

18. Ecclus. 50:25f.

19. *Kidd.* 76a; *Hullin* 4a; *Niddah* 56b; *Berakot* 47b; *Mas. Kutim* (*ed.* Higger), 1:10, 17; 2:1, 8.

20. [G. Uhlhorn, "Dositheus, The Samaritan," *The New Schaff-Herzog Encyclopedia of Religious Knowledge,* III, 495].

CHAPTER FIVE

Pp. 102 — 129

1. *Erub.* 100b; *Pesik. Rab.* 5.

2. "Asarah Yeridot", *Abot d'R. Nathan,* ch. 33.

3. *Mid. Tehil.* 9; *Sukkah* 52a; Ginzberg, *Legends,* I, 120-4; 125-40; V, 148-166.

4. *Ibid.,* I, 120f.; V, 130.

5. *Ibid.,* I, 126ff.

6. *Ibid.,* I, 145ff.

7. *Gen. R.* 26:4; *Makkot* 23b.

8. *Gen. R.* 39, 43; *Num. R.* 8:10, 14:7; Ginzberg, *op. cit.,* I, 186-192.

9. [*Gen. R.* 39:14; *Pesik. R.* (Buber), 180a; *Tanh.* (Buber), 32a; Ginzberg, *op. cit.,* pp. 203ff.].

10. [Ginzberg, *op. cit.,* pp. 217-220; *Baba Bathra* 91 a & b.].

11. [*Gen. R.* 53:13]; Romans 4:11, 18; Gal. 3:6f.; James 2:21f.; Koran, Sura 2:118, 3:58-60, 4:24, 6:162, 16:121.

12. *Gen. R.* 59:11; Yoma 28b; [Ginzberg, *op. cit.,* I, 383 and V, 304].

13. *Gen. R.* 42:8; [Ginzberg, V, 233]; *Mid. Tehillim,* 34, (Buber), p. 246.

14. *Mid. Tehil.* 37, (Buber), p. 252; Hebrews 8:36; *Gen. R.* 43:8-9; *Nedar:* 32 a & b;[Adolf Harnack, "Monarchianism", *The New Schaff-Herzog Encyclopedia of Religious Knowledge,* VII, 455].

15. *Gen. R.* 19:13; 84:2; Ginzberg, *op. cit.,* I, 393f.; *Gen. R.* 93; *Shab.* 33b.

16. [Ginzberg, *op. cit.,* I, 346, 421; see Ginzberg's corrective note, V, 322, n. 318].

17. [Ginzberg, *op. cit.,* II, 242, 308, 250f., 296; I, 396; V, 381; *Gen. R.* 73:9, 84:9; *Yoma* I, 6].

18. Ginzberg, *op. cit.,* II, 33ff., V, 333f.; *Sotah* 10a; *Gen. R.* 85:8f.

19. *Sanhedrin* 99b; Ginzberg, *op. cit.,* II, 76, 136, 172f., V, 374; K. Kohler, "Asenath", *The Jewish Encyclopedia,* II, 172-6.

20. *Mid. Tadshe* on Exod. 1:15; Ginzberg, *op. cit.*, V, 393, n. 17; *Vayik. R.* 1:3; *Megil.* 13a; *Der. Er. Zuta* 10:1.

21. *Moed Kat.* 16b; Josephus, *Antiquities* II, 9 and 11.

22. *Sh. R.* 1:38; *Yalk. Shemot* 168f.; Jellinek, *B. H.*, II, "Dibre hayamim lemosheh."

23. Ginzberg, *op. cit.*, III, 63f.; *B. Bathra* 109b; *Zebah.* 116a; *Deut. R.* 1:4; *Sota* 43a.

24. *Megil.* 14b—15a; *Zebah.* 116b; *Ruth R.* 2:1; *Bam. R.* 8:10.

25. *Horayot* 10b; *Megil.* 14a; *Nazir* 23b; Ginzberg, *op. cit.*, IV, 37f.; *Ruth R.* 2:9, 12, 23-5; *Sota* 42b, 47a.

26. *Yebam.* 77a; II Sam. 24:18-25; I Chron. 21:18-26; *Ab. Zar.* 24b; Jos., *Antiquities* VII, 13:4, VIII, 6-8.

27. *Yebam.* 76a; *Sh. Hash. R.* 11:10; Ginzberg, *op. cit.*, IV, 170f.

28. [*Yebam.* 76a]; *Sanh.* 102b; Ginzberg, *op. cit.*, IV, 271.

29. [I could not find any source for Raisin's reference to Elijah as a proselyte. Is it possible that our author had a dim recollection of the tradition which said that the widow at Zarephath was not a Jewess (Luke 4:26), and confused this tradition with Elijah? See Ginzberg, *op. cit.*, VI, 318, n. 9. Raisin might also have had some recollection of the Tosafot on *Kidd.* 71a, where Rabbi Abraham Ger speaks of the widow of Zarephath as a proselyte; I am indebted to my colleague, Rabbi Solomon B. Freehof, for drawing my attention to this Tosafot].

30. *Yalk. Jonah* 550; *Megil.* 16b; Ginzberg, *op. cit.*, IV, 246f.

31. Ginzberg, *op. cit.*, VI, 171, n. 12; IV, 322f.

32. [Ginzberg, IV, 347 and VI, 434f.] *Gittin* 57b.

33. *Sanh.* 107; *Sota* 47a; *Num. R.* 7:5; *Yalk.* 229 on 2 Kings; Ginzberg, *op. cit.*, IV, 300f.

34. *Gittin* 57b; *Ekah R.*, Intr., 23.

35. *Bab B.* 91b; *Sota* 11a; *Yalk. Jer.* 323.

36. [*Sefer Masaot R. Benjamin, Frankfurt a. M.*, 1904]; M.A. Ginzberg, *Debir*, (Warsaw, 1883), I, 96-101; "Rechabites," *The Jewish Encyclopedia*, X, 341f.

37. J. J. Williams, *Hebrewisms of West Africa*, [1930, pp. 159-185]; Sidney Mendelssohn, *The Jews of Africa*, [1920, pp. 4-32].

38. Jacques Faitlovitch, "The Falashas," *American Jewish Year Book*, [1920-21, pp. 80-100]; [D. Aescoly, *Sefer Hapalishim*, Jerusalem, 1943].

CHAPTER SIX
Pp. 130 — 153

1. Dan. 3:1-12; G. E. Tabuis, *Nebuchadnezzar*, (New York, 1931).

2. Ez. 13:18f.

3. Jer. 8:19f.; Ez. 12:22f.; 37:1f.

4. Ez. 44:7-9; 47:22f.

5. Ez. 7:1f.; 24:18f.; 33:25f.

6. Ez. 11:15f.; 18:2f.; 37:16f.; 38:16, 20; 39:23; 17:22-24; 25-32; Jer. 27:5; 29:7; 42:10f.; 16:19-20.

7. See Targum, Rashi and Radak on Jer. 10:11.

8. Dan. 2:28, 37; 3:16f.; 4:19f.; 5:17f.; 6:26; Psalms 69:8f.; 119:41f.

9. Ezra 1:2-4; Josephus, *Antiquities*, XI, 5:1.

10. Isa. 13-14:1f.; Haggai 2:7; [Zech. 8:20-23].

11. Zech. 14:9.

12. Isa. 66:1; 43:21; 42:1-12.

13. A. Kuenen, "National Religions and Universal Religion", in *Hibbert Lectures*, N. Y. 1882, pp. 117-40; Godbey, *op. cit.*, pp. 568f., is of the opinion that the Great Comforter was one of the Fearers of the Lord, not himself a Judaean; [Isa. 52:10].

14. Isa. 52:13 and 53; 49:6; 55:1f.; 45:4ff.; 46:1f.

15. Isa. 56:1-7.

16. Isa. 60:1f.

17. Isa. 65:16; 65:23.

18. Psalms 113; 126; Mal. 1:11; Psalms 47:10 should perhaps read *im* instead of *am*, ["The princes of the peoples are gathered together with (*im*) the God of Abraham"]; Psalm 118:1-4; Psalm 117.

19. C. G. Montefiore, *Hibbert Lectures*, 1892, pp. 229, 337. *Cf.* Ex. 4:24ff.; Dt. 10:16; 30:6; Josh. 5:2-9; Jer. 4:4; 9:24f.; Ez. 44:9.

20. Ezra 9 and 10; Neh. 10:1f.; 13:24ff.; *Kidd.* 69b-70a; *Horayot* 13a.

21. Neh. 3:4, 21; see *Hashiloach* XL, 140f.

22. Isa. 63:15f.; Ps. 22; 39:13f.; 69:7f.

23. Mal. 2:11f.; 16f.; 3:17 and 20; *Megil.* 15a.

24. Ruth 1:16f.

25. Esther 8:17; 9:10, 15f. Josephus, *Ant.* XI, 6:13, adds that "many even of the other nations circumcised their foreskin for fear of the Jews"; Ginzberg, *op. cit.*, III, 62f.

26. Nahum 3:1-19; *Taan.* 16a; *Yal. Jon.* 550:8 (end); *Tan. Vay.* 8 (end).

27. Prov. 1:7; 8:12; 6-7; Job. 1:6; 28:12, 28; 42:7f.; Ps. 2:11; 34:12f; 62:13; 67:2-8; 103; 115:4-8; 145:9.

28. Psalms 45; 68:32; 87. T. K. Cheyne, *Jewish Religious Life After The Exile*, N. Y. 1898, pp. 126f.

CHAPTER SEVEN
Pp. 154 — 172

1. Haggai 2:9; Ezra 3:12; *Sota* 48b.

2. *Abot d'R. Nathan* 5; Josephus, *Ant.* XVIII, 1:2-5; [*Aboth* 1:3].

3. *Sota* 22b; Josephus, *op. cit.*, XIII, 5:9; *War*, VIII, 2-14; [H. Graetz, *Geschnichte der Juden*, III³, (Leipzig, 1877), pp. 90-109, 648ff.; Philo. *Legat. ad Cajum*, secs. 36-41, (*ed.* Mangey, II, 584-586)].

4. [Emil Schürer, *A History of the Jewish People in the Time of Jesus Christ*, (Edinburgh, 1924), II, 2, pp. 220-242; I Macc. 15:16, 22, 23, *ed.* Charles, p. 121].

5. [Deut. 33:19; Tobit 13:2f., (*ed.* R. H. Charles), p. 235].

6. *Gen. R.* 28:5; *Aboth* 1:12; Matth. 23:15; Acts 15:21.

7. I Macc. 12:19-23; Josephus, *op. cit.*, XII, 3:2, 10; XIV, 8:5; I Esdras 3-4, [*ed.* Charles, pp. 30-32].

8. II Macc. 3:31ff.; 8:36; 9:28; Ecclesiasticus 36:1-17; 37:25; 40:13f.; 44:1f.; 50:5-10; *cf. Sanh.* 100b.

9. *Shabb.* 115a-b; *Sota* 32a-b; Godbey, *op. cit.,* pp. 646ff.; Josephus, *Contra Apionem,* II, 40; *Antiquities* XIV, 7:2; Augustine, *De Civitate Dei* VI, 10; *Kidd.* 73a; S. Schechter, *Documents of Jewish Sectaries,* (Cambridge, 1910); G. F. Moore, "Covenanters of Damascus", *Harvard Theol. Rev.,* Oct., 1911.

10. Acts 2:1-11.

11. *Yebam.* 48a-b; *Horayot* 13a; *Kidd.* 69a-b; 72b; *Kohel. R.* 4:3; *Lev. R.* 32:4; Ezekiel 16:4f.

12. *Kidd.* 73a-74a.

13. *Yebam.* 16b; *Kidd.* 17b; 70b-71a; *Pesahim* 62b; Josephus, *Contra Apionem,* I, 7; Josephus, *Ant.* XVI, 1:2; XX, 7:1f.; *Horayot* 13.

14. Tacitus, *Hist.* 5:5; *Yalk. Berakah* 961.

15. *Berakot* 19b; *Yebam.* 79a; *Yer. Hagigah* I, 37; *Yer. Bob. M.* II, [5, 8c, line 21].

16. [Josephus, *Antiq.* XIII, 9:1; *ibid.,* 11:4; F.J.F. Jackson, *Josephus and the Jews,* (N. Y., 1930), pp. 113-118].

17. [For a critical estimate of the traditional Jewish historical judgment of Herod, see Jackson, *op. cit.,* pp. 127-136].

CHAPTER EIGHT
Pp. 173 — 203

1. *San.* 41a; *Shabbat* 14b; R.T. Herford, *The Pharisees,* (New York, 1924), pp. 26, 112; *Pesahim* 57a; *Yoma* 39b; Josephus, *War* VI, 5:3; II Esdras 2:8f.; 6:17-28; 7:33-8, 105; 13:16f.

2. [R.H. Charles, *The Book of Enoch Or I Enoch,* (Oxford, 1912), 10:9, 13, 16, 21f., pp. 23f.; Jubilees 37:18-23 (*ed.* Charles), pp. 68f.; Josephus, *Antiq.* XIV, 9; XVII, 10; XVIII, 1; *War* I, 10; II, 4, 17].

3. J. Cohen, *The Deicides,* Eng. Trans., London, 1872, pp. 12-26; D.F. Straus, *The Life of Jesus,* Eng. Tr., 1902; Jos., *Antiq.* XVIII, 3:3; *Menah.* 110a; Matt. 5:17-19; 22: 36-40; 23:22; *Shabbat* 31a; G.F. Moore, *Judaism,* (Cambridge, 1927), II, 86f.; *Sanh.* 98b; *Echah R.* 2:5; *Erubin* 13b; *Ab. Zar.* 17a; *Sota* 22b; *Berak.* 28a; *Yoma* 72b; *Kohel. R.* 4:2; 5:3; *Taan.* 22a.

4. Matt. 10:5-6; 15:21-26.

5. Matt. 24-5; Mark 13:21f.; Matt. 16:31f.; Mark 8:27-30; Luke 9:18-21; F.J. Gould, *Hist. of Rel.,* (London, 1897), III, 254; Acts 10-11; see Jellinek, *Beth Ham.* V, 60-2; VI, 9-10; [H. Vogelstein and P. Rieger,*Geschichte der Juden in Rom,* (Berlin, 1896), I, 165-169].

6. [R. Akiba, at a later date, saw in Bar Kokba the promised Messiah and the fulfillment of the prediction in Numbers 24:17, ("there shall step forth a star out of Jacob"),—and R. Akiba was certainly not read out of the Synagogue, *Jer. Taanit* 68d]. Acts 5:34f.

7. Acts 22:3f.; J. Klausner, *Historia Yisraelit,* Second Ed., (Jerusalem, 1935), IV, 77f.

8. Acts 9; 23:9; 26; I Cor. 15:28; Romans 1:16; 2:9f.; 9:3-5; I Cor. 9:19-22; Colos. 3:11; Gal. 2:15; *Mid. Mishle* 9; *Niddah* 61b; I Cor. 9:19; Acts 4:36f.; 11:26;

16:1-3; Gal. 5:2f.; Renan, *St. Paul*, Eng. Tr., pp. 37-49, 90-101, 203; Gal. 2:3f.; I Cor. 9:1f.; II Cor. 11:5; 12:11; Acts 13, 14, 15:36f.; 16:14f.; 17:1-4, 7; 18:1-8; I Cor. 1:14; Acts 17:36f.

9. Acts 11:28; 21:10f.; II Pet. 2:15; Jude 11; Acts 21:21; Renan, *St. Paul*, p. 158, says: the expression, "synagogue of Satan" [Rev. 2:9, 3:9], refers to Judaeo-Christians of Smyrna and Philadelphia, probably Paulinists, "who say they are Jews but are not;" Acts 21:27f.; 23-26; I Cor. 16:22; Acts 28:25-28.

10. II Tim. 1:15; 2:18; 4:16; II Peter 3:3f.; I John 2:19; III John, verse 9; Renan, *St. Paul*, 299f.; Romans 16:17f.; I Cor. 1:10f.; 5:1f.; II Cor. 12:21; Ephes. 4:28f.; 5:3f.; I Thess. 4:3f.; *Sanhed.* 63b; Renan, *op. cit.*, pp. 196f.

11. [I Cor. 16:22]; II Peter 3:3f.

12. *Sota* 41a.

13. *Bam. R.* 8:2.

14. H. Graetz, *Monatsschrift*, (1881), pp. 289-94; *Yoma* 71b; *Abot* 1:10f.; *Berakot* 19a; Joseph., *Antiq.* XIV, 9:4.

15. *Shabbat* 31a; *Abot* 1:12f.

16. *Hagigah* 9b; *Abot* 5:25; *Kidd.* 10b.

17. *Cf.* Exod. 18:20; Deut. 47:26f.; *Kidd.* 2b; *Jer. Hag.* 2:31, translated by C.C. Starbuck, in *Andover Review*, April, 1884; G. Klein, *Der aelteste christliche Katechismus*, 1909, pp. 214f.; C. Taylor, *The Teaching of the Twelve Apostles*, (1886); *J. Q. R.*, N. S., Jan. 1915, p. 478; G.F. Moore, *Judaism*, (Cambridge, 1927), I, 188.

18. Moore, *op. cit.*, Vol. I, p. 330f.; *Hulin* 44b; *Yebamot* 47b.

19. Jos., *War* I, 20:2; VII, 3:3; [Moore, *op. cit.*, I, 348-353]; B.J. Bamberger, *Proselytism In The Talmudic Period*, (Cincinnati, 1939), pp. 230f.; Jos., *War* II, 19:2f.; IV, 9:3, 5; VII, 2:1; 5:6; 8:1. *cf.* Klausner, *op. cit.*, IV, 188f.

CHAPTER NINE

Pp. 204 — 243

1. *Gittin* 56b; Jos., *War* III, 8:9.

2. *Shabbat* 49a; 116a; *Yoma* 11a; *Ketubot* 3b; *Mekilta*, on Exod. 20:20 [*ed.* Lauterbach, II, 276ff.]; Graetz—Rabinowitz, *Dibre Yeme Yisrael*, II, 250f.

3. *Abod. Zar.* 18a; "Mid. Eleh Ezkerah," in Jellinek's *Beth Hamidrash*, II and VI; Eisenstein, *Otzar Midrashim*, 439-50.

4. *Yebamot* 61a; *Mas. Soferim* 15:10; *B. Bathra* 16b; M. Lazarus, *The Ethics of Judaism*, (Phila., 1900), I, 65ff., 256-265; J.Z. Lauterbach, ["The Attitude of the Jew Toward the Non-Jew"], in *C. C. A. R. Y. B.*, XXXI, (1921), 213-15.

5. *Pesahim* 118b; *Exod. Rab.* 35:5.

6. *Shabbat* 13b; *Sanh.* 58-9; Graetz—Rabinowitz, *op. cit.*, II, 89, n. 2.

7. *Hagigah* 13a; *Sanh.* 59a; *Gittin* 45b; *Yalk. Ki Tissa* 391; *Yebamot* 109b, and see *ibid.*, 47b, in Tosafot beginning "Kashim . . . ." [The editor of this work is convinced that all scholars of the past have overlooked the obvious interpretation of R. Helbo's remark. The best explanation is that of W.G. Braude, *Jewish Proselyting*, (Providence, R. I., 1940), p. 42, who says that the remark was an oblique reference to the penalties which Christian Emperors began to impose on Jewish proselytes. R. Helbo had in mind the danger to which the Jew who received proselytes exposed

himself. R. Helbo's remark was a cryptic allusion to political dangers resulting from the growing intolerance of the Christian Emperors].

8. [Bamberger, *op. cit.*, p. 161]; *Pesahim* 87b; *Sanh.* 98a; *Megillah* 6a; *Levit. Rab.* 13:5 (end).

9. *Num. Rab.* 8:1f.; *Yalk. Hoshea* 533; [*Sanhedrin* 59a; *Ab. Zar.* 3a; *Sanhedrin* 17a; S. Lieberman, *Greek In Jewish Palestine*, (N. Y., 1942), pp. 15:28; *Yer. Demai* IV, 6, 24a].

10. *Num. R.* 5:3; *Exod. R.* 19:4-5, [commenting on Job 31:32 and with reference to I Sam. 2:36; see also Braude, *loc. cit.*].

11. [*Ecc. R.* 11:2].

12. [*Lev. R.* 1:2; *Tanh. B.* 32a]; *Mas. Gerim* (ed. Higger), pp. 76-9.

13. [See Ginzberg, *Legends*, III, 182-188, 205, 341, 454; IV, 307; VI, 31f.].

14. *Num. Rab* 8:2-10; *Yalk. Mishpatim* 349; [*Pesahim* 87b].

15. [*Num. Rab.* 8:1].

16. [*Ibid.* 8:9 and 10].

17. [*Ibid.* 8:2-4; *Mas. Gerim* (ed. Higger), pp. 77f.; a full statement is in the *Mekilta* on Exod. 22:20, (ed. Lauterbach), III, 138-141].

18. [*Tan.*, on "Lek leka", 6, (ed. Buber), 32a; *Mishnat R.E.*, (ed. Enelow), pp. 302-4; *Num. Rab.* 3:2].

19. *Cant. Rab.* 1:22; *Tan.*, on "Behaaloteka", 4, (ed. Buber), 24a; [The quotation, p. 219, seems to be a mosaic of *Gen. R.* 39:18, rendered freely by our author.]

20. [*Nedarim* 32a; *Sanhedrin* 99b; Bamberger, *op. cit.*, pp. 65f.].

21. *Singer Daily Prayer Book*, pp. 48, 76f.

22. [*Berakot* 28b; see A.Z. Idelsohn, *Jewish Liturgy*, (N. Y., 1932), pp. 102f.].

23. *Berakot* 28a.

24. [*B. Bathra* 60b; *Shab.* 153b; *Gen. R.* 64:8; *Sanh.* 105a; *Abot* 2:11].

25. *Yebamot* 46a; *Gen. R.* 46:2; *Ruth R.* 2:9.

26. *Sanh.* 107b (in *Hesronot Hashas*, Cracow, 1893, p. 50); *Ruth R.* 2:17; *Num. R.* 8:4; *Bekhorot* 30b. This rigorism, however, was applied by some also to born Jews; see *Sanh.* 111a.

27. *Ab. Zar.* 17a.

28. *Jer. Kidd.* 65b; *Yebamot* 24b; *Yalk. Bo* 213.

29. [*Pesik. R.* 167b]; *Ber.* 57b; *Ab. Zar.* 24a; *Lev. R.* 2:9.

30. *Yebamot* 48b; *Gen. R.* 47:12.

31. [Our author's statement that circumcision of a *ger* could be performed on the Day of Atonement has no ground in the Halakah (see Simon Duran, *Tashbaz*, I, 21); even baptism of a convert could not take place on the Sabbath, according to *Yebamot* 46a. I am indebted to my colleague, Rabbi W. Leiter, for these two references]. *Yer. Yebamot* 8:1 [Wilna, 1922, p. 87].

32. [*Yebamot* 78a]; *ibid.*, 47a-b; *Mas. Gerim* 1:1, [ed. Higger, pp. 68f.]; *ibid.*, 4:5 [ed. Higger, p. 79]; Maim. *Issure Biah* 13:6.

33. [Bamberger, *op. cit.*, pp. 63f.; Maim. *Issure Biah* 14:10ff.]; *Yoreh Deah* 269:1-9.

34. [Bamberger, *op. cit.*, pp. 161-169, and especially Ch. V, "Status of Converts in Jewish Law," pp. 60-123].

35. [*Ibid.*, pp. 77f.]; *Yebamot* 76b-78b; *ibid.*, 48b; [*Gerim, ed.* Higger, pp. 72f.].

36. [*Yer. Shabbat* 6:8, (*ed.* Krotoschin), 8d].

37. *B. Metzia* 58b; 596; *Yalk. Mishpatim* 349; I. Bernstein, *Juedische Sprichwoerter,* (Warsaw, 1905), p. 64; *Ab. d'R. N.* 1; *Horayot* 13a.

38. *Ab. Zar.* 19b; [*Lev. R.* 16:2].

39. *Abot* 2:14; *Lev. R.* 2:9.

40. [*Meilah* 17b; Bacher, *Ag. Tan.* 35, pp. 285ff.]; *Taan.* 23a [*ed.* Malter, p. 167].

41. *Pesik. R.* [*ed.* Friedmann, 56b-57a].

42. *Mid. Haggadol* (*ed.* D. Hoffman), Berlin, 1913, p. 17; *Sanhedrin* 64a.

43. *Nedarim* 50a; *Yebamot* 98a; [L. Finkelstein, *Akiba,* (N. Y., 1936), p. 210].

44. *Shabbat* 33b [see Rashi's explanation, *ad. loc.,* of "ben gerim"].

45. *Zohar* 1, 10a.

46. [*Ab. Zar.* 3a]; *Sanh.* 38b; 39b; 90b; *Bezah* 25b; *Shabbat* 67a; *Ab. Zar.* 18b; *Gen. R.* 4:3; 70:7; Bacher, *Ag. Hattan.* II, 1, *cf. B. B.* 10a on R. Akiba; *Gen. R.* 65:16; *Exod. R.* 13:1; *Ruth R.* 2:14; *Hagigah* 15a-b.

47. *Shabbat* 33b; *Pesik. R.* (*ed.* Friedmann), 103b.

48. [*Gen. R.* 68:4; 4:6; 17:7; 25:1]; *Gen. R.* 14:8.

49. [Bamberger, *op cit.,* p. 254, but see p. 259, n. 6; and Hyman, *Toldot Tannaim VeAmoraim,* III, 998, col. 2]; *B. Bathra* 8b; [see also *Sanh.* 96b and Gittin 57b].

50. *Yer. Bik* 1:4, *Demai* 6:1, *Ab. Zar.* 1:9, *Yebamot* 11:2. [Benjamin bar Ashtor is mentioned in *Yer. Bik., loc. cit.,* as a descendant of converts].

51. *Pesahim* 113b.

CHAPTER TEN

Pp. 244 — 264

1. *Pesahim* 87b; *Berakot* 24b (Rashi); *Megillah* 29a; *Gittin* 6a; *Ketubot* 110b-111a; *Levit. R.* 7:3; Jacob Mann, "Gaonic Studies," *H. U. C. Jubilee Vol.,* [Cincinnati, 1925], pp. 257f.; *Godbey op. cit.,* pp. 60f., 611; *Sanh.* 38b; *Ge. R.* 74:5, 12. and II, 2, p. 279.

2. *Sukkah* 20a; *Gittin* 88a; *Tanh.,* Noah, 3; *Kidd.* 69b-71b.

3. *Gen. R.* 48:9; J. Darmesteter, *La Zend-Avesta,* (Paris, 1893), Intr.; I. Broydé, "Mandaeans," *Jewish Encyclopedia,* VIII, 286-8; M. Gaster, ["Parsiism in Judaism"], *Hasting's Enc. of Rel. and Ethics,* IX, 637-40.

4. [K. Kessler, "Mandaeans," *The New Schaff-Herzog Encyclopedia of Religious Knowledge,* VII, 146-51; A. Harnack, "Manichaeism," *Encyclo. Britt.,* (11th ed.), XVIII, 572-8].

5. [Graetz, *Geschite der Juden,* IV², 296, 307, 352, 363, 366, 382; S. W. Baron, *A Social And Religious History of the Jews,* II, (2), 182-5].

6. L. H. Gray, "Jews in Pahlavi Literature," *J. E.,* IX, 462-5; J. Darmesteter in *R. E. J.,* XVII, 168-76, XVIII, 1-15, XIX, 41-56; *J. Q. R.,* I, 223.

7. [*Gittin* 16b-17a; Graetz, *loc. cit.,* pp. 291, 402]; *Ab. Zar.* 30a; *Shabbat* 129a; *Jer. Shabb.* III, 6a; *Bab. M.* 70b, 119a; *Sanh.* 9a; [Graetz, *loc. cit.,* pp. 288, 293f.].

8. *Ab. Zar.* 76b; *Kidd.* 70a-b.

9. *Yebamot* 16a-17a.

10. [Graetz, *loc. cit.*, pp. 297-9]; Graetz-Rabinowitz, *Dibre Yeme Yisrael*, II, 368-70.

11. *B. Bathra* 8a, 10b; *Taan.* 24b; *Zebah.* 116b; [*Nidd.* 20b]; *Sanhedrin* 46b; Godbey, *op. cit.*, p. 170.

12. [Graetz, *loc. cit.*, p. 382]; *Zebahim* 19a; *Berakot* 34b; *Sanh.* 97a-98b. [Graetz, *op. cit.*, V², 23-27; n. 8, 393-396].

13. *Kidd.* 72a-73a; *Berakot* 17b.

14. *Kidd.* 71b; *Yebamot* 45b-47; *R. H.* 17a; *Shabbat* 109a; *Taanit* 26a; *Yebamot* 46-7.

15. [*Jer. Kidd.* IV, 1, 65b; *Num. R.* 8:2; *Lev. R.* 3:2].

16. *Ecc. R.* 7:19, *cf. Shabbat* 31a [for similar story about Hillel].

17. *Ab. Zar.* 64a; *Yebamot* 22a; *Kidd.* 76b.

18. [Bamberger, *op. cit.*, pp. 225-228].

19. Josephus, *War*, II, 20:2; IV, 9:11; V, 2:2; VI, 6:4; *Gen. R.* 46:8; *Bab. Bath.*

CHAPTER ELEVEN
Pp. 265 — 291

1. [Psalms 119:46]; *Menorah Journal*, August, 1929, pp. 197-209.

2. Isaiah 19:16-25. The original for "Ir Hazzedek" was probably *Ir Haheres*, "city of the sun," or Heliopolis (Godbey, *op. cit.*, pp. 189f.).

3. Godbey, *op. cit.*, pp. 137, 596f.

4. I Macc. 10:57f., 15:23; II Macc. 1:10; Jos., *Antiq.* XII, 1:1; XIII, 10:4; *Contra Apionem*, 2:5.

5. *Antiq.* XI, 8:4-6; *Yoma* 69a [*cf. Meg. Taanit*, 3]; *Lev. R.* 13, toward end.

6. *Ab. Zar.* 10a; Reinach, in *R. E. J.*, 1902, pp. 161-4; [E. Schürer, *A History of the Jewish People in the Time of Jesus Christ*, (Edinburgh, 1924), I, 1, p. 297 and II, 2, pp. 279].

7. Philo, *Against Flaccus* 8, *De Legatione* 20; Jos. *Antiq.* V, 1; XIV, 7:2.

8. [L. Ginzberg, "Aristotle in Jewish Legend"], *Jewish Encyclopedia* II, 98f.

9. Bottarel, *Sefer Yezirah* 26b; Isserles, *Responsa* 6; Bartholocius, *Biblia Magna Rabbinica*, (Rome, 1675), I; [N. Bentwich, *Hellenism*, (Philadelphia, 1919), pp. 70-77].

10. [E. Zeller, *Grundriss der Geschichte der Griechischen Philosophie*, (Leipzig, 1886), pp. 96ff.].

11. Frederic Huidekoper, *Judaism at Rome*, (Boston, 1900), pp. 2-4, 29.

12. Acts 10:19f., 13:7, 14:8f.

13. Jos. *Against Apion* I, 22, II, 17, 37, 40 [Schürer, *op. cit.*, II, 2, pp. 304-8].

14. Jos. *Ag. Apion* I, 22.

15. Bentwich, *op. cit.*, pp. 136, 199-202.

16. *Idem*, pp. 138, 217, 219.

17. *Idem*, pp. 207-10.

18. Wisdom of Solomon 8:7, 10:7, 14:12f.

19. H. M. Bate, *The Sibylline Oracles*, (London, 1918), Or. 3:810f., 4:1-25.

20. Oracles: 218-47 (Bohn's Tr.).

21. Or. 4:1-35.

22. Or. 3:762-5.

23. Or. 5:484-506, 3:715-23, 779.

24. [Schürer, op. cit., II, 3, pp. 159-168]; Graetz, Dibre Yeme Yisrael I, 396.

25. Bentwich, op. cit., index on "Septuagint"; [Sota 49b]; Mas. Soferim, (ed. Higger), 1:7-8, pp. 100-106. [See, and as a corrective of the popular view about the rabbinic attitude toward Greek, the very significant sections, "The Greek of the Rabbis," and "The Greek of the Synagogue," in S. Lieberman, Greek in Jewish Palestine, (N. Y., 1942), pp. 15-67].

26. Meg. 9a-b; M. L. Margolis, The Story of Bible Translations, (Philadelphia, 1917), pp. 29-38, [especially p. 35].

27. Bentwich, op. cit., pp. 157f.; Bentwich, Philo-Judaeus of Alexandria, (Philadelphia, 1910), pp. 81f.; De Vita Mosis 2:18; De Posteritate Caini 22, 24, 45.

28. De Monarchi 1:7; De Nobilitate 6, [quoted in Bentwich, Philo-Judaeus, p. 244].

29. [De Vita Mosis II, 2-9, in F. H. Colson, Philo, (London, 1935), Vol. VI, pp. 455-475 (The Loeb Classical Library); Bentwich, Philo-Judaeus, pp. 79f.].

30. Godbey, op. cit., p. 209; R. E. J., 1885, p. 305; J. Ency. II, 212 and VI, 514; [Colson, op. cit., De Vita Mosis II, 4, p. 459].

31. Jos. Ant. XIX, 5:2-3; [Contra Apionem I, 23, 25, 26].

32. [Jos. War VII, 10:3-4; Graetz, Dibre Yeme Yisrael II, 59, 83; Acts 4:36, 11:19, 13:5, 15:39].

CHAPTER TWELVE
Pp. 292 — 329

1. T. Reinach, Textes d'auteurs grecs et latins relatifs au judaisme, p. 259; Pliny, Natur. Hist. XIII, 4, 46 [quoted by Max Radin, The Jews Among the Greeks and Romans, (Philadelphia, 1915), p. 196]; Horace, Sat. I, 4, [18, quoted by Radin, op. cit., p. 247]; II Tim. 3:6f.; [Acts 16:20f.].

2. Jos. War II, 12:7; Ant. XV, 10:1; XVIII, 6:4; Yer. Berakot 9a.

3. Renan, Saint Paul, (Eng. Tr.,), London, p. 54.

4. Berakot 8a; Ps. 128:2; 145:18; Dt. 6:7.

5. Ab. d'R. N., c. 16 [ed. Schechter, 32a and n. 11]; Kidd. 40a; Gittin 58a.

6. [Yer. Bab. M. 2, 5, 8c].

7. [Yoma 84a].

8. [Radin, op. cit., pp. 224f., gives the relevant detailed passage from Cicero's speech in behalf of Flaccus (Pro Flacco, 66-69)].

9. [Bentwich, op. cit., p. 216; Radin, op. cit., pp. 300 and 338]; Bamberger, op. cit., p. 232 [quoting Yer. Nazir 8, 1, 57a]; Dion Cassius 46, 6.

10. Semahot c. 8; Ab. Zara 17b-18a; Sanh. 14a; "Midrash Ele Ezkerah," in Otzar Midrashim (N.Y., 1915), p. 443.

11. Ab. d'R. N. c. 17.

12. Taanit 29a.

13. Taanit 18a.

14. Ovid, Art of Love I, 75-6; Horace, Sat. I, 9, 61-72; Persius, Sat. VI, 319-26 (Gifford's Tr.); [Radin, op. cit., pp. 250ff. and 321f.].

15. Juvenal, *Sat.* VI, 778-87 (Gifford's Tr.); [Radin, *op. cit.*, pp. 323f.]; *Sibyl. Oracles* VII, 132-8.

16. [Margolis, *op. cit.*, pp. 26-43].

17. In *R. H.* 17b this matron's name is given as Valeria.

18. *A. Z.* 54b-55a; *Mekilta* 20, 5.

19. *Koh. R.* 9:3; Jellinek, *Bet Hamidrash* V, 132.

20. *Tanh. Tazria* 5; *Sanh.* 65b; *B. B.* 10a; *Tanh. Terumah* 3; Bacher, *Ag. Hat.* I, 2, 40f.

21. *B. K.* 38a; see Bamberger, *op. cit.*, p. 233, [quoting *Sifre D.* 344 on 33:3].

22. *Koh. R.* 1:28; *Lev. R.* 13, end.

23. *Oracles* 8:50-67, 141-5, 169-70; Suetonius, *Augustus* c. 94.

24. *Oracles* 3:337-64.

25. *Ibid.*, 3:46-54, 663-71; 7:108-12.

26. *Ibid.*, 2:6-33; 2nd Esdras [IV Ezra in Charles] c. 11; see Huidekoper, *op. cit.*, pp. 130f., n. 38.

27. *Against Apion* II, 2:24; 29-33; 37, 40.

28. [Radin, *op. cit.*, p. 224]; Graetz, *Dib. Yeme Yisrael* II, 24; Leroy-Beaulieu, *Israel Among the Nations*, (N.Y., 1900), pp. 103f.; M. Gaster, "Spread of Judaism," in *The Jewish Library*, (1st Series, N. Y., 1928), p. 124.

29. Juvenal, *Sat.* 4:230-5; 14:96-106 (Gifford's Tr.).

30. *Clementine Homilies* V, 2-26; *J. E.* I, 668.

31. H. Vogelstein and P. Rieger, *Geschichte der Juden in Rom*, (Berlin, 1896), I, 92f.; Schürer, *Geschichte*, III³, 483f. (Leipzig, 1909).

32. Pliny *Nat. Hist.* VII, 18, 3; Dio Cassius 59, 6 and 29; Tacitus, *Annals* 5, 8.

33. Tac., *Annals* 13, 32; *Antiq.* XVIII, 3:5.

34. Graetz, *Dib. Yeme Yisrael* II, 206.

35. Vogelstein and Reiger, *op. cit.*, I, 74; *Yebamot* 46a; *R. H.* 17b; *Mas. Gerim* 2:4.

36. Tacitus, *Annals* 13, 45; Jos., *Life*, Par. 3; *Antiq.* XX, 8:11.

37. Eisenstein, *Ozar Massaot* (N.Y., 1926), p. 75; Vilney, *Legends of Palestine*, (Phila., 1932), p. 143; [Graetz, *Geschichte*, IV², pp. 485f.]; *Ab. Zar.* 10a; [S. Krauss, *Antoninus Und Rabbi*, (Frankfurt a.m., 1910), pp. 43 and 67; Bamberger, *op. cit.*, pp. 248-50.]. *Gen. R.* 11:4; *Lev. R.* 10:4.

38. *Sanh.* 91a-b; *Ab. Zar.* 10b; *Lev. R.* 3:2; Bacher, *Ag. Hat.* II, 2, p. 131, n. 22; [*Yer. Megil.* I, 13, 72b].

39. [Graetz, *op. cit.*, IV², pp. 112-116; Bamberger, *op. cit.*, pp. 238-43.]. *Ab. Zar.* 11a; *Megil.* 3a; *Gen. R.* 70:5; *Pesik. R.* (ed. Friedmann), 116b-117a; *Tanh. Mishpatim*, Par. 5; *Yalkut Beshal.* 229.

CHAPTER THIRTEEN
Pp. 330 — 352

1. [*Sanh.* 105a; *Ab. Zar.* 64b; Maim. *Melakim* 8, 11; *Sanh.* 59a, 71a; D. Hoffman, *Der Shulchan Aruch und die Rabbinen ueber das Verhaeltniss der Juden zu Andersglaubigen*, (Berlin, 1894), pp. 144ff.]. *Hullin* 13b. By *minuth* the Rabbis referred to those who accepted some, if not all, of the moral teachings of Judaism. They also used the terms *Kuthim, Zadukim, Apikorsim, Kofrim*, etc., indiscrimin-

ately. [These words need qualification. See the definitive statement by I. Broyde, "Min," *J. E.* VIII, 594f. The meaning of "Min" must be related to the epoch to which the particular passage *in context* belongs. See also Graetz, *Geschichte* IV², 47, 48, 81, 104ff., 433f.].

2. [The examples of rabbinic exegesis and the *haggadot* transmitted by Justin give evidence of the general tendency, almost in all times, for Christians to turn to rabbis for additional light on the O. T. writings. See A. Lukyn Williams, *Justin Martyr, The Dialogue With Trypho,* (London, 1930), pp. 33, 72, 80, 110ff., 118, 129 — see especially the footnotes on each one of these pages. See also H. Hailperin, "The Hebrew Heritage of Mediaeval Christian Biblical Scholarship," *Historia Judaica* V, 2, pp. 133f., 153f. "Origenis Epistola ad Africanum," *Opera Omnia* (Berlin, 1847), I, Par. 7, col. 62f.; Par. 8, col. 63; Par. 6, col. 62; "De Principiis," *op. cit.,* I, c. 3, Par. 4, p. 74; Graetz, *Geschichte* IV², 232 and G. F. Moore, *Judaism* I, 165 and n. 1. On Jerome, see S. Krauss's admirable article in the *J. E.* VII, 116 and M. Rahmer, *Die hebräischen Traditionen in den Werken des Hieronymus* (Breslau, 1861), pp. 8, 9 and 11].

3. Acts 28:17-23.

4. *Sanh.* 59a; *Num. R.* 8:2; *Exod. R.* 15:23; *Shabbat* 118b; M. Friedlander, *The Jewish Religion* (London, 1927), p. 3; *Sanh.* 99a; I. Husik, *Sefer Ha-Ikkarim,* (*Book of Principles*), by *Joseph Albo,* (Phila., 1920), I, 44-7.

5. *Ab. Zar.* 16a-17b, 27b; *Ecc. R.* 10:7.

6. Acts 21:20; Jos., *Antiq.* XX, 9:1.

7. 2 Tim. 3:16; Mat. 24:20; Jerome on Ezekiel 16:16 (*cf.* Mat. 9:16); Renan, *Origins of Christianity,* (London), VI, 150-3; Graetz, *Geschichte* IV², 81.

8. A. Harnack, *Hist of Dogma* I, c. 6; J. H. Kurtz, *Hist. of the Christian Church* I, Sec. 28, Sec. 33; Harnack, *op. cit.,* III, 14-20; I John 4:2f.; Jerome, *Dial. adversus Lucifer,* Par. 23; "Docetae," in *Cath. Ency.* V, 70f.

9. Renan, *op. cit.,* Bk. VI, pp. 177f.; *idem,* c. IX-X.

10. *Jewish Ency.,* V, 681f., "Gnosticism".

11. [G. Krüger, "Marcion, Marcionites," *Schaff-Herzog Ency.* VII, 172-4].

12. [F. W. Farrar, *History of Interpretation,* (New York, 1886), p. 165, n. 3; W. Walker, *A History of the Christian Church,* (N. Y., 1921), pp. 61f.]; Matt. 26:28; Mark 14:24.

13. [Schürer, *op. cit.,* II, 3, pp. 35, 41, 70f., 81f., 109; G. F. Moore, "Apocrypha," *J. E.* II, 5].

14. Mark 4:38; 10:18; 13:32; 14:36, 38; Matt. 5:43f.; 23:23f.; see [E. A.] Abbott and [W. G.] Rushbrooke, *The Common Tradition of the Synoptic Gospels* [London, 1884]; E. P. Gould, *The Gospel According to St. Mark,* (N. Y., 1896), p. 186; Mark shows his ignorance of the Jewish law by making Jesus tell the Pharisees that "if a woman put away her husband, and be married to another, she committeth adultery" (10:12) — which was unknown in Israel. [For a corrective of Raisin's statement here, see I. Abrahams, *Studies In Pharisaism And The Gospels,* (Cambridge University Press, 1917), pp. 66ff., and H. L. Strack and P. Billerbeck, *Kommentar Zum Neuen Testament Aus Talmud Und Midrasch,* (Munich, 1924) on Mark 10:12, Vol. II, pp. 23f.].

15. Luke 3:37; 9:52f.; 10:13-15.

16. John 7:19, 22; 8:17; 10:34; 11:50f.; 17:25.

17. Epistle of James 1:24, 27; 2:19-22; 5:10-12. For Jewish parallels to James' teachings, see Kohler in *J. E.* VII, 68-70.

18. Hebrews 5:10; 7:12-22; 10:28f., [and the whole of ch. 11]; see Graetz, Eng. Tr., II, 370-2.

19. *Sanh.* 38b-39a; *Gen. R.* 8:8, 9:14; *Shabbat* 152a; *Pesahim* 56a; 87b; *Ab. Zar* 6b; 17a; *Sukkah* 48b.

20. *Ab. Zar.* 4a; 27b-28a; *Ecc. R.* 1:25; *Shabbat* 116a-b; *Yoma* 57a; *Berak.* 12a; 28a.

21. III John 9, 10, 12; Dio Cassius 68:32; Eus., *Hist. Ecc.* 8:2.

22. [A. Lukyn Williams, *op. cit.*, chs. 16 and 17, pp. 32-36; Ch. 1, pp. 1ff., *et passim*].

23. [*Ibid.*, pp. XXII; 110-17; 124ff.]; Tertullian, *Adv. Prax.* 16; *Adv. Judaeos* 9.

24. [A. Lukyn Williams, *op. cit.*, chs. 19-23, pp. 38-49; Chs. 134 and 135, pp. 276ff. and 278ff.].

25. [*Yer. Hag.* 77a; *Sifre* (*ed.* Friedmann, Wien, 1864), Par. 112, p. 35a; see the authoritative and all-inclusive article on "Allegorical Interpretation," by L. Ginzberg, in *J. E.* I, 403-11; for an enlargement and corrective of Raisin's judgment here, see H. Hailperin, "Intellectual Relations Between Jews and Christians," in *University of Pittsburgh Bulletin,* (Vol. 30, No. 2, 1933), pp. 130 and 137].

26. [A. Harnack, "Didache," Schaff-Herzog *Ency.* III, 420-24, and H. Achelis, "Apostolic Constitutions And Canons," *ibid.*, I, 245f.].

27. *Sibyl. Oracle* 2:241-5; *Cohortatio ad Graecos* c. 38; A. Baumstark, *Revue Biblique,* April 1906, pp. 253f.; Fouard, *St. Peter,* (N. Y., 1893); Jos., *Antiq.* XVIII, 63.

28. *Epistle of Barnabas* 4, 6f.; *Cohortatio* c. 13; Huidekoper, *op. cit.*, pp. 501f., n. 26; Harnack, *Expansion,* I, 34, 65f.; C. H. Moehlman, *The Christian-Jewish Tragedy,* (Rochester, N. Y., 1933), pp. 206-11.

VOLUME TWO

VOLUME TWO

CHAPTER FOURTEEN

Pp. 355 — 374

1. St. Augustine, Epistle 1; [*The History of the Decline and Fall of the Roman Empire by Edward Gibbon, Esq., ed.* H. H. Milman, (Philadelphia, 1872), II, 325-41 and III, 131-163].

2. [This paragraph is wholly that of the editor—one of several radical changes in the *corpus* made necessary by the requirements of coherence and continuity. The appeal to the O. T. and to the wider Jewish intellectual *milieu* by Christians of all persuasions is a constant throughout the history of Jewish and Christian relations].

3. [Sanh. 39a; see Gibbons, *op. cit.*, II, 297-369; A. Harnack, *History of Dogma*, (Boston, 1899), V, 140-203].

4. [James Parkes, *The Conflict of the Church and the Synagogue*, (London, 1934), p. 303].

5. [James Parkes, *The Jew in the Medieval Community*, (London, 1938), p. 102; Graetz, (Hebrew), II, 440f., *Geschichte* IV², pp. 389f. and 395; Clyde Pharr, *The Theodosian Code And Novels And The Sirmondian Constitutions*, (Princeton Univ. Press, 1952), 16.8.7, p. 468, and 16.8.21-29, pp. 469ff.].

6. [Graetz, *Geschichte* V², 36f.].

7. [*Ibid.* V², 17-19; Parkes, *Conflict*, pp. 246-255].

8. [Parkes, *Conflict*, p. 250; Gibbons, *op. cit.*, IV, 527-34].

9. [*Ibid.*, pp. 160f., 163-168, 210ff., 160ff., 110, 105].

10. [*Ibid.*, pp. 210ff., 283-85].

11. [*Ibid.*, pp. 285-294].

12. [*Ibid.*, pp. 294, 263, 166ff., 331, 235, 238, 207, 166-168, 244, 193].

13. [*Ibid.*, pp. 263f., 238].

14. [*Ibid.*, p. 401].

15. [*Ibid.*, pp. 212ff., 353, 355, 360ff.].

16. [*Ibid.*, pp. 394-400].

CHAPTER FIFTEEN

Pp. 375 — 407

1. Graetz, (Hebrew), III, 73f.; Israel Benzew, *Hayehudim Baarab*, (Tel Aviv, 1931), pp. 7f.

2. Benzew, *op. cit.*, pp. 81f.

3. Graetz, (Hebrew), III, 92f.

4. Laurence E. Browne, *The Eclipse of Christianity In Asia*, (Cambridge University Press, 1933), pp. 14-18; [Godbey, *op. cit.*, pp. 178f.].

5. Graetz, (Heb. Tr.), III, 84f., 404ff.

6. [Graetz, *Geschichte*, V², 77-80]; W. Robertson Smith, *Religion of the Sem-*

ites, (London, 1907), pp. 70f. and 109f.

7. [Graetz, *loc. cit.*, pp. 81ff.].

8. Graetz, (Heb. Tr.), III, 78-87; [Graetz, *Geschichte*, V², 95ff.; 100ff.; *The Koran*, (*ed.* Sale), all of ch. V, pp. 97-117, especially p. 110].

9. [*Koran, op. cit.*, p. 10].

10. [Graetz, *Geschichte*, V², 103; *Koran, op. cit.*, ch. LIX, pp. 527f.].

11. Benzew, *op. cit.*, pp. 163f.; [Graetz, *loc. cit.*, pp. 93f.].

12. Benzew, *op. cit.*, pp. 177ff.; [Graetz, pp. 110ff.].

13. [Sale, "Preliminary Discourse," *op. cit.*, Sec. VII, pp. 158-161].

14. A. Geiger, *Was Hat Mohammed Aus Dem Judentume Aufgenommen?*, [Bonn, 1834]; A. Guillaume, "The Influence of Judaism On Islam," in *The Legacy of Israel*, (Oxford, 1927), pp. 129-171; [D. S.] Margoliouth, *Mohammed And The Rise of Islam*, (London, 1905).

15. Renan, [*The History of the Origins of Christianity*, (London, 1890), Pt. 6, p. 154].

16. [*The Koran*, (*ed.* Sales), pp. 14ff.].

17. Browne, *op. cit.*, pp. 39f., 48f., 51f., [88].

18. D. Menant, *Le Parsis*, (Paris, 1898); *The Great Religions of the World*, (N. Y., 1901), pp. 109-38.

19. Browne, *op. cit.*, pp. 112f.

20. *Ibid.*, pp. 57f.

21. J. Finkel, *Three Essays*, (Cairo, 1927), pp. 17-20; Browne, *op. cit.*, pp. 53f., 106f.

22. Browne, *op. cit.*, p. 132.

23. *Ibid.*, pp. 110f.; Migne, *Patrologia Graeca*, 94:1586.

24. Browne, *op. cit.*, pp. 118 and 120.

25. "Kitab Masalik an-Nazar," (tr. S. A. Weston), *Journal Oriental Society*, 1903, pp. 363, 375, 381; Browne, *op. cit.*, pp. 118f.

26. Browne, *op. cit.*, pp. 121f.; I. Goldziher, *Vorlesungen über den Islam*, (Heidelberg, 1925), p. 109.

27. Graetz, (Heb. Tr.), III, note 11, pp. 412ff.

28. *Ibid.*, pp. 170-2, 428-31.

29. *Ibid.*, pp. 431ff.

30. *Ibid.*, pp. 453-4.

31. Jellinek, *Beth Hamidrash* III, 78; Eisenstein, *Ozar Mid.*, (N. Y., 1915), p. 555; A. H. Silver, *A History of Messianic Speculation in Israel*, (N. Y., 1927), pp. 36f., [43f.].

32. *Taam Zeḳenim*, (1854), pp. 59a-61a.

33. [I. Abrahams, *Jewish Life In The Middle Ages*, (London, 1932, *ed.* Cecil Roth), pp. 116f.].

34. Graetz, (Heb. Tr.), III, 38, 396; Migne, *op. cit.*, 12:265 [i.e. *M P G*].

35. J. D. Eisenstein, *Ozar Vikuchim*, (N. Y., 1928), pp. 310-15.

36. Graetz, (Heb. Tr.), III, 498f., [Harkavy's Additions].

37. Ginzberg, *Legends etc.*, IV, 324f.

CHAPTER SIXTEEN
Pp. 408 — 446

1. *Sanh.* 110b.—111a.

2. II Kings 17:6; II Esdras 13:39-47.

3. *Ekah R.* 5:2; Jos., *War* VII, 5:1; Pliny, *Nat. Hist.* XXXI, 2; Koran, Sura VII, '159.

4. Graetz, (Heb. Tr.), III, 268f.; A. Epstein, *Eldad Hadani,* (Pressburg, 1891); *Ency. Brit.,* 14th ed., *s. v.* "Prester John"; Eisenstein, *Otzar Massaoth,* pp. 38, 84, 113ff.; J. Jacobs, *Jewish Contributions to Civilization,* (Philadelphia, 1919), pp. 122f., 138, 194f. [In this connection, see the important contribution of L. Rabinowitz, *Jewish Merchant Adventurers — A Study of the Radanites,* (London, 1948), pp. 9ff. and the whole of Pt. II, pp. 108-197].

5. Godbey, *op. cit., pp.* 357f.; T. Holdich, "Afghan Claims to Descent From Israel," in *The Nineteenth Century,* July, 1919, pp. 111-5.

6. Godbey, *op. cit.,* pp. 372, 388.

7. *Ibid.* pp. 289-90; *J. E.* II, 440f., art. "Bagratuni"; J. J. Williams, *Hebrewisms in West Africa,* (N.Y., 1931), pp. 133f.

8. Eisenstein's *Otzar Massaoth,* p. 64.

9. [Godbey, *op. cit.,* pp. 337ff.].

10. *Ibid.,* pp. 17, 317, 344, 353ff. [Ezekiel Moses Ezekiel, "Beni Israel," *The Universal Jewish Encyclopedia,* II, 173-6; by the same author, "India," *ibid.,* V, 553-6].

11. [Godbey, *op. cit.,* pp. 355ff.]; *Tageblatt,* Aug. 1, 1922.

12. Godbey, *op. cit.,* pp. 422ff.; A. M. Hyamson, *New Era Illustrated Magazine,* 1905, pp. 400-4. [Cordier and Kohler, "China," *J. E.,* IV, 33-38; B. Postal, "China," *The Universal J. E.,* III, 156-9].

13. "Salem Shaloam David," *J. E.,* X, 650.

14. D. A. Brown, in *The American Hebrew And Jewish Tribune,* Jan. 27, '33 and Feb. 10, '33; Z. Kasdai, *Miyarkete Tevel,* (Jerusalem, 1914), II, 28f.

15. Godbey, op. cit., pp. 423f.; S. Sapir in *Tageblatt,* Sept. 21, '23.

16. Godbey, *op. cit.,* pp. 424f.; Williams, *op. cit.,* pp. 184f.

17. N. Slouschz, *Travels in North Africa,* (Phila., 1927), pp. 185, 336f.; Godbey, *op. cit.,* pp. 18f.

18. Godbey, *op. cit.,* pp. 19, 91f., 204f.

19. *Vayik. R.* 17:6; Slouschz, *op. cit.,* pp. 257f., 287f., 433. [*J. E.,* I, 226, "Africa"].

20. Slouschz, *op. cit.,* pp. 41, 228f., 345.

21. *Yebamot* 63b; Slouschz, *op. cit.,* pp. 111 and 219; Godbey, *op. cit.,* pp. 224f.; *Menahot* 110a; Commodianus, *Instruction* 24:11-14, 37:1-13. [The book by Paul Emanuel Lo Bagola, describing the Bnai Ephraim, was published by Knopf, New York, 1930].

22. Phoenicians, in Greek *Phoenikoi,* means "red"; Williams, *op. cit.,* pp. 252f.; Slouschz, *op. cit.,* pp. 110f.

23. [A. Lukyn Williams, *Adversus Judaeos,* (Cambridge Univer. Press, 1935), pp. 312-338].

24. Schlouschz, *op. cit.*, pp. 220, 231; Gibbon, IV, 469.

25. J. W. Draper, *History of the Intellectual Development of Europe*, (New York, 1875), I, 338; I. Goldziher, *Moham. Studien*, II, 777f.; Browne, *op. cit.*, pp. 60f.; S. Lane-Poole, *A History of Egypt in the Middle Ages*, (London, 1925), pp. 125f.; *Journal Asiatique*, (1877), I, 377f.; I. M. Robertson, *A Short History of Freethought*, [London, 1906, I², 261f.].

26. Graetz, (Heb. Tr.), V, 74f., 167, 380f.; I. Benjamin, *Mas'e Israel*, (Lyck, 1859), pp. 82f.; C. Roth, *A History of the Marranos*, (Phila., 1932), p. 6; L. W. Schwartz, *The Jewish Caravan*, (N.Y., 1935), pp. 311f.; Oskar Mann, in *Great Religions of the World*, (N.Y., 1901), pp. 53f.; E. D. Ross, *Idem*, pp. 189f.

27. E. G. Browne, *The History of the Bab*, (Cambridge, 1893); S. K. Vatralsky, "Mohammedan Gnosticism in America," in *Amer. Journ. of Theology*, (Jan. 1902), pp. 57f.; J. E. Esslemout, *Baha'u'llah And The New Era*, (N.Y., 1937), pp. 265f.; also translated into Hebrew, (Haifa, 1931). There have always been translations of the Bible into Persian, beginning with a Pahlavi version in the Sassanid period, to the Jacob Tawns translation into modern Persian at the beginning of the sixteenth century, published in the Polyglot Pentateuch, Constantinople, 1546, down to Simeon Hakam's rendition, Jerusalem, 1901-3. P. Grayevsky, *Hagerim*, (Jerusalem, 1932), I, 8, 9, 12-15, 20f.; II, 8, 11, 13, 15.

28. Gibbon, III, 232f.; C. A. Scott, *Ulfilas, Apostle of the Goths*, 1885.

29. Graetz, (Heb. Tr.), III, 71f., 148-51.

30. [Graetz, *Geschichte*, V², pp. 66, 141-6].

31. Renan, *Judaism As Race And Religion*, pp. 22f.; *R. E. J.* XXVII, 9.

32. Gregory of Tours, *Historia Francorum* VI, 17; Graetz, (Heb. Tr.), III, 61f.

33. J. Haccohen, *Emek Habakah*.

34. [Parkes, *Conflict*, pp. 324, 342f.].

35. Gross, *Gallia Judaica*, p. 404; Zacuto, *Yuhasin* (London), p. 84; [Rabinowitz, *op. cit.*, pp. 18, 159f., 183-5; for a critical estimate of the tradition about a Rabbi Machir who was summoned by Charlemagne from Babylon, see S. Dubnow, *Weltgeschichte des jüdischen Volkes*, (Berlin, 1926), IV, 109. Prof. Louis Ginzberg once told the present editor that later generations undoubtedly confused Charlemagne with some other emperor who influenced some Jews in Italy to settle along the Rhine. This happened about two hundred years after Charlemagne. To base history on a later story is the way of legends. That is to say, they transferred a later historical fact to an earlier supposed event].

36. Graetz, (Heb. Tr.), III, 235ff. [S. Katz, *The Jews in the Visigothic and Frankish Kingdoms of Spain and Gaul*, (Cambridge, Mass., 1937), pp. 85ff.].

37. Graetz, (Heb. Tr.), III, pp. 240f.; [Migne, *P L*, 194:72f., 74f.; 104:86, 87ff., 107].

38. Graetz, (Heb. Tr.), III, pp. 250f.

39. *Ibidem*, pp. 247ff., 207f.

40. [Graetz, *Geschichte*, V², pp. 366f., 495f. For a sound corrective of what Raisin says here, see Guido Kisch, *The Jews in Medieval Germany — A Study of Their Legal and Social Status*, (Chicago, 1949), pp. 135-9].

CHAPTER SEVENTEEN
Pp. 447 — 466

1. Gibbon [ed. Milman, Phila., 1872, Vol. III, pp. 520-37], Ch. 37; H. Hallam, *The Middle Ages*, Bk. 7, Pt. 1; Lecky, *Hist. of European Morals*, [N. Y., 1886, Vol. II, pp. 183-8].

2. H. O. Taylor, *The Mediaeval Mind*, (London, 1938), I, 488f. [and 373 f.].

3. J. L. Mosheim, *Ecc. Hist.*, on 9th, 10th, 11th and 12th centuries; J. C. L. Gieseler, [*A Text Book of Church History*, (New York, 1865), II, pp. 30-8, 146-51, 188-92]; James Bryce, *The Holy Roman Empire*, [New York, 1930], p. 161; [W. Walker, *History of the Christian Church*, (N. Y., 1921), pp. 204ff.].

4. [Bryce, *op. cit.*, pp. 159f., 170f.]

5. Charles Mills, *History of the Crusades*, I, 5, 15, 24; Gibbon, chs. 57-8.

6. A. C. Krey, *The First Crusade*, (Princeton, 1921), pp. 38f., [48f.].

7. J. W. Draper, *op. cit.*, II, 56; Gibbon, ch. 60; Draper, II, 135f.; F. C. Connybear, *Key to the Truth*, (Oxford, 1878); Mosheim, *Ecc. History*, IXth cent., II, 5, [ed. A. Maclaine, New York, 1859, Vol. I, pp. 327-334].

8. C. Schmidt, *Histoire de la secte des Cathares ou Albigensis*, (Paris, 1849); [Walker, *op. cit.*, pp. 235f., 249].

9. Gieseler, *op. cit.*, [II, 549-56]; H. C. Lea, *A History of the Inquisition of the Middle Ages*, (N. Y., 1888), I, 89f., 563f.; II, 290f., 569f.

10. Hallam, *op. cit.*, [New York, 1837, pp. 504-7]; P. Melia, *The Origin, Persecutions, and Doctrines of the Waldenses*, (London, 1870). John Milton was of the opinion that the Waldenses were the guardians of Christianity in its pristine purity. Their name, pronounced Vaudois, became synonymous with witchcraft.

11. Taylor, *op. cit.*, II, [pp. 368-85].

12. Mosheim, *op. cit.*, [I, pp. 341, 364, 380f.].

13. [Walker, *op. cit.*, pp. 260, 283]; C. Ullmann, *Reformers Before The Reformation*, [Edinburgh, 1855], II, 13f.; Mosheim, *op. cit.*, [I, 360-4, 376].

14. *Pirke Abot* 2:8, 4:12, 6:4; Matt. 16:14, 19:21; Luke 9:3, 14:33.

15. C. A. Addison, *The Knights Templars*, (London, 1854); Taylor, *op. cit.*, I, 547f.

16. Taylor, *op. cit.*, I, 318, 491f.; II, 55-64.

17. Vogelstein and Rieger, *op. cit.*, I, 214f.

CHAPTER EIGHTEEN
Pp. 467 — 500

1. *Shire Solomon b. Judah Ibn Gabirol*, (Tel Aviv, 1925), No. 9; Singer, *Daily Prayer-Book*, p. 90; Eisenstein, *Ozar Massaoth*, p. 44; Silver, *Messianic Speculation etc.*, pp. 49f., 58f.

2. Parkes, *The Jew in the Medieval Community*, pp. 65f.

3. *Ibid.*, p. 77; [J. R. Marcus, *The Jew in the Medieval World*, (Cincinnati, 1938), pp. 115ff.; Graetz, *Geschichte*, VI^2, pp. 91-100; A Kober, *Cologne*, (trans. S. Grayzel), Philadelphia, 1940, pp. 15-20; Graetz, *Geschichte*, VII^2, 277ff.].

4. S. Bernfeld, *Sefer Ha-Dema'ot*, (Berlin, 1925), I, 143f., 207; Silver, *op. cit.*, pp. [59], 77f.; J. Mann, in *Hattekufah*, XXIII, 243f.

5. [Graetz, *Geschichte*, VI², pp. 269-72; J. H. Greenstone, *The Messiah Idea in Jewish History*, (Phila., 1906), pp. 141f.]. J. Mann, in *Hattekufah*, XXIV, 341f.

6. Eisenstein, *op. cit.*, pp. 36f.; Maimonides, *Iggeret Teman*, (1875), pp. 50f.

7. *Zohar*, II, 7a-10a. [Raisin's quotation is a summary of the text].

8. *Ibid.*, I, 38b, 95a-b, 117a-118a, III, 167b-168a. Sometimes, however, the Zohar discriminates against *gerim* as in I, 25a; II, 37a.

9. *Ibid.*, III, 236b-237a. [I could not find Raisin's quotation from Isaiah 11:10, in this connection, in the Zohar text].

10. Silver, *op. cit.*, pp. 87f.; Graetz, Heb. Tr., V, 182f.; Vogelstein and Rieger, *op. cit.*, I, 249. [J. L. Blau, *The Christian Interpretation of the Cabala in the Renaissance*, (New York, 1944), pp. 15f., 22, 40, 46].

11. [A. A. Neuman, *The Jews In Spain*, (Philadelphia, 1942), II, 113f.; *Adret*, I, 548; *J. E.*, I, 98, s. v. "Abraham of Avila."]

12. [Graetz, *Geschichte*, VI², 166f.; S. Grayzel, *The Church And The Jews In The XIIIth Century*, (Phila., 1933), pp. 87-147].

13. Parkes, *Med. Comm.*, pp. 42f., [58, 85f., 152]; Grayzel, *op. cit.*, p. 93 [Pope Innocent III was repeating here the precise language of several predecessors].

14. Parkes, *op. cit.*, pp. 79, 81, 142f.; Graetz, Heb. Tr., IV, 107f. [For an authoritative and definitive statement on "Chamber Serfdom" and the theological-juridical concept of *Servitus Judeorum*, see G. Kisch, *The Jews In Medieval Germany, A Study of Their Legal and Social Status*, (Chicago, 1949), pp. 129-168].

15. [Parkes, *op. cit.*, pp. 118, 138, 140].

16. L. I. Newman, *Jewish Influence On Christian Reform Movements*, (New York, 1925), pp. 61f. [For a corrective of this section, see H. Hailperin, in works cited in note 1 of Editor's Preface, *supra*, p. 799, especially in *Historia Judaica*, V, 138ff. and 148ff.].

17. Graetz, Heb. Tr., V, 102f.; Eisenstein, *Ozar Vikuhim*, (N. Y., 1928), pp. 81f. [See F. I. Baer, "The Disputations of R. Yechiel of Paris and Nachmanides" [Hebrew], in *Tarbiz*, II, p. 176].

18. Graetz, *loc. cit.*, pp. 122f. [See A. Lukyn Williams, *Adversus Judaeos*, (Cambridge, England, 1935), pp. 259f.].

19. Graetz, *loc. cit.*, pp. 273f., 396f. [See the important footnotes in A. Lukyn Williams, *op. cit.*, pp. 261-66].

20. [A. Lukyn Williams, *op. cit.*, pp. 233-40]. J. Jacobs, *Jewish Contributions To Civilization*, (Phila., 1919), pp. 155f.

21. Parkes, *op. cit.*, pp. 31f. Steinschneider and others maintain that the letter was really written by a fourteenth century Dominican of Spain. Parkes [p. 31, n. 4], however, is convinced that the document was composed by a rabbi of Spain who became a convert to Christianity in the eleventh century. [See also Lukyn Williams, *op. cit.*, pp. 228-32. On Raymond Martin, see the authoritative and accurate statement of George Foot Moore, "Christian Writers On Judaism," *Harvard Theological Review*, Vol. XIV, No. 3, (July, 1921), pp. 203-5, and the excellent study of S. Lieberman, "Raimund Martini And His Alleged Forgeries," in *Historia Judaica*, V, 87-102; see also Lukyn Williams, *op. cit.*, pp. 248-55].

22. [Grayzel, *op. cit.*, pp. 61-9; Kisch, "The Yellow Badge in History," *Historia Judaica*, IV, 95-144].

23. [Kisch, *op. cit.*, pp. 277-85; Parkes, *op. cit.*, pp. 142f.; Kisch, "Studien Zur Geschichte des Judeneides im Mittelalter," *H U C A*, XIV, 431-456].

24. Parkes, *op. cit.*, p. 126; M. Lowenthal, *The Jews of Germany*, (Phila., 1936), p. 125.

25. *B. Kamma* 84; [*B. Bathra* 90]; I. Abrahams, *Jewish Life in the Middle Ages*, [*ed.* C. Roth, London, 1932, pp. 257f.]; Grayzel, *op. cit.*, p. 46, n. 24. [C. Roth, *A History of the Marranos*, (Phila., 1932), pp. 11-53, 99-145; Parkes, *op. cit.*, pp. 338ff.].

26. Parkes, *op. cit.*, p. 144.

27. *Sefer Hasidim*, 377.

28. Newman, *op. cit.*, pp. 240f. [and 403-29; see, in this connection, Hailperin, *H J*, V, 147, and also in *Rashi Anniversary Volume*, N. Y., 1941, pp. 126f.].

29. [Newman, *op. cit.*, pp. 401f.].

30. [See *Tos.* on *Kid.* 71a and *supra*, ch. V, n. 29, p. 805]. D. Yellin, *Kobez Teshubot Harambam*, I, 158ff.; Graetz, Heb. Tr., IV, 335.

31. J. Mann, in *Hatekufah*, XXIV, [337f.].

32. Eisenstein, *Ozar Mass.*, p. 75.

33. Bernfeld, *op. cit.*, I, 170, 313, 318f.; II, 40. A. Neubauer, "La Memorbuch de Mayence," *R E J*, 1882, p. 413.

34. C. Roth, in *B. B. Magazine*, Feb. 1935, p. 160.

CHAPTER NINETEEN
Pp. 501—527

1. [Parkes, *op. cit.*, pp. 51, 142, 154, 156f., 296f.].

2. [H. Denifle, "Die Handschriften der Bibel-Correctorien des 13 Jahrhunderts," *Archiv für Litteratur und Kirchengeschichte*, (1888), IV, 263 and 471; J. H. Bridges, *The 'Opus Majus' of Roger Bacon*, (London, 1900), I, 66f.].

3. S. Berger, *Histoire de la Vulgate [pendant les premiers siècles du moyen age]*, Paris, 1893; H. Hailperin, "The Relations of Christian Scholars to Jewish Scholars and Rashi's Influence on Christian Biblical Commentators" (in Hebrew), *Proceedings of the Rabbinical Assembly of America*, VII, (1941), pp. 215-23; L. I. Newman, *op. cit.*, pp. 64ff.; *Zohar*, II, 43b, 212a; III, 65a. [See Hailperin in, "Nicolas de Lyra and Rashi," in *Rashi Anniversary Volume*, (N. Y., 1941), pp. 115-47; S. Berger, *Quam notitiam linguae hebraicae habuerint Christiani medii aevi temporibus in Gallia*, (Nancy, 1895), pp. 32-45; J. L. Blau, *op. cit.*, pp. 12, 15f., 27f., 39f., 51, 54f., 83f.].

4. J. Jacobs, *Jewish Contributions etc.*, pp. 138-63; [E. R. Bevan and C. Singer, *The Legacy of Israel*, (Oxford, 1927), pp. 216-38].

5. [Bevan and Singer, *op. cit.*, pp. 189f., 257-71; for a corrective of the popular conception of Maimonides' "influence" on Christian scholastics, see Hailperin, "Maimonides in History," in *A Rabbi Teaches*, pp. 154-71].

6. [Kaufmann Kohler, "Disputations," *J. E.*, IV, 617f.].

826   GENTILE REACTIONS TO JEWISH IDEALS

7. Graetz, Heb. Tr., VII, 145f. 164f.; *J. E.*, II, 254; *ibid.*, IV, 617f. [Graetz, Geschichte, VIII², 407ff.].

8. *J. E.*, VII, 269f.; Gross, *Gallia Judaica*, pp. 252, 438.

9. [*Selected Essays of James Darmesteter*, (ed. Morris Jastrow, Jr.), London, 1895, pp. 266f.].

10. Lea, *op. cit.*, III, 10. [L. I. Newman, *op. cit.*, pp. 70f.; Walker, *op. cit.*, p. 280].

11. I. Loeb, *La Controverse Religieuse* [*Entre les Chrétiens et les Juifs du Moyen Age*, Paris, 1887], pp. 26f.

12. Newman, *op. cit.*, pp. [60f.], 325, 346. [Grayzel, *op. cit.*, pp. 31f., 339f.].

13. J. Fuenn, *Kenesseth Yisrael*, pp. 358f.; Eisenstein, *Ozar Vik.*, pp. [94-104], 118f.; Graetz, Heb. Tr., VI, 87f., [90].

14. Graetz, *loc. cit.*, pp. 89, 410f., [419f.].

15. Eisenstein, *op. cit.*, pp. 236f.; J. Kaufman, *R. Yom Tov Lipmann Muehlhausen*, (in Hebrew), [N. Y., 1927], pp. 1-109.

16. Leo VIII, Epistle XIV.

17. Joseph Jacobs, *The Jews of Angevin England*, (N. Y., 1893), pp. 7, 78, 86f., 90, 93, 269, 45, 94, 153, 165, 207, 215f.

18. *Ibid.*, pp. 7-12.

19. *Ibid.*, pp. 179, 92f.

20. *Ibid.*, pp. 45f., 146.

21. *Ibid.*, pp. 256f.; J. Jacobs, *Jewish Ideals*, (N. Y., 1896), pp. 192f.

22. Jacobs, *The Jews of Angevin England*, pp. 22f., 99f., 112.

23. *Ibid.*, pp. 113f., 122. [See also M. Adler, *Jews of Medieval England*, (London, 1939), pp. 128f.].

24. Jacobs, *Jews of Angevin England*, pp. 105-7, 259, 283f. [Ephraim's account of the persecutions in Germany, France and England is not the same as the *Emek Habbakah* (as mistakenly stated by Raisin). The account by Ephraim of Bonn was printed for the first time as an *appendix* (!) to Wiener's German translation of Joseph ha-Kohen's *Emek Habbakah*, Leipzig, 1858].

25. Jacobs, *op. cit.*, pp. 284, 216; J. J. Walsh, *The Thirteenth, Greatest of Centuries*, (N. Y., 1912), p. 177. [Adler, *op. cit.*, p. 24].

26. Parkes, *The Jew in the Medieval Community*, p. 157; Graetz, Heb. Tr., V, 171f., 233f., 237. [Adler, *op. cit.*, pp. 62f., 279ff., 95-103; Parkes, *op. cit.*, pp. 328, 361, 334f.]. Milman, *History of the Jews*, (1878), pp. 548, 551.

27. [Parkes, *op. cit.*, p. 374; Graetz, Heb. Tr., VI, pp. 71f.].

CHAPTER TWENTY
Pp. 528 — 563

1. J. W. Draper, *The Intellectual Development of Europe*, (N. Y., 1918), II, 28f.; Graetz, *Heb. Tr.*, IV, 197f.

2. [A. A. Neuman, *The Jews In Spain*, I, 4, 233; II, 217, 221, 227f., 229; Graetz, *Geschichte*, VII², 385ff., 407f.; Parkes, *Med. Community*, p. 189].

3. [Neuman, *op. cit.*, I, 65; II, 153; C. Roth, *A History of the Marranos*, pp. 14f.].

4. Roth, *op. cit.*, pp. 17f., 21ff., [24].

5. M. Lowenthal, *The Jews of Germany*, (Phila., 1936), pp. 87f.

6. Graetz, *Heb. Tr.*, VI, 255-8; Roth, *op. cit.*, pp. 34, 38f.

7. Roth, *op. cit.*, pp. 42-4; Graetz, *loc. cit.*, pp. 313f.; Roth, *op. cit.*, pp. 22f., 272.

8. Roth, *op. cit.*, pp. 100-2; B. Braunstein, *The Chuetas of Majorca*, (1936), p. 25; Roth, *op. cit.*, pp. 27f.

9. Godbey, *op. cit.*, p. 339; Roth, *op. cit.*, pp. 74, 394; Braunstein, *op. cit.*, p. 30, n. 108; Graetz, *Heb. Tr.*, VI, pp. 309, 335, 348, 353, 450f.; E. N. Adler, *Auto de Fe And The Jew*, (London, 1908), p. 60. [Joseph Sarachek, *Don Isaac Abravanel*, (N. Y., 1938), p. 43].

10. Roth, *op. cit.*, p. 198; Graetz, *Heb. Tr.*, VI, 69, 156, 376; Roth, *op. cit.*, pp. 60, 394; Graetz, *loc. cit.*, pp. 392f., 460f., 381; [Roth, *op. cit.*, pp. 55-60; Godbey, *op. cit.*, p. 246].

11. Roth, *op. cit.*, p. 385.

12. *Ibid.*, pp. 168f.; Braunstein, *op. cit.*, pp. 56f., 96f.

13. Braunstein, *op. cit.*, pp. 80ff.

14. Roth, *op. cit.*, pp. 67f.

15. *Ibid.*, pp. 34f., 64f., 71f.

16. *R. Abraham Ibn Ezra*, (ed. D. Cahane, Warsaw, 1894), II, 78f.; M. Liber, *Rashi*, (Phila., 1906), pp. 67, 163f.

17. D. Yellin and I. Abrahams, *Maimonides*, (Phila., 1903), pp. 38f.; S. Asaf, in *Zion*, V, 61f.; H. J. Zimels, *Die Marranen in der Rabbinischen Literatur*, (Berlin, 1932).

18. Responsa of *Ribash*, 4, 5, 11, 12, [1, 6, 14, 43, 52]; *Rashbaz*, p. 14, Para. 44; p. 28b, Para. 227; Edelman, *Hemda Genuza*, pp. 14f. [A. M. Hershman, *Rabbi Isaac Perfet And His Times*, (N. Y., 1943), pp. 70f., 120, 217f.].

19. M. Kayserling, "Marano," *J. E.* VIII, 319.

20. Abravanel, Intro. to Book of Kings. [Sarachek, *op. cit.*, pp. 163-212].

21. Roth, *op. cit.*, pp. 146ff.; Silver, *op. cit.*, pp. 143f.; Greenstone, *op. cit.*, pp. 191ff., [194-199].

22. [Graetz, *Geschichte*, VIII², 372.; Roth, *op. cit.*, pp. 147f.].

23. Roth, *op. cit.*, pp. 149f.; M. Kayserling, *Geschichte der Juden in Portugal*, (Leipzig, 1867), pp. 82, 291f.

24. Roth, *op. cit.*, pp. 151f., 170.

25. *Ibid.*, pp. 158f., 307, 340.

26. *Ibid.*, p. 159.

27. *Ibid.*, pp. 155f.; Menasseh b. Israel, *Mikveh Yisrael*, XVIII, 63-4.

28. Roth, *op. cit.*, pp. 43, 161f.

29. Braunstein, *op. cit.*, pp. 60f.; *Taanit* 22a; M. Gaster, *Maaseh Book*, [Phila., 1934], I, 72f., II, 488f.; Jellinek, *B. Hamidrash* V, 156, VI, 60f.; Eisenstein, *O. Mid.* II, 557f.; Vogelstein and Rieger, *op. cit.*, I, 257; J. Blieden, in *Haleom*, Oct. 24, 1907; Jellinek, *op. cit.*, VI, 137f.; [M. Guedemann, *Erziehungswesens u. Kultur d. Juden in Italien*, (Wien, 1884), pp. 82f.].

30. [Guedemann, *op. cit.*, pp. 79f.]. Vogelstein and Rieger, *op. cit.*, I, 296f.; Samuel Schwarz, *Os Cristãos-Novos em Portugal no século XX*, (1925). [Roth, *op. cit.*, pp. 363ff.; "Marranos," in *Universal Jewish Encyclopedia*, VII, 366ff.; I. Elbogen, *A Century of Jewish Life*, (Phila., 1944), pp. 556ff.].

828 GENTILE REACTIONS TO JEWISH IDEALS

CHAPTER TWENTY-ONE
Pp. 564—584

1. Eisenstein, *Ozar Mas.*, p. 114.

2. Graetz, *Heb. Tr.*, VI, 240f., 428. [*Eng. Tr.*, IV, 273].

3. *Ibid.* (*Heb. Tr.*), VII, 238, 423; Roth, *op. cit.*, p. 325; I. Aboab, *Nomologia etc.*, p. 308.

4. [Roth, *op. cit.*, pp. 199, 202f., 205, 207; Marcus, *The Jew in the Medieval World*, pp. 411-17; Roth, *Doña Gracia*, (Phila., 1947), pp. 83-121 and Roth, *The Duke of Naxos*, (Phila., 1948), pp. 3-38].

5. [Roth, *Marranos*, pp. 86, 148, 322-38].

6. J. M. Robertson, *A Short History of Freethought*, (N. Y., 1906), I, 417f.; Renan, *Averroes*, pp. 301f., 333f.; J. Burckhardt, *The Civilization of the Renaissance in Italy*, (Eng., Tr., 1892), pp. 51f.; Dante, *Inferno*, Canto X. 14-5, 118 (*cf.* II. 9, IV. 5); M. Landau, *Die Quellen des Dekameron*, (1884), p. 182; Schechter, *Studies in Judaism*, 1896, pp. 207.; Boccaccio, *Decameron*, 1st Day, second and third stories; Wuensche in Lessing-Mendelssohn Gedenbuch, 1879, pp. 329f.; Walter Pater's essay in *Renaissance*, 1878; Benrath, *Bernardino Ochino of Sienna*, 1876, pp. 268f., 287f. [Blau, *op. cit.*, pp. 21-30].

7. A. Gordon, "The Sozzini And Their School," in *Theol. Rev.*, 1879.

8. [M. Stern, *Die Stellung der Päpste Zu den Juden*, p. 33, No. 21; *cf.* No. 31].

9. Graetz, *Heb. Tr.*, VI, 268, 444; Responsa Maharik, 88, 149.

10. [Cecil Roth, *Venice*, (Phila., 1930), pp. 237, 288]. Roth, *Marranos*, pp. 211, 214f.

11. Draper, *op. cit.*, [N. Y., 1904, II, 214, 220f., 258, 263ff.].

12. Graetz, *Heb. Tr.*, VII, 244ff. [Roth, *The History of the Jews of Italy*, (Phila., 1946), pp. 288ff., 294ff., 303f.].

13. [Graetz, *Geschichte*, IX², 481].

14. [See, in this connection, M. F. Modder, *The Jew in the Literature of England*, (Phila., 1939), pp. 257f., and E. N. Calish, *The Jew in English Literature*, (Richmond, Va., 1909), p. 144].

15. Roth, *Marranos*, pp. 5, 198.

16. *Ibid.*, pp. 209f.; S. Bernstein, in *Shomre Hahomoth*, (Tel Aviv, 5698), pp. 49f.

17. Vogelstein and Rieger, *op. cit.*, II, 382f.

18. [Roth, *Marranos*, pp. 209, 219].

19. Roth, *Venice*, pp. 242f.; Graetz, *Heb. Tr.*, VII, 380, 383f.

20. Roth, *Marranos*, pp. 212f., 396, [312, 316].

21. Roth, *Venice*, pp. 68, [242]; Roth, *Marranos*, pp. 214, 300, 303, 395. [See also Graetz, *Geschichte*, IX², 315, 468].

22. Thomas M'Crie, *Reformation in Italy*, (1856), pp. 96f.; John Owen, *Sceptics of the Italian Renaissance*, pp. 201f. [W. E. H. Lecky, *Rationalism in Europe*, (London, 1910—two vols. in one), I, 252; II, 33ff.; Graetz, *Heb. Tr.*, VI, 164].

23. Roth, *Venice*, p. 158; Roth, *A Jewish Book of Days*, (London, 1931), pp. 211f.; Grayevsky, *Hagerim*, pp. 6, 15.

CHAPTER TWENTY-TWO
Pp. 585 — 620

1. It is interesting to note that while the first product of the printing press in Italy was a letter of Indulgence by Nicholas V, and a call to take up arms against the Turks (1454), and in Spain a tract on the Conception of the Virgin (1474), among the Jews it was Rashi's commentary on the Bible, in Spain, and a Spanish translation of the Scriptures in Italy. [It is possible that the Hebrew printing presses were established in Spain before reaching Italy. But the earliest dated Hebrew book now extant was the commentary of Rashi on the Pentateuch, Reggio di Calabria on the Straits of Messina, 1475].

2. [Lecky, op. cit., II, 52f.].

3. L. I. Newman, op. cit., pp. 463, 471, 483, 494.

4. [Lecky, op. cit., I, 373f., 383].

5. S. M. Jackson, Heroes of the Faith, (N. Y., 1901); Newman, op. cit., 454f., [469, 472, 482, 492].

6. [Newman, op. cit., pp. 498f.]. H. M. Baird, History of the Rise of the Huguenots, (London, 1880), I, 25f., 44f.

7. Baird, op. cit., pp. 52f., 67f.

8. [Jakob Guttman, Jean Bodin in seinen Beziehungen zum Judenthum (Breslau, 1906), denies that Bodin's mother was a Jewess]. Lecky, Rationalism, [ed. cit., I, 87-95]; Owen, Sceptics of the French Revolution, 1893; J. S. Bloch, in Jewish Forum, March, April, May, 1937.

9. Baird, op. cit., I, 87f., 102, et passim.

10. Ibid., pp. 397f.

11. Institutes, II, c. 1, Paragraph 8, cs. 13f.; III, cs. 36f.; IV, c. 1, Paragraph 7f., cs. 15f.; Willis, Servetus and Calvin, 1877; Newman, op. cit., pp. 588ff.

12. Lecky, [loc. cit., II, 42, 46ff.].

13. G. Deutsch, Jew and Gentile, (Boston, 1920), pp. 52f.

14. Roth, Marranos, pp. 222f.

15. Graetz, [Geschichte, X^2, 141f., 291f.; C. Roth, "Leone da Modena and the Christian Hebraists of His Age," Jewish Studies in Memory of Israel Abrahams, (N. Y., 1927), p. 384]. Roth, in J Q R, XXIII, 139f.; J. E., IX, 532.

16. Roth, in The Current Jewish Record, July, 1932, pp. 13f.; Opinion, N. Y., April 18, 1932.

17. Roth, in B'nai B'rith Magazine, Feb., 1932, pp. 170, 177.

18. Roth, in B'nai B'rith Magazine, March, 1935, pp. 190f.

19. P. Grayevsky, Hagerim, I, 18, 24. [Universal Jewish Encyclopedia, IV, 382; Aimée Palliére, The Unknown Sanctuary, (N. Y., 1929)].

20. Froude, Life and Letters of Erasmus, (London, 1894).

21. J. Ten Briuh, Kleine Geschiedenis der Nederlandsche Letteren, (1882), pp. 86f.

22. [Graetz, Geschichte, X^2, 2ff.; Roth, Marranos, pp. 238-41].

23. Adler, in Transactions of the Jewish Historical Society of England, 1893-4.

24. A. Wolf, The Oldest Biography of Spinoza, (N. Y., 1928), pp. 19f.; H. A. Wolfson, The Philosophy of Spinoza, (Cambridge, Mass., 1934), I, 14, 19, et passim; Robertson, History of Freethought, II, 197f.

25. Roth, *A Life of Menasseh Ben Israel,* (Phila., 1934), pp. 44f., 65, 87f.

26. *Ibid.,* pp. 109f., 112f., 115f., 117f., 119f.; M. Kayserling, *Sephardim*: [Romanische Poesien der Juden in Spanien, 1859], pp. 209f.

27. L. W. Schwarz, *Memoirs of My People,* (Phila., 1943), p. 89; Graetz, *Heb. Tr.,* VIII, 219f.; Roth, *Marranos,* pp. 245f., 333.

28. Roth, *Menasseh Ben Israel,* pp. 127f.; Graetz, *Heb. Tr.,* VIII, 224f.

29. Graetz, *Heb. Tr.,* VII, 376; VIII, 162f.; Roth, *Menasseh Ben Israel,* pp. 126f.

30. Roth, in *B'nai B'rith Magazine,* Feb., 1935, pp. 120, 161.

31. B. Krupnik, *Maaseh Beger Zedek,* (Berlin, 1921), pp. 15f.; *Die Yiddische Welt,* (Johannisburg, 1862), "Gere Hazedek."

CHAPTER TWENTY-THREE

Pp. 621 — 643

1. A. Sorel, *L'Europe et la Revolution Francaise,* (1885), I, 458; *Emek Habaka* (*ed.* Wiener), p. 37. [Max Grunwald, *Vienna,* (Phila., 1936), pp. 2, 73].

2. Grunwald, *op. cit.,* pp. 5-8.

3. [*Ibid.,* pp. 20, 28, 48].

4. *Ibid.,* pp. 30f.; S. Bernfeld, *Sefer Hademaot,* (Berlin, 1934), pp. 166f.

5. Grunwald, *op. cit.,* pp. 34ff., 148f.

6. *Ibid.,* pp. 130ff., [307, 430-7].

7. *Ency. Britt.,* 13th ed., s. v. "Pisa" and "Constance, Council of."

8. *Ibid.,* s. v. "Huss;" D. S. Schaff, *John Huss,* (N. Y., 1915).

9. Count Luetzow, *Bohemia,* (London, 1896); Count Luetzow, *The Life And Times of John Huss,* (London, 1909).

10. Hamilton, *A History of the Moravian Church* (Bethlehem, 1900).

11. Bax, *Rise and Fall of the Anabaptists,* (London, 1903).

12. *Jewish Ency.,* "Bohemia," III, 287.

13. Newman, *op. cit.,* pp. 450f.

14. Graetz, *Heb. Tr.,* VI, 137f.; *Jewish Ency., s. v.* "Prague."

15. Grunwald, *op. cit.,* pp. 108f.

16. *Ibid.,* pp. 366-70.

17. In the province of Styria, one hundred and seventy Jews became Christians, twenty-one Christians became Jews between 1890 and 1902. From August 1, 1919 to July 31, 1929, five hundred and sixty-seven men, four hundred and eighty-one women and eighty-eight children were converted (*J. D. B.* Oct. 30, 1929 and July 30, 1928). Miss Gold, the beauty "Queen of the Universe" who first came to the U. S. as "Miss Austria" was on the side of her paternal grandmother of Christian descent. According to a list published in the Budapest *Egyenlöség* there were in Czechoslovakia in 1935 (*Amer. Hebrew,* August 7, 1936): One hundred and thirty-five Jewish converts to Christianity and fifty Christians to Judaism. For the last six months of 1937 there were two Jewish converts to Christianity, against three Christian converts to Judaism (M. A. Tannenblatt in *Amer. Israelite,* February 25, 1926 and November 24, 1927; *Jewish Examiner,* May 5, 1935; *Amer. Hebr.,* November 6, 1936 and February 26, 1937. Five Bohemian Christian families embraced Judaism at the beginning of 1936 (*J. D. B.,* July 24, 1933 and December 3, 1934).

18. A. Harkavy, *Hayyehudim Usefath Hasslavim*, (Vilna, 1867), p. 116; N. Samter, *Judentum und Proselytismus*, (Breslau, 1897), pp. 23f.

19. [S. H. Fritchman, *Men of Liberty, Ten Unitarian Pioneers*, (Boston, 1944), pp. 20ff.; E. M. Wilbur, *A History of Unitarianism*, (Cambridge, Mass., 1946), pp. 222-26, 230f., 302-5; Newman, *op. cit.*, pp. 422f.].

20. [Wilbur, *op. cit.*, pp. 367ff.; Fritchman, *op. cit.*, pp. 31-44].

21. M. Gaster, "The Spread of Judaism Through The Ages," in *The Jewish Library* (ed. Leo Jûng, New York, 1928), pp. 147ff.; G. Bader, "A Kristlicher Shomer Shabbos," in *Tageblatt*, February 15, 1916.

22. It is interesting that this R. Abraham interprets R. Helbo's unfriendly [?] statement that proselytes are as painful to Israel as leprosy for the reason that they are usually more observant, and hence make the indifference of born Jews more conspicuous. Tosafot, *Kidd., s. v. Kashim*, 70b. [But see my note 7 of chapter 9, *supra* p. 808].

23. A. M. Haberman, *Nashim Ibriyot b'Tor Madfisot*, (Berlin, 1933), pp. 13f.

24. *Teshubot R. A. Eger*, (Warsaw, 1834), 30b, paragraph 41; Gaster, *op. cit.*, p. 149.

25. *Hashahar*, II, 272; III, 334f.; *Amer. Israelite* November 28, 1912; *J. Daily Bull.* April 13, 1928; Samter, *op. cit.*, p. 38.

26. *B'nai B'rith Magaz.*, January, 1938, p. 163.

27. According to the Report of the Chief Rabbi of Hungary, there were the following conversions to Christianity or Judaism (including reverts):

1914—Jews to Christianity,   532; Christians to Jews, 104.
1920—Jews to Christianity, 1,401; Christians to Jews, 234.
1921—Jews to Christianity, 1,200; Christians to Jews, 332.
1922—Jews to Christianity,   437; Christians to Jews, 185.
1923—Jews to Christianity,   158; Christians to Jews, 237

(183 women).

Tageblatt October 27, 1922; *Jewish Ency., s. v.* "Banoczi," II, 496. [See also Elbogen, *op. cit.*, pp. 190, 492; Israel Cohen, *Jewish Life in Modern Times*, (N. Y., 1914), pp. 300f.].

28. *Tageblatt* July 17, 1924.

29. [This story is not known to me. (H. H.)].

30. *Maaseh Rab*, or *Ezba Elohim*, (Koenigsberg, 1857); A. R. Malachi, "Ger Zedek," in *Haddoar*, December 18, 1936.

CHAPTER TWENTY-FOUR

Pp. 644 — 670

1. [*The Cambridge Modern History*, (N. Y., 1934), II, pp. 142-173].

2. L. Geiger, *Johann Reuchlin*, (Leipzig, 1871), [pp. 205-54].

3. J. S. C. Abbott, *Hist. of Christianity*, (Portland, Me.), pp. 420f.; H. C. Lea, *A History of Auricular Confession*, (Phila., 1896), [I, 511, 515f.].

4. H. Barge, *Andreas Bodenstein von Karlstadt*, (Leipzig, 1905).

5. H. S. Burrage, *A History of the Anabaptists in Switzerland*, (Phila., 1882), [pp. 83f., especially footnote 1].

6. [*Cambridge Modern History*, II, 222ff., 226f., 229, 319, 322f., 611].

7. Newman, *op. cit.*, pp. 617f.; Graetz, Heb. Tr., VIII, 130f.

8. Graetz, *op. cit.*, VII, 142f., 417.

9. [J. R. Marcus, *The Jew in the Medieval World*, pp. 167f., quoting Luther's "Von den Juden und Ihren Luegen"].

10. J. Kaufman, *R. Yomtov Lipman Muelhausen*, pp. 66f.; Grunwald, *op. cit.*, pp. 102ff.

11. C. Roth, *Jewish Contribution to Civilization*, (London, 1938), [pp. 108f., 312f.]. [Graetz, *Geschichte*, XI, 8f., 32ff., 66-74, 140f., 171ff.].

12. G. Karpeles, *Heinrich Heine's Memoirs*, (London, 1910), I, 172.

13. [J. R. Marcus, *The Rise and Destiny of the German Jew*, (Cincinnati, 1934), pp. 28, 34ff., 74, 147, 153].

14. B. D. Weinryb, *Jewish Emancipation Under Attack*, (N. Y.), pp. 14f. [I. Elbogen, *A Century of Jewish Life*, pp. 162ff., 706f.].

15. Donath, *Geschichte der Juden in Mecklenburg*, (Leipzig, 1874); *J. E.* VIII, 541, *s. v.* "Michel Jud;" [*Ibid.*, X, 152f., *s. v.* "Prado, Moses"]; Samter, in *Monatsschrift* XXXIX, p. 178. [J. R. Marcus, *The Jew in the Medieval World*, pp. 414f.].

16. Graetz, *Heb. Tr.*, VIII, 305f.; Samter, in *Monatsschrift* XXXIX, 221f.; Eisenmenger, *Ent. Judentum* II, 996; J. M. Toledano, in *Mizrah Umaarab*, (Jerusalem, 1930), pp. 40f.

17. Prof. Will, *Lebensgeschichte Brent's*, (Anspach, 1791); *J. E. s. v.* "Typography" and "Halle-on-the Salle."

18. Biberfeld, "Joseph Abraham Steblicki," in Berliner's *Magazin* XX, 181f.; Neustadt, *Joseph Steblicki* (Breslau, 1894); D. Zamosz, *Ger Zedek* (Breslau, 1816); A. M. Herzberg, *Der Neue Jude*, (Glauvitz, 1845).

19. Roth, *Marranos*, pp. 301, 341. [Graetz, Geschichte, X², 21f.].

20. Grayevsky, *Hagerim* I, 21f.; II, 9, 12; *Haolam*, (1932), p. 618.

21. Her autobiography, *Ich Suchte Dich* (1898), was translated into Hebrew (*Bikashticha*, Tel Aviv, 1932) by Dr. Israel Schapira.

22. Samter, [*Judentaufen im 19 Jahrhundert*, (Berlin, 1906), p. 38], gives these statistics of converts:

Prussia, 1875-94 — 184
Berlin, 1872-94 — 126
Germany, 1890-94 — 79

23. *J. D. B.* August 31, 1933, September 1, 1933; *Amer. Heb.* February 28, 1936; *J. D. B.* July 4, 1934, March 31, 1935, April 21, 1935; *Jewish Forum*, December, 1935, p. 290; *Amer. Hebrew* February 21, 1935—p. 6, November 1, 1935—p. 10.

CHAPTER TWENTY-FIVE

Pp. 671 — 723

1. V. Krasinski, [*Historical Sketch of the Rise, Progress, and Decline of The Reformation in Poland*, London, 1838], I, 29f.

2. [See *Encyclo. Brit.*, *s. v.* "Casimir III," (Chicago, 1949), IV, 965].

3. Krasinski, *op. cit.*, I, 143.

4. *Ibid.*, pp. 345f.; [*Ibid.*, (London, 1840), II, 362-400].

5. S. M. Dubnow, *History of the Jews in Russia and Poland*, (Phila., 1916), I, 35, 40-58.

6. [*Ibid.*, pp. 47f.]. Graetz, *Heb. Tr.*, VIII, 101.

7. Dubnow, *op. cit.*, I, 81f.

8. G. Bader, *Dreisig Doros Idden in Poilin*, (N. Y., 1927), pp. 215f.; Marcus, *The Jew in the Medieval World*, pp. 179f.

9. Dubnow, *op. cit.*, I, 144ff.

10. N. Hanover, *Yeven Mezulah*, (Warsaw, 1872), 7b-8a, 19a. [Dubnow, *op. cit.*, I, 151f.].

11. Graetz, *Heb. Tr.*, VIII, 229f., 546f.

12. [Graetz, *Geschichte*, X^2, 333-40].

13. [*Ibid.*, pp. 417-29].

14. Dubnow, *op. cit.*, I, 136.

15. *Ibid.*, pp. 137f.

16. Deutsch, *Jew and Gentile*, p. 62.

17. [Dubnow, *op. cit.*, I, 79f.].

18. *Tageblatt* (Anna Constance). [The editor finds it necessary to state here that the present chapter presented the greatest difficulty in tracing Raisin's sources. All of our author's footnotes were in his own handwriting. He refers several times to his "typed notes"—which no one in the family, up to the time of this writing, has been able to find. Are we to surmise that he perhaps never was able to revise his notes for the typist? Raisin's numbered footnotes were not in order to correspond with the typed MS. given to the editor].

19. B. Krupnik, *Maaseh b'Ger Zedek*, (Berlin, 1921), pp. 15f. [Israel Cohen, *Vilna*, (Phila., 1943), pp. 73f., 484ff.].

20. Godbey, *op. cit.*, pp. 257f.; Dubnow, *op. cit.*, I, 19ff.; Graetz, *Heb. Tr.*, III, 199f., 340f.; N. Slousch, "The Origin of the East European Jews," *Menorah Journal*, (Oct. 1923), pp. 255f.

21. A. Harkavy, in *Hammagid*, 1877, p. 357. A similar saying obtained among the Jews of Italy. There it was rendered, "Out of Bari shall go forth the Torah, and the word of the Lord from Otranto." S. Schechter, "An Unknown Khazar Document," *J. Q. R.*, (N. S.), III, 181f. [See Dubnow, *op. cit.*, I, 26f.].

22. Among the Jews it was rumored that the Grand Duke rejected Judaism because it prohibits the eating of pork, and Mohammedanism, because it is against the drinking of liquor. [See Dubnow, *op. cit.*, I, 30f.].

23. [R. N. Bain, "St. Vladimir," *The Encyclopaedia Brittanica*, (11th Ed.), XXVIII, 168].

24. [Dubnow, *op. cit.*, I, 242].

25. [*Ibid.*, I, 29, 35ff.].

26. [*Ibid.*, I, 243, 247f., 255, 259f.].

27. [*Ibid.*, I, 358f., 378, 392f., 386ff., 348, 396f.; II, 74, 18-27].

28. [*Ibid.*, I, 27ff.].

29. [*Ibid.*, II, 103f., 207-9, 184-190, 245-357; III, 9-22, 93, 141]. Max Lilienthal, in *Occident* V, 252, 296.

834   GENTILE REACTIONS TO JEWISH IDEALS

30. [Dubnow, *op. cit.*, II, 151, 205, 241f.; "Constantin Abba Schapira (Schapiro)," *U. J. E.* IX, 389].

31. [Dubnow, *op. cit.*, II, 333ff.]. De le Roi, *Juden-Mission*, (Leipzig, 1899), 1², 204.

32. Z. Kasdai, *Hamityahadim*, (Haifa, 1916), pp. 5f. [Dubnow, *op. cit.*, I, 36f.].

33. Dubnow, *op. cit.*, I, 249-57. [Graetz, *Heb. Tr.*, VIII, 447f.].

34. Dubnow, *op. cit.*, I, 401ff.; S. Anski, *Die Gerim Fun Idishen Kwall*, Nos. 1 and 2.

35. *Tageblatt*, Feb. 3, 1920. [Dubnow, *op. cit.*, III, 10].

36. Kasdai, *op. cit.*, 26f., 44f.

37. S. Ginzburg, in *Forverts*, July 3, 1932 and July 10, 1932.

38. J. Boyarsky, in *B'nai B'rith News*, May 13 [?]. *Special Notes* [The editor has been compelled to decipher as best he could the rest of Raisin's sources for this chapter. These notes, in the original MS. were not arranged in order. They are as follows: *Tageblatt* 12/29/16, 3/21/23; A. Parri, in *The Jewish Tribune*, (N. Y.), 5/27/27, pp. 24, 43; M. Elkin, in *Menorah Journal*, Aug., 1927, pp. 347f.; *Tageblatt*, 9/29/12, 1/20/20, 3/7/23, 10/11/23, 3/27/24; *Jewish Daily Bulletin* 2/17/28, 3/29/28, 12/23/31; R. Breinin, in *Tageblatt* 2/9/21, 2/10/21, 1/17/24; *Amer. Israelite* 4/10/24; *Tageblatt* 3/8/23, 4/29/24; *Jewish Tribune* 12/22/22; *Young Israel*, Feb. 1924, p. 12; *Amer. Hebrew* 7/30/37, p. 2; G. Bader, in *Tageblatt*, 6/24/24; Bader, in *Tageblatt*, 7/9/24; *The Jewish Forum*, May, 1934, pp. 145f. The editor cannot vouch for the accuracy of these transcribed references because of the difficult penmanship in this section of the original footnotes and because of the several omissions].

CHAPTER TWENTY-SIX
Pp. 724 — 755

1. H. Hallam, *Middle Ages*, (N. Y., 1900), III, 107f.; Newman, *op. cit.*, pp. 222ff.; [M. Guedemann, *Geschichte des Erziehungswesen Und Der Cultur der Juden in Frankreich und Deutschland*, (Wien, 1880), pp. 35f.].

2. J. R. Green, *A Short History of the English People*, (N. Y., 1900), III, 290f.

3. "Lollard" may mean a hymn singer, or an idle babbler, probably a nickname given by the Church (Mosheim, 14th century, Part II, c. 2, Par. 36).

4. D. Hume, *Hist of England*, (Phila., 1836), I, 408f.; R. L. Poole, *Wycliffe And The Movements For Reform*, (London, 1889); G. M. Trevelyan, *England In The Age of Wycliffe*, (London, 1904).

5. [See the editor's several contributions to this historical idea, *supra*, p. 799, n. 1].

6. Th. B. Macaulay, *Hist. of England*, [N. Y., Harper and Bros., 1899, I, 84].

7. *Ibid.*, [p. 121]; Green, *op. cit.*, II, 139f.

8. Green, *op. cit.*, II, ch. VII; Wilbur, *op. cit.*, p. 278; Foxe's *Book of Martyrs*; W. W. Confort, *Just Among Friends*, (N. Y., 1941).

9. A. N. Brayshaw, *The Quakers*, (N. Y., 1938); Hume, *op. cit.*, I, 696.; W. B. Selbie, in *Legacy of Israel*, (Oxford, 1928), pp. 407f.

10. Macaulay's Essay on Milton, *The Nineteenth Century And After*, vol. LXXI; M. Raisin, *Milton* (in Hebrew), p. 33; Robertson, *op. cit.*, II, 30f., 116.

11. Wilbur, *op. cit.*, pp. 296f.

12. *Ibid.*, pp. 324f.; Robertson, *op. cit.*, II, 126f.

13. Macaulay, *op. cit.*, V, 226f.

14. Hume, *op. cit.*, I, 612, 619, 693f.

15. [*Dictionary of National Biography*, Vol. 58, p. 212].

16. N. Sokolow, *History of Zionism*, (London, 1919), I, 42f., 47f., II, 207f.; Silver, *op. cit.*, pp. 172f.

17. [Sokolow, *op. cit.*, I, 19, 44; II, 182f.]; Roth, *A Life of Menasseh Ben Israel*, (Phila., 1945), pp. 176f., 195f., Roth, *Marranos*, pp. 261f.; Green, *op. cit.*, II, 154f.

18. E. N. Adler, *London* (Phila., 1930), pp. 91f.; Roth, in *B'nai B'rith Magazine*, (March, 1935); M. F. Modder, *The Jew in the Literature of England*, pp. 36f.

19. [C. Roth, *The Jews of Medieval Oxford*, (Oxford, 1951), pp. 24f.; Roth, *A History of the Jews in England*, (Oxford, 1941), pp. 134f., 140ff., 147; Andrew Marvell, "To His Coy Mistress," in *Oxford Book of English Verse*, (Oxford, 1939), pp. 399f.].

20. Modder, *op. cit.*, pp. 102f., 150, *et passim;* E. Heine, *The British Nation Identified With Lost Israel*, (London, 1871); W. H. Poole, *Anglo-Israel*, (Detroit, 1889); C. A. L. Tutten, *Our Race*, (New Haven, Conn.).

21. [Modder, *op. cit.*, pp. 83ff., 373].

22. S. Schechter, *Studies in Judaism*, Third Series, (Phila., 1924), p. 163; De le Roi, *Michael Solomon Alexander*, (1897); [Modder, *op. cit.*, pp. 194f.].

23. Adler, *London*, pp. 91f.; Roth, *Menasseh Ben Israel*, pp. 187, 194.

24. *The Jewish Chronicle* 7/2/1882.

25. I. Solomons, in *Transactions of Jewish Historical Society of England*, VII, 222f.; Adler, *London*, pp. 127f.; *Dictionary of National Biography*, XXII, 197f.

26. L. Wolf, *The History And Genealogy of the Jewish Families of Yates and Samuel*, (London, 1901), pp. 2, 11; Adler, *London*, p. 123.

27. B. A. Elzas, *A List of Converts to Judaism in the City of London, 1809-1816*, (N. Y., 1914); C. Roth, "If England Had an Aryan Test," in *B. B. Magazine*, (June, 1934), pp. 315, 331f.

28. *Tageblatt* 9/11/33; *J. D. B.* 9/11/33, 11/19/33.

29. Modder, *op. cit.*, p. 379; *Jewish Chronicle* 12/8/1899.

30. M. Oliphant, *Memoirs of the Life of Lawrence Oliphant*, (London, 1891); [Sokolow, *op. cit.*, I, 207ff.].

31. *Jewish Quarterly Review*, London, 2/23/1906; E. N. Calish, *The Jew in English Literature*, (Richmond, Vir., 1909), p. 192.

32. *Tageblatt* 10/23/34; *J. D. B.* 7/30/28, 8/15/28; *Amer. Israelite* 10/9/24, 12/6/29.

CHAPTER TWENTY-SEVEN
Pp. 756—795

1. S. Oppenheim, in *Proceedings of A. J. H. S.*, XVII, 53f.; R. Gottheil, *ibidem*, VIII, 131f.

2. A. Brenner, in *Menorah Journal*, Jan., 1929, pp. 12f.

3. C. Adler, in *A. J. H. S.*, XVII, 27f.; Brenner, *loc. cit.*, pp. 19f.

4. Roth, *Marranos*, pp. 157f.

5. Brenner, *loc. cit.*, pp. 18f.; A. Parry, in *Jewish Tribune*, 8/24/28; Gottheil, *Proceedings, A. J. H. S.*, VIII, 19f.

6. Bab, "Marrano Survivors in Chile," *Amer. Hebrew* 1/19/34; S. Oppenheim, "The Jungles of Yucatan," *B. B. Magaz.*, 1933 (?), pp. 160f.; *J. D. B.*, 6/16/35.

7. C. Roth, *Marranos*, pp. 285f.; *A. J. H. S.* IV, 3f.; VIII, 129f.

8. E. R. Clinchy, *All in the Name of God*, (N. Y., 1935); S. H. Cobb, *The Rise of Religious Liberty in America*, (N. Y., 1902).

9. O. S. Straus, *Origin of Republican Form of Government*, (N. Y., 1926).

10. A. Kohut, *Ezra Styles and the Jews*, (N. Y., 1902).

11. I. Goldberg, *Major Noah*, (Phila., 1936), pp. 114f.

12. E. M. Wilbur, *The First Cent. of the Liberal Movement in Amer. Rel.*, (Amer. Unitarian Ass'n., Tract No. 289); Wilbur, *op. cit.*, pp. 290f.

13. F. E. Evans, *Shakers*, (Albany, N. Y., 1858); Orson Pratt, *The Divine Authenticity of the Book of Mormons*, (Utah, 1891).

14. J. E. Talmage, *The Articles of Faith*, (Salt Lake City, 1899).

15. *The Jewish Forum*, June, 1922, p. 212.

16. *Jewish Exponent* 3/18/1889; *Year Book, C. C. A. R.*, 1891, pp. 36, 66f.; *ibidem*, 1892, pp. 15f., 33f.; D. Philipson, *The Reform Movement in Judaism*, (N. Y., 1931), pp. 137, 369f.; E. Felsenthal, *Bernhard Felsenthal Teacher in Israel*, (N. Y., 1924), pp. 217, 247.

17. [*U. J. E., s. v.* "Jacob Mordecai," Vol. VII, p. 644].

18. E. D. Cowen, in *Amer. Hebrew* 4/14/16, 3/29/18.

19. [*Charleston, S. C.*] *Sunday News* 3/24/1907.

20. Morais, in *The Jews of Philadelphia*, [Phila., 1894, pp. 379f.] and *The Amer. Jewish Annual*, 1886.

21. E. Lieberman, in *Amer. Hebrew* 8/21/25; H. A. Potarikin, in *Jewish Tribune* 7/26/29. [Sokolow, *op. cit.*, I, 136f.].

22. S. Talpioth, in *Tageblatt* 3/21/24; S. Petrushkin, in *Der Tog*, 10/12/27; *Occident*, 1852, p. 360.

23. *Occident*, 1855, pp. 134f.

24. *Tageblatt* 10/13/10; *J. D. B.* 2/8/29.

25. *Tageblatt* 10/3/10.

26. *Die Warheit* 1/29/15; *Morgen Journal* 6/22/15; *Tageblatt* 4/1/13.

27. *Tageblatt* 9/4/23; 12/27/23; 9/8/25.

28. *Tageblatt* 1/1/17.

29. *Morgen Journal* 7/15/38.

30. *J. D. B.* Dec. 17, 19, 1928;*Tageblatt* 8/26/19; *Jewish Monitor* 1/19/17.

31. *Amer. Israelite*, Oct. 1922.

32. *So. Israelite* 5/5/27; *Der Tog* Jan. 14, 1928; R. Benjamin, in *Hatekufah*, XVIII, 420, 422; *Tageblatt* 4/17/24; *Jewish Tribune* 4/6/23; *J. D. B.* 6/20/34.

33. *The American Israelite* 3/28/30; *Southern Israelite*, Feb., 1931, p. 6.

34. *The Jewish Exponent*, (Phila.), 4/3/36.

35. A. Levinson, "Negro Jews," in *The Jewish Forum* V, 185f.; B. Z. Goldberg in *B. B. Mag.*, August, 1927; A. Green, in *B. B. Mag.*, Jan. 1933; P. Mack, in *J. D. B.* 1/22/34; 2/18/29; 1/18/34; *Amer. Hebrew* 12/15/33; *Lit. Digest* 3/2/29; *Amer. Israelite* 3/5/31; *Morgen Journal* 1/15/29. [See *U. J. E., s. v.* "Negro Jews," Vol. VIII, p. 145].

36. [The last two paragraphs of this concluding chapter are the words of the present editor. It is also to be noted that some of the footnote references in this chapter to Jewish journals and newspapers were not arranged seriatim by the original author.]

INDEX

INDEX

"R." preceding a forename=Rabbi

"(RE)"=Roman emperor